S0-AHJ-933

AN HISTORIAN'S CONSCIENCE

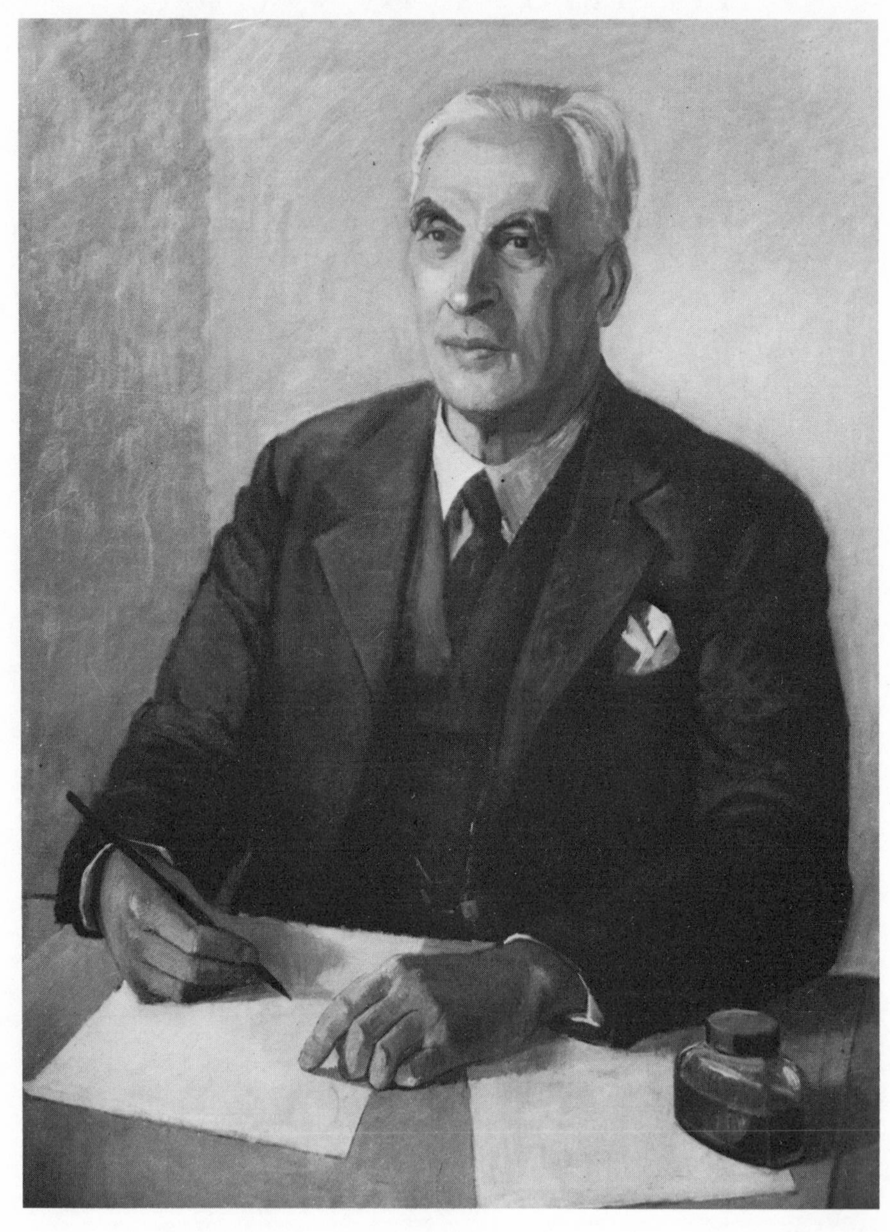

Arnold J. Toynbee, a portrait by Lawrence L. Toynbee, painted in 1955, in the Toynbee Room, Chatham House

AN HISTORIAN'S CONSCIENCE

The Correspondence of Arnold J. Toynbee and Columba Cary-Elwes, Monk of Ampleforth

Edited by
Christian B. Peper

Foreword by
Lawrence L. Toynbee

BEACON PRESS · BOSTON

The publication of this book has been assisted by the
Harvard Divinity School.

Beacon Press
25 Beacon Street
Boston, Massachusetts 02108

Beacon Press books are published under the auspices
of the Unitarian Universalist Association
of Congregations in North America.

Printed in the United States of America

92 91 90 89 88 87 86 8 7 6 5 4 3 2 1

Library of Congress Cataloging in Publication Data

Toynbee, Arnold Joseph, 1889–1975.
An historian's conscience.

Includes bibliographical notes and index.
1. Toynbee, Arnold Joseph, 1889–1975—Correspondence. 2. Toynbee, Arnold Joseph, 1889–1975—Religion. 3. Cary-Elwes, Columba, 1903– —Correspondence. 4. Historians—Great Britain—Correspondence. 5. Benedictines—Correspondence. I. Cary-Elwes, Columba, 1903– II. Peper, Christian B. III. Title. IV. Title: Correspondence of Arnold J. Toynbee and Columba Cary-Elwes, monk of Ampleforth.
CB18.T65A4 1986 907′.2024 85-47952
ISBN 0-8070-5000-8

Text design by R. Williams

CONTENTS

ILLUSTRATIONS

Photo gallery follows page 320.

ACKNOWLEDGMENTS

Facile princeps comes Columba Cary-Elwes, O.S.B., in his unique role as correspondent and commentator; his ubiquitous hand appears as "C.C.E." in numerous footnotes to identify, clarify, and supply nuances and in various Annexes to add invaluable supplements. Inspirer and co-worker, subject and object, he has been an ever-present help during five years of travail. Lawrence Toynbee read the manuscript, made many suggestions, and supplied vivid recollections of his father; his liberal attitude toward the publication of the letters combined filial piety with respect for truth. Margaret Toynbee, Arnold's sister, contributed family memories and a ready response to every question. Posthumous recognition surely must be given to Veronica Toynbee who devoted the years that followed Arnold's death to collecting and putting in order his manuscripts and papers.

More general but not less grateful acknowledgments are owing to the many who assisted and encouraged the work: to Alexander Murray, grandson and literary executor of Gilbert Murray; to Louise Orr, in late years Arnold's secretary and helper; to Admiral Sir James Eberle, G.C.B., Director of the Royal Institute of International Affairs, who has made available the resources of Chatham House; to Dorothy Hamerton, archivist at Chatham House, who was of great help in tracing persons and events; to Mrs. Philip (Sally) Toynbee, who gave much information about Philip and his children; to D. S. Porter, of the Department of Western Manuscripts at the Bodleian Library, who has been most helpful in making its resources easily available; to S. Fiona Morton whose *Bibliography* enables one to chart a course within an immense corpus of publications and to ascertain the published material resulting from various of Arnold's many journeys and lectures; to the Warden and Scholars of New College, Oxford, for permission to quote from Guy Cheesman's unpublished diaries; to George Rupp, then Dean, and to Roger Martin, Associate Dean of the Harvard Divinity School, who gave timely support to the project, and to others, *quam multa in silvis autumni frigore primo/lapsa cadunt folia* . . .

Finally, I must acknowledge my dependence on the quietly persistent help and encouragement of my daughter, Anne Peper Perkins, and of my wife, Ethel, who spent so many hours with me in the Bodleian examining and transcribing a sometimes difficult (though beautiful) script and whose almost unerring eye for the written word has corrected many an error.

INTRODUCTION

Arnold Toynbee has defined a history of the world which puts "first things first" as "a continuous series of meetings with God" (20 October 1959). A study of Toynbee's life and work must include his encounters with Absolute Reality. These letters may serve as a thread of Ariadne in the labyrinthine ways of Toynbee's conscience.

Religio Historici

Toynbee had "an ordinary Anglican upbringing at home and at school" (5 August 1938). During his five years at Winchester, compulsory services included a Saturday liturgy in honor of the Theotókos, with hymns in the traditional Latin (11 July 1974). But about the time when he went up to Oxford as an undergraduate in 1907 he drifted into a state of "disbelief in the existence of any transcendental reality, life or personality" (5 August 1938), a "typical reaction" (*Comparing Notes*, p. 9).

Courtship

In 1912 Toynbee became a fellow of Balliol. The early letters in the *Prolegomena* reflect vividly the youthful scholar living at the apogee of the British Empire like one of Matthew Arnold's "young, light-hearted masters of the waves." Our second letter describes his first visit to Castle Howard under the wing of Gilbert Murray, who many years before had come as a young don to marry the daughter of George Howard, later the 9th Earl of Carlisle (West, *Gilbert Murray*, pp. 25–33); here Arnold and Rosalind, the daughter of Gilbert and Lady Mary Murray, will spend their honeymoon.

In the letter of 9 March 1913 we see the dawn of his love of Rosalind; and, finally, in the letter of 13 June 1913, his rejection, despair and acceptance, a letter that now is seen to mingle threat with promise.

Marriage

Rosalind, daughter of doctrinaire post-Christians, had not been baptized; the wedding was in a registry office. Arnold's sister, Margaret, recalls that her mother did not permit her and her sister Jocelyn to attend. The picture of the religious atmosphere of Castle Howard may be completed by Margaret Toynbee's account of a conversation with Lady Carlisle (Rosalind's grandmother) in which, when Margaret said she was a Christian, Lady Carlisle replied, "Fancy your believing all those fairy tales."

Return to Faith

Toynbee's recovery of a belief in God in 1930 "came through an experience of help in withstanding a very strong temptation . . . but had probably been long in preparation" (5 August 1938).

Rosalind's Conversion

Meanwhile Rosalind had become increasingly drawn toward the Catholic Church; and in 1932 she entered the Church, an act which "produced disquiet and foreboding" in Arnold (20 September 1944). Rosalind brought their youngest son, Lawrence, into the Church, and he was enrolled at Ampleforth College, conducted by the Monks of Ampleforth Abbey, near the little village north of York, in Castle Howard country, near Rosalind's Ganthorpe Hall.

A.J.T. and C.C.E. Meet

Columba Cary-Elwes was a master at Ampleforth when he and Toynbee met in the monastery in 1936, where they discussed the Lübeck incunabulum (17 December 1966). Here the mature historian and the younger monk, both *nel mezzo del cammin*, commenced a friendship and correspondence that extended (with one curious lacuna in 1945) to Toynbee's death, 39 years later.

The Correspondence Preserved

Each, except for apparently deliberate exceptions, preserved the other's letters. After Toynbee's death his widow, Veronica, and Columba placed all the then available A.J.T.–C.C.E. correspondence with the Bodleian. Unfortunately, when Columba had come to the United States in 1955 to found the Saint Louis Priory, he had left Arnold's earlier letters (1937–55) at Ampleforth in "safe-keeping." For many anxious months these letters were *introuvables*; at long last a diligent novice found them in the attic; and the writer recalls the happy day when he met Columba with the letters at Oxford and turned them over to the Keeper of Western Manuscripts. To this corpus have been added occasional letters like Rosalind's (17 June 1943), which form part of the *res gestae*. The *Prolegomena* contain a few excerpts from Toynbee's correspondence with his lifelong friend Robert Shelby Darbishire; these, too, have generously been placed in the Bodleian by the Darbishire family and Veronica.

It will be noted that a number of letters are listed as "missing"; these include the lengthy "autobiographical" letter Arnold wrote Columba in 1943 about his relations with Rosalind; Arnold asked Columba to return this letter and presumably destroyed it; certain of Columba's letters, including some written during the "time of troubles" in 1943, also are missing. On the whole, however, the corpus remains remarkably intact and presents a uniquely comprehensive picture of Arnold Toynbee's conscience.

The editor has rectified certain minor and obvious abbreviations, ellipses, ampersands, oddities in spelling and other concomitants of spontaneous letters, standardized dates (for example, 12 September 1950 for 12th Sept. 1950), and generally italicized words in other languages and titles of publications; Columba has made a few minor corrections, chiefly of his poems.

An Eighteenth-Century Parallel

There is a curious parallel to this unbroken series of letters in the correspondence of another man of letters with another Yorkshire clergyman: Horace Walpole and the Reverend William Mason exchanged frequent letters from 1763 until the year before their deaths in 1797. Needless to say, the eighteenth-century letters were concerned with more mundane matters than theology.

The Correspondents

Not the least interesting facet of our letters is their reflection of the relationship between the writers. The younger monk revered the older historian as a distinguished scholar; Arnold, with characteristic humility, sees Columba in the role of spiritual counselor: ". . . you are my most direct door to God" (3 September 1939). Columba's early attempts to bring Arnold into the Church as a latter-day Saint Augustine were frustrated by Arnold's refusal to abandon his "intellectual freedom." But the correspondence remained an exchange between equals, united by a deepening friendship which transcended the conceptual theological differences, and the influence of each upon the other is reflected in increasingly similar terminology.

A Philo-Catholic

Although the statement of 5 August 1938 (his *apologia pro religione sua*) remained that of Toynbee's essential positions, the letters of the years from 1938 to 1947 show him at his nearest approach to traditional Christianity; "I certainly am, and shall remain, a philo-Catholic . . ." (14 July 1944); and this is apparent in Volumes IV through VI of the *Study*: "And now, as we stand and gaze with our eyes fixed upon the farther shore, a single figure rises from the flood and straightway fills the whole horizon. There is the Saviour" (*Study*, VI: 278).

A Follower of Symmachus

The basic conceptual barriers remained and in later years became more fixed. As a believer in the value of symbol and myth Toynbee was profoundly affected by archetypal phrases: among these was the reply that the fourth-century pagan orator Quintus Aurelius Symmachus made to the Christians as he urged restoration of the statue of Victory to the Senate House, *Non in uno itinere potest perveniri ad tam grande mysterium*. Toynbee insisted that no revelation was unique; "if the revelation of the One True God is to be accessible to all men, it has to be diffracted" (*Study*, VII: 443).

This remained an unbreakable barrier against Toynbee's acceptance of the unique role of Christianity: "Uniqueness, as you point out, is the stumbling block for me" (10 October 1959). This was reinforced by his ever scrupulous care lest his own

Christian indoctrination prejudice his conclusions: "Brought up as you and I have been, within the Christian circle, how can we know that the other religions are not alternative roads to a single god?" (13 April 1949).

Toynbee acknowledged his debt to Cardinal Newman in seeing in cosmic revelation "an economy of truth" (*Study*, VI: 538); and in the passions of Tammuz, Attis, Adonis, and Osiris he could find "a foreshadowing of the Passion of Christ" (*Study*, VII: 423); and this is expressed explicitly in the letter of 14 May 1940. But he remained syncretistic to the end: "My knee bows, like every Christian's knee, at the deed of self-sacrifice, done for love of us men and for our salvation, that is recited by Saint Paul to the Philippians. For me, the doer of this deed is one presence in more than one epiphany. It is Christ, and, because it is Christ, it is also the Buddha and the bodhisattvas" (*Study*, XII: 102; *The Litany: Study*, X: 143–44).

But though Toynbee could not abandon the dictum of Symmachus, Columba was able to profit by it in an increased appreciation of cosmic revelation. "God has left his imprint everywhere on the things He has made" (7 July 1959).

Marcion and Evil

The problem of evil, not mentioned in the *Apologia* of 5 August 1938, became increasingly intrusive. Here the archetypal phrase was that of Lucretius, a poet who supplied more texts to the *Study* than did Virgil: *tanta stat praedita culpa*: the universe cannot have been divinely created for our benefit, *it is so loaded with fault*. Arnold raises the question early in writing about his estrangement from Rosalind: "It is certainly an evil and therefore cannot, in itself, be God's will . . . Does submitting to God's will mean acquiescing in something that cannot be God's will? This baffles me" (23 February 1944). At one time he found a reconciliation: "This paradoxical truth that Love is inseparable from the Almighty Power put forth in Creation is visually portrayed in Medieval Western Christian *mappae mundi* in which the latent figure of Christ Crucified holds together and sustains the World" (*Study*, IX: 401).

But in later years Toynbee became increasingly of the mind of the second-century heretic Marcion, who held a dualistic view that the God of Power of the Old Testament was other than the "stranger God" of Love of the New; "I am also a Marcionite in believing that love is not omnipotent, whereas you are presumably an Irenaean. (I cannot reconcile omnipotence with beneficence). I believe in the Agony in the Garden and in the Crucifixion, but not in the Resurrection . . ." (25 January 1972).

Le coeur a ses raisons que la raison ne connaît point

Perhaps the most illuminating light these letters cast is not so much upon the historian's formal (and, indeed, protean) theologizing, but upon his heart; for *le coeur* is here revealed as that of an *anima naturaliter Christiana* in its response to suffering: at his son Tony's death, "I felt myself come face to face with God, and realized that, from now on, I should be dealing about Tony with God, and not with Tony himself" (19 March 1939); when he writes about his estrangement from Rosalind: "I have been able, by God's mercy, to pray to God more actively and fruitfully than I ever have since I was a child" (25 February 1943); his prayers before the altar of Sainte Thérèse at the Sacré-Coeur (5 October 1947); upon hearing of Rosalind's death: "Yes, I love Rosalind with all my heart, and I love Veronica, too, with all my heart, because the heart can give the whole of itself to more than one person; this is one of the things in which love is unique and in which the First Epistle General of Saint John speaks one of the ultimate truths when it identifies love with God" (11 May 1967).

Je veux montrer à mes semblables un homme dans toute la vérité de la nature; et cet homme, ce sera moi.

Unlike Rousseau, Arnold Toynbee, despite his voluminous writings, was reticent about many facets of his personal life. These were revealed behind the veil of allusion and poetry, much of the latter in the decent obscurity of a learned tongue.

Here we have the vivid and fresh accounts rendered to Columba, *solus cum solo*, of Arnold's acceptance of Tony's tragic death; his travail and suffering through the three years that followed his separation from Rosalind; the beginning of a *vita nuova* with Veronica; his relationships with his children. Here are glimpses of an England preparing for war; London during the Battle of Britain; and afterward, all the color and glitter of the historian's many travels and triumphant career. Here are recorded the immediate impressions of books and men and cities and the works of man, in which he took such an eager interest. *πολλῶν δ' ἀνθρώπων ἴδεν ἄστεα καὶ νόον ἔγνω*. Some of the material that was incorporated into the *Study* and other works, including the travel books, has its primary source in these letters; indeed, in the give and take of the correspondence we may see the important Volume VII taking shape and being affected by Columba's contributions and reactions.

But, above all, the *homme dans toute la vérité de la nature* here appears living and moving and having his being not in self-centeredness but in love; here is a partial revelation of the smiling, courteous, humble scholar, always ready to listen, whom we knew and revered. *And gladly wolde he lerne and gladly teche.*

Columba's Contribution

Columba's letters again hold interest not only in their theological content and in their relation to Arnold's; here too we find contemporaneous insights into England at war; the multiple affairs of a great Abbey; an intimate glimpse of Hilaire Belloc; the founding of the Saint Louis Priory and School; the making of *China and the Cross*; the effects of Vatican II and the controversial encyclical *Humanae Vitae*; ecumenical work and pilgrimages; missions *in partibus infidelium*; the emerging world of Africa: Kenya, Cameroon, and Nigeria, so recently torn by civil war. Here is the portrait of a follower of St. Benedict carrying the Rule, which played so great a part in civilizing Europe, into the world-wide *oikoumenê* of the Twentieth Century.

Epilogue

Arnold Toynbee retained to the end the role of the bodhisattva which he had described in the *Apologia* of 5 August 1938; he held that "the impulse of an ex-

Christian on the run to find a hiding-place in Christ's riven side ran directly counter to the spirit and significance of Christ's incarnation" (*Study*, IX:632). The intellectual problems remained: "I hold to my liberty to follow wherever the argument may lead me (and it may never stop keeping me on the move)" (16 September 1953). This role was intensified by his belief in the value of suffering epitomized in Aeschylus' πάθει μάθος: "The attitude towards suffering is, for me, the acid test, and on this I am Christian, not Buddhist" (16 September 1953).

Thus, he remained without commitment except that of his dream of 1936 where he "was clasping the foot of the crucifix hanging over the high altar of the Abbey of Ampleforth and was hearing a voice saying to him *Amplexus expecta* ('Cling and wait')" (*Study,* IX:634–35).

Columba completely understood: "You have followed truth as you see it—and, in my terms, God already loves you infinitely for that" (20 January 1972).

There can be many interpretations of the words which Arnold spoke, so unexpectedly, to Columba at their last meeting on 18 September 1975 (6 November 1975). It was Veronica's opinion that this was an act of courtesy and love to Columba. To the writer a more likely explanation is that it was this, and more: by affirming the Trinity Arnold was saying, Yes, this is *one* aspect of the Ultimate Reality. Another interpretation, less likely, but one we cannot conclusively reject, is that Arnold was telling Columba that his mission was ended and that he had doffed the role of bodhisattva: "In my end is my beginning."

FOREWORD

Lawrence L. Toynbee

Early last summer, sitting in my borrowed office high above Olive Street in St. Louis and reading these letters and trying to help with the footnotes and any other information I could conjure up, I began to realize how little I had known my father during my youth and—much more important—to appreciate him. To me as a boy he was a rather remote figure totally immersed in the production of *The Survey of International Affairs* and devoting the best of his time to his *magnum opus A Study of History* (known to his family as the "Nonsense Book"). He was miserable about my eldest brother's death, distracted by Philip's outré behavior (which now with hindsight, and seen in perspective, seems quite understandable but was then to him quite exacerbating), and probably felt isolated from me as I had been swept away into the fold of the Catholic church by my mother in prep school days (i.e., in England under twelve). There was an enormous difference in age; and also my father's mind was essentially an intellectual critical one, whereas my own interests were already moving towards what is—for want of a better word—creativity. Even in maturity I felt a gulf between us, in that he saw pictures in an historical way rather than as things of value in themselves.

My parents were not, as they would say here in Yorkshire, "well suited." I as the youngest and, by her, most spoilt was inevitably drawn into my mother's ambit and not really allowed to see my father's qualities. She tended to belittle what he did—to make me feel that he was slightly ridiculous—which in practical matters indeed he could be. I deeply regret that I was in a way prevented from appreciating him sooner.

When he decided to retire to Yorkshire, and lived with us while he was waiting to move into the cottage which had been built and prepared for his retirement, I felt that we got much closer, but this was cut short by his stroke and lingering death.

The loving care and trouble shown in the collection and editing of these letters between two such good and charitable minds has been to me, as it must be to all who read them, a revelation.

At the end of the *Study of History* my father wrote a litany embracing all the Gods and religions of the civilized world. When I first read it I thought it stupid—now I understand, a little.

But it is really Catholicism and its attractions and repulsions which are the subject and continuous topic of this correspondence.

To read in a week a series of letters covering nearly forty years is not ideal, and I feel sad that Fr. Columba, whom I regard as a most dear and respected friend, is inevitably upset by my following in my father's footsteps, at least in rejecting the exclusive claims of any particular religion.

A very distinguished man, who perhaps should remain anonymous, suggested that this series of letters should really be called "the conversion of Father Columba." It is certainly true that his contributions over the years became more and more ecumenical (in the very best sense of the word) and less and less the liberal but nonetheless fundamentalist opinions of Ampleforth as I knew it as a boy. Of course his impressive faith has not altered at all, but his tolerance and understanding of other views has greatly expanded, and I cannot but feel that my father's influence is clearly there. His rational and sympathetic outlook was bound to find a response in a mind as appreciative, warm and charitable as Fr. Columba's.

Ganthorpe Hall
Autumn, 1984

CHRONOLOGY

	Arnold J. Toynbee	*Evelyn Columba Cary-Elwes*
1889	Born, 14 April.	
1890	Rosalind Murray born, 17 October.	
1902–7	Winchester.	
1903		Born, 6 November.
1907	Balliol College, Oxford. Loss of faith.	
1908	Harry Valpy Toynbee's illness commences.	
1910	Article on Herodotus in *Classical Review*.	
1912	Fellow of Balliol (1912–15).	
1911–12	*Wanderjahr* in Italy and Greece; British Archeological School, Athens.	
1913	"The Growth of Sparta" in *Journal of Hellenic Studies*. Marries Rosalind Murray.	
1913–14		Attends École St. Michel in Brussels; escapes before the German army arrives, August 1914.
1914	*Greek Policy since 1882* (Oxford pamphlet). Antony Robert Toynbee born.	
1914–22		Ampleforth College.
1915	Commences war work; assists Lord Bryce. *Armenian Atrocities.* *Nationality and the War.* *The New Europe.*	
1916	*The Destruction of Poland.* Theodore Philip Toynbee born.	
1917	*The German Terror in Belgium.* *The German Terror in France.* *The Murderous Tyranny of the Turks.*	
1918	Political Intelligence Department, Foreign Office.	
1919	Peace Conference in Paris: member, Foreign Office Section, British Delegation (December 1918–April 1919).	

	Arnold J. Toynbee	*Evelyn Columba Cary-Elwes*
1919	Koraes Professor of Byzantine and Modern Greek Language, Literature, and History. *The Place of Medieval and Modern Greece in History*: inaugural Koraes Lecture.	
1921	In Anatolia as special correspondent for the *Manchester Guardian*. *Alexander and Hellenism.*	
1922	Lawrence Leifchild Toynbee born. *The Western Question in Greece and Turkey.*	In French vineyards: Champagne, Cognac, Bordeaux, studying wines.
1923		Threadneedle St. Bank of New South Wales, City of London;
1924	The Koraes Chair resigned. *Greek Civilization and Character.* *Greek Historical Thought from Homer to the Age of Heraclius.*	Benedictine novice at Ampleforth; discovers the Rule of St. Benedict, the three Francises—Assisi, Xavier, de Sales—and Ste. Thérèse of Lisieux.
1925	*The World After the Peace Conference.* Director of Studies, Chatham House. *Survey of International Affairs, 1920–23* (introductory vol.).	Simple monastic vows.
1925–26		Studies philosophy, *The City of God*, Newman's *Essay on the Development of Christian Doctrine*.
1926	Rosalind's *The Happy Tree*. *Survey of International Affairs*, 1924.	
1927	*Survey of International Affairs*, 1925, vol. 1.	
1927–33		Undergraduate at St. Benet's Hall, Oxford (1927–30): B.A. and M.A. in modern languages (with honors); solemn monastic vows; discovers Blaise Pascal, San Juan de la Cruz.
1928	*The Conduct of British Empire Foreign Relations since the Peace Settlement.* *Survey of International Affairs, 1926.*	
1929	Trip to China and Japan: July 1929–January 1930; temptation resisted. *Survey of International Affairs, 1927, 1928.*	
1930	Return to belief in an ultimate reality. *Survey of International Affairs, 1929.*	A founder of the Quadragesimo Club at Oxford (with Henry John, S.J.).
1930–33		Theological studies at Blackfriars, Oxford, under Hugh Pope, O.P., Bede Jarrett, O.P., and Thomas Gilby, O.P.: the *Summa Theologica*.
1931	*A Journey to China*, an account of the 1929 trip. *Survey of International Affairs, 1930.*	
1932	*Britain and the Modern World Order.* *Survey of International Affairs, 1931.* Rosalind enters the Catholic Church.	Visit to Spain: Burgos, Cartuja de Miraflores; Monastery of Santo Domingo de Silos.

	Arnold J. Toynbee	*Evelyn Columba Cary-Elwes*
1933	*Survey of International Affairs, 1932.*	Ordained priest at Ampleforth; monastic librarian, until 1937; commences teaching at Ampleforth; French, Spanish, political philosophy, religion.
1934	*Survey of International Affairs, 1933.* *A Study of History*, vols. I–III.	
1935	2d ed. of *Study.* *Survey of International Affairs, 1934.* Lawrence enters Ampleforth.	In charge of Helmsley Parish until 1937.
1936	*Survey of International Affairs, 1935*, vols. 1, 2. A lecture by Hitler. *Amplexus exspecta.* C.C.E. and A.J.T. meet at Ampleforth.	Visits Abbé Joseph (Cardinal) Cardijn, founder of Jocistes, in Brussels.
1937	*Survey of International Affairs, 1936.*	House master (St. Wilfrid's), until 1951. Second visit to Spain, during the civil war: Burgos, Salas de los Infantes, again visits Monastery of Santo Domingo de Silos.
1938	*Survey of International Affairs, 1937*, vols. 1, 2. 5 August, "Statement" to C.C.E.	
1939	A Study of History, vols. IV–VI. Rosalind's *The Good Pagan's Failure*. Director, Foreign Research and Press Service, R.I.I.A. (1939–43). Return to Oxford and Balliol. Antony dies. Sarah Edith Toynbee dies.	Stays with the Toynbees at Oxford.
1940	"Christianity and Civilization," the Burge Memorial Lecture at the Sheldonian Theatre, 23 May.	
1941	*Survey of International Affairs, 1938*, vol. 1. Harry Valpy Toynbee dies.	
1942	Trip to United States by *Clipper*; November, parting from Rosalind.	
1943	Director, Research Department, Foreign Office (1943–46). A.J.T. returns to London; the three years of the pending divorce commence.	*The Beginning of Goodness.*
1944	Sylvia Payne consulted.	
1945	Interruption of letters between A.J.T. and C.C.E.	
1946	Civil divorce became final, 13 August; annulment (in Westminster Chancery), 13 December. Marries Veronica Boulter. Resumption of letters to C.C.E. *Abridgement* of vols. I–VI of *A Study of History*. Member, British delegation to Peace Conference in Paris.	

	Arnold J. Toynbee	*Evelyn Columba Cary-Elwes*
1947	Lectures at Harvard, Montreal, Princeton, Bryn Mawr, and Union Theological Seminary.	Charles Cary-Elwes dies.
1948	*Civilization on Trial.* 10 June, awarded Doctor of Letters (*honoris causa*) at Cambridge by Jan Smuts, as chancellor.	
1949		Comprehensive critique of manuscript of *A Study of History*, Part VII: *Universal Churches*. *The Times* correspondence: "Catholicism Today."
1950	Preface to C.C.E.'s *Law, Liberty and Love*	Ecumenical Meeting at Grottaferrata. *Law, Liberty and Love.*
1951	*Survey of International Affairs, 1938*, vol. 2; introduction by A.J.T. Visit to Spain; Madrid lecture, 25 October.	Prior of Ampleforth, until 1955; ecumenical meeting in Switzerland.
1952	"The World and the West"—Reith Lectures Broadcasts. *Survey of International Affairs, 1939–1946: The World in March 1939* (with F. T. Ashton-Gwatkin).	*Ampleforth and Its Origins.*
1953	The European Round Table Discussion in Rome, in October; the *sacro speco.* *Recovering Europe's Sovereignty*—written on A.J.T.'s return. *Survey of International Affairs, 1938*, vol. 3, ed. by Veronica.	Ecumenical pilgrimage to Rome.
1954	*The Counsels of Hope*—Toynbee-Jerrold controversy. *Survey of International Affairs, 1939–1946: Hitler's Europe,* ed. by A.J.T. and Veronica. *A Study of History*, vols. VII–X.	
1955	Albany, New York speech: "Man at Work in God's World in the Light of History"; *Survey of International Affairs, 1939–1946: The Realignment of Europe*, ed. by A.J.T. and Veronica; introduction by A.J.T. Retires as Director of Studies, Chatham House.	Assists in the foundation of the St. Louis Priory and School; prior until 1967.
1956	*An Historian's Approach to Religion.* *Survey of International Affairs, 1939–1946: The War and the Neutrals*, ed. by A.J.T. and Veronica. Awarded the C.H. Journey round the World (20 February 1956–3 August 1957).	*The Sheepfold and the Shepherd.*

	Arnold J. Toynbee	*Evelyn Columba Cary-Elwes*
1957	*Christianity among the Religions of the World.* Gilbert Murray dies. Abridgement of vols. VII–X of *A Study of History*.	*China and the Cross.*
1958	*East to West.* *Survey of International Affairs, 1939–1946: The Eve of War, 1939*, ed. by A.J.T. and Veronica; A.J.T. wrote the introduction. *Survey of International Affairs, 1939–1946: The Initial Triumph of the Axis*, ed. by A.J.T. and Veronica; several parts by A.J.T. First visit to the St. Louis Priory.	
1959	*Hellenism.* *A Study of History*, vol. XI.	
1960	*Civilization on Trial.* Tour of India, Pakistan, and Afghanistan. *One World and India.* *A Study of History: Abridgement*; complete in 1 vol.	
1961	*Between Oxus and Jumna.* Second visit to the St. Louis Priory.	Edythe Isabel Cary-Elwes dies.
1962	*America and the World Revolution* (University of Pennsylvania addresses).	
1963	*Comparing Notes*—with Philip. Third visit to the St. Louis Priory.	
1964	*Janus at Seventy-five.* African tour.	
1965	*Between Niger and Nile.* *Hannibal's Legacy.*	
1966	*Change and Habit.* Tour of South America.	Lectures at St. John's Abbey, Collegeville.
1967	*Acquaintances.* *Between Maule and Amazon.* *Cities of Destiny.* Rosalind dies. Third trip to Japan.	Return to Ampleforth. *Monastic Renewal.*
1968	*Man's Concern with Death.* The *éloge* at the Institut de France.	
1968–70		In Uganda, Kenya, Tanzania: conferences with missionaries in Kampala and Nairobi; the Masai Missions, Peramiho, South Tanzania; at Pan-African Bishops' Conference; visit of Paul VI. Works at keeping the major seminary near Nairobi afloat—1969–70.

	Arnold J. Toynbee	*Evelyn Columba Cary-Elwes*
1969	*The Crucible of Christianity: Judaism, Hellenism and the Historical Background to the Christian Faith*, ed. with contributions. *Experiences.* *Some Problems of Greek History.*	
1970	*Cities on the Move.*	Return to Ampleforth. Visit to Saint Louis Priory.
1971	*Surviving the Future.* *An Ekistical Study of the Hellenic City-State.*	
1972	*A Study of Toynbee*: The Oxford University Press and National Book League Exhibition. *A Study of History* (rev. and abridged).	
1973	*Constantine Porphyrogenitus and His World.*	Return to Africa (West); Bamenda, Cameroon; assists in the foundation of the major seminary.
1974	*Toynbee on Toynbee* (with G. R. Urban). The *Ad Portas* address at Winchester. Stroke, 2–3 August.	Nsukka, Nigeria: assists in the foundation of the Monastery at Eke, near Enugu.
1975	C.C.E.'s last visit, 18 September. Death, 22 October. Memorial services at St. James's, Piccadilly.	Visit to England. Return to Eke, near Enugu, Nigeria; conferences to theologians at Bigard Major Seminary, Enugu, 1975–77.
1976	*Mankind and Mother Earth*; *Choose Life*; the Toynbee-Ikeda dialogue.	
1977		Assists transfer of Eke monastery to Ewu, near Benin City.
1978		Retreats in Australia; return to Ampleforth.
1979–80		Visitation of Benedictine Monastery in Manila; lectures, conferences in Australia.
1980	Veronica dies.	
1981	*The Greeks and Their Heritages.*	First visit to India; speaks at Hindu, Muslim, and Christian conferences on prayer at Asirvanam Monastery, Bangalore.
1983		Second visit to India; gives series of conferences at Asirvanam; visits Bede Griffiths at his Christian Ashram, Shantivanam.

O N E

PROLEGOMENA

1910–19

First visit to Castle Howard; the courting of Rosalind Murray; Tony and Philip as children; World War I begins; the Peace Conference; postwar depression; doubts about the Koraes Chair.

Saturday 10.55 [March, 1910] Balliol

Dear Darbishire,[1]

I am afraid you won't get this by Sunday. I have been having three days of upsets: I was going in for the Jenks, and my Mother[2] was coming to Oxford, and then I was not going in because she was coming, and she was not coming because I was going in. Finally, she is here and I am doing the Jenks, and here are some minutes before bedtime to write to you in. The Jenks lasts 24 hours, and contains three comps, which are anathema, and one ancient history paper, for whose sake I endure them. Most excellent Fluffy:[3] I made cautious enquiries, and discovered that our prey means to go to Whitby, I think it was, next vac. He talked about Italy, and said he must try and get there cheaply before schools. If he has certain moneys of his own therefore to expend, he had better lump them with the "prize" and really achieve Italy. But nothing can be done till the prize is actually won and awarded.

A.L.[4] went off to the States a few days ago—about two months of lecturing, in the fashion of H.A.L. Fisher,[5] and I am going off to-day week with Gilbert Murray[6] to Castle Howard,[7] a fenced city of his parents-in-law, somewhere in Yorkshire. I wonder if Lady Carlysle (is it so spelt?) will be in residence,—like Lady Mary,[8] I am told, plus temperance, raised to the tenth power. It will be very amusing and delightful.

Have you had such glorious weather as this? I walked with my Mother to Godstow this morning, and there was not a cloud, and Port Meadow was covered in a silvery mist, and the floods half out, and centre-boards sailing on the river (I was in one yesterday: they are superb)—it is simply wonderful Spring all at once.

I sympathise about the Comedy: I lost my one chance of seeing Coquelin[9] in *Cyrano de Bergerac*, because I could not bestir myself to seek out a theatre somewhere the other side of London—and then the poor man went and died within a few months, just to teach me what an ass I had been. The similes are painfully realistic.

"The Relation of Art to Truth;" do that—I had to write three hours of it yesterday afternoon, and it gave me a headache.

Yours v. sincerely,
Arnold J. Toynbee[10]

1. Robert Shelby Darbishire (1886–1949); son of Godfrey Darbishire, an English civil engineer who came to America and married Anne Shelby, a member of a well-known Kentucky family. Robert Darbishire attended Rugby and Balliol College; returned to Kentucky in 1910; later taught at Athens College in Greece; he was one of A.J.T.'s closest friends at Oxford; cf. A.J.T.'s *Experiences* (London, 1969), pp. 24–25, 33, "my fellow Balliol man and life-long friend Rob Darbishire."

2. Sarah Edith Toynbee (1859–1939); daughter of Isaac Edwin Marshall (1814–64), a manufacturer of railway carriages in Birmingham; entering Newnham Hall (later College), Cambridge, in 1876 (at the age of seventeen), she read for the Cambridge Historical Tripos and was placed in the first class in 1879; for several years before her marriage in 1887, a history mistress at the Tottenham High School for girls; *True Stories from Scottish History* (London, 1896); *Men and Movements in British History* (London, 1904). Her daughter, Margaret Toynbee (letter of June, 1984 to C.B.P.), recalls: "I am sure that Arnold owed his early interest in history to my mother. She made the past come alive for children, and I can never remember a time when I was not wrapped up in it!"

3. Henry William Carless Davis (1874–1928); historian, Fellow and History Tutor at Balliol (1902–21); Professor of Modern History, Manchester University (1921–25); Regius Professor of Modern History, Oxford, 1925–28).

4. Arthur Lionel Smith (1850–1924); Balliol College; Jowett Fellow, tutor, dean, and, finally, Master of Balliol College (1916–24); *Church and State in the Middle Ages* (Oxford, 1913).

5. Herbert Albert Laurens Fisher (1865–1940); historian and politician, warden of New College, Oxford (1925–40); *A History of Europe*, 3 vols. (London, 1935).

6. George Gilbert Aimé Murray (1866–1957); then Regius Professor of Greek at Oxford; *Euripides and His Age* (London, 1913); *Five Stages of Greek Religion* (Oxford, 1925); a founder of the League of Nations Union; president (1947–49) of the United Nations Association; cf. Francis West, *Gilbert Murray: A Life* (London, 1984).

7. Castle Howard, the home of Rosalind Murray's maternal grandparents, George James Howard, the ninth Earl of Carlisle (1843–1911), and Lady Carlisle (Rosalind Frances Stanley, daughter of the second Baron Stanley of Alderley) (1845–1921). Work on Castle Howard was commenced in 1700 and continued intermittently over a long period, during which alterations were made to the original concept of Sir John Vanbrugh (who was assisted by Nicholas Hawksmoor); the west wing was designed by Sir Thomas Robinson, an amateur architect and member of the Howard family; cf. Nikolaus Pevsner, *Yorkshire: The North Riding* (London, 1966), pp. 106–18. Castle Howard appears as the seat of the Marchmains in the Granada production *Brideshead Revisited*.

8. Lady Mary Henrietta Howard (1865–1956), the eldest daughter of the ninth Earl of Carlisle, wife of Gilbert Murray.

9. Benoît-Constant Coquelin (1841–1909); created the part of Cyrano in Rostand's play in the Théâtre de la Porte-Saint-Martin; A.J.T. was an undergraduate at Balliol in 1909.

10. This letter and the following one were not dated by year. All available evidence points to 1910.

Castle Howard
York

12 March [1910]

Dear Darbishire,

So many thanks for your invitation, but now I am here I find I am miles away from Manchester—only about forty miles from the East Coast, so I am afraid I ought not to come back round by you.

It is a great and marvellous place, early 18th century style on the vast scale, with pictures and lakes and statues and libraries and all manner of things.

Lady Carlysle is obviously a mighty force, but not, perhaps, so formidable. Would though that I was less entirely at sea about politics[1]—domestic matters, I mean, for I only read the foreign sheet of the *Times*, while police-courts, cabinet crises, football leagues, and such "own dirty linen" I eschew. However, I shall doubtless know plenty about home politics before I go away. Do you like Canalettos? They cover all the walls in the room where we eat—I won't call it the dining room, for there are at least twenty like it. There are also Wattses,[2] and crowds of nice solid books of the eighty years ago kind.

Altogether, it is more peaceful, and less of a "fearful" joy than I expected.

How noble of you to do Truth and Art for me; but really you would not have liked it if you had had it set down before you to work three hours in the sleepiest part of the day. One always envies the toils of other people.

What good Sunshine. I thought Yorkshire would be frozen at this time of year, and certainly it grew colder and colder in the train yesterday. But the Sun makes up for all.

I will tell you more of the happenings here before I go away—which is, I believe, on Friday.

Yours v. sincerely,
Arnold J. Toynbee

1. Lady Carlisle was intensely interested in social causes; cf. West, *Gilbert Murray: A Life*, pp. 25–27.

2. George Frederick Watts (1817–1904), a popular Victorian painter of allegories and portraits.

9 March 1913 Balliol

Dear Rob,

The spirit very much moves me to talk to you, and having finished my collections, and totted up all the marks, and notified that I will give them back tomorrow morning, I am free. I did collections solidly yesterday (24 papers altogether, which take longer than you would expect) with intervals of seeing people: three men to lunch, for instance, which makes 30 this term: then I had tea at St. Hugh's to arrange work with my first woman pupil in Roman history: and then I dined with the Murrays and there was Rosalind Murray,[1] and since that the inner parts of me have been whirling round and round somewhere at the back of the parts that have been correcting these foolish collections, and I am moved to write to you because I want to talk, and certainly can't bend myself to Aeneas Poliorceticus.[2] I object to being run away with by myself, and not to be able to do the job I want to at the moment. I have only seen Rosalind Murray three times since the June before last: namely, 2½ hours last night, 2½ hours one Sunday night last term, and about 2½ seconds in the distance at a meeting the other day (which suffragist meeting I undertook, on that chance, to attend as a steward or chucker-out, in case of a row—but there was not any: only about 25 males to 250 females, and said males all obviously converted already: they made one commit oneself by presenting a great bunch of colours and a safety pin). Last June I worked a canoe with her for a day up the Cherwell. What is the use of five hours in a year and a half? All the same, I think I know her fairly well—pick up where I left off: but I want more. I am always being crossed. Whenever they have asked me to stay with them, I have always been in bed, or abroad, or obviously needed by my Mother. I was almost tempted to falling the other day, but when my Mother has just moved into this new house at Southwold, it is up to me to go and keep her company. But I might have gone three weeks to Italy with them. It is simply damnable to do one's proper job, and then feel sulky about it inside. But these stingy hours are no use: you want to live with people for a time, in order to get further with them. Better luck in the summer perhaps. It is exasperating not to know what is in the other person's mind, or rather, to know their mind more or less, except just so much of it as concerns you; it is 5 to 1 they think just nothing of you at all: but if only you knew. But you can't do that without really seeing something of them. How monstrous it is, to stalk about this quad being gnawed at inside, while the person you want to be stalking about with is just 15 minutes off: and then not to be able just to go and say: "Come and stalk with me": moreover she is only in Oxford a few days at a time—otherwise in London, or with a brother up at Barrow.

Meanwhile back to the books, and write a great history, and get made a professor, and gain moneys (I have ensured my life anyway, which is so much to the good): and meanwhile see her when you can: that probably won't be for three months now: meanwhile work, and don't gnaw yourself like a fool. I am going to adjourn, because I seem to be writing to myself instead of you, Rob.

However, meanwhile I have had lunch in Hertford and paid three calls, and been to chapel, and talked ¾ hours of College business, and stoked people up with port, and been to an organ recital in New College Chapel—that ante-chapel is the best thing in Oxford, after their cloisters. Stapledon[3] was up the other day, and an elder brother of Reginald Sharpe,[4] for degrees—but they never let people know beforehand, and I did not see them.

I have acquired a woman pupil, which will bring me moneys and be an interesting job too: I want to see if it is all a lie that the ordinary run of them work like automatons: I am expecting the "words of wisdom" as Ashby would call them, to be taken down in shorthand almost before they are out of my mouth. I have written a great work on the Spartan army, which Guy Dickins[5] is at present examining: I am still running after all knowledge, and buying books faster than I can read them: it is like taking a second helping before you have finished your first; but you know you have half secured it, anyhow, and fancy it is half inside you.

I wonder when I am going to see you again: I have been wondering if the sick sheep are triumphantly cured—it would be as fine as the doctors in the Adrianople trenches.[6] Yannina has fallen, hurrah, since I wrote last: isn't it one up for the poor old Dagoes? The other people have had a grim time at Scutari, and if Austria stops them getting it, it will be a most damnable business. Mrs. Atchley nearly came up here last week, by the way, but the elder daughter was not well. They are apparently going back to Athens in the Summer. I suppose the young one stays here. I should like to be talking to you, but I have drenched you with fair bucketsful of slops as it is, though it is only the written word. I am going to know all about the Roman Empire down to Diocletian, before I come back here. But life is not in books, and what on earth one would do if one were left staring face to face with them, and all the living people gone, I don't know. But they are one's job—sort of energy-machines. Have you ever read Reid's[7] "It is never too late to mend"? Well, goodnight, and write again soon, even though I have been in arrears lately.

Affectionately,
Arnold J. Toynbee

Address till April 14th Kingsthorpe
Reydon
Southwold
Suffolk

1. Rosalind Murray (1890–1967).

2. Aeneas Poliorceticus: Aeneas Tacticus of Stymphalus, general of the Arcadian Confederacy in 367 B.C., wrote military treatises, one on the defense of fortified positions, hence the name "Poliorceticus" (siege-wise).

3. William Olaf Stapledon (1886–1950); Balliol College, Oxford; received his M.A. in 1913; extramural lecturer in psychology and philosophy, Liverpool University; *A Modern Theory of Ethics* (London, 1929).

4. Reginald Lawford Sharpe (1886–1959); solicitor in Bombay (1919–48). His elder brother, William Seaford Sharpe (1879–1956), Balliol College; received his M.A. in 1913; served in World War I in Malta, Egypt, Lemnos, and Gallipoli; returned to career as solicitor.

5. Guy Dickins (1881–1916); fellow of St. John's College, Oxford (1909–16); *Hellenistic Sculpture* (Oxford, 1920).

6. In the First Balkan War between Bulgaria, Serbia, and Greece, on the one hand, and Turkey, on the other (1912–13), the Greeks took Janina on 5 March 1913; the Bulgarians took Adrianople on 26 March; and on 22 April the Montenegrins took Scutari but gave it up under Austrian threats.

7. Thomas Mayne Reid (1818–83); a favorite author of A.J.T.'s youth; cf. A.J.T.'s letter of 19 April 1947, below.

13 June 1913 Balliol

Dearest Rob,

No, I have not written to you for a month, or rather ten years: meanwhile, she loves me and is going to marry me. I saw her several times at Howard the beginning of this term, more often than I had seen her at all since I came back and I just could not stick it any longer. One Wednesday, it must have been four Wednesdays ago, I knew suddenly that at 5:15 next day I was going to go to her Father and Mother and clear it up. I thought she was tuberculous; she is not. I also thought my Father's[1] breakdown might affect me. It does not! I went to see his doctor about that the next week, on the Thursday: Rob, that is the grimmest thing I have ever had to do, and I hope I shall never have anything like it again: you see, they trusted me absolutely to find out the truth from him (they only went to see him themselves, *after* she had found she wanted to marry me): so it was not merely that one had to hold oneself from pleading one's own cause, but I had to be on the lookout all the time to be sure he was not hedging, or in the least uncertain. I was sure, though (he is a very jolly, straight forward man with a smile, and that helped). Only he said I must never overwork, or even do extra work, as my father's case did show I had a tendency to nerve-exhaustion, though it is not a mechanically hereditary thing: it depends entirely on myself—on whether I play the fool or not. I thought that dished me. I had meant to make the extra money by extra work: you see, my Mother and sisters are a first charge on me, and I am in my Father's place towards them. This just stopped that: it was in the morning: I had been going on to talk to her that afternoon, (I had told her the Sunday before, that I should be in London on business that day, and would come to talk with her if the business allowed: the business was the doctor, of course: it was awfully hard to get that out in a casual sort of voice: I think I almost funked it): then I wandered about the Parks of that town trying to make myself go back first to see her people and tell them the doctor's opinion did dish me after all, though it was on the money and not the health question. I was hideously tempted to speculate on my energy and power of solid horse power work, knowing I was now free from that horrible hereditary shadow. It was quite childish. But about lunch time I arrived at the Admiralty, and made a man there called Gleadowe[2] come out and have lunch with me, and I talked it out with him (or at him) and that screwed me to the point of telegraphing to put her off and coming back here by the next train. Then they told me that the extra work did not matter, because she had moneys, and that I might go ahead: I had not thought much about moneys before, because the health question loomed before everything. So the next morning I went up again to see her (she lives in a flat near Baker Street): I went straight out as if I were wound up by clockwork and said just what I wanted to say. She was absolutely taken by surprise and could hardly speak a word. I had not expected that: I had thought she would be calm and very kind, and that I should go to pieces, unless she saved me from that by dealing very kindly with me. But it was like knocking her down. I have told you before that I have kept this absolutely to myself during these three years. I had not somehow reckoned on moving her. I just went away thinking that would help her most: it lasted three minutes. I came straight back to Oxford: that was three weeks ago today. Then I waited. Luckily I had just taken a share in a canoe on New College ground. On Sunday afternoon came a letter from her Mother, saying there was no hope: on Monday morning a letter from herself: but I had got over the worst by then: first of all one can do nothing but look back, and that is terrible pain: it is folly, but one can't help it. I walked round New College Cloisters that evening: the shadows of the open-work in the windows are wonderful on the grass, when the sun begins to get low, and it is a real Summer evening. I got to sleep all through, because I was very tired, but waking up early was terrible, on that Monday morning especially: one is not quite master of oneself at those weak hours before dawn, and pain has its way with one. The rest of Monday I was dead: I could not look forward or backward: I just toiled on as many pupils as I could, and waited for the time to pass. I thought it might last months: but when I got out of bed on Tuesday morning, I suddenly looked ahead and saw I could not live in College for ever like Sligger[3] (or not like him, for the fellowship you have with undergraduates seems to give him the equivalent of what then I had lost). So I determined I would become thorough master of this job, get made junior dean, become a trained teacher, and get a grip of history, so as to have a real trade, and then do work like my Father's or something where human life and sorrow comes in. I wrote to Zimmern[4] and told him he must help me get a footing in some such work within the next half-dozen years, it was curious: I myself was altogether looking backwards, but I saw that as long as you were actually alive you could always build up work ahead of you, which would keep your forces in working order even if your life faced the other way. I had to begin from the very foundations; you see, on Monday my work went absolutely. I saw it was not the centre of my life, nor ever could be (I mean, History): that discovery alone was perhaps worth that week. The rest of the week I spent in that canoe, and took care never to be alone. Nobody in Balliol suspected there was anything amiss with me. I asked my Mother to come the next week, and she arranged to: I knew by then that I could hold out till she came, and that after that I should be on my feet again: I was going to do things instead of learning things. Then on the Saturday (the Saturday before last) there was a note from her Mother saying she wanted to see me again. My mind was so turned the other way (for I knew that if my mind allowed itself to hope for a change, I should do nothing else all my life but go on hoping) that I did not realise what that meant. I came to their house that evening: then she just came into the room and said she had changed her mind. She had gone back to her flat in London that week, and on Friday her mind had come clear; she had had as bad a week as I. At first we neither of us knew where we were: we knew it was real, but we could not take it in. Now we have, and it is real and solid and absolutely good. I am not the same man who wrote to you last. I lost her first and then found her, and those two changes have made me a different person: this is beginning again, only I am looking forward now as I never have done before.

The College have been delightful. I expected a grim fight with them like fighting dogs in Greece, but they suddenly seemed full of affection and good-will, and they have made no obstacles at all:[5] not a trace of grumpiness, though I am making myself an awful nuisance to them. And everyone else is the same. This added love and kindness on top of the wonderful thing itself is almost overwhelming.

She has been spending the middle parts of the weeks alone in her flat again, in order to recover her breath: she is coming down again this evening. My dear Rob, there is nothing more to write for you can't put feelings into words, not unless one is a poet, like you: it is as horrid as not being able to draw outlines of Greek mountains when you see them and suddenly want to: but there it is: so you must just do the imagining of it yourself.

You shall now hear from me at the normal intervals, nor, Rob, will you hear less or be more distant from me. And as soon as possible you must know her: we must come to Kentucky or you hither.

Your affectionate, as always,
Arnold J. Toynbee

She was 22 last October, I 24 in April, so we are the right sort of age.[6]

1. Harry Valpy Toynbee (1861–1941), from 1881 to 1908 he had been a social worker in the Charity Organisation Society; cf. A.J.T.'s *Experiences*, pp. 297–300.

2. Reginald Morier Yorke Gleadowe, (1888–1944); New College, Oxford; master, Winchester College; Slade Professor of Fine Arts, Oxford (1928–33); head of Honours and Awards Branch, Admiralty; designer of the *Stalingrad Sword*, given by King George VI to the people of Stalingrad, and presented by Winston Churchill to Marshall Stalin at the Teheran Conference on 29 November 1943: "When . . . I handed the splendid weapon to Marshall Stalin, he raised it in a most impressive gesture to his lips and kissed the blade. He then handed it to Voroshilov, who dropped it" (W. S. Churchill, *Closing the Ring* [Boston, 1951], pp. 363–64).

3. Francis Fortesque Urquhart (1868–1933); dean of Balliol (1916–33); articles in *The Catholic Encyclopoedia* (New York, 1907–13); chairman of the board of the faculty of modern history (1927–29); cf. Christopher Hollis, *Oxford in the Twenties* (London, 1976): "The Catholic Dean of Balliol (he was known as Sligger, he once told me, because in his youth he was supposed to be very sleek, and the sligger was a corruption of the sleeker.) . . . a man of many virtues and much piety" (p. 12).

4. Sir Alfred E. Zimmern (1879–1957); then ancient history tutor at New College; A.J.T. attended his lectures in 1909; his *The Greek Commonwealth* (London, 1911) "has a quality that I also find in my Uncle Arnold's *The Industrial Revolution*, and, on a much grander scale, of course, in Gibbon's *The History of the Decline and Fall*" (A.J.T.'s *Acquaintances* [London, 1967], pp. 55, 49–61 *passim*).

5. In *Acquaintances*, A.J.T. recalls that, "till at least half way through the nineteenth century, one of the conditions for holding an Oxford college fellowship had been celibacy" (p. 27).

6. The marriage was performed in a registry office. This raised an issue that later appears more significant: On 23 August 1913 Rosalind wrote A.J.T.: ". . . Grandmother [Lady Carlisle] suddenly wrote suggesting that we should be married in Castle Howard chapel . . . she was evidently very much worked up and excited at the plan, but we have said it was too late to change again—that was right, wasn't it? And what would your mother have thought if we had changed back to church again, just because Grandmother suggested it? She has written me *such* a nice letter, and says that she would much rather we kept to the Registry if we feel it most truthful"; and on 27 August 1913, Rosalind wrote: ". . . your Mother has written that she would rather not bring Jocelyn and Margaret—Dad has asked her to reconsider it, and

explained that there will really be nothing to shock them in the Registry, but I suppose she can't change her mind . . . it looks as if she would have preferred the Castle Howard wedding after all . . . I can't understand its mattering so much either way . . ."

5 Sept. 1914 10 Holland Park W.

[We are here because our Oxford doctor volunteered, and has gone out to Belgium in men's kit to give anaesthetics].

Dearest Rob,

This at last in answer to many of yours. First the good. Antony Harry (my father) Robert (yourself)[1] was born on Sept. 2, 10:30 P.M. after only five hours labour, which is amazing considering the vastness of his skull and the fact that he is a first child: she is doing splendidly: so gloriously happy and proud of him (for he is very big and strong and placid: weighed 8 lbs.—one above the average—and knows how to suck without being taught. It is a glorious mystery how we have produced such a little sturdy between us.) Seeing them together, she lying at peace (the war forgotten) gazing at him, and he asleep with lots of movements going across his face, and his little hands clutching and waggling—the hands are the best of his many beauties—it's just the thing that makes life utterly worth living even in this great darkness that has settled over us here—I wonder if the fringe of it is falling upon you: Kentucky and all America seem such a wise happy place to us here: but it is the "joy that a new man is born into the world"—which he will jolly well have to take as he finds it and leave better than he found it. All is peace and beauty inside this house, and I am longing for you to look in and share it: I am sure it is like dipping into the waters of life: I wish I could show you what it is like, but I can't do it by words. Meanwhile, there is the war. Firstly, I am convinced that our Government had to do it: tell me if the "White Paper" they have published is circulating in America. It is simply the diplomatic documents bearing on the crisis printed in chronological order without comment, ending with our ultimatum. If it is true, it is to my mind absolutely convincing: and I cannot believe those documents are false (I am pretty clear there are no omissions either: there is a perfect sequence). If that is not being read in America, get hold of it, and make other people read it too: we can't put our point of view better. Meanwhile, we are going in for this war with all our might: there has been no excitement even, let alone Jingoism: travelling by train during mobilisation was wonderful (I had to take Rosalind from York to Oxford, and started with trepidation). People are contemplating a very long war: we hope it won't be, but we shall go right through with it to the. . . .[2]

1. Antony Harry Robert Toynbee (1914–39).

2. Dysentery, contracted in his walking tour through Greece in 1912, incapacitated A.J.T. for military service; A.J.T.'s *A Study of History*, 12 vols. (London, 1934–61), X:236–37; during the war he worked for the Government, chiefly on Turkish affairs, and wrote a number of ad hoc works: *The Treatment of Armenians in the Ottoman Empire, 1915–1916* (London, 1916); *Turkey: A Past and a Future* (London, 1917); and see works listed in the Chronology, above.

Boothby House
Brampton, Cumberland

21 July 1919

Dear Rob,

Your letters are good, and the one I got this morning bucked me up to write—which is also good, for I am in a tepid state, in which doing anything is an effort, and income tax forms, passbooks and railway time-tables a torment. One must simply wait till it wears off, and Rosalind is in the same case, as a result of babies and maids and housekeeping under war conditions. The babies, though, are full of beans and busy with battleships, trains and God: I saw Philip[1] the other day rolling along a roll of wire rabbit-netting and chanting: "I am being God rolling the night away." What fun, you will be able to see them now, if Armenian relief trundles you across the Atlantic—Tony speculative and wrapped up in his own ploys, and Philip matter-of-fact and sociable: they are good friends, in spite of being opposites, or perhaps because of it, as they have not each got the same corners to rub off against the other. It is almost incredible that in these years that have gone like clockwork standardised, Tony has lived through most of that part of one's life which seems as long as all the rest put together—in fact, infinite.

Well, yes, I am depressed: partly because when the pressure of the war is taken off one goes flying all over the place, every part of one spinning a different way. Partly because one is disappointed pretty badly at the Conference.[2] Partly—which is really the same thing—that one had made believe during the war that one was building something up, and not merely assisting at a catastrophe, and now it has all fallen flat, and one sees the war for what it is—pure destruction. One had the pathetic delusion that because it wasn't one's fault one ought to be able to make some good come of it.

My particular mania is dislike of the professorship[3]—I feel uprooted and bewildered; I can't turn back from my war-plough, and everything is in such flux that I had to take the professorship without knowing whether the other would come to anything permanent or not. If it did, I suppose the professorship could be abandoned, or I might find it was what I wanted after all! Anyway, I am in a loathsomely neurasthenic and self-concerned condition. All the same, this Eastern business is there to do; do you realise that the whole Moslem problem is now virtually on the back of the British Empire, with appalling possibilities if we don't balance it right? We had our peace—bonfires last Saturday, but we are only at Act III about—no further. Islam and Tropical Africa and Labour—all the great international forces that the President has failed to sweep into the League of Nations net—blind, mass-forces like winged-bulls, which will stampede and trample things to bits if we don't admit their right to live. But I am not going on talking about politics.

I have been reading lots of miscellaneous history—chiefly medieval or agrarian; also lots of Plato; also Herodotus: like going into a grocer's and devouring tongues and cheeses and soap at sight. Well I *am* glad the Relief Committee are really on the way to bringing you across[4]—Give me early news of your starting. It will be so good to see you because we haven't seen each other since the war, and it will make the war drop out between. In hopeful moments I wonder if the war isn't negative, just like St. Augustine's Evil—just a blank or absence of normal life, which will vanish if one happens to have come through to the other side.

I agree about humility. The Quakers are really right, and Tolstoy: in fact Christianity: it is ultimate truth, but also, of course, it is the last ditch.

Affectionately,
Arnold

1. Theodore Philip Toynbee (1916–81).

2. The Inter-Allied and Associated Powers held their first plenary session in Paris on 18 January 1919; the draft treaty was handed to the German delegates 7 May 1919. A.J.T. had attended from December 1918 to April 1919 as a member of the Foreign Office section of the British delegation; here he became acquainted with T. E. Lawrence; cf. *Acquaintances*, pp. 178–97.

3. The Koraes Chair of Byzantine and Modern Greek Language, Literature, and History, University of London; A.J.T. held this chair from 1919 to 1924. In 1921 he visited the scene of the Graeco-Turkish War (1919–22) as the *Manchester Guardian*'s correspondent and reported Greek atrocities in his *The Western Question in Greece and Turkey* (London, 1922); as a consequence, he resigned the chair. This crisis led to his new career at Chatham House.

4. Darbishire went to Constantinople in 1919 to work in Near East relief.

TWO

1937–39

Columba Cary-Elwes, O.S.B., then thirty-three, and Arnold J. Toynbee, forty-seven, have met at Ampleforth, where Lawrence, A.J.T.'s youngest son, is a student; the letters commence and increase in ease as the friendship grows; A.J.T.'s pivotal statement of his religious position; Tony's death: "from now on, I should be dealing about Tony with God"; Rosalind's Good Pagan's Failure; *the civil war in Spain; the coming world war; A.J.T. goes to Oxford to direct intelligence services; the first air raids; a Catholic country house.*

Ampleforth Abbey
York

27 January 1937

Dear Professor Toynbee,

Thank you very much for your most generous gift to the library. Really, to be quite continental in my expression, your presence here was gift enough.

I wonder whether you have heard of or seen Mr. Eppstein's book *The Catholic Tradition of the Law of Nations*.[1] It contains things that interested me very much, especially Vitoria's[2] teaching on colonization. I enclose a copy of *The Christian Democrat*[3] which quotes from it. If it seems interesting from those quotations, perhaps you would like to borrow our copy some time.

Your talk on the wireless was first-rate. There are saints living now. I think I met one in Belgium in the summer.[4] One died in Canada the other day, one of your beloved "Canadiens",[5] (see Le Figaro Jan. 26th).

I remember you and your family, for the present, daily in my Mass. The reason is manifold, but I think we see things in the same light, though, I, an ignoramus, dare say so, and therefore wish you well in every way.

Yours sincerely,
Columba Cary-Elwes, O.S.B.

P.S. No answer expected.

1. John C. N. Eppstein, *The Catholic Tradition of the Law of Nations* (London, 1935).

2. Francisco de Vitoria, O.P. (ca. 1485–1546), humanist and theologian of Salamanca; author of *De los Indios (de Indis)*, concerned with the moral issues involved in the Spanish colonization of America; before Grotius, a founder of modern international law; *Relecciones teológicas*, a modern critical edition (Madrid, 1960).

3. A monthly paper published by the Catholic Social Guild at Oxford.

4. Abbé Joseph (later Cardinal) Cardijn (1882–1967); before World War I founded the association of factory workers in Brussels known as the Jeunesse Ouvrière Chrétienne. "He gave me three hours of his time." (C.C.E.)

5. "A.J.T. had deep appreciation of the powerful influence the cultural integrity of the French Canadians would exert on the continent." (C.C.E.)

3, Melina Place
St. John's Wood, N.W.8

31 January 1937

Dear Father Columba,

Thank you very much for your letter of the 27th and particularly for the last paragraph. Your remembering us in your Mass gives me great happiness, for I can most sincerely say for myself—as well as for my wife and for Lawrence,[1] about whom you would be able to take it for granted—that I do see things in the same light as you do, and though this is not at present possible to say about Philip[2] and Tony,[3] that only means that they have perhaps even more to gain from your remembrances than the rest of us.

I am so glad you thought my talk was all right. I have been amused, since, at being asked by several people, in most genuine surprise, what I meant by talking about saints in modern France and Italy (the assumption obviously being that for saints, like monks, the verb must be in the past tense only, and not in the present or the future). But from my own experience till a few years ago I should say that it was quite true that, for the non-Catholic World, the notion of nineteenth-century France being notable for its saints is very surprising. And yet I daresay, some thousands of years hence, the saints will be the only nineteenth-century French men and women whose memory will still be living. I think one of the most saddening things in history is the contrast between the ultimate destiny of the political and economic action on the surface, which makes such a stir at the moment and then is so quickly forgotten, and the spiritual life underneath which makes its effect almost unnoticed.

Thank you so much for these two numbers of *The Christian Democrat*. The summary of Vittoria's findings is particularly interesting, and I shall pursue the subject in Eppstein's book, which so far I have only glanced at and not read—but I need not ask you to lend it me as it will be in our library at Chatham House.

By the way, I shall be posting Delehaye[4] back to you tomorrow, but I will keep Lagrange's *Le Messianisme*[5] a bit longer if I may.

Thank you, once again.

Yours very sincerely,
Arnold J. Toynbee

1. Lawrence Leifchild Toynbee (1922–); A.J.T.'s youngest son; Rosalind Toynbee had become a Catholic in 1932; Lawrence, a student at Ampleforth (1935–41), was being reared in the Catholic Church.

2. Theodore Philip Toynbee; A.J.T.'s second son; then at Christ Church, Oxford; cf. A.J.T.'s letter of 21 July 1919, above.

3. Antony Harry Robert Toynbee; A.J.T.'s first son; cf. A.J.T.'s letter of 8 September 1914, above.

4. Hippolyte Delehaye, S.J. (1859–1941); president of the Bollandists, editors of the *Acta Sanctorum*; author of numerous hagiographical studies; *Les Légendes hagiographiques* (Brussels, 1905); *Les Origines du culte des martyrs* (Brussels, 1912).

5. Marie Joseph Lagrange, O.P. (1855–1938); biblical scholar; appointed to the Biblical Commission in 1902; author of commentaries on the four gospels; *Le Messianisme chez les Juifs* (Paris, 1909); founder of the École Pratique d'Études Bibliques (1890) in Jerusalem and of the *Revue biblique* (1892); influential in bringing the church into the stream of modern biblical scholarship.

Ampleforth Abbey
York

7 February 1937

Dear Professor Toynbee,

Very many thanks for your letter, which gave me immense pleasure, especially what you implied. But perhaps I make you imply what you did not intend. For the moment I am keeping my inferences to myself; and having your sanction to add, what Dr. Barnes would call the magic of prayer to your hard reasonings, you cannot blame me for wanting you to see things in the same light precisely as the monks, descendants of S. Columba, saw things finally at Whitby, as you so beautifully explained in one of your footnotes in the *History of Civilization*.[1]

The book has arrived safely, thank you very much. Also, it was very thoughtful of you to have returned those two copies of the *Christian Democrat*, I really did not expect it.

Please excuse this delay in answering your letter. I have had flu. This is my first day up.

Please give my kind regards to Mrs. Toynbee. I shall make a special effort over Philip and your other son whom I have not yet met. The Mass is the thing, and to humble us, that humblest creature, Mary.

Yours very sincerely,
Columba Cary-Elwes, O.S.B.

1. "I meant *A Study of History* and was referring to Vol. II: 334–40." (C.C.E.)

3, Melina Place
St. John's Wood, N.W.8

14 February 1937

Dear Father Columba,

I hope you are all right again after the flu. It seems to be not of the worst kind this year, but it has a way of turning nasty if the patient doesn't show it a proper respect.

About my position—or, rather, the direction in which I am moving, let me tell you, in a word or two, all that I know about it myself, and that is that I am on the move, and have been so for the last year or two, after having been stationary for something between 20 and 25 years, ever since I was an undergraduate.

I can see what I am moving *towards*: and that is, as you rightly read from my last letter, the position in which you yourself have always been, and which was once the position of the whole of the now broken-up world out of which we have all of us come—you and I and Philip alike.

But I don't yet know where I shall end up or when I shall get there (this sentence is logically indefensible, but I think, all the same, it makes sense!).

My sensation is rather like what one has if one jumps from a fair height into deep water and goes down and down, but at last feels that the movement is reversed and that one is now rising.

At first I found this sensation very surprising. For one of the oddest things about the Liberal rational paganism (which I dropped into as a matter of course, out of an ordinary public-school Anglican upbringing) is that it feels itself to be self-evident and the last word in human enlightenment, and I think this characteristic of it was common to my generation (the last to be just grown up before the outbreak of the war) and the generation of, let us say, the Restoration and the Revolution of 1688, which was the age, I suppose, when this Weltanschauung first prevailed as a reaction against the Wars of Religion.

In England, where this outlook has lasted for so long and counted for so much, it is a massive and formidable heritage—if one happens to be one of the people who have inherited it, as most of the living generation of "intellectuals" in England have. To go back to my simile, I have heavy boots on, with a great weight of water in them, so, though I may be moving up, I can't expect to move very fast. Nor—and about this I do feel sure—ought I to speed myself up by kicking off the boots and letting them sink to the bottom. For I have not been under water for nothing, and my business now is to bring up the boots as well as myself.

This is, as I now see (though I had no notion of this when I started work on it) what I am trying to do in my "nonsense book" (as the Study of History is called in the family). I am trying to digest a large lump of the modern knowledge and understanding of the material world which has grown up (so vigorously, but yet so lopsidedly and without deep roots) during the last 250 years, and to re-place it in the Christian setting from which it has broken out. (I suppose this is what the Schoolmen did succeed in doing with Aristotle). As I get on with this work (and I have an almost painful inward "urge" to get on with it) I shall get, I believe, *pari passu*, a clearer knowledge of the road that I myself am travelling.

All this may seem rather odd to you, for I am like a hermit crab who has crawled out of one shell without having yet crawled into any other, while you are like a crab who has had a native shell of his own ever since he can remember.

Yours very sincerely,
Arnold J. Toynbee

Ampleforth Abbey
York

23 February 1937

Dear Professor Toynbee,

Your last letter gave me very great joy. It was most kind of you to have bothered to write such a frank and personal account. You probably cannot conceive how consoling it was to an old crab who, as you so amusingly said, had never been out of his shell. It is encouraging to one's own judgement to find someone who has been through the intellectual jungle of Liberalism coming out and saying about it what one had always thought it to be, cf. Leo XIII's encyclical on the subject *Libertas Praestantissimum*.[1] To boys your judgement, as being that of one who has lived these theories and found them wanting, will be much more forceful and convincing than mine, say, as I have only had a walk round, as it were. Your lecture next autumn must be on these lines.

I stole your crab simile for a class the other evening, but turned it into a tortoise. The Catholic tortoise sees other creatures rushing past him full of new enthusiasms, and feels tempted to imitate and follow down some inviting valley. Occasionally the other creatures come back and beat the old tortoises on their shell and they cover up and even stay still. But the tortoise wins in the long run because the other creatures, though going much faster, go the wrong way.

The way the Liberal paganism of which you speak touches the average educated Catholic is like your experience, but whereas the Protestant school boy gives way, more than 90%[2] of ours do not. Speaking from experience, the "world's" thoughts looked so enticing and plausible and were presented with so much glamour and freshness, whilst the Church's thought looked so old and worn. One just trusted the Church and only gradually, it is still going on, the reasoned basis for the traditional view becomes evident and real, through history, daily life and the fruits of the other becoming apparent.

I often tell the boys they must be in their small way S. Augustines, because the Vandal is knocking at the gate as he was in S. Augustine's day. They must pass on, over the chaos that is coming, our Catholic inheritance and all that is good in their age. So, when reading your "nonsense book" I saw you were in a way doing the same thing, but this time on the grand scale, it looked like the long awaited City of God (revised edition 1937–).

Please God you will achieve the great design, lose nothing of God's teaching, like those giants S. Augustine and S. Thomas, and like them embrace all the knowledge of your time in the synthesis only possible to truth, natural and supernatural. You may be assured of at least one reader for the three volumes which are I hope soon to appear.

Yours very sincerely,
Columba Cary-Elwes, O.S.B.

P.S. My kind regards to your wife.

1. Issued 20 June 1888; on the nature of liberty.

2. "Were I writing this today, the percentage would be considerably lower." (C.C.E.)

Ganthorpe Hall[1]
27 July 1938 Terrington, York

Dear Father Columba,

Here is the letter for the B.M.[2] It is an amiable place: they contrive to make the reader feel that it is their pleasure to serve him, and not just a bore.

I am sorry, though, that the Spanish journey seems likely to be off, for it would have been a greater change.

As to the argument about Spain,[3] I don't believe any of us know enough about the facts to argue with much authority; all that matters is that you and I can argue, without breaking any bones, about these, I am sure very ephemeral, current politics.

Your prayers I am conscious of—as well as deeply and humbly grateful for, as a precious gift which I have done nothing to deserve (but, then, I suppose it is impossible to deserve gifts that really are precious).

If the state of mind necessary for membership of a church depended only on one's being aware of the existence and presence of God as one can see this shining through the lives of one's fellow human beings, my acquaintance with the community at Ampleforth would long ago have been enough to open the door to membership of the Church for me.

But though this may be—and, I personally feel, is—the heart of the matter, there are, I know, also important concrete conditions—not merely a submission to rules of life (which would probably not be a very serious obstacle when one is thinking only of the rules laid upon the laity), but also an acceptance of intellectual beliefs; and this last point is the crux for people with my intellectual heritage and background, which is that of the pagan modern scientific mind.

This mind has broken out of the Church and has been ranging very far afield for some centuries now; and as far as I know, in myself, what it is feeling, it is now in a painful and difficult dilemma. It doesn't know how to reconcile its new knowledge and outlook with Christian doctrine; at the same time it feels that, if ever it cuts itself right off from its Christian roots, it will wither. The question it is asking is "Can a man enter a second time into his mother's womb and be born?" That is, I believe, the supreme question of the present age, and I am in the dark about how it will be answered, and how soon. One can only go on working away at it, in the conviction that this is one's own most important business.

Yours ever,
Arnold J. Toynbee

1. Ganthorpe Hall; the eighteenth-century residence in the village of Ganthorpe, conveyed, together with the village, to Rosalind (Murray) Toynbee by her mother; here the Toynbees spent their summers. See "Ganthorpe: An Elegy and Dedication," in A.J.T.'s *Experiences*, pp. 393–401; cf. Pevsner, *Yorkshire: The North Riding*, p. 165.

2. The British Museum (reading room); now part of the British Library.

3. The civil war (1936–39) was a source of bitter contentions, ideological, political, and religious.

13, Elm Park Gardens
30 July 1938 Chelsea, S.W.

Dear Professor Toynbee,

Very many thanks for your letter of introduction to the B.M. Director. I sent it off and got a 6 months permit to read there. It is still uncertain whether I'll have occasion to use it properly as the Spanish journey still hangs fire.

I see Philip got a second. I am very sorry, and hope he will not attribute it to bourgeois preconceptions of history on the part of the examiners![1]

The rest of your letter gave me great consolation as I wondered whether you were still struggling in the jungle or rather giving up, although I could not believe the latter had occurred.

Of course you have to be born again, like Nicodemus with his preconceived notions,[2] S. Paul with his and the great S. Augustine[3] with his, and like S. Thomas Aquinas bringing the whole mediaeval world to rebirth. I always think of those crises when thinking of yours because each in its way bears some likeness to yours.

My part in this rebirth is no doubt to pray, but if it would give you any satisfaction to tell me the intellectual misfits between the modern pagan world and the Christian mind, please do. I am so naïf as not to be able to see any real contradiction between what is good in the modern pagan outlook, and Christian belief; but perhaps I am too ready to throw overboard what does not fit of the pagan outlook! Write me a letter telling me the salient intellectual difficulties as you see them; it would be most instructive for me and perhaps not a bad thing for you. But no doubt you have already done this with someone else, Fr D'Arcy[4] or another who would make some attempt at reply. I almost certainly would make very little.

I venture to make this suggestion because, for reasons only known to Providence and yourself, you have told me rather a lot about yourself, and I am intensely anxious to understand you and your "modern pagan" outlook in order to help, if not you, then others.

My kind regards to Mrs. Toynbee.

Yours sincerely,
Columba Cary-Elwes, O.S.B.

1. Philip Toynbee had joined the student section of the Communist party of Great Britain when he was at Christ Church, Oxford, in 1935; Philip was the first and only Communist president of the Oxford Union (1938); David Walker, *The Oxford Union* (London, 1984), pp. 111–12; Philip left the party in 1939 when the Soviet Union signed the Non Aggression Pact with Hitler's Germany; the Pact was signed 23 August 1939; on 1 September Germany, and on 17 September Russia invaded Poland.

2. John, 3:1–21.

3. Saint Augustine of Hippo (354–430); cf. *A Study of History*: "A classic example of a work of metahistory . . . is Saint Augustine's *De Civitate Dei*" (XII:229).

4. Martin Cyril d'Arcy, S.J. (1888–1976); philosophical theologian; master of Campion Hall, Oxford (1933–45); provincial of English Province (1945–50); *The Nature of Belief* (London, 1931); in his *Reconsiderations* A.J.T. frequently refers to D'Arcy's *The Sense of History: Secular and Sacred* (London, 1959); cf. *A Study of History*, XII:10, and passim.

Ganthorpe Hall
Terrington, York

5 August 1938

Dear Father Columba,

Here is my statement; I have waited a few days to let it take shape in my mind. I think that, as I have put it now, it does represent my position fairly clearly, and also (I hope) frankly and sincerely. I have never tried to set it out before.

Your concern for me is a large gift which I accept with gratitude and at the same time with humility—because there is no return that I can make for it (I know, of course, that you are not thinking about a return!).

In trying to put my state of mind into words, I have tried above all, to make it plain, for your use. So I have not wrapped anything up, or used any "tact" or "diplomacy", but have treated you as both a friend and a "pro" who wants to know the facts and whom one therefore need not be afraid of "hurting" (in the conventional sense).

I don't believe you will be hurt, because there is no hostility in me either towards the Church or (this I really needn't say!) to you. Indeed, how could one feel hostile towards those from whom one has received nothing but kindness?

Yours very sincerely,
Arnold J. Toynbee

5 August 1938

The Gulf between the Modern Western Paganism and Catholic Christianity, as it appears to A.J.T.

(i) *Different degrees of pagan remoteness from the position of Catholic Christianity:*—

(a) A disbelief in the existence of any transcendental reality, life or personality;

(b) A belief in the existence of some kind of transcendental reality, without the belief in the existence of God;

(c) A belief in the existence of a transcendental reality and life, and in the existence of God—but this without being convinced of the unique or absolute truth of the formulations of these beliefs in the doctrines of either the Christian churches in general or of the Roman Church in particular.

(ii) *Experience of A.J.T.*

After an ordinary Anglican upbringing at home and at school, A.J.T. drifted out of Anglican Christianity into position (i) (*a*) about the time when he went up as an undergraduate to Oxford in 1907, and recoiled from (i) (*a*) to (i) (*c*) in 1930. His loss of belief was by infinitesimally gradual stages, though it was borne in upon him in the end by the shock of finding that someone very close to him whom he had always believed to have religion, had found his faith a broken reed in a very grave mental crisis. The recoil in 1930 was superficially more abrupt, and the recovery of a belief in God came through an experience of help in withstanding a very strong temptation.[1] But the change precipitated by this experience had probably been long in preparation.

(iii) *Obstacles in the Way of A.J.T.'s passing from (i)(c) to the Catholic Position.*

(a) *Intellectual Obstacles*:—

1. To a historian's eye, the propagation and the survival of Religion in general, and of Catholicism in particular, have been—and are—contingent upon mundane historical causes: some trivial, some unedifying, all natural. (E.g. Gibbon's explanations of the spread of Christianity through the Roman Empire; the political reasons why China and Japan are not Catholic countries to-day; the political reasons why to-day Belgium is Catholic but Holland Protestant, England Episcopalian but Scotland Presbyterian.).
2. To a scientific observer's eye, the mode of operation of Nature—Spiritual as well as Physical—is prodigality and manifoldness, not uniqueness or economy.

> And not through eastern windows only,
> When daylight comes, comes in the light.[2]

On this showing, a belief in the existence of an Other World and of God does not lead on to a belief that either Catholicism in particular or Christianity in general is the only way in which the transcendental reality and the transcendental personality will have discovered themselves to Mankind on Earth. The postulate that it is possible to discern a sharp line between an absolutely true and a decidedly erroneous conception of God and of the Other World, does not carry conviction. It seems more likely that, if a light from the Other World does irradiate this World, it floods in along an infinite number of beams, and that, if these beams are unequal with one another in brightness, this difference of luminosity is not clear-cut, but is graded in an infinitesimally fine gradation of degrees. (E.g. the difference between Christianity and the Mahayanian Buddhism would appear to be one of degree and not one of kind; and the spiritual insight and experience that have been won by Syrian prophets and Indian saints have not been beyond the ken of Greek philosophers and Chinese sages.).

3. In an anthropologist's eye, it seems unlikely that God, in putting Mankind into communication with Himself through concrete channels, will have limited his action by making certain particular channels into unique and exclusive means of grace. This is an obstacle to a belief in an exclusive incarnation of God in Jesus, or in an exclusive Real Presence in the Host, or in an exclusive supernatural faculty in a duly ordained Catholic Christian priest to serve as the intermediary on Earth between his fellow men and their common Creator.
4. The common outcome of these three considerations is to make it seem

not impossible that Catholicism is *a* revelation, but most improbable that it is *the* revelation, of God.

(b) *A "Professional" Obstacle* (for want of a better name).

This obstacle would not arise unless and until the intellectual obstacles disappeared; but, if these did disappear, and if, therefore, it were open to A.J.T. to move, for his own part, from (i)(*c*) to the Catholic position, he would then find himself faced with a choice between two alternatives that might, very likely, turn out to be incompatible with each other. In so far as he is conscious of having any religious or pastoral mission, this mission is to help his fellow pagan "intellectuals" to move to position (i)(*c*) from position (i)(*a*). He thinks he knows the road, because he has travelled over it himself, and to map out this road has been, for some time past, one of the deliberate aims of his research and writing. But, if he himself moved on from (i)(*c*) into Catholicism, this, as far as he can see, would bring his "mission to the heathen" to an end, because the pagan intellectuals would then at once write him off as a fellow who had "gone soft-headed" and was no longer to be taken seriously. He would lose all authority in their eyes.

At this point, if he ever came to it, A.J.T. would therefore have to make the choice between being (in Buddhist terms) a "Bodhisattva" or an "Arhat". The Arhat is a practitioner of Buddhism who, having arrived at the threshold of Nirvana, goes on to take the next and final step into a state of being, or of not-being, which is the goal of existence both for himself and for his fellow creatures, but which, in the very act of its being attained, will preclude him from ever doing anything more to help his fellows to make progress on their own journey towards the same goal. The Bodhisattva is a potential Arhat who, upon arriving on the threshold of Nirvana, refrains—for the reason just given—from stepping over, and deliberately prolongs his own period of servitude to "the Wheel of existence" for the sake of remaining in a situation in which it will continue to be possible for him to help his fellows forward. The Arhat's choice is the Hinayana; the Bodhisattva's is the Mahayana. At present, A.J.T. would make the Bodhisattva's choice if he had to choose between these two courses.

1. In *Experiences* A.J.T. describes his temptation in his poem "ΓΡΑΜΜΑΤΙΚΟΣ ΜΙΝΟΤΑΥΡΟΣ": "22 December 1929, at sea between Wei-hai-wai and Shanghai" (pp. 389–90); and his rescue: "I was in a moral conflict between the better and the worse side of myself, and this at a moment when the better side was fighting with its back to the wall. . . . it felt as if a transcendent spiritual presence, standing for righteousness beyond my reach, had come down to my rescue and had given to my inadequate human righteousness the aid without which it could not have won its desperate battle" (p. 176). A.J.T. was a member of a group attending the third biennial conference of the Institute of Pacific Relations in Kyoto; cf. *A Journey to China* (London, 1931) in which he recounts his trip (July 1929–January 1930). Eileen Power (1889–1940) also attended the conference; she was a noted medieval historian (see, e.g., her *Medieval People* [London, 1924]), "as beautiful and incisive as her legend claims": John King

Fairbank, *Chinabound* (New York, 1982), p. 27. A.J.T. wrote his wife, Rosalind, from Mukden, that he had fallen in love with Eileen but had not told her so and that he would see Eileen again in Shanghai; Rosalind responded with two understanding letters: "I hope she doesn't feel the same, for that would make it all more serious. I am not afraid that you will want to leave me and go off with her. . . . I feel you might feel much more seriously in love with her in China, by yourself, like that, than you ever would have meeting her quite as much at home. And if you did become really much in love with her, it would be a very unhappy thing for all three of us. . . . I think possibly your feeling like this now is a sign of your having grown up or woken up more—and if it makes me feel less sure of you and take you less for granted (as it will!) that will be good too in the end. For it wasn't natural really that you should never be interested in anyone except me, nor attracted by anyone else, without my taking any trouble. Now, probably, I shall take more trouble to keep you and please you, for people are like that, I am sure, even sophisticated people like you and me. . . . I think your analysis of Eileen's attraction for you is probably right. I expect her 'childish quality' does give you something which I don't. . . . I believe if you did run away with her you would 'get through' it in a very short time, for I don't think you would get to unexplored depths. I don't think the depths are there, but I think she is a nice person, and you might stay quite fond of her, though not excitedly so" (R.T., 11 December 1929); "Even if you have had it out with her, as I feel may well have happened—it may do her more good than harm in the end, for I think it is just this sort of spiritual experience that is lacking in her, and she might become a much fuller and finer person if she was awakened" (R.T., 14 December 1929). The experience is only obliquely reflected in the Chapter on "Yin and Yang" in the *A Journey to China*, pp. 216–19, where he finds that the "male human being looks like a single creature" but is two, "a human being and a bull."

Without A.J.T.'s letter, we may still assume securely that "Eileen" was Eileen Power.

2. Arthur Hugh Clough, "Say Not the Struggle Naught Availeth," *Oxford Book of Victorian Verse* (Oxford, 1968), p. 327.

13, Elm Park Gardens
Chelsea, S.W.

Sunday 7 August 1938

Dear Professor,

This letter cannot be an adequate reply to your letter for which very many thanks. I feel almost ashamed for having butted in like that; but it is most revealing. My first impression was: how well Leo XIII understood your position;[1] and then thousands of ideas went tumbling over each other. Unfortunately I have no time to sort them and send them by post, as I am off to Spain tomorrow! Perhaps it is providential, as my ideas would not be particularly illuminating.

I shall quietly go on praying for you to integrate all your ideas and reach what I believe is that integration: the Church. How well I see your difficulties and divergences now. Thank you.

I know you will follow truth; and whether you come into the Church or not, we shall, God granting us perseverance in our quest, meet in heaven; which is what I want.

Yours very sincerely,
Columba Cary-Elwes, O.S.B.

1. "Leo XIII was to me an exemplar of a Christian leader with a mind open to the world outside the church." (C.C.E.)

13 September 1938 Ganthorpe

Dear Father Columba,

I have just finished reading the article [1] with great enjoyment and interest—I do hope we shall manage to get it published, because what you have to say is so directly at first hand, and you are so manifestly not "tendentious".

It would, I should think, be more useful, from your point of view, not to preach to the converted (I am sure you could easily get it published in the English Catholic Press) but to get it into some Liberal paper whose readers will come to it with an anti-Franco bias. I could try either the *Contemporary Review* (a monthly) or the *Spectator*.

I cast it up at about 4200 words, which would, I think, make one *Contemporary* article (perhaps with a few cuts) or alternatively three articles in a weekly.

I have gone over it and made—largely from a now fixed habit in editing my collaborators on the *Survey* [2]—a number of, I hope not too impertinent, suggestions.

Mostly these are on mere points of expression, but in some cases I have made suggestions for toning down any symptoms (very slight!) of what to a Liberal reader might look like prejudice.

I am an old hand at toning down, and I do know that quite slight verbal changes often make just the difference between opening the reader's mind to you or closing it against you.

If you care to glance through my suggestions and let me have a fair copy, I should suggest my showing it to the *Contemporary* first, as it is pleasanter to get it published in one lot and not in installments.

Why not come over to lunch with it yourself, and then we could talk over any moot points? I will suggest a time when my wife comes in—I never know our time-table myself.

Your prayers have, I have no doubt, done good to my "nonsense book" already, and will do more.

Yours ever,
Arnold J. Toynbee

Yes, Bar Sauman,[3] wasn't he, the Uighur Nestorian Monk? There was quite a strong tincture of Nestorian culture in the Mongols—e.g. they use the Syriac alphabet—written vertically like Chinese!

1. "An article on Spain—the Franco half—after my visit there in August of that year." (C.C.E.)

2. A.J.T. for many years edited the *Survey of International Affairs* issued under the auspices of the Royal Institute of International Affairs.

3. Bar Sauman or Sauma (d. 1294), a Nestorian monk from China who traveled to Rome in 1287.

Ganthorpe Hall
Terrington, York

26 September 1938

Dear Father Columba,

I am returning the article to you herewith for the moment, because I am going up to London now, to my Institute, and the ms. will be in safer keeping with you.

If peace is saved this week, I will see you on Sunday after Mass and take the ms. back to "place", as we had arranged. But we know nothing of what, by next Sunday, the state of this World may be.[1]

I feel, you know, that in spite of all the intellectual complications and obstacles of the present world my beliefs and faith are not at bottom different from yours, even though I may not find the intellectual bridge between them. And anyway you know what I feel about your concern for my soul.

Yours ever,
Arnold J. Toynbee

1. The crisis, arising from the German demands that Czechoslovakia surrender the Sudetenland, reached its climax on 24–29 September 1938; on 29 September, the Munich concessions were made.

Saint Wilfrid's House
Ampleforth College, York

27 September 1938

Dear Professor Toynbee,

Leave taking is what both of us seem to have thought of simultaneously, as I too intended wishing you "farewell" in this present peril, a precautionary farewell!

Your little beginnings of an act of faith have given me great peace and joy. Thank you for bothering to tell me. Please if you are faced with immediate death throw your great but tiny-in-God's-creation mind to the winds and embrace in thought and unconditionally that crucifix you have in your study, as a sign of handing yourself back unconditionally to God. He will understand and then solve your difficulties.

If it is any consolation to you in the coming strain, I repeat what you must know, that you have been one of the greatest inspirations in my life, your idealism, your intellectual courage.

I enclose a picture as a symbol of my regard and as a permanent petition to Our Lady for you in your search for Wisdom.

Yours very sincerely,
Columba Cary-Elwes, O.S.B.

Please God you will be cheerfully talking to us on Monday.

P.S. Thanks for the article. It must wait. How distant all that is now.

Saint Wilfrid's House
Ampleforth College, York

3 October 1938

Dear Professor Toynbee,

Just a line to thank you for giving us all such an interesting lecture. The boys were most thrilled, naturally, by your account of London. Most people were very consoled by your relative optimism. I found the whole thing most interesting.

The strange thing about that week is that one feels as though we have all been through a war, without having done so. One feels quite different, as though life, everything, is more precarious; or perhaps we have come through realising once and for all how precarious life and all always has been.

Please excuse more—Corneille calls!

Yours ever,
Columba Cary-Elwes, O.S.B.

Ganthorpe Hall
Terrington, York

24 October 1938

Dear Father Columba,

I am so very sorry that I have drawn blank with both the *Contemporary* and the *Spectator* (you will have got the ms., with the editors' letters, which I left at the Monastery yesterday, with the book on Père Lamy,[1] which we read aloud with great pleasure—he was as you described him).

No doubt you will find plenty of Catholic papers eager to take your article, but it is always more profitable to preach to the *un*converted, if one can get the entrée: I wish I had managed to do that in this case.

We waited a bit yesterday morning after Mass in the hope of catching sight of you, but we thought that perhaps the boys' retreat kept you busy.

We go to London for the winter (less tragically than last month!) on Friday.

Is there any chance of your coming to London at Christmas? And staying with us, if you do? You may be sure that you would be welcome.

Yours ever,
Arnold J. Toynbee

1. Le Comte Paul Biver, *Père Lamy, Apostle and Mystic* (Introduction by Jacques Maritain), trans. (London, 1936).

Saint Wilfrid's House
Ampleforth College, York

25 October 1938

Dear Professor Toynbee,

I am so sorry to have missed you. I went straight up to St. Wilfrid's and settled down to preparing, or rather putting the last order into jottings for a retreat over at

Gilling,[1] which I gave yesterday. The result was that I never saw the ms. or the book till this morning.

You have been most kind in trying to get my article published; no one could have tried harder. Thank you very much. It is a pity neither periodical would bite, and the letters refusing were interesting. I may send the article to the *Catholic Herald*, or the *Clergy Review*.

It is very kind of you to invite me to your house in London. I told Fr. Abbot and he said, if at Christmas, he would let me loose in/on London, by all means. The "if" is the key word. There is, however, a chance of my going up for the Old Boys' dinner in January; if so, then may I write and suggest myself?

I often think about the Winchester attitude to life and find that if it and the English generally believe in half measures in religion, they go against the founder of Christianity. But sometimes I think that we believe in complete surrender but hate emotional frills. After all it is not so long ago since the Puritan and Catholic martyrs. Was Campion[2] continental or just first class English? And the phrase keeps on echoing in my brain "I would that thou wert either hot or cold . . . etc".[3] Why then are we English lukewarm? Riches, power, maybe, or is it native to us? I think the first two give sufficient explanation. Further, in any country the average man still remains mixed in his motives and off and on in his zeal. What is wrong, I am sure, is to take mediocrity as the ideal. Could it be due to pride, a hatred of finding oneself falling below the point aimed at? These are just the thoughts that have been through my head, and I take the liberty of unloading them on you.

So glad you liked Père Lamy. He was very pessimistic wasn't he? But so sublimely simple.

Once again many thanks for the trouble you took over my article, also for inviting me to Melina Place.[4] I hope that comes off.

When I last met you behind the monastery it seemed you were tempted to Anglicanism. Whatever you do will be sincere and that will satisfy me; but it did urge me to more prayer, even a special Mass. So, it is an evil . . .

Yours very sincerely,
Columba Cary-Elwes, O.S.B.

1. Gilling Castle; an Elizabethan building on a fourteenth-century tower house; the great chamber completed in 1585; with eighteenth-century additions; now the lower school of Ampleforth College; cf. Pevsner, *Yorkshire: The North Riding*, pp. 167–69.

2. Edmund Campion, S.J. (1540–81); executed at Tyburn.

3. Rev. 3:15–16.

4. A.J.T.'s London residence.

Ganthorpe Hall,
Terrington, York

28 October 1938

Dear Father Columba,

A line, before we start south, to say that you will be equally welcome at Christmas or in January or at both.

Your question: Are the English Laodiceans superficially only, or fundamentally?—I won't start on now, or this evening I should still be sitting at my desk here instead of in a lecture-room in Nottingham.

My own answer is "only superficially".

Well, au revoir.

Yours ever,
Arnold J. Toynbee

Saint Wilfrid's House
Ampleforth College, York

20 December 1938

Dear Professor Toynbee,

I feel rather like a sponge after it has been squeezed out, so please excuse the futilities that will no doubt follow.

Firstly, thank you very much indeed for being so generous and kind as to send me 1937's *Survey*.[1] In spite of the stress of this last week I have not been able to resist the temptation of dipping into it frequently. It is rather like carrying on a conversation with you. This time you do the talking (on Spain), last time I did. Perhaps you will be glad to hear that I do not think you have been sufficiently pro Franco, as it will prove to you that you have kept a judicious balance. And on the whole I have to admit, that is the case; though I should like to see a distinction made between the killing by the Franco-ists of the rather criminal "Red" elements and the cold-blooded killing by the Red elements of very peaceful citizens. Also, no one ever mentions it, but *can* the 'government' be exonerated from blame as the Anarchist and Communist elements *ex professo* believe in slaughter as a pre-requisite of the 'change' they wish to effect. However, the broad lines and the introduction to the war I found profoundly true and interesting: Spain was/is a misfit in modern Europe; and you were very fair to the Church, especially to the Jesuits, and that was a real pleasure.

The section on the purge in Russia was an eye opener to me, and madness is the word that comes. There is no *a priori* reason why madmen should not get control of governments and we should expect such a thing to happen, but it is hard to have to admit such a frightful calamity.

I am leaving North Africa till after Christmas.

I am so glad you have given such prominence to the Van Zeeland report;[2] that again is an after Christmas fare.

Christmas, A very happy one to you and all the family. I hope you get deeper and deeper dug into its healing peace-giving depths. Tomorrow I say Mass for you and your family. But first and foremost for you.

Yours very sincerely,
Columba Cary-Elwes, O.S.B.

1. *The International Repercussions of the War in Spain (1936–7)*, vol. II of the *Survey of International Affairs, 1937* (2 vols., by A.J.T., assisted by Veronica M. Boulter [London, 1938]), was entirely devoted to the Spanish civil war.

2. The Van Zeeland Report to the governments of France and Great Britain concerning obstacles to free trade; see the *Survey of International Affairs, 1937*, 1:86–96.

31 December 1938 Ampleforth Abbey, York

Dear Professor Toynbee,

Very many thanks for your lovely and truly Christmas card. A happy New Year and may you be spared the necessity of writing a 2 volume *Survey* of 1939.

I have had a lot of travelling to do these last few days and carried Vol ii about with me and read it almost word for word until you got to the bit on the Non-Intervention Committee.[1] I retract what criticism I made previously. I think you have been marvellously fair. It all gave me a wonderful sensation of balance and even of distance from the events, as though you really were looking on dispassionately.

The parts I liked were the spacious introduction. In that I want enlightenment on what you really mean by 17 Century outlook. Also, I felt you would have liked to have said the Spaniards were lucky to have escaped the modern spirit.

The bit on English Conservative opinion[2] made me laugh and think, particularly the footnote on p. 155, because I used to use the argument you rebut. You held your peace very well. I think you are right.

The introduction to the interests and motives of the powers too set me thinking and took me right beyond the present problem to the bigger ones of indifferentism and enthusiasm. G.K.C. says somewhere he could only now defend a religious war. Your quotation from the *Osservatore Romano* was one of the most interesting in the book (p. 134).[3] Your footnote on the parliamentary game of government and opposition was amusing too. In fact I fairly revelled in it as a display of your mind and was also sadly interested in its brilliant exposition of the WAR. May it very soon cease.

The section on Italian aspirations and designs for the first time awoke in me a real understanding of our perilously thin line of communication East and West.

In the summer when we next meet you must explain more in detail who these strange syndico anarchists are, what they intend. You called their movement religious. Did you really mean it, or was the word used only analogously?

Perhaps this meandering letter may interest you as a sample of one kind of repercussion from your *Survey*.

Yours very sincerely,
Columba Cary-Elwes, O.S.B.

1. Compare *Survey of International Affairs, 1937*, II, pt. 3, sec. 2:222–376.

2. Compare ibid., p. 154, n. 1; here A.J.T. questioned the British Conservative opinion that, after accepting Nazi and Fascist assistance, the Falangists would not permit the Germans and Italians to retain any hold on Spain. In the event, A.J.T.'s fears were not realized.

3. A.J.T. quotes the statement that "all wars are really wars of doctrines" from "an article published in the *Osservatore Romano* of that date [8 January 1937] in which the accents of a pre-Voltairean Western Christendom made themselves heard once more."

Saint Wilfrid's House
23 January 1939 Ampleforth College, York

Dear Professor Toynbee,

Lawrence tells me you have retired to bed exhausted. I am so sorry, but it must be the exhaustion after achieving something, the pang, of book-bearing, as he tells me that the long awaited vols 4, 5 and 6 are in the world. It gives me immense pleasure to hear that. May the thoughts enshrined there become flesh and bone of the English mind (rather mixed metaphor) and radiate more and more widely and never dimly. We must ask God in his Wisdom to make use of your book for his purposes. It is a great immortality to go on influencing men for good and through some, hundreds, thousands and in the end millions of others.

This must be a letter which gives you no worry, that is, you must be under no obligation to answer it.

Volume II of the *Survey* (or is it Vol I the non-Spanish one?) has been keenly scrutinised, particularly the part on China by Br. William Price.[1] He told me he found it most interesting. He was out in China for many years. The section on the Van Zeeland report[2] was very interesting, but made sad reading. The Russian section is hair raising.

We are all looking forward to the "Rosalind Murray" production.[3]

Yours very sincerely,
Columba Cary-Elwes, O.S.B.

1. William Price, O.S.B. (1899–1971); a scholar of Corpus Christi College, Oxford; a first in jurisprudence; entered the Catholic church at Oxford; legal adviser, then director, of British American Tobacco Co., in Shanghai; in 1933 became monk at Ampleforth College; head master (1954–64).

2. Compare C.C.E.'s letter of 20 December 1938, above.

3. Rosalind "Murray" was about to release *The Good Pagan's Failure* (London, 1939).

3, Melina Place
5 February 1939 St. John's Wood, N.W.8

Dear Father Columba,

At last I am writing to you: it has not been out of my mind, but being laid up and then catching up again have kept me busy. I did have to go to bed, and then it turned into flu: the result, I think, of extra hard work during the crisis, and another bout of it in November, on top of my ordinary work. But I am now gradually getting up to normal level again.

What you wrote about the *Survey* pleased me a lot, of course—particularly your feeling that it gave you a certain sense of distance from the events; for that is perhaps the chief test of success in trying to write the history of what happened only yesterday, and this in one's own world.

By the seventeenth-century spirit I meant the pre-utilitarian spirit: the conviction that the things to spend oneself on are spiritual ideals—as opposed to the modern spirit, which thinks this attitude not only silly but dangerous, and believes that "practical" material ends are alone worth striving for.

There is a historical and moral crux about this, because the modern attitude is a reaction against the Wars of Religion (now returning!) which was in one sense a right reaction. You *can't* achieve spiritual aims by the use of force. The crux is that, in a world where force is still used for achieving whatever your aims may be, it is hard to see how you are to say that it must be renounced for just the aims that seem to oneself the really important ones. All the same, I am sure the history of religions proves it true that "all they that take the sword shall perish with the sword"[1]—well, there is a long piece about that in one of the forth-coming volumes of my "nonsense-book"; I wonder what you will think about it.

You may have seen that my wife's book[2]—coming out in a few weeks—has been "serialised" in the *Tablet*. I have hopes that the book may make a hit, for the subject is certainly one which people are confronted with now, and the book is written with great sincerity and straightforwards, from a double knowledge—which I daresay few people happen to possess—of both the "good pagan" world and the Christian one.

I am grateful to you, as always, for your good wishes for my book and for me. Parts of my book will be in harmony with your outlook; other parts you may, I am afraid, feel discordant. I am in a kind of limbo or "no-man's-land" between two worlds, as you know—feeling my way in what is probably a typically English fashion that I am often impatient with when I see it in other Englishmen!

I can't tell what road I shall find myself travelling along, or where it will take me, but I do know, for certain, that your good wishes and prayers for me are not in vain.

Yours ever,
Arnold J. Toynbee

1. Matt. 26:52.
2. *The Good Pagan's Failure.*

S. Thomas' Day — Saint Wilfrid's House
7 March 1939 — Ampleforth College, York

My dear Professor Toynbee,

I missed you by a few minutes after I had seen Fr. Abbot on Sunday. He seemed to think the best time for you to spend your week here would be Holy Week, that is approximately 2nd April (Palm Sunday) to the 10th (Easter Monday). The place is big enough for you to be as social or as retiring as you wish. The following week he did not say impossible but seemed to prefer what I have suggested. As you can imagine, I am delighted. If Holy Week is inconvenient do not hesitate to come the following week or two weeks later (not Low week).

I read "Miss Rosalind Murray's" article[1]—extracts in the *Tablet* with very great pleasure and interest and am reading Fr. Paul's copy when he finishes. There are some telling phrases and it is all so true, to be screamed from the house tops. The mob rule section was most disturbing.

I don't often get angry with the English mind but Basil Selincourt in the *Observer*[2] made me abnormally irritated to put it mildly. It reminded me of two sayings, Pascal's when he saw light: "Dieu d'Abraham, Dieu d'Isaac, Dieu de Jacob, non des philosophes et des savants"[3] . . . and St. Bernard's in that hymn:

"Jesus spes poenitentibus
quam finis es petentibus
quam bonus te quaerentibus!
Sed quid invenientibus?"

It seems so extraordinary that anyone could conceive perfect religion to be just the seeking. If others claim they have found, then surely the claim should be examined. It either is or is not true, and what one wants or feels about it is beside the point.

You may be sure that when your Nonsense Book comes out I will not feel irritated, because I know any differences we still have are due to no insincerities but ultimately to misunderstandings, and perhaps God waiting.

Didn't you feel the brilliance of that event, the election of the Pope?[4] For me it seemed to shine out against our murky world with immense light, so glorious, so eternal. I longed for it to open your eyes to the divine origin of the Church, so that it would outweigh all the failures of us its wretched members. Communion of Saints! Yes, but only in the making.

I shall not pursue our discussion of religious wars until I see your book, because you have already answered there, no doubt, all my arguments. As you know, my instinct and the New Testament seem to be against it, though the latter is none too clear. Reason seems to justify such a war in defensive cases. Meanwhile I am digging about trying to disprove your universal negative: "no religious war has ever had good results!"

Your volume on Spain[5] is in continual use among the boys in my house. They are writing essays with its help on all the aspects of the war. Thank God the end is in sight; and Spain may yet be for the Spaniards.

I gave my first talk on China and the Church today.

Yours very sincerely,
Columba Cary-Elwes, O.S.B.

Excuse the effusion about the Pope. It has gone like wine to my head.

1. From the forthcoming *The Good Pagan's Failure*; see A.J.T.'s letter of 5 February 1939 above.

2. Basil de Selincourt ("Faith in the Unknown," *Observer* [5 March 1939]) had reviewed *The Good Pagan's Failure* with asperity: "Those, like Miss Murray, for whom the face of truth seems not to have changed its lineaments in two thousand years, we cannot envy, though their simplicity may bring them joy."

3. A reference to Blaise Pascal's (1623–62) *Memorial* of his mystical experience of 23 November 1654 (see *Oeuvres complètes*, ed. Louis Lafuma [Paris, 1963], p. 618).

4. The election, on 2 March 1939, of Eugenio Pacelli as Pope Pius XII.

5. *Survey of International Affairs, 1937*, vol. II; cf. C.C.E.'s letter of 20 December 1938, above.

3, Melina Place
8 March 1939 St. John's Wood, N.W.8

Dear Father Columba,

I was delighted to get your letter this morning. I very much appreciate Father Abbot suggesting my coming in Holy Week—if I shall not be in the way, of course. I shall be very glad to be with you then, so I am writing to him, accepting with gratitude.

I will come over on Palm Sunday from Ganthorpe—where I shall be from about the Thursday of that week.

As I am in a rush with proof, I won't at the moment write about the other things in your letter—except to say how pleased I am that you like my wife's book. I have felt sure all along that it deserved to be a success, and that it would be one; and this seems to be coming true.[1]

Yours ever,
Arnold J. Toynbee

1. The first edition of 1939 was followed by reissues in 1943, 1948, and 1962.

3, Melina Place
19 March 1939 St. John's Wood, N.W.8

Dear Father Columba,

Of the many letters that my wife and I have had, yours has helped me the most,[1] and it is the first that I am answering, because, about this as about so many other things, I find myself able to open myself to you quite freely and easily.

The assurance of God's mercy—which you so rightly put first—did come to each of us while we were watching Tony[2] dying on Wednesday morning. It came through a change in Tony himself. He was an over-sensitive boy, who had been hardening himself, at the expense of other sides of his life and character, for the last ten years; but on Wednesday we found him gentle and loving again, as he had been as a little boy, before he was fifteen. We felt that, before he had left this life, he had been allowed to enter on, and we had been allowed to see him enter on, a happier chapter of life than the last one. This was very merciful to all three of us.

As he was leaving this life, I found myself once again, as one is always doing with one's child, projecting myself along with him, to launch him and guide him on this new stage of his journey, as one has done on so many earlier stages, when he had been sent to school or to China. One's own impetus, this time, was far greater because the change, and the distance he was going, were so much greater for him than ever before. But this time, for oneself, it was very different. At earlier stages, this launching and guiding had been unhappy. He was never able to face life with normal ease, or to take the ordinary fences at the ordinary stages; so we were always in the position of having to spur him, while he was resenting in us what it was our duty to do for him. Doing our duty by him, as far as we could, meant an alienation of him from us; and while we took this as being all in the day's work, and while we did, anyway externally, bring him along up to this point and get him into a career in which his superiors write to us of him as a promising young civil servant, still the success was very imperfect and the relation rather miserable. On Wednesday, this conflict between our duty to him and our personal relation with him disappeared—I suppose, because the issue of our trying to get him to take up his responsibilities, which had been between us for so long, was now no longer there because he was leaving this life. This time, as I was straining forward to do what I could for him, instead of finding myself up against Tony himself in the unhappy way which I knew so well, I felt myself come face to face with God, and realised that, from now on, I should be dealing about Tony with God, and not with Tony himself.

Between that moment and the time when I got your letter, I began to do several things:—

(i) to offer to God anything that I had managed to do for Tony during his life here;

(ii) to realise the extreme inadequacy of what I had done, and to offer to God my repentance for that;

(iii) to tell myself that, being human, I am bound to be imperfect in everything that I do, and that, though I must be penitent for my imperfection, I must not have the presumption to suppose that, even with the best human will—which, no doubt, one never has—I could have done for Tony those essential things that each of us must do for himself, and which lie wholly between oneself and God.

(iv) then I have prayed God to use these offerings of mine, if he will, as part of his means of carrying to completion that change in Tony of which he allowed us to see the beginning on Wednesday morning.

When I got your letter, I found—I hope I am right about this; I believe I am—that I was already doing some of the things that you were telling me to do. The explanation is that you had already been influencing me, by your prayers and your friendship, before this happened. I am like someone who, after having been given artificial respiration for a long time, is now just beginning to breathe by himself. You have known, I am sure, all along, that I have realised what you were doing for me, and that I have been grateful.

I hope to be at Ampleforth at the beginning of next month as you had so kindly arranged with Father Abbot. It looks, though as if, after all, there may be war, and that will keep me at the Institute, if it does break out. So all the more in case we do not meet in the near future, I have been wanting to write to you.

Yours ever,
Arnold J. Toynbee

1. Missing.

2. Tony had shot himself; he was commencing a promising diplomatic career which had taken him to China; after an attack of rheumatic fever, he returned to England to work in the Foreign Office in the consular service; Lawrence recalls that the immediate cause of the suicide was a quarrel with his fiancée. In *Acquaintances*, chap. 21, A.J.T. described Tony's coming to a

"dead end" in his classical studies at Winchester, his interest in (quick command of) German, and his enrolling in the University of Bonn in 1933. A.J.T.'s elegiac poem "Ganthorpe," written in 1943, contains several reminiscences of Tony; see A.J.T.'s *Experiences*, pp. 393–401; cf. Philip Toynbee, *Part of a Journey* (London, 1981), p. 102, and passim.

[*postcard*]

Expédié par A. J. Toynbee
Grande Hotel
Bandol, Var,[1] France

4 May 1939

We are leading a lazy life here, in a very pleasant place, and it will have done us good. At first, when one suddenly stops one's ordinary activities, one feels other things more acutely; but I think it is a necessary stage, though a painful one, to face what has happened and to take it up into one's life, and, for this, a time of quiet and withdrawal seems to be needed.

The people here are kind and agreeable, and the atmosphere peaceful: international politics seem a long way off, in spite of Toulon being one's nearest town, and the gun-practice often in our ears.

It was a pleasure for us to have Lawrence with us for the first week.

I wish I had your company; but anyway you are much in my thoughts.

Yours ever,
A. J. Toynbee

1. Bandol, on the coast north of Toulon.

Saint Wilfrid's House
Ampleforth College, York

24 July 1939

Dear Professor Toynbee,

It is quite possible that we shall not meet for some time, in spite of hopes and wishes to the contrary; so I am writing you a note as a token of my feeling of deep gratitude and immense pleasure at receiving vols 4, 5, and 6 of *A Study of History*. In any case I would like to have my thanks down on paper.

Wednesday I shall take them into my little chapel and offer them up at Mass together with you and all your desires to God, for him to do his will in them and you.

I realise now how true and necessary for me is Christ's own phrase "He who is not against me is for me",[1] and that we are each given in accordance to God's wisdom what he wills. You should take F. Baker's[2] advice and pray to God for half an hour a day. As this is unsolicited advice, treat it as it deserves.

I hope that in your Survey for 1938 you will give us at least a foot-note on Yugoslavia explaining its origins as one thing. We get very little news about a strong

Catholic minority, that seems to get a bad time there. Perhaps this would be too much mere internal affairs and not fit matter for the *Survey*.

Ever yours affectionately,
Columba Cary-Elwes, O.S.B.

1. Mark, 9:40; Luke 9:50.

2. Augustine Baker, O.S.B. (1575–1641), wrote treatises on prayer; these were reduced to one volume and published as *Sancta Sophia* (1657); modern edition by Francis Gerard Sitwell, O.S.B., *Holy Wisdom* (London, 1961).

Ganthorpe Hall
Terrington, York

25 July 1939

Dear Father Columba,

I hope it will not really be long before we meet again; I may see you this afternoon at Ampleforth, and I hope you will soon be over here again.

You show a forbearance and understanding towards me that I am very humbly and affectionately grateful for. The spirit in you which makes this possible for you is something that I can at any rate recognise and admire and do my best to respond to. I say no more than "do my best", because our relation is a one-sided one; you do the giving and I do the taking, and generally this is an unsatisfactory kind of relation, in which no good comes to the mere taker; but I do not feel this about my relation with you, because, as far as I can succeed in taking something from you, I may perhaps, in the end, be giving something in return. And anyway there cannot be much wrong with a relation that is based on affection and sincerity on both sides.

I shall now try and take your advice about setting aside that half-hour a day for prayer—perhaps partly in the form of using some book like the *Imitation*[1] or the *Spiritual Exercises*.[2]

I am writing this note in case I don't after all, see you to-day.

Yours affectionately,
Arnold J. Toynbee

1. The *Imitatio Christi* of Thomas à Kempis (ca. 1380–1471).

2. Saint Ignatius Loyola (1491–1556) wrote the *Spiritual Exercises* as a handbook for four weeks of meditation on sin, Christ's life, his passion, and risen life.

Sedgley Park College
Prestwich, Manchester

23 August 1939

Dear Professor Toynbee,

You are never out of my mind for a day, and as the clouds settle down round us, you are for ever more present. I feel I must write.

I have read the fifth volume of your last three first. You said that our friendship was no giving on your part; well, it is untrue, as the riches of your mind are poured out there and came to me as a precious gift. Now I understand a little, no, enormously, more the world outside my tortoise shell! And much better lots of things inside it. This, I mention not for the purpose of discussing the book but to show you that as always friendship is reciprocal.

May God keep you and your family safe together with our England and our inheritance, even if great Babylon falls; that is, safe to fulfill our mission in his plan.

Oremus pro invicem,

Yours ever,
Columba Cary-Elwes, O.S.B.

London
(Temporarily)

30 August 1939

My dear Professor Toynbee,

I am almost convinced that war is almost inevitable. We may both be killed, or one of us; so I want to make quite certain that our friendship, so strangely guided by God, should have the effect He wants. You seem to regard me more than I deserve. There is nothing in me except what God placed there, so do not let our friendship stop at me but let it lead as it should, and in spite of my shortcomings, on to God; as it ever has done me. For I never think of you but I think of God's design in you, which you must fulfill.

Then this terrible thing: war. England, after God and Christ's Church is what we both love more than any other thing this side of death. You have great responsibilities. I will pray for you. We must keep rancour out, preserve peace of soul and love, in spite of, and against all the anger that may be let loose. You must do this, and hold the mob at the end from losing the peace. I know you love Christ's Church because this thought came to me; although you would not mind a Liberal free-thinker turning Catholic, indeed thinking it a gain, you would hate me turning apostate.

Please God a synthesis will come to your soul, and having sought peace and pursued it, you will find it.

Yours in *Caritate Christi*,
Columba Cary-Elwes, O.S.B.

Kind regards to your family.

Chatham House
10 St. James's Square
London

3 September 1939 12:50 P.M.

Dear Father Columba,

Your letter of the 30th August reached me here yesterday, but I haven't had time to ring up anyone of your surname in the London telephone book to get track of your London address, and I probably don't have time—even if you are still here. So for the moment I will just write to you at Ampleforth, in between odd jobs.

Besides feeling you one of my closest and dearest friends, I also feel that you are my most direct door to God. To have that door is a boon which I know I can't do anything equivalent for, either to God or to you. I just accept it and try to use it to the full.

If you were not in London this morning you may be amused to hear that we had our first air-raid warning within 10 minutes of the end of the P.M.'s speech. Nothing came over, so I suppose they were intercepted, or else it was a false alarm.

This Institute has turned into a sort of supplementary political information department for H.M.G. at a place which I hope to be able to tell you later. It is an enormous relief to all of us here that our job will still, as in peace time, be to try and tell the truth, and that we are not having to do propaganda. I got this point settled about a year ago, and we have been making our practical preparations ever since September, so we have been able to be quick. Our library and most of our staff are now already at work in our new quarters, and today only three of us are here in St. James's Square as a sort of rear-guard.

I am at the head of our war-time organisation:[1] will you pray for me and my colleagues that we may keep our souls free from all evil feelings (a) for the sake of our own souls (b) for the sake of our job, which, as you will see from my account of it, can only be done properly by people who are in a good spiritual state of charity, without animus or rancour.*

I am very grateful for your faith that I am "on the side of the Angels". Myself, I sincerely believe that I am, because I believe that the intellectual level, on which I do not believe in a number of things in the Creed, is a rather superficial level. What you say is quite true: I should be deeply sad and upset if (supposing this were conceivable) you ceased to be a Christian, and should be full of joy if my father-in-law[2] or Philip became one.

I didn't altogether keep to my resolution of doing spiritual reading for half-an-hour a day, but, since I came up here the Saturday before last, I have read most of the *Imitatio* in intervals between all kinds of hard work, including the loading of five lorries. I have read it, not for knowledge or scholarship, but for the most important side of A.R.P.,[3] and, while I was squatting in the basement here last night and Sunday morning, after the sirens went, I did feel less unready for sudden death than I should have felt a year or so ago. And for this I am indebted to you more than anyone.

I wonder if you are opening the school at once. I suppose it is important to provide as many billets as possible in the country for children; and boarding schools can help in this by reopening early.

The crucifix in the Abbey, hanging above the altar,[4] is printed very clearly on my mind and often presents itself there when I am free from the moment-to-moment jobs.

God Bless You.
Yours ever,
Arnold J. Toynbee

*This will be particularly important if, as I hope, we have something to do with the peace settlement as well as with the war.

1. A.J.T. was director, Foreign Research and Press Service, Royal Institute of International Affairs, 1939–43; director, Research Department, Foreign Office (1943–46). In the autumn of 1939, the Chatham House staff and its library of press archives were moved to Oxford, where A.J.T. directed a staff of experts who reviewed the clippings from newspapers from all over the world, including enemy and occupied countries. From these were composed running summaries of events, which were distributed on a weekly, fortnightly or monthly basis, chiefly to governmental offices. In 1943 the work was continued at the Old Stationery Office in London; the summaries have been reprinted in 27 volumes entitled *Review of the Foreign Press 1939–45*, published by Kraus International Publications, Munich.

2. George Gilbert Aimé Murray, O.M.; cf. A.J.T.'s letter of March 1910, above; reared as a Roman Catholic, he had long since abandoned his belief and practice; cf. *The Good Pagan's Failure*, p. 10. Although he was anointed at his death in his daughter Rosalind's presence, his return to the Church has been questioned; see the *Tablet* (29 June 1957), p. 603; and West, *Gilbert Murray: A Life*, pp. 245–50, for a discussion of his death; cf. Gilbert Murray, *An Unfinished Autobiography*, ed. Jean Smith and A.J.T. (London, 1960), pp. 212–20, for A.J.T.'s summary.

3. Air raid precautions.

4. In *A Study of History*, A.J.T. tells of his dream, in the summer of 1936, that he was "clasping the foot of the crucifix hanging over the high altar of the Abbey of Ampleforth and was hearing a voice saying to him *amplexus expecta* ('Cling and wait')" (IX: 634–35).

Ampleforth College
York

10 October 1939

My dear Professor Toynbee,

It is ages since I have written to you, and we must converse somehow, so here is a little news, jottings.

We had our dress rehearsal air raid warning last night. The school and staff were all in shelters in six minutes. It was not perhaps quite sufficiently a surprise so we cannot guarantee such speed every time.

I see your ministry has been under fire of criticism.[1] It is difficult to disentangle the case, but from here it looks as if the papers want more rope for cock and bull stories; or is it that it is a very subtle way of making the M. of I. appear in the character almost of an infallible pronouncer of true news. Intentionally or not, that has emerged. All to the good. However, I expect your section is rather remote from the Dailies and more concerned with neutral countries. I like the poem in the *Tablet* this week on the subject.

I suppose we are now on the brink of the real war, edging sadly into the blind part of it and wondering at what point we will come out. One's mind is too full of thoughts to put them down almost. But I am so glad you will, God willing, have a finger in the last act of the tragedy, and let's hope the first of a new birth. But how can sense come out of this rage. If it goes on more than 6 months we are doomed; or is that too pessimistic? How can federal Europe come out of war in two camps?

I read much of Vol IV of the *Study* this last month and it has put my patriotism to the test.[2] You are dead right on that point. How poignantly it all reads now, now sadly true the Greek analogy. Nevertheless we are right to love England best after the whole world, which is God's Church in fact or "*in potentia*", provided we love it in a Christian way. Love anything the wrong way, and it strikes back and kills. You would, I know, agree there.

Yes, of course, you are on this side of the Angels. Already your book is deeply imbedded in the modern mind. I have heard echos many times recently, and lastly in a book review of "*The Rise of European Civilization*" where the reviewer suggests a better title would be The Decline and Fall and many other things.

I must be honest and admit sadness over the adoptionist[3] point of view you seem to take up. I feel that in fact these people who held it ceased to believe Christ was God, it being so difficult to see what to do with the individual person, the entity, who was Christ before the adoption; it leads to dualism and then Christ would be just like us with grace. All that section made me see the clamouring necessity for a teaching body to decide now. But the Angels and God and the saints look not at what you hold but, in your case, being still on the journey, to that marvellous desire for God and Truth and so endearing courage to express your findings. The section on Hildebrand is profoundly interesting and moving too.

Here is that book on Pascal which has suddenly turned up. It is sending coals to Newcastle sending it to Oxford, more especially as you could easily get it in the original from the Taylor; but I said I would send it, and you might like to dip into it.

Please give my kindest regards to your wife and her mother whom I was so pleased to meet last time at Ganthorpe.

Bootham[4] has quietly slipped into place. I hear rumours we are to play them at soccer, and other rumours of a demonstration against blood sports at our first meet, the latter passing off very quietly, Ampleforth being mildly shocked! and amused.

We must pray all the day long, loving God.

Yours ever,
Columba Cary-Elwes, O.S.B.

P.S. Thanks for no. 1 of your war time publications.[5] The boys are devouring it and the blue book.

You must at most send me 2 small pages in reply some day.

1. See next letter.

2. "The Intractability of Institutions," in *A Study of History*, vol. IV, esp. pp. 206–14, where the inability of the parochial Greek states to form an international community is discussed.

3. A.J.T.'s "adoptionist" point of view is explicit in *A Study of History*, VI: 268–75; for a reference to the historic adoptionist theories, see *The Oxford Dictionary of the Christian Church*, ed. by F. L. Cross (London, 1958), pp. 18–19.

4. Bootham School, a Quaker boys school at York, took up residence at Ampleforth for about a year, expecting that York would be subject to aerial attack.

5. The Chatham House pamphlet *World Order Papers, First Series*, with an introduction by Viscount Samuel (London, 1940); six papers; these had been circulated before publication among members of the Institute.

Chatham House
Balliol College
Oxford

19 October 1939

Dear Father Columba,

Now it is the 20th, because, as soon as I had set pen to paper, some work turned up and another twenty four hours went by. We work hard here, which in one way is just as well. By the way, we aren't part of the M. of I. (fortunately for us), and our job has nothing to do with "publicity" or "propaganda": we try and state the truth to government departments who want it for strictly private use—truth in wartime being, like petrol, a luxury which is a government monopoly.[1] To be trying still to discover and present the truth—even if it is only the truth about the very ephemeral and earthy things that matter to the people who have to take public action in war, is a consolation because one is being allowed to do something that is in essence the same as one's ordinary occupation.

I find it very odd being installed here, for, when war broke out in 1914, I was a fellow and tutor of Balliol, and the wave that washed me out of this college then has now washed me back again. Perhaps I shall pass the next 25 years here till a third war washes me away to who knows where. I have a very fine company of able and learned men—mostly professors—working round me, and I hope we may succeed in forming a sort of oasis of intellectual honesty, and I hope also of Christian charity, in the great desert of the war-mind.

Today I turned aside from my daily round for an hour and gave a university lecture in Balliol Hall—standing on the spot where I gave my first lecture of all, more than 26 years ago. If I weren't such a firm disbeliever in the cyclic theory of the universe, I should be almost bamboozled into thinking that my life had come round full circle and that I was now again an undergraduate of this college (we lunch and dine in Hall) with hopes of becoming a fellow the year after next.

My wife found this kind of work strange at first, but she is now getting used to it, and her particular job—which is to follow the *Osservatore Romano* and the Catholic Press of the world—is congenial to her, more or less. Anyway, without such a job, she would feel rather lost without any household at Ganthorpe to look after.

I am most grateful for the book on Pascal. I came away with no more than half a dozen books in my suitcase—not knowing, when I left Ganthorpe in August, whether it was for three days or three years, and not packing a heavier load than I could carry myself at a pinch. As it has turned out, it may, I suppose, be three years. Among what I did bring were Saint Augustine's *Confessions*, *Pilgrim's Progress*, Saint Ignatius's *Spiritual Exercises*, the Book of Common Prayer, and the *Imitatio Christi*.

We are in digs at No. 3 Ship Street—a quiet place, within a stone's throw of my office in No. 15 staircase in the garden-quad in this college, and with a benign landlady; so we are well housed—in spite of our London house standing empty and Ganthorpe being stuffed with Yorkshire Hussars (to whom, I hear, the Monastery and not Father Quirk,[2] ministers—thus perhaps settling the delicate question of the debatable ground between your respective dominions).

You are very kind about my nonsense book, and of course bound not to like the Adoptionist passage. *Homo Occidentalis longe antehac dechristianisatus* has a very stiff back, because it is now about 250 years since he has bowed down and worshipped; so, when he tries to touch his toes again, his fingers at first get only as far as his knees; but the man is at any rate trying to bow himself now, and with practice, he may get further—though perhaps he will not again make exactly the same kind of gesture of worship as in the old days. Still, what his body does is only an outward expression of what his heart feels, and if his heart is inclining to God, perhaps God will have mercy on him. Do you know a man called J. H. Oldham,[3] who has just started publishing a weekly *Christian News Letter*? Here is a copy of the first number. Beneath the difference of doctrine and discipline, he stands, I believe, for the things you stand for at Ampleforth—things that are now perhaps going to be tested by a much more open and violent attack than they have been exposed to under a more passively pagan liberal dispensation.

God Bless You, and write again when you have the time.

Yours ever,
Arnold J. Toynbee

1. Perhaps a reminiscence of G. B. Shaw's "Truth telling is not compatible with the defence of the realm" (*Heartbreak House* [1919], rev. standard ed. [London, 1931], preface, p. 39).

2. Gerald Quirk (1882–1978), born in York and educated at Rockwell College, Ireland, and by the Benedictines at Douai, France; then serving as parish priest of Malton, Yorkshire.

3. Joseph Houldsworth Oldham (1874–1969), secretary of the World Missionary Conference (1908–10) and of its Continuation Committee (1910–21); in 1939 a member of A.J.T.'s "team"; he edited the *Christian News Letter* (1939–45); T. S. Eliot took part in editorial conferences and on occasion was guest editor.

Ampleforth Abbey
York

3 November 1939

My dear Professor Toynbee,

Fr. Justin sent me a line about a Spanish correspondent for you. I am writing to Fr. Sebastián Ruíz, Sto. Domingo de Silos, Provincia de Burgos asking him to act.[1] I suggest you should write immediately explaining what you wish him to do and explaining how it can not be harmful. It would be best for him to correspond directly with you.

There is another friend who might be useful, a young judge, now in Madrid but perhaps you only wanted the religious angle through Silos, having plenty of others in other ways. I would quite willingly get him in touch with you too.

I can just imagine your feelings when standing in Balliol Hall lecturing. I would have remained dumb. It is a good case of Withdrawal and Return, and I only wish you were to stand more often there and be the philosopher to the future Kings.

Your section on detachment and the following Transfiguration in vol 6 are indescribably great.[2] You put the process and conclusion, and it satisfies me who somehow seem to have reached the same conclusion without the process, if you see what I mean.

I read the passage on SS. Benedict and Gregory [3] to my political philosophy class the other day. They loved it.

Apart from the places where we obviously disagree—and the curious thing is that those parts could be omitted and it would not break the Synthesis—the "Study" reminds me of St. Thomas' *Summa*, only this time in History: the evidence of truth, the inevitableness, the joy of it. It makes me laugh. I wonder whether you ever feel like that.

There is only one place where, I think, unwittingly you mis-state Catholic doctrine, that is grace; and I venture to think that the reason was you were getting it from S. Augustine—safe enough, you will say; yes, but he developed, as he fought a rearguard action against Faustus and others.[4] I venture to think you would find food for thought in Billot [5] on the subject *De peccato Originali*.

Being yourself you almost never say an inaccurate sentence I suppose. But the implication is that Original sin is positive, a thing passed on. Really, to my mind it is just a failure to pass a thing on (grace) leaving man unbalanced.

Perhaps you don't want to be bothered with my very unscholarly remarks. But perhaps also it is good for you to have a change of thought; as I can imagine you working yourself to death at your work.

Pascal is dwarfed by the companions he has on your shelf but strangely enough you remind me of him, though in different spheres.

Those articles by your wife are a good idea and inspired me with a scheme which, of course, I have not carried out, namely to persuade people to pray every day during the war for the Germans. It would be a practical way of preserving our love of enemies and of doing of good to those that do us harm.

If this war becomes fierce and lasts three years, we are in for martyrdom; let us hope it will be a clear case and not some mixed political motive!

I teach Lawrence a little now, translation from the French. His command of English is better than mine, but we get on, and he will learn a few things.

There is still the false security, the occasional awareness of war. Our food is still much the same though the butter looks queer occasionally.

I have not said Mass for you for some time and will tomorrow.

Yours very sincerely,
Columba Cary-Elwes, O.S.B.

P.S. I am very glad your work is not M. of I. I knew you were not propaganda, but it is best to be quite independent and free to find truth.

Many thanks for the Christian newsletter. I may persuade myself to get it for the house.

1. Augustín Sebastián Ruíz Gutiérrez, O.S.B. (1897–1978).

2. "Transfiguration," in *A Study of History*, VI:149–68; and see "The God Incarnate in a Man," in *A Study of History*, VI:259–78, which ends with the poignant recognition of Christ:

"And now, as we stand and gaze with our eyes fixed upon the farther shore, a single figure rises from the flood and straightway fills the whole horizon."

3. "A Pair of Saviours," in *A Study of History*, III: 264–69.

4. Faustus of Milvius, a fourth-century Manichaean under whom Saint Augustine studied and whose teachings he later attacked in *Contra Faustum Manichaeum*.

5. Maxime Louis Cardinal Billot, S.J. (1846–1931); French theologian, lecturer at the Gregorian University, Rome; *De personali et originali peccato* (Rome, 1912).

Saint Wilfrid's House
Ampleforth College
York

29 November 1939

My dear Professor Toynbee,

It is strange that you should enjoy my babblings, but you have said so, and therefore in another spare ½ hour I write; not now expecting any answer as I know your business is too pressing and the strain too great to give leisure for or pleasure in, letter writing.

It was a great pleasure seeing your wife and hearing of you. I can't help wondering how your mind sees all this if it is the same mind now as wrote vols IV, V, VI. We must according to the latter mind be rapidly heading for that universal state, which seems to grip so hard its poor victims as to leave them no escape except death by strangulation; and further what good can come from force. But there I think you were never very fixed in your opinion; namely the evil of war, but kept at the back of your head the possibility of a just war occurring. This, I think—wretched I who am far removed from all this—started as a very just war, and could still remain so; but, here I agree with the "Study mind", the chances are excessively remote. So I pray for a quick war and one in which peace is achieved by negotiation before exhaustion. If that does not happen, and I am terribly afraid it will not, then if we live, we will see your diagnosis come true and have to prepare for the coming of desolation.

I wrote in my last letter of how you might be the philosopher to our kings. It amused me after to find (vol VI) that philosophers never came off! Well then, you must be the saint—easy said. But it was you that first spoke the word in this context. For this, may I tell you what is needed—provided you do not expect me to show the way—? You must give up all (your baggage) and follow Christ, who did; and S. Paul who did; and S. Augustine who did especially in the matter of Holy Scripture; and S. Francis who did; and S. John of the Cross who did; and who all *received* back a thousand fold. There is a marvellous passage in "The Hound of Heaven" which I would love to quote to you, but have no copy handy.[1] Perhaps you remember it. But read it when you are going to do the deed of 'losing all to gain all'.

When your wife was up we discussed one or two misprints. I found one or two others since:

Vol IV p. 151 n.2. Barère also spelt Barrère some lines down.

Vol VI p. 629 col. 1. Wars: General . . . . twice the phrase "peace settlement" following—(the 2nd looks unnecessary.) Also, wanting to read to some boys passages on just and unjust peace settlements I could not, from the pages here referred to, find the long account I knew existed of the Peace of 1783. This at length I found on p. 149 Vol. IV. Please include this in next edition which I hope will soon be needed.

Philip's marriage gave me a premonitory fear when I saw it in the papers, and Lawrence confirms my fears.[2] I am so sorry. You seem to be suffering in your own lives all that the modern world has given us of its cruellest. Perhaps God will give grace to the two young people despite their refusal to admit the need. God bless them.

I must stop.

Yours ever very sincerely,
Columba Cary-Elwes, O.S.B.

P.S. No answer yet from Spain. I am convinced that in order to get letters safely and in which our correspondents will dare speak their minds they must somehow get into the Diplomatic bag. I hope you soon get this.

1. Francis Thompson (1859–1907); "The Hound of Heaven" (1895), *The Oxford Book of Modern Verse* (London, 1970), pp. 54–59, at p. 59: "All which I took from thee I did but take, / Not for thy harms, / But just that thou might'st seek it in My arms."

2. Philip's marriage to Anne Barbara Denise Powell (1920–); dissolved in 1950; of this marriage were born Josephine Laura Toynbee (1943–); New Hall, Cambridge; married Francisco Campos Inchanrreque, and then David Lambourn; and Polly Toynbee (1946–); married Peter Jenkins (now a writer for *The Sunday Times*); reporter, the *Observer* (1968–71); feature writer, the *Observer* (1974–76); *A Working Life* (London, 1970); now a columnist and feature writer for the *Guardian*; "the most radiantly easy of all my children" (Philip Toynbee, *Part of a Journey*, p. 368). "I had heard that Philip's wife was a baptized Catholic and that the marriage ceremony was only civil." (C.C.E.)

The Royal Institute
of International Affairs
Balliol College
Oxford

4 December 1939

Dear Father Columba,

Bless you for going on writing to me when I don't answer: I now seem to have twenty minutes, but I can't count on them—I am always in John Gilpin's[1] position nowadays.

Perhaps one difference between the saint and the philosopher is that, while the saint drops all his baggage, the philosopher drops all except his intellectual baggage. Take myself: at the moment I have no house, no servants, no books, and, being busy, I can put up with the loss without any great exercise of virtue; but if I were called on to give up my free study of and speculation on, the universe, I should still have the impulse to defend my mental property, and shouldn't feel any sense of sin in doing so. Would it be a sin? And is the intellectual baggage an impediment? Well, you have read my empirical conclusions about the barrenness of philosophers compared with saints—and now my customers arrive at the counter, just as I thought I was off to the Bell at Edmonton. . . .[2] And now my time is up, but I will post this now and will take the next opportunity to continue. The director of the wartime organization of Chatham House is still, you see, the same mind as the writer of the Study of History.

Yours affectionately,
A.J.T.

1. William Cowper, (1731–1800), "John Gilpin's Ride."
2. Ibid.

Ampleforth Abbey
York

22 December 1939

My dear Professor Toynbee,

Business first. Still no reply from my friends in Spain.[1] Yesterday, however, I got a letter from another one who said that my letter had reached his and my friend (the latter asking for information). So perhaps soon there will be a reply. But what is so upsetting is that the one who wrote, in his letter, said he had already written FOUR times to me since the war began. Now, I have received exactly none of those letters. The question is: are our censors or Spanish ones stopping them? And if ours, can we persuade them to let them through?

One good bit of luck, I have found the address of the Canon of Burgos Cathedral with whom I stayed. But I intend not to write until we are more sure of not perhaps queering our pitch for good and all. If I write now and am not trusted somewhere on the way then the Canon's letters and mine will be intercepted *et puis, voila tout*!

May the work of Chatham House prosper and help by truth being disseminated even to the small extent allowed, to hasten on the conclusion of the war.

My father has been very ill and still is.[2] You might pray for him and my mother[3] who loves him just the same as 40 years ago when they married. I have been staying with them in Lincolnshire in my cousin's house[4] where they are for the duration. You might be interested in an account of its day; it is very much the old Catholic tradition—though our family is mostly Newman convert period. There is a lovely chapel imbedded in between the three sides of the house. Of course it has the blessed Sacrament. My uncle, a Jesuit missionary,[5] is chaplain and rather ailing but very active. There are lots of children and a French governess—Action française, reads Gringoire,[6] rather pacifist. The servants are Catholic. There is Mass every morning; all the household attend and this includes the servants, but all of them cannot. Then in the evening there is the Rosary heralded by the gong at 6:45. It is so charming to see the mothers and fathers teaching the little tiny ones their prayers and making little visits to the crib; and to see the natural way everyone goes to the chapel at night to say night prayers.

Whilst I was there half the house was down with measles and we had little processions led by the children taking Communion to the sick.

This may all sound very dull to you, but I write it because I do not think it will; it may be the passing of something very typical of the old English Catholic tradition, so naturally and supernaturally religious, yet much huntin' and fishin' too.

You must not feel obliged to answer my epistles. Many thanks for your last letter, all the more so as I know how busy you are. That letter did open up big questions and in a Christmas letter one hasn't much time to write one's mind, there are so many other letters to write but I must have a shot, your opening was too good a one to be missed!

No, of course you must go on exploring; that is what your mind is for, and ours too to hear what you have found. St. Augustine remained inquisitive, and I fail to recollect how many questions St. Thomas set himself. However, there was bound to be a 'however'—both these sages being at the same time saints included in their weapons for settling problems certain principles which were not in themselves discoverable by their reason alone, some truths which they took on faith. To those outside the Church this seems a cramping of the field of action, to those within a great saving of time and therefore opportunity for more extended exploration with more certainty of success.

This you know as well as I do; but underlying it is something, I wonder whether you appreciate as I or any Catholic does, namely the necessity, for our world's survival, of accepting authority in religious matters.

It seems to me that the withdrawal motif has a very profound intellectual significance. The saints of the Church went into their desert and came back more subject to the Church, humble, obedient, and, in that obedience, strong; other men, with seeds of greatness, withdrew and came back a law unto themselves—Hitler. It is not the withdrawal that produces the good effect, but only the dynamic energy; it is the obedience found in the withdrawal that turned that energy into real lasting worth.

The non-Catholics writing on Saints stress all kinds of things but not the thing they stress themselves above all, namely obedience; and they know best the country they have traversed.

What makes me gloomy sometimes about the future is that though Hitler may be bad, will the infusion of Federal Democracy into his dechristianised new world put Germany right? Can it even keep us right? Who is to say what is right, what wrong when all external voices are silenced and each man become a law unto himself? It is Babel in the moral sphere.

There may not be an authority that deserves to be obeyed; but the Church has consistently claimed to be so, has allowed worlds to slip through its fingers because it would not change its views, and it claims that there are sound reasons for accepting the claim, historical reasons. True, it may be natural for religion to arise at the time Christ taught, and as you say, it would not be beyond God's wit to choose a suitable time. On your showing we either float with Peter or we sink and if the latter, then I wish we could both live to see a prophecy I am prepared to risk! That Europe will again only rise by another Boniface or Gregory, a Catholic from distant lands; a strange Catholicism no doubt, with Mass in a barbaric tongue and a strange new philosophy in its train, an unintelligible jargon, and music from the East and architecture from the West; but so long as the truth had the same meaning, though differently decked out, we could both go up to a crucifix and say "ever new ever old". But the only authority we know or will know in our lifetime, I imagine, is the Catholic Church as it is now. I wait patiently for God to call you into it in his own good time, to be a leader of your generation, someone who will dare to face the fact of our ancestors' sin of "I will not serve" and counter-act it.

You do not mind my writing like this I am sure. It sometimes seems to be written between every line you write yourself.

A happy Christmas, full of God's grace and some peace.

My kindest regards to your wife, and Lawrence.

Yours affectionately,
Columba Cary-Elwes, O.S.B.

One day you will say, 'This fellow is a pest'; but before that, write and say the feeling is coming on, and I will write on other things.

1. Compare C.C.E.'s letter of 3 November 1939, above.

2. Charles Cary-Elwes (1870–1947); Stonyhurst College; civil engineer in India; in the wine trade in London; he revivified the Order of the Knights of Malta in England.

3. Edythe Isabel, (1876–1961); daughter of Sir John Roper Parkington.

4. Elsham Hall, near Brigg, Lincolnshire; home of Colonel Robert Geoffrey Gervase Elwes, D.L., J.P. (1890–1956); eldest son of Gervase Elwes (1866–1921) of Billing Hall, the singer; and of Lady Winefride Elwes, née Feilding (1868–1959). Colonel Elwes served in World War I as captain in the Northamptonshire Yeomanry and major in the Tank Corps and in World War II as staff colonel.

5. Cuthbert Cary-Elwes, S.J. (1868–1945), at one time a missionary in British Guiana.

6. *L'Action Française*, the journal of the militantly nationalistic movement of the same name, dominated by Charles Maurras; the journal was condemned by Pius X in 1914, as confirmed by a decree published in 1926; cf. *Survey of International Affairs, 1929*, by A.J.T., assisted by Veronica M. Boulter (London, 1930), pp. 483–88; *A Study of History*, VII: 520–21, n. 4. *Gringoire*: a right-wing journal.

THREE

1940–42

A.J.T.'s forebodings during the brooding early months of the war; peaceful Yorkshire; the invasion of France: "The tide is full against us now"; Dunkerque; the moral collapse of France; critique of Pétain; a glimpse of Hilaire Belloc; the battle of Britain; London in wartime; A.J.T.'s difficulties with his colleagues; the church "a pure stream in a muddy ditch"; contrasting attitudes to Russia, now in the war; Lawrence in the Coldstream Guards; A.J.T. flown by Clipper to the United States, "a middle-class terrestrial paradise."

3 Ship Street
14 January 1940 Oxford

Dear Father Columba,

I haven't had time, for weeks, to write—not even to ask you to go on writing, all the same, to me. But you will have guessed the reason why you haven't heard from me, and you won't, I know, weary of well-doing, for your letters are a great help to me, as well as a great pleasure.

Another pleasure that my wife and I have been having is Lawrence's being here for the holidays. It has turned out very happily: though we are camping in digs, he has been thoroughly enjoying himself, seeing a good deal of some Ampleforth friends, making new friends, and working hard at his painting. All this has given one a feeling of something normal and healthy and prosperous going ahead.

I have been having rather an anxious time, trying to pilot our ship through the mine-fields of questions in Parliament and letters to the *Times*. I had been on guard against the war-spirit's breaking out in hatred of the Germans, but, so far, all the hate has been inter-English—department back-biting department, and individual individual. One has twinges of regret for one's ordinary life and work, in which one's relations with one's neighbors are usually so friendly and pleasant—but no doubt the truth is that, if one can carry on the present unpleasant job without biting back or returning the bad feelings, one is doing the most useful thing that one can at the moment.

The Government, I think, are being brave in trying to wake people up to the unpopular realities, out of the dream of "normality" into which they have dozed as a result of the quiet opening of the War. It seems unlikely that Hitler will submit to perishing without having first tried every kind of frightfulness, and therefore unlikely that the first four months of the War give any indication of what now lies before us.

My own expectation still is that we are in for very great tribulations. These will, I fancy, refute, rather conclusively, the modern illusion that an earthly paradise (Capitalist, Marxian, Fascist, it doesn't matter which) is just round the corner, and that to run round and harvest this is the supreme end of Man. In this way, calamity may open the way for a return to God, but, merely because this way is opened again and other ways are choked up with ruins, it does not follow that we shall take the right road. In other words, there will be an opportunity, but it will need the utmost efforts of all men of good will to get Mankind to take it.

Well, this is just a scrawl to signal to you that I am alive and that I have you in my thoughts.

Yours ever,
Arnold J. Toynbee

Ampleforth Abbey
York

19 January 1940

Dear Professor Toynbee,

It was a great pleasure receiving your letter, and particularly to hear how you have enjoyed having Lawrence home.

I have followed, off and on, the letters about Chatham House and admired your restraint in not answering.[1]

Your remarks about great tribulation and the aftermath, I am afraid, are likely to prove true. Though sometimes it seems to me that Hitler's idea in the West is a kind of Chinese Wall, and then to behave as he likes behind it and Eastwards. This more especially as Russia is showing her usual ineptitude for war. But in either case the cost is economic ruin all round, and that might appear a good thing considering how purse-proud we are with even economic instability. It is interesting to hear others and oneself talk about the ruin of our civilization when they mean the crumbling of buildings and economic bankruptcy; one might justly though paradoxically say that the flourishing condition of super building enterprises and super banking were signs not of civilization but of its breakdown. Though that too is simpliste, because I suppose a truly Christian state could make use of all this ingenuity. S. Augustine in his *Confessions*—which I have recently been re-reading through your inspiring enthusiasm for that book—has little use for intellectual flirting with the natural sciences. One wonders whether he had a glimpse of the topsy turvidom that might result somewhat on the lines of your Chinaman on the English steamship. Can we pick up a thing that has been warped by centuries of mishandling and just put it right, or must we begin again? *Study of History* mind please note.

Among the people staying at Elsham (Lincs) was a Mrs. Pollen (née Baring)[2] who knows your wife slightly, I think. I bring her up because she told me that one of the books that she thought fitted her case (and that of her set) before becoming a Catholic was, *The Good Pagan's Failure*. She was very enthusiastic about it. Another book that appealed to her very much was Noyes' *The Unknown God*.[3] It is a pity you have no time to read because I should be interested to hear what you thought of Fr. Aelred's *The Love of God*[4] just published by Longmans.

I must stop my burbling and get on with one or two jobs. It still gives me a deep sense of union with you to mention your name daily at Mass and to feel that perhaps in some way your work is made even more Catholic than you will yet allow it to be in theory by that fact of a Memento.

My kindest regards to Mrs. Toynbee. No more news from Spain, though I have written again.

Yours affectionately,
Columba Cary-Elwes, O.S.B.

1. In *The Times* of 8 November 1939 and 9 December 1939 were letters concerning salaries at Chatham House.

2. Daphne Baring Pollen (1904–); wife of the sculptor Arthur Pollen; daughter of the third Baron Revelstoke; niece of Maurice Baring.

3. Alfred Noyes (1880–1958); *The Unknown God*, 2d ed. (London, 1934).

4. Aelred Graham, O.S.B. (1907–84); prior of Portsmouth Priory, Providence, Rhode Island (1951–67); *The Love of God* (London, 1940); *The End of Religion* (London, 1971).

3 Ship Street
Oxford

3 February 1940

Dear Father Columba,

Here is a scrap of time for writing you a line as a signal that you are constantly in my thoughts, however seldom one can get pen to paper, nowadays, for one's private correspondence with one's friends.

I was very sorry to hear about your father, and I have been praying for him, as you asked—intermittent and feeble prayers, I am afraid, compared to yours. I have also prayed for your mother, for whom his illness is probably a greater ordeal than it is for him.

I am surrounded by illness at the moment—mostly not serious, I am glad to say, but just the result of long bad weather on top of long overwork.

I have just been seeing an old Russian friend[1] of mine who is one of the noblest and most Christian-minded people I know. He is now for the second time in exile—having first lost everything in 1918, then had a job at the London School of Economics and been superannuated, and finally retired several years ago to share a house with some old cousins of his on the Karelian Isthmus, within a mile or two from Viborg! He has now lost everything again, and is still entirely free from bitterness or resentment. Experiences like his are a very searching test of one's character, and I have known few exiles who have stood up to the test completely, as he has. I hope we may do as well if our turn comes.

I, too, finished re-reading the *Confessions* the other day, having begun early in September and continued in odd moments. The last book drags a bit, but the discussion of the nature of Time[2] is fascinating, though of course not in the same way as the autobiography. If I live, I hope to re-read it several times.

Well, now I must sign my letters. I am really writing in Balliol, but, if you write to me there, it is automatically opened and registered, so I write as from 3 Ship Street.

Yours ever,
Arnold J. Toynbee

1. Baron Meyendorff (1869–1964); see A.J.T.'s *Acquaintances* (London, 1967), chap. 17; the Finnish war with Russia soon after was ended with the cession of the Karelian Isthmus and other territories to Russia; with Norman H. Baynes, Meyendorff wrote the chapter "The Byzantine Inheritance in Russia," in *Byzantium*, ed. by Norman H. Baynes and H. St. L. B. Moss (London, 1948), pp. 369–91.

2. Saint Augustine, *Confessions*, 11.14–30; A.J.T. contributed "Time" and "Pre-scientific Conceptions of Time and Their Influence" to the *Encyclopaedia Britannica*, 15th ed. (Chicago, 1974), 18:410, 411–13; and cf. *A Study of History*, 12 vols., VII:293–305, 452–54.

Saint Wilfrid's House
Ampleforth College, York

5 February 1940

My dear Professor Toynbee,

I appreciate very much your affection in finding time to write to me. I am sure you are all working yourselves to death. We live so secluded here that it still is hard to make real all these horrors and to appreciate the sufferings such as those of your Russian friend. He is more fortunate than many refugees, he has such kind friends. There is something about those people who remain serene in their sorrows which makes one worship God. I found that in Spain, as I listened to the quiet grief-stricken accounts of people whose experiences were almost past belief. That absence of hatred for the doer was so like our Lord.

What a man S. Augustine was. I would not have been surprised to have heard that the whole of Italy and Africa had followed him. At any rate his whole world did for centuries after. I have just been reading the staggering section on memory. He was only trying to make the mind puzzled—and amazed—mine was already in a whirl after the first few paragraphs. There were one or two passages that seemed to me to fit the world from which you are emerging. Do you remember:

> "For it is one thing from the mountain's shaggy top to see the land of peace, and to find no way thither; and in vain to essay through ways impassable, opposed and beset by fugitives and deserters, under their captain 'the lion and the dragon'; and another to keep on the way that leads thither guarded by the host of the heavenly General"
>
> End of bk VII

and the other bit which must have given you courage (I see it is in a footnote in my edition and from *de Doctrina Christiana*)

> "For as the Egyptians not only had idols and heavy burthens, which the people of Israel were to abhor and avoid, but also vessels and ornaments of gold and silver and apparel, which that people, at its departure from Egypt, privily assumed for a better use . . . at the command of God . . . So all the teaching of the Gentiles not only hath feigned and superstitious devices . . . it also containeth liberal arts fitter for the service of truth, and some most useful moral precepts . . . etc. . . . These the Christian, when he severs himself from their wretched fellowship, ought to take from them for the right use of preaching the Gospel."

There is justification, from one who knows, for your effort to retain the good of the last 300 years.

Both these passages made me pause a long time, and long for their fulfillment in your case and in that of all your friends.

You will be pleased to hear that in at least one school your book is already being used, though in a small way. I take a few potential scholars once a week for sociology. We begin with *The Code of International Ethics*.[1] They have already done *Rerum Novarum*,[2] *Quadragesimo Anno etc.*;[3] I thought a dose of the *Study*, using it for showing how we have got to our present impasse, a good idea. So we read extracts, trying to give a bird's-eye view of the Rise, Poise, Breakdown of our World. The disintegration may be performed before their very eyes. I find the chaos which was the seed-bed of Christianity fully described, but the first period very scantily. I suppose it will come in Vol. VII, now in America.[4] I cannot nail you down to the beginning of the second period, unless it is Constantine. But these I will only read later on. It is the last stage we are interested in—interested is not the word, passionately, hopelessly, almost despairingly concerned in. I hope to explain the Italian experiment, the Papal failure—with a few caveats, I think perhaps you do not sufficiently state the fears the Popes had that the Councils would usurp power by refusing the personal prerogatives of the Papacy. It is a pity the Vatican Council had to pack up in such a hurry before it could lay down the prerogatives—always admitted—of the Church as a whole. We will read all the facts on Parochialism, which are hard truths; on industrialism, on the Mother of Parliaments, in fact all my favorite bits. Then, perhaps, one day you will come and solve our difficulties that will crop up as we read.

You are very disturbing by your historical rules. According to one of them Germany ought to win this bout. Doesn't it look as if, on account of all the prayers, God is trying to give us time to think, (with) this impossible weather even for fighting?

My father's state of health is stationary. He is pretty bad. How I love to hear you have prayed for him and for my mother. As you say, she feels it dreadfully.

Did you see Miss Barbara Ward's article in the *Christian Democrat*?[5] She wants us to be kind to Liberals. We are.

Yours affectionately,
Columba Cary-Elwes, O.S.B.

1. *The Code of International Ethics*, published by the Catholic Social Guild, produced by European Catholic Sociologists (Westminster, Md., 1953).

2. *Rerum Novarum*, issued by Leo XIII, 15 May 1891; the classical statement of the traditional teaching concerning relations between employer and employee and the problems of social justice.

3. *Quadragesimo Anno*, issued by Pius XI, 15 May 1931; an elaboration of the themes of *Rerum Novarum*.

4. A.J.T. had sent his original notes to the Council on Foreign Relations in New York, to await peace.

5. Barbara Ward (1914–81); (Baroness Jackson of Lodsworth); assistant editor, the *Economist*; *The Rich Nations and the Poor Nations* (London, 1962); professor, international economic development, Columbia University (1968–73); chairman, Institute for Environment and Development (1980–81); active in Catholic circles. She was a friend of the Toynbee family; stayed at Ganthorpe Hall on several occasions; Lawrence remembers her teaching him to dance in the drawing room at Ganthorpe.

Ampleforth Abbey
York

11 February 1940 Sunday

Dear Professor Toynbee,

How wonderful! I immediately went off to Fr. Abbot to find out whether it could be done, and he said most certainly. He is afraid that the 14th is not a good day as we will still have many "chapter fathers" from the missions in until the 15th (morning) so suggests you come on the 15th when everything will be all clear. However, if it is rather inconvenient staying in London, I could easily put you up in a spare room in S. Wilfrid's, if you didn't mind, from after having returned to undergraduate life, returning to schoolboy life for one night. Do just as suits you best. Say what train you are coming by and we will meet you at the station.

I read the account of the discussions in the House about supplies for Chatham House, and was very pleased to see it all settled at last. It must be a great relief to you.

¡Hasta la vista!

Columba Cary-Elwes, O.S.B.

The Royal Institute
of International Affairs
Balliol College, Oxford

7 March 1940

Dear Father Columba,

This has been my first chance of sending you a line since we said good-bye in the guest room the Wednesday before last—which already seems ages ago, but I must send you just a word of affection and gratitude before I am immersed again.

I have printed on my mind's eye the crucifix[1] in the church, and on my heart my feelings for you and for my other friends in the monastery, by whose kindness I have been made to feel at home there.

I must go off to receive a posse of V.I.P.'s who are bearing down on us seeking material, I suppose, for further parliamentary questions. I beard them to-night, show them round to-morrow, go up to London to-morrow night, and take Saturday's aeroplane for Paris.

What a life: but one can still think of your life and take pleasure in it.

Yours affectionately,
Arnold J. Toynbee

1. See A.J.T.'s letter of 3 September 1939 above.

Elsham Hall
15 March 1940 Brigg, Lincolnshire

My dear Professor Toynbee,

I would have written before but as you see I am with my father again and I knew you would send me a line. It was only forwarded to me yesterday. Many thanks.

My father is now very weak indeed, though he may yet recover. He is quite resigned, more than resigned for heaven. He almost longs for his favorite Saints to come and take him there.

It was one of those special gifts of God your being able to come up to Ampleforth and our being able to have you with us. Sometimes I wonder whether I should be more militant and bring up the problems that keep you from the Church, but deep down I think you are still in the stage of clearing the ground of débris and not quite able to see. But one day you yourself will see the City, the débris being cleared away. It did make me sad to feel I could not understand your miracle difficulty, and I have prayed about it and think now it is more understandable, very understandable. Perhaps you would like to read my thoughts.

I tried to find an analogy. This is what I thought of. Suppose one knew lots about Napoleon but not his Egyptian expedition, and took it for granted that such an enterprise was fantastic, and then someone said it had occurred. What would one do? I presume, begin *a priori* by saying the thing was too unlikely to be worth considering and then go into the evidence. In fact did he? I need not explain the analogy. (I don't know in fact whether the Egyptian expedition was odd or not, but it does not matter for the analogy. You probably know any number of extremely unlikely doings of people that have actually happened).

My old Jesuit uncle when I spoke about the problem, putting it in your way: the extreme unlikeliness of the spiritual breaking into the natural material order, said, among other things, that he thought prayer would solve the problem, I think because prayer is the bridge between the natural and supernatural, the human will being caught up into the realm of God's will which is the source of all the laws, not laws of nature but the way God decided things should normally work. Fr. Raphael[1] had an interesting point of view. He said that as Protestantism dropped further and further into naturalism, or just "leading a good life, imitating Our Lord, according to one's lights" the need of the miracle vanished, the natural order needed none, it was its own announcer. But grant GRACE, the raising of man to a new level, the super-man, but in the Christian dispensation not only super-man but super-spirit, God-like man level, the need for miracles is inevitable, because the natural order cannot explain or guide to such a thing. A miracle, he would say, was a sign that a bridge had been put across between the world of man and nature and the world of God's own mysterious Life.

The usual reaction to the problem is to produce 1st or 2nd hand miracles. Here, everyone knew people who had been miraculously cured. I shan't recount these. But in the night before last an Ampleforth old boy now a sub-lieutenant in the 60 Rifles came to tea and supper. Casually, he mentioned he had been to France and Lourdes and that he had been cured. There was great delight and we got him to tell us the story; it is so perfect an example that I must put it on paper.

At the age of 15 he was suffering from tuberculosis and was at Ampleforth, he had got to the permanent temperature, dry cough to choking, black in the face stage. He was not told what he had. He was shown to a specialist who reported T.B. and bad. His parents arranged for him to go to Lourdes with some friends in a pilgrimage. He was not told why. He rather objected, he disliked the discomfort, disliked the "friends" and felt the care which was taken of him unnecessary and irksome. He got there, disliked the commercial side very much, felt extremely ill very often. After 5 or 6 days he was persuaded to have a dip in the baths. He did it very unwillingly and not thinking it was to much purpose. The thing was very unemotional, he was suddenly pounced on by the attendant who ducked him. He was irate. However, it was done. Two days later he no longer had any cough, he went for a walk in the Pyrennees, got lost, has been perfectly well ever since. He went to the specialist. He admitted the cure, was very angry and refused to admit the cause, and called it inexplicable. It is a good example isn't it? I hope you haven't got bored and stopped reading.

Enough for miracles.

This Finland collapse[2] makes me feel as though I and all Englishmen have taken part in a murder. It is too dreadful to contemplate, comparable only to the Austrian disaster.

If you keep your mind on Christ crucified as you say you do, you and your friends who are Christians and still powerful may yet save us. S. Gregory pray for us. Have you seen the *Tablet* of last week all about S. Gregory?[3]

Yours affectionately,
Columba

1. Fr. Raphael Williams, O.S.B. (1891–1973); monk of Ampleforth; professor of philosophy and watercolorist.

2. On 12 March 1940, the Russians breached the Mannerheim Line, and Finland accepted peace terms negotiated at Moscow.

3. Gregory I (ca. 540–604), monk; pope; doctor ecclesiae; see the *Tablet* (9 March 1940), pp. 220–24; A.J.T. describes his achievements in *A Study of History*, III: 267–69.

Ampleforth Abbey
6 April 1940 York

My dear Arnold,

I am tired of calling you Professor etc.; the only thing that kept me from changing was your still calling me *Fr.* Columba; you had therefore better drop the Fr. I do also wish Arnold were more Christian—I mean the name—perhaps the J. is the 19th Century way of hiding, yet keeping, deep down our Christian origin.

At last the boys have gone. Two of mine are prone in the infirmary with diptheria but now are nearly well. My father is much better, even sitting up. But with heart cases: better today and bad the next is the rule.

You will be amused to hear and see that I chose the enclosed as the Higher Certificate class Prose piece for the Prize exam.[1] You will notice one word is changed to help them on to a French word, "enrichment" for "enhancement"—embellishment, had I thought of it, would have helped even more. One or two sentences I left out to save space and retain a complete thing. Herewith also the best boy's answer. It might distract your mind a little.

When I was at Elsham we listened one day to the *Dream of Gerontius*[2] coming over the wireless. I took down a copy from the shelf, it had been Gervase Elwes'[3] and apparently given him by Mary Gladstone.[4] In it was a letter from Newman to some obscure person. I liked it so much that I sent it to the *Tablet*. You will find it in D. W.'s *Talking at Random*[5] page. I wonder what you think of its history and also what Rosalind thinks of its theology. Far too predestinate I'll be bound. It is true Newman's beginnings were Calvinist—I think I'm right. He also seems to have more use for the energies of the Jesuits than for that of the more obscure but equally ubiquitous monks in the earlier days. All the same it is rather fine and suits our day better than his own. But it is hard to be still. I forgot to mention in my miracle story that the boy did not know he had the disease nor that he had been cured till three months after his return to England. All he knew was that his cough had gone—he became aware of the fact.

I cannot understand why people are not more clear-headed about the motives of this war. Lord Elton's letter in the *Times*[6] was a fine recall to Christ but not a true exposition of our aim. It seems to me that we—having fought or at least striven spiritually to preserve Catholicism in Europe and failed—are now at the next stage down the cliff, fighting or striving spiritually to preserve the Natural Law, natural justice as against force. And even the fact of brotherhood of all men which in fact came to us through Our Lord is, I suppose, acceptable and self-evident to all who believe in God. Or perhaps we can only be sure of it from the fact that Christ said he came to save all men.

The only people who can have no logical part in this war are the anti-moralists. I was going to say atheists, and perhaps truly, but somehow they seem to preserve the idea of the brotherhood of man.

I told my S.J. uncle I was reading Léonce de Grandmaison's[7] book *Jésus Christ* vol. ii and it turned out they had been great friends. In fact the four inseparables in their student days were de le Taille,[8] Grandmaison and Lebreton.[9] He has a great opinion of the sanctity of Grandmaison. Even then, he said, Grandmaison seemed to have read every book on his subject, Catholic and otherwise. He had a high opinion of your friend Ed. Meyer,[10] for all his contradicting him. They, all four, talked metaphysics all day and were ardent Thomists (please note) of the Dominican persuasion, leaving Suarez[11] high and dry. When the exams came round there was a great set to on the subject, but they held their own—and were not cast out of the Society! All this partly just gossip, partly to persuade you one day to read vol. ii of Grandmaison's good book.

I almost forgot to say I had received at last another letter from Spain, here is a transcription of the relevant passage.

This letter must now stop.

Yours affectionately,
Columba Cary-Elwes, O.S.B.

1. Compare *A Study of History*, IV : 59: the description of autumnal foliage in the Connecticut Valley.

2. John Henry Cardinal Newman (1801–90); *The Dream of Gerontius* (London, 1866).

3. Gervase Elwes (1866–1921); a cousin of C.C.E.'s father; he was the first to sing the chief part (Gerontius) in Elgar's oratorio *The Dream of Gerontius*.

4. Mary Gladstone Drew (1847–1927); the second daughter of William Ewart Gladstone; cf. *Letters of Lord Acton to Mary, Daughter of the Right Honourable W. E. Gladstone* (London, 1904).

5. *Tablet* (6 April 1940), p. 336; "D.W." was Douglas Woodruff (1897–1978), the editor (1936–67).

6. In his letter to *The Times* (2 April 1940), Lord Elton said, "Against a fanatical paganism, we cannot victoriously defend the Christian heritage without setting ourselves to recover the Christian faith."

7. Septime Léonce de Grandmaison, S.J. (1868–1927); *Jésus Christ, sa personne, son message, ses preuves*, 2 vols. (Paris, 1928); trans. Basil Whelan, Ada Lane, and D. Carter as *Jesus Christ, His Person, His Message, His Credentials*, 3 vols. (London, 1930–34).

8. Maurice de la Taille, S.J. (1872–1933); *Mysterium fidei* (on the Eucharist), 3d ed. (Paris, 1931).

9. Jules Lebreton, S.J. (1873–1956); *Histoire du dogme de la Trinité des origines au Concile de Nicée*, 8th ed. (Paris, 1927); trans. A. Thorold (London, 1939).

10. Eduard Meyer (1855–1930), historian of the ancient world; frequently quoted by A.J.T.; *Geschichte des Altertums* (Stuttgart and Berlin, 1884–1902).

11. Francisco de Suarez, S.J. (1548–1617); Spanish theologian who wrote commentaries on the *Summa* but whose system differs in some respects from that of Saint Thomas Aquinas.

Ampleforth Abbey
York

22 April 1940

Dear Arnold,

No letter from you does not give me a feeling that you have forgotten me, so do not worry at receiving another without having answered. All I think is that you must be what my brother calls—though probably quoting P. G. Wodehouse—up to the antlers in work.

I missed Hitler's birthday and only heard faint echoes this morning. So I missed yours. I can't think why we do not make more of them when grown up, they are very salutary reminders. Perhaps, that is exactly why; we do not want to be reminded.

I shan't say Mass for you tomorrow, it being S. George's Day and obviously reserved for all England, or the next two days, as I will be with my Father—who is much better—but on Friday when I return here.

We had the most perfect day last Monday, a week ago. You would have enjoyed it. It was a clear and cold day, the sky light blue, but not a misty blue, and buxom clouds with a rather piercing wind, but exhilarating. We went straight up to the Beacon Farm,[1] then over the heather towards the Rye[2] down into its valley. There in a sheltered spot we sat watching the running water for a bit and pushed on towards Rievaulx[3] where we had a sandwich lunch. So fortified, we clambered up one of those gashes in the valley side on the left, back on to the moor and walked on and on, spotting deer on our right till we reached the Goremire[4] road well beyond Tom Smith's Cross. One aeroplane sped over us going Norway-wards, and we said a prayer for its safety. Then we made our way down towards Wass[5] and Byland[6] where, through the largesse of Fr. Abbot we had an excellent tea, and so home and to bed.

No, not immediately to bed; in fact, I was detained long after supper by P. Antonio[7]—the Basque priest, still in mild exile—who had come for a week. He still knows no English, still has no use for Franco. I managed to get him to explain how it was he came over with so many Communist children. Originally, the shipload had been arranged by the Catholics among themselves; but, when the "Rojos" heard, they insisted on anyone going, in fact, whoever put their names down first.

This holidays I have put into some sort of shape my little "paper" on the Christian Assaults on China.[8] A very sketchy affair, but interesting to the general public that knows nothing of these things. It is now on its way to the Clergy Review and may be printed. I draw the analogy between China now and England in S. Gregory's Day and quote your little bit about the latter, a mild tribute to one of my inspirers in this Chinese venture. I have also translated lots of passages from P. Ricci[9] so that I need not refer to the texts again. Now I need to get to a big library for the Franciscan period and for all the Jesuit "relaciones".

This is all about myself, excuse.

From here, the war seems to be going on rather well, despite Denmark.[10] Norway may give us our opportunity. Can't you understand S. Joan of Arc better now, as the champion of moderate nationalism (patriotism)? Now that we are pooling economic and politic life with France, we should pool saints. S. Joan is the saint of the moment, not that she would not be in favour of a Federation of Europe now, but not by force or by exterminating the patriotic spirit. She was not afraid to use force to deter aggressors.

It would be terribly against the grain for me to have to share in a war against Italy. I cannot believe Mussolini will have the temerity to venture further than he has, provided we are determined enough. He can't have his people behind him. That is merely how I feel.

Well, this letter is too long for you to read already, so I must stop.

Yours affectionately,
Columba Cary-Elwes, O.S.B.

1. Beacon Farm, on the hill behind Ampleforth Abbey; in the Middle Ages the site of beacons lit to warn of enemy Danes or Scots.

2. The Rye flows thirty-five miles into the Derwent through a series of scenic valleys.

3. Rievaulx Abbey (*Rye Vallis*), a Cistercian foundation colonized from Clairvaux in 1131; completed in the thirteenth century, destroyed under Henry VIII.

4. The Goremire Road runs to Sutton Bank overlooking Goremire Lake, past the grave of Tom Smith, an eighteenth-century hanged highwayman; the Ampleforth boys held an annual picnic not far from the lake.

5. Wass, a small village near Coxwold and Byland Abbey.

6. Byland Abbey ("bella landa nostra") was founded in 1171 by monks of the order of Cîteaux; at the dissolution of the monasteries (1539), the abbey was plundered, and, like the Colosseum in Rome, it became a quarry; the west facade, with a great opening for a rose window, and part of the walls survive.

7. P. Antonio had been exiled by General Franco because of his Basque separatist views.

8. Later to grow into *China and the Cross* (New York, 1957).

9. Matteo Ricci, S.J. (1552–1610), missionary to China who adapted Christian teachings to Chinese molds; his work was later frustrated by opposition in Rome. Cf. *A Study of History*, VII: 441–42.

10. On 9 April 1940, the Germans occupied Denmark without formal resistance; Norway was still resisting, but effective defenses were broken by 30 April 1940.

Ampleforth Abbey
5 May 1940 York

My dear Arnold,

I cannot write you a long letter just at the moment, but I send two things; one may at least amuse you on account of its temerity, *The Philosophy of History*, written long before I had heard of the *Study*; and the other is for Rosalind who asked for it! It is an incredible piece of translation and a pretty incredible piece of S. Augustine;[1] but she said she did not mind how bad it was. Some day, I should like them back.

We are having some lovely days when, as so often here, the air seems golden.

Today is the feast of the English Martyrs. I always have to pull myself up about martyrs, especially those of long ago, because my tendency is to imagine them not ordinary people. The English ones are just sufficiently modern to give me the necessary shock—their cold-blooded courage.

The Norwegian Campaign is depressing people here—but, perhaps, unduly because, after all, the landing in the South[2] was only a daring shot in the dark. Still I should not like to be at Narvik next winter.

Herewith another letter from my Spanish friend. I had written putting our case very strongly. Anyway, it got to him.

Yours ever,
Columba CE, O.S.B.

1. "I think this was a translation (done by me) of S. Augustine's treatise on predestination, which was a letter to his friend Bishop Simplicianus, entitled *De diversis quaestionibus ad Simplicianum*, M.L. vol. 40, tome 6 of *Opera Sancti Augustini*." (C.C.E.)

2. Anglo-French expeditionary forces had landed in southern Norway in April 1940 but were compelled to withdraw on 3 May 1940.

Ampleforth Abbey
York

12 May 1940

My dear Arnold,

At 9:15 this morning the local Bobby came to the House and told me that "Oswald"[1] had to go off with his brother to be interned. There was no saying no. We told them as gently as we could, gave them some books which could last for some time, and off they went with a Bootham boy at 10:15 A.M.

Both of them were very brave about it, particularly Oswald. They expect to be interned for the duration; but one of the officials seemed to think they might be back in a few weeks.

So the war has begun in earnest[2] and your prophetic mind proving true that the fortress theory of last war is proving out of date; I sincerely hope the War cabinet theory will not prove true as well.

We had full pontifical ceremonies this morning and I thought how often you had been present in the past and how you were in some way present this morning—the feast of the Holy Spirit—and how the sequence is your prayer, that lovely thing composed by an Englishman; and I asked the Holy Spirit to give you his gifts and his Fire and fearlessness and his Light.

I read occasionally your Summa Historica as a substitute for the living voice, and re-read yesterday the section on *The Reign of the Mock King*.[3] The resemblances "*sautent aux yeux*," and one feels inclined to agree with the terrible hypothesis that the soldiers did this rite as a "bright idea". For me it came as a flash of insight: here is another example of how Christ's life seems to catch up and bind to itself all the past—bad, by suffering it and good by transforming and transcending it.

Thank you for yet another insight for me.

Yours affectionately,
Columba Cary-Elwes, O.S.B.

P.S. Please excuse writing—vile nib. You must not write unless really rested.

P.P.S. At present we see no way of preventing this internment, perhaps you have power to get them back, or at least Oswald.

1. Oswald Wolkenstein Rodenegg and his brother Christoph, refugees from the Nazis, had left the Jesuit school at Kalksburg, Austria, and entered Ampleforth in January 1939, under Rosalind's wing.

2. On 10 May 1940, German armies had invaded the Netherlands, Belgium, and Luxembourg.

3. *A Study of History*, annex II to V. C (ii) (*a*), "Christus Patiens" (VI: 376–539).

The Royal Institute
of International Affairs
Balliol College
Oxford

14 May 1940

Dear Columba,

Up to the antlers[1]—and over—I certainly am, but I must just seize a moment to write to you, who are never weary of well-doing in writing to me and praying for me.

About the Wolks, Rosalind has asked a friend of hers who is a big gun on the Catholic Refugees Committee to go straight to Sir Alexander Maxwell[2]—a big-wig in the Home Office (big enough to have common sense and human feeling) who himself arranged for the Wolks to be admitted in the first instance. One can't say, in present circumstances, whether this is likely to have an effect. As the Home Office know all about the Wolks, and as they have been in the School since before the age of 16, and were planted there by us and not by any grown-up refugee who might be fifth-column, the case is clear; but the sudden swing from a foolish slackness about aliens to a sudden severity may override sense and justice. H.M.G., I believe, have known all about parachutists for months past, and ought to have made a review of all aliens long ago, and in that case the Wolks would no doubt have been given a clean bill of health. I feel very unhappy about them—there is something innocent and full of good will in both those boys—vastly different though they are from each other in other ways. They had acclimatised themselves to English life so wholeheartedly. It is, of course, only a minor misery in proportion to the rest, but it is a real one.

Well, Hitler has staked everything, and we must face the possibility that he may win and that Religion and Freedom may be suppressed all over Europe—temporarily, but for a time that might still run into hundreds of years. If we can stem the tide, then I should say Germany was certain to collapse before the end of next winter. Well, the battle is joined, and, whatever may be the issue in this chapter, we may be certain that, in the long run, God will not let the gates of Hell prevail.

I find myself more exercised over the future if we win—as I believe we shall do by a hair's breadth—than if we are smashed. If we are smashed, it is all very simple for us—we have no material power to do well or ill; but, if we win, what are we to do with a Germany that has done this?

Rosalind thanks you for the thing you sent her, and I thank you for your own paper—though I (15th May—I got interrupted for the rest of yesterday) will confess (and in the circumstances, without shame) that I haven't yet been able to read it.

About the reign of the mock king, I am diffident about offering any explanation of those anticipations, in history, of the Incarnation and the Passion which I have discussed in that Annex. For myself, I think the rationalists' explanation is, if at all true, only a part of the truth and that not the most important part. The simile in my mind is that of dawn before sunrise: the Light spreads over the sky before the Sun himself appears: but this is only an image.

Now I must go to a committee. This being 11:45 on Wednesday 15th May, I expect to see the main action fought, not in front of Brussels, but on French soil between Meuse and Moselle. I think the Germans will dent the Maginot line here, and that we shall perhaps pull back to the Franco-Belgian frontier between the Meuse and the Sea. If Hitler does not get a complete military decision now, I think he will collapse next winter—but we shall have a gruelling time meanwhile.

Yours affectionately,
Arnold

1. Lawrence recalls that A.J.T. read P. G. Wodehouse to the family.

2. Sir Alexander Maxwell (1880–1963), K.C.B.; permanent undersecretary of state, Home Office (1938–48).

Ampleforth Abbey
York

29 May 1940

Dear Arnold,

The tide is full against us now, but please God it will turn. You were right about Sedan, but even you with all your uncanny foresight could scarcely have foreseen the disaster. This battle in a new edition of the *Study* will have to be added to the David and Goliath section, as a complete revolution in technique. One wonders whether small sea craft will do the like revolution in the Channel.

The part of your letter I was most grateful for—apart from the fact of the letter at all, which was an undeserved sign of your affection, was the bit about the Annex. It somehow brought peace to Volume VI and that section of the letter is inscribed at the end of the Volume.

Someday I will show you all my remarks on each "correspondence". But here I must record the thought: you must not be too hard on the words "He who is not against me, is for me",[1] as you yourself will come under that category! Thank God for his broadmindedness.

If we lose, you must finish your work; and we all must transcend the mundane level and achieve liberty of spirit even in chains, and not try and turn the tables yet again by force. Should we win you must prevent the annihilation theory getting hold; as for the form of the political structure in Europe, we would have to take the rôle of Universal State. And, having said that, have I signed our death warrant?

Perhaps I am wrong, but I feel convinced that all these political and economic contrivances for our safety are as useless as the Maginot line, leaving us with false security. We must get a moral order first, i.e. unity of purpose, a seeking of God, and the right way. And for this we need unity of teaching, yes *teaching*, because even you, with all your knowledge self-taught, admit to be still groping. In other words we need a Revelation, or isn't it: we need the power to accept the Revelation already given. I know you agree, and we storm heaven for grace as S. Augustine the great did with tears, longing to walk over the water to Christ.

But meanwhile the immediate problems call for a solution. Act, in them, as though you were in a Catholic world, and on its principles. After all, even if you cannot see it all, still, it is the only coherent plan of action; and Our Lord will say at the end—if the Catholic theory is right—"He was not against me".

P.S. The above is an absurd letter telling *you* what to do. Still I leave it as it stands, being the ideas inspired by thinking on your letter, and the desires arising from those thoughts.

There is no news except that a Catholic prep school—Avisford[2]—is arriving in a day or two and is occupying, this term, the gym, the underworld of the theatre and the infirmary. Bootham next term, if it comes, are going back to York.

No more news of the Wolks, though Fr. Raphael and Fr. Peter saw them the day before they left York.

I am afraid the 'hate campaign' has started in earnest in the press and the boys find it hard not to want to torture Hitler as we wanted to do to the Emperor William.

I wish you all God's blessings on your work, and hope you have succeeded in making your team work as you wish.

My introduction to Christian Missionary efforts in China was refused by *Clergy Review* and *Dublin*, though C. Dawson[3] said some kind things about it.

Punishment and yet with mercy they should suffer—but war is punishment enough in all conscience.

Are the Germans merely acting like external proletariat—war bands? Should we vacate a Christian world including the Rhine, Bavaria, Austria, Hungary and let them come in after. The difficulty is: are we Christian? With Wells and others so noisily broadcasting the futile 19th century stuff. Back again we get to the need for conversion, "*Jerusalem, Jerusalem, convertere ad Dominum Deum Tuum.*"[4]

Yours affectionately,
Columba, O.S.B.

1. Mark, 9:40; Luke, 9:50.

2. Avisford Preparatory School; near Arundel; founded in 1922 as a preparatory school for Catholic boys; closed in 1973.

3. Henry Christopher Dawson (1889–1970); historian; *The Making of Europe* (London, 1932); *The Gods of Revolution* (London, 1972); Charles Chauncey Stillman Professor of Roman Catholic Theological Studies, Harvard Divinity School (1958–62).

4. A coda to the Lamentations of Jeremiah, recited during the last three days of Holy Week.

Ampleforth Abbey
York

16 June 1940

My dear Arnold,

It must be quite a time since I wrote—and what hair-raising things have occurred since. Italy's entry in the war makes nonsense of any attempt to show that this war is between people inside a wall and the barbarians without, these latter are now evidently within as well. The only solution is the one I came across again in the "nonsense book", the proletariat turning to Christ. I have the utmost confidence they will; and feel we should turn all our energies to help; I only wish I were a member of that class like abbé Cardijn of the Jocists.

I hear you gave a lecture on Christianity and civilization,[1] and how I wish I had been there. You could not conceivably just send me the MS. I suppose, and I promise to return it.

The poor Wolks are still in his majesty's keeping only more so, as now they have left York. Oswald wrote me such a nice letter, saying how he loved Ampleforth, how terribly he missed daily Mass, not realizing, before he had it no more, how much it had meant to him.

What a wretched wireless address by Duff Cooper on the Italians.[2] But how hard it is to keep oneself free from the war mind; and how humanly impossible for the soldiers—or is their problem more God's love in the midst of this crying misery. I feel my mind slipping down to a mild form of hate, i.e. a refusal to accept the Germans back into the Brotherhood after the war. If we win we will have to create a Universal State and so make them physically innocuous, and who knows but the 2,000 years of grace may yet turn that U.S. into a Christendom.

My relief was great on hearing that Paris had been saved a siege,[3] though it looked like a sign that the French resistance was nearing its end. I may be wrong, but it seems we will soon be fighting alone.

You will be glad to hear that my father is now so well that he is leaving Lincolnshire, and with my mother going off to Bournemouth. I would not have thought it possible three months ago.

These chaotic times give one a more acute appreciation of S. Benedict and his character and his little Rule. One feels quite akin in outlook, whereas before it was difficult. I sit down daily and read, or rather ponder over, it for 1/2 hour and marvel at the *long view* he preserved through and through. Listen to our Master, God "*ut ad eum per obedientiae laborem redeas, a quo per inobedientiae desidiam recesseras*", is the motif. But a 20th century S. Benedict might put *idolatriae* in the place of *inobedientiae* for we still worship idols—ourselves, or money, or state, or race, or class, whilst in his day those idols perhaps were crashed already.

This may be terribly platitudinous to you. It is just me.

Another personal thing which war has made plain to me is the peace that comes through having given things up. I have nothing to lose but my life. The only belongings I worry about are the letters you have written me which I have preserved for obvious reasons. And then the thought of the misery of the millions wandering the highways of Europe homeless pulls me up, and I wonder how I would stand that. From this way off, I should like to take the place of one, as some early Christians would exchange themselves with Christian slaves. It is terrifying to be left so safe in the strife—but perhaps it will not be long before we are caught in War's embrace. Let us go on praying for one another.

My kindest regards to Rosalind.

Yours affectionately,
Columba, O.S.B.

No answer expected except the MS.?

1. The Burge Memorial Lecture, "Christianity and Civilization," delivered in the Sheldonian Theatre, Oxford, 23 May 1940: "At a critical moment . . . in the history of both the lecturer's own country and the world"; reprinted in *Civilization on Trial* (Oxford, 1948), chap. 12, pp. 225–52.

2. On 10 June 1940, Italy declared war on France and Great Britain; Duff Cooper, minister of information, broadcast a speech in which he said: "Italy has never won a war without assistance, except against the unfortunate Abyssinians. . . . In her struggle for independence in the last century she was assisted at every turn, both by Great Britain and by France. . . . Italy, the heir of Rome, allied herself with those very barbarians who destroyed the Roman Empire, and is assisting them in their second attempt to wipe out civilization. . . . [Mussolini] will increase the number of ruins for which Italy has long been famous" (*The Times* [11 June 1940]).

3. On 14 June 1940, Paris fell.

Ampleforth Abbey
York

[Autumn 1940]

My dear Arnold,

It was very pleasant to see the well-known writing. These letters keep our two worlds together, you in cosmic battles, I in a quiet backward teaching French irregular verbs whilst the aeroplanes buzz overhead; but also in the cosmic battle in another plane, trying to get the Principalities and Powers of the better sort on our side. Or should one say trying to get us and keep us on their side?

You will be amused to hear that after reading an article by Arnold Lunn[1] on Spengler I took up my pen to defend you from the accusation of treating him cavalierly or superficially. I remembered discovering, *en passant*, quite a lot about Spengler[2] from reading the "nonsense book" so I had a look again and there it was, pages of it. So I wrote to the *Tablet* and said so. But the editor will not have room to put it in. One thing struck me, that you did not mention Spengler when dealing with Gobineau;[3] I remarked, either because you felt that, having cut the root, the branches died, or because, as according to A Lunn, Spengler's *race* theory is more idealistic and not bloody—I was going to say and leave it so.

A thing I should love to do would be to "Everyman"—if one can use the verb—the *Study of History*, in the form of selections which would yet keep the structure, the thread. One day it will be "Complete in 10 volumes" in Everyman; but it is a bit complicated for everyman but so good for everyman. I for one walk in its broad highways and get new co-ordinations from its view-points time and time again. For instance, a boy read a paper on the political background to Dante's life, and was cursing Boniface VIII and Popes generally for supporting the towns against the Emperor. And suddenly I saw he was all wrong—the boy—that the Popes were nursing the New Idea against the old order that was changing; that despite Boniface's harshness his battle was our battle saving government from pure laicism, keeping God in politics. This may be wrong, one day you will tell me. But suppose Boniface had been suave, would Europe have survived in unity? Or would *suavitas* have been a medieval Munich? And was not he bound to fail? No, I suppose not, divinely speaking.

We had *Murder in the Cathedral*[4] this time last week. From the very first word spoken it gave that impression of grandeur, spaciousness, that is as rare an experience as vulgarity is common. Occasionally I thought it degenerated, though others thought it fitting, I mean the swinging of the golf club; but other parts were three dimensional, most of the Chorus "Clear the air, clean the sky, wash them, wash them . . ." and one of the Knight's speeches at the end, the one which showed how modern Englishmen had a share in the Murder. To my mind he—Eliot—did not bring out enough the tragedy of Dis-Union symbolised in the martyrdom. But I suppose holding views he does, he would not.

Now I must say good bye, keep you alive in my mind in my prayers, and especially your work. "Living and partly living" as the play would have it, striving to perfect the microcosm, the little world of self as the only way—and the best way—to do good to others left to us. I salute the dweller in the sub-basement of your mind and await the time when it can turn out all the lodgers.[5]

Yours affectionately,
Columba

1. Sir Arnold H. M. Lunn (1888–1974), founder of Alpine Ski Club (1909); Catholic convert, controversialist; *Come What May: An Autobiography* (Boston, 1941).

2. "Saeva Necessitas," in *A Study of History*, IV: 11ff., quoting at length O. Spengler (1880–1936), *Der Untergang des Abendlandes* (Munich, 1920); A.J.T. here refers to him as "our most celebrated post-war exponent of a philosophy of history."

3. Le Comte J. A. de Gobineau (1816–82); *Essai sur l'inégalité des races humaines* (Paris, 1853–55); cf. *A Study of History*, IV: 40n., and VI: 216–17, where A.J.T. says, "But this amiably academic French political *jeu d'esprit* [Gobineau's racial theory] began to breed a violence of its own when it passed out of de Gobineau's hands into those of a Nietzsche and a Houston Stewart Chamberlain."

4. T. S. Eliot (1888–1965); *Murder in the Cathedral* (New York, 1935). This places this letter in the autumn and long after Dunkerque, 4 June 1940: "an old Ampleforth boy, Michael Birtwistle, who had escaped to England from the beach in a small boat was beside me during the performance and finding the play irrelevant." (C.C.E.) Colonel Michael Birtwistle (1920–) served with the Gurka Parachute Regiment (1943–44); wounded in Burma; served the rest of the war in the War Office; later commanded the duke of Lancaster's own yeomanry; high sheriff of Lancashire (1978–79).

5. This letter must have followed A.J.T.'s letter of 10 October 1940, below.

F.R.P.S.
Balliol

Sunday 23 June 1940

Dear Columba,

Well, here is another chance to write to you: by now you will have seen Rosalind, and will have got a copy of my lecture in print, which I posted to you the other day.[1]

I have just been listening to the 9 A.M. news that the Bordeaux Government have accepted the German armistice terms—which no doubt include the surrender of the French fleet and empire as well as the army and metropolitan France. Our Prime Minister has rightly called on Frenchmen to revolt against the Bordeaux Government's decision; some of them will; if the bulk of the French Navy does, we can still be fairly confident about the next chapter; and anyhow, with our own strength, we ought to be able to beat Hitler off this summer and drag him through another winter.

The moral, even more than the military collapse of France means, I suppose, the end of an epoch. The national state is over, and we are now going to have a world state—established by Hitler if he smashes us this summer, or by the English-speaking peoples if we beat Hitler. The next chapter will perhaps be more interesting and fruitful: when the political waves have died down, religion will sail the seas again: A.D. 1940 = about 40 B.C.

My colleagues here are taking it all very quietly and stout-heartedly, and in London, last Wednesday, when I went up for a committee, everything was normal: none of the ghastly atmosphere of London in September 1938.[2]

This reversal of the engines from making material comfort to destroying it is a terrible form of spiritual cure, but it *is* a spiritual cure all the same—or rather, a preliminary external treatment to make it easier for the soul to do what only the soul and God together can do, that is, help the soul to find its way to God.

Yours affectionately,
Arnold J. Toynbee

1. Compare C.C.E.'s letter of 16 June 1940, above.
2. See A.J.T.'s letter of 26 September 1938, above.

Ampleforth Abbey
York

24 June 1940

My dear Arnold,

Many thanks for your lecture.[1] Reading it was one of the most wonderful moments of my life. I experienced—or almost—what Pascal called "*Joie, pleurs de joie*". Nothing grated; everything sheer delight. How the hosts of the Past must have breathed in peace in hearing your true return to the motto "*Dominus illuminatio mea*". What a magnificent and fortifying emendation that is "Our winding sheet, the Kingdom of God". P. Ricci, too, will smile on you for interpreting his mind so rightly. The Mass, also, is just as you say, the summing up and rectifying and spiritualising of all past sacrifices. The parts that appealed most were, first when you showed how our Time of Trouble is for a deeper understanding of the Kingdom of God, your insistence on Original Sin, and the grand ending giving the Catholic teaching on Salvation for all men—a thing S. Augustine seems to have been shaky about.

Fr. Abbot[2] was delighted with it, and Fr. Paul[3] is reading it now. I hope to read it to some boys.

In my heart of hearts and therefore only for your ears, I am afraid we are in process of losing this war unless some unforeseen things happen. I only venture to express this—which may be legally treasonable, I don't know—in order to suggest to you to be doubly brave when the time comes, if it does, and do what Leopold the King[4] did, and General Pétain[5] is doing, before the homage paid to national pride is too exorbitant. Sometimes I feel that way very strongly, and consider that great injustice is done to these peace makers, and at others I hesitate. But the opinion is strengthening in my mind that the cause is just, that we all should have fought as we did, but that there is a limit even to the good of physically resisting evil. It would require a brave man or an utter coward to come to terms in the event of collapse. I hope, if necessary, you will go into the breach.

The losing or the winning of this war must be for us who have a glimmering of understanding of God's almost inscrutable designs, a sharing through suffering, which in general we deserve, in the Passion of Christ, a denuding ourselves of worldliness. "*Christus obediens usque ad mortem* . . ."

I saw Rosalind for a short time, and she told me of the calamity at Ganthorpe,[6] I hope it was not in the end found serious. But soldiers are inconsiderate people.

We have some humorous interludes in the general tragic expectancy. Fr. Raphael[7] is reputed to have remained glued to a telephone from 11.30 P.M. to 4 A.M. waiting for the all clear to be given and then at 9 sending a message to find out whether he could be released from his vigil as no message had even come then. In fact it came a few minutes after 4 A.M. Up to now our alarms have been academic affairs as nothing has happened near us. But there is no guaranteeing that will continue here or anywhere else.

One never knows, this may be the last letter to reach you for a long time if the threat of invasion becomes a reality. I feel a bit like Bernard* showing Dante around and now handing him over to our Lady. She and the saints who now are in heaven lead you on to the deepest understanding of her Son and their Lord.

Yours affectionately,
Columba, O.S.B.

*Without the Saint!

1. The Burge Memorial lecture; see C.C.E.'s letter of 16 June 1940, n. 1, above.

2. Abbot Herbert Byrne, O.S.B. (1884–1978); Abbot of Ampleforth (1939–63).

3. Paul Nevill, O.S.B. (1882–1954); headmaster of the school at Ampleforth at the time and until his death.

4. On 28 May 1940, Leopold III of Belgium ordered his army to cease fighting.

5. On 17 June 1940, Pétain sued for peace.

6. Lawrence recalls that, when troops were billeted in Ganthorpe Hall, many family possessions, including wine stocks, were placed in the attic, which was sealed; an antiaircraft soldier posted on the roof looked into the attic and saw wine bottles; the troops broke into the attic and in the course of the invasion vandalized and destroyed various family papers, including letters and poems written by Tony.

7. Raphael Williams, O.S.B.; cf. C.C.E.'s letter of 15 March 1940, above.

Ampleforth Abbey
York

6 July 1940

Dear Arnold,

We have had a melancholy week indeed. But I personally have no doubt we did right to blow up the French fleet.[1] The more one hears of the Pétain government the less one likes it. I thought and still think, they had to come to terms, because of the imminent danger in France of famine, pestilence, anarchy. But what I cannot understand is why these Frenchmen outside the clutches of Hitler should pay the slightest attention. What handle has he over them? If ever you write, I should love some explanation and comment on all this. Though the utter breakdown of the French I expected.

Thank God the Pope—though indirectly—has spoken plainly to America and so to us all about the duty to fight.[2] There seem to have been lots of pacifism in Catholic American Universities as in all the rest of the U.S.A., sedulously encouraged no doubt by the Germans.

Now that the French Navy has been disposed of we should feel more secure, as you say. That reminds me, thank you so much for your last letter which crossed with mine. You are right as usual about finding God, no one can really help in the last analysis, it is too intimate a thing; and I feel at times I have intruded too far and only made things more difficult. But that lecture which I have now read and re-read four times calms my misgivings by proving that I have not done irreparable harm.

I think the story of Justinian's wife superb[3] and the emendation better and the—but it's no use going on, I should just describe the whole thing. Fr. Stephen[4] has read it with delight. He thought the only thing suggestive of unorthodoxy was whether Moses and Abraham existed. But you of all people are a believer in things being done, especially on the great scale, by individuals.

There is one curious omission when you justify the Hierarchy; namely, the reason for instituting it which must have been in the divine plan: to teach! Perhaps you thought that might raise too many immediate objections in your audience's mind—and it must have been a very mixed audience.

I had a curious experience the other day. A "Mirfield Father" an Anglican divine, a young man, very keen on Eastern theology, no doubt most learned, came over to see Fr. Aelred,[5] who brought him up to S. Wilfrid's to see me. We had a long and very friendly chat. But afterwards he said to Fr. Aelred he supposed I must be very bitter about the Anglican Church! Asked why, and he replied that people put down your lack of enthusiasm for the established church to Ampleforth and me! I admit not to be enthusiastic myself, but I wonder whether we ever mentioned it except to talk in "praise" of the Archbishop of York. My own interpretation of your attitude, if asked, would be that you see it all as part of the Nationalist outburst from unity. Personally I am very sorry for them and long to rope them back into unity, feel even inclined to do as S. Augustine suggests to his local heretics: that they should keep the episcopal sees if they would return to the unity of faith. The difficulty today is the diversity of faith among them and lack of discipline, no corporate action seems possible. Return of England to the faith is one of the things I should like to have the courage to die for.

Yours ever,
Columba Cary-Elwes

P.S. Have you seen that Dawson is editor of the Dublin Review?[6]

1. On 3 July 1940, the British fleet had sunk or crippled a great part of the French fleet in Oran, Algeria.

2. *The Times* (5 July 1940) reported that an "American speaker" in a Vatican broadcast had said: "It is clear that we have been allowing our unreasoned fear of what we call entangling alliances to obscure an obvious duty of charity towards the defenders of our own cause, which the Pope has called the cause of universal morality."

3. Theodora, in a time of crisis, had told Justinian she would not flee, because *καλὸν ἐντάφιον ἡ Βασιλεία* (empire is a fine winding sheet). This and the question of Abraham's and Moses' historicity are set out in A.J.T.'s "Christianity and Civilization" (see *Civilization on Trial*, pp. 225–52). Later A.J.T. presumes Moses' historicity in his letter of 23 August 1964, below.

4. Stephen Marwood, O.S.B. (1890–1949) monk of Ampleforth, master of Lawrence Toynbee's house, St. Oswald's House.

5. See C.C.E.'s letter of 19 January 1940, above.

6. See C.C.E.'s letter of 29 May 1940, above.

The Manor House
Mells, Near Frome[1]
Somerset

(written during the Battle of Britain, Summer 1940)

My dear Arnold,

It seems a long time since I have seen you or written. That little glimpse of you and your life at Oxford was a great pleasure, especially our little family Mass. It was the first time you had shared in mine by being there.

After leaving Oxford I was at Bournemouth, as you know, for a couple of weeks. Although there were air and sea battles frequently, and only a few miles off, Bournemouth remained undisturbed; we scarcely heard a shot and I only saw one German plane. Whereas here we get warnings at least twice a day, this being on the way to "somewhere".

I was very disappointed in *The Times*' latest effort to give us some idea of what our Peace plan would be. It seems so pathetic that people should still be defending free markets when it could now only matter to the few rich men that own the giant concerns of 20th century industry. It is precisely this cave man spirit about markets—grounded on a topsy-turvy set of values, gold first, God second—that starts wars. The ordinary man wants security. If we are going to live in this internationalised world it will have to be organised just as strictly as the old guild towns were, don't you agree?

This house belongs to Mrs. Asquith, it used to belong to the male descendants of "Little Jack Horner" but they died out.[2] When I arrived Mr. Belloc[3] was staying. He has gone now, but fortunately I did get a glimpse of him, even if only in his old age. He seems very aged now, walks with difficulty and with the help of a massive notched stick, more like a club with a huge knob. His whole appearance is picturesque; first of all sea boots, of a very refined sort, baggy trousers, black clothes, extremely uncomfortable looking collar, a cloak, and side whiskers, and a felt hat, shapeless and battered and treated with contempt, shoved into a pocket or sat on under the slightest provocation. But his appearance is neither here nor there. His talk was very much the stuff one would expect from the man who walked the Path to Rome.[4] He was feeling very much at home at Mells, would break out into little French ditties, roll off great pieces of the *Chanson de Roland* pronounced as it should be, and recite or sing some of his own humourous verses. He would occasionally burst out into a dogmatic statement that there never could have been more than 6,000 armed Danes in England at one time. He is very sad about the plight of France,[5] pities Pétain and thinks that the only thing that could have brought the French colonies to heel was a threat by Hitler to massacre the French in France. The only good he can see from that catastrophe is the death blow to the "Grand Orient" and the continental Freemasonry which depended upon it.[6] He would not have it that the French national spirit was killed, and he repeated several times "civil war is a chronic disease with the French", they would get over it. And on the last evening of his stay he said a thing which gave me great pleasure; he said he never thought that he would live to see the turn of the tide back to the Church, but now he has, and there were almost tears in his eyes, and he sang a Salve Regina he had heard in Saragossa. I now feel that whenever I pick up any of his books I will hear his intonation and know the spirit in which he wrote it. Another thing he said was that he did not think his historical writings had had the slightest effect on the academic world. I told him for his consolation that you admired him a lot and thought many of his fundamental theses right. He was pleased but incredulous. He said that personal contact was the only thing which did any good and went into ecstasy over Soeur Thérèse. He was on his way to Oxford, and I almost suggested his going to see you in Ship Street, but then he changed his plans, so I said nothing.

I am staying here a week perhaps longer, partly holiday—which I do not need—partly for usefulness, saying Mass and acting as chaplain to the little community of Catholics here. Mells is just another little oasis of Catholic life, with its Catholic chatelaine and little chapel in the grounds and children who breathe the Catholic atmosphere with every breath they breathe. One wonders whether that could be transposed into an industrial setting. It has been done by the saints, but as a *tour de force*.

You must be in the thick of work again now that the war has restarted, and I wonder what you think is likely to happen. I think Hitler is bound to take the plunge of invasion, but is leaving it very late. You won't have time to read any more, so I must stop my babbling.

Yours affectionately,
Columba Cary-Elwes, O.S.B.

1. Mells is a stone-built village, once the property of the Abbots of Glastonbury, fifteen miles south of Bath; the manor house in the village has belonged to the Horner family since the dissolution of the monasteries: little Jack Horner's "plum."

2. Not true: Katherine Asquith (1885–1977), the widow of Raymond Asquith, was Miss Katherine Horner, daughter of Sir John Horner; she was a convert to the Catholic Church; Raymond Asquith was the uncle of Jean Constance Asquith, who married Lawrence Toynbee in 1945; cf. A.J.T.'s letter of March 1969, below.

3. Joseph Hilaire Pierre Belloc (1870–1953); Catholic historian, controversialist, poet, friend of G. K. Chesterton: the "Chesterbelloc."

4. *The Path to Rome* (London, 1902), an account of the young Belloc's pilgrimage, on foot, from Toul to Rome.

5. This would seem to date this letter some time after Pétain's capitulation and the signing of the armistice on 22 June 1940.

6. "Le Grand Orient de France," the French Masonic establishment.

The Royal Institute
of International Affairs
Foreign Research and Press Service
Balliol College, Oxford

14 July 1940

Dear Columba,

At last I am able to write—what with civil service red tape, which I dislike enormously, and various communal activities to keep my colleagues going—which I like very much—my leisure is infinitesimal. I started with a sports club (punts, canoes and tennis). Now I have got a service going in Balliol Chapel, and allotments on the college cricket field, and find people in the mood for both! I must say, in these times, I am glad to be here and not in London, where we could have done none of these things corporately.

The foundering of France is indeed a portent. I believed that in our lifetime we should see the establishment of a universal state, but I believed in this as an astronomer believes in a predicted eclipse: my calculations led me there, but I didn't see how we were going to get there. Now, when a national will and consciousness like that of the French crumples up in a few days, there is no familiar land-mark of the modern world that may not be uprooted.

I am glad the Cardinal[1] has put out his démenti of the Vatican's supposed eulogy of the Pétain—or rather Laval—regime. There is some intellectual, and perhaps also moral, falsity at the root of Pétain's attempt to make an apologia for his policy in terms of religion. He says France must embrace suffering (in terms of humiliation), but what he has actually done is evading suffering (in terms of sticking out the war). Christ could take his suffering in terms of humiliation because he had never accepted the life of worldly pagan prowess. But if ever one has accepted it, and profited by it—as every nation has that has been a Great Power—then the one moment when we shouldn't have second thoughts is the moment of trial. Leonidas might have been a conscientious objector; but having accepted Spartanism and marched to Thermopylae, he surely did right to stay. If he had turned tail then, he would have become a bad Spartan and would have had a very poor chance of becoming a good Christian. I like the line in the speech of the old Retainer in *The Lay of the Battle of Maldon* (where there may be another battle now any day): "Mood shall be the more, as our might faileth"[2]—I have put it on the title page of the first three volumes of the nonsense book.

Now my breathing space is up, but I have managed to finish this letter.

Yours affectionately,
Arnold J. Toynbee

1. On 22 June 1940, Cardinal Hinsley stated, "We in this country are the more closely united to you [France]" (see *Tablet* [29 June 1940], pp. 624–25); and on 15 July 1940, Cardinal Hinsley wrote to *The Times* that "certain papers" had quoted statements purporting to come from the Vatican, which were not official utterances: "We are fighting for centuries of Christian freedom against the brute violence of enslaving paganism."

2. Quoted in the title page of vol. I of *A Study of History* as "*lessens*."

Ampleforth Abbey
York

18 July 1940

Dear Leonidas,

Please get me a 3rd single to Thermopylae, and may I be in your carriage?

That is how I feel, and thoroughly agree with your piercing diagnosis of the LpAéVtAaLin fiasco. One cannot help sympathising with Pétain and giving him the benefit of the doubt; but in the long run he is not perhaps saving the soul of France but its Nationalism, and poor France will yet need another operation, before that cancer is removed entire. If one could be sure of motive in the nation's conscience I suppose it would be possible to lay down arms, as France has done, to save the good; but Eliot's lines keep recurring to my mind:

> The last temptation is the greatest treason:
> To do the right deed for the wrong reason.[1]

The chances, in the circumstances, of doing the deed for the right reason, are very few. That is how I rationalize your intuitive conviction that we always have to give up all to gain all.

Must we have a universal State no matter who wins? It is an admission of failure, isn't it? I liked so much Pius XI's principle, when speaking of Corporativism and nationalisation, the principle of subsidiary function; namely that a bigger entity should not undertake what a small one can reasonably do.[2] In the political order nations can be efficient provided the economic side is kept free, don't you think? They must be free to enforce common interests. And, the mind replies to itself, then whoever has that force, controls not only economics but all the rest, and sovereignty in Europe can really no longer exist. But again force should not be the enforcer, but some of the Christian virtues. We go on coming back to "conversion of manners";[3] given that, a Universal State would be unnecessary.

I hope you have put your sports club and Balliol Chapel service under the patronage of S. John Bosco,[4] it all sounds the same thing as his ventures in Turin, though with a different setting, dons instead of ragamuffins, city of spires in place of industrial chimneys. When I first read the news, it gave me a bit of a shock which does show a rooted antipathy to heretical worship! But I think it fine and will do lots of good, and is perhaps a repayment on your part of that *servitus mentis* you owed to God from your undergraduate days. I will be quite frank. The Mass seems to me so integrating, vital, strong, that all else especially Non-Catholic worship seems like moonlight to sunlight. I was afraid it might draw you away from the spring of grace, this Balliol chapel. But I came to see that in essence you were praying the Mass even there, in fact everywhere. The Mass being the external expression in symbol of the giving of himself and of us back to God by Christ; in symbol and in fact, the fact being the INTENTION of Christ once and forever fixed. So you can, so long as you linger on the edge of the City, be one with the spiritual act, as no walls of stone can or need separate us. You in Balliol are sharing in Calvary as I do in S. Wilfrid's chapel. But one day I humbly hope to give you the sign of that oneness in spirit: Holy Communion. I will pray hard for your Balliol worship, Balliol come home to God.

I am going to see my father and mother in Bournemouth after term, perhaps I might go through Oxford; would it be possible to put me up, or at least share a meal in your busy day. If Fr. Justin (McCann)[5] is still at Oxford I would stay with him naturally.

I really do feel now that any day the great trial, our Thermopylae may come. Even the thought strips one of the falseness of all these worldly thoughts and standards one has, and makes one feel the stronger like your Maldon hero.

Au revoir, at least across the gulf of war, unless I am given time to get south.

Yours affectionately,
Columba, O.S.B.

1. Eliot, *Murder in the Cathedral*, p. 44.

2. In the Encyclical *Quadragesimo anno*; cf. C.C.E.'s letter of 5 February 1940, above.

3. "Conversion of Manners" is one of the three monastic vows, imposed by the rule of Saint Benedict, the other two being obedience and stability.

4. Saint John Bosco (1815–88), founder of the Salesian order.

5. Justin McCann, O.S.B. (1882–1959), monk of Ampleforth, was master of St. Benet's Hall, the Benedictine house in Oxford.

Ampleforth Abbey
York

10 September 1940

My dear Arnold,

I meant to write to you on S. Augustine's feast, because you were very much in my mind, and I hope in his too, that day. You at any rate had the better thing, my Mass.

We have just come out of retreat given us by a Downside monk, Fr. Dunstan Pontifex.[1] It was very good, recalling one to the fervour of noviciate days. I thought especially good his insistence on the Holiness of God, as something awe-inspiring and also humbling; making me turn to God for comparisons and putting me beautifully in my place—very nearly nowhere. I find we live in so criticising an age that I spend my time summing people up—public figures, judging the motives of their actions as though I had the whole thing mapped out before me, as God must have, and I certainly have not. We are always being given violent and crude and unkind judgements of people and peoples in the newspapers, and it becomes second nature. I am going to try not to be caught up in this pestiferous habit. This arose out of Fr. Dunstan's reminder that we are 'near nothing' and we ourselves have got to imitate the perfection of God who is infinitely merciful. There are some, Hitler and Co. who clearly are very wicked and we are bound to state, but even him God still has mercy on. I like S. Francis of Sales' treatment of all this in the *Introduction to a Devout Life*[2]—do dip into it if you have the time. His spirit is so gentle and peaceful and witty and psychologically probing. Read *troisième partie*, of course in French. You are sure to have read it already.

Fr. Dunstan also said a few stimulating things about the Order. He said it has passed through as great storms as this before, but thought that today what it stood for: just by living its life, was more needed now than ever. He meant, Order resting on God—*Nisi Dominus* . . . . and family spirit. He said we were a microcosm of the world, the *Domus Dei* in the *Civitate Dei*.

Please God you will be able to finish Vol. 7 which will be your *de Civitate Dei*.

What I often pray for you is that the two worlds you live in, *Civitas Hominum* and *Civitas Dei* will not be so segregated as to make the two together impossible. I mean—may I say this?—that like S. Augustine, the *whole man* does everything in you, setting up infinite stresses and strains. At times these might seem unbearable, and you might be tempted to give or break and throw away one half of you. I pray God always that you will rest always in his loving kindness trusting him to draw you out of the storms and set you in calm seas in his own good time.

You looked so drawn and tired at Oxford ~~I felt the~~ strain was being too much. Great our trials but greater the LOVE of GOD for US.

I wish I could have gone to Oxford on my way, but it would have meant another three days, and my only excuse for being away from Ampleforth in these days was being useful in parish work saying Mass for this little community at Mells, so that I felt I could not leave them before the appointed time.

I wonder what you make of the latest phase of the war. It is becoming more bestial hourly, we are sinking deeper until, O my God, what? We must be very humble and perhaps He will shorten the time.

My desires for Peace proposals before Armistice have waned, partly because the people concerned cannot be consulted (cf. letter in the *Times*)[3] and partly because I am sure there are plenty of people with good schemes (your friend especially) and that it is far more important to get the Christian God-fearing background which once acquired would probably make even the less good schemes work.

I must stop. Was the rumour correct that you were coming up? Please do.

Yours affectionately,
Columba Cary-Elwes, O.S.B.

1. Dunstan Pontifex, O.S.B. (1889–1974), monk of Downside Abbey in Somerset; titular prior of Canterbury.

2. Saint Francis de Sales (1567–1622); bishop of Geneva and, with Saint Jane Frances de Chantal, co-founder of the Visitandines; *The Introduction to the Devout Life* was a spiritual treatise published in 1609–19; the *troisième partie* deals with the practice of virtue.

3. Letters to *The Times* in response to a leading article of 30 August 1940, in which it was suggested that one should now make plans for postwar reconstruction.

Ampleforth Abbey
York

28 September 1940

Dear Arnold,

Just a few lines, first of all, to ask you if it would not be too much of a business to send me the 'Pascal' I lent you some time ago. I would not bother you except that I am reading a selection of the *Pensées* with some H.C. boys for the summer exams and need it for the good notes it has.

It will be interesting to see how the boys take to Pascal, and it will be interesting trying to get him 'across'.

We are now well launched on our new term's journey. The London boys are very relieved to be back into quiet. It really has been a very fearful experience for them. But they say they got accustomed to it, even the whistling bombs and the shrapnel falling like rain. The sirens themselves seem to be the most terrifying thing, except for the bomb whose sound continuously gets louder until the crash.

I have just read Mgr. Knox's pamphlet *Nazi and Nazarene*[1] and think it very good indeed. Its theme reminds me of those three young German Catholics you once told me of who could not decide which course to pursue: keep clear of the unclean thing, or join it in order to influence it. It is only too evident now that there can be no compromise. But still we must not degrade ourselves by intentionally killing innocent people.

I hope my surmise is true, that we have gained a great victory this summer by staving off invasion and holding more than our own in the air. Bravery is more plentiful than ever.

Can we still hope for a German crack in the Spring? If you are hopeful, do express it in a little note should you have time to write one.

Laval is emerging as you promised. If only the Germans would behave according to type in France and then even Pétain would throw in his hand, and Morocco could be freed.

Yours affectionately,
Columba, O.S.B.

1. Ronald Knox (1888–1957); chaplain to Catholic undergraduates at Oxford (1926–39); *Nazi and Nazarene*, Macmillan War Pamphlet no. 5 (London, 1940); *Enthusiasm* (Oxford, 1950).

The Royal Institute
of International Affairs
Chatham House
St. James's Square
London, S.W.1

10 October 1940

Dear Columba,

For days, at Oxford, I have had a sheet at my elbow with "Dear Columba" written on it and no more. This morning I am in London for a committee, and have shaken off the "one damned thing after another" which is one's job while one is on the spot; so here is a chance to write to you: I did post the Pascal book to you the other day: I haven't, I am afraid, yet managed to read it—my reading nowadays is fragmentary, and even when one does the London journey by train, one is beginning, now, to be cheated of reading-time by the blackout on the way home. London, as one sees it driving in, looks much as usual: the smashed houses aren't appreciably more than those that in ordinary times are always being pulled down by the house breakers to make way for bigger and better buildings. The people look a bit tired, but quite placid. All the same, I think an enormous peaceful social revolution has begun, and I hope we shall be able to deepen it into a spiritual revolution as well. This war, which began so tamely, looks as if it might now sweep away barriers between classes and nations that looked, only a year ago, immovable. One thing that is hopeful is that, in spite of the suffering, there is very little sign of hate springing up. Rosalind has started working in London for the *Sword of the Spirit*[1]—fitting offers of housing—room in the country to homeless families in London. I am a bit sorry to have her in what is rather greater danger—the danger has a certain amount of fascination for her—but she was getting restive in sedentary work at Oxford, and wanted a change. My own work goes on as usual—full of jolts and jars, like all war work, but it keeps going and produces results which, I believe, are useful. I never expected to turn into even a temporary administrator: it is a good discipline, especially at my age when one might easily grow incapable of doing anything except what one has actually been doing during the past twenty years. Meanwhile, somewhere in the sub-basement of my sub-conscious, I expect my mind will work on—I hope some day the subterranean thoughts will come to the surface!

Please go on writing to me, however poor a correspondent I may be, perforce.

Yours affectionately,
Arnold J. Toynbee

1. The Sword of the Spirit was inaugurated under the auspices of Cardinal A. Hinsley in 1940 to promote justice in the war, and the peace to come, by prayer, study, and action; Christopher Dawson was active in its inspiration and operation.

Ampleforth Abbey
11 October 1940 York

Dear Arnold:

I am so sorry to have put you to all the bother of sending me the book on Pascal; and I was horrified to see it! I had given it to you and you must, at least, have thought it odd my writing for it as though it were mine. There must be some ambiguity in my last letter, as what I really wanted was the Pensées de Pascal (Hachette, little olive green book). Don't bother to hunt for it because we shan't be doing the Pensées in class for a bit, and I will try and get another copy.

Your work must be tremendous now; the Middle East is one of your subjects. The crisis of crises is upon us, and I trust and know you will have your full share in winning through.

The material havoc has begun in earnest, and we must try and keep Pascal's *Ordres* before us, that a mountain of masonry in ruins is not equal to one just liberty kept intact.[1]

I have been re-reading the *Confessions* again recently, especially the story of *Simplicianus and Victorinus* (Bk8).[2] That is what I pray for now—that you too will see that "Walls" do not matter in the Church founded by Christ.

Yours affectionately,
Columba, O.S.B.

P.S. No answer expected—I know how tremendously busy you are.

1. Inspired by "Tous les corps, le firmament, les étoiles, la terre et ses royaumes, ne valent pas le moindre des esprits. Car il connaît tout cela, et soi, et les corps rien," Blaise Pascal, *Oeuvres Complètes*, ed. Louis Lafuma [Paris, 1963], *Pensées*, no. 308 [Brunschvicg no. 793], and *passim*.

2. Saint Augustine, *Confessions*, 8.1–4.

Ampleforth College
York

21 November 1940

My dear Arnold,

Rosalind told me in utter confidence about the momentous work in which you are engaged.[1] I can't tell you what pleasure it gave; for it seems to me that this is the work for which Providence fitted you out, with your knowledge of the past and of the immediate past, or present, with your eagerness to do God's will. I have scarcely ceased praying for God to guide you since I heard the fact, and have put a notice on the monastery board asking prayers for a special intention, got the boys to join in too. One can conceive of no stage in the war more vital than the one at which we have arrived: laying down conditions of a possible peace. The history of the future depends on it.

In my ignorance I would not make any suggestions, except that you really do consider how Jesus Christ would view your plans, how they are conducive to the salvation of souls. You know as well as I do, you taught it me, that it is the long view—the one that goes straight to the spiritual profound motives—that is the only one of any value, the rest will succeed and pass.

The other thing—and this too I say quite simply—do not leave out the Holy Father—the Papacy. If there is to be appeasement, if not with Hitler, then with the German people, the Pope is a rallying point. He has been a Father to us all. It is all very well for Patriarchs from Greece or Canterbury to cry out for condemnations. He is, every priest is, an instrument for the saving of souls. I would do penance all my life if I felt you were giving due place to the one possible rallying point for peace, true peace.

This sort of letter should be destroyed, it is too personal perhaps; but I know you do not mind me speaking my mind, I speak to the tenant in the sub-basement. *Regina pacis, ora pro nobis*.

How wonderful it would be if you could come up here and spend a few restful days. Fr. Abbot gives you a definite invitation. He says, bring Professor Clark,[2] too, if he would like to come. You, he would not mind coming up over Christmas, being so much an old friend, but if you come up together, this term or after January 12th. My own idea is you should come up separately, otherwise it would not be half so good for either of you. Please let me know as soon as convenient, as then, I am sure, Fr. Abbot would not send me off anywhere during that period if I told him when it was.

I have just read a very interesting life of St. Wilfrid,[3] apparently by one of his immediate disciples, Eddius. It emerges there how near a thing the Celtic alternative was in Britain. Only his superhuman perseverance kept the connection with Rome unbroken. One little incident amused and surprised me. When putting his case before the Pope and bishops, they suddenly broke off into Greek making some joke. It must have made Wilfrid feel very provincial. On every page of that life there is a great reverence for the Apostolic See; and the necessity of order.

The letter I wrote in your defence to the *Tablet* was not accepted because it was too long and A Lunn had only attacked you very much in passing. Douglas Woodruff wrote and said he would accept a shorter letter, but it seemed scarcely worth just knocking down A.L., the first letter gave some positive information by quoting from the Nonsense Book. So I did not go on. It emerged that D.W. has also read all 6 volumes through.

Yours affectionately,
Columba Cary-Elwes, O.S.B.

In my Mass on Sunday for Peace, you and Ld X will have a very large place.

1. A.J.T. was to serve as a member of the British Delegation to the Peace Conferences to be held in Paris in 1946.

2. Sir George Norman Clark (1890–1979), then (1931–43) Chichele Professor of Economic History and Fellow of All Souls College, Oxford; later Regius Professor of Modern History and Fellow of Trinity College, Cambridge (1943–47); provost of Oriel College, Oxford (1947–57); *The Wealth of England* (London, 1946).

3. Saint Wilfrid (634–709), Bishop of York; a leader at the Synod of Whitby; life by his contemporary Stephanus Eddius of Ripon; *The Life of Bishop Wilfrid*, text, translation, and notes by Bertram Colgrave (Cambridge, 1927).

3 Ship Street
Oxford

5 December 1940

Dear Columba,

I got that far six weeks ago: now for another shot.

I don't, alas, see any prospect of getting up to Ampleforth for Christmas, but I might manage it sometime after the 12th January, which is the other time you suggest. Will you tell Father Abbot that I am deeply grateful for his personal message, and that Ampleforth is the one place where I feel I could get a real holiday—by which I mean an inward spiritual holiday in which one can get away from the daily dog-fight and then come back into it better prepared to fight it in the right spirit.

I lead a curious life, nowadays, such as I never dreamed of before: in snatches I deal direct with eminent men over quite important affairs, and manage, with my colleagues here, to do some good work for them. But most of my energy still goes in fighting with beasts at Ephesus:[1] defeating and wasting intrigue and backbiting. During these first fifteen months of the war, I have been kept so busy resisting these attacks by other Englishmen that I have been given little chance of doing my proper job of fighting the Germans in my part of the battlefield.

Whether the present state of interdepartmental warfare is normal or abnormal, I don't know: in the last war I was only a junior, and this kind of thing passed over my head. I suspect that, where political power is, there intrigue and perfidy are also always to be found—politics being one of the slum areas of human affairs that has never yet been cleaned up; at least, that is my reading of history, and this is now confirmed by what I find in my present job. I suspect that all this is worse in war-time, when people in general are more pugnacious and less scrupulous than in peace time; but I think one would probably find it like this at all times, if one were normally engaged in my present kind of work.

In feeling like this about the job, I am not at all repining at it. I feel it immensely worth-while to do, in itself; and it is also all grist to my mill as a historian.[2] Ordinarily I lead a sheltered life, working among people all of whom I have a respect and affection for, and this under conditions in which ambition and struggle for power don't come in at all. Now I have to swim in the great ocean of sewage and keep my head above the rather evil-smelling waves. If it were for a personal career, I should sooner or later be "too proud to fight"; but luckily, as it is, I have to do the job as a duty to Chatham House and H.M.G. and my colleagues here, so I can do it with a certain amount of disinterestedness. Perhaps in this I partly delude myself, because one has an egotistic interest in making a success of any job that one has in hand. Still, it is true that my treasure isn't in being an administrator, but in writing the nonsense book and the survey of international affairs. As far as I can make out, I am not doing badly in the administration; at any rate, I am holding my own. And, besides the nasty business of fighting, there is the job of trying to help one's colleagues to do their work and to cope with their personal troubles; and this is so plainly worth doing that it much more than compensates for the rest.

Well, as you see, I am getting a second education—just at the right age, when one might go stiff if one wasn't shaken up and re-exercised.

At the moment I am tied by the leg here till certain troubles are cleared up, but I hope that may happen before the end of this month, and then I will suggest a date for coming to Ampleforth: I shall come, if possible, soon after the 12th January. You are much in my thoughts, though I so seldom get time to write. But if I manage to come next month, we can walk and talk.

I haven't yet spoken to Clark[3] about the invitation to him: I think we should anyway have to come at separate times, as it would be difficult for both of us to be away from here at the same moment. But I will talk to him about this now.

Yours affectionately,
Arnold J. Toynbee

1. 1 Cor. 15:32.

2. A.J.T. surely had in mind a favorite passage from Edward Gibbon's *Autobiography*: "The captain of the Hampshire Grenadiers . . . has not been useless to the historian of the Roman Empire" (cited in *A Study of History*, X:98).

3. Cf. C.C.E.'s letter of 21 November 1940, above.

The Royal Institute
of International Affairs
Foreign Research and Press Service
Balliol College, Oxford

24 January 1941

Dear Columba,

You will have had my telegram: I heard suddenly today that my father is probably dying, so I shall probably be going tomorrow to see him; anyway I must stand by till I see how it turns out.

But in any event my coming to Ampleforth is only postponed: I will give you another date as soon as I can.

My father, poor fellow, has been an invalid, and a very sad one, for thirty-two years and is now, I think, eighty-two, so it is no occasion for sorrow if at last he is given his release.[1] Like Jean Valjean[2] in the galleys, living through the Revolution and Napoleon and not realising them, so my father has lived through all these wars and revolutions without being really aware of anything that has happened, public or private, since 1908.

Such things are grievous and hard to understand; but I suppose they would fall into proportion if one could see them in the setting of the great Whole of which they are fragments.

Yours affectionately,
Arnold J. Toynbee

1. Harry Valpy Toynbee; cf. A.J.T.'s letter of 13 June 1913, above.
2. Hero of Victor Hugo's novel *Les Misérables* (1862).

The Angel Hotel
Bridge Street
Northampton

25 January 1941

Dear Columba,

I got here an hour or so ago and found that my Father had died last night. I have had a last sight of him, looking peaceful, as the dead do.

He is to be buried on Wednesday. If I may, I shall come up to Ampleforth on Thursday or Friday.

A bomb crater in the garden of a mental hospital makes one realise that this is a war from which nobody is exempt.

I very much look forward to seeing you.

Yours affectionately,
Arnold J. Toynbee

3 Ship Street
Oxford

12 February 1941

Dear Columba,

Here I am in St. James's Square, just out of a committee, accompanied by a tiny chest and waiting for the car to Oxford. I have plunged back into the swirl, but now have my head above water, thanks to my time in the monastery. It seems impertinent for a guest from outside, like me, to claim any great effect from sharing in the community's life in such a superficial way for so short a time; but it does have a tremendous effect; above all, it puts things in their place—I mean, puts them into their true spiritual proportions to one another. In this, as in so many things, the war, in the way it has of obsessing one's mind and filling one's horizon, is only a heightening of ordinary life in peacetime, coming to and fro beween the monastery and war work, one feels the contrast in a more than usually sharp way.

You were wonderfully good in finding snatches of time for me to see you in. Will our next meeting, I wonder, be at Ampleforth or at Oxford?

Yours affectionately,
Arnold J. Toynbee

Ampleforth College
York

18 February 1941

Dear Arnold,

It was very nice of you to bother to write to me when you had so much work on hand, to say nothing of your letters for Fr. Abbot and Fr. Wilfrid. All the time you were here I felt that I was very stingy with my time. But what you really wanted, and got—thank God—was a pervading spiritual Peace. Some people go in and out, or rather up and down in spiritual insight, but I imagine what you discover you retain for good, it is built in to the existing fabric; and I feel you took a big internal step in this your last visit; and there it waits to be told us in due time. That I hope also. The Church waits on the other side of the river, and you seem to wait too on your side. Each longing for the other. I feel a worm not being able to help; and yet know that God will dry up the river or make you plunge across in his own time. Any shortcomings you may see in the Church in me, us, attribute to our failure to represent Christ adequately, not to his life in the Church. We can't help putting obstacles to that life and so making a caricature of it. I see that Henri Bergson [1] was received some time before his death, but kept it to himself in order not to hurt his fellow Jews. Azaña [2] too was received (or reconciled). That makes three strange brothers in Christ, with Niemöller. [3] But what joy.

It is not fair to talk to you on these lines, because in talking you are put in an unfair position; but my writing, you can behave as you like without offending me.

Fr. James [4] has just been in and I told him I was writing to you. He asks me to thank you very much for your letter.

You will be interested to hear that your talk to the "Voyageurs" set off Ryan [5]—the smaller one who impressed you—to found another society whose whole object is to be 20th century—Our World. He was there as a visitor. So I am being roped in as a president for yet another society. In some ways it would be best to amalgamate the societies, but 20 members might be too many.

We all hope Professor Clark will be able to come up soon.

My kindest regards to Rosalind.

Yours affectionately,
Columba Cary-Elwes, O.S.B.

1. Henri Louis Bergson (1859–1941); intuitional philosopher; *L'Evolution créatrice* (Paris, 1907); influential among "modernists" of the Catholic Church; an inspirer of Jacques and Raïssa

Maritain; see *A Study of History*, X:236, where A.J.T. acknowledges his debt to Bergson, particularly to *Les Deux Sources de la morale et de la religion* (Paris, 1932); Bergson was not received into the Church: "He did not wish to do so while his people, the Jews, were being persecuted" (T. Hanna et al., *The Bergsonian Heritage* [New York, 1962], pp. 91–92).

2. Manuel de Azaña y Diaz (1880–1940), prime minister (1931–33) and later president of the Spanish republic until his resignation in Paris in 1939. I question now the truth of that assertion. (C.C.E.)

3. Martin Niemöller (1892–1984), then in a Nazi concentration camp; president, World Council of Churches (1961–68); he did not become a Catholic.

4. James Forbes, O.S.B. (1913–80); guest-master at Ampleforth; historian, connoisseur of porcelain; later Master of St. Benet's Hall, Oxford.

5. Gerald Valentine Ryan (1922–44), Kitchener scholar, New College, Oxford; lieutenant in the Rifle Brigade, killed in action in Belgium; the Voyageurs: a discussion club in St. Wilfrid's House.

S. Wilfrid's
Ampleforth College, York

10 March 1941

My dear Arnold,

I have been very remiss, but not through lack of wanting to write. We have been snowed up with illness, and still are. But the storm in this house, at any rate, is abating. Your visit already seems ages ago, a little oasis of joy in rather a grinding term. I shall always look back on that evening in my room with unmixed pleasure. Lamb[1] has completed his essay on Islam, but refuses to touch it except in its beginning i.e. the first 30 years or so. The Voyageurs will have to use question time to bring it to the present day. We had an interesting talk by Babington[2] on Italy. The point that struck me was that "The Party" had already become a race apart. From early childhood the boy is taken from his family, segregated. This, I think, might have very great results, for instance make the break between Italians and Fascists very easy.

You must be very pleased, as I am, over President Roosevelt's last speech.[3] He usually means what he says, and if we get guns, food and ships, IN TIME, then perhaps we might say the war is virtually won.

I still think in spite of your reassuring remarks that we are slipping into a vindictive attitude towards the Germans; we are fighting the Germans certainly. But are they consciously doing evil? The majority must be hoodwinked by their propaganda. That being so, we must not talk of punishing THEM but the Party, which is the villain of the piece.

Another point which perhaps Professor Baynes[4] could make crystal clear for us. Did the Germans ever hand over their freedom to Hitler in a free vote? There were so many elections forced on the Germans by the Nazi tactic of bringing voting into disrepute that it is difficult to remember the sequence of events. But my bad memory seems to record that Hitler got into power on a bare majority and then by the usual methods in continental democracies gone to seed, "persuaded" the people to give him a huge vote of confidence. If this were the case, it would mitigate the crime of the German People in allowing themselves to be governed by thugs!

In order to help the 20th Century society, I read some back numbers of the *Survey*, and came across 1933, the "parting of the ways" volume.[5] A boy is using it to write a paper just on 1933. How revealing and prophetic that volume is. I expect the reviews of it were the usual stuff, "unduly pessimistic outlook." It has proved only too true, and a monument to your foresight.

Do you never have time to read? If you have, do read Lagrange O.P. on Prophecy (1906 Revue Biblique).[6] You would agree with it, I am sure. It is magnificent. The Blackfriars Library is sure to have it. That reminds me have you seen Fray Columba?[7]

The valley is very different now to when you were last here. There is a white mist, at midday receding to the horizon, and green, ever so green fields, but the grass still short, and the rooks are more noisy, and at least one blackbird and one thrush have sung outside our windows. Everything indeed peaceful, serene. But the other night we were shaken by a couple of land mines between Brandsby and Sutton. They did no damage.

This afternoon I am off to preach in the village on the text "in whom we have redemption". It is one of a series, and I am precluded from talking of the Passion, as that is coming later. My point will be that Christ's life also was redeeming. In a sense more redeeming than anything, because he was in his life doing God's will all the time, to make up for our almost continual failing to do so in intention and in fact. Even Our Lord's death was redemptive in its living part, that is: Christ's active will of acceptance. Christ was loyal to God—obedient too; loyalty I suppose is loving obedience.

I must stop. Please accept these pensées as they spill out of my mind onto the paper, as a sign of my not forgetting you ever.

Yours affectionately,
Columba, O.S.B.

1. Osmer Ogilvie Lamb (1922–43), scholar, Peterhouse, Cambridge; lieutenant, Intelligence Corps; killed in action in the Isle of Leros.

2. George Francis Paul Emil Gothard Babington (1925–), a member of the school.

3. On 11 March 1941, the U.S. Congress passed the Lend-Lease Act.

4. Norman Hepburn Baynes (1877–1961), barrister-at-law; Byzantine scholar; then working with A.J.T. in the Royal Institute of International Affairs; cf. A.J.T.'s *Acquaintances*: "His published work is all magnificently scholarly in quality. . . . He died without having given to the public the masterpiece that he was qualified to write" (pp. 59–61). Baynes and H. St. L. B. Moss, eds., *Byzantium* (Oxford, 1948); cf. A.J.T.'s letter of 3 February 1940, above.

5. *Survey of International Affairs, 1933*, by A.J.T., assisted by Veronica M. Boulter (London, 1934).

6. Cf. A.J.T.'s letter of 31 January 1937, above.

7. Fray Patrick Columba Ryan, O.P. (1916–); an old Amplefordian; a Dominican of the English Province; son of Sir Andrew Ryan, K.B.E. (1876–1949), in the Levant Consular Service; chief dragoman (counsellor) of His Majesty's Embassy at Constantinople (1921).

Ampleforth College
Tuesday in Holy Week (8 April 1941) York

My dear Arnold,

I must write you a line, before the great ceremonies begin which remind us of our Redemption, to say that as we approach Easter and the three last days before it, you become more and more present in my prayers, your well-being and that of your work, the present work, and the ultimate work you are designated for.

The boys having gone, we are having a delightful calm. I have almost completed my St. Wilfrid, and feel I might even begin on the Christian Approaches to China.[1] Meanwhile you must be weighed down with Balkan problems.[2]

The ecclesiastical cycle of feasts in all this turmoil has on me the effect of showers of rain on a landscape that needs the rain; but some part is ready, other parts are not. The steady beat of the Church's story told in music goes on through the years, at the same time as the unsteady, riotous, noise of guns and bombs; but at last the steady beat will be heard alone—please God.

You will be glad to hear that your "Study" is now in Fr. Bruno's[3] hands. I am guiding his "First Steps", or 'Study' without tears. He is after your views on the Old Testament. He also has your last lecture.

Talk about Indian Summers, this Spring was a fraud. It began—you remember my last letter—but we have now gone back to a diet of east winds and snow.

I must close being called off to plant 'earlies' and anything else we dare put in. The wire has not arrived and rabbits have a taste for promising young shoots.

Yours affectionately,
Columba Cary-Elwes, O.S.B.

1. This became C.C.E.'s *China and the Cross*.
2. On 6 April 1941 German armies invaded Yugoslavia and attacked Greece.
3. Bruno Donovan, O.S.B. (1911–67); novice master and student of scripture at Ampleforth.

The Royal Institute
of International Affairs
Foreign Research and Press Service
10 April 1941 Balliol College, Oxford

Dear Columba,

You never weary of well doing, while I have left at least two of your letters unanswered; so I am seizing time to write you a line now after having got, this morning, the letter you wrote me on Tuesday.

I believe, like you, that the Church's music will last, and that the noise of the World will gradually die away and in the end be silent. In the historical sense, the dreadful things that are happening now are insignificant—though in the absolute sense the good and evil deeds that are being done have an eternal effect, which is not wiped out.

To change the simile, the Church's life is like a pure stream running into a muddy ditch full of silt and flotsam. In the end, we believe, the pure water is going to scour out the ditch, so that the ditch will have in it nothing but the pure clean running water of the stream that is now pouring into it. Meanwhile, the pure water is being contaminated with the foul water into which it has been injected, and its flow is being cumbered up with all the silt and flotsam that it has found in its path.[1]

In the Church as it is, which part, exactly, is the pure water, and which part is the silt and flotsam that has been accidentally picked up by it and is being only temporarily carried along with it? That is the puzzle to me.

Religion being for some reason (perhaps because it has to appeal to the masses) very dependent on tradition and custom, it is particularly hard, in religious things, to sift out the accidents from the substance.

I shall be thinking of you these next days—as I am always doing when I get my head above water and shake myself free for a moment from current work.

Yours affectionately,
Arnold J. Toynbee

1. Compare *A Study of History*, where A.J.T. expands this simile into a picture of the Nile carrying alluvium in suspense: "It is only when the flotsam is able to sink from the intellectual surface of the psychic stream to the well-springs of lowly folk-lore and lofty poetry in the Psyche's intuitive and emotional depths that this sediment can fertilize the Psyche and that, in virtue of this fruitful disentanglement of two fortuitously intermingled elements, the heavenly water of spiritual life can regain its original purity" (VII : 456). And cf. A.J.T.'s letter of 31 August 1947, below.

St. Wilfrid's House
Ampleforth College, York

13 April 1941
Please forgive a lot
of the obvious bore.

My dear Arnold,

As always, so this time, the sight of an envelope addressed in your hand gave me a great start of pleasure. I take this pause before the initial turmoil of term to thank you and to write a few pages full.

This business, problem, of the essential and the unessential in religion interests me too. Strangely enough Fr. Lawrence Bévénot[1] started the discussion a day or so ago over spades we were wielding on my house garden plot. By the end of it we were both reconstructing the liturgy, specially, according to our tastes, pruning, transposing, and I changing the language. The trappings of our liturgy will one day be changed—as they have been changed before. What I meant in my last letter was that the steady beat of the worship of God would go on, under, through and above the noise of guns, bombs, planes. To confine ourselves to the liturgy for a moment, it was good to find John of Montecorvino writing home from Peking that he had said Mass in the Language of his princely convert George (including the Canon)—Uighur I presume (?).[2]

Sometimes I feel a bit savage about the out-of-dateness in Church matters, but then I think we should treat this as we do the foibles of an old and loved person. The person I think of most readily in this connection is the old Abbot Matthews,[3] who had lots of funny ways, and ideas one might describe as die-hard and old fashioned, but one loved them in him. So with the Church, it bears down from past ages, modes of thought (transubstantiation), ways of behaviour, styles in dress, which in a brand-new thing would be laughable, but in an old are lovable. They remind one of victories won and yet more glorious defeats—transubstantiation, the Thomist synthesis; the Douai version, the persecutions. The beech tree with its old leaves, delighting the eye, but to give place soon to new leaves—but the same beech.

To decide what is ephemeral and what permanent is difficult for all of us, but more so to the individualist in religion, because he has to start at the beginning, and might do it several times in a life time. For me and any other Catholic it is simplified by the fact that in some very few cases the Church has said—this is permanent, definite. The thing that still strikes me about the Church's attitude is, how few things she has put her foot down about. The definitive pronouncements of the Church are very few, but they are fundamental. I am sure the more profitable approach to the "ephemeral or permanent" problem is, not to ask: What is ephemeral? but to ask: What do *we know for certain to be permanent*, and what for certain are ephemeral.

I wonder what your list would be? Here are some of mine, just for the interest of the thing:

Permanent.	*Ephemeral.*
1. That God is.	1. The philosophic language describing him (Greek terminology).
2. Some attributes [Good [Just [Merciful [All Knowing [All Powerful [Infinite	2. The philosophical adjustments of these to each other which are only approaches.
3. That God prepared the way for a later revelation by being attentive to the Jews.	3. Much of the Old Law, much of the terminology.
4. That God sent a messenger Christ.	4. The language our Lord spoke is not now exactly suited to our methods—the parable is difficult for Westerns.

5. That Christ's word must be taken as TRUE (There is sufficient evidence to make that conclusion in general) We have no right to pick and choose because that would be exactly contrary to Christ's evident attitude towards his own message.

5. The Gospels as they stand are not exactly as written, but the modifications are immaterial. We are too near the originals to allow for changes of doctrine. *Securus judicat orbis terrarum*.[4]

6. That Christ was not two people but one. But He had all that men have, is a man, and is God. (leave out 6 for the time being)

6. The Aristotelian exposition is the best so far, but there may be a better.

7. Christ, God's messenger founded ONE body, to be in some mysterious way his Body.

7. Vast quantity of flotsam here. At times, in certain ways:
   a) Ecclesiastical dress & vestments
   b) Language.
   c) Parochial government
   d) Liturgical anomalies (Easter Sunday celebrated on Holy Saturday morning)
   e) Uneducated clergy
   f) Church mixed up in social environment, feudalism, capitalism
   g) Italian Popes (Not essentially a bad thing)
   h) Superstitious laity
   i) Irreligious ministers of God—beginning with Judas, ending with us all in various degrees.
   j) The wrong interpretation by individuals of the teaching; the failure to live up to the teaching. The failure to teach in individual cases.

8. That his body was meant to TEACH. And if it was to teach, then:
   a) there were truths that needed teaching
   b) People had to accept being taught
   c) We had to be sure that we were getting sound teaching.

9. That his teaching, if followed, would lead to sanctity.

—And, that "holiness" is a mark of the Church, you are ready to admit. God's relations with men are to make them holy. That is the supreme test. There are good men and bad men everywhere, but great saints, on and on, and in the most difficult circumstances, over and over again. Jesus Christ, God, shines through many members of his Church. It is the supreme test. How futile all the above lists are, as straw, compared with the lists of saints.

What did they care about the 'ephemeral'; some of it, I suppose, helped them, some did not, as for instance S. Augustine and music.[5] The truths of faith are the only not ephemeral part of religion, facts which remain; but these truths are wrapped up in changing forms, some clearer than others.

I do not think, either, that because we decide that a thing is ephemeral, it is to be cast out. Certain liturgical forms are helpful to the majority and the others have to put up with those parts. The Church contains many of the few intellectual people that are, and many of the simple. It must teach the simple by images—obvious, no need to go further. S. Benet Biscop and his pictures.[6] I wonder whether they were good or bad art? They were the best he could get, no doubt.

Just as the political world is crumbling for lack of unity, so has the religious world crumbled for the same reason. We must return *sicut natos ad matrem* to Rome; or rather to the One Church that is not only in Rome, but in England, all over the world, '*sicut natos ad matrem*'.

I have had a very peaceful holiday, except for the worry of the war, the seriousness of the situation as it is evolving. God will not desert us. He could, might, on the field of battle; but whatever happens we may yet put our trust in him.

Please God, you still have some say in the affairs of state. *Some political thoughts*:

I consider the idea of bombing Rome as ridiculous if logically examined. Germans bomb Athens, we bomb Italian Rome. Not Italian Rome, but OUR ROME. I cannot believe it is seriously meant. If so, then suddenly a real depravity is present in high places.

Provided we fight foot by foot everywhere we should just have time to get America's aid. People are too pessimistic about the Middle East calamities.[7] This is partly—and I speak as one suffering under the arrangement—because we cannot (must not) be told the truth. That should be impressed on us: that we must not expect to know the truth till that particular round is over.

I must stop.

Yours affectionately,
Columba C.-Elwes, O.S.B.

1. Ludovic Lawrence Bévénot, O.S.B. (1901–); Ampleforth monk; musician, a founder of the Society of Saint Gregory to promote plain song and the new liturgy; now on parish at Cardiff.

2. John of Montecorvino, O.F.M. (1247–1328); first archbishop of Peking.

3. J. E. Matthews, O.S.B. (1871–1939); Abbot of Ampleforth.

4. Saint Augustine, *Contra epistolam Parmeniani*, III.3.24.

5. Saint Augustine, *Confessions*, 10.33.

6. Saint Benet Biscop (ca. 628–ca. 690); abbot and founder of Wearmouth and Jarrow monasteries; formed libraries; taught the Venerable Bede.

7. Compare C.C.E.'s letter of 8 April 1941, above.

The Royal Institute of
International Affairs
Foreign Research and Press Service
Balliol College, Oxford

5 May 1941

Dear Columba,

This is not an answer to your last letter but just a line of sympathy over the accident.

In war time one is less prepared for misfortunes that have nothing to do with the war, and this tragic misfortune was not in the ordinary picture of the risks of civil life.

I am very sorry.

Yours affectionately,
Arnold J. Toynbee

S. Wilfrid's

May 1941

My dear Arnold,

Thank you so much for your sympathy for us all.[1] It was so good of you to remember us in spite of your world worries, as they must be becoming; though, light is coming in the west.

In spite of one's certainty that these beloved children have gone to heaven, that accident was such a "back-hander", such a bolt from the blue that the shock was terrible. I say "was", as one's balance is restored. For the parents it is still, one knows, a dead weight. But they, every one of them, were heroic and Christ-like to a marvellous degree, especially the Pierlots, who could only utter words of thanks to God for allowing their two to have had a chance of being here at least a little time. One tried to console them all and oneself with the CERTAINTY that they are not really separated from us, or only by the senses. Nature is very strong, and even I, who only had—at any rate not a parental affection which is like a vice gripping—felt the strain of it. They will all rest in peace.

Professor Baynes[2] will have great fun finding out from Hess[3] whether his learned guesses were correct. What an amazing incident. The wildest theories are current: the first 5th columnist; he was off to America, to Ireland; he is "scramming", he has lost his reason; he has found his reason. I suppose you know; perhaps we shall. At all events it is another example of the least expected happening.

Excuse more. I am determined this should go by this post.

Yours ever,
Columba Cary-Elwes, O.S.B.

1. The school train from King's Cross bringing the boys back to school caught fire, and nine boys were burned to death and others injured. Among the dead were two sons of Hubert Pierlot, then in exile; Pierlot had become prime minister in Belgium on 18 April 1939.

2. Compare C.C.E.'s letter of 10 March 1941 above.

3. On 10 May 1941, Rudolph Hess (1894–), deputy führer and leader of the Nazi Party, landed by parachute in Scotland.

Ampleforth College
York

Eve of the feast of Corpus Christi
11 June 1941

My dear Arnold,

Tomorrow is so very much your feast, after your mention of it in that superb lecture you gave last year in the Sheldonian Theatre[1] that I must send you a letter.

You will find enclosed a litany of Christ's names to be found in the New Testament. A book I once read in Sto. Domingo de Silos by Luís de León[2] called *Los Nombres de Cristo* gave me the idea of collecting for myself all the names I could. This is a preliminary list as I have not been very carefully through the Acts. But I know you would like them. It is also partly to encourage you in your resolution of prayer made now how many years ago? And now almost impossible. What I do is just to take one of these names and repeat it many times. It is an Old English method of prayer, suggested to me by *The Cloud of Unknowing* which I expect you know. But do you remember the key passage about the presence of God "If thou desirest to have this intent lapped and folden in one word, so that thou mayest have better hold thereupon, take thee but a little word of one syllable, for so it is better than of two; for the shorter the word the better it accordeth with the work of the spirit . . . and such a word is this word God, or this word Love . . . This word shall be thy shield and thy spear, whether thou ridest on peace or war" c.7.[3]

I think that a lovely passage, don't you? As the years go by I hope to do a little commentary on many of these Names.

You remember the talk about subsidiary function. The article eventually got written and appeared in the May number of Blackfriars.[4] I received a message from the Cardinal[5] through my cousin Val Elwes[6] saying he thought it excellent. That gives me more pleasure than I can say, as it gives a sanction to lots of ideas I have been propagating; and, as they resemble many of your basic ideas, it confirms me in my incurable admiration for them too! This *entre nous*.

The speech of Mr. Churchill was just what was wanted.[7] We have not the facts to judge by and he cannot afford to give them to us. It does present a problem, namely how can democracy truly exist in war? We have to trust the P.M. and if he fails us, then, by the time we really get to know it will probably be too late. An inevitable situation but unfortunate.

You may be interested in a letter I received from one Vincent Cronin[8] an old boy of this House and son of Dr. Cronin[9] of *Citadel* fame. The latter is now on the American M. of I. The remarks on America are as follows:—

"As regards America and the war, I am convinced that Roosevelt is doing everything in his power to get help over to Britain, but he is doing it very slowly, for this simple reason. A large number of Americans are just too stupid to realise that the war in Europe is as much their war as England's, so step by step he is sending over more ships and more planes and gradually increasing help to Britain, without actually making one big move at one time, which would stir up these people and make them react violently. The labour question in this country is in a shocking situation, comparable with that in France before the last war move by the Nazis, and the number of strikes in the defense productive factories is simply appalling. The slightest thing Roosevelt does sets off fireworks among the workmen and the unionists. I think Roosevelt will eventually work up to convoying ships across the Atlantic, but he will have to do it slowly. If Roosevelt declared war now, the division of interventionists and isolationists would be so great that internal strife would result and production would come to a standstill. Perhaps it would be months before Britain got more aid." May 10, 1941

You know all that, but it does confirm. I must stop.

Remember me to Lawrence and Rosalind and to Miss Boulter and Miss? Bridget [10] and Professors Clark and Baynes.

Yours affectionately,
Columba Cary-Elwes, O.S.B.

I shall remember you extra specially at the repetition of the Last Supper and the re-presenting of Calvary.

1. The Burge Memorial Lecture.

2. Luis de León (1528–91); Spanish Augustinian friar; for *De los nombres de Cristo*, see Félix García, O.S.A., ed., *Obras Completas* (Madrid, 1951), pp. 386ff.

3. *The Cloud of Unknowing*, an anonymous work of mysticism, was edited from the British Museum's Harleian ms 674 by E. Underhill (1912; 7th ed., London, 1970), pp. 81–82.

4. C.C.E., "A Principle in Sociology," *Blackfriars* (May 1941), pp. 245–53.

5. Arthur Hinsley (1865–1943).

6. Monsignor Valentine Elwes (1898–1966); then the cardinal's secretary; at one time chaplain at Oxford; son of Gervase Elwes.

7. On 10 June 1941, Winston Churchill took part in the debate in the House of Commons over the British loss of Crete; reported in *The Times* (11 June 1941).

8. Vincent Cronin (1924–); author of numerous works on European history and civilization; he was then a student at Eliot House, Harvard University (1941–43); joined the Rifle Brigade; after the war took a degree in Greats, Trinity College, Oxford; *The Florentine Renaissance* (London, 1967); *Napoleon* (London, 1971).

9. Doctor Archibald J. Cronin (1896–1981); *The Citadel* (London, 1937).

10. Bridget R. Reddin (1895–1981); A.J.T.'s secretary who typed the "nonsense book"; she had been Lawrence's nurse; see A.J.T.'s acknowledgment in *A Study of History*, X:240; her letters to C.C.E. will appear herein from time to time.

Ampleforth College
York

2 July 1941

My dear Arnold,

Ever since the Russian development I have been meaning to write, but I am glad I waited as ideas have clarified. My first impression was one of immense relief, as in it

I saw the end of the Bolshevist regime, and a final "all in" solution of Europe's life to come after we have beaten the Germans. Everyone I suppose felt, before, that any balance in Europe created after the war would be precarious with Russian saboteurs on the Eastern border. My second reaction was a great fear that Churchill might go too far in support of Russia. Clearly every Russian man and woman has a right to defend the home, the land they live in, and to that extent an unjust regime could fight a just war. But would the Russians stop at that; if they got a chance they would sweep across Eastern Europe; in any case they have already behaved in the same way as the Germans in Finland and Poland. My third reaction was one of immense relief when Mr. Churchill spoke.[1] He dissociated himself utterly from that vile regime, and promised to help the Russian people. It still leaves difficulties. You cannot help the one without helping the other. The ideal thing to have done, it seems to me, would have been to be grateful that Hitler had made another enemy for himself, promised help to Russia only on certain conditions e.g. the Lothian five points (or was it four?),[2] and promise of final withdrawal from Poland, Esthonia, Lithuania, Finland. In any case I see not the ghost of a chance for the Russian armies against the German, and (for Hitler) it would have lost him all the propaganda value of his attack. The situation reminds me of the remark by the Bp. of Winchester quoted in the Introduction of *Contemporaries of Marco Polo*: "Let those dogs devour each other and be utterly wiped out, and then we shall see, founded on their ruins, the universal Catholic Church, and there shall be one shepherd and one flock", a particularly cynical remark in his case.[3] But in this case it is difficult to see which of the "dogs" is the worse.

My final opinion has come to be that we should have kept these two wars separate, but that, as in fact we cannot help the Russians, our cause is not lowered in moral standard. This is only my view and most others here seem to think we should not look a gift horse in the mouth.

I have written all this just to give you grist for your mill. What I hope will happen is that the German onslaught crack—blow up—the Bolshevik regime but not destroy the Russian armies which will carry on.

My plans in the summer are as follows, a retreat to nuns at Enfield in the last week of July, ten days in Bournemouth with my father and mother and then to Seel St. Liverpool, for the rest of the time. I felt one could not galavant about these days and that our mission priests needed a long earned rest; so if you hear that the Catholic Presbytery in Seel St. Liverpool, has been blown up, you will know what has happened to me; and if in time I get to heaven my prayers there will prove more useful to you than the ones so painfully and fitfully made here.

We read together, four or five boys and I, the David and Goliath section of the Study.[4] It was a most fruitful source of discussion for discovering the essential point in the German stage in technique. We decided that they had done with armoured vehicles what the Mamluks had done with armoured knights against the free-lance French and Tartar. But also they had co-ordinated arms, perhaps the next state is "a men-of-all-trades"; but please God it will be rather 'Farewell to Arms'.

How well one can understand the rise of stoicism, fatalism, now; it is the educated man's solution; the educated man who has lost his religion. We do seem in the toils of inexorable fate, playthings of the things we have made; first of economics gone mad; now of democracy gone mad (crowd worship of Hitler); of machines gone mad. Equally well, better, I feel the return to sanity will come, the return to God.

Lawrence looks very well and from all accounts has enjoyed his Oxford term; he is still bursting with enthusiasms.[5] He gave me news of you, which I was very glad to have; and let that be an excuse for you not to write yet awhile. I know you are tremendously busy, but I know you probably have a page of letter half written, do not feel bound to write, or else I will feel I am putting an unfair burden on you.

Yours affectionately,
Columba Cary-Elwes, O.S.B.

1. Winston Churchill's broadcast of 22 June 1941.
2. Philip Henry Kerr, Marquess of Lothian (1882–1940); ambassador to the United States (1939–40); in a famous address to the organization known as the "Pilgrims," he attributed the long peace of the nineteenth century to the Monroe Doctrine and Britain's "paramount navy," a stable world currency based on gold, relatively free trade, and free immigration into the New World; cf. *The American Speeches of Lord Lothian* (London, 1941), pp. 1–19.
3. Manuel Komroff, *Contemporaries of Marco Polo* (London, 1929).
4. A.J.T.'s "The Nemesis of Creativity, David and Goliath," in *A Study of History*, IV:431–65.
5. Lawrence had four terms at New College before joining the Coldstream Guards.

3 Ship St.
Oxford

5 July 1941

Dear Columba,

The unwritten letter didn't even begin to get onto paper this time till now (Saturday 10.0 PM—but in this double summer-time we can't believe in clock time). But I know you know that you are in my thoughts and that dumbness doesn't mean forgetfulness.

Rosalind and I are coming up north this next Wednesday the 9th—staying at the Guest House at Castle Howard[1] till the 15th, and then, I hope, she is coming for two nights to Ampleforth, and I for at least one—it might be two, but it depends on whether a pending appointment falls on the 17th or 18th. Anyhow I should like to spend the night of the 16th in the Monastery, if I may. And if you can raise a bicycle I hope to see you over at the Guest House before that—or vice versa come and see you at Ampleforth if I can find wheels at Castle Howard.

As to my feelings about the Russians:[2] I don't think Communism is going to come out of this war without being greatly changed: the Russians will have had the experience of all the other nations—of being attacked without provocation—and I think they will have suffered so much that they will stop being the peculiar people that they have been for these last 24 years and will become more or less ordinary again. I expect, for instance to see Hitler and Stalin compete with one another in restoring the Orthodox Church, and though neither will mean it seriously the Church may be restored all the same. On the analogy of China, I think there may be a puppet Nanking government, in Moscow and a patriot Chungking government at Omsk[3]—but the Russians are putting up a much tougher resistance than I had imagined they could.

Well, I look forward immensely to seeing you.

Yours affectionately,
Arnold

1. Compare A.J.T.'s letter of March 1910, above.
2. On 22 June 1941, the German armies invaded Russia.
3. The Japanese set up a puppet government of China at Nanking in 1938; the Chinese government withdrew to Chungking after the fall of Hankow.

The Royal Institute
of International Affairs
Balliol College, Oxford

21 July 1941

Dear Columba,

Just a line to say how much I hope to see you on your way back from Bournemouth, and how much happiness I got from those two days at Ampleforth last week.

Please go on writing, and be sure that your letters are read and pondered over even when they are not answered!

As usual, I am writing in very great haste, between a train and a committee.

God Bless You.

Yours affectionately,
Arnold J. Toynbee

5 August 1941 Enfield Convent

My dear Arnold,

I am just coming to the end of my retreat to these nuns and feel at liberty to write.

The poor nuns had a land mine in the road opposite their front door. The whole place including their just completed school came down on their heads. They struggled out into the street and another fell, plus bombs. Those demolished the Catholic church and presbytery opposite. Not one of them was even seriously injured. But the church the presbytery and convent are not there to see. Half the school survived as a wreck. This was some months ago. They are quite cheerful and seem to take it all as a gift.

On the other hand I had a letter from an old boy, a doctor in the London Hospital—Whitechapel, who has been through every blitz. He wants revenge; but being muddled-headed, wants it on the people who never did it. I am quite sure that the time has come for one of our most prominent men, preferably Mr. Churchill, to say something like the following: "I know, in the heat of the moment, even responsible people have said that we must punish the German people, we must given them what they have given us. What we meant to say was that we will punish the Nazi leaders and willing tools. That was our early cry and we repeat it. We want to free the ordinary decent Germans and everyone else from this mad gang. We know there are decent Germans. Hitler only got into power by a bare majority. The others were terrified of the prospect in spite of fair promises. Once in power, who was to stop him? All those who voted against then, would be more against, now; I believe all plebiscites after H. came to power were cooked, or by threat; and how many must now be gulled by his propaganda. We have allies among the Germans as well as among the other Europeans." I think that, unless something of the sort is said very strongly, the tone of the average mind will sink, and again we will be faced by the intelligent few who want a fair peace and the blind, enraged, multitude crying out for vengeance on all and sundry. Hitler in *Mein Kampf* was very accurate when he said our propaganda won by concentrating on the Kaiser and not on the German people. We should concentrate still on those responsible: the Hitler gang.

Giving this retreat has opened my eyes again to the futility of logic for persuading—an exaggeration perhaps. But when one considers the Old and New Testaments from this point of view and searches for one single bit of logic, the fact scarcely seems an exaggeration. I came to wonder whether we are not too attached to the Thomist, or rather mediaeval systematisation. The thing that first struck S. Augustine about the Bible—if I remember correctly—was its apparent uncivilisedness, its lack of logic one might say. So in this retreat I have been trying to understand the Hebraic mind, or better the technique of persuasion used by God through the medium of the Hebrew writers, seers, prophets. It is just beginning to be plain to me that it is the same method as the poets use, something deeper than "ratiocination", a mixture of insight and symbolism. Now the modern world is so bound up with Reason and logic, "hard facts", the practical, that all this means nothing, and never more so than in the liturgy. Now, I am also beginning to see that the liturgy is the carry-over into our world of this ancient secret of knowledge. Just as in the Bible you have to look twice to get the deep meaning, the longer the gaze—in a certain spirit—the deeper the meaning, so with the liturgy. It is like looking for hidden treasure. I wonder whether all this makes sense. I was encouraged on this line by finding a copy of Luís de León's *De los Nombres de Cristo*[1] in Foyle's second hand department. It was very lucky, as Blackwell's told me it was unobtainable. This book is just one example of the same thing: this symbolism of Names, like the Dionysian book on the divine Names. I used rather to poo poo this type of thing. But now I think, it isn't logical, that is to be granted, but in a mysterious way it has a profundity that logic has not.

This has helped me over the obscurities of the liturgy. They make one search, and the finding is more affecting and real than a bold statement or act would be. I am sure I have S. Augustine with me and have discovered a key to the treatment by the Fathers and the Saints of the Bible; and am consequently highly delighted; and so you have suffered this.

The City of London was a sorry sight, a real ruin, but it was cheering too to think this great capital had withstood all that. It makes the City a noble thing, when it was a bit sordid before. As for the rest, particularly Oxford St, I was agreeably surprised how very little damage has been done; but I have not yet seen the East End.

Tomorrow I go off to Bournemouth for a week. My kindest regards to Rosalind and to Lawrence.

Yours affectionately,
Columba, O.S.B.

1. Compare C.C.E.'s letter of 11 June 1941, above.

A note

6.10 P.M.
14 August 1941
Eve of the Assumption

St. Mary's Priory
Talbot Rd.
Cardiff

My dear Arnold,

I do not know whether you are with Mr. Churchill in Mid-Atlantic! but must write a line immediately, having just heard the Peace Principles, to say that they are magnificent, please God realisable.[1] That is my first impression, and I am sure it will be a permanent one. Thank God we have produced them and that they are so utterly free from vengeance or propaganda. They sounded noble, magnanimous, and are so. I like the disarmament section specially. I will study them more and give you further "thoughts of the man in the street (cloister)" on them.

Here I am in Cardiff staying at one of our missions, St. Mary's, for the space of ten days.

What a wonderful gift to the world those Peace Principles are, for the feast of the Assumption.

One day you will tell me what part you had in the proceedings. I can see the hand of God in it all. "*Nisi Dominus aedificaverit domum. . . .*"[2]

Yours affectionately,
Columba

1. Winston S. Churchill and Franklin D. Roosevelt had met in Placentia Bay, Newfoundland, 9–12 August 1941 and had issued a joint declaration: the Atlantic Charter.

2. Psalm 127. A.J.T. had placed this, in English, at the title page of his *Study of History*, vols. IV, V, and VI.

Ampleforth College
York

10 September 1941

My dear Arnold,

First let me thank you and Rosalind for your most hospitable reception of me—as always. It is a joy seeing you. Secondly, on my arrival here I found a parcel from the O.U.P., and what should it be but the *Survey* for 1938.[1] You are kind. Thanks very much indeed. It is a great temptation to devour it now, but I shall have to put the desire aside, except for the chapter on Austria which I shall read as soon as I can, by snatches. These volumes since 1933 are like acts in a cosmic tragedy. Is the survey being written for 1939 or has it to be abandoned?

I think you were right about the Catholic position usually being between two extremes. We both revolted against the idea that evening because of the context in which it came and the parallel it implied. I don't think the Church took the central position in order to reconcile, but because truth so often is central between extreme views. The odd thing is that those positions once central are now extreme, one side being abandoned by those outside the Church. Nor was the Catholic position central until there had been a rhythm of four moves, a swing to minimise, a reaction, an exaggeration of the reaction and finally a retracing of steps to the central. All that taking many years and so guaranteeing the truth—finding motive, and putting out of account the expediency motive of Our Mother the Church.

I suppose friends have intuitive ways of knowing each other's minds and I felt you had travelled a long way to the Church since the war, that Reason is losing its preeminence and faith has come already. One day I hope you will say with S. Augustine that you have done enough answering questions, that there is enough reason to make all objections, however plausible, insignificant, that you will not be "always learning, and never able to come unto the knowledge of the truth".[2]

How insignificant did that suggestion seem to the Protestants, which we read in the Preface to the 39 Articles:[3] not to express contrary views on faith and yet to hold them. Yet how tremendous for the world has been the result, the faith of Englishmen has crumbled away and who can build it up again. It was a revelation to me of the importance of principles, so intangible yet so active—like yeast. I would like to think that the Atlantic Charter will prove to be the principles on which we shall act. But the principle of compromise in truth which led to indifference did not come from that expression in the passage we read, though it was encouraged by it, but must already have been well embedded in the minds of men. Can we say the same of the principles of the Atlantic Charter? I don't think so. We are learning by suffering that the old ways led to destruction, but unless someone expounds the nature of these principles in relation to our past mistakes and experiences, they are likely, I think, to remain a dead letter. There is the true use of propaganda. The machine must be turned on to explain to the common man the lesson seen by the wise. I don't see why Chatham House should not do a bit of that, probably in the style used for cabinet ministers and others, that is, the simplest and shortest.

Yours affectionately,
Columba Cary-Elwes, O.S.B.

P.S. St. Jerome and the Canonical Books. (I take this straight out of Hugh Pope's Aids to the Bible)[4]

1. He did hold the views mentioned in our reading.
2. He changed his views to the standard Catholic view later in life.
3. His friend St. Exuperius seems to have been worried by his views and asked Innocent I for a decision on the matter. Innocent gave the full list.

Securus judicat orbis terrarum, we always reply against one Father. Just as S. Thomas was wrong on theological points, so must be St. Jerome on scriptural ones, so as to save us from thinking either infallible in his own sphere!

I have written this useless foot-note so it had better stand, I can't re-write the whole letter.

1. A.J.T., assisted by Veronica Boulter, *Survey of International Affairs* (1938) (London, 1941).
2. 2 Timothy 3:7.
3. Compare John Henry Cardinal Newman, *Tract XC* (London, 1841); and *Apologia pro Vita Sua* (London, 1864), pp. 158–72, where Newman argues that the Thirty-nine Articles did not oppose Catholic teaching and "but partially" opposed Roman dogma.
4. Hugh Pope, *The Catholic Student's "Aids" to the Study of the Bible*, rev. ed., 3 vols. (London, 1926–38).

Ampleforth College
St. Francis 1941 (7 October) York

My dear Arnold,

I have just received a letter from Mgr. Ronnie Knox saying he intends to dispatch to you a copy of his version of St. Matthew. I hope you encourage him for all you are worth in the sense of sound modern English.[1]

I enclose with this letter the now to me very precious MS. of a chapter in the hypothetical book: *Christianity in China*, the chapter on the Franciscans. I showed it with trepidation to Fr. Abbot, with trepidation because he is very exacting, and he really did seem to find it interesting. So I hope I shall not disappoint you. But it will not be news to you as it mostly was to him. When you next have time, after reading it, do please criticise it.

In the holidays I looked at Giles on Confucianism and its Rivals[2] and Granet: *la Pensée Chinoise*.[3] The former I found fascinating, and I want to read more on the

Mahayana Buddhists. Anyhow I have committed myself to reading a paper on religious thought in China to the Historical Society and am making it the first draft of a chapter for the book, which will have to be written on the Chinese religious and philosophical atmosphere which the missionaries encountered. The Franciscans seem to have been impressed by the Buddhists—I must add a section on that—whereas P. Ricci was anything but impressed.

How strange the different reactions of people to the same thing. Professor Murray seems to have been overjoyed at that meeting of Scientists.[4] I was profoundly depressed. It did not seem to me to be a meeting of Scientists but of doctrinaires, Negríns[5] and Maiskys[6] and H. G. Wells[7] and even Smuts[8]—a great man—roped in. I cannot understand all this talk of loving freedom with a representative of Russia in an honoured position. I can't stand the 19th century smugness of the whole proceeding. Obviously something has gone wrong with the world based on 'science' and not 'morals.' The whole proceeding was a Left affair with a political leaning, when it might truly have been scientific, a little apologetic, a little chastened. Historically I suppose we are to blame in being too smug also and not baptising science as St. Thomas baptised Aristotle. I wonder what you really thought of it all, the old slogans and the rest.[9]

The school term is in full swing, most horariums are fixed irrevocably, school societies are grabbing nights for their meetings. The Voyageurs, the one you have frequently addressed, began well last night with a talk on 'le proche Orient' from Br. Gilbert,[10] only three weeks ago Mr. Montgomery, just back from Angora as attaché or secretary to our Embassy there. His talk was most entertaining, but he kept off politics, which disappointed the boys a bit.

I have read of the *Survey* the part on Austria, which I think I already told you made me feel I was reading an Act of Cosmic tragedy. I read with very great interest the parts on American public opinion. I found that most revealing. The Spanish part was good, but just a polishing off. Mr. Charles Edwards[11] has run off with it, so that my reading has stopped there. The Austrian story exemplifies the truth of Shakespeare's division of men, some of whom have greatness thrust upon them. I feel the Cardinal of Vienna was the most tragic figure of them all.[12] You were most fair, so fair and uncondemning, that the tragedy of it stood out even more clearly. I thought then, and re-reading the story makes me more convinced that the break occurred there. Other doubtful things had been done before, but that was brigandage on the grand scale: Hitler walking in.

So the war goes on; and as you expected the USSR is giving more and more religious freedom, and the Poles are saving their population—or half of it. But the rest of Europe I think is being prematurely encouraged to open revolt. We are making Mola's mistake of boasting about a fifth column in the enemy Madrid.[13]

Some articles are appearing in the *Times* on the Atlantic Charter. I think the equating of order and freedom an excellent idea. I hope they go on stressing the necessity for economic order (or freedom).

I must stop. You have not time for such long letters. I pray daily for you and daily thank God that through people like you England is being preserved from losing touch with its Christian heritage.

Yours affectionately,
Columba, O.S.B.

1. Ronald Knox in 1938 had been commissioned by the English hierarchy to translate the New Testament into the modern vernacular. It was published in 1945; his translation of the Old Testament followed in 1948 and 1949. See his *On Englishing the Bible* (London, 1949).

2. Lionel Giles, *The Sayings of Confucius* (London, 1907).

3. Marcel Granet, *La Pensée Chinoise* (Paris, 1934), "Évolution de l'humanité," vol. 25b, secs. 1, 25.

4. The Council of the British Association called a council to consider the role of science in world planning after the war; it adopted a Charter of Scientific Principles; cf. *The Times* (29 September 1941).

5. Juan Negrín (1891–1956); premier in the Spanish republican government from 1937 to 1939.

6. Ivan Mikhailovich Maisky (1884–1975); Soviet ambassador to the Court of St. James (1932–43); journalist; member, Academy of Sciences; *Memoirs of a Soviet Ambassador: The War, 1939–43*, trans. A. Rothstein (London, 1967).

7. H. G. Wells (1866–1946); A.J.T. speaks of his "intuitive genius" in *A Study of History*, VIII: 53n. Wells presided over a section of the council.

8. General Jan Christian Smuts (1870–1950); South African statesman and author of *Holism and Evolution*, 2d ed. (London, 1927).

9. "My animus against the meeting was misplaced, as its purpose was to break down, if only in a small way, the barrier between Communist absolutism and the Western belief in freedom of thought and expression." (C.C.E.)

10. Brother Gilbert, Msgr. Hugh Edmund Montgomery (1895–1971); Winchester, Christ Church, Oxford; had just returned from service in the Foreign Office at Ankara; after some months at Ampleforth he decided to become a diocesan priest; at the suggestion of the British government, was sent to Rome where he lived in the Vatican during the war; afterward a priest in the Birmingham diocese.

11. Thomas Charles Edwards (1902–77); an outstanding history instructor at Ampleforth College.

12. Theodor Cardinal Innitzer (1875–1955) who made an ill-fated attempt to conciliate the Nazis; cf. *Survey of International Affairs, 1938*, vol. I, by A.J.T., assisted by Veronica M. Boulter (London, 1941), pp. 242–56.

13. General Emilio Vidal Mola (1877–1937); commander of Franco's northern army during the first year of the Spanish civil war; reported to have used the phrase *la quinta columna* in a radio address. See *The International Repercussions of the War in Spain (1936–7)*, vol. 2 of *Survey of International Affairs, 1937*, 2 vols., by A.J.T., assisted by Veronica M. Boulter (London, 1938), p. 59.

Ampleforth College
York

7 November 1941

My dear Arnold,

It is ages since I wrote and I am sorry, as I have no sufficient, or over sufficient reasons as you have. Sometimes I think the reason why I don't start writing is that the things I want to say are too big to be thrown down haphazard in the "odd half hours", or the more or less tired evenings. That is really a poor reason, because I know you will understand that.

The *Survey 1938* has proved more interesting than ever. I found that the first part on economics was full of good things; particularly the dissertation on Autarky and Sovereignty—German interpretation. It really made me feel very sorry for the Central Europeans. An impasse had clearly been reached before the war. The recent speeches by Mr. Sumner Welles [1] and the President are clarifying the air, preparing our minds as they should for the right solution: the world for all without favour. BUT who is going to guarantee that the ideal will be put in practice. That to me is the haunting, really haunting problem. What chance have we really got that a clique will not break in and prevent good intentions being made effective. The only guarantee we have is universal suffrage. But how often has that been deceived? Really, the crowd should never have elected Baldwin in. I suppose the great ray of hope is that the Crowd on the other side Atlantic did vote in Roosevelt. But there again he is being thwarted all the time. Millions of lives are being lost and will be because democracy cannot be in a hurry.

This is all a bit depressing, and only one side of the picture. Even grown ups learn lessons, and two wars should be a big enough one.

I noticed in a review of books, that someone said Peace was our aim—in Society. Was it Mr. Lionel Curtis? [2] I wonder whether that is what we should *aim* at. Isn't it rather like aiming at pleasure? We should aim at something more concrete, being just and being loving, and these two in union produce Peace.

Another thing that struck me in the *Survey* was the account of all this international raw material control. Perhaps someday you will devote a whole or large part of a *Survey* to these institutions, their history, their constitutions, their power, their possibilities. In the past they appear to have been a mixed blessing, but the future may have something great in store for them.

My talk, or paper, on Chinese thought, "went off with a bang," if Chinese thought does that kind of thing. In my reading up for it I found two curious points (a) that Taoism seemed very like Buddhism, *première manière*, wondered whether there could be a connection, (b) that Granet [3] seems to have a special idea about Taoism, namely that it was not primitively a philosophy but a mixture of extasy and "recettes" for a long life. If that were true, it would make hay of most ideas about Taoism.

Another point I discovered was that P. de la Vallé Poussin [4]—who is an authority isn't he?—thought Nirvana primitively did not stand for utter negation. If that were so, it seems to me, you could make out a very good case for Mahayana being a true derivative of the primitive form of Buddhism. But of course I am a hopeless amateur.

Ever since that conversation under the trees at Castle Howard last summer, I have been pondering on the meaning of the Love of God. Perhaps you would like to see something I wrote, with that conversation in mind, but as part of this little treatise I am concocting on 'The Names of Christ'. I have written several others: Christ the King, *Heres Universorum*, Bread of Life, Christ the Priest, The Lord, *Logos*, *Agnus Dei*, Son of Man; but in a way this is the best. I will not be offended if you don't read it. Just send it back sometime with the Franciscan Essay. In a sense the thing is a conversation with you. Many of my thoughts are prolongations of our talks, and many of my prayers also. Indeed I am sure that our community of mind is really in our prayers; that you approach more nearly to the plunge of faith by prayer than by anything else; so please let me have the cheek to sermonise you. Pray to Our Lord for light. I always find that prayer solves problems in the same sort of way as the sun dissolves the mist. When I think of you daily at Mass, it is so that you will completely accept Christ's divinity and authority and finish your great book in utter harmony with the Church; so that like another "*Civitas Dei*" it will build up our world again on the spiritual Authority of S. Peter, fisherman, but prince of the Apostles, instrument of Christ, servant of the servants of God.

Yours affectionately,
Columba, O.S.B.

1. On 7 October 1941, Sumner Welles, secretary of state, read to a meeting of the National Foreign Trade Council a letter from F. D. Roosevelt to the effect that, after the war, "we must make sure that no effort will be spared to place international commerce on a basis of fair dealing, equality of treatment and mutual benefit" (*The Times* [8 October 1941]).

2. Lionel George Curtis (1872–1955); a founder of the Royal Institute of International Affairs; he sought the transformation of the self-governing countries of the British Empire into a "British Commonwealth"; *Civitas Dei*, 3 vols. (London, 1934–37); *Civitas Dei, the Commonwealth of God*, 1 vol. ed. (London, 1938); see A.J.T.'s *Acquaintances*, chap. 10, "Lionel Curtis," pp. 129–48; with A.J.T. at Balliol during the war.

3. See C.C.E.'s letter of 7 October 1941, above.

4. Louis de la Vallée Poussin, *Nirvana* (Paris, 1924); *Bouddhisme*, 4th ed., Études sur l'Histoire des Religions, vol. 2 (Paris, 1925).

3 Ship St.
Oxford

14 November 1941

Dear Columba,

I got much happiness from your letter of the 7th, as I do from all your letters, and I return the enclosures (*not* unread!) herewith.

I entirely agree that our aim, in public affairs, should not be just peace, which is a negative good; it should, as you say, be justice and love; and if we attain these, peace will incidentally follow, though the way to them may be not peace but the sword. To reach something worth reaching, one generally has to aim at something else that is a long way above and beyond.

Taoism: I think the original philosophy was an independent flowering, in China, of the same ideas and practices that, in India, became Buddhism; but it was afterward influenced by Buddhism itself when that came to China, while the Taoist Church was a still late imitation—almost caricature—of the Mahayanian Church.

I am very glad the talk on Chinese thought made a hit.

As for prayers, thanks to what you do for me I am having a sort of "artificial respiration"—the kind of thing that, sooner or later, starts one breathing on one's own; at least so I think and hope, though neither you nor I can foresee exactly what kind of breaths I shall take if and when I do get going.

This is my usual scrawl in my usual haste.

Yours affectionately,
A.J.T.

3 Ship Street
Oxford

5 December 1941

Dear Columba,

Of course I can put you up here at the beginning of January, and please make it more than one night if you can. I do look forward to this.

I would have written before, but I have been overtaken—and am still laid by the heels—by some kind of gastric trouble which has been going the rounds here. Though tummy-ache and starvation diet are unpleasant in themselves, I daresay it is quite good for one in other ways to have a compulsory break in the daily round of war work.

Incidentally, I have at last an opportunity to start reading your "preliminary essay".

Lawrence is coming up to Ampleforth at the beginning of next week for the beginning of his vac. I am very much pleased that he flies back at once, each time, to a place which has done so much for him and which ought to make the whole difference to the rest of his life—I believe the influence of Ampleforth will do that.

Yours affectionately,
Arnold

35, Ashley Court
Morpeth Terrace
S.W.1

31 January 1942

Dear Columba,

Well, these three weeks have been one of the times of my life, to which I shall look back as a precious thing in my memory.

One thing that I am specially happy about is that you and I can talk about everything completely frankly—including things on which our minds don't agree. There is not, I am sure, the same disagreement in any point between our hearts.

Father Abbot, when I said goodbye to him, was particularly kind, and told me to propose myself whenever I had the opportunity and that he would tell me frankly if the dates didn't happen to be convenient. I am of course very pleased about this, and shall certainly do as he said, without hesitation.

It is a good thing now to get back to work. I am fitter—thanks to Ampleforth—both in body and in spirits than I have been since the beginning of the war, and it is time to get into harness again, with all my colleagues plodding along in harness all the time, without having been out at grass, as I have been. But I hope I shall keep with me—and renew in future visits—the sense of the eternal behind the temporal which you always have at Ampleforth through the school's depending on the monastery and the monastery on the *opus Dei* in the Church.

Our ordinary world is a Wellsian little world now—feeling itself big because it has expanded in its three dimensions, and quite unaware that it is really dwarfish and myopic through having lost its spiritual dimension. I shall try, as far as I can, with thoughts of Ampleforth in my mind, to live in the spiritual as well as the material dimension.

I shall be finishing your ms. on Christianity in the Far East and sending it you back in a week or so, though I shall no longer be master of my own time as I have been for these last weeks.

God Bless You,

Yours affectionately,
Arnold

Ampleforth College
York

9 February 1942

My dear Arnold,

I was glad to get your letter, and am amazed at your energy in writing to us all. People really did appreciate it. The great thing is that you really have had a rest and a spiritual tonic. The news that Fr. Abbot wants you to come whenever you feel like it, is splendid. You must excuse the scrawl, I am writing with a nib several inches long in the point.

The results in argument of your talk are only now beginning to die down. We held another little meeting last night to wind up the discussion. The general opinion seemed to be that we had in Europe, anyway, the danger of a Russian rather than a Western control. They also seemed to be keen on preserving old, political boundaries, though giving up economic ones, and yet unwilling to hand our Power, or military control to a supra national entity. The plea for the old political sovereignties was that we should otherwise all be communised. Once or twice too the despairing remark was made that no one with this power will be just, whoever has it in this post Christian, a-moral world, will use it for the advantage of his section and not for the advantage of the whole. So we come back to Religion. But all the first part of the discussion, the shrunken world part, they accepted; they saw the need for economic order.

Meanwhile we have to win the war, and prepare our spirits for the post-war world.

It is a strange thing that the discovery that our views were so divergent rather tightened the bonds than slackened them between us. The reason is I think that we both realise that below, under or within the outer casing of difference there is a fundamental unity of idea and purpose. I do think the level on which we differ important, because it is an out-work of the defenses, it is part of the structure; but the part about which we agree, without perhaps finding common language, is far more important. I liked the description of Fr. McNabb quoted in the *Tablet* this week. "Perhaps the reason why we give the title 'mystery' to such an obvious thing as a Birth or a Scourging is that what is obvious and visible in it is as nothing compared with what is not obvious nor visible."[1] All the pages of Tanqueray[2] are answers to people who are using the language and technique that he uses in return; it is true, but not the essence. What you call myth perhaps is the other part, the mystical side that the Latin mind tends to ignore without denying. I am sure by myth you don't really mean that the things did not happen, but that that is not half so important as what they signify.

I am trying to persuade people to let 100 Y.C. Wkrs[3] descend upon us next holidays. It is not as easy as I first hoped. The History of the Church is going well. The Vision of Constantine and its significance was well received, also the meeting of Leo and Attila. We now move on to Ireland.

I continue storming heaven for you not only to get more and more truth but also for you to get it in time to use it to the fullest and not like S. Augustine cry out too late (not in this case have I loved Thee) but seen Thee.

Yours affectionately,
Columba

1. Vincent McNabb, O.P. (1869–1943); well-known preacher, writer, and controversialist, especially at the Catholic pitch in Hyde Park.

2. Adolph Alfred Tanqueray (1854–1932); a dogmatic theologian; *Synopsis theologiae dogmaticae*, 20th ed., 3 vols. (Paris, 1925). Indigestible because of its excessive tidiness, when theology is a mystery. Arnold found it distasteful. (C.C.E.)

3. Young Christian Workers, the English version of the Abbé Cardijn's Jeunesse Ouvrière Chrétienne; cf. C.C.E.'s letter of 27 January 1937, above.

Ampleforth College
York

4 March 1942

My dear Arnold,

It seems, and is, ages since I last wrote to you; it is not for not wanting, but time is more elusive than ever. I have about 10 hours more teaching this term, which means about 20 hours more work.

You will be interested to hear that the Young Christian Workers are coming here 100 strong and more in the holidays. They will be housed in these two houses, SS. Wilfrid and Edward. They arrive on a Saturday morning and leave on Sunday and Monday. It ought to be an interesting meeting, as these youths come from all over England and will give one some idea of what the working youths are thinking—or at least saying—throughout the country. (Low Sunday week-end)

The other interesting item is that we are getting on with our co-operation schemes with Nuffield College's Reconstruction Survey. The London man and the Liverpool one have both written now to say that they will welcome help. So quite a number of boys are volunteering, or thinking of doing so, to help in the holidays. In our complex life it is just that sort of work which is truly charitable, and let us hope the experiment comes off. One wonders what a S. Gregory would have done in our circumstances. So long as things had not quite broken down he might have done precisely that. These thoughts pass through my head these days. What can I do? And the answer is every time: prayer first; though sometimes there comes a desire to join in the fray, especially when things as now seem to be going so very badly; the empire is apparently going smilingly to its death. But that is too pessimistic and the long view gives us victory, but oh! after how much toil, through failure beforehand to prepare. The toil is understandable, which comes from the ordinary clash of war, but the one that comes through laziness or incompetence drives to despair. All this above is due to Singapore.[1] I think it will prove a far greater defeat than the battle of France, because the latter was a try-out, we were learning; whereas Malaya should have been a try-out after we had learnt. However, that is not really my province; still the fact that my mind runs like that may show which way the wind is blowing.

I enclose a list of some of the names you wanted: All your friends are well and the novices still there, including Br. Gilbert, so far, but perhaps not for long.

I finished the 'Title of Christ' *Heres Universorum* a few weeks ago, and found the prophets so full that it all had to be cut and many choices made, whilst the other religions' contributions or fulfilments in Christ's teaching had to be very summary and useless enough. Now I am thinking about, and hope to jot down some thoughts on, Christ 'The Suffering Servant' 'The Man of Sorrows.' It appears to me at the moment as a subject in which '*tout est dit*,' and also one on which only those who have heroically shared in His Sorrow, can effectively speak. Nevertheless we can and should all ponder it.

Our conversations often come to my mind. Your suggestion of a pilgrimage to Rome has come to symbolise for me the time of the future peace. I can think of few things which would give me so much pleasure. Then the discussions we had stand round in my memory, the various points crystalizing. I don't think we stood the strain—if any—of difference because, as I suggested in my last letter, we were fundamentally at one on the subjects we discussed. I think we are fundamentally at variance in the realm of thought, you being at the moment a Protestant; but because we are one, yes, but in another order, that of charity and grace. All the same, I think probably you were putting your extremest views to us, which you have held, or might hold, rather than those you firmly do hold; and that faced with an agnostic you would probably appear to him a Papist!

The point that I have thought a bit on is the typical example: the Virgin Birth. I know that even if I could prove it to you so as to make you admit that one point, the principle of private judgement would still hold, yet there are two obstacles which hold you back, it seems to me, not just the one. The principle of private judgement yes; but encouraged and nourished by a disinclination to believe particular points which appear unlikely, un-divine; and suppose these supports were taken away, it further seems to me, your clinging on to private judgement would not be so desperate. Thus, this doctrine of the Virgin Birth is not merely an example of a refusal to accept authority but also a stumbling block in itself; and it might therefore be worth while clearing these particular things up. That being the case I suggest—in my ignorance—this. The doctrine of the Virgin Birth is comparable to much in the O.T. as a fact true, but as a fact not very important, its importance being in its symbolism. For the people of the period, and God was manifesting his power in a particular period, such a thing would have great significance, it is what would be expected if God were to appear—it even seemed to have been prophesied in Isaias. It even has significance for us as a symbol or sign that the Coming was not at the age of 30, but at the first instant. When we consider—I think this true—that the doctrine is deeply embedded in the earliest doctrinal stratum it does take some power away from the Adoptionist thesis. I know this is all very unscholarly; but I venture *in caritate*. I must stop.

Yours affectionately,
Columba, O.S.B.

1. On 15 February 1942, the Japanese had captured the British bastion, Singapore, by land, taking 60,000 prisoners.

The Royal Institute
of International Affairs
Foreign Research and Press Service
Balliol College, Oxford

18 March 1942

Dear Columba,

I have just written a personal letter to poor Hugh Montgomery,[1] following up a business one from our administrative officer. After looking over our position as it is at present, we have very regretfully come to the conclusion that we have really nothing suitable to offer him. He is, characteristically, very modest in the kind of thing he offers to do, but, after all, suppose we had a junior vacancy in any of his fields—and we have not even that—it would not be suitable to offer it to a man of his age and standing, who has been a professional diplomat.

I wish I could have been of some help to him, over this, at a moment when he must be sad—sad, but, I hope, not downcast, for to stay the course of the noviciate, starting in middle life, must, I think, be a most extraordinary feat, and no one need be downcast at finding that, after all, he can't rise to it.

If anything turns up, here or anywhere else that I know of, which might be suitable for Montgomery, I will let him know.

This is an opportunity to write to you: I have left your letters unanswered for the usual reason that my nose is to the grindstone. I am quite prosperous, thanks to

Ampleforth. I am still at 3 Ship St., where my landlady Mrs. Pristly treats me kindly, giving me meals at home now, which is a great relief from fatigue; and I spend most week-ends in London with Rosalind. Our work here for HMG is going well and is always increasing.

About my intellectual outlook, I am very glad that the full extent of its difference from yours has now come out, as we have thrashed things out this last time we have been together. I should have been pretty sad if I had thought that this was going to affect our friendship, but I am sure it won't.

Though we can't reconcile the ways we formulate things intellectually, there are deeper levels—ways of feeling about things, objects which are one's aim in life—at which we don't need reconciliation, because there is no disharmony. No disharmony, it is true, but great disparity in spiritual prowess between a parachutist like you and a pedestrian ground-staff man like me.

Now I must get back to work.

God Bless You.

Yours affectionately,
Arnold

1. He had just withdrawn (as Br. Gilbert) from the Ampleforth novitiate; for his career, see C.C.E.'s letter of 7 October 1941, (n. 10) above.

Ampleforth College
York

Palm Sunday (29 March) 1942

My dear Arnold,

I was so glad to get your letter and to know you had written to Br. Gilbert. He was a bit blue at going but he did amazingly well to have stayed the course so long. I did not anticipate you would have anything for him immediately, but some day—things and people change so quickly now—you might be able to help him. I see you say you will.

So you are back in Ship St. and having meals there. That should be a relief, provided you can really get away from work when you get there.

We have had two very interesting visits recently. The first was from Barbara Ward,[1] whom I had not met before. She gave a very good lecture to the boys on the Church and the modern Crisis. Her point was that we should mix in and influence our surroundings not only as Catholics, but as citizens with a very clear idea of the Natural Law, a ground which we share with most other Englishmen and women. We saw a lot of her, and her social ideas were very stimulating and I found myself agreeing with almost all she said. I think perhaps I would not go quite so far in the direction of State control, it always seems to be so deadening, legalistic, unimaginative.

The other person was Professor J. H. Jones[2] of Leeds who is the local "Local Investigator" for the Nuffield Survey[3] that we are hoping to help with. Personally I am torn between two convictions. One is that the whole immense social structure will fall about our ears, and so why worry! The first half of the above statement is deep inside me; the second half is superficial and wicked anyway. The second is that so long as the old punt floats, with all its leaky rivets loose, we must help to bail out the water. This picture comes to me a lot; we had a corrugated iron-bottomed punt at Foss lake here when I was at school, and I can remember so well the bailing out process. We had to, we were in the boat. So we must for all we are worth help the salvage and then even hope to recondition the old thing later.

I liked Prof. Jones very much indeed. A quiet, sincere and very clear-headed person, and practical in his suggestions. We are going to do a try-out in "Statutory Social Services." What an unspectacular way of giving one's neighbour a cup of water; but perhaps Our Lord will see it as a very good way when the time comes.

Perhaps you do not have time to read the *Times*. Did you see those astonishing articles of the week before last on Monetary[4] reform and International Trade. It seems to me that if the *Times* dare be so revolutionary there is hope. Those articles also made me realise that perhaps the "cranks" of my generation are to be the prophets of the next. I was always afraid that those theories were really "cranky" though they looked so obviously right. A book that has confirmed me in the acceptance of that revolutionary idea is "*Wall St. under Oath*," by Counsel for the Senate Commission on Banks etc. set up after Wall St.'s crash (1933?), a certain Mr. Pecora;[5] you perhaps have read it; if not, do look at it. It would be light relief as well as a revelation of the ways of big business.

I must close down, not only my letter, but my mind, for the time being, on the mundane things and get deep into Holy Week; and I wish you all the graces you need from the Passion and Resurrection of Christ. The Cardinal was right, we should close down our clamour for a span and recognise that the ultimate victory comes from God and from a change of heart.

Really I am beginning to be very sorry for Churchill. The noise of suggestion, counter suggestion, of criticism and counter criticism, instead of dying down, is growing. Is this the *reductio ad absurdum* of Democracy, that there is so much initiative, so much self expression, so much freedom of speech, that nothing gets done, no cooperation. I am beginning to see how the saying is true: the best is the enemy of the good. Anyhow this little station is closing down on that line of talk.

Sir Stafford Cripps[6] seems a good man. I am beginning to have great hopes in him.

Well, I must stop. We will be united in thought and prayers and longings for God's will in our world, during this next week.

Yours affectionately,
Columba, O.S.B.

P.S. The Chatham Hse *Russia* pamphlet[7] I like *very* much. It under-does, as the *Tablet* says, the difference between Marxism and its present system. But anyone can see the difference.

A dios!

1. Cf. C.C.E.'s letter of 5 February 1940, above.

2. John Henry Jones (1881–1973); professor of economics and political science and head of the Economics Department, University of Leeds (1919–46).

3. Nuffield College was the center from which was prepared the *Beveridge Report*, which became a blueprint for British postwar social welfare.

4. The leading article "World Trade after the War" appeared in *The Times* (24 March 1942); cf. *The Times* (25 March 1942).

5. Ferdinand Pecora (1882–1971); counsel to the U.S. Senate Committee on Banking and Currency (1933–34), which made investigations that led to the creation of the Securities and Exchange Commission.

6. Sir Richard Stafford Cripps (1889–1952); intellectual leader of the British Labour Party; emissary to India during the war to attempt (unsuccessfully) to secure the cooperation of the Nationalist leaders; ambassador to Moscow (1940–42); chancellor of the Exchequer (1947–50); a fellow Wickhamist, A.J.T. praises him in his letter of 16 November 1947, below.

7. Kathleen Gibberd, *Soviet Russia, an Introduction* (1942; rev. ed., London, 1946).

35, Ashley Court
Morpeth Terrace
S.W.1

Easter Day, 5 April 1942

Dear Columba,

I was pleased to get your Palm Sunday letter (I was fortunate enough to be born on Palm Sunday—'89—an auspicious day to be given). Here is my chance of answering while I am still on my Easter holiday: I have been thinking of you during the week.

It is an excellent idea for the School to take a hand in the Nuffield survey: it is a practical, non-controversial way of getting a glimpse of the world and of doing something to help it. The scientific approach is neutral ground, of a convenient kind, as far as it goes (it doesn't, of course, go all the way, but is apt to collapse under one's feet when one gets to the really interesting and important stage of the journey).

We are cooperating a good deal ourselves, at the F.R.P.S.[1] with Nuffield, in the borderland country between international and home affairs.

Barbara Ward, I imagine, cooperates with Caesar with a good deal of zest. I am not so enthusiastic myself, for the reason you give, that *étatisme* is so sub-human and so uncreative (it is the genuine "dead hand"). But though I don't love Caesar, I think he has a big job to do, in the next chapter of history, in cleaning up the mess and in making sure that applied science is going to be a cornucopia and not a *flammenwerfer*. I think Caesar will succeed, within his own limitations, and will make the world materially peaceful and prosperous. Hundreds of millions of Chinese, Indians, Russians, etc. will be raised to the present standard of living of trades union labour in the United States. That is right and necessary, and those remarkable articles in the *Times* will help it on its way. But we must hope that, when they have all got their material standard of living, they won't be long in finding that it is dust and ashes.

I have your Far Eastern Christendom ms. here with me, but am being extremely lazy about turning my mind to anything.

Rosalind sends her love,

Yours affectionately,
Arnold

1. Foreign Research and Press Service, Royal Institute of International Affairs, of which A.J.T. was director (1939–43).

Ampleforth College
York

21 April 1942

My dear Arnold,

Many thanks for the MS. and for, I am sure, far too kind a criticism of it; but you did promise to be truthful about it, so it cannot be so bad. My real aim in writing this little history is I suppose to inspire others with a zeal for the Conversion of China, and so the 'romance' or 'epic' quality (small e) you find in my MS. is in place and one day may do some good. Your approval has urged me to persist, and the next section I am going to tackle will be the Nestorian twilight, as here again the documents are limited and manageable; and meanwhile I can collect books on the Jesuit period. And whilst I do all this, the most glorious period of the Chinese mission, or should we now call it Church, seems to have begun, if the stray news one hears is true. *Deo gratias*.

The Young Christian Workers' week-end spent here went very well and profitably to all parties, not least to us. There is something refreshingly downright and simple and strong about the faith of those young men which was an inspiration to me. The question is, can these save the situation in time. There is a race going on, corruption on the one hand and resurrection on the other. One only has to talk with those boys—from all over England and from all kinds of industrial work—to realise that now not only Truth has gone but also Morals; that for all our education the masses do not think, or perhaps mostly they have no tools with which to judge matters morally. On the other hand these Y.C.W. are not only keen but they have the knowledge. They knew what they were about. S. Joseph—your patron saint—a worker will surely get graces for them—and for you—to-morrow, his feast day.

Everyone is very well here except Fr. Wilfrid[1] who jumped over the brook, or tried to, and sprained his ankle. The novices are still with us and I have been lucky enough to see a lot of them as Fr. David[2] has been away and I helped to look after them. Your friend Br. Mungo[3] is still as lively as ever. We went for one long ramble: Helmsley: then due north up a dale, where we lunched, then left up on to Moorland and down into Rievaulx where three bathed, then over the moors and down into Byland where we had tea and across the valley avoiding the road, home.[4] It was a lovely day and I wished you had been with us. You are still one up in letters, so you will get another fairly soon.

Yours affectionately,
Columba, O.S.B.

P.S. I am so glad you wrote to Hugh Montgomery as he took a great liking to you, and if you put in your letter to him what you put in yours to me it would have consoled him a lot.

He has I believe already started at the Beda (Upholland?) to train for the secular priesthood.

1. Ian Wilfrid Mackenzie, O.S.B. (1911–); an Ampleforth monk; now on parish duty in Preston.

2. David Ogilvie-Forbes, O.S.B. (1904–1985); for some years novice master at Ampleforth, including the year when Cardinal Basil Hume was a novice (1941–42); he then went to one of Ampleforth's parishes where he took up the Y.C.W. movement, the English version of Abbé Cardijn's *Jeunesse Ouvrière Chrétienne*; cf. C.C.E.'s letter of 27 January 1937, above.

3. Robert Kentigern ("Mungo") Devlin, O.S.B. (1922–82); monk of Ampleforth; had recently read history at Oxford; in later years on parish in Warrington. Saint Kentigern was also known as "Mungo."

4. Compare C.C.E.'s letter of 22 April 1940, above.

Ampleforth College
York

13 May 1942
Eve of the Ascension

My dear Arnold,

It seems ages since I last wrote, and it is a long time, I am sorry.

Since I last wrote I have been in London and wondered whether you were there at the same time—the last week of April. The reason was to help my father and mother in a heartbreaking business of selling up all the furniture in the house. It was my first experience of auctions and Jews on the business side. The place seemed infested with them; and though one knew they were children of God, they looked unpleasant and the circumstances were not likely to make them seem friendly. I begin to see why people have an unreasoning dislike for them; they tend to come in at the death. Anyhow the sale, if not good, realised some money. The incident is the culmination of a purifying of my father and mother, who together have gone through one great sacrifice after another. They were wonderful; God be praised.

I spent two of the nights I was there with one of Fr. Gabriel's cousins,[1] a complete business man was what I had always thought him; but I found to my amazement—even though I did know a little before going—that here was a business man turned saint or almost. His wife had come back into the Church before she died through the intercession of Soeur Thérèse[2] and now her husband (after business, i.e. 5 PM onwards) wherever he is spreads devotion to the Little Flower either by persuading priests to encourage the devotion or by going to the hospitals and houses of the poor, particularly those with cancer and showing them how to love suffering. It was a great blessing for me to have come in such close contact with him. All his business efficiency and push were now transformed into spiritual equivalents. Case of etherealization![3]

While both novice masters were away I was asked to look after them for a week, and I had an opportunity of finding out how they were. All were in excellent spirits, especially your friend Br. Mungo. I believe Montgomery has gone to the Beda.[4]

Everyone delighted with Rosalind's first instalment of her new book,[5] I one of them. One always feels like saying: how true! I must keep that fact to the fore, yet one goes on forgetting. I am so glad you are keeping well and that your work is so much sought after.

Yours affectionately,
Columba, O.S.B.

1. Gabriel Gilbey, O.S.B. (1914–77); Ampleforth monk; became the ninth Baron Vaux of Harrowden.

2. Sainte Thérèse of Lisieux (1873–97); known as "the Little Flower," the saint of renunciation in little matters. "Je vais faire tomber un torrent de roses." A.J.T.'s devotion appears in his letter of 5 October 1947, below.

3. Compare "Etherialization," in *A Study of History*, III: 174–92.

4. The Beda, the English seminary in Rome for late vocations, was transferred temporarily to England.

5. *Time and the Timeless* (London, 1942).

3 Ship St.
Oxford

19 May 1942

Dear Columba,

I was very glad to get your letter, with Saint Ignatius's prayer.[1] Rosalind gave me this a long time ago: I shall now again start saying it daily. It is one of those rare forms of words that are the perfect expression of what they set out to say—and what this prayer expresses is one of the deep truths that one ought to confess to continually.

I am sorry about your parents' house: seeing furniture being sold, when one has been familiar with it for years, is bound to give one a terrible twinge, though it is no doubt purifying, as you say, because it cuts one of the bonds that bind us to this world. I was much interested in your story of Father Gabriel's cousin.

It is now Rosalind's turn to be laid up: she is in the same nursing home in Highgate as I was, and it is the same complaint, namely simple tiredness. She has been there a fortnight and is staying, I am glad to say, over the next week-end! Writing books and working in the East End, on top of doing one's own cooking and living through the Blitz, has been—not surprisingly—too much for her. I hope she will now take things a bit easier.

I am so glad you liked the first instalment of the new book: it is worth while being laid up if one's work is of some use to other people.

I have no particular news of myself, except that I am still busy and still prosperous.

Yours affectionately,
Arnold J. Toynbee

1. "Suscipe, Domine, universam meam libertatem . . ."; see *A Study of History*, VII: 518.

Ampleforth College
York

16 June 1942

My dear Arnold,

It is just ages since I last wrote, reasons various. The thing that gets me down is lots of necessary but tedious letters, and there have been lots. Your present life must be full of them. They leave one too exhausted for anything else.

Many thanks for your last letter. I knew you would like that prayer; but how extraordinary that you had picked on it specially before. I say it every day after Mass. It is one of those prayers I hope to mean more and more, rather than already fully manage. Or better, we mean the words but fail to live up to them in practice.

I am so sorry Rosalind has had a break-down. It is not surprising; and if she has been well looked after—as you were in that Convent, given real rest, I hope by now she is right as rain. I suppose there is no chance of your both coming up here in July for a few days rest.

We live here in almost unbelievable remoteness from the war and its horrors. The peaceful exterior is shattered by still very occasional "red warnings" at night. Shattered is too strong a word. But it almost answers the need to describe one's feelings, at the news of some old boy being killed. The human make-up refuses to be rational and faithful and groans at such news even though one can be morally certain these boys have gone to heaven, and even though we know God wants them there, not here.

I came across a wonderful phrase in a letter of St. John of the Cross[1] the other day. He was writing to someone who did not like to see him so ill-used by his brethren. The end of the letter runs "Where love is not, put love, and you will draw out love" "A donde no hay amor, ponga amor, y sacará amor". It seems to me a principle which covers everything, particularly one's relations with people and also of course circumstances no matter how unpleasant; for these ultimately derive their reason from the loving hand of God.

Two boys of S. Wilfrid's, for whom I had real affection are lost, one for certain, the other, I am afraid, probably. Both were in the R.A.F. Please say a prayer at Mass particularly for their parents.

We had our Goremire day[2] as usual. Machine-gun firing was stopped for the day in the locality. On the feast of Corpus Christi I biked with a group of boys to Fountains.[3] It is now almost as lonely and remote as it must have been when the monks first went there from S. Mary's York. The buildings beat Rievaulx[4] but not the atmosphere. There is something exquisite about the latter.

There were even some stray parents here at the Prize day functions. Fr. James[5] and Fr. Robert[6] produced Twelfth Night. The stage effects were as usual particularly pleasing. One of the electricians however caused an unexpected diversion by falling down from the switchboard platform. He was not hurt.

The boys who did some surveying for Nuffield College, were very kindly received by Mr. Mitchison[7] and they apparently did some useful work for him, and he was pleased. They, the boys, certainly learnt a lot from the experience, not least the conditions in which the poor live.

I have read recently a book by Dorothy Day[8]—have I told you already?—called *House of Hospitality*. If one can judge of a person by the written word I should say she was a saint. There is the real thing: complete trust in God, complete love of her neighbour, the intellect fully at work, but completely subordinated to Charity. It made one feel a worm and made one praise God, that yet another clear manifestation of his grace had been given us. If Canon Cardijn[9] and his jocistes are the equivalents of the Jesuits for our world, then Dorothy Day and her group are the Franciscans.

Gandhi is a fascinating person. I am beginning to disentangle my mind on his attitude. His is a solution which ignores one side of the problem.[10] One is very tempted to agree with him, that to stoop to violence is to be smeared with the same grime as one's opponents; on the other hand to refuse—when others are concerned—is to shut one's eyes to that half of the problem which is: how to preserve the rights of one's community to live, and freely? One should fight and at the same time know—and act upon it—that fighting alone will not get the result. The difficulty remains that it is almost humanly impossible to fight and at the same time preserve the balance of one's mind.

On the other hand, this war may go on so long that all rancour and hatred will be worn out; but so too may be the desire for justice and even more important: desire for Love. The world is bound to the wheels of the monstrous monster states and crushed as they move to the fight. The Germans must know now that they can't win. Why do they go on? Because they cannot expect any justice if they stop now. Are they right? No one knows, because no one knows what we would do, were the Germans to lay down their arms to-morrow. So it will go on. This is a bit lugubrious. I had better stop.

I have written one or two more Titles of Christ. One the Faithful Witness. The point that struck me was that the Buddhists discovered grace, the need for it, and individually achieved it; but that a faithful—absolutely reliable witness, was lacking to them. Christ, being heaven-sent, is that faithful witness, who does not merely preach: "come and try and see for yourself, the proof is in the having"—which is good and conclusive enough to those who do, perhaps—but "I guarantee by my credentials that this cannot be wishful thinking." All very amateurish this must seem to you.

My only other literary excursion was a sermon I preached at the Junior House. It was on S. Peter and the Unity of the Church; and I imagined us both—leaving you out of the wording!—at the tomb of the Apostle and thinking on all those great saints who had knelt there before us. S. Augustine, S. Leo, S. Benedict, S. Wilfrid, S. Ignatius, and what they had asked. Please God one day we really will be there together, and get what they asked for, in our measure.

Boys have just come in—cricket. I must stop.

Fr. Stephen is very well:[11] Fr. Paul[12] *un peu souffrant*—his unfortunate sinus. All the Rodeneggs' clothes have been sent to their father. I heard from Oswald[13] some weeks back. He seems now really happy again. I hope it lasts and that the Japs do not harry them that side of the world.

Fr. Alban[14] is full of gardening work, all kinds of succulent vegetables are coming up in his allotment. Fr. Bruno[15] digs in S. Wilfrid's plot occasionally. He is happy as can be teaching the juniors S. John's Gospel. Fr. Aelred[16] I scarcely ever see to speak to these days. Fr. Barnabas[17] is very busy too. I saw a large load of books returning from the binders. The novices are all there, brother Ian[18] quite settled. No novices for the coming years.

You will never read all this. Pray for me at Mass, the centre of Our life.

Yours affectionately,
Columba, O.S.B.

1. San Juan de la Cruz (1542–91); the great Spanish mystic; founder of the Discalced Carmelites; *Vida y Obras completas*, ed. Crisogono de Jesus (Madrid: B.A.C., 1973), p. 382, carta 27.

2. Compare C.C.E.'s letter of 22 April 1940, above.

3. Ibid.

4. Ibid.

5. Father James Forbes; cf. C.C.E.'s letter of 18 February 1941, above.

6. Father Robert Coverdale (1912–84); many years bursar-procurator at Ampleforth.

7. Compare C.C.E.'s letter of 29 March 1942, above; five Ampleforth students prepared a study of Boys' Clubs in London under the category of "voluntary social services: youth organizations."

8. Dorothy Day (1897–1980); pacifist; worker among the poor in New York; *House of Hospitality* (New York, 1939).

9. Abbé Joseph Cardijn; cf. C.C.E.'s letter of 27 January 1937, above.

10. Mohandas K. Gandhi (1869–1948); in 1942 Gandhi had demanded immediate independence for India, had been arrested, and was later released.

11. Stephen Marwood, O.S.B. (1890–1949); house master of St. Oswalds.

12. Paul Nevill, O.S.B. (1882–1952); then head master of Ampleforth.

13. Oswald and Christoph Rodenegg; cf. C.C.E.'s letter of 12 May 1940, above; H.M.G. had sent these internees to Australia.

14. Alban Rimmer, O.S.B. (1911–84); onetime editor of the *Ampleforth Journal*.

15. Bruno Donovan, O.S.B.; cf. C.C.E.'s letter of 8 April 1941, above.

16. Aelred Graham, O.S.B.; cf. C.C.E.'s letter of 19 January 1940, above.

17. John Barnabas Sandeman, O.S.B. (1910–80); professor of moral theology to the young monks and teacher of classics in the school; also monastery librarian.

18. Russell Ian Petit, O.S.B. (1922–); Ampleforth monk; at St. Louis Priory (1956–71); now on parish duty at Bamber Bridge, Preston.

Ampleforth College
3 July 1942 York

My dear Arnold,

Your life must be at fever heat at this present crisis[1] and I thought I would just send you a line to show I have not forgotten you.

My last letter must have read very oddly when you got it. How far we seem now from assured and inevitable victory! All the same—and knowing extremely little about it—I think this reverse is only a reverse and not a collapse. It is a new element in war, that one, perhaps a very little, mishap should upset the balance over the whole Near East. I mean our 200 tanks falling into a trap. The disparity of arms before and after a defeat in the old days would not have made all that difference would it? One always had time far away at the base to create new armies. But now the speed gives no respite. All the same, this business is terrible, and all one's friends and relations out there must be going through terrible days. '*Dios sobre todo*' as the lay brother at Silos[2] in Spain used to say to me during the Spanish troubles.

All my sympathy goes out to Churchill and the generals and very little to their critics. The unpredictable will happen. Do you remember your own remarks on the subject! (*Study*, Vol. I, p. 301), "the outcome of an encounter cannot be predicted and has no appearance of being predetermined, but arises, in the likeness of a new creation, out of the encounter itself." I may be misusing your idea; but this campaign does seem to fit it. No one seems to blame. Or do you think I am wrong! Obviously there are times when the whole management may have been wrong, but this time does not seem one of them. It beats me why always people take it for granted that a battle was lost owing to the failure of the general or government. A stray bullet might have hit the one advance scout who could have spotted the ambush. This just to let off steam and show you which way my sympathies lay before Churchill's speech, and more since. Meanwhile the Germans may have reached Alexandria, and you realise all the implications so much more fully than I, Turkey, West Africa, Iraq and so on. Still, the Germans are not there yet and only in Egypt.

Lots of old boys come up for two or three nights, either just on leave or just joining up, one or two from Oxford and Cambridge. You remember G. V. Ryan[3] who went to New College, he is here at the moment, and Lamb[4] arrives next week, while the fire-eating Foll[5] came last week-end from his training "ship" King Alfred. They *all* are amazingly cheerful and keen and Catholic as well. It is a real consolation to be served at Mass by these young men.

If you want ½ hour's relaxation—besides wading through this—read Fr. Louis d'Andria's[6] fantastic article in the current number of the Ampleforth Journal on 'The Serious Side of Chess'.

Field Marshall Lord Birdwood[7] is inspecting the corps tomorrow, and this evening there has been a 'wartime' guest room dinner at which the cadet officers are present. He is going to talk for an hour to the contingent after the inspection.

Lawrence has been distinguishing himself. Do congratulate him from me. I hope Rosalind is quite well again. My kindest regards to them both.

I see your Burge[8] lecture is again quoted in this week's *Tablet*. It is a *great* pity it, the lecture, is out of print. Is there any chance of its being reprinted?

My prayers are always with you and my thoughts.

Yours affectionately,
Columba, O.S.B.

1. On 21 June 1942, Rommel again had captured Tobruk in the new German drive which was only checked at El Alamein, within seventy miles of Alexandria.

2. Santo Domingo de Silos, Benedictine Monastery in the mountains of Old Castille; cf. C.C.E.'s letter of 3 November 1939, above.

3. Gerald Valentine Ryan; cf. C.C.E.'s letter of 18 February 1941, above.

4. Osmer Ogilvie Lamb; cf. C.C.E.'s letter of 10 March 1941, above.

5. Cecil Foll (1923–); survived the war and sent two sons to Ampleforth. All these were members of St. Wilfrid's House and known to A.J.T. from Voyageur meetings.

6. Louis d'Andria, O.S.B. (1880–1945); monk of Ampleforth; learned historian, respected by A.J.T.

7. Lord Birdwood (1865–1951); Field Marshal William Riddell, who commanded the Australian and New Zealand Army Corps (ANZAK) in the First World War.

8. Compare C.C.E.'s letter of 16 June 1940, above.

35 Ashley Court
Morpeth Terrace
S.W.1

12 July 1942

Dear Columba,

I have a long letter and a short one of yours in my drawer, unanswered, but I won't try to answer either of them properly now, as I am hoping to come to the monastery—I believe Father James is arranging this—from the 25th July to 2nd August (Rosalind will be staying in the village). We are going up this next Saturday the 18th to the Gate House, Castle Howard. We are both quite ready for a holiday, in spite of both having had rest cures since this time last year.

Bun[1] went to Pirbright[2] yesterday—along with some other Ampleforth boys, I am glad to say, as it is less formidable when you start in company with your friends. I think the Army will be a much better education for him than Oxford; and, as the good life is more important than the long life on earth, this reconciles me to what is the first step towards his hazarding his life like all the other millions of young men. I hope he will both be educated and be given a long enough life in this world to do some of God's work in it.

Yours affectionately,
Arnold

1. Family name for Lawrence.

2. Pirbright, the Guards' Armoured Training Wing.

Hotel Hermitage
Nashville, Tenn.

24 September 1942

Dear Columba,

Your letter was waiting for me when I arrived at St. Louis the night before last; along with letters from Rosalind and Lawrence: all very welcome.

After spending a clammy and strenuous fortnight trotting round "official circles" in Washington, I took to the air, starting by getting myself catapulted in one day from New York to Houston, Texas. I go via Denver and Salt Lake City, to the Coast before returning to New York.[1]

I like the Americans and am thoroughly enjoying myself—not at all disdaining to enjoy the flesh pots, among other things. But how terrifying and puzzling it is. The Americans, by the exercise of the Puritan virtues, have conjured into existence a middle-class terrestrial paradise. Food, hotels, pullmans, airliners, air-conditioning, and so on; it is all perfect after its kind, and good; and yet, though good in itself, it puts up a veil between men and God. At present, this paradise is unshattered, and I find it hard to conceive what will happen when it is suddenly broken in upon by the ordinary sorrows of life; e.g. all the mothers and wives, who are going to lose their sons and husbands—something against which neither plumbing nor air-conditioning is any earthly good. I believe they will rise to it, for they are a great nation, and there is a kind of innocence about their sybaritism; it isn't as vicious as its feebler counterpart in Europe. But I get, again, the sensation of two incompatible walls towering along side by side for the moment—but only for the moment; they can't both of them last.

Your bicycle journey[2] was a more daring affair than my round-trip by air. I am glad it was such a success.

Yours affectionately,
Arnold

(Will you tell Father Abbot that, so far, I haven't been able to pay my respects to Saint Anselm's Priory,[3] Washington. Everything is on a vast scale. I asked the Dean of the Catholic University at Washington about it but to him it was just one of 20 or 30 religious houses).

1. A.J.T. had flown to the United States on the *Clipper*, arriving on 24 August 1942, for a two-month stay, at the invitation of the Rockefeller Foundation and the Council on Foreign Relations.

2. Ampleforth to London in two days; it was wartime, and therefore no traffic.

3. A Benedictine foundation made by Fort Augustus Abbey in 1924; in 1949 the priory was granted independent status, and in 1961 it was raised by John XXIII to the rank of Abbey.

Ampleforth College
York

27 September 1942

Dear Arnold,

I wonder whether you have got back yet. The six weeks you promised yourself in the U.S.A. must be up by this time, so I am writing. Did you influence Lord Halifax[1] to make that fine speech or encourage Mr. Myron Taylor[2] on his way to Rome? Whether you did or not those were two encouraging signs after a rather bleak period with the T.U.C.[3] laughing a Catholic speaker to scorn when he suggested that Catholics should be allowed to keep their own school. It is all part of the topsy-turvidom of our world. Which side is going to win? The Christian or the pagan. We know the ultimate answer but I, for one, have doubts about the immediate future. But I repeat that Lord Halifax's speech was grand. Yet we are very "Protestant" in our politics: you cannot guarantee that what one spokesman says is what the others hold by.

The great thing is that we must not be cowed to silence because of the noisiness of the Left. In this connection, have you ever thought of publishing together some of your lectures and broadcasts connected with the return to religion, for instance that Christmas broadcast of some years ago and the Burge Lecture (now out of print). Wouldn't they make ideal material for the series in which *Time and the Timeless* appeared. In fact I should like to see that lovely part of the *Study* on Charity[4] taken bodily out and printed separately. But perhaps now my suggestions are getting wild.

Meanwhile Ampleforth is living its life in peace—owing to the heroism of the young everywhere. The school is bigger by 25 than last year; our staff adequate. All your many friends are well. Fr. Bruno is promising to come and dig in S. Wilfrid's garden; Fr. Aelred[5] is awaiting the publication of some *Meditations for Wartime*; the novices were all simply professed with solemnity the day after the boys returned. The Prior officiated, as the Abbot is in Ireland.

Fr. James is busier than ever and Fr. Paul rather fit; Fr. Stephen snowed under with fitting everyone out with his time-table. So that now the engine is under way and steaming out of the station for its 1942–1943 journey.

I was at Leyland for ten days helping in our parish there. It is I imagine a typical wartime war-working town. Everything seemed to be going like clock work; hundreds and hundreds of people carried every morning and night to and from the great Chorley armament factory. The war was taken for granted and a new routine set in which seemed to suit everyone. But this is a superficial opinion really, as I did not get sufficiently in touch with the people. An odd conversation or two is not much to go on.

What a beautiful book Rosalind's is.[6] It fits our discussions at more than one point. The one that struck me forcibly was that the liturgy is not exactly old fashioned but timeless. We have both been a bit too ready to scrap it—or perhaps only I have. Another point was something with which I agree almost violently: that Truth is eternal and changeless, that therefore historical truth is so likewise. A thing either happened or did not. Either Christ was God or not, did or did not found a church, make definite dogmatic statements or did not. Therefore that to be certain about the FACT is the only thing to bother about; whether it was likely or not, not really being the problem. Having said this, I feel I may be just beating the air; that is, you don't really hold the opposite, and to imply you do is to malign you. Yet I think there is some truth in saying that part of our problem—debate—is connected with an *a priori* approach on your side to a matter of historical fact.

I do hope Lawrence is getting on. All my best wishes to you all and prayers *in quantum possum*.

Yours affectionately,
Columba

1. Edward Frederick Lindley Wood, Viscount Halifax (1881–1959); Viceroy of India; Foreign Minister; Ambassador to Washington (1941–46); on 20 September, on his return to London, he had broadcast to the American people: "We know that, stripped of accidents which have brought this or that nation into war, the real issue for us is whether Christianity and all that it means is to survive" (*The Times* [21 September 1942]).

2. Myron C. Taylor (1874–1959); chairman, United States Steel Corp. (1932–38); personal representative of Presidents Roosevelt and Truman at the Vatican (1939–50).

3. The Trades Union Council.

4. *A Study of History*, VI: 164–68.

5. Aelred Graham, O.S.B.

6. *Time and the Timeless*.

Ampleforth College
York

23 October 1942

My dear Arnold,

I like to think that your influence has been behind all this public profession by statesmen of their belief in God and Our Lord, in the traditional truths. Perhaps I exaggerate your direct influence, but not I think the permeating one. I had a good example of that the other day when visiting a boy in the Purey Cust Home in York. He was recovering from appendicitis and reading the 1st three Vols. of *A Study of History*, volumes he had bought for himself. Nothing gives me more joy either than reading two passages from Vol 6. to my Religious Instruction set, the ones beginning *11. Transfiguration* p. 149 and p. 276 "Who is this god. . . ."

Perhaps we will perform the unbelievable feat of returning to our origins after all; and if we put the pieces of broken china together, God will so weld them, merge them, that it will all not be a cracked thing but one whole, a perfect thing without blemish, spot, wrinkle. Even at this state there is nothing inevitable in history. It is at such instants as these that I personally appreciate the free will of men. We have to make decisions, the roads are clearly marked—dangerous but right, easy but wrong. We cannot foretell the results of choosing which we do.

I wonder what you think about all this talk of punishing those responsible? Personally I think it better to punish individuals who may have been responsible than a whole nation and its descendants for something at any rate the latter could not be responsible for at all. Peace treaties usually punish the future and so always give the losers a just grievance.

John Somers Cocks[1] (now in the Foreign Office and just returned from Finland) was here a week ago. He put the Russian outlook rather starkly. He said they still regarded war in the old fashioned sense: I win and take the prize; you lose and that is the end. He is not optimistic about justice in East Europe. I hope you meet him sometime; he was here at school in my time.

Mr. Churchill I notice is still adverse to promoting post war plans. It surprises me that he cannot give more weight to other peoples' efforts, not by doing anything in that line himself, but simply by giving them the prestige of his approval. General Smuts, one supposes, would be a very good person to busy himself with that kind of thing if he were keen.

ALL the plans, the very best, are going to be worthless without men living by Christian justice and *love*; and although plans are very important, the latter are more so. I feel more and more moved to concentrate on the latter, so many are caring about the former. If we could only get a few—among them ourselves—really loving God; he will save our City. *Nisi Dominus*. . . . So, my prayers join with yours, so that your plans may be God's plan.

Yours affectionately,
Columba, O.S.B.

1. John Sebastian Somers Cocks (1907–64); Amplefordian; Balliol College, Oxford; Foreign Office (1941–43); Tehran Embassy (1943–47); H. M. consul-general, Naples (1959–64).

Ampleforth College
York

6 November 1942

My dear Arnold,

On Wednesday your letter airmailed from Nashville, arrived. Very many thanks. I can imagine your pleasure and interest in doing the extreme distances in the U.S.A. in a day, a kind of experimental verification of what you told the boys here: that the world had shrunk.

The American scene must be a fascinating and mystifying one. What will happen to it all? You did not quite say, but implied a thing that 'beats me,' the very people who are Christian or Catholic even are building the earthly paradise. I suppose the early medieval church was *en passant* building an earthly paradise in the eyes of some celtic backwoodsmen. In Europe the paradise was (is) being built by *ci-devant* Christians and with no other aim; in America it is being built by the still Christian. Their aims are unrelated, God on Sunday, earth all the rest of the week. You can have seen how far they were really worshipping Mammon, and whether, when the crisis comes, they will see their errors. One day you must tell me the probable answer they will make. You say you believe they will rise to it. Is that wanting them to, or really having grounds for hope?

As compensation for not having you to talk with, I read the *Study*. It acts like a ferment in the mind. The "*Tanqueray*"[1] approach to apologetics made no appeal to you—and perhaps it makes none to anybody—it is the bare bones. This has been on my mind. It is not the only one, as perhaps I admitted. The early Christians had the fulfilling of prophecy; then Pascal had the corresponding of the doctrine to the facts of human nature "*la grandeur et la misère de l'homme*."[2] *The Study* opens up yet another way, the correspondence between our nature which is to Love and the Christian message, which is Love. "*Deus caritas est*," the Holy Eucharist—the Love Feast—; the Crucifix 'greater love than this no man hath'; the saints, witnesses of divine love in the world; Creation an act of love '*maxime liberalis*'.[3] And so on. All the rest is true, but on a lower level, necessary foundation, but only means to the building of the City, which is a city wholly of Love.

This must do for the moment. I am 39 today, that is I begin to be 40, and hope God will give me grace to make better use of this decade than of the last.

Love,
Columba, O.S.B.

1. Compare C.C.E.'s letter of 9 February 1942, above.

2. Compare Pascal's *Pensées*; in Lafuma, ed., *Oeuvres Complètes*, "Misère," sec. III, nos. 53–75 (Brunschvicg nos. 429 and various), pp. 506–09; and "Grandeur," sec. VI, nos. 105–118 (B. nos. 342 and various), pp. 512–13.

3. A phrase in the *Summa Theologiae* of Saint Thomas Aquinas to explain why God created the universe: "Ipse solus est maxime liberalis" (He is generous to the limit) I, 44.4.

Ampleforth College
York

22 November 1942

My dear Arnold,

I want very much to write to you, but feel it will be such a poor thing, after such strenuous days—beating the clock—I scarcely dare. You must be very irritated by my inept remarks at times. The reason is I have not time to think.

I shall be in Rothiemay[1] for Christmas. My consolation is that Christ taught us not to want our own will, but what he sends. In any case one carries within the true and permanent happiness. I know we shall be united during this season as ever before, please God more. So, as each year Christ's coming is commemorated, it is not a man becoming a God, but God becoming man, which was inconceivable to the Greeks and blasphemy to the Jews. But it did make the pagan dream come true: our becoming like God, having through Our Lord a communion with God-man. The strength of the saints is Christ REALLY living in them, working through them not by example but by action. Here I am preaching at you, and you know this as well as I. I want you to believe it. Blessed are those who have not seen, yet believe.

There is an interesting article in the *Times* which I cut out because it fitted in with my previous letters. Perhaps you have read it. I find it very interesting, because expressing very well what is just wrong, so it seems to me. First of all, Our Lord was really referring S. John to a prophecy (Isaias) and his fulfillment of it. Then don't you agree that his order is wrong? One begins by seeing the fruit: that it is good—the saints; and then goes into the credentials. But, ultimately after all our searchings it is humility and God's loving hand that draw us over the threshold.

Mr. Eden is optimistic if he thinks he is going to dispel our fear of Russia by blustering.[2] I am afraid that the peace will be ruined by the fundamental dishonesty of the Russians. The thing is logical. Enlightened self-interest does not work. We must give all our energies to holding the City of God, spreading its light.

All graces you need for Christmas is my prayer, God's cause upheld throughout the coming year also.

Yours affectionately,
Columba

1. Rothiemay, the home of Colonel Forbes, father of Ian George Forbes, O.S.B. (1902–), Ampleforth monk, who served as Chaplain to the first, sixth, and seventh Brigades of Guards in North Africa and Italy; awarded the M.B.E. (Member of the Order of the British Empire) and M.C. (Military Cross); Rothiemay was in the remotest Highlands of Scotland, a castle by the river Deveron; a Catholic house with a private chapel that served the scattered Catholics of the neighborhood.

2. Anthony Eden had sent a message to the Soviet Union on its twenty-fifth anniversary; he referred to "the spirit of the Anglo-Soviet Treaty of last May, which ensures that our two nations, both during the war and for the next 20 years, will march together for the benefit of human progress and liberty" (*The Times* [7 November 1942]).

Ampleforth College
York

2 December 1942

My dear Arnold,

Even though this will be worse written than even the last few, I must send you a line, while a few minutes to spare remain.

Mundane things. I remember when staying at Mells[1] during the Battle of Britain being told by a French lady in the house—acting governess—that Darlan had said then to a mutual friend that whatever he did or said, he must trust him; and that he, Darlan, would snatch the chestnuts out of the fire at the end; that he, Darlan, would appear the arch-enemy, but that it was all a subterfuge. I believed the story for a year, then gave up, and now it seems true. Even so, it is a curious technique.[2]

The *Times* has been extremely informing of late on the American scene, but the conclusions to be drawn are depressing. It would seem that the USA is not prepared to come into the outside world and help except in philanthropic ways. But what is needed is economic cooperation between governments or combines watched over by governments. You must have lots to say on that subject. Are we going to return to international economic competition, only this time more highly organised. Mr. Churchill reminds me—only on the political plane—more and more of Abbot Edmund,[3] a wonderful practical judgement which he cannot fully explain. Thus on this matter of post-war reconstruction, he seems to have stuck his toes in; and, you know, probably rightly, as we are all squabbling about reform already. Look at the storm brewing up about education. Still, I think, and sincerely hope, he is giving *you* all the encouragement and help you need. It is one thing having Tom, Dick and

Harry discussing and squabbling, and another you quietly getting a scheme going behind the scenes.

I am giving a talk on Akbar[4] to a little society to commemorate his 4th centenary. It is strange to think that he and S. John of the Cross began their lives in the same year. One doing his greatest work in a prison, the other making himself a god on a throne. The "nada" and the "all." The first the truth, and truth coming through in the long run.

I said I thought we could persuade to the Church by love, in my last letter. I don't withdraw that; but truth has the primacy never the less. This lovely thing, it is true? Its loveliness perhaps is a guarantee of its truth. But appreciation of beauty is always somewhat subjective, so we have to do the spade work of going to the credentials in the end. Truth likewise must be above liberty. No one wants to be free of truth. Thus, in my small way, I have no desire to get outside your framework of history which cries out that it is true in the main. So you should not feel confined by submitting to revealed truth which also in the main cries out that it is true.

Besides, and I have tried this idea before, (but you have shied at it) obedience is love. When we love we want to put ourselves wholely at the disposal of God. Without a revelation this would be hard except in glaring instances. But with Christ and his Church we can show our love all the time in hundreds of ways and in all our faculties: mind and will. This is the way the saints looked at obedience. But obedience has a bad press now, as something servile. It is the pledge of love, the opportunity.

I write all this hoping it will not hurt. This is the way we talked, and I carry on our interrupted conversation.

Fr. George[5] was up a week ago, before going abroad somewhere. He said that Lawrence was doing well. I hope that is true, it is so long since I heard. Anyway he and you all have a share in my poor prayers which do, I believe, become of value *per Christum Dominum Nostrum*.

Yours affectionately,
Columba, O.S.B.

1. See C.C.E.'s letter written during the Battle of Britain, Summer 1940, above.

2. On 8 November 1942, the U.S. forces landed in French North Africa; on 1 December 1942, Admiral Jean-François Darlan (1881–1942), who had represented the Vichy government, assumed authority as chief of state with the approval of Britain and the United States; he was assassinated on 24 December 1942.

3. Abbot Edmund Matthews, O.S.B. (1871–1939); headmaster at Ampleforth from 1900–1924; Abbot from 1924–39; "A sturdy Lancashire man whose practical 'political' judgment was almost unerring, though his reasons seemed inadequate." (C.C.E.)

4. Akbar (1542–1605); ruler of the Mogul Empire in India.

5. Ian George Forbes, O.S.B.; see C.C.E.'s letter of 22 November 1942, above.

30 December 1942 Rothiemay

My dear Arnold,

Here I am in the peaceful atmosphere of a Scottish Castle with all day to write to you in.

This may reach you on New Years' Day. I wish you every grace and blessing for the coming year; no doubt even more exacting than the last, especially for you, as the goal of all of your labours approaches.

I hope you have seen the Pope's Christmas message.[1] He is on your side, or rather you have proved to be on his; and that is a good omen. There is a ring of hope in his words which gave me joy. He sounds as though convinced now that the end is in sight, and the right end.

To explain some of my remarks in that last frantic letter before Christmas. May I ask you a few questions about Russia. 1. Has Stalin signed the Atlantic Charter? I just don't know. 2. Have all the Polish priests taken to the East by the Russians, and not liberated when the Polish soldiers were, have they been freed? 3. How did the Russians treat the Lithuanians, the Latvians, the Ukrainians when they took those parts? (We could discover their "Liberal" intentions by studying those examples). 4. If Stalin has signed the Atlantic Charter, is religion given as free a hand as anti-Christ? I am not doing this in order to "show up" the Russians. I honestly don't know.

It seems quite clear that the Russians are no longer the backward (in war capacity) nation they have been for so long. Therefore in peace too their power of industrial recovery will be equal if not greater than ours. Can we therefore still say: *they* will be too weak to concern themselves with anything beyond their frontiers. I can see them sweeping over Roumania and Hungary; and what will even be left to Poland?

The Americans are very good at educating their public at the moment; Roosevelt is a past-master. We should prepare the public mind for a just peace. Is there any way of avoiding the newspaper rant such as that at the end of the last war?

I am convinced that our attitude to the Italians is wrong. We should, surely, be saying: you never meant to come into the war, that is why you don't fight, and not because you are cowards. All but your silly Fascists are pro-Allied Nations.

Have you any time for relaxation? I know you love the modern saints; well, read a beautiful book called *The Song of Bernadette*.[2] It is her life told most movingly. I know you would love it, and it would be such a change for you from international affairs in the political sense. I have at last read a big piece of Tolstoy, Vol I of *War and Peace*. It interested me very much, but never stirred me as some books do. One looked at it dispassionately and said, Yes, that is a marvellous description of a death—Pierre's father; or those must be the sentiments of a young soldier faced with his Emperor; that drunken scene by the window is brilliantly vivid. Of course my memory for names is bad, these Russian ones make it even more difficult. Then it all seems formless—but then, I have only read Vol I. It is a grand description of what *is*, especially of the emotions; but there is no heavenly music in it. The *Song of Bernadette*, on the other hand, I am starting to read again.

As ever, every success in your great undertakings, and health to carry them out, and grace to see and do exactly what is right.

Yours affectionately,
Columba, O.S.B.

P.S. Don't get worried about not answering. I can wait. The world's business presses.

My host is Colonel Forbes,[3] Fr. George's father. He is a real Highlander, plays the pipes before dinner, wears highland dress all the time. The place is covered with swords—his father was in the Indian Mutiny, he himself in Ladysmith, his grandfather at Waterloo. The carpets are all tartans. There is a chapel in the House.

1. The Pope had said, "It is only through an intelligent and generous sharing of forces between the strong and the weak that it will be possible to effect a universal pacification in suchwise as not to leave behind centres of conflagration and infection from which new disasters may come" (*The Times* [29 December 1942]).
2. Franz V. Werfel, *The Song of Bernadette*, trans. by L. Lewisohn (London, 1942).
3. George Forbes, D.S.O. (1875–1954); cf. C.C.E.'s letter of 22 November 1942, above.

FOUR

1943–46

*The long agony of parting from Rosalind; "*Qua cursum ventus*"; Veronica's role; vain hopes of reconciliation; "the door should still be open"; Rosalind's marriage that was no marriage; grounds for annulment; "man married to goddess"; Niebuhr and Catholicism; visits to a psychoanalyst; A.J.T.'s hopes for Russia; the flying bombs; the unexplained breach in the correspondence; A.J.T.'s sorrow; the resumption of letters in June 1946; the final decrees of annulment and divorce; A.J.T. withdraws from government service.*

Ampleforth College
York

19 January 1943

My dear Arnold,

This is the last day before term and I have a great desire to write to you once again before the stresses of the term make my mind scarcely my own.

How is the great work for the pacifying of Europe and the world getting on? I pray and you work, and sometimes echoes of your work reach us. I liked that article that Monday in the *Times*[1] on the public services of Europe. We also want, on so much higher a level, the people of the world to be able to live in love with one another, to be able and to want to praise God. When will all this come about? We are not consumed by this desire; we have it. But if we have it, then it should be so tremendous, that we should be prepared to do anything for its accomplishment. I am lukewarm, and every one seems like me. Not every one, but so many. I pray for you, who have such vast opportunities, to be a shining light. It is the only thing that really matters, the changing of men's hearts, including my own. I realise how wretched I am in this—divided in allegiance—by reading the lives of the saints, and just now that of St. Catherine of Siena.[2] What a zeal. Where is that zeal today?

Suppose God in his mercy changed the hearts of the rulers of Russia, what an immense good. The people of Russia have suffered so much and been so brave, they must have great natural goodness, and surely will be rewarded. Our lukewarmness is, I am sure, greatly due to that longing to see results. We are few, we feel almost alone against a whole world of unbelievers, and that our little heroisms will sink into insignificance. What God wants is that we should do the whole right and then HE will, in his own time, reward it beyond all bounds. I feel that Satan works in the contrary direction with similar technique. When a man gives himself over to a great passion—pride of power—though the price seem impossible, he gets it (Hitler).

You must pray for the completion and goodness of a little booklet, *minimum opus*,[3] I am writing; and even write me some advice if you ever have time now (the latter I don't expect). The aim of the booklet is to give an outline of how to live for God *in the world* and especially for young men. The idea being that most books are written on that subject with an eye to religious, priests or nuns. The circumstances of a life in the world give different kinds of opportunities for different virtues to those that occur to monks, also different dangers and obstacles.

I have been asked by Mr. Charles Edwards on behalf of the Archbishop of Edinburgh to write a book (for 16 yr. olds) on what he calls Civics.[4] Am I qualified? Have I the time? I haven't accepted or refused yet. One hates beginning and then abandoning. I give myself till 1950! to finish China. It is hard to get the books.

Although you cannot be present at my Mass, where all your intentions and you yourself willy-nilly are offered to God, source of Love, love itself, join yourself in spirit to that ½ hour when I am sure Our Lord is specially supporting you. It would give me great comfort to know that you consciously join with me in that act of sharing by our giving of ourselves to God, in Christ's most perfect giving. This is put very badly. I want you positively, actively to share in my Mass.

News. Fr. James has been very busy arranging week-end retreats here, first for men then for officers. They both were a great success. Br. Ian[5] is recovering from jaundice. The new book of Fr. Aelred is almost out. Fr. Stephen is well.

There has been a little and very good skating, black ice; but now a thaw. I have been down to say Mass in the village and had breakfast with an old school mistress. At the age of 13 she taught 45 children and did this till 17. Then at a salary of £34 per annum she had in her first year a class of 117 children. That was in Wigan among the very poor when the Catholics had not aid from the state to speak of. She did it quite obviously for the love of God. A wonderful person. Next time you come we must go and see her.

Au revoir

Yours affectionately,
Columba, O.S.B.

1. "Europe's Public Utilities," *The Times* (11 January 1942); the correspondent suggested: "There might be a separate central European Utilities Council with subsidiary corporations for each of the separate services."

2. Saint Catherine of Siena (1347–80); a Dominican tertiary who went to Avignon and persuaded Gregory XI to return to Rome.

3. C.C.E.'s *The Beginning of Goodness* (London, 1944).

4. Archbishop Macdonald, O.S.B., of Edinburgh (monk of Fort Augustus) had suggested that C.C.E. and Charles Edwards write this book, to be used in the schools as a counter to a civics book proposed by the public educational authority; after completion of the book and A.J.T.'s preface, the educational authority abandoned the project; and the book was never published.

5. Ian Petit, O.S.B.; cf. C.C.E.'s letter of 16 June 1942, above.

As from 3 Ship Street, Oxford
Yatscombe
25 February 1943 Boar's Hill, Oxford

Dear Columba,

In your affection and your charity you will have known, I think, that my long silence—longer even than usual—has not been due to callousness or forgetfulness. You have been much in my thoughts, as usual, and I have been grateful for your unwearying good will in going on writing when I haven't written to you.

I have, it is true, been particularly busy in my work. After more than three years out in the cold, my colleagues and I at Balliol have had what is quite a success. The Foreign Office has decided to incorporate us into their organisation as from the beginning of April; they are amalgamating within another organisation of theirs; and they are almost certainly going to move us up to London. All this is giving me a lot of work, as you may imagine. It is welcome work, and also it isn't the cause of my long delay in writing.[1]

The reason for the delay is that I couldn't write to one of my most intimate friends without telling him something which I can hardly bear to write and which it will grieve you terribly to read.

A breach which, in spite of efforts on both sides, has long been widening between Rosalind and me, has now come to a final break. There, now I have told you. I won't go into details at present, if you will forgive me, except to say that it was the prospect of my moving back to London that brought things to a head, so that a success in my work is bound up with a very awful calamity in Rosalind's and my lives.

The knowledge of your loving-kindness towards me, and your constant prayers for me, has helped me a lot during these four months since I got back from America. I am now "acquainted with grief".[2] I have had trouble before, but none like this.

I have been able, by God's mercy, to pray to God more actively and fruitfully than I ever have since I was a child, and I believe this will remain with me. I am able to meditate on the first half of the Lord's Prayer. My praying is a crude and rudimentary spiritual activity by comparison with anything that you are accustomed to in yourself or your brethren. I try to do three spiritual acts:—

First, to think and feel the comfort of the paradox in the combination of "Father" with "Heaven". Where you might expect to find nothing but merciless unapproachable impersonal forces, you actually find a person who, while as formidable as the astronomical universe, is, again by paradox, not only formidable but also loving and tender: one can turn to Him.

Second, to make the invocation "Hallowed be thy name" into an act of opening oneself and submitting oneself to God. Here I always think—this may seem incongruous, but it is a simile that helps me—of the turning on of the red light that tells one, when one is broadcasting, that one is now *en rapport* with one's audience; the little room in which one is sitting seems like the same little box as before, but, when the red light is on, one knows for a fact that one's voice is passing, beyond the walls of that little box, into the ears of an unseen audience beyond. If one calls on God sincerely and whole-heartedly, one not only puts oneself *en rapport* with Him, but, in the same act, one submits oneself to accept his will and to do one's best, oneself, to carry it out, because one's relation to God is in this unlike one's relation to human beings: if one really is *en rapport* with God, that in itself makes one want to do His will: the two things are inseparable.

Third, "thy kingdom come" means the same thing, not only as "hallowed be thy name", but also as "thy will be done in Earth as it is in Heaven". Here is another paradox: in so far as earth is changed, by the doing of God's will there, to become more like Heaven, Earth becomes an almost unrecognisably better place. And yet, at the same time, this process of getting better is—on Earth—inevitably a process of pain and travail, just because Earth, where by nature God's will is hardly done at all, starts by being such a different world from Heaven, where it is done perfectly and without strife. To bring Earth into conformity with Heaven, our Earthly life has to be wrenched round, and there is grievous pain in that.[3]

Well, God Bless You.

Yours very affectionately,
Arnold

1. A.J.T. became director of the Research Department of the Foreign Office in 1943 and held this post until 1946.

2. Isa. 53:3.

3. Compare A.J.T.'s discussion of the Lord's Prayer in his *Experiences*, pp. 167–72.

3 Ship Street
Oxford

4 March 1943

Dear Columba,

Your two letters[1] have given me great help and comfort, as your prayers do all the time.

I certainly will come—or rather propose myself for coming—to Ampleforth at the first opportunity, but this won't, I am afraid, be until the dust has settled after the move: perhaps late May or early June.

Further about what has happened to Rosalind and me: for the general cause, read a poem by Arthur Hugh Clough beginning "As ships becalmed at eve" (no. 749 in the Oxford Book); it describes what has happened exactly.[2]

God Bless You,
Arnold

1. Missing.

2. See Arthur Hugh Clough's "Qua Cursum ventus," in *The Oxford Book of Victorian Verse* (Oxford, 1968), p. 324; the opening stanza reveals the theme: "As ships, becalm'd at eve, that lay / With canvas drooping, side by side, / Two towers of sail at dawn of day / Are scarce, long leagues apart, descried."

3 Ship Street
Oxford

24 March 1943

Dear Columba,

Will you let me know exactly what Rosalind told you when she came up to see you? Your friendship matters so much to me that I want to clear anything up that can be cleared up, and I am not sure, from what you write in your letter of the 22nd,[1] exactly what she did say. She would not, I am sure, mind your telling me.[2]

God Bless You.

Yours affectionately,
Arnold

1. Missing.
2. "I did not feel free to report to A.J.T. Rosalind's confidences at this meeting." (C.C.E.)

3 Ship Street
Oxford

29 March 1943

Dear Columba,

This is only a preliminary answer to your second letter:[1] I can't forbear to thank you for it straight away, nor can I answer it adequately on the spur of the moment: in fact, I can never answer it adequately. It is a letter that is also an act, and an act that will have a most important effect, for good, on my life.

I have shown it to Veronica,[2] and she feels the same as I do about it.

As I expect Rosalind told you, Veronica never in the least degree came between Rosalind and me. Down to the moment when I spoke to her, she had been praying every day that Rosalind and I might be reconciled. And I did not speak to her until I believed that a reconciliation between Rosalind and me was no longer possible. Until I had come, very slowly and through great pain, to that belief, the possibility of being married to anyone but Rosalind hadn't entered my head.

About your letter, the only other thing that I will say at the moment is that you have shown an understanding, and a loving kindness, which quite knocked me over.

Yours affectionately,
Arnold

1. Missing.
2. Veronica M. Boulter (1897–1980); daughter of the Rev. Sidney Boulter, Rector of St. Peter's church, Poulshot, Wiltshire; Newnham College, Cambridge; first class honors, but no degrees were then awarded to women; assistant writer and subeditor, with A.J.T. of the *Survey of International Affairs*; V.M.B. also contributed articles under her own name; during the war, publication stopped; after resumption in 1951, V.M.B. variously acted as co-writer and editor or as sole editor; the masterly indexes to *A Study of History* were her work; cf. "Acknowledgements and Thanks," in *A Study of History*, X: 241–42; cf. A.J.T.'s *Experiences*, pp. 78–80: "To this day, if I open some volume of our *Survey* at random and glance at the page, I am unable, as often as not, to tell whether that page was Veronica's or mine," ibid. p. 79.

3 Ship St.
Oxford

21 April 1943

Dear Columba,

I was very glad to get your letter of the 19th:[1] God bless you.

I am in the course of writing you a very long letter, giving a detailed history of, and reflexions on, my relations with Rosalind. It is going to be a great help to me to do this. I am still drowned in work, as my personal troubles hit me at the same moment as the pressure of work arising out of our change of status and our move. So I may not be able to finish the letter for some weeks. But it will reach you sooner or later.

Don't worry about anything you may have said in your earlier letter about the possibility that Rosalind might have been given different advice. I will take it as never having been said, and hope this may set your mind at ease.

I deeply value your prayers.

Yours affectionately,
Arnold

1. Missing.

As from 3 Ship St.
Oxford

31 May 1943

Dear Columba,

My letter has grown into an autobiography; I am not shy of unloading it on you, because I know you care about Rosalind and me and all concerned—but don't try to digest it except at your leisure (of which, I know, you have too little anyway).[1]

I should very much like to come up to Ampleforth for my summer holiday—if that were convenient—i.e. for ten days to a fortnight—any time from about the middle of July onwards when I should have the best chance of seeing something of you.

God Bless You.
Yours affectionately,
Arnold

1. "At A.J.T.'s request this 'autobiography' (except the statement of faith of 5 August 1938, above) was returned to him." (C.C.E.) See A.J.T.'s letter of 30 March 1944, below; the "autobiography" is now missing.

3 F Morpeth Terrace
S.W.1

17 June 1943

Dear Columba—

I had been meaning to write to you for some time, and now I have just heard, through a mutual friend, that Arnold is going up to Ampleforth in a week or so. You can imagine that I am very glad indeed to hear that. I have seen nothing of him, nor heard except in this indirect way through 3rd persons (apart from one or two purely business notes on Income Tax, etc); and it seems unnatural and somehow artificial to keep up this absolute break, though I suppose he must do it for legal purposes. However, I am very thankful that he will be seeing you, and I assume talking out his real position. I keep wondering about that. For, as I think you know, I do most truly want his good, and in so far as I am able, I want to further it; but I can't feel clear in my own mind about his projected new marriage—how far he still really wants it and means to go through with it, and how far it will be a good thing that he should do so. You see the particular reason why I was going to write, before I heard he was going to you, is that his fundamental objections to it, seem likely now to be removed—in particular the one he pointed out—of its preventing his coming into the Church at some later time; for after all the original counter-advices, it now seems *almost* certain that our marriage was *not* valid, and that I shall get an annullment before long, without its even having to go to Rome. The ground is one which you also were the first to suggest—that I was not baptized when it took place, in 1913.[1] Mgr. Scanlan,[2] who is, I understand, *the* authority in canon questions, seems pretty certain about it. He said it seemed a very clear case of fact, and it is now under consideration by Fr. Geraerts[3] who is the official who has to prove it valid if he can. I have seen him too and answered all his questions; and although he was more non-committal than Mgr. Scanlan, he didn't seem to find any hitch, and I am now just waiting to hear from him again.

I haven't as yet written to Arnold about this, as I wanted to wait till it was quite definite; but he had better know before he talks his position over with you, so I will either write or try to see him. I don't suppose he will think it of any importance; he will consider it 'just a quibble', as he did before when I suggested the possibility to him, but, of course, it does make the whole difference, if only he could see it.

It has been an almost bewildering relief to me to find that, after all, the feeling I have had for so long of never having been really married to him, was, almost certainly, justified, although on quite different grounds from what I thought of, as indeed fortunately it now appears on *both* grounds. They seem to think it very astonishing that Fr. Steuart[4] did not realise this invalidity from the beginning; and the only satisfactory explanation would be that it was a 'providential' oversight—in view of how things were going to turn out later (so Arnold's refusal to re-marry me, was also providential). It is really all very queer, for I have brought up this question several times, feeling so queerly uneasy as I have, and always it has been turned down or brushed aside, till it seemed that my 'scruple' must be groundless. To me all this makes it seem much more clearly God's will that we should separate—that we were not meant to go on together—whatever the next phase for either of us may be; but I doubt if Arnold will see it so.

I had also meant to ask you to tell Fr. Stephen,[5] if you please would, for people in general are getting to know now—at least that we have parted, and I should like him to know the truth about it.

I should be very glad to know what you think about the annullment—and when you have seen Arnold—what you think about his marriage? Not that I would try and stop it, if he wants it—but I should like to be able to feel more hopeful about it—now that the way is cleared for it—than I do.

I am sure that you won't mind my bothering you with all this.

I should be very grateful for your prayers, and for Fr. Stephen's.

Yours ever,
Rosalind Toynbee

1. For many centuries a "diriment impediment" to a valid marriage was held present when an unbaptized person married one who had been validly baptized; this had been recognized in the canon law in force at the time of the marriage in 1913. The impediment in itself invalidated the marriage; the behavior or attitudes of the couple were not pertinent. Since 1918 the canon law has been changed to apply the impediment only to a case where one had been baptized in the Catholic Church. This served to validate a great number of marriages. "Also A.J.T. had written to Gilbert Murray before the marriage that if the marriage was not a success, they would get a divorce." (C.C.E.) In the event, the annulment was granted by the Metropolitan Tribunal of the archdiocese of Westminster on 13 December 1946 on the grounds that the marriage entered into on 11 September 1913 in a registry office and dissolved by a civil decree of divorce on 13 August 1946 had never been valid canonically, because at its inception Rosalind (unlike A.J.T.) had not been baptized.

2. Monsignor James Scanlan (1899–1976); later Archbishop of Glasgow.

3. The defender of the bond was Canon John M. T. Barton (1898–1974); it was his task to point out any flaws in the proofs of Rosalind's not having been baptized. Canon Joseph Geraerts (1899–1979) was the *officialis* or presiding officer of the tribunal, who issued the decree of nullity.

4. Robert Henry J. Steuart, S.J. (1874–1948); of the Farm Street Church in London; writer of spiritual treatises; much sought for counseling; *World Intangible* (London, 1934); his *The Inward Vision* (London, 1930) had been quoted in *A Study of History*, I: 282.

5. Stephen Marwood, O.S.B. (1890–1949); house master of St. Oswald's, Ampleforth.

18 June 1943 At 4, Sussex Square, W.2

Dear Columba,

You put a labour of love into your letter.[1] There was complete understanding, charity and sympathy in it, and there was not a word in it that hurt; if you had been talking instead of writing, I should have said, at every sentence, "go on, and God Bless You."

I would now like to carry on the conversation by talking—which we shall be able to do so very soon on the 10th July, being three weeks off to-morrow.

The crux lies in the relation of Rosalind's religious development to her established relations with other people—me in particular. The way you put it in the last paragraph but one of your letter expresses exactly what I meant to say in my letter. Our relation was, as I see it, part of her and my rightful scheme of things, and any change from that is a breaking of the scheme or framework within which her perfection should be built up. This repudiating of a framework of human relations which already exists, and rightfully exists, is of course different from what a monk does when he renounces in advance the possibility of making for himself a not yet existing framework of human relations. Because this act of renunciation may open the way to God, it does not follow that the act of repudiation opens the way! And then too, as you say, a monk doesn't deny the lovableness of the things he has given up.

When we talk, I will take up the question you ask—would I take Rosalind back now, if she came?—and I think after that (the two things hang together), I shall be able to say whether I should like you to show my long letter to Father Steuart and/or to Rosalind herself.

I am very sorry to hear the news of Father Vincent McNabb's[2] death. He must have been a great and noble man.

God Bless You. I am full of gratitude for your affection and help, which have no limits.

Yours affectionately,
Arnold

1. Missing.
2. Vincent McNabb, O.P.; cf. C.C.E.'s letter of 9 February 1942, above.

19 June 1943 At 4 Sussex Square, W.2

Dear Columba,

Our letters keep crossing: I have just had yours of the 18th.[1]

It was a quite unexpected lifting of the clouds—I am sure, from the way you write, that there *is* a lifting, though I cannot guess at what the new element in the situation is. Probably you will be able to tell me when I come: till then, I won't ask.

But I shall meditate your three chapters of the Paradiso.

Your letter has brought great comfort to Veronica and me.

Yours affectionately,
Arnold

1. Missing.

22 June 1943 As from 4 Sussex Square, W.2

Dear Columba,

Since I answered your letter in which you said you had had a note from Rosalind, I have seen an old school-fellow of mine and common friend of Rosalind's and mine, Dick Gleadowe,[1] who had been seeing Rosalind; and he told me that she had said to him that she would like to see me.

This was, I think, practically a message through him to me, and I want to make sure I don't do anything that might seem like rebuffing her. I want to see her, but I would very much like to have seen you first, as I feel I am in the dark about her state of mind, and I feel you could throw light on this for me. I should be better prepared in every way to see her if I had first talked over the whole thing with you, as I am eager to do.

I wonder though, in view of what you say in your letter about her note having cleared up your doubts (and she mentioned to my friend D.G. that she had just written to you), whether her need to see me might possibly be urgent: whether she might be on the brink of some perhaps irrevocable decision about which she wanted to talk to me before she took it (all this is guesswork).

From anything that you know, do you think it is important that I should see her without waiting till I have seen you? And if you think it is all right to wait, will you send her a line to tell her that I do mean to see her and to explain that I want to see you first?

If she were to have a change of heart, the door isn't closed against her. I don't want to write about this more precisely, but I will explain, when I come, what Veronica and I mean by that.

Yours very affectionately,
Arnold

1. Reginald Morier Yorke Gleadowe; cf. A.J.T.'s letter of 13 June 1913, above.

As from 4 Sussex Square
London, W.2

29 June 1943

Dear Columba,

I was sad to leave you at King's X yesterday, though I can look forward to seeing you again so soon.

God Bless You for coming; it must have been very difficult to manage it in the middle of term. The journey wasn't in vain, though in one sense nothing came of it. But it was right that Rosalind should know, before she finally puts the annulment through,[1] that Veronica and I wouldn't stand in the way of a restoration of the marriage if Rosalind felt that this was what the love of God pointed out to her as her path towards spiritual perfection. No one could have painted the possibility to her so well as you. It doesn't seem to come in, at all, into her own picture of what might be possible. This is puzzling to me, for the reasons I put at the end of my long letter. But there is really no doubt about the fact.

Your advice to look now towards the future is right. Though my life is cut in two, I shall survive; for, though God has taken Rosalind from me, he has given me Veronica and my friends and my work. The first thing, almost, that I remember is being told by an evangelical great-uncle that we were not brought into the World to be happy, and my thinking to myself: "No doubt that is true, but I am only three, and it is rather early to be told it!"[2]

Thank you and God Bless You.

Yours affectionately,
Arnold

1. See R.T.'s letter of 17 June 1943, above.
2. Compare A.J.T.'s *Acquaintances*, p. 1.

2 July 1943 At 4 Sussex Square, W.2

Dear Columba,

You did all that you could have done, and if you, for whom God's will *is* sufficient, could not succeed, it means that no human being could.

When Rosalind sees me—and I think it is nicer for me not to ask her to see me before she herself wishes—I shall tell her again what you told her: that if, at any time before the three years beginning last November run out,[1] her religious life takes a turn which makes her want to restore our marriage, the door will be held open by both Veronica and me.

From what you found when you saw Rosalind, this seems most unlikely to happen, but I feel it very important, all the same, that the door should still be open and that Rosalind should know it, because, after all, there is no miracle that God's grace can't do.

It was kind of you to write again, for you must indeed have awful arrears of work. I was very much touched by your making the time to come and help us.

On the 10th I will take the train from York at 3.15 p.m. which gets me to Gilling at 5.25 via Malton and Pickering. I look forward very eagerly to coming to Ampleforth.

Yours affectionately,
Arnold

1. A.J.T. was proposing to secure a divorce on grounds of desertion for three years.

Yatscombe
3 July 1943 Boar's Hill, Oxford

Dear Father Columba,

Many thanks for Arnold's letter, which I return herewith; I will not make any comments of my own on the situation between two people to whom, like you, I am deeply attached, except to say two things. First, I quite agree with you in dismissing the point about the "quest of spiritual perfection"; and secondly, that I believe that

Arnold's acceptance of the attitude of "man married to goddess" is largely responsible for putting the relations of the two in a false position from the beginning.

Yours sincerely,
G.M.[1]

1. Gilbert Murray.

Ampleforth College
York

25 July 1943

Dear Columba,

I found Duncombe Park[1] still open, so I walked home by the way up past the Castle[2] and out through the Nelson Gate,[3] after having tracked down some boiled sweets for Father Alexius[4] in Helmsley. You must have had a fine view of Teesdale from the head of Bilsdale.[5] This morning I have had a walk with Father Stephen: he knows the essential facts, but, if he would care to see the long letter[6]—sometime when he has the time to look at it—will you let him see it, warning him that it is *ex parte*, though not written deliberately so. I shall be writing to you again after I have seen Rosalind ca. Thursday. Meanwhile, thank you and God Bless You, my dear friend and guide.

Yours affectionately,
Arnold J. Toynbee

I am carrying off the Spanish Saint John of the Cross, as I find I can understand it sufficiently to spur me, if I have the time, to get grammar and dictionary and master it properly. I am beginning with the "pensamientos del santo" at the end: an anthology of short sentences.

1. The nineteenth-century seat of the earls of Feversham, the house by a local architect, William Wakefield, the design perhaps by Vanbrugh; the park "one of the most extensive and boldest landscaping enterprises of England" (Nikolaus Pevsner, *Yorkshire: The North Riding* [London, 1966], pp. 139–42); the Duncombe Terrace looks down on the ruins of Rievaulx Abbey.
2. Helmsley Castle; see Pevsner, op. cit., pp. 188–89.
3. Nelson Gate, or Arch; see Pevsner, op. cit., p. 142.
4. Alexius Chamberlain, O.S.B. (1878–1965); monk of Ampleforth.
5. Bilsdale is the high end of the Rye Valley.
6. Among those returned to A.J.T.; cf. A.J.T.'s letter of 31 May 1943, above.

As from 7 Trevor Street
London S.W.7

29 July 1943

Dear Columba,

I did see Rosalind the night before last, with the result that you and I both expected: that is, the same result as when you saw her. There is no change.

I told her I had been praying that God would bring about whatever was spiritually best for her, and at the same time praying that I might make this prayer for her disinterestedly. I told her that I was trying to "fold the wings of desire" for her and for my past life if it was God's will that I should lose both, but that if, at any time before the three years came to an end, she herself felt, with love on her side, that it was God's will that the marriage should be fully restored, both Veronica and I felt it right that the marriage should be restored in that case, and that I should then receive Rosalind with love, mingled with grief at the loss of Veronica.

She said that she could not bring herself to think of restoring the marriage now, and that she believed that nothing short of a miracle would ever make her change her mind about this. The offer to me to live apart but visit her by invitation was still open, but her life spent from me would then still be her real life, and she strongly advised me not to think of trying this but to regard the whole question as closed and to turn all my thoughts and feelings towards marrying Veronica.

She spoke of Veronica with kindness and regard, admiring her willingness to let me go, if this had to be, for the sake of doing right.

She said that she thought my conscience about holding the door open for her (Rosalind) to come back was really an unquenched desire in me for her, masquerading as conscience.

This may be so, or at least partly so, considering the weakness of one's nature and its capacity for self-deception.

My conclusion is (may I have your opinion on this?) that I ought now to regard the point of conscience as being set at rest—after all, Rosalind does now know that the marriage can be restored, if she wills, any time between now and November 1945—and that I ought to concentrate my prayers and efforts of will on unloosening my hold on my past with Rosalind and grasping hold of my future with Veronica. Veronica has gone to the utmost lengths of willingness to sacrifice herself in order that what is right shall be done, and I believe it was right of me to accept this from her for the sake of conscience. But it would be very wrong that I should cause her to suffer, not for my conscience but for my unquenched desires—specially for a lingering desire for something which, by God's will, it is beyond my power to have.

During the night Veronica, she tells me, had a scruple arising from Rosalind's having questioned, in her talk with me, whether I was really holding the door open for a restoration of the marriage so long as I was regarding myself as engaged to Veronica and was spending so much of my time with her as I do. It occurred to Veronica that it might be our duty to part for a time, and to work on different jobs in different places, in order to make sure that the door *was* being held open for Rosalind. But, as Rosalind held out no hope that she would come back through the door, however genuinely it might be held open, and as she advised, and hoped, that I should marry Veronica, I think this scruple of Veronica's goes beyond what conscience requires. Do you agree?

The meeting between Rosalind and me was very sad but friendly and, at moments, even affectionate.

God Bless You for your help to me.

Yours affectionately,
Arnold

As from 22 Brown St., W.1
Pad. 0698

23 August 1943

My dear Arnold,

You will see from the above that I am on the point of arriving in London. I shall be staying with my cousin Lady Winefrede Elwes[1] from Wednesday night till Saturday morning next. Could we see a little of one another? I know you must now be head over heels in work, but perhaps I might just come round for half an hour.

My evenings are booked up, not the lunch hour. The difficulty of both is that it is impossible to get meals anywhere.

Anyhow, this is a warning, and perhaps by the time I have arrived you will have thought out a plan.

I am anxious to know how you are as it is sometimes since either of us wrote.

The war is so swiftly moving to its climax that a letter of one day seems past history the next. But I must say the Italian situation seems to have been badly handled.[2] Yet, what can I know about it all? We are completely at the mercy of our government over foreign affairs which have to be conducted more or less in secrecy.

You will be glad to hear that my little booklet on the *Beginning of Goodness* is complete as far as matter is concerned. It now remains to persuade the Censors that it is orthodox and the publishers that it is printable!

More news and views when we meet. But I will quite understand if it is impossible.

Yours affectionately,
Columba, O.S.B.

1. Winefrede Mary E. Elwes (1868–1959); seventh daughter of the eighth Earl of Denbigh and Desmond; wife of Gervase Elwes of Billing Hall, the diplomat and singer; with Sir Richard Elwes, *Gervase Elwes, the Story of His Life* (London, 1935).

2. The allied forces had completed the conquest of Sicily with the fall of Messina on 18 August 1943.

As from 7 Trevor Street
London, S.W.7

29 September 1943

Dear Columba,

I have been carrying your letter of the 9th September[1] round in my pocket, re-reading it from time to time, but just now finding the moment to write to you.

The presence of God everywhere—the thought that struck you most during the retreat—is a particularly apposite thought for me. As you guessed, I am far from being back at normal: I am still struggling with waves of pain at the cutting of my earthly roots; I am still earth-bound, tied to Ganthorpe and the human recollections of thirty years with that patch of country and Castle Howard. The terrible strength of its hold on me shows, I think, that you are right: the purpose of the calamity is to detach me from idolatrous worship of the creature and liberate me for making God himself my centre of attachment.

I am ashamed because, even within the limited "Good Pagan" horizon, leaving God out and limiting myself to the side of worldly values, I have a greater earthly treasure, in Veronica's love for me and the opportunity I have of giving her what I have failed to give to Rosalind, than in the empty husk of the last thirty years of my life.

I am trying to loose myself from the hold of this by writing a poem about it.[2] I didn't start the poem in cold blood as an exorcism, but I hope, when I have written it, I shall find that it has that effect. I have often noticed that some field of knowledge, or set of problems, that has bothered me for years stops troubling me as soon as I have written it into the Nonsense Book. Perhaps the poem will do something of the kind.

I am, fortunately, able to pray all this time, and this, with the love and kindness of my friends, is keeping me going. I must take each wave of trouble as it comes and concentrate on getting through just that, without looking too far ahead. But I think, as Churchill says of the War, that my heaviest fighting is still to come.

Yours affectionately,
Arnold

1. Missing.
2. A.J.T.'s "Ganthorpe: An Elegy and Dedication," in *Experiences*, pp. 393–401.

7 Trevor Street
London, S.W.7

16 November 1943

Dear Columba,

When next you write, tell me the date of the Feast of All Monks, for I should like to remember you specially on future anniversaries and in war time we can't reckon how long a letter has taken en route from Ampleforth to Trevor Square.

I am much touched and pleased with your wanting to dedicate "The Names of Christ"[1] to me, though it is an inverted kind of dedication, as I am a recipient, not a giver, of spiritual guidance and inspiration from you: such start as I have made comes partly from you, whom God has given me for my friend, and partly from my experience of life, which is also God's gift. This second gift, unlike the friendship with you, is a mixture of grief with happiness. I am beginning to learn to be grateful for the grief as well as the happiness, because there are things that one can only be taught through grief.

This, as you saw, is part of what I was trying to say in the poem. God gives us the gift of his creation to enjoy in the right way: that is, always for His sake and in relation to Him and as a medium for the partial revelation of Himself. If one enjoys these things in the wrong way—for one's own sake and in relation to oneself and as idols obscuring instead of revealing the real God—then (though this is hard) one has to be thankful to God for taking these things away, if this is the only way one can learn one's lesson.

Since I wrote the poem I have read T. S. Eliot's *Little Gidding*,[2] which is also a wrestle with the problem of desire, and a notable large book (Hibbert Lectures) by the American Protestant theologian Reinhold Niebuhr called *The Nature and Destiny of Man*.[3] I hope you will get this book for the monastery library, for, though Niebuhr isn't a Catholic, he isn't, as a theologian, a Protestant either, and he has a powerful mind which knows how to put the fundamental and permanent problems of theology in terms which modern man can take, without watering it down or giving anything away.

The central theme of the book is a definition of sin as a refusal by man to recognize and accept his own finiteness, so that he tries to build a (necessarily fragmentary and imperfect) universe round himself, instead of entering into the true universe that has its centre in God. This is perhaps one of those truths that are so simple and fundamental that it is a great achievement to express them in terms that will grip: and this, I think, Niebuhr has achieved.

The theme of the book came home to me because my attempt—expressed in the Greek poem at the beginning of the *Study*[4]—to make a harmony of my life and work has been broken up, and I now see that at any rate one cause of the smash has been that I tried to build, pagan-wise, round selfish desire (Ἔρως) instead of round un-self-seeking love (Ἀγάπη). I also see that to transmute desire into true love for other people—and this is what we try to do—is so difficult that it can't be done by human effort without God's grace.

All this, I wrestle with in my prayers, which are gradually taking shape round what I hope—though I am only groping—are the main things that one ought to pray for.

As to titles for your book,[5] I think "A Layman's Life" might be a little empty to the reader. While written for the layman the problems are at bottom—though not of course in all cases on the surface—the common spiritual problems of all human beings. What about "The Challenge of Life"? But "challenge" is perhaps too favorite a word with me.

I think you are too gloomy about the Moscow Conference[6] and the state of France. I think the French (though at the moment they are behaving badly and foolishly in the Lebanon)[7] are getting over their divisions. The new life and leadership is coming from the Resistance Movement in France itself, which has been started by young men whose names will suddenly become famous, like those of Michael Collins[8] and the other young leaders of Sinn Fein after the last war. These young men will unite France, and for them de Gaulle is the symbol of their cause (in spite of his obvious personal limitations) because in the darkest hour—the supreme time of testing—he alone refused to capitulate.

About the Moscow Conference: it seems to me that the question whether or not we are going to avoid a third and final world war depends largely on whether Russia and America can manage to work in partnership to run the world in a more or less decent way, and I think the Conference has laid some good foundations for this. What has been said about the rights of smaller countries—by the Conference collectively and by Stalin individually—is surely notable and encouraging. There is no evidence that the Russians want more than their 1939 frontier, and, as far as "Eastern Poland" goes, the Russian claim is surely much better than the Polish. The interwar frontier was imposed on Russia by Poland by force of arms at a moment of Russian weakness, and it put millions of White Russians and Ukrainians under Polish rule.[9] The Ukrainians, at any rate, have been badly treated by the Poles, and undoubtedly would resist coming under Polish rule again. But I don't think the Russians have any intention of asking for Polish-inhabited territories.

Yours affectionately,
Arnold

1. C.C.E.'s "The Names of Christ" appeared in thirteen articles published in *The Life of the Spirit*, a Dominican (Blackfriars) review, from July 1946 to April 1949.

2. (London, 1942).

3. Reinhold Niebuhr (1892–1971); American evangelical theologian; professor at Union Theological Seminary, New York (1928–60); *The Nature and Destiny of Man*, Gifford Lectures, 1939, 2 vols. (London, 1941–43); cf. *A Study of History*, VII: 508.

4. "ΣΥΓΓΡΑΦΕΩΣ ΒΙΟΣ" in *A Study of History*, I: ix–x.

5. *The Beginning of Goodness.*

6. The conference of the three foreign ministers, Anthony Eden, Cordell Hull, and V. M. Molotov, held in Moscow beginning 19 October 1943.

7. On 11 November 1943, the French arrested the president of Lebanon after the Lebanese Chamber of Deputies proclaimed independence; on 27 November, the French withdrew their opposition.

8. Michael Collins (1890–1922); a leader of the Sinn Fein; with Arthur Griffiths, he negotiated the treaty that granted Ireland dominion status as the Irish Free State; on Griffith's death Collins became head of state and of the army; ten days later he was assassinated by members of the Republican army.

9. On 18 March 1921, (in the treaty of Riga), "the Poles had exploited politically a capricious turn in the tide of the fortunes of war in order to force upon the Soviet Union a Polish-Soviet frontier—drawn some 150 miles east of the ethnographic Curzon Line, and bringing about 4½ million Ukrainians and 1½ million White Russians under Polish rule" (A.J.T. in *Survey of International Affairs, 1939–46: The Eve of the War, 1939*, ed. A.J.T. and Veronica M. Toynbee [London, 1958], p. 11).

Saint Wilfrid's House
Ampleforth College, York

18 November 1943

My dear Arnold,

All Monks comes on the 13th November. Thank you ever so much for your letter and all its parts. You underestimate the spiritual power of the *Study* and the influence it has had on my mind and on the *Names of Christ* therefore.

Your reply to my political questionings was very very welcome, and relieves me a good deal; particularly what you say of France and of sovereign States in which I have a big belief—within limits. I hope you are right about Russia. The point about the Polish frontier has very solid weight; but I hope the Ukrainians will be allowed to save their souls and not forget they ever had any.

Fr. Aelred has a copy of the book you mention. I shall read it. Meanwhile I have read again *Little Gidding*. It is obscure, very, but some light has penetrated, especially the Desire part, which is good. No sooner read than I had to write one myself. Is it poetry? I don't know. Is it beauty? I don't know either. I think it has the beauty of truth.

THE TAMING OF DESIRE 18-11-43

There is no escape from Desire
For to desire to escape is Desire.
Desiring self is death,
Whereas we were made for life.

There is no escape from Desire,
But we may change the object
As an archer changes his aim
As a plane changes direction.

Our sin is to desire for ourselves alone,
To be locked in a self embrace
Which blinds and tastes of ashes—
That burns up our being.

The spirit in man has insatiable desire.
A divine longing making it
return to its Beginning,
To God, The First and the Last.

When we love without consideration
Creatures: self, others, glory,
Or gold, then we mistake,
Poor fools, the shadows for Reality.

Setting up an idol, as the Jews did
of old in a desert to worship,

We manufacture a god; and it crushes us.
It crushes and kills that desire.

Then we either despair or return,
Return to the God that first made us;
But not unless He lift us, willing,
Out of the bog by the power of his GRACE.

We learn the lesson by pain,
Self-inflicted, unforeseen but deserved,
That creatures are symbols only,
Not God, to be loved, not adored.

Yours affectionately,
Columba, O.S.B.

Saint Wilfrid's House
Ampleforth College, York

20 November 1943

Dear Arnold,

It is marvelous to think that you really can, probably, write a preface for the Civics book.[1] Here is my copy, the one you read before, still uncorrected except for that phrase about Gt. Britain allowing immigration into its colonies. The question of emigration is too big to be opened up in a paragraph. Perhaps you might say something in the preface.

I have not seen C. Edwards since your reply, but he will, I know, be overjoyed.

I must rush off to Sat. Benediction.

Yours affectionately,
Columba, O.S.B.

1. Compare C.C.E.'s letter of 19 January 1943, above.

8 December 1943

7 Trevor St., S.W.7

Dear Columba,

I have not yet managed to re-read the typescript in order to write the introduction, but I hope to get down to it this week-end or the one after.

I am writing now to ask you to think of a book that you would like to have from me as a Christmas present. Will you send me a choice of several, as they are apt to be out of print nowadays?

My work is still keeping me quite busy, and this is good. In myself, I am in the same state as before, fighting a very difficult battle with myself to make myself give up my own will and accept God's, and to exchange desire for a disinterested love of other people. The battle goes on and on and up and down in the background, while the foreground of my mind attends to my work. If I win, I shall have done it largely through your help.

Yours affectionately,
Arnold

Saint Wilfrid's House
Ampleforth College, York

Saturday, 11 December 1943

My dear Arnold,

Thank you very much for your letter. It is very kind of you to want to give me a book for Christmas. I find it difficult to choose. Here are a few suggestions:

Boswell's *Dr. Johnson*
The Eagle and the Dove Sackville West
The Nature and Destiny of Man R. Niebuhr
(I don't know the price of the last)
Travels of Marco Polo (Everyman edition)

So there you are. Please don't worry if you cannot find any of them.

I am not surprised that you have not had time to re-read the MS. Your life must be exceedingly full at present what with all the conferences.

General Smuts' speech was most interesting.[1] People misread him on France. Quite obviously, if we are not going to be a first class power, neither is France compared to the new giants. How perfectly his speech fitted into your section on the Balance of Power in Vol. III of the *Study*.

Smuts' speech was, to my reading of it, an admission (a) that the League without power was a failure (b) that the only alternative was a return to the Balance of Power. There is a third alternative in theory: of a League with power. But if that is still unrealisable so much the worse for us. It is tragic that we must be forced back to the Balance of Power when all is set for the real solution.

I am sure you do love people for their sake, and are not so far from your goal as you think. Be at peace and trust in God's grace to tide you over all the crises as they come. This Christmas time must be one of much grace for both of us. *Oremus pro invicem* as the saying is.

The Names of Christ has reached the next stage—that of being passed by the local censor. Soon I hope to send it to a publisher, presumably Burns & Oates.

Yours affectionately,
Columba, O.S.B.

1. General Smuts, on 8 December 1943, had spoken at Cairo: "The old order into which I was born lies buried in the western desert. . . . The significance of this war is that it is the first step towards the greater liberty which is coming to us" (*The Times* [9 December 1943]).

7 Trevor Street
3 January 1944 London S.W.7

Dear Columba,

Here at last is my preface: only a midget one, I am afraid—so, if it is not the kind of thing that you and Charles Edwards want, scrap it without hesitation.[1]

I haven't taken up the question of emigration, because it seemed rather arbitrary to single out just that particular point of detail for comment. But I do think that, in your text, you ought to distinguish between the problem of migration and the problem of non-self-governing dependencies: the two have very little to do with each other now that all the "white man's countries" overseas have become fully-self-governing states. The closing down of immigration by the overseas countries after the last war is, in my opinion, a notable sin of theirs which has been one of the main causes of the present war. After this war, it is possible that the tide of emigration from Europe, which has been dammed out of America, may flow into Russia.

I have told Blackwell's to send you Niebuhr's[2] book, and they have written to say that only vol. ii is at present in print, but they have sent me an invoice for both vols., so will you let me know whether the pair, or vol. ii only, arrives?

Is there a story of a dove whispering the word "*concede*" in the ear of Saint Gregory the Great? Rosalind sent me a Christmas card—a reproduction of a fifteenth century illumination—with this in it. I don't think she was meaning it as any kind of message from her to me. Still, I should like to look it up. If you don't happen to know about it, could you suggest where I could trace it?

Lawrence was passing through London the other day—in better spirits, I am glad to say, than for a long time past. He will, I suppose, be in the Second Front.

With prayers and good wishes for the New Year.

Yours affectionately,
Arnold

1. Compare C.C.E.'s letter of 19 January 1943, above; the book was never published; A.J.T.'s preface has vanished.

2. *The Nature and Destiny of Man*; cf. A.J.T.'s letter of 16 November 1943, above.

4 January 1944 Ampleforth

My dear Arnold,

I am back from Burnley[1] and find your lovely present awaiting me. Already I have dived into Vol. I and find it most illuminating. His interpretations of Marxism and Romanticism, of the rationalists, of Rousseau, are most most interesting; and summed up so often in brilliant and penetrating phrases: "half truths set against half truths". "Modern man has an essentially easy conscience".

His analysis of sin is excellent, will his analysis of grace prove so fruitful? It is useful to read a book with which one does not quite agree, it usually results in some more intimate understanding of the truth. Looking at Vol. II I see he has some hard knocks at the Church and its teaching on grace, but probably the Church and her teaching elude him. I shall let you know what I think when I get there. Meanwhile thank you very much for this real mind-stimulant.

Fr. Bruno has recovered and is back here, battered in body and tired in mind, but not permanently affected.[2]

How are you? I hope Christmas time, in spite of the pressure of work, has been the occasion of real enlightenment. I love the feast of the Three Kings. The presents brought have such rich symbolic meaning for today. If only we could offer the gold back to God, so that we do not turn it into our god; if only we could not worship creatures, ourselves, and then offer our deaths or our life in dying, back to God. Gold, incense, myrrh. It depends so much upon our rulers, upon the Kings of this world. I can see faint hope of peace unless combined with all this wise thinking and planning in the economic and political spheres, we have yet wiser thinking in the spiritual. How are we going to get back a community consciousness for behaving with justice and love. Self interest is rarely enlightened until after the crash.

All success and blessings for you and your work in 1944, and peace of mind in so far as struggling man can have it before the fullness of the sonship of God, which we hope to reach in heaven.

Yours affectionately,
Columba, O.S.B.

1. Burnley in Lancashire. "I was giving a short retreat there." (C.C.E.)
2. Bruno Donovan, O.S.B.; cf. C.C.E.'s letter of 8 April 1941, above.

5 January 1944 York

My dear Arnold,

Very many thanks for your kind preface summing things up very clearly and simply. Mr. C. Edwards is away, but I am sure he would approve, and so have sent the type-script straight off to Edinburgh.[1]

By the time you get this you will know that both volumes of Reinhold Niebuhr have arrived. It was very kind of you to give me so handsome a present.

At first I had no success with your problem of St. Gregory and the dove; but Fr. Barnabas[2] put me on the track by sending me to Schuster's *The Sacramentary*, a 5 volume work of historical comments on the Roman missal.[3] I quote from Vol. 1 where he is commenting on the 1st Sunday of Advent:

p. 323

"In the later Middle Ages there was a widely spread custom, at the opening of the Liturgical year, of singing certain verses before the Introit in honour of St. Gregory the Great, the inspired compiler of the Antiphonarium which still bears his name: *Sanctissimus namque Gregorius, cum preces effunderet ad Dominum ut musicum tonum ei desuper in carminibus dedisset: tunc descendit Spiritus Sanctus super eum in specie columbae et illustravit cor ejus. Et sic demum exorsus est canere ita dicendo: 'Ad te levavi*, etc."

The *Ad te levavi* is, of course, the Introit of the Mass. In your card "*Concede*" has taken its place. Now one is guessing. Presumably the artist is imagining St. Gregory as being inspired to write a prayer beginning with the word 'concede'. There are several which so begin. I suggest as the most likely the standard one for feasts of Our Lady.

Concede nos famulos tuos, quaesumus, Domine Deus, perpetua mentis et cordis sanitate gaudere: et gloriosa beatae Mariae semper Virginis intercessione a praesenti liberari tristitia, et aeterna perfrui laetitia. Per Dominum Nostrum Jesum Christum, Filium tuum, qui tecum vivit et regnat in unitate Spiritus Sancti Deus. Amen.

So there probably was a very kind thought behind the sending of the card, but no relenting.

All best wishes for the Epiphany.

Yours affectionately,
Columba, O.S.B.

The end of Europe's war seems in sight, we must *all* pray for true Peace.

1. For the fate of this project, see C.C.E.'s letter of 19 January 1943, above.
2. John Barnabas Sandeman, O.S.B.; cf. C.C.E.'s letter of 16 June 1942, above.
3. Ildefonso Schuster, *The Sacramentary (Liber Sacramentorum)*, trans. Arthur Levelis-Marke, 5 vols. (London, 1924).

Yatscombe
10th January 1944 Boar's Hill, Oxford

Dear Columba,

Thank you and Father Barnabas for answering my query. As you say, there was a kind thought behind the card. I am so glad both vols. of Niebuhr arrived after all. He is a man of character who knows his theology, and he has no soft interpretation of it for the modern world.

A.J.T.

Feast of St. Benet Biscop
12 January 1944 Ampleforth

My dear Arnold,

Today is the end of the holiday and so the end of any considerable leisure for some time; therefore I am writing you my thoughts on "*The Nature and Destiny of Man*" helter skelter before being engulfed in the "particulars". I have read only as far as "The destruction of the Catholic synthesis" in Vol. II. Were I to wait till having finished the volume many of my clear judgements on the whole might be forgotten.

It has been an exhilarating experience and helped to shift emphasis. I think the best part of the book is the analysis in the abstract of the Sin of pride. The half conscious, half unconscious will to power. It is nothing new, being extraordinarily well put also by St. Thomas. But R.N. uses the technique of modern psychology very effectively. He is, of course, perfectly right that innate in man is the will to domineer, what St. Thomas calls the excessive desire to exalt oneself beyond creaturehood.

When R.N. gets going on Catholic theology, much as I hate to contradict so learned a man, and your opinion of him, I am afraid for honesty's sake I must proclaim that he is a veritable morass of errors. The funny thing is that what he calls his own view is very often the Catholic one in fact, and then he states a completely misconstrued Thomist or Augustinian or Catholic theology in general, and rightly condemns it. But it was not Catholic.

1. R.N. says that the Catholic view of original sin is one of privation rather than one of corruption. True, if by corruption he meant Reformation and I suppose Calvinist theology: total corruption. *But* we mean privation of that wonderful thing 'original justice' which included the loss of *Integrity*—that key word, not I think even mentioned in R.N.—and this is the equivalent of his section VII, Vol. I, Man as sinner (*i.e. still*). We are according to Catholic doctrine still prone to sin, even after having returned by God's loving mercy to grace. Yes, even prone to mortal sin. But by this same grace—with God all things are possible, as today's gospel says—we can avoid mortal sin.

2. It follows from the above, in all books of Catholic doctrine, St. Augustine etc. that this state of perfection which we are in, please God, is perfect in a very limited sense. To say that either St. Augustine or St. Thomas would hold the following: "sins which remain are 'venial' rather than 'mortal'" (Vol II, P. 140) is simply not true. The whole point of confession is to elicit sorrow for mortal sin and receive pardon. This is the strangest accusation from the Protestant angle.

3. Consequently he seems to me to misjudge the Catholic attitude towards "perfection", "Image of God" and so on. No Catholic following the Church's teaching would dream of imagining himself perfect in fact, or safely so until in the arms of God. (P. 146 Vol. II) Neither St. Thomas nor any other Catholic would dream of believing we got absolute conformity with God. Man's life is continuously FREE to follow or to refuse God's will. The grace is there but it does not force us.

[The odd thing is that I am stating what R.N. calls his doctrine, yet I have known it all my life as a perfectly normal Catholic.]

4. Then the problem of Predestination and Free will. The only presentable statement of it is the Catholic one as he more or less admits (c.p. 121, Vol. II), and then he boggles at the fact that all the ends do not fit. When in all the rest of the volumes he rather delights in belittling intellect. And so do we. We of all people admit mystery; we do not claim to rationalise all the revealed truths and leave out those we can't. We just try and understand as best we may.

5. His attitude towards the Church as such is very interesting. I do think,

however, that it is derived more from unconscious Protestant prejudice than he thinks.

a. We do not claim to have all truth. All that the Church claims is to *preserve* what was revealed. It claims no power of positively creating new truths. Infallibility is a negative power of not mistaking the truths passed on from the Apostles and Christ. And when I read R.N. it gave me great sadness to think that if he were right then everyone else must have been wrong; all these centuries, and therefore, how absolutely necessary in the historical order for some extrinsic guide.

b. Again, of course, we do not think the Church 'perfect' in the sense he makes us. We know how imperfect it is, both in its Popes, priests and layfolk. But it has this limited perfection of aiming at it, and being linked with God through grace.

c. Nor, as you know if R.N. does not, does the visible Church claim an exclusive list of all the saved. She, the Church, is a battered ship, her sailors are poor folk, history proves how poor. She is immersed in history, as R.N. truly said, she suffers, she sins. But Christ loves her and gives many in her much grace. Her members are very conscious of sin, of their own sins; so much so that the world is often shocked by her austerities. Of course, she is tempted to pride, but that does not disprove her mission, it only proves her humanity, just as her crown of saints proves God with her, just as her stability in storm proves the same.

d. I acclaim the title of Vicar of Christ for the Pope. Anyone who does Christ's work could be so called, but he who is preeminently doing his work might especially. It is a tremendous and terrifying truth that we can be instruments of God even in a small way. Such a title would humble and not exalt, just as the title of priest does. Fancy being a priest, a mediator between God and men. Yet the truth is there, as we see it.

To say we deify the Church either in theory or in fact is not true. All men may be saved. Many a time I must have written to you saying how sure I was that you were in the love of God so long as you were in good faith. Those who have been set before us by the Church, the saints, have shown most universal love and special tenderness for those outside the Church.

Truth is a fierce thing and, though we would be the last to claim the last word, we do claim that truth is one; and though what we know is limited, it is true. That accounts for the horror among the saints for heresy from the beginning of the Church—e.g. St. Ignatius of Antioch[1]—to this day. It also accounts for the excesses when fallible men confuse the untruth with the person holding it and perhaps in good faith. For instance, I have a horror of what I call the errors in this, in many ways, fine book. That is why I felt very sad reading parts of it.

Looking back on this I find it a veritable outburst, but I hope in charity. He holds one view, I hold the opposite about the Catholic Church. But his theology, when not imputing things to the Church, seems very Catholic. Curiously his view of mysticism seems almost Buddhist. The Catholic view is not *unity* of mystic with God, but *union*. He chooses the late German mystics for his texts and they are notoriously exaggerated in their statement on "unity"; but even they can be exonerated from holding such a view, while the mainstream: St. Augustine, St. Bernard, St. Teresa, St. John of the Cross and St. Francis of Sales are quite clear on the point.

Well, even if I had more to say, I had better stop, as you can't possibly have more time to read!

Will this upset you? I hope not. The time of milk for babes has gone. You must be fed on the strong meat of the beginning of truth.

Yours affectionately,
Columba Cary-Elwes, O.S.B.

1. Saint Ignatius of Antioch (ca. 35–ca. 107); Bishop of Antioch, martyred at Rome; author of surviving letters long the subject of debate between Catholic and Protestant scholars; he warned against a Docetic heresy and insisted on the reality of both the divinity and the humanity of Christ.

Ampleforth Abbey
York

13 January 1944

My dear Arnold,

When all is said on the theoretical side to disprove the statements of R. N. upon the Church, there is something to be said for them in fact.

We do tend to be so overjoyed with grace and the new life, the regeneration, that we forget sin.

We do tend to be blind to those big social sins, the community sins and confess little peccadillos.

We do tend to consider ourselves as the only ones with truth and all else error.

We do tend to think that when we have our moral theology books, the last word has been said.

Whereas, we are smeared with present sin. We are not sufficiently on fire against the mighty injustices which we have a share in allowing. We do forget that others are seeking the light and do find some, to which we are blind, at least temporarily.

So please counter yesterday's letter with this. He, R. N., is a brave man who is trying to break the bonds of mere traditionalism; in that he is much to be praised. Truly we must live more by love, more by humility, more by trust as well as faith which is a firm hold on revealed truth.

Yours ever,
Columba, O.S.B.

7 Trevor Street
London, S.W.7

17 January 1944

Dear Columba,

I was overjoyed to get your second letter because the first had left me rather sad—if even you were touched by that Pharisaism which, I am sure, is not only not an inevitable accompaniment of Catholicism but is a first-class sin against its principles, but which, all the same, does seem to be a sin to which Catholics are particularly prone. If they could all say to themselves daily what you have written to me in that second letter, Catholicism might quickly achieve its hopes and expectations of converting the world—breaking down, by love and humility, the wall which now, alas, divides so many Catholics from non-Catholics who are wrestling, in their own way, with the world's sins and sufferings.

Yes, Niebuhr is a brave man pioneering in the wilderness, and therefore, as you say, he is much to be praised.

Yesterday (Sunday) afternoon I talked to a group of Westminster boys on what H. G. Wells would call "the shape of things to come", and got comfort and encouragement from being able to get into touch with them and give them something. I started thinking about what I should say when I was walking back up Sloane Street to 7 Trevor Street from a fire-watching night at the office, and I was then quite defeated in trying to turn my mind broody and creative—being imprisoned in one of those self-centred states of anguish in which I often start the day. But after breakfast I did break out of it, partly by praying for other people in trouble—for one, that poor young farmer at Ganthorpe who has lost his wife—and partly by taking pen in hand and putting a blank sheet of paper under my nose after breakfast. The battle is severe, and I am often forced to the ground, but so far God has helped me, each time, to get up again and go on.

Yours affectionately,
Arnold

2 February 1944 Ampleforth
Feast of the Presentation

My dear Arnold,

Just a few scraps of thoughts, partly to show you I think much about you, and also to carry on this analysis of pride.

Would you concur with this? We have set up a logical structure which is logically sound, and answers all attacks on the logical plane. This we had to do out of charity to the logicians and in defense of our own fold who might be led astray by false logicians. But we suffer from the danger of thinking that this scaffolding, this outwork is the City of God, when it, the City of God is really a compound of the power of Christ and visible men working, they through an organisation, which in essentials he founded. We are in danger of confounding an outwork of this organisation with the thing itself.

Few will enter the Church by the narrow gate of logic, though it must be there. Many will enter through the wide avenue of Charity lined with trees of humility.

I must stop as I have much to do.

In union of love of God,

Columba, O.S.B.

Saint Wilfrid's House
6 February 1944 Ampleforth College, York

Mrs. Toynbee came in today and said she would not write a statement of her side of the story concerning the break between her and Arnold. She told me to record the following:

a. That the facts as recorded in A.J.T.'s M.S. can bear a different interpretation more favorable to her.

b. That the reason there given that she wished to lead a higher life and so broke away, is not true.[1]

Columba Cary-Elwes, O.S.B.

1. This is a memorandum, not sent to A.J.T.

23 February 1944 7 Trevor Street, S.W.7

Dear Columba,

I have added you to my prayers as well as my praise. I can't help feeling that it is a kind of private joke between God and me that I should be presuming to pray for you. But I know, of course, that, while you seem to me—and indeed are—at a very different spiritual level from myself, no human being is good enough in God's sight to be able to do without the prayers of any other human being. So I override my shyness of praying for you, and allow myself the happiness of doing it.

Yes, I meant you to keep the manuscript.[1] It will be a unique one, as you are the only person to whom I could write on paper, uncensored, my prayers exactly as I pray them.

As you see, there are two main things for which I pray for God's help: (i) to have no hostile or resentful feelings towards anyone, but only loving ones; (ii) that my love may be as pure as possible, by which I mean: disinterested and, as far as necessary, self-sacrificing, not self-regarding or seeking consolation or satisfaction for myself.

I find (a) comparatively easy, but (b) enormously difficult.

Also, the estrangement between me and Rosalind and the break-up of our family is a wound that won't heal, and I am puzzled about how to take it. It is certainly an evil and therefore cannot, in itself, be God's will; it is an evil of the moral and spiritual kind, not of the material kind which one might understand being subjected to as a means of education and purification. Does submitting to God's will mean acquiescing in something that cannot be God's will? This baffles me.

I was on the point of putting pen to paper to write you this letter on Sunday night (in the office, where I am writing now) while I was fire-watching, when the sirens went, and a few minutes after, I came within a few yards distance of being removed from the map. It was a mighty bang. God Bless You.

Yours affectionately,
Arnold

1. Returned; whereabouts now unknown; see A.J.T.'s letter of 30 March 1944, below.

7 Trevor Street
12 March 1944 London, S.W.7

Dear Columba,

Your letter of the 24th February [1] did help me a lot. What you are getting at is, I think, that one's priority concern ought to be about what is most in our power and is therefore our chief responsibility, and that is how we ourselves behave—which we can to a large extent control—and not what happens to us from outside, which is hardly in our control at all. I am now trying to look at it in this way when I am crushed and almost driven mad by the awful evil of my family being broken up, and Rosalind and me being estranged from each other, and Veronica having been involved in this largely by my act, when my will is only to do her good, as hers is to do me good. If it *is* beyond human power to put this right, then I suppose it isn't capitulating to evil, but is doing the only good left to be done, if one tries to take the evil fact in a good way.

What I am trying to do is to take it wholly with love. I am under no temptation not to love Rosalind, and this is, I think, very hard on Veronica, for whom it would have been much easier if I had turned against Rosalind and been filled with animus towards her (not that Veronica has ever shown any sign of wanting me to do this!). What I do find supremely difficult is to love Rosalind so purely that, if it were finally proved that the best thing for her is to be completely parted from me in this world, I should want this to be so in spite of its being to my own destruction. In aiming at love that is 100 per cent real love and naught per cent selfish desire, one is aiming, I suppose, at love as only God has it. One can never reach that completely in this world, and never begin to approach it without asking for, and being given, God's grace.

The other day I was dining with an old friend of Rosalind's and mine whom I hadn't seen since the catastrophe, who knows the story down to, but not including, my having asked Veronica to marry me. She is a person of character and religion, not a Catholic, but with a sister-in-law who is a convert. When I told her that I would mend the break in my marriage with Rosalind if I could, she said to me: "Who is her spiritual adviser? Why don't you go straight to him and have it out with him? In a sense it is he, not Rosalind, with whom you are dealing." I daresay, in what she said, there is a certain amount of Protestant misconception of the relation of a spiritual adviser to the person advised. I imagine that, in theory anyway, he tells her the principles that apply to her case but leaves the actual application to her conscience and judgment. All the same, I have no doubt that Father Steuart [2] has been a very important factor in Rosalind's relation to me, as she certainly believes that all the steps that she has taken have been approved by him.

I am a good deal exercised about this, because I do feel, as I am sure you do, that trying to accept God's will in evil that we can't mend does not dispense one from doing every mortal thing in one's power to try and mend the evil. Therefore, if there is here a stone left unturned, I ought to turn it.

Till lately, it wouldn't have been likely to help much if I had had an interview with Father Steuart, because I did have an animus against him, though not against

Rosalind. I felt it was the old story of the Jesuit being given a welcome in the house (I did always give him a sincere welcome) and then making mischief. Happily, in my prayers, over many months, I have now conquered that, by putting to myself (i) that I have only had a second-hand account of Father Steuart's attitude, and, though I am sure Rosalind didn't in any way consciously misrepresent it, it would be only human for her to want to believe that her action was covered by Father Steuart's authority, so that I ought to suspend judgment about his attitude in the absence of any sure knowledge of it; (ii) that no doubt Father Steuart, whatever line he may have taken, was aiming only at Rosalind's good (whether he was right or wrong in his judgment of what was her true good being a different question, one of the head and not of the heart); and, as what I want to want is Rosalind's pure good, I am aiming at the same aim as he is, and so have no quarrel with him; (iii) then, when I have meditated on these points, I turn my will towards embracing Father Steuart in my love for my fellow-creatures.

I could now, I believe, meet Father Steuart without anything but good will towards him, so that the meeting wouldn't be shadowed by ill-feeling, as it might have been at an earlier stage.

This being so, I should go to see him without hesitation, if it weren't for the effect on Veronica. To her, it would be bound to cause very great anxiety and distress, because the only reason for the meeting would be the possibility of reopening the whole question. If there were a real possibility of mending the breach between Rosalind and me, I should feel that this was the first consideration, while feeling very deeply my sin in having involved Veronica in this suffering. But if nothing were likely to come of it, it would be useless and wrong to expose Veronica to this pain. In the present situation, the suffering which is bound to fall on Rosalind, Veronica and me does, I believe, fall mainly on me, as I pray every night that it may do. I don't want to shift the burden to other shoulders out of weakness or selfishness.

If I did see Father Steuart, I should have the following things to say to him:—

(i) I do love Rosalind whole-heartedly, and am heartily sorry for my sins and shortcomings towards her in the past, which I try to see and amend.

(ii) Though I am not, I believe, likely to become a Catholic myself, I have nothing but good-will towards Rosalind's Catholic life and her Catholic friends.

(iii) Though our civil marriage is a true marriage for me, I recognize that, in default of previous baptism, it is not one for her under canon law, and I should be glad to put this right for her by our having a Catholic religious marriage, if the other obstacles to a restoration of our marriage were removed.

(iv) The one condition—and of course this is a big one—that I ask for on my side is that our marriage shall mean sharing life and home. (I don't mean by this that we should be under the same roof 365 days in the year, or that I should be in the relation to her which she has called "possessive dependence".)

Don't try and answer this letter in a hurry, but I should like your advice. It may be that I am merely following a will-of-the-wisp.

Yours affectionately,
Arnold

1. Missing.
2. See R.T.'s letter of 17 June 1943, above.

30 March 1944 7 Trevor Street, S.W.7

Dear Columba,

Thank you, with all my heart, for your letter written on Passion Sunday,[1] and for the copy of the *Beginning of Goodness*[2] which you sent me on Saint Gregory's day and which I have been reading in snatches (as it was, I think, written to be read).

In order to find the peace that you pray that I may find, I have to do two things: (i) submit myself to the will of God in general; (ii) get light on what the will of God is in this particular case.

As a means to this second end, I must see myself through Rosalind's eyes. In your letter you lifted a corner of the veil with a characteristically tender hand, but, as you say, you haven't, yourself, seen the whole of that picture. I must try to see the whole of it, notwithstanding the pain, because I think, if I can see it truly, I shall learn either that it is best for Rosalind that I should pass out of her life (and then I can concentrate on the task of loving her unselfishly enough to renounce her, a very difficult task but possible to strive for if we were sure that it was right) or else that it is best for her that our marriage should be restored if I can change myself in such-and-such a way (and then I can concentrate on changing myself in that way, and grapple with the terrible problem that would raise about the relations between Veronica and me). It is quite true that I couldn't make a success of marrying Veronica if I still loved Rosalind in the earthly way, and of course, if I have to aim at loving Rosalind in the purely heavenly way, I don't know where that may lead me: it may not be compatible with ordinary life in the world.

Between writing and getting your answer, I was advised by the Murray's family doctor, Mrs. Nasmyth, to see a psycho-analyst, Mrs. Payne,[3] to whom Rosalind went more than once in the past, with good results, and who thus knows the earlier chapters of the story. I am going to her first because I think she can help me to see the rest of the picture of myself through Rosalind's eyes; I may go to see Father Steuart later. Meanwhile, in case she wants to see documents, could you send me by registered post my very long letter to you, the poem, and the prayers? I think it is best, if one does see a doctor, to tell him all one can. I shall send them back to you eventually. Thank you and God Bless You.

Yours affectionately,
Arnold

1. Missing.
2. Compare C.C.E.'s letter of 23 August 1943, above.
3. Sylvia May Payne (1880–1976); chairman of directors of Institute of Psycho-Analysis, (1944–47); "The Myth of the Barnacle Goose," *International Journal of Psycho-Analysis*, Vol. 10 (1929), pp. 218–27. See A.J.T.'s acknowledgment in *A Study of History*, X: 237.

4 April 1944 7 Trevor Street, S.W.7

Dear Columba,

Your letter,[1] with its packet, arrived just in time for me to leave the papers with Dr. Payne—at my first appointment with her this afternoon—to read over the Easter Holidays.

I liked her and felt confidence in her power to help me. She won't undermine my religion; I am pretty sure she won't try.

God Bless You.
Yours affectionately,
Arnold

1. Missing.

16 May 1944 Ampleforth

My dear Arnold,

It is too long since we have written to each other. The last was over your going to see the psychologist doctor. I have been praying hard that this resulted in some relaxation of mental pain; in some decision, or some hope of reconstruction.

Then on Sunday, in the *Observer*, I saw that your "child" Chatham House was growing;[1] that tomorrow there was going to be a grand opening of the second house. You will be there and all your friends—save me. But I rejoice in your success in that from here. Space is of no moment.

The war is reaching, has reached the final stage in Europe unless some unforeseen calamity occurs. England, at the moment, to me is like a lot of people probing about in the dark, whispering to one another. The Germans might yet save their souls by letting us in; but I fear me it will have to be a bloody business.

Perhaps it is fitting that the slaughter should occur during Paschal time when we remember with gratitude that God has promised and shown us a better Resurrection.

My silence is partly due to my having to rush to Bournemouth at Easter, and on my return being piled up with odd jobs I should have done before. It is not due to forgetting you and all your burdens.

I know a book which would give you happy relief and relaxation, the biography of that valiant and happy man G.K.C., recently published by Sheed & Ward, and written by Maisie Ward.[2] It is a beautiful piece of work.

Ampleforth as peaceful as ever, a little more isolated, though old boys come in from everywhere, including occupied Europe, for a few hours, and then vanish again into the "daylight night" which England is.

We are full to bursting—with boys. Next autumn there will be 40 more boys than we have ever had before. I think it is a sign that God wants us to do this work. There is no doubt that England will need men who believe in God, in right doing, in values above money-grubbing.

I am aghast at the Machiavellian technique of Stalin even as it is put in our very polite press. To call it Machiavellian is giving it too subtle a name. There is more effrontery than that. Fancy, after having signed the Atlantic Charter, running its relations with Poland by means of newspaper articles in the Sunday *Observer*. I have a great love and longing for the Russian people but an intense fear for Europe from the Russian leaders. Whence all the fratricidal divisions in Yugoslavia Greece, etc?[3] I can't help seeing the hand of the Soviet. Perhaps you can allay my fears.

I must stop now.

Yours affectionately,
Columba, O.S.B.

1. Number 9, St. James's Square, had been given to Chatham House by Sir Henry Price, a member of the Council; both No. 9 and No. 10 had been designed, ca. 1736, by Henry Flitcroft (1697–1769), the architect, probably, of No. 10 Downing St. The extension of Chatham House was formally opened on 18 May 1944.

2. Maisie Ward, *Gilbert Keith Chesterton* (New York, 1943).

3. In Yugoslavia, Josip Broz Tito, partisan leader, was at odds with the royalist resistance leader Drazha Mihailovich. In Greece, the rivalry between the National Liberation Front (EAM) and the government in exile was to result in the revolution of 3 December 1944, which followed the German withdrawal.

19 May 1944 7 Trevor Street, S.W.7

Dear Columba,

I was so glad to get your letter of the 16th. I hope the sudden rush to Bournemouth didn't mean that your father was ill again. Perhaps you were just getting in a visit to your parents "while weather permitted".

I am in the middle of my treatment by my psycho-analyst, Mrs. Payne; she is not giving me a full-dress analysis but what I believe they call "therapeutic talks". I like these and have confidence in her, and she has already succeeded in relaxing the tension very considerably, though of course I have relapses.

She thinks, as I know you do and Rosalind's parents do, that it is unlikely, to the extreme, that Rosalind's mind and feelings will change, and what she is trying to do is to help me to arrive at a psychological acceptance of the loss, and hence a release for starting a new chapter of life with Veronica. She says I am "suffering from a sense of guilt" (by which she means an irrational sense of guilt, not that I am guiltless). She thinks that my present wound, in addition to its own formidableness, has drawn to itself the effects of earlier wounds—particularly the time, when I was 19, when my Father went out of his mind and my Mother became entirely absorbed in him, so that I then virtually lost my Mother (with whom I had had a particularly close relation till then). She brought me to see a syllogism in my unconscious mind. "My Father got my Mother's attention by going out of his mind; if I go out of my mind now I shall get my wife's attention back." It is like the false reasoning of savages which the anthropologists tell one about. It is a great help to catch this savage part of oneself at its tricks.

All this is being useful. It doesn't touch religion or morality, but perhaps it will help one to apply them rationally, more free from irrational associations and phobias. I am going on with this treatment, and though I can't yet, any more than before, see the issue out of my afflictions, I am at any rate no longer stuck in an impasse in which the tension was piling up.

Yes, it is an unpleasant moment, while we are all waiting for the storm to burst and the heavy casualties to begin. At Ampleforth, I am afraid, you have so many hostages given to fortune.

I am glad that Monte Cassino is now out of the fighting.[1] It already meant much to me, long before I knew Ampleforth. It has been ruined before; it will rise again.

About Stalin, I think you are hard on him, as you know, and oversuspicious. His terms to Finland were exceedingly moderate;[2] his proclamation to the Roumanians[3] was just what we would have wished, and, towards Poland, he has claimed a frontier line which, after all, was laid down not by him, but by British experts at a time when Russia was weak and helpless, as being the right frontier, on ethnographical grounds, between Russia and Poland.[4] As for the Greeks and Jugoslavs, they have suffered from violent internal dissensions for centuries, long before Russia had anything to do with them. One doesn't need to postulate a Russian factor in order to account for the present situation in either country. My own belief is that Russia will not seek to go beyond her 1940 frontiers *unless* there is a revival of the old "cordon sanitaire".[5] It would only be in that case that she might conceivably try to defend herself by taking the offensive first. In the last resort, all depends on whether Stalin and the capitalist core of the Republican party in the U.S. can or can't get on together. If they can't we shall have a third world war and then a Pax Americana or Pax Russica. What we are fighting for now is another chance of building a world order which, instead of being imposed by a single Power (Germany, if she were to win this war, or America or Russia if there is a third war), will be cooperative and will therefore leave room for a great deal of liberty in the world as well as the necessary minimum of order. Don't let us force Russia to play the part of Rome in spite of herself. She could be poked into doing that, but it would be very perverse of us to poke her.

Well, I shall give you further news of myself when I see how this treatment turns out. I am very thankful for your prayers, and I do pray for you every day, very humbly.

Yours affectionately,
Arnold

1. Monte Cassino fell 18 May 1944.

2. On 12 March 1940, after the three months war, Finland accepted a peace, negotiated at Moscow, in which the Karelian Isthmus, Viborg, and territories aggregating 16,000 square miles were ceded to Russia, the Finns to be resettled in Finland.

3. Vyacheslav Molotov, on 2 April 1944, in announcing the entry of the Soviet army into Roumania, stated that the Soviet government "does not pursue the aim of acquiring any part of Roumanian territory, or of altering the social structure of Roumania as it exists today" (*The Times* [3 April 1944]).

4. The Curzon Line of 8 December 1919.
5. "Quandoque bonus dormitat Homerus," Horace, *Ars Poetica*, 359.

7 Trevor Street
26 May 1944 S.W.7

Dear Columba,

Here is a letter to you from Bridget[1] which is characteristic of her nature. The only reason why the cheque is mine and not hers is because I managed to insist on that. My only fear is that, what with what you have been doing anyway for years, this may monopolize (if in such things there can be monopolies) almost the whole of your offices.

My treatment is going well, with certain inevitable set backs that haven't stopped the general movement forward. Dr. Payne's general line, as I have said, is to help me to accept the present situation (i) as, in all human probability irreversible, (ii) not as the equivalent of my own death, which is how I have been taking it, but as a loss which, though very grievous and formidable, still needn't and mustn't stop me from starting a new chapter of life. She is also trying to help me to see Rosalind not as a goddess, but as a human being with limitations and frailties like my own. If I do see that R. may have taken her religion in a partly mistaken way, that won't, of course, turn me against religion in, say, you or in Bridget.

God Bless You.
Yours affectionately,
Arnold

1. Bridget R. Reddin; cf. C.C.E.'s letter of 11 June 1941, above. The letter requested a novena of masses in honour of Saint Thomas More for the spiritual and temporal welfare of the Toynbee family and particularly "for Mr. Toynbee's intentions."

Saint Wilfrid's House
June 1944 Ampleforth College, York

Dear Arnold,

Just a line to say that I will put all my heart and soul into this prayer of oblation, of petition and of praise and of reparation I am doing in the Mass with you and for you all.

These are the crucial days, not only the invasion but all the stirring of minds planning peace. Here again I am with you, and would not hurt you for a moment. The Americans have begun, and well, to enquire as to the true form the organs of peace should take. It is a subject we never broached except in those discussions on Sovereignty. I feel it requires first a disentangling of what is internal politics and what is international, and that these things have not been clearly set out. Once nations little and big can see that certain things are not purely internal but international then you can begin to create the necessary machinery—e.g. international trade perhaps should be internationally controlled and not be individualistic. We are so far behind our desires in our understanding of these things.

God give you the gifts of the Holy Spirit; wisdom, understanding.

Yours always affectionately,
Columba, O.S.B.

P.S. Hugh Montgomery[1] has just wired from the Vatican "*Laqueus contritus est et nos liberati sumus*," were his words. I think Cassino was worth Rome[2]—it really came to that, but very, very sad.

1. "Then at the Vatican studying for the priesthood and acting as a liaison between the British government and Pius XII, who had become his close friend when Montgomery was in the Foreign Service in Germany and Eugenio Pacelli was Papal Nuncio." (C.C.E.) Compare C.C.E.'s letter of 7 October 1941, above.

2. A spoonerism for Rome was worth Monte Cassino; *"Paris vaut bien une Messe."*

3 July 1944 — 20 St. Stephens Gardens, W.2

Dear Rev. Father,

Thank you for your letter. Yes I wish we had got in touch long ago, because Mrs. Toynbee talked out her mind to me before she left Oxford, when it was all happening. I got the impression then that she resented Mr. Toynbee's friendship with Miss B and I thought it was pure imagination. It was only last summer I discovered that Miss B cared for Mr. Toynbee and that that really was the cause of Mrs. Toynbee's annoyance. I knew that Miss B was indispensable to Mr. Toynbee and could see no way out of the difficulty. I also got the impression, in spite of anything Mrs. Toynbee might say, that she cares for Mr. Toynbee and I always hoped that after the war, when we got away from the war work she would come round. I told Mr. Toynbee that and tried to keep up his spirits, but the tide was against me. He has been psycho-analysed into an engagement with Miss B in spite both of his heart and his conscience. He said to me a few days previously that Mrs. Toynbee had not done the right thing and he did not want to clinch it. However it is done now and humanly speaking it is only wishful thinking to think that it can be undone. I have told Our Lady I can do no more and it must be her responsibility. I am afraid I don't agree with you that there can be any possibility of a conversion if there is a second marriage, for two reasons. First because Mr. Toynbee feels that the Church has taken his wife from him (did he get any chance at all to defend his case?); and secondly even if he did discover that the Roman Catholic religion was right his wife would see to it that he did not become a Catholic.

I feel sad about the conversion.[1] I have been praying for it for 14 years in the hope that the Study of History would serve God's cause. I made a sort of vocation of it, but my prayers must have been presumptions. But that is not the reason that makes me go on wishing for the impossible. It is having to watch the heart of so kind and gentle a person being broken and feeling that the Catholic Church will get blamed. I also feel that Mrs. Toynbee has no idea of the moral consequences to herself and her children of what she has done, and that it ought to have been pointed out to her. If it had she might have thought twice.

Besides plagueing Our Lady all day and every day I have been treking out to Fr. Vincent McNabb's grave every Sunday and asking him to make it his first miracle. It will have to be a big one, I'm afraid, but we have till nearly the end of the year, I think, to go on praying.

I don't know whether Mr. Toynbee has much use for the Catholic point of view on politics but I think from the spiritual point of view your letters help him.

I hope you will forgive me for all this, it is such a relief to be able to talk about one's worries.

Yours very sincerely,
Bridget R. Reddin

1. "Bridget Reddin watched with growing interest Arnold's increasing concern for spiritual things, the Church in particular, as the work on *A Study of History* progressed. She was a simple Irish Catholic." (C.C.E.)

9 July 1944 7 Trevor Street, S.W.7

Dear Columba,

I have been meaning for a long time to write but have been occupied with my daily round: doing my business in the office, going to my psycho-analyst and so on.

I had been thinking whether I shall ask to come to Ampleforth again for my summer leave, and have decided not to ask to this year because of the nearness and sharpness of the associations with Ganthorpe. My relation with Ampleforth is, as you know, one of the things I prize most in this life, and I shall never let go of it, but I believe it is better not to come this year. That Alice-through-the-looking glass view of the Sheepwalk and Slingsby Banks[1] might undo me while I am still struggling to gain my spiritual independence—not, of course, independence of God, but independence of human beings and objects, like Rosalind and Ganthorpe, which one can only gain through dependence on God.

Will you be passing through London at the end of the term? Bridget, as well as I, hopes you are, for, if you are, she has asked me to say that she would like to see you (I think, to say something to you about Rosalind and me).

The psycho-analyst is helping me: in the first place, she has helped me relax the tension which went on growing until I couldn't see any issue from it but a catastrophic one; in the second place, she is helping me towards psychological maturity, which, if I can attain it, may, in time, I think, help me to take the fences that lie ahead of me.

The flying bombs are a strange experience:[2] life is quite ordinary, except that one does not know from moment to moment whether oneself, and one's friends and colleagues, may not be suddenly obliterated. This is something that one soon learns to digest, and it is wholesome food for people brought up in the Victorian age, as it contains an antidote for the materialistic security that makes one forget God.

Besides that, it is a personal boon to me, because I find I am not at all frightened and am able to do my work just as usual, and this is balm for a wound from which I have been suffering since, during the first Blitz, Rosalind wanted me to throw up my government work, which was then in Oxford, and join her in London. I refused, because I felt I ought to stick to my job, and she taunted me with being afraid of the Blitz. The barb stuck, but now, when my job requires me to be in London, I find I am not afraid, and this is healing that particular wound.

I don't know whether Lawrence is still in this country or is in the Battle of Caen.[3] When last I heard of him he was expecting to cross at any moment. He is much more prosperous than he was a year or so ago. He has proved a good officer, and has been fortified by this.

How are your parents? Perhaps you will be passing through London to visit them during the holidays. I shall be here till the 4th or 5th August, when I shall be going to stay for a fortnight with Constance Howard's mother[4] in Cumberland. I hope we may meet either before or after that.

I pray for you, as you asked, but with diffidence and humility, every night.

God Bless You.
Yours affectionately,
Arnold

1. Sheepwalk and Slingsby Banks: near Slingsby visible from Ganthorpe.

2. The flying bombs were first launched on London from cross-Channel emplacements on 13 June 1944.

3. On the day of this letter, British and Canadian troops captured Caen. Lawrence recalls that at the time he was "nearby—actually Caumont, next door." He was commanding a troop of Churchill tanks.

4. Lady Constance Howard (1898–1964); daughter of the tenth Earl of Carlisle and cousin of Rosalind; a member of the Chatham House staff (1937–52). A.J.T. wrote her obituary in *The Times* (11 September 1964): "Though Constance Howard had not had a university education, her family was the equivalent of a university for the study of contemporary affairs at first hand, and this informal but effective way of getting familiarity with current history proved its worth when she entered this field of intellectual work." A contributor to the *Survey of International Affairs* (see her "The United States of America," pt. 7 of *Survey of International Affairs, 1939–1946: The Eve of War, 1939*, pp. 587–618). A.J.T. lodged with Lady Constance and Heather Harvey during much of the three-year period when the divorce was pending.

As from 7 Trevor Street, S.W.7
(Oxford & Cambridge University Club
Pall Mall, S.W.1)

14 July 1944

Dear Columba,

Our letters crossed: we were each thinking of the other.

My course is set on trying to recover the wish to live, and to learn, late in life, to stand on my own feet. This is something that I must try to do anyway, whether Rosalind and I come back to each other or whether we are parted irrevocably and I eventually marry Veronica. But there is no door shut on Rosalind, and there will not be till the three years have run out. If, at any time, our marriage could be restored on the terms of a proper marriage—I mean sharing a common home and life, and sharing them on a footing of equality—I would open my arms to Rosalind, both because I love her and because I should think this right. And Veronica would think it right too—given those conditions—though this would bring great suffering on her, and on me at having been the bringer of it.

Also, if the spiritual side of the marriage could be restored, I would make the legal side perfect for Rosalind by being re-married to her with a Catholic marriage. Marriage, as I see it, has, in order to be right, to be right both spiritually and legally in the sight of both parties. My present civil marriage with Rosalind is legally right in my eyes but not in hers; therefore, I would remedy it legally for her, if this were the only obstacle to its being restored.

The other side—which I call the spiritual side—only comes right if one shares a common home and life on a footing of equality—by which I mean that neither must treat the other as a heretic or an outsider; each must love the other with a love that can embrace the other's creed and outlook, even if one does not have the same creed and outlook oneself.

About myself and Catholicism, I have thought a great deal in retrospect, and I don't believe I ever could have, or could, become a Catholic myself, because I am a Protestant about the central point of Catholic doctrine: the Real Presence and the powers of the Priest—powers which all flow from his ability to perform the miracle of the Mass. My love for Rosalind and my submissiveness to her will and her leadership have been so great that it is extraordinary that I did not follow in her wake. The temptation was very strong, because being married to her was my most precious possession in this life. My inability to perjure myself, even for the sake of saving that, was, I feel certain, something good in me.

But if I am not, and perhaps never could be, a Catholic, I certainly am, and shall remain, a philo-Catholic—for Rosalind's sake, for your sake, for Ampleforth's sake, and for the sake of my Catholic friends (such as the Mathew brothers)[1] and the Catholic saints whom I reverence and admire. Where reason and conscience forbid one to cross a gulf, Love can still carry one across. I can be, and am, philo-Catholic for love of Catholic persons—thereby following, I think, the genius of Christianity, which has taught us that our personal relations with a person, Christ, can carry us beyond the points at which reason and conscience give out.

I am not being turned anti-Catholic by the fact that Rosalind's conversion has turned out tragically for me, because I think this is not the fault of Catholicism but is the result of the interaction of Catholicism with Rosalind's character. There is nothing in Catholicism—nor in my attitude towards Catholicism—that *need* have produced this result, and I do not know of any Catholic friend of Rosalind's or mine who isn't sorry at what has happened.

You see, I am not embittered and haven't hardened my heart. I wouldn't, even if I could, recover the will to live by turning savage. But I haven't yet found a way—I am still wrestling with my problem: relaxed from extreme tension, thanks to my kind and helpful psycho-analyst, but still sick. At least though, I am now making a fight for it instead of lying paralysed and waiting for either insanity or suicide to swoop on me—which was my previous state.

How quaint it is, writing a letter like this with the alerts going on and off. Now I shall walk home across the Parks and go to bed.

I am very sorry I shan't see you. God Bless You.

Yours affectionately,
Arnold

1. The Mathew brothers: Archbishop David Mathew (1902–75); Bishop in ordinary to H.M. Forces (1954–63); Archbishop of Apamea; Assistant at the Pontifical Throne; historian of the English Reformation and post-Reformation; *Lord Acton and His Times* (London, 1968); and Gervase Mathew, O.P. (1905–76); Byzantine scholar; lecturer at Oxford University; fellow worker with G. S. P. Freeman-Grenville in the study of Islamic penetration of East Africa; with David Mathew, *The Reformation and the Contemplative Life* (London, 1934). The Mathew brothers were of an old recusant family.

26 July 1944 7 Trevor Street, S.W.7

Dear Columba,

How splendid that we shall meet now after all, if only for a few hours.

I would have met you at King's X, but I have two men lunching with me, and as it is about work, and one of them is a stranger, I can't put them off, unfortunately.

So come to the *Stationary Office*, on the East side of Prince's Street, running between the Central Hall and Birdcage Walk, at right angle to B.W., at its eastern end. If you have heavyish luggage, bring it round by inner circle, going east from King's X, to Westminster Station—quite close.

Ask for Miss Reddin—I will arrange with her tomorrow—and shall probably be back soon after you arrive. I shall be able to see you off at Waterloo later, and will look up the trains to Bournemouth.

You will find London quite normal: the flying bombs have now been digested by the public.

I have just come in after dinner, and will run out now and post this so as to speed it off first post tomorrow morning.

How much I look forward to seeing you.

Yours affectionately,
Arnold

9 August 1944 7 Trevor Street, S.W.7

Dear Columba,

You nearly saw the last of me, for at 2 : 30 A.M. last Thursday we were blasted by a bomb that fell not much more than eighty yards from the house. It is an odd experience to wake up finding glass and plaster falling all over you. At first it looked a wreck, but the damage turned out not to be serious, and nobody had even a scratch: the worst part of it is the indescribable dirt. Where the bomb actually landed, everything is laid flat.

There is news from Lawrence in Normandy dated 2nd August—quite up to date.

For Rosalind and me to come together again, two things are necessary: on my side, I must grow out of what she called my "possessive dependence" by becoming adult (as my psycho-analyst calls it) or (as I call it) by becoming dependent on God more, and on human beings less. On Rosalind's side, what is necessary is that she should see that the spiritual perfection, which she is so genuinely seeking, is incompatible with spiritual pride and self-will (which are the exact antithesis of being spiritually perfect).

At present I can see only the part and not the whole. I can see that, if Rosalind and I could come together again, that would be right and should be done. But this could—after what has happened—break up Veronica's life (though, in spite of that, Veronica too thinks it would be right). How can good come through the suffering of an innocent and loving person who, through her lovingness, has been involved in Rosalind's and my sin?

My sin was that, after Rosalind had refused me a home, I broke away from her and turned to Veronica. The cause (though not excuse) was that being refused a home where one has a right to have a home gives one an enormous shock. When I recovered from the shock, I opened the door again, as you know, to Rosalind with Veronica's blessing (though it was a dreadful ordeal to her, and cost her a great deal). Except for that time, I haven't, I believe, gravely sinned against Rosalind. What was awkward in me, as a husband, was not wilful sin but the psychological immaturity which I am now trying to remedy by treatment. If, however, what is right did happen, and Rosalind and I came together again, I should have sinned most grievously against Veronica by having broken down the barriers that formerly lay between her and me in the good and affectionate but limited relationship which we used to have. And, as a consequence of that sin (for which Rosalind is, of course, partly responsible, besides me), there would be very great suffering for Veronica and for me.

I am so very glad you saw your brother,[1] even though only for a few hours.

Well, one can only try to do what one sees as right, even if one can't see all the consequences as being right.

Yours affectionately,
Arnold

1. Lieutenant-Colonel Oswald Cary-Elwes (1913–); Lincoln Regiment; in the Special Air Service; often behind enemy lines helping the French underground; *croix de guerre avec palme*.

8 September 1944 20 St. Stephens Gardens, W.2

Dear Rev. Father,

Your letter to Mr. Toynbee which he received yesterday was a terrible blow to him. He came into my room first thing and showed it to me and asked me what I thought had happened to make you change your mind between writing your previous letter and it. I said I had no idea.

He then asked if you meant that while he holds his present convictions he could not (a) be reconciled to his wife and family, (b) be friends with you and the fathers at Ampleforth, all of whom he loves. I said I would write and ask you.

I asked him if he found your friendship a help and he said most emphatically yes, the greatest help, and added something about a saintly person which I can't quote exactly.

I think I told you what Mrs. Toynbee said about your having a good influence on him.

Would you mind sending a line in answer to his queries and please forgive me for bothering you.

Yours sincerely,
Bridget R. Reddin

7 Trevor Street
London S.W.7

20 September 1944

Dear Columba,

Your letter of the 5th September was, of course, as painful for me to read as it was for you to write.[1] Also (but this is only a small point) it took me entirely by surprise, as previous letters and meetings had not given me any expectation of it. I know, from experiences of my own, that things that have long been brewing in the depths of one's psyche sometimes do suddenly erupt, and I expect this is what happened in this case. Inevitably, I had a great shock, and that is one reason why I didn't answer immediately. The other reason was that I was then meditating another interview with Rosalind. I had this last Sunday. I will tell you about it at the end of my letter. Meanwhile, Bridget has shown me your letter to her in answer to one from her to you, and I am now really answering both these letters of yours.

Here, as truthfully and accurately as I can put it, is my own account of my approach to the Catholic Church:—

(i) My first approach was for Rosalind's and Lawrence's sakes after their conversion. But for Rosalind, it seems unlikely that I should have encountered the Church except in the most casual and superficial way. Her conversion, as you know, produced disquiet and foreboding in me.[2] I resolved to overcome these feelings (i) out of loyalty to Rosalind and affection for her (ii) out of concern for Lawrence, because we all know that it is of vital importance for a child's well-being that he should have no sense of any breach of solidarity between his parents. These motives were not, I should say, self-regarding, because at that time I was not acutely aware of any danger of my family breaking up; they were "family regarding": a combination of love for my wife and my child with a sense of my duty to God towards them—a duty which ought to make me able to rise above my traditional Protestant prejudice against Catholicism.

My attitude at this stage must be something quite familiar to members of the Community who are concerned with the School. So many of your boys have one parent who is not a Catholic. If a majority of the non-Catholic parents did not take some such line as this, there would be estrangements and break-ups of families which, I am certain, you would deplore.

(ii) The second stage was that, through making this friendly approach to the Catholic Church for Rosalind's and Lawrence's sake, I came to admire and love it, or (to be more precise) at least one Catholic institution (Ampleforth) and a number of individual Catholics (above all yourself; besides you, many other members of the Community; and also other Catholics outside Ampleforth, such as the Mathew brothers). At Ampleforth I realized that I was at one of the windows through which God's light shines into this world. I felt it when Father Paul took Philip and saved the situation for him.[3] I felt it when I myself was allowed to come and stay in the monastery. I felt it in Father James. I felt it, of course, most intimately and intensely in my friendship with you. It seemed to me that this revelation, through Ampleforth, of some of God's goodness and truth was an unsought and unexpected reward which had been given to me for having taken Rosalind's and Lawrence's conversion with love and sympathy and not with hostility.

The longer I have been in this relation to Ampleforth—and, as you say in your letter to Miss Reddin, I did come right into the heart of Ampleforth and into your heart especially—the more I have felt myself in communion with God, through, and thanks to, Ampleforth. There has been no change in me from a movement of approach to a movement of shearing off. My movement has been one of steadily closer approach, but all the time on what I should call the institutional, as opposed to the doctrinal, plane. On—I don't know whether you yourselves would call it the most important belief, but what is, I imagine, uncontestedly the distinctive belief of Catholicism (in contrast to other forms of monotheism like Protestantism, Judaism and Islam)—I mean the belief in trans-substantiation and the consequent belief in the powers of the priest—there had been no shearing off because there had never been any approach.

Now I know—and not merely know as an external fact but understand, I think, to some extent "from inside", so to speak—that, for Catholics, this distinctive belief, which I do not share, is the foundation and the driving force of the life and works which I admire and love. You are bound to ask me "How can you say that the fruit is good when you do not accept what we Catholics believe to be the roots of the tree on which the fruit grows?" My answer is something like this: "It is not uncommon in this world, where so far there has never been unity in people's beliefs about fundamental things, for us to admire and love the life and works of a person, or an institution, without believing the beliefs which he or they have believed to be the source of the things in them which we admire and love. Catholics are probably in this puzzling predicament in relation to, say, Socrates or the Buddha. It *is* puzzling because (and here I profoundly agree with Catholics and differ from "good pagans") it seems impossible that there can be good life and works without a foundation of true belief. My own explanation of the puzzle is that there *is* a fundamental agreement about truth between myself and the Catholics whom I love and admire, but that this agreement is at a different level from—or, to say what I mean in less contentious terms, through a different medium than—the doctrinal one." If it was solely for me to pronounce on this, I should say, therefore, with complete sincerity, that you and I were of one faith in spite of differing in our beliefs about the distinctive doctrine of the Catholic Church. But of course it is not just for me to say; and you, as a good Catholic, say the opposite emphatically. One of the characteristics of the Catholic Church is that it tests agreement and disagreement sharply and uncompromisingly in doctrinal terms. My attitude is Modernist to the nth degree, and so, for Catholics, it is non-Catholic. Therefore I see that what looks to me like an imperfect and irrational unity between you and me may look to you like an utter and irreconcilable difference when you face the fact of what my doctrinal position is. And if, in this situation, you feel, as you do, that your duty is to break off your relations, and Ampleforth's, with me—well, I know that this is a very painful thing which you are doing because you believe it to be right, so I respect your act, as characteristic of what I love and admire in yourself; and I shall continue to love and admire you while suffering the great pain of this break in the expression, through personal intercourse, of a friendship which has become one of the most precious things in my life.

Now I wonder if you can enter into the inwardness of my non-belief in the distinctive Catholic doctrine (a non-belief which is the negative aspect of a positive belief, unformulatable in doctrinal terms, but nevertheless incompatible with this Catholic doctrine). If I had persuaded myself (and I have an ingenious mind) that I did believe this doctrine, I should have salvaged my relations with you, with Ampleforth and perhaps even with Rosalind—and these are the precious things in my life, not my intellectual prowess, which I use as a gift given me by God to use, without finding in it my personal happiness. Don't you see that all my personal interests pointed the path which, for quite different and entirely spiritual reasons, you have prayed that I might follow, and that, in refusing to take it in spite of the enormous personal losses which this refusal has brought upon me, I have been resisting a severe temptation and have been doing my duty—a very difficult duty, I have found it—to God as that duty appears to me? If I were to persuade myself against my true conviction, to you it might seem (at any rate, at the moment) like a surrender of pride to Christian humility, but for me it would be a selling of my soul and a betrayal of God. I should be a liar and a hypocrite—pretending to be a Catholic and not being one truly on the Catholic Church's own terms (which, of course, the Church alone is entitled to lay down) of genuinely believing the beliefs which, for a Catholic, are the obligatory test of faith. If I had taken this line, then, so far from coming nearer to you and your brethren who do hold these beliefs with whole-hearted sincerity, I should have moved right away from you. I should have been nominally one of you, but under false pretenses. It would have been an odious deception of myself and some of my best friends. Had I done it I should have lost my self-respect. I feel sure that you would feel the same if you could imagine yourself in my situation.

Therefore I must now lose—not your friendship and affection, for I know I have not lost that; and also not your intention towards me in your daily Mass, which I treasure because I do to some extent understand, from inside, both the intention and the spiritual travail in which it is put into action; but I must lose the personal intercourse with you and with Ampleforth.

About this, I will repeat more or less what I wrote in an earlier letter: my own feelings towards you and towards Ampleforth remain unchanged; I remain a "philo-Catholic"; I am not embittered.

As you consulted the Abbot before writing your letter of the 5th September to me, I should be glad if you would show him this letter of mine or tell him the gist of it—whichever you think better. As you and he know, I am sure, I have a very great respect and regard for him, so that I would like him as well as you to know where I stand.

God Bless You.
Yours affectionately,
Arnold J. Toynbee

The history of Chinese philosophy has just reached me,[4] and I am posting to you *Saint John of the Cross*. I had the volume with me on my holiday.

Confidential

Post-script. Thanks to Veronica's having made it possible completely to re-open the door for a reconciliation between Rosalind and me, I have been able to clear up my relations with Rosalind finally—so far as can be foreseen.

I wanted to have this final meeting because (i) *both* of us (we agreed last Sunday), in the action we successfully took in November 1942[5] had been to some extent carried away by forces inside us which were not fully under the control of our rational wills, and such action, when it entails serious results, ought to be re-considered calmly and rationally after an interval; (ii) two new facts had entered into the situation (a) the relief of strain on Rosalind through Lawrence's life no longer being in danger[6] (b) the improvement in my psychic condition through the "work" I have been doing with Dr. Payne; (iii) no important new facts are likely to enter in after this, so far as can be foreseen, so that there seemed to be no reason for delaying an attempt to arrive at finality in ourselves—though legally, of course, the door will remain open till the end of the three years.

So I asked Rosalind to meet me, and we had a long and friendly meeting, as a result of which it appeared that there was no likelihood of a reconciliation and that we had better now look definitely towards a future in which our marriage would not be restored. This conclusion did not turn at all upon my relation with Veronica. It turned on the following points: (i) we agreed that a restored marriage could only work on a footing of equality between us; (ii) Rosalind has no feeling at all for me corresponding to my love for her;[7] (iii) therefore, for her, there could be no gain, and only loss, in coming together with me again; (iv) thus there could be no equality in the relations between us.

This is put very briefly and baldly, but it gives the heart of the matter.

A.J.T.

1. This letter has not been found. In it C.C.E. apparently told A.J.T. that he would no longer correspond with him. C.C.E.'s letter in answer to Bridget Reddin's letter of 8 September 1944 also is missing. "The gap in our correspondence was my doing, and I regret it now. The whole episode escaped my memory. We seemed to slip back into our old relationship so easily. Arnold was so forgiving. All I can go on now are the letters that have survived. Mine, in reference to the break at its start, have not survived. Arnold must either have destroyed or mislaid them. I venture a reconstruction on the evidence available. (i) I found myself being the confidant of both Arnold and Rosalind at the critical moment of the break-up of their marriage. It seems that relationship between Arnold and me was restored when the break was complete. (ii) Mother Abbess Elizabeth of the Workington community of Poor Clares was regarded by many of us as a mystic and visionary of a high order. See my letter of 26 February 1947, below. Apparently she had persuaded me that to allow Arnold to continue his close association with Ampleforth and me was to give him a false sense of belonging to the Church. (iii) Fr. Abbot seems to have come in as an arbiter of what I should do, and I followed his decision. I feel much confusion and sorrow as I contemplate the harshness of my behavior, and I do not attempt to exonerate myself for my part in the distressing hurt Arnold must have experienced as a result of my action. The amazing thing is the completely Christian reaction on his part; and perhaps we can now take consolation that the situation resulted in such profoundly Christian letters from him." (C.C.E.)

2. For an account of A.J.T.'s first reaction to Rosalind's conversion, see Rosalind Toynbee's "Finding Life and Light," in *The Road to Damascus*, ed. John A. O'Brien (New York, 1950): "I asked my husband then if he agreed to my going to see a priest, and suggested one or two whose books I had happened to read. He objected strongly, saying that if once I saw a priest he knew I was 'done for', and that it would be 'intellectual suicide.' . . . Then suddenly, quite unexpectedly, he relented; without my saying anything more about it, he came in one day and said he had been wrong, that I should be free to see a priest if I wished to, and that he had in fact arranged an interview for me, through his secretary, who was a Catholic" (p. 133).

3. For a detailed account of Philip's experience at Ampleforth, see A.J.T.'s letter of 23 October 1961, below.

4. Hu Shih, *Religion and Philosophy in Chinese History* (Shanghai, 1931).

5. The separation.

6. Lawrence had been shell-shocked and withdrawn from the front.

7. In a letter of 24 September 1944 to Gilbert Murray, A.J.T. reports this meeting and says: "Rosalind was kind but very clear: she has no affection for me, no pleasure in my company, no interest in my work. . . . if she could conceive of loving me at all, it would be in the sense in which the saint loves the universe."

Ampleforth College
Eve of Pentecost (8 June) 1946 York

My dear Arnold,

You are constantly in my thoughts and in my prayers; always at Mass I mention your name in the commemoration for the Living. There is a soul whom I know is most dear to God who offers up great suffering for the well being of your soul.

I do not want this letter to be the beginning of a renewed correspondence, but only as a proof to you, on this feast of Divine Love, of my love, and desire to see you in the one Fold of the One Shepherd, Jesus our Lord.

My history of the Church in China goes on at a snail's pace, but it goes on. Those articles on the Names of Christ, which you saw, are to be published—in extracts—in the new spiritual Review "*Life of the Spirit*"[1] beginning July—published by Blackfriars.

I pray for your work, the *Study* and the Peace. We must get as much justice as we can, and never pretend that failure to achieve full justice is right, but admit the wickedness in compromises forced upon us.

Your devoted friend,
Columba, O.S.B.

1. Compare A.J.T.'s letter of 16 November 1943, above.

8 Abington Villas
13 June 1946 London, W.8

Dear Columba,

I was very glad indeed to hear from you. Your letters[1] reached me this morning at a critical moment in my life.

After I had made a number of further attempts to get a reconciliation between Rosalind and me on the basis of the normal relations between husband and wife (I am talking about spiritual relations, not physical), I divorced her for desertion on the 27th May. All the facts, including the one involving a third person, were stated in Court.[2]

I am now trying to start life from the beginning again. At the moment, I am going to and fro between London and Paris on peace-making work,[3] but by September I shall be back at Chatham House, to start work again on the *Study* and the *Survey*.

My feelings towards you remain just what they were, as I believe yours do towards me. I also continue to believe that you and I have, at bottom, the same faith, and that this fundamental agreement matters much more than the differences on the surface. But I cannot overcome these surface differences by saying I believe what I do not believe: that would be untrue and wrong, and it would therefore drive us apart instead of bringing us together. I might have been tempted, all the same, to do this if I had been a cynic, because my relation with you and Ampleforth and my relation with Rosalind are things of supreme value to me which I have now, at least outwardly, lost.

You are constantly in my thoughts and prayers.

God Bless you.
Yours affectionately,
Arnold J. Toynbee

1. One, at least, is missing.

2. The civil decree absolute of divorce was entered on 13 August 1946; Rosalind's decree of annulment was entered on 13 December 1946; see her letter of 17 June 1943, above.

3. A.J.T. was a member of the British Delegation to the Peace Conference held 29 July–15 October 1946 in Paris. The conference dealt with treaties of peace with Italy, Roumania, Hungary, Bulgaria, and Finland.

Hawksfield
5, Bradmore Way
Brookmans Park, Herts

3 October 1946

Dear Rob,[1]

Your announcement of Elizabeth's[2] marriage reached me just after I had been married myself: last Saturday, Veronica Boulter—my partner at Chatham House and then in the Foreign Office for the last twenty-two years—and I were married after a long time of uncertainty and tribulation.

When Rosalind would not bring herself to live under the same roof with me, after I came back here from the United States in the autumn of 1942, I asked Veronica if she would marry me if ever I were free honourably to ask her, and she said she would. After that, I was attacked by conscience and hounded by the past, and Veronica, on her own initiative—though it mattered very much to her because she has a great love for me—set me free to be reconciled with Rosalind if I could, and stuck by me while I tried, as I did by my best, half a dozen times, but always without success.

Last May I divorced Rosalind for desertion. Now Veronica and I are married, and I am very happy—able once again to live in the present and the future and to remember the past without being tormented.

We had a civil marriage in the Kensington registry office, and then went on to Winchester, where an old school fellow and friend of mine, Eddy Morgan,[3] who is now Bishop of Southampton, gave us a service in the chantry in the cloisters of College.

We are out of govt. service and back at Chatham House, and I am giving a course of lectures at Bryn Mawr between the 10th of February and 17th March, 1947. Veronica is coming over with me. Will you be at Beach Point? May I bring her to see you?

The ebbs and flows in life are strange. During the past few years, I have been in sight of the madness that overtook my father and the suicide that overtook Tony. Now I am on an even keel again.

I must now catch my train; I have become a commuter for the present, but we believe we have secured a house in London. Meanwhile, we are having a honeymoon in Veronica's house here, clearing out the cupboards, blacking the shoes and doing all the little chores that it is a happiness to do together. But I must rush for King's X.

My love to you, and best wishes to Elizabeth and the whole family.

Affectionately,
Arnold

1. Robert Shelby Darbishire; cf. A.J.T.'s letter of March, 1910, above.

2. Elizabeth Darbishire (1921–), the eldest daughter of the Darbishires.

3. Edmund Robert Morgan (1888–1979); Winchester; New College, Oxford; Suffragan Bishop of Southampton (1943–51); Bishop of Truro (1951–59); *The Catholic Revival and Missions* (London, 1933); *The Ordeal of Wonder* (London, 1964).

Ampleforth College
York

17 December 1946

My dear Arnold,

Here is Christmas and I shall write to you for that great feast. All blessings for it, to you and Veronica—I hope she does not mind my calling her that as I know you as Arnold.

I saw the notice in the *Times*, and pray for you to have joy and peace together.[1]

Now the Nonsense for Short, or without tears, has come.[2] The reception of it I cannot describe. It is all you, but it and what is to come I know is part me, even if it does not always agree with my way of looking at it. Part me, by my cooperation in prayer.

Then today came your lovely Christmas card, and a gentle act of reverence to Mary. Of course, all ways are different; and for each soul the secret is different.[3] The way of mysticism is a secret way and the Church in that stands as a safety appliance to save us from deception and illusion. The Hindu pantheists I feel would have been more, much more, illumined, had they only known the humility which comes through belief in creation. But I say: follow your reason and your illumination but in humility, and the ways we go will meet at the end and may be earlier. Unconsciously perhaps even you have been preserved from error by the mental atmosphere created by the Church with its affirmations. Every saint's way is different: S. Francis of Assisi, S. Thomas Aquinas, S. Benedict, Soeur Thérèse, S. Augustine, the Curé (of Ars).

I have had a little time to see what Somervell has been able to include in 6 in 1, and I approve over and over again: some of my favorite passages, "As we gird up our loins . . ." p. 527, the passage from Machiavelli and about him, and of course, the pair of Saviours. You[4] left out that wonderful quotation from Acton's memorandum; the end of "the Intoxication of Victory" is there. Poor Hilaire Belloc, his life-in-death drags on, and soon he will have the vision of that Church whose human instruments irritated him so much.[5] The Nestorian abortive civilization could not be included but it was an exciting chapter in the original, if complex. Therefore I think it will be a great asset, this abridgement, thank you for sending me a copy.

Fr. Dunstan[6] has gone and I now do most of the Spanish, particularly the Golden Age, and have become enthralled by the Catholic revival in the 16th and 17th Centuries. Combined with that I am going to teach my religious instruction set Church history of the period. There seems but one book on the Counter-reformation as a whole.

The Chinese studies crawl, but I have written part I of the Jesuit section and hope to do part II shortly. Part I is really P. Ricci.[7]

As spiritual reading I have followed up an idea I had on Obedience. What the Benedictines gave Europe, essentially and not *per accidens* such as agriculture and work, was Obedience. Not slavish obedience but loving obedience as to God. Then I followed this up and found a sequence of degeneration: Rabelais and obedience, Gibbon and obedience, J. J. Rousseau, then Leo XIII and obedience. And having written 30 pages I hope to have it printed somewhere.

My point is that obedience to God is liberty because it is following Truth, and obedience to God through appointed men also. But the alternatives are anarchy or slavery. I believe that a solution which can be acceptable to modern men, of Obedience and Liberty, is the root solution.[8]

So the U N O deliberations are not completely a failure, and even there is hope if words mean action. But we have had too many words to let us be deceived now, and we, or I, at any rate, wait for facts.

You are too busy to write but I know you would like to hear from me. Christ is *Via, Veritas, Vita*. He will support you and lead you the way he wills and I leave you in his care.

Yours affectionately,
Columba, O.S.B.

1. The notice of A.J.T.'s marriage to Veronica; cf. the preceding letter.
2. D. C. Somervell's *Abridgement* of vols. 1–6 of *A Study of History* (London, 1946).
3. On his Christmas card, A.J.T. had inscribed "uno itinere non potest perveniri ad tam grande secretum," a favorite quotation from Q. Aurelius Symmachus (ca. 345–ca. 402), a public servant, orator, champion of the pagan Senate, who sought the restoration of the altar of Victory in the Senate chamber in his plea (*relatio tertia*) to Valentinian II, in which he uses this phrase.
4. "A.J.T. told me that Somervell had a free hand, therefore the 'you' should have been 'he,' that is, Somervell." (C.C.E.)
5. Somervell included (without divulging his name) Belloc's statement (not in the original *Study of History*) that the proof of the divinity of the Church was "that no merely human institution conducted with such knavish imbecility would have lasted a fortnight" (*Abridgement*, p. 359).
6. Dunstan Pozzi, O.S.B. (1880–1962); monk of Ampleforth. "He had started the Spanish

studies at Ampleforth; when he went on one of our parishes (St. Mary's Workington), I was the one available to take over." (C.C.E.)

7. See C.C.E.'s letter of 22 April 1940, above.
8. This study ended in *Law, Liberty and Love* (London, 1950), to which A.J.T. wrote a preface.

Hawksfield
5, Bradmore Way
Brookmans Park, Herts

24th December, 1946

Dear Columba,

I am certainly not too busy to write. And your letter was the best thing that has come to me for Christmas, by a long way. Thank you for your blessing on Veronica and me—the thanks come from us both. I hope we may have joy and peace together, as you pray for us. If God wills, I think we may, as we each have something to give to the other.

I am glad, too, that you can make Symmachus's words your own. It should indeed be possible, for by the end of the 4th century the religious pagans and the Christians were not far from one another in spirit—however bitterly they might feud about whether the golden statue of Victory should or should not remain in the Senate House (the Christians were then still the iconoclasts).

I agree, of course, about humility. Man goes to disaster whenever he mistakes himself or his works for God. The next idols of the kind will, I dare say, be the Unconscious and Atomic Energy. Of course, when we have comprehended them, one will find that they are no more identical with God than the sun and moon are. Each time that Man mistakes a creature for God and brings suffering on himself thereby, he has a chance of learning more about the nature of God—even if it is only the negative discovery that, after all, God is not this or that one of His works.

I am glad you like the *Abridgement*.[1] I think, myself, that Somervell has done a wonderfully skilful piece of work (very largely, by the way, because of humility in the doing of it).

Yes, willing and loving obedience to God has been the spiritual power that has made the Benedictine Order able to do all that it has done—the incidental practical fruits as well as the spiritual example and leadership which is, I suppose, the Order's central purpose and achievement. The crux here is, of course, that while, on the one hand, no human society can prosper unless the human members recognise that their leading fellow-member is God, this membership and leadership of God has, in this World, to be represented by human institutions, and to receive obedience, in the name of God, from their fellow-men is a tremendous ordeal for the "appointed men." It is the severest temptation to which any human being can be exposed, because it is constantly suggesting that he himself is divine. Hence it is here that you get some of the most sensational cases of ὕβρις and downfall: *corruptio optimi pessima*.

Rabelais, Rousseau, Gibbon and the rest were, I would say, reacting against what (with respect!) had been a bad case. This explains their attitude—and the blame for their having been thrown into this negative and uncreative attitude has to be divided between them and those representatives of the church whose shortcomings had scandalized them.

I have been out of government service since August, and started with a month on my cousin's sheep farm near Kirkby Stephen in Westmorland.[2] The wheels are not yet turning very fast, but my mind is more at peace again and therefore once more in a brooding and creative state, and, though most of my time so far has been spent on my Chatham House work (we have to get the *Survey* going again after a break of seven years), I have worked through my notes for Parts VI to X inclusive, and have brought them alive again: in fact, I have already given a course of lectures at Birmingham on VI to VIII (mostly on VII), and I am giving one on IX at Bryn Mawr College in Pennsylvania in February and March. Veronica has never been to America before, and, each of the four times that I have been there, I have travelled alone, so going there together will be a treat for both of us.

After that, we hope to get into a house in London that I have succeeded in buying freehold: 45 Pembroke Square, Kensington, W.8. This house from which I am writing is Veronica's, where she lived before the war, but going up and down every day is a bit of a strain, and also shortens the day's work too much. Meanwhile, we are very happy here.

I am now just going to start writing Part VI: at the tail end of August I did write the first four sheets of ms., just enough to hook it on to the close of Part V. You are quite right about the Nonsense Book having you in it. And perhaps there is a bit of me in your Chinese Work. If you can bring Father Matteo Ricci into people's minds again, that will be a great deed: he is the type of great missionary for his extraordinary gift of entering into the souls of the people to whom he was delivering the message, and so learning how to give them the message in language which they could take.

Well, God Bless You.

Yours affectionately,
Arnold

1. Lawrence recalls being told that A.J.T. had had no knowledge that Somervell was writing the *Abridgement* until the manuscript arrived with a letter asking his permission to publish; at first indignant, on reading the manuscript A.J.T. recognized it as a work of scholarship and understanding and gave it his full recognition.

2. Raven Frankland (1918–); Raven was also a land agent who acted for A.J.T. for his Cumbrian property; his brother, Anthony Noble Frankland (1922–), was deputy director of studies at Chatham House (1956–60); director of the Imperial War Museum (1960–82); named as an executor and trustee under A.J.T.'s will: sons of Edward Frankland (1884–1958), A.J.T.'s first cousin; cf. A.J.T.'s letter of 24 October 1958, below.

FIVE

1947–50

Renewal of life after the divorce; the trip to Kentucky; the gradual healing of the wound; The Broken Trunk*; the Mother Abbess loses stature; the resumption of theological discussions; A.J.T.'s dislike of Pharisaism; his prayer at the altar of Ste. Thérèse at Montmartre; the visits to Princeton; Communism in Europe; Westmorland vacations; A.J.T.'s queries about Pascal; advice concerning C.C.E.'s* Law, Liberty and Love*; C.C.E. prepares A.J.T. for his trip to Spain; the Chicago lecture; ecumenical beginnings in Rome; the decree of the Assumption debated; Christmas in New York.*

Saint Wilfrid's House
Ampleforth College, York

26 February 1947

My Dear Arnold,

I enclose a letter from the Poor Clare Abbess[1] of Workington. I have only the very vaguest idea as to what she is writing to you. I am convinced that she speaks by the guidance of God.

For about three years I have known her and been her director. So as to give you confidence in her wisdom I must tell you—but quite privately—that I think her a great mystic, as wise and love-inspired as St. Catherine of Siena[2] and as matter of fact and as near God as St. Teresa of Avila.[3] Though in herself she is just a simple lower middle class Cockney with very average education, I believe the above because I have tried her in humility and obedience with the utmost severity and she has come through with shining virtue. I have seen her in ecstasy many times, speaking with Jesus and Mary, and suffering the Passion with Jesus. I cannot describe how wonderful those experiences were, or how completely genuine they were. Over and over again she has shown her wisdom in the advice she has given, and which she simply tells has been given her by Jesus.[4]

So now, the two most wonderful people I know—both with mighty missions from God—are meeting through this letter. Please God, may you understand and act on whatever she has said. If you saw her you would be convinced; for ever since I have known her she has prayed and suffered for you night and day.

I close this letter with a repetition of my unshakable affection and regard for you and Veronica.

Columba, O.S.B.

1. Elizabeth, abbess of Workington; see n. 1 to A.J.T.'s letter of 20 September 1944, above.

2. Saint Catherine of Siena (1347–80); cf. C.C.E.'s letter of 19 January 1943, above.

3. Saint Teresa of Avila (1515–82); Carmelite reformer and mystic who, from her own experiences, gave vivid descriptions of the degrees of prayer; *The Interior Castle (Las Moradas del Castillo Interior)* (1577); the tourist in Rome will know her through Giovanni Lorenzo Bernini's masterpiece in Santa Maria della Vittoria.

4. "Arnold was patient; I was wrong. The case of Sister Elizabeth is one of the most puzzling, as later she came into opposition with Bishop Heenan of Leeds. She lived in retirement in a Poor Clare Convent (Liberton) in Scotland for a number of years until her death. Of all the experiences of the saints and mystics that are least dependable, 'locutions' and ecstasies come first, as they can come from self-inducement—in all good faith. Saint John of the Cross was forever telling Saint Teresa that ecstasy is a weakness and that locutions 'could be of the devil.'" (C.C.E.)

28 February 1947 20 St. Stephens Gardens, W.2

Dear Rev. Father,

Since I heard that Mr. Toynbee was likely to be visiting Ampleforth again I've been wanting to write to you about his difficulties, so the other day I turned to the Little Flower and asked her to advise me what to do. She didn't keep me long waiting for an answer!

This is Mr. Toynbee's attitude as I see it:

To God

Mr. Toynbee has *no* faith—no more than an Ancient Greek or an educated China man. He said to me once in an argument that it is not possible to get into touch with God. The Bible is just a mixture of myth, legend, folk lore, whatnot. There is nothing in the *records* of the time to show that it is true. (I think personally, it is a mistake to encourage people in that state of mind to attend Catholic services).

To the Church

Mr. Toynbee's whole attitude to the Church is based on *Fear*. He sees it as we see Communism: a vast powerful organisation run by crafty men, mostly foreigners, who are out to "get you" and once they have got you, its goodbye to your freedom. (I said this to Mrs. Toynbee and she admitted that it was true.) Unless and until Mr. Toynbee's fears are removed it is useless to talk to him about the Catholic religion. Ampleforth, and you in particular, were helping about this, so I was very sorry when he was cut off. I never allow Mr. Toynbee to think I want his conversion.

Mr. Toynbee has another great fear: that of being alone—hence the second wife.

He is a very conscientious person but the one thing for which I respect him most is that he is such a hard worker. I think the only way to get at him is through his book. He is out to find the truth, he thinks he can do it himself and the best thing is to let him *think* he can.

As to the position at present, I'm not quite so worried since Theresa took the reins. You heard about the pact of course. The turning to St. Theresa was a direct answer from Our Lady, but I won't bother you with the story now. I am wondering what St. Theresa will do next and am getting a bit impatient. (Every so often I go to Our Lady, and to her, and say, "Look here, if you don't give me some encouragement I'm giving up," and they always answer).

I think Mr. Toynbee is feeling better and has got over the parting from Mrs. Toynbee a bit. The trip to the U.S. has taken his mind off his troubles. I believe it is being a great success.

I enclose an offering for Mass in honour of St. Theresa that she may get on with the good work.

As for myself, I'm heading downwards I'm afraid, so please remember me in your prayers.

Yours very sincerely,
Bridget R. Reddin

P.S. No answer necessary.

Ampleforth Abbey
York

Holy Saturday (5 April) 1947

My dear Arnold,

I have a spare half hour in this stress-full week-end—boys going, ceremonies, guests. I have prayed much about you since I sent that letter of Mother Abbess, for though I have practically no idea of its contents, I do know that the words are mighty, and that they may even cause you pain. But of this I am sure, they will cause healing pain.

I wish you deep joy in the Resurrection and Redemption and specially Love in Truth, which is real love; all else is make-belief.

Dr. Coomaraswamy[1] wrote to me a few weeks ago. His positions seem analogous to yours. Sincere and groping, but perhaps more satisfied than you. I wrote him a long reply which I hope did not hurt him or the cause of Mother Church. If you meet him do explain that I am what I am and no great brain, nor considered such in the Church, or else he may judge it by me.

The chapters on the Friars and P. Ricci in China have been seen by Carter, of Carter and Hollis, who is enthusiastic about them. That is very consoling to me and a great incentive. I owe to you more than to anyone that I pushed on in spite of obstacles. Now I think the book may be written and published after all. It must be that one I shall offer "To A.J.T.".

We have abbatial elections in 10 days time. Pray for us.

Fr. Raphael[2] has been very ill but has recovered. Old Mrs. Nevill[3] died a week ago. Dr. Vidal[4] lost his (lay) son in a car accident at the same time.

Have you read Hugh Dormer's Diaries?[5] They would give you real joy and remind you a little of Ampleforth.

God bless you and guide you to the fullness of Truth, which makes all men free who find it.

Yours affectionately,
Columba, O.S.B.

1. Ananda Kentish Coomaraswamy (1877–1947); curator of Asiatic art, the Museum of Fine Arts, Boston, since 1917; *Hinduism and Buddhism* (New York, 1943).

2. Raphael Williams, O.S.B. (1891–1973); monk of Ampleforth, artist, philosopher.

3. Anne Fenwick Nevill (1852–1947); the mother of Paul Nevill, O.S.B., headmaster of Ampleforth.

4. Alan Vidal, M.D. (1880–1956); University of Edinburgh; D.S.O. (Companion of the Distinguished Service Order) for World War I services; the school doctor at Ampleforth from 1928 until his retirement; the surviving son is Francis Vidal, O.S.B., a monk of Ampleforth.

5. Hugh Dormer (1919–44); Amplefordian; captain, Irish Guards; killed in action in the Normandy landings; previously had been seconded for a special mission to blow up works in the Clermont area; this he did, and in the process wrote a diary (*Hugh Dormer's Diaries*, ed. Patrick Barry, O.S.B. [London, 1947]).

Care of Robert Shelby Darbishire
Beech Point, Stanford R 2
Kentucky, U.S.A.

19 April 1947

Dear Columba,

The last time I was in America, a letter of yours reached me at St. Louis and made me feel at home in a strange land (strange in spite of Captain Mayne Reid's "The Boy Hunters," which I daresay you read, as I did, when you were small).

I have had two letters from you on this journey,[1] and the one you wrote on Holy Saturday has reached me here, where I am very much at home—staying with an old Balliol contemporary of mine who is one of my closest friends (Tony was named Robert after him).[2]

I am also at home in this country, which is like a piece of green and unspoiled England, only a shade more luxuriant.

The peach blossom has come out while we have been here and the limestone beds are full of running water, and the early green fields are stuffed with lambs, piglets, calves and foals: in fact, it is an unspoiled piece of the pre-industrial, pre-atomic world. The people's religion is old-fashioned too: the aristocrats are Presbyterians, the rest are Methodists and Baptists. There is also a sect called Christians, *sans phrase*, because they believe that very soon all other sects will be converted to their way of thinking. My friend's cook is one of these, and, after reading a review of the *Abridgement* in the New York Times, he asked Rob if I believed in Hell Fire.

We have had a strenuous time but an interesting one—being here at a moment when Americans are very conscious of being at a turning point of their history.

What good news about Carter and Hollis. It will be splendid to have the book published. I am on the track of several American books on the subject, which I will lend you if I get hold of them.

My best wishes to Father Raphael for his convalescence. Please tell Father Paul how sorry I am about his mother's death. And give my love to Father James.[3] I wasn't pained by Mother Abbess's letter. I will write to her at leisure.

Yours affectionately,
Arnold

1. In February and March 1947, A.J.T. had given a series of lectures at Bryn Mawr College; he had also delivered lectures at Union Theological Seminary, New York, Harvard University, Princeton University, and the University of Toronto.

2. Robert Shelby Darbishire; cf. A.J.T.'s letter of March 1910, above, and the letters following.

3. James Forbes, O.S.B.; cf. C.C.E.'s letter of 18 February 1941, above.

Ampleforth College
York

7 May 1947

My dear Arnold,

I do not know where you are so I send this to Chatham House, expecting you will have returned.

Your letter I take to be not only a description of spring, but also of a renewing of spirit, and I rejoice.

The Mother Abbess who sent you that message is a Poor Clare. It is the order which has preserved a wonderful simplicity and takes one back to the ideal atmosphere of S. Francis of Assisi. They practise absolute poverty, their ways are simple, they think of little else than the Love of Jesus and praying and suffering for their neighbours and themselves. The Mother Abbess, through me, has become spiritually closely united to your spirit praying for you and suffering for you daily. She has read only *Christianity and Civilization* which I lent her. Her insight into it and you is almost entirely supernatural because she has no learning except that of the Cross and the Saints.

Here is a slip of paper[1] on which I wrote what you see! The ordinary histories did not make much sense, so I turned to the *Study*, and sure enough the tangle was disentangled, but I think there were these details wrong. As there is bound to be another edition very soon, perhaps this is the moment. Aragon and Castile are in this business splendid examples of your thesis.

Going to Beccles, where my father and mother now live, I had a good picture of the religious situation. A Christian Commando (man) and young Methodist woman opposite me, a young Anglo-Catholic on my left. We discussed reunion. I did my best to prevent their schemes developing into all abandoning their belief, to agree with the one who held least. It was very friendly, a new spirit and certainly there was union in Charity if not yet in Truth. Do tell me what you think of the spiritual condition of U.S.A. A mouthful. Thank you so much for thinking of the Chinese field of my work, and collecting books.

If you still like my letters, I am prepared to begin a series. No one can now say your friends in the Church have ever persuaded you. I leave the persuading entirely to the Holy Spirit and your resolve always to Love and cleave to Truth.

Yours ever,
Columba, O.S.B.

1. Missing.

45, Pembroke Square
Kensington
London, W.8

Sunday, 18th May 1947

I am winding up the last chapter in my life—a long one—and opening a new chapter. Veronica and I have just moved into this house, and I am sorting out papers that have been in store since 1939.

This bundle[1] contains all the letters I ever had from Rosalind, from the day she accepted me after all—the 31st May, 1913—until our breach in November, 1942. The only letters missing are those I had from her during my visit to America in the summer and autumn of 1942. Coming back to England by air under war restrictions, I had to leave my papers behind.

I remember these letters so clearly; for instance, the funny sizzling noise made by the gas in her letter of the 11th of June, 1913.

I do not want these letters to be destroyed at my death. I want them to be kept and handed down to one of our grandchildren: Josephine or Polly or Rosalind, or one not yet born. I want the letters to pass into the hands of a member of the family who is far enough removed from Rosalind and me not to feel the grief of what has happened to us, and yet near enough to us to feel compassion for us.

My love for Rosalind always remained what it was from the first, but this does not mean that I am less the cause than Rosalind is, of our marriage breaking down. Till the challenge of 1942–1946 gave me the choice of growing up or perishing, I remained a child: not an equal partner for her. I do not know—and no one will ever know—whether Rosalind could have had a happy lifelong marriage with someone else, or whether there was some latent strain in her that would have broken out at this stage of her life in much the same way, whoever had been her husband. I only know that she has been unfortunate like so many members of her family, and that I failed to save her from this misfortune.

May God pity and forgive us both, as He has, I believe, shown mercy on Tony.

God Bless You, Rosalind. You came into my life, and went out of it again, like some fairy creature from another world. I know how much you gave me; perhaps I did give something to you—more than you thought when you were looking back over our lives in 1942. I love you, and I am very sorry—towards God and towards you—that I failed to be the husband that you felt you wanted.

Arnold Toynbee

1. This covering note and the bundle of Rosalind's letters were among A.J.T.'s papers and now are at the Bodleian.

Saint Wilfrid's House
Ampleforth College, York

S. Augustine's Day (2 June) 1947

My dear Arnold,

The time has come for you to visit us again, if you would. I invite you with all my heart. This morning Fr. Aelred gave me a note saying that the best weeks were

(1) 13th June for about 10 days

(2) 1st July–18th July

The latter dates would suit me best in some ways. But I expect you need a holiday now.

A happy feast for tomorrow St. Bede,[1] the patron of historians. (Transferred)

I must close now. My kindest regards to Veronica.

Yours ever,
Columba, O.S.B.

1. The Venerable Bede (ca. 673–735); biblical scholar and father of English history; his remains are in Durham Cathedral, of which C.C.E. was to be named titular prior.

Saint Wilfrid's House
Ampleforth College, York

17 June 1947

My dear Arnold,

I wrote some two weeks ago, but as I addressed the letter to your home address, as I know it, Hawksfield, you may have moved, and the letter not been forwarded.

The letter was an invitation to come and stay here. Originally I suggested two series of dates, but the earlier is past; there remains the later, i.e. any period within the two weeks, 1st July–18th July.

I hope you can come for at least some of that time.

There are many things we can talk about, and we might revive those meetings in the evening with the boys.

Br. Kentigern will be back from Oxford having done his history finals. Fr. Aelred is looking forward to seeing you and many others. So I hope you come.

God bless all your undertakings. My kindest regards to Veronica.

Yours ever,
Columba, O.S.B.

Saint Wilfrid's House
Ampleforth College, York

18 June 1947

My dear Arnold,

Grand. Yes those dates suit, if they are on the short side.

We shall have a car at Gilling to meet the evening train unless we hear to the contrary.

You will be here for the feast of St. Benedict, and you and I will keep it as the 14th centenary of his death—though this feast is really the 'Translation'[1] and the centenary is by the learned to be kept in 1950.

At any rate all the abbots are congregating in Rome this autumn for the purpose.

Do you remember we promised each other we were going to go to Rome one day together . . . I am going to Spain this summer.

Yours ever,
Columba, O.S.B.

1. "Here 'Translation' means the translation of the bones of Saint Benedict from Monte Cassino to Fleury, the abbey of Saint Benoît sur Loire, in the eighth century when some pilgrim monks went to the former, found it in ruins, and carried the relics away. The monks of Monte Cassino strongly contest the story as a legend." (C.C.E.)

As from 45 Pembroke Square
Kensington W.8

18 June 1947

Dear Columba,

You will have had my telegram and learnt that your guess about my silence was right. Your first letter (forewarded from our previous address: I think the tenants must have been away) reached me at 45 Pembroke Square this morning, by the same post that brought your second letter to Chatham House.

I hope my suggestion of July 10–14 still fits. I would have liked to propose a rather longer stay, but we are still entangled in arrears of work and engagements that filled up while we were in America.

I don't think I need to tell you that your letter gave me great happiness, and that I immensely look forward to seeing you again, as well as my other friends at Ampleforth.

Though it is only a few days, they will mean a lot to me.

Veronica and I both appreciate your kind messages to her.

Yours ever,
Arnold

45 Pembroke Square
London W.8

24 June 1947

Dear Columba,

I wonder whether, one of the days I am at Ampleforth, you would care to ask George and Christian Howard[1] from the Gatehouse, Castle Howard, to come over.

If that were convenient, I should like to see them, and it would be nice for him to be in touch with Ampleforth, as his father[2] was. Perhaps you know him already.

I am so much looking forward to coming.

The Rockefeller Foundation have just made a most generous arrangement for releasing most of my time for the next five years to finish the nonsense books.

God Bless You.
Yours affectionately,
Arnold

1. George Anthony Howard (1920–84); Lord Howard of Henderskelfe; major, the Green Howards (1939–45); fought in Burma; chairman, British Broadcasting Corp. (1980–83); the owner of Castle Howard; nephew of Lady Mary Howard (Murray), Rosalind Toynbee's mother. Rosemary Christian (1916–), his sister, a deaconess of the Church of England.

2. Geoffrey William Algernon Howard (1877–1935); son of the ninth Earl of Carlisle; a Lord Commissioner of the Treasury (1915–16).

Ampleforth College
York

27 June 1947

Dear Arnold,

Thank you for your note. I told Fr. James[1] about the Howards. He is seeing them and doubtless will arrange something.

How marvellous about the Nonsense Book. I must pray harder than ever. It must not be half good, but just good, *simpliciter*.

God bless you and it.

Columba, O.S.B.

1. James Forbes, O.S.B., then guest master.

Ampleforth College
York

1 July 1947

My dear Arnold,

That is much better. Yes, we can put you up for a week.[1]

Fr. James has not yet arranged about the Howards but I have reminded him.

The House monitors punch in the evening you arrive, though we have tried to change the day; it was impossible. So do not be surprised if you do not see me till after ten; and if I get a puncture—we go to Nunnington of all places!—later than that.

Don't forget China, and also ideas on *Law, Liberty and Love*, which is my spiritual puzzle at the moment.

Also: is the basis of every civilization *faith*?, by which I mean unhesitating conviction of the whole body of the people in certain fundamental theological (purpose-in-life) philosophical and moral truths. It seems to be true for us, for Hindus, Muslims (followers of) Confucius, (of) Jesus of course, what of Egypt, Assyria?

Your affectionate friend,
Columba, O.S.B.

1. When Rosalind heard of this trip to Yorkshire, she urged A.J.T. not to go to Castle Howard or Ganthorpe: the country people would talk. "It is impossible to explain the subtleties of a complicated situation to those village people. . . . It was real happiness to me the other day to see your new delightful home and think of you and Veronica happy in it." (2 July 1947).

45 Pembroke Square
London W.8

17 July 1947

Dear Columba,

Here are three poems,[1] which will tell you my feelings better than I can in a letter.

Those four days were happy and sorrowful—but sorrowful in retrospect and happy in prospect.

I have read and re-read your sonnets,[2] and have entered into the feeling of them.

I have only one small technical point to raise; some of the lines are short of a syllable or two. Was this syncopated effect intentional?

I shall be anxious to hear how you find your parents. And I hope the journey to Spain is only deferred.

God Bless You.

Yours affectionately,
Arnold

1. Two, " *῎Ανδρες ἀνασπαστοί, φῦλον τάλαν, αἰνὰ παθόντες*" and "*O silvae, silvae, raptae mihi, non revidendae*," were published in A.J.T.'s *Experiences*, pp. 401–3; the latter was also published in *A Study of History*, VII: xiii–iv. The third, unpublished and titled "The Broken Trunk," follows.

2. One of C.C.E.'s sonnets begins on page 194.

The Broken Trunk

I

We took the unfamiliar track
With the familiar places behind us:
Ampleforth, Oswaldkirk, Stonegrave
And the crown of Hawnby Hump
Rising as it used to rise to my eye
Through my study window at Ganthorpe.

The track seemed aimless
Yet it led us on—
Past the war-built watchtower,
With its windows scanning the twelve winds,
And down into the unfamiliar wood
Ravaged by axe and tractor,
Till suddenly, in front of us,
Rose up the unforgetable bare brow
Of the ridge of the Morpeth Plantation,
Drawing its sharp line across the sky
Like the beautiful bows of a leopard-swift warship;
And, as we climbed to the point where I have so often sat,
I found my feet treading the ground in which my spirit is rooted—
Rooted like a tree whose trunk, hurled to earth by the storm,
Could not draw, in its fall, the roots up with it,
So indissolubly are they wedded to the soil;
Broken, like the trunk
When trunk and roots are riven asunder perforce.

II

Sitting once again on the old man's barrow,
Meditating in unison with him,
As I have communed with him a hundred times before,
I remembered that here
I had once been inspired to sing my song of broken lives.

I had sung of victoriously twice-born souls,
Who glorified God
By harvesting the ineffable fruits
Of His loving chastisement.
These men served the Lord:
By drinking of the cup of which He drinks
They ministered to His work of creation.

And I remembered how I had smiled to myself—
Amused, relieved, yet also in some measure wistful—

At the thought that God, in sparing me their stripes,
Had counted me unworthy to be numbered in their company.
I had not been parted from my Beatrice,
I had not been exiled from my Florence.
Secure in the blessings of This Life,
I should live and die no Dante, no Thucydides,
Never scaling the heights of agony;
Never beholding the beatific vision
From the lonely summit of the terrible peak.

O God, I was a harp in Thy hands,
And Thou hast broken my strings,
And now Thou biddest me play for Thee new music on a stringless lyre
Or be forever silent.

My God, I will follow Thy hard commandment,
Since Thou hast not left me without a sign.
For, as we rested on the brow of the hill
And gazed across Frier's Moor to the far-away four trees
That denied me the sight of the gables of Ganthorpe,
I smelled the sweetness of clover,
And saw at my feet a smiling pasture—
Fairly flowering clover and tenderly shooting grass—
On the beloved slope where, in the days of my innocence,
All had been coarse grey bent and barren bracken.
The tempest of war which had shorn away the trees*
Had restored its proper beauty to an unkempt country-side.
The Lord hath given; the Lord hath taken away.
O Lord, in Thy might and Thy mercy,
Help me to make Thy music on my broken strings.
In these latter days Thou hast marked me too as Thine;
Thou hast printed on these ageing hands and feet
The stigmata of Thucydides and Dante.
Make me too Thine instrument, as Thou madest them.

III

O Lord, I have been inditing of a trivial matter,
For what loss would it be if one harp were missing
From the symphony of Thy creation's praise of Thee?
Thou never lackest instruments for making what music Thou wilt.
O Lord, it matters not at all
Whether I make music for Thy glory or fall sorrowfully dumb.
O my God, Thou hast shown me Thy will:
To do righteousness in the sight of the Lord,
That is the true end of Man.

O God, I will open to Thee the heart that Thou readest undeclared.
I have done evil in Thy sight.
Distraught like a child at the height of manhood,
I set myself a share from which there was no sinless issue—
I could not but sin against one of Thy children.

O Lord, I am seeking to declare the truth,
And, if I lie, Thou knowest.
O Lord, I took Love for my guide
And Love counselled me
To choose the greater Love and the lesser wrong:
"Thou shalt not sin against Love"; "Love will not be denied".
Yet, O Lord, for the wrong that I have done,
I must suffer the** penalty.
My strings are broken, my roots are riven, I bleed.
O Lord, I bless Thee for these Thy grievous wounds;
For whom the Lord loveth He chasteneth
And scourgeth every son whom He receiveth.

Arnold Toynbee
16.7.47

*In the copy of "The Broken Trunk" in his unpublished notebook, A.J.T. added: "Making havoc of the lives / Of men and nations," after line 11 of this stanza.
**In his notebook A.J.T. changed "the" to "Thy." In a letter to C.B.P. of 22 October 1977 Veronica wrote: "I have been looking at *Experiences* again to-day, and I am quite relieved to see that his selection of poems to be printed omitted that sad English poem dated July 1947. I think this must have been written after a visit to Ampleforth and a walk round Ganthorpe (probably with Father Columba) and it reflected the acute feelings of loss which he still felt, at that time in those familiar surroundings, (we must have just returned from America and all the hullabalou about the Somervell abridgement). The omission of this poem when he was making his selection of poems for printing some twenty years later shows, I like to think, that his feelings of loss had faded by then, and that he had found happiness with me."

SONNET

Christians, Co-heirs with Christ, God's Son, arise!
For Christ, our Pasch, the Lamb of God, has made
Oblation, holocaust, and so repaid
The debt, by due and worthy sacrifice;
And now has risen from the dead, the New
And Perfect Man. His wounds did not depart—
Those signs of victory—nor pierced heart,
To signify what death He chose in lieu
Of us, to win the power and show the Way

To heaven's battlements, where angels wait
And saints, in dazzling ranks to celebrate
The faithful soul's first homing holiday.

Christians arise! Take Faith, have Hope, be brave!
Win triumph here and Life beyond the grave
C.C.E., Easter, 1946

Ampleforth College
York

20 July 1947

Dear Arnold,

Just a few lines, which *deo volente*, may have a chance of spreading into a letter. Thank you very much for your Ganthorpe poem. It is a lovely one, much more so than the first,[1] deep, as the Christian soul can be. I am going to read it many times; but first I shall pass it on to Fr. Barnabas.[2]

The syncopated effect in mine was intended; perhaps it is too daring; and in any case I intended to keep the number of syllables even when shifting the stress, and I see I have not. Thank you for pointing it out; a final edition will smooth these things out.

My explanation of my past action[3] will seem very bewildering to Veronica and I hope you can explain what a Catholic can feel in regard to a mystic and one he considers a saint. Perhaps she knows St. Catherine of Siena. It is something like that. Of course she will keep this always as our private affair, because the world will never understand. My own fear at the time was that you would wash your hands of the Church for good and all, as being something which was too cruel—in my person—to be in the charity of God. But you did not; because, I suppose if you have not faith in the Church, you have kept faith in me: trusting without understanding, and hoping one day to have all explained.

Several people here—including Fr. Paul—remarked how wonderfully better you looked in health after 4 days here.

I must stop and watch diving.

God bless you both,

Yours affectionately,
Columba, O.S.B.

P.S. I can't tell you how glad I was to hear that your marriage was all clear. No one knew here until you told me.[4]

1. Compare the "first" "Ganthorpe" (1943) in A.J.T.'s *Experiences*, pp. 393–401.

2. Father John Barnabas Sandeman, O.S.B.

3. See n. 1 to A.J.T.'s letter of 20 September 1944, above; this passage indicates that, during the Ampleforth visit of 10–14 July 1947, C.C.E. told A.J.T. about the abbess's advice that the correspondence end; and see A.J.T.'s letter of 24 July 1947 below.

4. "I meant that, from a Christian point of view, because of Rosalind's getting an annulment, Arnold's 'second marriage was genuine.'" (C.C.E.)

The Royal Institute
of International Affairs
Chatham House
10, St James's Square
London S.W.1

24 July 1947

Dear Columba,

I was very glad to get your letter. The poem came from the heart.

I have been trying to think why it was that your breaking off relations with me did not have the effect that—very reasonably, I think—you thought it might have. I should say they were:

(i) Love and admiration for you.

(ii) Love and admiration for the whole Community at Ampleforth.

(iii) Perhaps strongest of all: a deep sense, which I have always had, of the sinfulness of belligerency and animosity. If ever I am in hostile relations with somebody (which is often inevitable, and sometimes one's duty) I can't rest till the breach of peace and charity has been healed.

This is one of the things I have suffered most from in my breach with Rosalind—of all people in the world, the one with whom I have most wished to live in love and charity.

The Reverend Mother's part in the story shall, as I promised, be secret from everybody except Veronica.

God Bless You.
Yours affectionately,
Arnold

Staithe House
Beccles

4 August 1947

My dear Arnold,

Here I am in Norwich, with my father in the hospital trying to recover from his operation. Today for the first time it looks as if he might. My address will remain Beccles till the end of August—.

In between going to the hospital and keeping my mother cheerful I have been reading *I Chose Freedom*.[1] It is not a cheerful book, and the sooner I finish it the better. But it is the best authenticated and complete picture of Russia I have read. God help that unhappy country and anyone within arm's reach. I suppose you have read it. It is all evil made into a good, and all good supposed evil, and consequently the canker of the world.

I passed on your poems to Fr. Barnabas and he read them; and I hope he wrote to you, because we had so little time to talk before you left that I got very little as to his impressions. He liked the Latin and Greek ones very much, but the English one not so well. He thought the focus was wrong in it; the personal sorrow perhaps too prominent. Perhaps my sonnets helped there.

I have been reading an Anglo-Catholic tract called *Catholicity*[2] and find it very enlightening upon their ways of thinking. It amazes me that they do not get to the point: did Christ found a Church with a living Teaching voice, or did he not? They all seem to beat about the bush, asking such questions as: should He do so? Like a detective asking whether people should die and not how did this death in fact happen.

But their criticisms of the Church were I thought in part justified. However, they made a curious parallel when they said the Catholics lacked wholeness as much as, say, the Lutherans. But the latter actually deny certain ancient doctrines, while the Church only did not stress some at particular periods.

I thought that your whole attitude had changed radically when you were last at Ampleforth and that your approach was not only one of *la raison* but also of *le coeur*[3] to things of faith.

Sometimes clever people have faith and do not realize it, thinking, particularly if they have only recollections of Low church "faith", that it is a feeling. Pascal with Chevalier's comments does, I think, give a true statement of the Church's view on faith.

As you know, I went up to see Mother Abbess at Workington, but my visit only lasted one day because, my father's operation impending, I had to rush South. We spoke about your visit. Among the things she said were that your remark about water divining and her power of discerning spirits was very true; it was very like that. She also said that one of her reasons for wanting you away from Ampleforth was, as you said, to force your hand! She thought you would never get any further towards the Church so long as you had the liturgy and the friendship which might seem sufficient to you and hide the gulf between everything and Faith. She says you will only be happy and at peace within the fold, and that if you take the step, then Truth will flood in and with it pure joy. She thinks you capable of great holiness and great good. And when she says 'great' and 'holiness' she means it. The matter of course is Doing God's Will and following Truth.

We talked about Henri Bergson;[4] she seemed to accept his behavior as reasonable—so do I. But she saw nothing comparable in your case, should it occur. His race was being persecuted.

Should I speak like this? I think so, because it is my thoughts. What she said I have thought for some time. But I would not have you move quicker than your mind can accept, nor more slowly. Truth—that is God—is the inexorable Master whom we must follow with love and without fear, because Truth and Love alone can, or even could, save our world; and time is short. You must waste no time finding it and publishing it; we are on the edge of an abyss worse than in the days of S. Augustine. He was fearless. I never think of either but I think of the other, him and you. God be with you. God speed.

Love,
Columba, O.S.B.

1. Victor Kravchenko, *I Chose Freedom* (London, 1947).

2. *The Catholicity of Protestantism*, ed. R. Newton Flew and Rupert E. Davies (London, 1950); a report presented to the archbishop of Canterbury by a group of Free Churchmen.

3. "Le coeur a ses raisons, que la raison ne connaît point" (Blaise Pascal, *Oeuvres complètes*, ed. Louis Lafuma [Paris, 1963], *Pensées*, no. 423 [Brunschvicg no. 277]).

4. Henri Bergson; cf. C.C.E.'s letter of 18 February 1941, above.

Howard Hotel
Bethel St.
Norwich, Norfolk

6 August 1947

Dear Arnold,

I have written you a long letter but don't like sending it to Chatham House, and, as I had to rush away here, I left your other address behind. It is not in the telephone book. So this note asking you to send a card giving the home address.

My father is struggling valiantly to recover from his operation, and we hope he will pull through.

My kind regards to Veronica, who I know will look after you. And I must say you looked more frail than when we had last met.

Also remember me kindly to Miss Reddin and I hope she is well.

Yours affectionately,
Columba, O.S.B.

45, Pembroke Square
London W.8

12 August 1947

Dear Columba,

I had your letter, and now I have just read the sad announcement in this morning's *Times*.

Your father must have been a courageous man—so I judge from the picture of him that I have from you.[1]

When someone of that character dies—even at a ripe age—it leaves a terrible gap, and though, for the person directly concerned, it may not be an altogether unhappy thing to part from this life, the loss to the people left behind is very great.

You will be glad to have been on the spot—though I can't help being very sorry about the postponement of your visit to Spain, from which you would have gained so much.

You are always in my thoughts, and will be particularly so during these next weeks.

I shall be writing you before long.

With much sympathy and affection.

Arnold

1. Compare C.C.E.'s letter of 22 December 1939, above.

At Holkes House
Cave-in-Cantwell
Lancashire

31 August 1947

Dear Columba,

You have naturally been much in my thoughts, and I was glad—and interested—to see the supplementary piece about your father in the *Times* the other day. So I was particularly glad to get your letter.[1]

How my book will stand 'the siege of battering days',[2] nobody can tell. The great thing, I am sure, is to be sincere, and to write the truth as one sees it. We all of us—even Saint Augustine, even Saint Thomas—are doing no more than add our thimblefuls of water to the river of understanding. Each contribution, even the greatest, is very small compared to the volume of the river, but there would be no river if there were not perpetual contributions from innumerable hands. I believe this is how a writer ought to look at his work: I think it is a humble attitude.

I have two notions about this business of man's getting at the truth, i.e. his taking the revelation that God offers him. The job is one of winnowing the grain from the chaff. How can one tell which is which? The only way to learn—and this is my second point—is through suffering, and that takes its own time: it can't be hurried.

Pride, like power, has an awkward catch about it: when you shoo it away from one place,[3] it lodges in another. Christians don't effectively become humble by transferring their pride to the Church, for the Church is a projection of themselves, and a man is still proud when he exercises his pride through the agency of an institution. Apply this to secular institutions—empires, clubs, schools, regiments—and it is evident. Now, the Church, too, is an institution on its manward-facing side, and I don't think it is exempt from this law.

All the higher religions make the same claim to the unconditional allegiance of all mankind, and declare that they have absolute authority. I think they are all revelations of different aspects of the same truth, and all of them are clogged with silt and flotsam that they have picked up on their way through the world. Gradually—through suffering—the water will be filtered.

Perhaps, in the end, they will coalesce. Perhaps one will absorb the others and will be influenced by what it has absorbed: as Christianity already has digested Judaism, Zoroastrianism, Isis and Osiris, Ishtar and Tammuz, the Magna Mater and Attis, and most of Greek philosophy.

You cannot assent to these ideas, but you can see that I can only follow the truth as I see it, and learn as much by suffering as God allows me.

Yours affectionately,
Arnold

1. Missing.
2. Shakespeare, sonnet 65.
3. A.J.T. obviously had in mind one of his favorite quotations: "Naturam expelles furca tamen usque recurret" (Horace, *Epistolae*, 1.10.24).

Ampleforth Abbey
York

4 September 1947

My dear Arnold,

I liked your last letter; it puts fairly and squarely your state of mind. The strange thing is that I can agree with almost all of it. But words are tricky and what you mean may not be what I mean, though we use identical phrases.

I love your attitude to your work; of course you should think like that; and I almost say, of course I think the way of my last letter, wanting the *Study* to be perfect in its degree.

I love the Church and it is an act of faith for me to affirm. Dross there is in the Church's theology. One has to distinguish I think between the defined doctrines and the expansions or excursions of particular thinkers or groups of thinkers.

I agree that the Church has swallowed Judaism whole, has digested Greek philosophers to suit its purposes. Zoroastrianism I should have thought, at least in its most fundamental, was rejected, first in Genesis by its affirmation of the creation of all things and again in the time of St. Augustine and his Manichean troubles. Isis and Osiris I thought you yourself have maintained were myths of the season's cycle: birth and death and birth again; and the idea of the cycle was used both by Christ and by S. Paul but as a figure and transcended. The Magna Mater and Attis I know nothing about. As a Catholic, as far as I know, it is not forbidden to believe that Christ made use of pre-existing revelations or insights into God's ways in order to make his own 'Way of Life' more intelligible to his hearers. In so far as all Truth is from God it seems to me inevitable that the more complete thing embraces all the previous incomplete expressions of it. But it is very difficult to say whether any are explicit borrowings or simply restatements of the same.

My stand-by in this is P. Pinard de la Boullaye[1] who gave a series of remarkable Conferences in Notre Dame—1934—which I got in France. His view seems to be that Christ could have borrowed from pagan sources but does not in fact seem to have done so, almost all being already in the O.T. or in fact original. As he was aiming at separateness from and not coalescing with paganism, clearly it would have been dangerous to show too many similarities underlying the muddled myths and his new teaching.

The chief and perhaps only point upon which we must for the time disagree is the phrase "Perhaps, in the end, they will coalesce", unless you mean it as Ricci meant to use Confucius's ideas as a *natural* basis for his superstructure on Chinese soil. But Hinduism cannot very well be digested by the Church except in some of its philosophy, and again in the natural order . . . But this is endless.

I have a beautiful prayer by St. Thomas for study—it is a bit long!

Here it is: Creator ineffabilis, qui de thesauris sapientiae tuae tres Angelorum hierarchias designasti, et eas super coelum empyreum miro ordine collocasti, atque universi partes elegantissime distribuisti: Tu, inquam, qui verus Fons Luminis et Sapientiae diceris, ac supereminens Principium infundere digneris super intellectus mei Tenebras, tuae radium claritatis, duplices in quibus natus sum, a me removens Tenebras, peccatum scilicet, et ignorantiam.

Tu qui linguas infantium facis disertas, linguam meam erudias atque in labiis meis gratiam tuae benedictionis infundas. Da mihi intelligendi acumen, retinendi capacitatem, ad discendi modum et facilitatem interpretandi, subtilitatem loquendi gratiam copiosam. Ingressum instruas, progressum dirigas, egressum compleas: tu qui es verus Deus et homo qui vivis et regnas in saecula saeculorum. Amen.

Yours affectionately,
Columba, O.S.B.

1. P. Pinard de la Boullaye (1874–1958); one of the great preachers during Lent in Notre Dame de Paris; see, e.g., his *Conférences de Notre Dame de Paris Carême, Jésus, lumière du monde* (Paris, 1934); *Les étapes de redaction des Exercises de S. Ignace* (Paris, 1945).

Saint Wilfrid's House
Ampleforth College, York

1 October 1947

My dear Arnold,

I wonder whether you celebrated yesterday in any way. It was the 50th anniversary of the heavenly birthday of your favorite saint—and one of mine—Soeur Thérèse. Anyhow, she will have remembered you. I am saying Mass for you on Friday, her feast day.

Dr. Coomaraswamy will now know that he exists.[1] I am saying Mass for him tomorrow. He was a gentle person and I am sure had many friends in heaven to help him along. What a dazzling awakening it must be to see all Truth in the vision of God. It is one of the thoughts that delights me about heaven: that we shall *know* what here we puzzled over. For instance, such things as I am puzzling over at the moment, where do all the primitive men fit in to the scheme of history, geology, chronology. It is tantalizing to know so little. My religious instruction set and I are enjoying ourselves studying Father Schmidt's theories on the religions of early Man.[2] Something of your sensation of continuity with them came to me as we burrowed down to those distant generations. It is wonderful that they had religion and were physically so primitive. It all confirms your thesis that command over environment even has a contrary effect, making men less God-seekers. In my search for information I came across a delightful little preface by l'Abbé Henri Breuil[3] on the relationship between the first chapters of Genesis and the discovered facts of the earliest times. He said in print very much what P. Schmidt said to you in conversation years ago in Vienna. (*Man Before History*, by Mary Boyle, Harrup).[4] It is only a child's book, but interesting for all that.

You will be glad to hear that B.O.&W. have made no definite offer over the Chinese History. I am rather relieved, as it does not commit me too early to anyone or anything.

How is the *Study* getting on? The school is back.

My best wishes to Veronica.
Yours affectionately,
Columba, O.S.B.

1. Compare C.C.E.'s letter of 5 April 1947, above.

2. Wilhelm Schmidt (1868–1954); *Ursprung der Gottesidee*, 12 vols. (Münster, 1926–55); *The Origin and Growth of Religion*, trans. Herbert Jennings Rose (London, 1931); A.J.T. cites Schmidt in *A Study of History*, VII: 760–66.

3. Henri Edouard Prosper Breuil (1877–1961); abbé and archeologist; professor of prehistory at the Collège de France (1929–47); founder of studies of art in the Stone Age; with L. Berger-Kirchner, *Franco-Cantabrian Rock Art*, in *The Art of the Stone Age* (English trans. A. E. Keep) (London, 1961), pp. 15–71.

4. Mary Boyle, *Man before History* (London, 1924).

45, Pembroke Square
London W.8

5 October 1947

Dear Columba,

I was reading your letter of the 4th September again and meditating on it when your last letter arrived. Yes, I am sure all is well with Dr. Coomaraswamy. The only misdemeanor of his I know of—and it was a mild one—was a sly attack on the Indian Muslims in a speech to an American audience in which he posed as the impartial sage above the battle. It was naughty, because the Americans were so easily taken in, and he ought to have known better, but it was a very human lapse, and the Muslims will survive it.

About our awakening to fuller knowledge, it is a puzzling thing for us, with our earthly faculties, to imagine; for it is difficult for us to think of eternity except as an afterlife, and yet it can't be that but must be an existence altogether outside the time sequence, in a higher dimension. One can say that in words, but not picture it to oneself. I suppose, in this life, one is potentially in eternity all the time, and is actually there if one ever has, in this life, a direct intuition of God.

You were very kindly tolerant of what I wrote about the relations between the different religions. Yes, there is a Catholic pride, which pulls non-Catholics up short, just as there is a Protestant's or rationalist's pride which hits a Catholic in the eye. It is elusive and insidious, because the proud Catholic transfers that pride from his own ego to the church in his own emotional attitude, yet doesn't get rid of the pride of doing that. It is something like the pride which the English used to take in the Navy or in the Empire: this is, of course, a gross and inadequate analogy, but I think it holds good on the point of the device of transference, and the catch in it. Perhaps the really pertinent analogy is with the pride of the Pharisees: they really had been the chosen people; they really had got God's law, and were following it. Yet Christ appeared, and they were caught out. They just couldn't imagine that there could be revelation and salvation outside their circle. I think we are always slipping into being Pharisees, and always being caught out over it by God. To judge by the New Testament, it is a very heinous sin—perhaps not because it is intrinsically so wicked, but because it is such an effective bar to further spiritual progress. No doubt there is mercy for Pharisees as individual souls, but, as heirs of the Promise, they are scrapped—I believe, always.

This applies to our situation to-day. There is no obligation on God to send us our next instalment of revelation through the Judaic religions. Judaism, Christianity and Islam may point out one facet of the truth about God and man and the universe. A Chinese would smile at the idea that salvation can be found out through revelations of Jewish origin—and he could support his argument by pointing to the vein of irony—the discomfiture of the Scribes and Pharisees who so reasonably are so sure of their own monopoly of truth and salvation—which is one of the main themes of the New Testament.

Meanwhile, I have been thinking about Saint Thérèse. One Sunday during the peace conference—I daresay I told you this—I found myself, with her in mind, walking straight out of my hotel after breakfast and making a bee-line across Paris via the Rue la Boétie to Montmartre, where, when I had climbed all those steps and walked into the church, my bee-line led me, to my astonishment, straight up to a statue of Saint Thérèse: I had no idea it was there: I don't think I had ever been inside the Sacré Coeur before. I stayed on that spot for several hours, praying in very great agony that the cup might be removed from me and that still, at the last moment, Rosalind and I might be reconciled. The prayer wasn't answered in that way: a direct request is a naïve kind of prayer, and seldom does—or deserves to—get a direct response giving what is asked for.

Perhaps that prayer of mine is now being answered in this way: St. Thérèse made her sainthood and of being a saint over the little ordinary things of life, and I have it much in mind to do my part in them, for Veronica, better than I did for Rosalind. This sounds prosaic, but I don't believe it is.

She and Gregory the Great and Saint Francis and Saint Ignatius are the saints whom I hold onto by the hems of their garments.

I was reading Thomas of Celano's[1] *legenda* of Saint Francis while we were on holiday in the North.

Go on with the Chinese history, and when the book is ripe, Burns and Oates will probably be eager to publish it.

The Nonsense book is on the move. I write a bit every morning nowadays. God Bless You.

Arnold

1. Thomas of Celano (ca. 1190–1260); the earliest biographer of Saint Francis, by order of Gregory IX; translated by A. G. F. Howell (London, 1908).

St. Wilfrid's House
Ampleforth College, York

St. Edward's Feast (13 October) 1947

My dear Arnold,

As you scarcely realize, it gives me increasing pleasure to get letters from you. Your last has been in my mind ever since it came; and I snatch this half holiday to reply to it.

Heaven. How we flounder in our thoughts upon it. I agree time ceases, yet somehow I think we grow and grow in insight before the wonder of God's majesty, Truth and Love. I have no doubt his Love will astonish and ravish us the most.

Catholic: Pharisees.

The interpretation of the sin of the latter is a little tricky, I think. However, it appears to be twofold (i) formalization: outward show, inward corruption; the futile attitude that if they fulfilled the exterior mechanical obligations, the inward spirit was not what mattered. The letter v. the spirit. (ii) The mistaken notion that their own doing got them to heaven. As they did not recognise themselves as sick, Jesus the physician could not cure them—they would not go to him.

Catholics—like everyone else—are prone to take outward conformity for inward intent. That is the nature of the beast.

Catholics do hold that *extra ecclesia non est salus*, and that the Church is *usque ad aeternum*. I believe both these propositions. Does that make me Pharisaic? That is what I have worried about and I think resolved.

The first proposition: *extra ecclesia, etc.* I do not hold this truth as perhaps the Pharisees maintained their equivalent; a) Everyone in the Church—visible organization—does not get to heaven. I am quite capable by my sins of not deserving to receive such a gift. Any moment by pride, disobedience, sensuality, I could fall to the lowest hell. God alone supports me. b) Millions outside this *visible organization* will see God face to face and be nearer to God than many who had a better chance, primitive pigmy, Hindu, Confucian, Russian Communist—*per accidens*—free mason, who knows no better. Every man has a chance of salvation. This is a dogma of the very Church which says *extra ecclesia* . . c) By outside the Church I would understand two things (1) if a man knows the church is the best instrument of grace founded by God, he should join it; and if he did not, for an unworthy motive, would forfeit his right to the Vision of God. (2) Those who are outside the visible organization but in good faith are *in fact* in the invisible Church, i.e. God gives them grace, which is none other than a share in his Life, won by Jesus upon the Cross of loving suffering. Therefore you, being in good faith, are in the invisible church sharing—up to a point in its hidden life—with Christ. Without that life no one is saved, for it is God's life by which we are made sufficiently like God to walk once again with him as Adam did in the garden.

I hold the second proposition *usque ad aeternum*, this with difficulty, because of the state of the world which seems so hostile and powerful. But by faith, I trust the Founder who promised it. Secondly because of the vast ages that stretch before us, perhaps; and if one for a second forgot the supernatural origin and nature of the Church (the God-life-in-the-world) one would be tempted to say: impossible. That sometimes accounts for the harshness of the expression of it. It is the voice of the little human mind of a soul with its back to the wall. Yet I hold it as a Truth because of the Promises of Christ: "the Gates of hell shall not prevail against it,"[1] "behold I shall be with you, even to the consummation of the world."[2] His sacrifice, "For this is the chalice of my blood of the New and everlasting Testament".[3] . . .

In this way we Catholics are not the Chosen Race, because not blood or the will of man saves us, or anyone, but the loving kindness of God; though we should do his will which among other things includes—as we think we see in the New Testament—submitting to a body which Christ left behind to preserve his precious, and ever threatened, Teaching.

Time's up.

P.S. I have tried to work out the connection between the Magna Mater and the Church.

Thank you for telling me about Soeur Thérèse and the Montmartre statue. She is sure to be looking after you, and St. Ignatius and the Great St. Gregory and the simple, loving St. Francis.

God bless you.
Yours affectionately,
Columba, O.S.B.

1. Matt. 16:18.
2. Ibid. 28:20.
3. Ibid. 26:28; Luke 22:20; Mark 14:24.

Saint Alfrid's House
Ampleforth College

All Monks (13 November) 1947

My dear Arnold,

Just a line on today's holiday—All Monks—to tell you I am still alive and not forgetting you.

You will be interested to hear that your thesis that the Roman Empire is the period of decadence under apparent glory always seems like an absurd paradox to the Classical Sixth. They cannot believe it. So you must somewhere in the 7–9 volumes show this very clearly. You give plenty of instances in 1–6 of the unrest *before* imperial times, but not much during them. Could it be that the peoples *were* content? Of course, if our own age can be shown to be a replica of Rome, the boys might then accept the thesis; they see that this age is one of apparent prosperity: buildings, roads, etc., and they might see under the mask of the Roman Pax also.

I listened in to the joint talk and wished I had known the others were on; so I missed your personal one on "Is there a Western Civilization"? I was disappointed in the joint effort, as it got nowhere. But my second thoughts were that this was as it should be. The answer was patent—and you, I thought, were leading us to it. Our civilization lost itself when it lost its faith. The odd thing was that no one said it. It sounded almost like a conspiracy. But it said itself in those little pauses!

Your voice comes through very truly. I could see you saying what I heard, and it gave me a great sense of nearness.

I am getting on with my essay on *Law, Liberty and Love*; and wonder whether you would like, or have time to look at the preface which is a very summary putting aside of Greece and Rome as the origin of the Western World's original belief in the liberty of men; and so preparing the way to show that it was derived from the Christian belief in the love of God for all men as displayed on the Cross.

Why does Professor Murray muddle myth and dogma? Myth has no reasonable grounds. Dogmas have, at least in Catholic theology they do. When you next meet him, do give him my best wishes and tell him how I respected his restraint in the *Times*.[1]

Would you agree that all the "Dying God" myths had in connection with Christian dogma was to prepare men's minds for the really spiritual significance of the Cross when it came? Men need a sign they can understand; and men's minds were prepared by the myths to expect God to die; but that he died for love of them was the revelation.

This is a scrappy letter. At least it is in its way a symbol of affection.

Yours affectionately,
Columba, O.S.B.

1. Gilbert Murray had defended the Marshall Plan, against Russian attacks, as "one of the most generous efforts ever made by any Government in history" (*The Times* [7 November 1947]).

45, Pembroke Square
London W.8

16 November 1947

Dear Columba,

I was so glad to get your letter; I never answered your last. We all seem to have less spare time than before. All the same, Veronica and I are happy and prosperous, and are getting things done.

I was at Oxford last week end, seeing Lawrence in his new house: 209 Woodstock Road.[1] I am very glad they are settled in—the more so as Jean is going to have another baby in March. Lawrence is having quite a success in getting commissions—for painting inn signs, which is rather fun, among other things.

I am interested in the difficulty of putting over my apparent paradox about the Roman Empire. I believe I am right. Perhaps the pagan literature, such as it is, of the Antonine Age—Apuleius,[2] Fronto,[3] Lucian,[4] for instance—gives a glimpse of the melancholy side of the picture. The savour had gone out of life before the crash came.

I am delighted that my old school-fellow Cripps[5]—for whose honesty, disinterestedness, courage, austerity and power of work I have a high regard—is now in the saddle. He comes of many generations of Crippses who have been to school at Winchester and then practiced at the ecclesiastical bar, but Stafford Cripps has struck out an individual line of his own without having lost the family tradition of solid virtue. I believe he will bring the real issue to a head—I mean the very difficult point that Labour, having come into power, have to work harder and live more austerely instead of enjoying the greater amenities that everyone expects to have when he comes into power. It is a difficult thing to put over, but I fancy Cripps, if anyone, may succeed in doing it. I don't think they would take it from a Conservative, because they would suspect his motives.

All the same, I have been interested to notice the amount of common ground between the two parties that has been established lately by R. A. Butler.[6] It is the English way to make politics a question of more or less and not a question of incompatibilities. Hence, I suppose, our comparative success in a field which is one of mankind's main failures so far.

What a political letter: I will now go and read a French book about the Praetorian Guards.

Write again,
and God Bless You.
Yours affectionately,
Arnold

1. Lawrence had received a diploma in Fine Arts from the Ruskin School of Drawing; became art master at St. Edwards School and visiting tutor at the Ruskin (1947–62); later lecturer in the Oxford School of Art (1960–63); senior lecturer in painting at the Bradford College of Art (1963–67); then director of the Art Centre at Morley College and director of the Morley Gallery (1967–72).

2. Lucius Apuleius (b. ca. A.D. 125); wrote the *Metamorphoses*, called by moderns *The Golden Ass*, a picaresque romance tinctured with religious allegory in which appeared, for the first time in classical literature, the story of Cupid and Psyche; cf. *A Study of History*, V:531–32: "Apuleius's pornographico-devotional romance."

3. M. Cornelius Fronto (consul, A.D. 143); baroque stylist who taught Marcus Aurelius; correspondence with his imperial pupil and others survives; cf. *A Study of History*, VI:81.

4. Lucian of Samosata (ca. A.D. 120–ca. 180); writer, in Greek, of philosophical and satirical dialogues; cf. ibid., pp. 133–34, for an extended quotation.

5. Sir Richard Stafford Cripps; in October had become minister for economic affairs, chancellor of the Exchequer in the Labour government; cf. C.C.E.'s letter of 29 March 1942, above.

6. Richard Austen Butler, Baron Butler of Saffron Walden (1902–82); chancellor of the Exchequer (1951–55); home secretary (1951–62); and foreign secretary (1963–64).

11 December 1947 45, Pembroke Square, W.8

Dear Columba,

Here is a premature Christmas card—Lawrence's work*—which I am sending you now because I want to know what book you would like for Christmas.

Would you care for C. Delisle Burns' *The First Europe*[1] which is just out?

It is about the transition between A.D. 400 and 800, with an eye on the parallel between that age and ours: not a history of events so much as an explanation of social and spiritual changes.

Burns was a Catholic priest who broke away and married and died early of consumption when he was spiritually on the return journey—not, perhaps, to the Church, but certainly to religion.

The book was written mostly under great difficulties and with much heroism, and will turn out, I should guess, to be a notable work.

Well, you may not fancy it or may anyway have other things you would like better. Do let me know.

All goes well with us. How is your mother getting on?

God Bless You.
Yours affectionately,
Arnold

*No, I would like better to send you the enclosed.

1. C. Delisle Burns, *The First Europe, a Study of the Establishment of Medieval Christendom, A.D. 400–800* (London, 1947).

Ampleforth College
York

S. Lucy's Feast (13 December) 1947

My dear Arnold,

Thank you very much for the Christmas card.[1] It inspired me to write a few lines, which I enclose as my Christmas present to you both. I rejoice in your mutual happiness.

I should love the book you mention, because, if you think so highly of it, it is sure to be of lasting value. As for the past history of the writer, who am I to judge him? And I can pray for him with every word of the book that I read.

You gave a talk which was referred to in the *Times* educational supplement. It interested me very much and I cut it out and kept it. We think on parallel lines and yet not the same. As we all are Christ: The New Man, I too believe we should accept all that any thinker has proposed, be he Confucius or an Indian philosopher. What is to be the rule by which we judge—our own reason or a faith once delivered to the saints—whether this new thing is to be incorporated or not? That is the point at which our ways diverge, I think. And will the new world now emerging come from your approach or mine? I think that your remarks in the *Study* about the "toughness" of the Jewish concept was—humanly speaking—why it survived in the contest. So—on the human seeming too—the "toughness" of the Catholic approach will outclass all contestants, yet at the same time accepting all that is good. That is my desire and would be my occupation if my time was my own, I mean to help create a new *Summa Theologica*, orthodox yet new. God bless you both and give you joy in Christmas time and in years and years to come.

Columba, O.S.B.

1. The card reproduced the *Madonna, Child and Angels*, a leaf of the Wilton Diptych, attributed to the English school of the late fourteenth century; in the National Gallery in London. C.C.E.'s poem:

English the Mother and the holy Child,
 The standard and the gorgeous marigolds,
English the face of angels there who smiled,
 Their golden hair, the dresses' faint blue folds.
Once English too the Faith serenely drawn:
 God manifest, God hid and lowly meek.
So end the Night for us and come the Day.
 We thirsting, with the hart, Life's waters seek.

1947

16 December 1947 45, Pembroke Square, W.8

Dear Columba,

Here is the Deslisle Burns. As you will see, he puts the Church up and the barbarians down.

I shall be interested to know what you think about his treatment of the Church's dilemma: (i) they couldn't hold aloof and just let things rip; (ii) they couldn't do business with barbarian war-lords without compromising with the world.

Merry Christmas,
Yours affectionately,
Arnold

Ampleforth Abbey
York

20 December 1947

My dear Arnold,

Here is a little book—our Country.[1] Thank you very much for *The First Europe*. It certainly is interesting and in "my period". But more of that later.

God bless you both and give you a very happy Christmas.

Yours affectionately,
Columba, O.S.B.

1. *The Ampleforth Country*, by "a Group of boys of Ampleforth College" (York, 1947); later amplified in the 4th ed. of 1966; a vade mecum for the neighborhood of Ampleforth.

Mount Saint Bernard Abbey
Charnwood Forest
Near Coalville
Leicestershire

30 December 1947

My dear Arnold,

A very happy New Year, and God's blessing upon your life and work during it.

No, I have not become a Cistercian. I am merely giving the monks here their annual retreat. They live in great austerity, much as St. Bernard did at the beginning:

rise at about 2 A.M., no meat, fish or eggs. Silence always—this is modified by the fact that they may talk to their immediate superior and the Prior and Abbot. The Rule is never relaxed, not even for Christmas. It is a life of faith, because they see no results, whilst we with our school see some; though I should be the first to agree that *our* results may well be due to *their* prayer and mortification.

It is an interesting place in which to read *The First Europe*.[1] One takes one's own monasticism for granted. This is like looking at a familiar landscape through a looking glass.

The book. I read most of it carefully and even marked passages in the margin with a pencil. Towards the very end I tired, and must admit not to have read some parts very closely. They followed well known tracks.

I can see what appeals to you and in what way it is a notable book. It casts aside the two favorite themes: the humanist classical one that all that is good in Europe comes from Greece and Rome, and Acton's strange aberration that the blond Saxon or at any rate our German cousins brought with them the seeds of the First Europe. It surprised me that he nowhere mentions Acton, and only you very much in passing, because he has obviously read you pretty thoroughly, while Acton's grand finale about "Render to Caesar . . ." in his *Essay on Freedom in Antiquity*—I think—clearly stuck in his gullet—to put it vulgarly.[2]

Those two recurring phrases "climate of opinion" and "moral authority v. authority of force" are very true, and in a way are the motif of the book. But unfortunately he has crowds of bees in his bonnet buzzing away, which in the end destroy almost the good. But of those buzzings perhaps later. I take it he recognises that (a) the Papacy and (b) the monks were the great architects of the First Europe. You of course have written as much, only better. Still this is a whole book proving it. So far so good.

Some strange points in the book.

I never have read anything quite so lacking in understanding of the sacraments and magic—I suppose that is the Bp. Barnes school.[3] He imagines that we believe the sacrament does the spiritual renewal, of course it is God who does. While magic is not, surely, his definition, anyway, but: thinking to force God's hand by man-made ritual.

By beginning at A.D. 400 he can conveniently avoid discussing the earlier evidences for the Papacy. His treatment leaves out of account S.S. Ignatius, Irenaeus, Cyprian and many others. It is things like that which destroy the value of the book. While his fantastic idea that Christ was later made into an incarnate God on the model of the Emperors, is scarcely worth bothering about, and makes one want to throw the book down! Had he gone into it, one could be patient, but he just throws it off as one of those established facts. How can anyone who faces the accepted dates of the N.T., in which Christ's divinity is stated over and over again, claim that this is due to an imitation of the very people who are killing all the chief Christians? And in any case how many emperors were divinified by the time the epistles of St. Paul were written? For in them the divinity of Christ is unquestionably affirmed. The only hope for fundamental truth and sanity in historical writing since the mists of Modernism—Loisy[4] and the like—is for some historian—and please God may it be you—to return to the question of the authenticity of the Gospels, examine them in all simplicity, without pre-conceived ideas. This work must absolutely be done; or men will live in a world—not of Truth, but of questions and possibilities.

Throughout LB's book, I am afraid, he shirks the problem in its historical setting: did Christ found the Papacy? I also think L.B. has got the wrong end of the stick about monks and hermits. They did not think themselves the only True Christians, but they were following options, counsels of the Gospels and of S. Paul. It is all there in black and white in the N. Testament. S. Paul on virginity says he gives no command on the matter.[5] (Jesus: "if thou wouldst be *perfect* go sell all . . .")[6] But again you have written magnificently on S. Benedict, and how all comes to him who gives up all for God. So I need not labour that point.

The Problem

The Church *always* gets contaminated by mingling with the world. Christ alone did not. But Christians for all their good intentions are weak. But that is no reason for not trying to convert the world. We should always try, trust God, and be sorry when we fail. The other side of the picture is this openly co-operating with evil doers in Governments. I think he exaggerates horribly and fails to realize that ALL MEN are evil doers, and that if we worked on his principle the Church would never co-operate. The same principle underlay the attack on Pius XI's attitude to Mussolini. The pope did not approve of all he did, but worked with him in what he did well. This was the principle of Our Lord, don't you agree, and the opposite one, the pharisees'. He goeth with publicans and sinners.

And yet, in spite of my disagreement with so much, I bear no ill will to the writer. I am terribly sorry for him. It has shown me how far one can go and how far many are away from the True story.

It is very simple—and you see most of it—but let me just once state it, for love of it.

Someone came on earth who by his life, works, death and resurrection, convinced his disciples that he was Almighty God in human form. It followed that everything he said and did was treasured as absolute truth. Could this not be the birth in the world outside Jewry of the idea of historical Truth? The disciples were determined to preserve that Truth. Each little heresy thought itself *The* Church—quite unlike the Protestant sects who believe there is *no* visible church.

It was this absolute conviction in the Truth of their way of life, derived from a divine master, which made it possible to create a new world out of one which no longer knew its own mind. Thus, not only the Papacy is infallible, but the Church cannot err either, was the theme.

The monks and the Papacy were two expressions of this absolute certitude, the former living it by example, the latter by precept. The Papacy was accepted as the Teacher because the Christian world believed it had divine guidance behind it.

I agree with you that men more willingly obeyed because also they loved the

Papacy which had been so good to them: given them the faith, helped them against poverty or oppression. But, for the fact of the Papal claim, one must simply be an historian and examine afresh the early evidence.

I have said too much. Yet in some way I think it interesting for you to have my almost immediate reaction to the book. I do not mean to be unkind.

It is possible that L.B. was one of the Philips de Lisle family which gave the ground here to the monks over 100 years ago?

God bless you and ever lead you towards himself, the fulness of Truth and Love.

Yours affectionately,
Columba, O.S.B.

1. Compare A.J.T.'s letter of 11 December 1947, above.

2. John Emerich Edward Dalberg, first Baron Acton (1834–1902); planner of the *Cambridge Modern History*; *The History of Freedom and Other Essays* (London, 1907).

3. Bishop Earnest William Barnes (1874–1953); bishop of Birmingham (1924–52); *The Rise of Christianity* (London, 1947), in which he rejected the miraculous.

4. Alfred Firmin Loisy (1857–1940); founder of modernism in France; *L'Évangile et l'Église* (Paris, 1902).

5. 1 Cor. 7:6

6. Matt. 19:21; Mark 10:21; Luke 18:22

Ampleforth Abbey
York

12 January, 1948
St. Benet Biscop.

My dear Arnold,

This requires no answer. It is a meditation on pride. This morning during holy Mass I receive an illumination of what you meant by pride in the Church. I was saying Mass in St. Benet's Chapel—the one with the altar stone of Byland.[1] Let me speak for myself—what others think or their motives I do not know. Yes, I am proud not of the Church but because I am in the Church, as though that was any merit to me. I neither deserve to have received that grace nor do I deserve to have kept it. I feel ashamed, and rightly, that I should feel anything but confusion for having been given by God so much Truth all my life and used it so ill. The pharisee in me is to think that I can be saved by knowing the Truth. It must be lived up to; and in any case, please God, I shall be saved by his great mercy.

That is the scandal in history too, a body which has been given so much light and lived so little in conformity to it. Let me acknowledge that fact: the Catholic Church may be Holy in ideal, but it has often been wicked in its members. But I am no one to lament the sins of others. My own arrogance is enough to turn people away. Knowing the truth is not enough. Therefore God surely will save all those who seek Him and ask his mercy. If you ever quote me in your book, if only in idea, let it be only this one thought that all the world is saved by God's mercy if the world asks for it. God does not ask knowledge but humility and love; knowledge of Him will come after that.

God bless you and your humble seeking.

Your friend,
Columba, O.S.B.

1. Byland Abbey; see C.C.E.'s letter of 22 April 1940, above.

45, Pembroke Square
London W.8

January 31, 1948

Dear Columba,

We sail on a Polish boat—the 'Batóry;—tomorrow week, the 8th of February, but, having just finished a draft chapter and got vaccinated and secured our visas and taught a newly arrived little Austrian maid how to lay the stove for the boiler, I have got my head above water again, so here is a chance to write a long-delayed letter in my little study here—with the sun pouring through the south window out of a wide sky which is a luxury in London.

Your meditation about pride made me happy—though I didn't need to hear it in order to know, as I have always known, that you are not far from the Kingdom of God.

Burns[1] was bound to annoy you, though you rightly kept your sympathy and charity awake while you were reading the book. He deserves regard, for he was writing under tribulation with great sincerity—exposing himself to be dismissed as batty by the people he had lived among since breaking away from the Church.

To you, such pioneering is at best superfluous, and at worst misleading, because, for you, the ground is already charted correctly, once for all. But you must remember that this is not so, today, for most of the world—indeed, never has been so; for Christians (including all the vanished ones) have never been more than a small minority of mankind in one corner of the world, so far.

We have now entered on a new great debate, like the one in the Roman Empire during the first four or five centuries, and Christianity may once again come out changed in outward form.

The crucial and immensely controversial question, of course, is what is the essence and what is the accretion of some particular time and place. This, perhaps, is the main subject of debate—for, though there are anti-Christs who deny the essence too, their colour is so plain, and their fruits are so obviously poisonous, that they are perhaps unlikely to prevail—at any rate, in the long run.

Since you wrote, I have read the Barnes[2] too, and he, too, is sincere. To you, he would be an atheist, I expect, but beware; for the Jews seemed atheists to Pompey,[3] and the fourth-century Christians to Julian.[4]

Well, from the 16th February onwards, we shall be at the Institute for Advanced

Study, Princeton, N.J., U.S.A. We sail from New York on the 7th May, but you will have heard from me long before then.

God bless you.
Yours affectionately,
Arnold

1. Delisle Burns; see A.J.T.'s letter of 11 December 1947, above.

2. Compare *A Study of History*, VII: 393, n. 1, where A.J.T. cites E. W. Barnes, *The Rise of Christianity*.

3. Gnaeus Pompeius Magnus (106–48 B.C.); stormed Jerusalem in 63 B.C.; cf. ibid., p. 463: "An Hellenically cultivated Pompey was dumbfounded at finding no material object of worship whatsoever inside the Holy of Holies of the Temple of Yahweh at Jerusalem."

4. Flavius Claudius Julianus (r. 361–363); the "Apostate"; *A Study of History*, V: 584.

Ampleforth College
York

S. Scholastica's Day (10 February) 1948

My dear Arnold,

Thank you for your really stirring letter. I agree the debate is as you say, What is the essence of Christianity? Even within the Church we can ask ourselves that. But, as you say, some things for us are already settled; and all the same, there remains the relative importance of certain Truths and how one looks at them. The presentation gets distorted: Pascal may have exaggerated in his attack on the "moralists", Escobar and his gang,[1] but he hit a nail on the head, one could turn casuistry into a fetish, a gargoyle of a substitute for the Love of God.

While I have not read Bishop Barnes, I can imagine myself thinking he was a near-atheist; and sometimes people are! But I admire his courage while doubting his wisdom or justice in staying where he is.

You will be glad to hear that I have written on: *Law, Liberty, Love*, a study in Christian Obedience, The Preface, The chapters on the Gospels, the Pre-Benedictine monachism, and St. Benedict's Rule. I am now faced with the Post-Benedictine creation of Europe and the second half of the N.T., as my immediate objectives. I wish you were here to canalize my work on the Post-Benedictine section. Perhaps on your return you will be willing to see the first draft.

I meant this to have been written before you left, to speed you on your way. Now it will have to fly over you to receive you on your arrival. I hope this trip will be even more profitable than the last.

All best wishes to you and Veronica.

Yours affectionately,
Columba, O.S.B.

1. "*Les Provinciales*: Cinquième et Sixième Lettres" (1656), in Lafuma, ed., *Oeuvres complètes*, pp. 387–97.

Institute for Advanced Study
Princeton, N.J. U.S.A.

22nd February, 1948

Dear Columba,

We arrived here the day before yesterday after a night (and two press conferences!) in New York, and a ten days' crossing. It was rough, and we were 48 hours late, and Veronica suffered a bit—worst of all, I am afraid, from my imperviousness (I noticed nothing, and wrote 40 pages of foolscap). We are installed in a very pleasant and convenient flat in the middle of Princeton, looking out into Palmer Square, with the statue of the Princeton Tiger (the university totem). We have also got a very pleasant room to work in at the Institute, and a bus to take us there—it has a campus of its own, out in the country—or alternatively one can walk there across four campi: the university's, the Presbyterian Theological Seminary's, the Graduate School's, and the Institute's.[1]

Housekeeping is, I hope, going to be easy for Veronica, with our midday meal at the Institute's canteen and a delicatessen shop, just below this flat, where one can buy anything you like, ready cooked.

As for the Institute, it is an epitome of the scholar's world, Chinese mathematicians, a Swedish philosopher, American and English epigraphists, of whom one is my old school friend Theodore Wade-Gery,[2] whom I fancy you met: he is professor of Greek history at Oxford: they are editing the Athenian tribute lists.

I have in my bag your Pascal, whom I propose to read in April, travelling to and from Birmingham, Alabama where I am giving some lectures.

Our little Austrian maid arrived ten days before we left, and we have left her under the care of a friend and colleague from Chatham House, who is living at 45 Pembroke Square when we are away. To poor little Nessi, England is an America—a land of inconceivable plenty; so all these things are relative. My goodness, what a pleasure to eat bananas—but I mustn't make your mouth water.

I am sure I shall be able to do lots of work here, and we shall certainly both enjoy the visit and be happy to come home at the end of it.

God Bless You.
Yours affectionately,
Arnold

1. During this visit to Princeton, A.J.T. delivered lectures in various cities; his address in Chicago was printed as *An Historian's View of American Foreign Policy* (Chicago, 1949).

2. Theodore Wade-Gery (1888–1972); Winchester, New College, Oxford; member, Institute for Advanced Study, Princeton, at various times (1937–61); Wykeham Professor of Ancient History, Oxford (1939–53); A.J.T. was traveling with Wade-Gery on the Orient Express in 1921 when he conceived of *A Study of History* (see p. ix of the preface to Vol. VII).

Ampleforth Abbey
York

16 April 1948

My Dear Arnold,

The written work recalls your voice and your gestures. Thank you for *Civilization on Trial*. It arrived the day after your own birthday, so you fulfilled an Eastern custom of giving presents not receiving them on *your* big occasion. The 14th you noticed coincided with the feast of St. Joseph, I wonder whether it did in 1889. Many happy returns of the day—if this is not too belated.

I have devoured the book. Some I knew and loved already, specially *Christianity and Civilization*; but much is new or in a new dress.

You make Islam the possible ground for the next religious recreation. I wonder whether it might not be in Catholic Eastern Europe or even Catholic China, submerged under the new colossus. You will have to answer this question for me: in the physical struggle does the more ruthless always win in the end? Thus will Russia win the physical battle in the end? To be conquered herself by those she conquers?

I took your book with me this evening—after reading it by the fire in the calefactory—into the Church and handed it to God, asking what was true, what nearly so. The question that I ask now always in regard to your mental probings is: in what sense could the message and *action* of Jesus Christ be modified. If truth is truth, it stays. If Christ is truth, he stays. But I see that truth can be set in new settings, can be joined with truth to make a third, not contrary but complementary to the first two. Thus the Jewish Christ is the Son of God, and becomes for the Greek: Christ, of the same *Nature* as God, another *person* to the Father. The truth remains but deepened, or one might even say a new understanding of the truth, more of the truth.

I remember Prof. Clark (G.N.?)[1] when he was here denying that truth had a history, when I thought it the only history worth bothering about! I, of course meant, our discovery of it. So I believe tentatively that a modern P. Ricci—of glorious memory, he—may state Christ's message in a new way and bigger way for us, without denying one iota of what he said. In a way this is being done all the time by all of us. I embrace your idea that we should be heirs of Confucius, the Buddha, Socrates, indeed of any man who has enlightened the world with truth. But I, as a follower of Christ, would put all these others on a lower plane, for they were admittedly human and fallible, and Christ divine. How does that seem to you? I should like to know very much. For me, and all of us, I suppose, there are three ways of judging, when these great men differ on vital points; the first to be judge oneself, the second to accept one as supreme, and any who differ from him to be discarded to that extent; the third to live in a twilight of true not knowing which to follow. Mine is the second. The first is almost impossible for the 2,000,000,000 men alive today. The third may be the only conclusion possible for most. I pray they will find the second.

This "A.J.T. for beginners," as you see, has roused me intensely and almost wholly to assent. I love those little autobiographical details, specially in regard to your mother. The way to approach history that you would like history written, I agree with of course, and hope that in my China book I will fulfill the desire.

Please give my greeting to Veronica; and I hope she is preventing you from lecturing too much; though, if this book is the result of such tours, I do not want her to prevent you too much either.

Spring is here gloriously, the Gilling woods are many greens; the cricket pitches are patches on the fields. Fr. Raphael has begun his coaching.

Fr. Alban, Fr. Barnabas, Fr. Patrick are avid to read the book.

God bless you and all your works,
in caritate Christi,
Columba, O.S.B.

P.S. I have written two poems, one on faith, one on following God's will, which you will see when you return.

1. Sir George Norman Clark; cf. C.C.E.'s letter of 21 November 1940, above. "We were discussing the relativity of truth, what is true for one age is not for another, a theme that A.J.T. developed on Pascal's famous *pensée*, truth being falsehood this or that side of a frontier, and Christianity being true for the West, but not for the East, where, say, Buddhism is the truth. G. N. Clark did not agree to that relativism, so I passed it on discreetly to A.J.T. A.J.T. refused the Regius Professorship later on for the same reason as that for which G. N. Clark gave it up: administration made original historical scholarship virtually impossible. A.J.T. told me it had been offered him, a tempting offer, as he might, according to his lights, have broadened the base of Cambridge historical scholarship away from the 'parochial West' to include the world." (C.C.E.)

Union Theological Seminary
80 Clermont Avenue,
New York, N.Y.

21 April 1948

Dear Columba,

I have just had your letter of the 16th about the book: I am so glad it arrived, and that you like it.

Here I am, with just time to write before going off to give the fourth and last of my lectures at Columbia on 'the prospects of the Western Civilization'.[1] It is on the conflict between the Heart and the Head. Someday you will see it in nonsense book form (Part XII).

To-morrow we go to Washington, and then for a week to Birmingham, Alabama, a steel town in the 'Deep South', where I am going to give another set of lectures. Then we come back, via my friend Rob Darbishire in Kentucky, to sail from New York on the 7th May.

We lost our hearts to Princeton, and are glad that we shall be coming back there for another such visit next spring. But I should be sorry, of course, to have my roots anywhere but in England.

On the whole I am an optimist about the possibility of avoiding the third and final world war, but I do hope America will use her authority in Italy and Greece to enforce there enough social justice to make a free enterprise society a more attractive alternative than a Communist society for the masses. So long as that is not done, there will always be a danger of Communism spreading. But I don't know whether the rather conservative middle class that governs America have the imagination to understand that something that may not be necessary in America may be indispensable in the different conditions of Western Europe.

Well, I wonder if liberal Catholics in Europe and America can't combine to put through a constructive social policy in the countries in no-man's-land.

With very best wishes from both of us,

Yours affectionately,
Arnold

1. Published as *The Prospects of Western Civilization* (New York, 1949) in an edition limited to 400 copies. And see "The Prospects of the Western Civilization," in *A Study of History*, IX: 406–644, and "The History and Prospects of the West," in *A Study of History*, XII: 518–36.

45, Pembroke Square
London W.8

Whitsunday 16 May 1948

Dear Columba,

I have been meaning to answer your letter of the 16th, but we were on the move for three weeks ending this last Thursday, when we arrived back home.

You should have seen me in the train, reading your copy of Pascal as we wound our way through the furry mountains of Central Tennessee. I really have read the Pensées now, after many dips into them. After this very long loan, I shall be sending them back to you when I have copied several passages for my own use.[1]

I want to see those poems you told me of, that you have lately written.

I am glad you liked *Civilization on Trial*.

As for the insistent question of Russia, I think the key to the situation is that (1) three quarters of the world is on the non-Communist side of the dividing line (2) the Russians are too weak militarily to challenge the Americans in war (3) the only method open to the Russians is their present one of missionary work (4) the rich and powerful minority that rules the non-Soviet three-quarters of the world has it in its power to sterilize this communist mission field by mitigating the moral and social evils which give the Communist propaganda its opening.

Russian Communism is a challenge to the rulers of the rest of the world.

Take Italy, where we have a short breathing space now owing to the results of the election.[2] If de Gasperi's supporters will allow him, he has it in his power to sterilize Italy against communism by building houses for the urban workers, carrying out agrarian reforms in the South, and putting down the black market. But if the well-to-do minority in Italy were to say to itself: 'The victory in the elections has made it unnecessary for us to do social justice,' then communism would eventually well up again, and this time with irresistible force, as underdog's only hope.

Personally, I am rather an optimist. I believe the historical mission of communism will prove to have been to put the fear of God into the hearts of the ruling minority outside the Russian sphere. If that did happen, it would be a happy ending.

If, though, the ruling element in America preferred to 'smash Russia' rather than do social justice on their side of the dividing line, I think the result would be a very ironic tragedy. I am sure the Americans could overthrow Russia in war—their superiority in military strength must be decisive—but the price would be the end of democracy in America and the destruction of Western Europe.

What do you think of this? Well, it is good to be home again.

Yours affectionately,
Arnold

1. In the event, A.J.T. quoted Pascal several times in *A Study of History* from vol. VII on.

2. In the first national election under Italy's new constitution, on 18 April 1948, the Christian Democrats won an absolute majority; Alcide de Gasperi (1881–1954); prime minister (1946–53); founded the Christian Democratic party in 1944.

Saint Wilfrid's House
Ampleforth College, York

Whitsunday (16 May) 1948

Dear Arnold,

Thank you for your cheerful letter from America. I hope you are right about peace. These dictators get mesmerised by their own theories, and even ordinary democratic politicians do who hear opposition. What it must be like for a person who never hears any is hard to imagine.

I hope you got my little note written on Easter Sunday;[1] it had an idea on the nature of Christianity which even after a few months still seems better to me than many other peoples' efforts to state it! I am in fact asking lots of people point blank what they think the essence of it is; and it is amazing how many different answers one gets even from Catholics: the idea of the distinction between Creator and creature; the vision of God; Grace; God's life in the soul; Redemption; God entering time.

Please tell me your impressions of Pascal. Would you say that in the tug of war between heart and head it was an early example of letting each go its own sweet way and living two lives? A thing easy enough to do when the divergence was so small, but impossible now. There must be a reconciliation. (Must I wait till Vol. IX before I see that lecture?).

Welcome home. I hope to be in London for a week from 27th July, so perhaps we can manage a meeting.

You must read *Ways of Confucius and of Christ*, by Dom Pierre Célestin Lou, ex prime minister of China.[2] It is all about the "marriage of two minds."

in caritate Christi,
My very best greetings to
Veronica.
Columba, O.S.B.

1. Missing.

2. Dom Pierre Célestin Lou, *Ways of Confucius and of Christ*, trans. M. Derrick (London, 1948); see n. 1 to C. C. E.'s letter of 22 August 1948, below.

Saint Wilfrid's House
Ampleforth, York

22 May 1948

My dear Arnold,

It was right that we should each write to the other on Whitsunday, for we know we are one by that day, though not visibly so.

Yes, I believe that justice must be done before the West is safe from the scourge, but I doubt if the Faith to be just is strong enough in Western minds; that fire which came into the world with Christ, and which we call charity is necessary too. What fearful straits our ancestors have led us to, some defiling their Treasure so that others threw it away; and here are we left, millions of blind men wandering in a forest. So I am not despairing; for the grace of God may raise up men and women to grasp this serpent of doubt and of dilatoriness; but in spite of spasms of "rapprochement," I see not only economic motives but also that ogre, the will to power—a thing I find terribly hard to understand, but a thing which seems to exist, and which may lead to war. *Dios sobre todo.*

Here are the two poems. They both had comments, but there is no copy of one and the poem is clear enough. The other is best understood with the comment first. This is the first final draft of it. Do keep them, and then you and Tim Smiley [1] share the comment. He, by the way, is a simple, clever, mathematical scholar, aged 16½–17.

In view of your search for 'the essence of Christianity' I think you should read, if you have not, Newman, who puts our point of view so beautifully, or Marín Sola O.P.[2] who does it so accurately (and aridly!).

Law, Liberty, Love have got to S. Thomas now.

Yours affectionately,
Columba, O.S.B.

1. Timothy John Smiley (1930–); Fribourg University; Clare College, Cambridge; professor of philosophy at Cambridge University (1980–); fellow, Clare College.

2. Marín-Sola F., O.P., *La evolución homogénea del dogma católico* (Valencia, 1923).

45, Pembroke Square
London W.8

19 June 1948

Dear Columba,

I have been meaning to write and hoping to know when I shall be in London or away, as you said you would be coming to London in July. Will that be at the end of the month when term is over? I now think we are almost certain to be here then, and we hope you will stay with us here.

Since I wrote last, we have been with my cousins in Westmorland,[1] looking at our two farms and cottage that they farm for us—on the banks of the River Lune, about four miles S.W. of Sedbergh. We were delighted with the farms themselves and with the country—it is high fells on the Yorkshire side of the River, and very pleasant broken hilly country on our side. The cottage is just right, and we have been trying to persuade the old lady who is now the tenant to let us have it during hay time, when she goes to her daughter's farm ten minutes away: but she is a shy bird, and won't, I think, agree—at any rate, not this year. So we shall probably stay here through the summer—especially as we are going for a month to Turkey in November.

With so much greenery and open space, front and back, this is half like being in the country, and we are very fond of it.

We have also been at Cambridge where they gave me a degree.[2] This was fun, as Smuts was being installed as Chancellor,[3] and Winston and Cripps[4] were in the party. I have been bowling away at Part VII of the Nonsense Book, working on such things as the conflict between Science and Religion, and the relation between Christianity, Hinduism, the Mahayana and Islam. You shall see it at some stage in typescript.

I like your poems, and the commentary on one of them. As you say, it is a poem on the commentary rather than vice versa.

We have just been visiting our old friend Norman Baynes,[5] the Byzantine scholar. He went under an operation expecting to die, and has come out to find he has a new lease of life. As a thank-offering, I am hoping he is going to precipitate several books which he owes to the world and which nobody but he can write.

I much look forward to seeing you.

Yours affectionately,
Arnold

1. The Raven Franklands; cf. A.J.T.'s letter of 24 December 1946, above.

2. Litt.D.

3. Compare C.C.E.'s letter of 7 October 1941, above; A.J.T. admired Jan Christian Smuts; cf. "Field Marshall Jan Smuts," chap. 13 of A.J.T.'s *Acquaintances*, pp. 169–77; and *A Study of History*, X: 234–35.

4. Sir Richard Stafford Cripps; cf. A.J.T.'s letter of 16 November 1947, above.

5. Compare C.C.E.'s letter of 10 March 1941, above.

Saint Wilfrid's House
Ampleforth College, York

27 June 1948

My dear Arnold,

It is very kind of you to offer to put me up; as you know it would be one of those great pleasures. But my mother is coming up to London too and we are going to a little hotel somewhere. I arrive on the 27th July, have a meeting on the 28th, am booked on the 29th and stay in London to the following Friday the 6th August, which would probably be my free day as my mother returns to Beccles that morning and I am staying Friday–Monday with a friend—Robert Wilberforce—in Essex somewhere. We should leave London probably in the early morning. That then is the pattern and as you are busy and I free, please you pick the day and the hour.

Your promise and offer to show me the VII Volume in typescript, as you knew it would, fills me with pleasure, but, as you perhaps cannot realise, with almost as much awe, for who am I to represent the Church in the Great Debate. But you do know my limitations and will make allowances.

Here is the commentary on the Faith poem.[1] You will see it is specially written for the boy who received the poem. He lent me the MS. for copying.

All graces suitable to the feast of SS. Peter and Paul. You have heard perhaps that the excavations under St. Peter's have revealed such wonderful evidence of S. Peter etc. that the Pope himself is producing a 5 volume work on it all.

My love to you and Veronica.

in caritate Christi,
Columba, O.S.B.

1. A commentary on a poem written by C.C.E. for a student concerned with the faith.

45, Pembroke Square
London W.8

9 July 1948

Dear Columba,

I have been waiting to answer your letter of the 27th June till I knew our plans.

We are hoping to stay a week or two at one of our farms in Westmorland, and the date depends on hay.

We may not go till the 17th August, but we may go on the 3rd. But anyway, even if we are not here on the 6th, can't we see you over the 30th July–2nd August?

It would be very nice if you would bring your mother to lunch or supper with us, and you and I might have a walk together, too, over the week-end. If we go on the later date, we can do something together on the 6th August as well.

Thank you too for the commentary on the poem.

We are going to stay this next week-end with Lawrence and Jean, to see my youngest grandchild Celia.[1]

Yours affectionately,
Arnold

1. Celia Toynbee Caulton (1948–); King's College, London University; she is a free-lance radio interviewer and producer; cf. A.J.T.'s letter of 30 October 1970, below.

Ampleforth
York

12 July 1948

My dear Arnold,

Thank you for the invitation. That is grand. I suggest Sunday, 1st August, lunch. If that does not suit please send me a card. I think we are free so far, because we have left the times to the last, but I can imagine us being very full of meals with various members of the family. We could go for a walk after, as you suggest.

Unfortunately I did not hear you on the wireless last night. We always have a House-masters' meeting at that time. I wonder whether you knew that you were speaking on St. Benedict's feast day. I had to talk to the Junior House—a thing I always find difficult but pleasing—on St. Benedict. As I had seen someone spinning and weaving in the age old way some days before, it struck me how much like that very early invention the Holy Rule was. The simple elemental *search for God*, upon which all other progress depends.

For the rest, until we meet,

Yours affectionately,
Columba, O.S.B.

P.S. I have just seen matron who heard your broadcast. She said that it began in a rather depressing way about breakdowns, collapses, and that she expected to hear that our Time had come, but that you ended on an (optimistic) encouraging note. *But*, she could not remember why you were not so discouraging as she expected you to be. Matron used to be at Gilling Castle. What strikes me as interesting is that she remembered only conclusions, not reasons.

1. Compare *The Listener*, 15 July 1948, Vol. XL, No. 1016, pp. 75–6, "Civilization on Trial": ". . . our fate is in our own hands. . . ."

The Royal Institute
of International Affairs
Chatham House
10, St James's Square
London S.W.1

14 July 1948

Dear Columba,

We look forward very much to seeing you and your mother at 45 Pembroke Square for luncheon Sunday 1st August. Come, if you can, by 1.0 P.M. as we shall probably be going to the restaurant in the block of flats just round the corner.

We were staying over the week-end with Lawrence and Jean, to see Celia Jane: a very friendly baby.

Well, how good it will be to see you—and, if the weather prevents us walking, we can sit and talk at home.

Yours affectionately,
Arnold

The Royal Institute
of International Affairs
Chatham House
10, St James's Square
London S.W.1

4 August 1948

Dear Columba,

Here is the Cambridge laudation: it pleased me a lot.[1]

I was so very glad to have that time with you on Sunday. It was all too short, but to be with your mother during just these days is certainly very much the first call on you, as you feel.

I shall be reading your ms. and hope to write a short foreword, as you ask. I very much want to, and, though the difference in our positions exists, and may be important, I don't think it is likely to prevent me from doing what I want.

As I expect you could see on Sunday, I am happy, but I have learnt that happiness in this world is provisional and precarious—in fact, every earthly summer is an Indian Summer.

My sense of the command laid on me to write out my book is as urgent as ever it was. As I see it, the book is a kind of thinking aloud of the thoughts of secularized Western Man now that he is near the end of his secular tether. Like happiness, such thoughts are provisional only. If they are timely, and helpful in moving the mass forward, even by an inch, that is enough reason for producing them with the sweat of one's brow.

You ought to read Tremaye's Life of William Temple.[2]

Yours affectionately,
Arnold

1. See A.J.T.'s letter of 19 June 1948, above; the citation concluded: "Hac usus ratione *ἰστορίης ἀπόδεξιν* condidit eruditione vix credibili confertam, tam rerum copia quam sententiarum varietate et sapientia mirandam, cuius cum ad umbilicos pervenimus. 'Sic' exclamamus, 'Sic rerum summa movetur / Semper, et inter mortales mutua vivunt.' Quid plura? Exegit monumentum aere perennius. Hoc nos quoque sertis debitis coronemus. / Duco ad vos / Arnoldum Josephum Toynbee."

2. William Temple (1881–1944); archbishop of Canterbury from 1942; *Readings in Saint John's Gospel*, 1st ser. (London, 1939), quoted in *A Study of History*, VII:429, 524–25; A.J.T. refers to him as "a leader of Christian thought and action in the generation of the wars of 1914 and 1939 whose untimely death had been a grievous loss to his contemporaries" (ibid., p. 429).

Staithe House
Beccles, Suffolk

9 August 1948

My dear Arnold,

I can't tell you how much I enjoyed seeing you both and of course especially our little talks. Your zeal for the essential is a great help to me; I love to see you searching for God with all your heart, it encourages me to do the same. The Love of God, that is all in all, the beginning and the end, the way and the means.

We all live as conscious pilgrims on this earth now, pilgrims who cannot even hope to see their fellow pilgrims for long; all human loves are fragile; but they will be completed and glorified in heaven, especially those which are loves of sacrifice, and all yours have been, including your friendship with me.

Our Lord who lives loves us all. I like the present tense, it makes it real. So do all the saints from Mary, his Mother onwards, your friends especially. So we can stand firm in trust.

Yours affectionately,
Columba, O.S.B.

The Royal Institute
of International Affairs
Chatham House
10, St James's Square
London S.W.1

10 August 1948

Dear Columba,

I was so glad to get your letter.[1]

I have begun reading the typescript, with full concurrence of mind, so far.

My colleague, Sir Paul Butler[2] is now back here, and says he would like to see the poor Korean (he was H.M. Consul-General in Korea himself), so I will try to fix this up.

Don't you think Cassian[3] *was* a Scythian = a native of the Diocletianic Roman province of Scythia = Dobruja. This was Latin-speaking in the interior and Greek-speaking on the coast. Aetius[4] came from next door, at Durostorum.*

Best wishes to your mother.

Yours affectionately,
Arnold

*And Saint Martin of Tours[5] from Pannonia, so the Latin-speaking Danubian provinces did quite a lot for Gaul.

1. Missing.

2. Sir Paul Dalrymple Butler (1886–1955); director-general, Far Eastern Bureau, Ministry of Information, New Delhi (1942–43); advisor in the Foreign Office (1944); Far Eastern research secretary of the Royal Institute of International Affairs (1946–48).

3. John Cassian (ca. 360–435); monk, "natione Scytha," who founded two monasteries near Marseilles; his *Institutes* (ca. 420–29) may have influenced the Rule of Saint Benedict (ca. 534).

4. Aëtius (d. 454) was a Roman patrician and general who, with Theodoric, King of the Visigoths, defeated Attila the Hun at Châlons (Mauriac plain).

5. Saint Martin of Tours (ca. 316–ca. 397); bishop of Tours; a patron Saint of France; "Saint Martin's cloak."

The Royal Institute
of International Affairs
Chatham House
10, St James's Square,
London S.W.1

16th August 1948

Dear Columba,

Here is a shot at a preface[1]—and, if it doesn't do, that doesn't matter.

I have posted the typescript to you at Straithe House separately.

I have also had a quarter of an hour with the Korean on his way to Sir Paul Butler.

To-morrow we go to

c/o Mrs. Shepherd
Hall Beck Cottage,
Killington,
Kirkby Lonsdale,
Westmorland

till the end of the month, so this is in haste, in the middle of a cleaning-up.

God Bless you.
Yours affectionately,
Arnold

1. A.J.T.'s preface to C.C.E.'s *Law, Liberty and Love* (London, 1950).

Staithe House
Beccles, Suffolk

22 August 1948

My dear Arnold,

You must be wondering whether your preface ever reached me. Thank you very much, it has; and it is a great privilege to have such a thing from your pen.

I saw it on the hall table before morning Mass and left it there before opening it, to offer whatever it contained—I mean the envelope—to God, wondering whether you had been able to do one or not. I read it after breakfast. My first impression was that you had weighted the scales heavily on the side of the Liberal Protestant, the "surrender" motif. Then I thought that that was a good thing because it would show a largeness of view and tolerance in both of us. I was a little disappointed you had not said the kind of thing usually found on a dust cover! "This book has a new approach to an old problem" or "This is the right kind of history, and though I do not agree" etc, you know what I mean. But the latter part of the book perhaps you thoroughly disapprove of. Do tell me privately what you think of it all. Is it too slight to have weight in "the great debate"? Is it too one sided or even unfair? Is it illogical or muddled? I would welcome, as you know, your impressions.

My Mother asked, having read your preface, though I have told her countless times before, whether you were a Catholic! So you see your work was nicely balanced.

Your preface has exposed two further weaknesses in the book.

1. Obedience to a superior, as you suggest at the end, *is* a means to an end. Loving obedience to God through a human superior is only one of the ways of showing our love of God. I shall make that clear somewhere.

2. Even obedience to God's will is also only one of the ways of loving God, the more fundamental being prayer, or the love of contemplation.

These things and an analysis of the "surrender" motif might come in my own little introductory pages.

I envy your striding over the high fells, with that springy turf under your feet and the champagne air in your lungs.

Next Sunday and for a week I shall be giving a retreat to some Carmelite nuns, 'sisters' of your friend Soeur Thérèse, at Carmel, Kirk Edge, Sheffield, 8.

On Friday I did a bit of sailing, we did not capsize, and most of the afternoon we were becalmed.

How do you like P. Célestin[1] now?

My kindest regards to Veronica.

Yours affectionately *in caritate Christi*

Columba, O.S.B.

1. Dom Pierre Célestin Lou, O.S.B. (1871–1949); Lu Tseng-Tsiang; Chinese foreign minister; representative at the Treaty of Versailles in 1919; became a Catholic and, on his wife's death, a Benedictine monk at the Belgian monastery of Saint André near Bruges; A.J.T. was about to read his *Ways of Confucius and of Christ*.

c/o Mrs. Shepherd
Hall Beck Cottage
Killington
Kirkby Lonsdale
Westmorland

24 August 1948

Dear Columba,

I certainly do think it is the right kind of history, and will say so, with all my heart, in a revised version (if I had kept my draft a day or two and had another go at it, I should probably have added this then, but I was in a hurry to get it off to you before I left London and you went to give the retreat.).

I think so because I think history is all really spiritual history—when you strip the rind off the kernel. It is the history of people's relations with God and, through God, with each other.

Here is exactly what I felt: I read it, as I said, with sympathy and much agreement; but, when I got to the first citations from Saint Thomas, I felt (as no doubt one often feels with him): 'Now he, in those few words, has got right down to the heart of the matter', and I then wished you had done just what you suggest doing, in the last paragraph of your letter, I mean, taken the subject in Saint Thomas's terms almost.

When you got to him, he didn't fit into your framework of obedience as something absolute, and you most honestly quoted the passage that you now more or less paraphrase at the end of your letter—and then went on to some other dicta of his which did fit your framework better. I know, from much experience, how one feels when one hits on something that demands a widening of one's framework and a re-casting of what one has written already. Writing is such hard labour anyway that one shies away from the task of having to re-think one's already ordered thoughts and break up the pattern that one has put together with such toil.

If one does make the effort, though, one is usually rewarded—and one often finds that the labour of re-casting is not so great as it looks like being, before one gets to grips with it.

In this book, if you start with Saint Thomas's thesis, as you have put it in your own words to me, and make this your theme, I think you will make two gains—the first gain a much greater one than the second, but the second, too, important.

1. If you make it clear that obedience to a superior is a means towards obedience to God, and that this, in turn, is a means towards loving God and serving Him for love, you will have taken the whole argument of the book two layers deeper.

2. If you want to convert the unconverted (and one isn't, after all, preaching to the converted) to understanding the value of obedience, you have more chance of doing so if you present obedience as a means to an end about which you and they are agreed—and Protestants do agree with Catholics that the end, for Man, is to love God ('What is the true end of Man?'—'To glorify God and enjoy him forever' is the opening of the Scotch Presbyterian catechism).

This is what I was driving at, at the end of my draft, in suggesting that Saint Thomas had stated the true end and had thereby set up a test of the value of the various means towards it.

There is a direct road to God in which Man has to be alone with God face to face; and there is an indirect road by which he approaches God with the help of other human beings. I believe we have to use both roads; and I also believe that Catholics and Protestants agree on this—what they have differed about is the relative importance of the two roads, but this is not an unbridgeable difference of principle; it is a difference over the practical job of spiritual pioneering, and can be reduced to terms of 'more' and 'less', as contrasted with 'yes' and 'no'.

Suppose, if you draft a new opening, and raise the main body of the ms. accordingly, you were to let me see the additions and changes and send me back my draft to make changes and additions of my own. I believe the story would then have a happy ending.

Father Lou is at my elbow, but I still haven't read him—what between walking in the country and writing notes for some Chichele[1] lectures (and Part

XI: Rhythms) which I am to give at Oxford in October. I shall be reading him in the next week or two and will write about him then.

It is lovely here: the banks of the Lune are very varied, and, a few hundred yards up stream, we can look over at a tip of Yorkshire where Lune and Rawthey meet. Across the Lune, eastwards, we look up at high fells which are the boundary between Westmorland and Yorkshire: on our side the hills are lower, and full of lanes and footpaths.

When we get a foothold of our own in this cottage, as we hope to do one day, you shall see it for yourself.

God Bless You.
Yours affectionately,
Arnold

1. "The subject of Part XI was my theme in a set of Chichele lectures delivered in the autumn of 1948 . . . ," *A Study of History*, VII: viii; cf. ibid., IX: 167–394, "Law and Freedom in History."

Poor Clare Convent
Scarthingwell Hall
Todcaster

26 August 1948

My dear Arnold,

I am writing before my recollection of Mother Abbess' reactions to your preface fade.

The first page obviously gave her great pleasure and she proceeded to quote from the same poem—of Tennyson I believe—that you used.

She liked particularly the passage "God's love for man can call out . . . etc". By the end she said she thought it excellent as a preface; it would set people thinking. She also thought you affirmed less than you believed—and I replied that you did not want to prejudice your own book which was to follow.

This is one of the stately homes of England in a state of complete dilapidation. Only Poor Clares would dare venture on living in it: no money, complete trust in divine Providence—and wonderful to say, it works.

I hope your holiday was a great success.

My constant prayers and hers for you and your book.

God bless you.

Yours affectionately,
Columba, O.S.B.

27 August 1948 Scarthingwell

My dear Arnold,

Thank you for your letter which got to the 'heart of the matter'; I thank you for being so straight. You are quite right, I have left an exaggerated view of obedience.

Therefore I will rewrite my preface and adjust the Benedictine part specially; add to and rewrite parts of S. Thomas; add the Love part to S. Francis.

Please could you return me my letter which you refer to in your last, because I must have expressed it very clearly there. You will get it back.

I shall send you your draft preface.

Yours affectionately,
in caritate Christi
Columba, O.S.B.

P.S. I had to rush this letter to catch the post and now find it was too late. I am so glad you have had a good little holiday.

1 September 1948 Hall Beck

Dear Columba,

Your letter has just caught me here before my cousin Helga Frankland[1] came to carry me off to Ravenstone-dale (I have been seeing Veronica off to London from Oxenholme earlier in the morning).

Here is the precious letter: sheet 3 is the passage.[2]

I am very glad indeed if my comments have been a help.

In haste,
Yours affectionately,
Arnold

1. (1920–) The daughter of Edward Frankland; an officer of the Nature Conservancy; cf. A.J.T.'s praise in *Experiences*, p. 294.

2. Compare C.C.E.'s letter of 22 August 1948, above.

Ampleforth College
3 September 1948 York

Dear Arnold,

Here is the reference to St. John of the Cross. "fragment of a letter to La Madre María de la Encarnación in Segovia. Madrid, 6 de julio de 1591."

The last and incomplete sentence runs:

Y a donde no hay amor, ponga amor,
And where there is not love, put love,

Y sacará amor . . .
and you will draw love out . . .

Obras de San Juan de la Cruz, editadas y anotadas por el P. Silverio de Santa Teresa. O.C.F., Tomo IV p. 287 (Burgos, 1931).

There was some other reference you wanted, but I cannot remember unless it was the title of Henri Bernard's book:

Le Père Mathieu Ricci et la Société Chinoise de son Temps (1552–1610) (Tientsin, 1937).

His other work has just arrived here from China:

Sagesse Chinoise et philosophie chrétienne, Essai sur leurs relations historiques. (Tientsin, 1935) pp. 1–277.

I enjoyed my stay at the Carmel very much and steeped myself in the spirit of the Great little Soeur Thérèse. I asked them all to pray for you and your work, without my mentioning any names. There they are perched up overlooking Sheffield and innumerable valleys and ridges over into Lancashire, completely cut off and seeking the one Thing necessary, God and his Holy Will. From there I came back here yesterday. All seem well, especially Fr Paul.

In caritate Christi
Columba, O.S.B.

The Royal Institute
of International Affairs
Chatham House
10, St James's Square
London S.W.1

7 September 1948

Dear Columba,

Your letter of the 3rd with the passage from St. John of the Cross and the reference to Henri Bernard arrived this morning.

Meanwhile, I have read Dom Pierre Célestin. He must be a very remarkable man: his countenance and his words fit one another. I am very glad he has gone back to China to work for the Church there—though it must have been a wrench for him to leave his Belgian cloister.

Could you find out for me, or put me on the track of finding out, whether there is any Catholic girls' club in our neighborhood? Does the pro-Cathedral, where you have said Mass when you have stayed at Pembroke Square, have one?

I ask because our Austrian maid, and her friend who is maid to our friends the Carlyles, five minutes away from us, go to Mass regularly at the Convent in Kensington Square, but the sisters haven't, so far, made any personal contact with them.

They do go to a Y.W.C.A. in Tottenham Court Road for German-speaking girls in London, but it would be good for them to meet English-speaking Catholic girls as well as non-Catholic German-speaking ones, and it seems a pity, when they belong to a church that bridges the gulfs between different nations, that they should not benefit by this.

If you can help me over this, I shall be grateful, for I feel it might make a great difference to the two girls if they could find some Catholic club not too far from us. Well, God Bless You,

Yours affectionately,
Arnold

Ampleforth Abbey
York

8 September 1948

Dear Arnold,

I have written to Canon James Walton of Our Lady of Victories and given the address and the facts. So you may expect a note or a visit in the near future.

Fr Aelred was *very* gratified to have a letter from you as he will probably write and say so! The international situation is perilous. I am afraid that the Russians, knowing we shall not move a hair's breadth in the direction of war will parley and go on with their plans, encroaching on the liberty of men everywhere within their reach. At what point do we and the Americans say: you must go no further? Should it be only when our own liberty is imperilled or sooner? The sooner the better. That is the tragedy of it, that we have to use force in the long run, and force will end in ruin; while if we do not use force it will end in servitude.

I find it very hard to understand hatred; it must be due to an accumulation of injustices suffered. But in the mass of the Russian people it can only be propaganda, as it is also in the West.

It is equally difficult to understand the lust for power. Is it an effect of fear in a world devoid of charity?

Yours affectionately,
Columba, O.S.B.

The Royal Institute
of International Affairs
Chatham House
10, St James's Square
London S.W.1

14 September 1948

Dear Columba,

Two queries (at your leisure).

(i) Can you give me the correct original Latin text of the prayer of Saint Ignatius: one sees it printed with variants?

(ii) 'O felix culpa'—reference? Saint Bernard? Anselm. What shameful ignorance. I should like the vol. and col. of Migne.

I am revising jots and tittles in Part VII.

Yours affectionately,
Arnold

45, Pembroke Square
London W.8

17 September 1948

Dear Columba,

Thank you so much for sending me what I asked for: I have already put it all in,[1] and this completes Part VII for typing.

I had no idea that *O felix culpa* went back so far: I had supposed it to be a phrase of one of the late Latin Fathers: 11th or 12th century.[2]

I am particularly glad to have the three versions of Saint Ignatius's prayer. What a contrast between the directness and informality of the Spanish original and the 'lapidariness' of the Latin version. The Spanish goes straight to one's heart: he is so much in earnest, and so sure of his own sincerity, that he speaks to God like man to man, and this is very sublime and very moving.

What a lot of trouble you took over these queries of mine. I am very grateful.

Yours affectionately,
Arnold

1. The prayer of Saint Ignatius Loyola appears in *A Study of History*, VII: 518, in Latin, Spanish, and English versions.

2. The liturgical text that includes "O felix culpa" appears in ibid., p. 568, n. 5. The text is found as early as the time of Alcuin (A.D. 804).

Ampleforth College
York

18 September 1948

Dear Arnold,

I am glad you were satisfied with my notes; it gives me deep pleasure to feel that even in a little way I am co-operating in the Nonsense Book, or rather the really sensible book on history.

Here now is the revision I have done; pages marked with a X are there either because of some modification or to give the context; the others are additions.

Now, I think, you have the completed work, and anything more I write will only be an amplification here and there.

I include also your first draft.

Please excuse more now; the boys are returning Tuesday and I wanted to get this off before they came.

Who should be the publishers—the more "heretical" the better, and of course the more notable. Longman?

Yours affectionately,
in caritate Christi,
Columba, O.S.B.

20 September 1948 45, Pembroke Square, W.8

The ms. has arrived safely, and I shall now study your revisions and revise my preface.

I wonder if Hodder and Stoughton—who sometimes publish religious and philosophical books—might be the people to approach.

A.J.T.

The Royal Institute
of International Affairs
Chatham House
10, St James's Square
London, S.W.1

29 September 1948

Dear Columba,

In a few days now I shall be getting back to your typescript and mine and letting you have them back.

Meanwhile, this is just to let you know that I have not yet heard from your friend at the Pro-Cathedral about the possibility of a club for our Austrian maid, about which you so kindly wrote to him—and I am keen to get her in touch with the English Catholic circles if possible.

God Bless you.
Yours affectionately,
Arnold

St. Jerome's Day (30 September 1948) Ampleforth

Dear Arnold,

Just a hasty note. I have written to the Rev. Mother, Kensington Square, asking her to get in touch. It will have to be through you as I have not the girl's name.

I await with tremendous interest the arrival of the package.

Here are a few odd pages which without changing the point of view amplify it and perhaps you should see.

Yours affectionately,
Columba, O.S.B.

11 October 1948 45, Pembroke Square, W.8

Dear Columba,

At last! Here are your revised sheets of typescript, and a new draft (as you will see, almost entirely new) for my preface.

Be as frank in telling me whether you like or dislike the preface as it now stands, as I have been in telling you what I think of the book.

I think your changes and additions—particularly the crucial ones on the relation between Obedience and Love—strengthen the book a lot and at the same time make it easier for your non-Catholic readers to take it—without being headed off the essential points by controversial secondary issues.

As you will see, my pencilled suggestions are few and not very important.

Introductory chapter I: God's Love for Himself: this is always startling for non-theologians till explained, and an explanation might make too big a digression. Therefore query: Omit.

Comparison between present state of Northern and Southern Europe. Invidious and also disputable. Therefore query: Omit.

Councils of Florence and Lyons. These are, I think, unfortunate instances to choose, as the Byzantines were victims of power-politics in both cases. They admitted Papal supremacy in order to get Western support. They did this without conviction; they were repudiated at home; and in the end the Eastern Orthodox Christians opted for 'the turban' rather than 'the tiara'.

Socialism versus Individualism. This is an afterthought and a parenthesis: it is not relevant to your thesis, and it is a terrific red herring, on which every unfriendly reviewer will pounce. Therefore I should leave it out.

That is all. I do hope the book will now have a smooth passage to press, and will be given the reception that it deserves (my new preface is an attempt to show why it does deserve a good reception).

Well, we are getting rather journey-proud before our next, to-day fortnight, for C'ple via Zurich—especially as I have four lectures to give before that, in Oxford on '*Recurrence and Uniqueness in History*.'[1]

Thank you again for all you have done about Catholic Clubs for Nessy. On Saturday we took her to call on the Mother Superior at Kensington Square, who is going to put her in touch with Father Foster's club (mostly Irish girls), and then we called on the Daughters of Mary Immaculate (Spaniards).

These new links will, I hope, make a lot of difference to the child.

Could you copy for me the *Pensée* containing the famous 'A meridian settles everything,'[2]—with a note of the *number* in Brunschvicg and the pages in B's edition? (no hurry about this).

God Bless You,
Yours affectionately,
Arnold

1. See n. 1 of A.J.T.'s letter of 24 August 1948, above.

2. "Un méridien décide de la vérité" (for Pascal's *pensée*, see Lafuma, ed., *Oeuvres complètes*, no. 60 [Brunschvicg no. 294]).

Ampleforth College
York

Saint Edward's (13 October) 1948

My dear Arnold,

I had been more or less overwhelmed in my prayers this morning by the thought of how good God was to make us two friends and then pat comes the envelope. Thank you first of all for your very wise suggestions, I shall follow them all. Perhaps in the case of Saint Thomas More I might substitute some 4–6th century Byzantine texts for unity, but I agree that at Lyons and Florence the Easterns were in a political fix.

The Preface is a gem, and I could not ask for anything better. So your labours—in the midst of so many more important ones—have come to a very happy conclusion. Now for a publisher. *Thank you very much indeed.*

Unfortunately I could not hear your wireless talk[1] but I read it yesterday. I agree with it all. Do you think men will ever reach up to the perfection of Christ's message, as the struggle will always remain between the goodness and the badness in all of us. Only those religions which do not demand much, can completely dominate a people. All we can expect is that the climate of opinion—or conviction—be on the side of Christ.

What wouldn't I give to sit at your feet at Oxford. God be with you there and also in your excursion through the iron curtain.

My love to you both *in caritate Christi*,
Columba

P.S. I shall be sending you the Pensée with this or tomorrow. Here it is. Today is a holiday, so I seize the opportunity.

1. Compare A.J.T.'s "A Western Tradition Is Still in the Making," *Listener* 40, no. 1027 (30 September 1948): 489–90.

The Royal Institute
of International Affairs
Chatham House
10, St James's Square
London S.W.1

14 October 1948

Dear Columba,

I am so very glad you like the preface, and thank you for the *pensée*. I am giving it, to quote, to an *advocatus diaboli* who is saying that religious allegiance is just a matter of geography (to which I have an answer: all this is in Part VII).[1]

For Lyons and Florence I would substitute something pre-Constantinian, from an age in which no one could say that the unity of the Church was un-spontaneous or was politically contrived. There are things in Irenaeus and in Cyprian (whom you note already).

After reaching up to the perfection of Christ's message: a Saint spends himself on tuning up his sinful nature to this pitch—and this is the greatest effort that any human being ever makes in this world. Perhaps, in later chapters of the story, more and more people will be devoting themselves to what, so far, has been the life work of a handful of saints scattered through the centuries.

Yours ever affectionately,
Arnold

1. Compare *A Study of History*, VII: 432 and n. 3.

[*Postcard*]

Ankara Palace Hotel
Ankara

4 November 1948

Here is the ancient citadel of Ankara overlooking the new city: a symbol of the World we are living in. We are off on Saturday to Boghaz Köi, Amasya, Sivas, Kaiseri, Adana, Konya. Cloudless weather, so far, and the very greatest kindness and hospitality.

A.J.T.

Ampleforth College
York

9 December 1948

My dear Arnold,

The wonder has happened. Hodder and Stoughton have accepted the book, *Law, Liberty and Love*.[1] They write "L.L.L. presents a case for unity alike with power and toleration. . . . We are complimented that both you and Professor Toynbee should have considered us in this connection. . . . etc". The letter is long, with technicalities about royalties, so I shall quote no more; and though I should like to send it to you, I must show it to Fr. Abbot and keep it handy. I know I have you to thank for this and it makes one more bond between us.

You must be back in England now and I wonder whether you got my last chasing you among the Hittite remains. It was to thank you for your card from Ankara.

Have you read Christopher Dawson's *Religion and Culture*.[2] I think it first class.

In the holiday—I hope to begin again on China—I am already seizing up with too many facts, don't know where or how to begin—meanwhile for my spiritual reading I am relating the Christ-given revelation to the other religions and hope to work '*legendo*' something permanent on "Christ, Heir of all things".

God bless you both.
Affectionately *in caritate Christi*,
Columba, O.S.B.

1. Published in 1950.
2. Christopher Dawson, *Religion and Culture*, Gifford Lectures (London, 1948).

11 December 1948

45, Pembroke Square, W.8

Dear Columba,

I was delighted to get your letter of the 9th with its splendid news about the book. No bit of news has given me such pleasure for a long time. I think the book will have an important non-Catholic public as well as the Catholic readers that it will have as a matter of course.

Your letter to me in Turkey hasn't turned up yet, but then we were very rapidly on the move. We came back from Athens the Thursday before last—in 8½ hours, leaving Athens at 2:40 P.M. and seeing Vesuvius before it got dark.

It has been a wonderful experience for both of us: it was Veronica's first sight of the Mediterranean, and I hadn't seen Athens since 1921, Knossos since 1912, or Boghaz Kale[1] ever—and B.K. is one of the Wonders of the World. I have done nothing for five weeks but drink in dust and impressions, and I have taken a lot of new cargo on board: I reverted to the age of 23, and indulged my passion for climbing citadels—above all, at Amasya. I did have fun.

Well, three cheers for Hodder and Stoughton.

Yours affectionately,
Arnold

1. Compare the reference to "Boghazqal 'eh offering a grander stage than Hisārlyq for the Second Book of *The Aeneid*" in *A Study of History*, X: 216.

Ampleforth Abbey
York

S. Thomas Day (21 December) 1948

My dear Arnold,

Thank you very much for the beautiful card and also for the verse—I am sure one of the reasons you had for sending it me. It makes me bold to suggest that you have reached another watershed and that the time has come for you to pray to Mary at any rate in the words of the Angel: *Ave Maria*, *Gratia plena*, *Dominus tecum*. She will give you greater insight into the ways of the loving God with men than all the books in the world—though I am not denying their use.

And as I think I know that your times of tribulation are not over, but may recur, a closeness to her and with her to Christ Jesus Our Lord in all simplicity will fortify you and make it possible to bear all with peace and win inward joy.

My present to you is a suggestion that you squeeze in to some Catholic Church before midnight and go to the Nativity Mass. I shall remember you specially then.

Your talk of climbing citadels reminds me of a Peruvian to whom I gave a letter of introduction to you. He has climbed most of the ones so far found perched up on the pinnacles of the Andes: Cuzco and all the other unspellable names. He is a real expert on the Inca period and on the whole country of Peru which he has tramped as you have tramped Greece.

You seem to have had a marvellous time.

God bless you both and give you both peace for Christmas.

Affectionately,
Columba, O.S.B.

Ampleforth Abbey
York

17 January 1949

My dear Arnold,

Here I am back after having been to London and not seen you. It was Old Boys' occasion, so I had to sacrifice other things and even other people.

H & S have sent off the book MS. to the printers so it is now on the way. All very exciting. I pray it will do good and not be damned by reviewers.

Talking of reviewers, the ones on yours[1] were very interesting and I expect very helpful to you. It was the Old Guard, so it seemed to me, not flexible enough to see things differently; and for that very reason most useful to you because they stated the positions.

I have been reading the One vol: *Golden Bough*.[2] It is beautifully written in parts and a mine of useful data but it is like a lumber room, everything in wild confusion, if P. Schmidt's[3] schematization means anything. Also I felt he lumped together things which were only physically, not ideally, similar.

You should look at the Hungarian news[4] in the last two numbers of the *Tablet* (Jan: 8th and 15th).

When is your Ms. coming? I am longing for it.

in caritate Christi,
Yours affectionately,
Columba, O.S.B.

P.S. I stayed with Michael Cubitt[5] whom I find is a keen member of Chatham House discussion groups. Syria, Palestine and Egypt are his specialties.

1. A.J.T.'s *Civilization on Trial.*

2. Sir James G. Frazer (1854–1941); *The Golden Bough, a Study in Magic and Religion*, 3d ed., 12 vols. (New York, 1935), abridged by Frazer in 1 vol. (London, 1922). *The Golden Bough* is widely quoted throughout *A Study of History*; and the influence of this work, as of Edward Gibbon's *Decline and Fall of the Roman Empire* (1776–88), is pervasive. A.J.T.'s later appraisal became more critical; cf. *A Study of History*, VII: 383–87: "[Alfred] Rosenberg and Frazer were both propounding an identical Gibbonian thesis," ibid., p. 385.

3. Compare C.C.E.'s letter of 1 October 1947, above.

4. On 27 December 1949, the Hungarian government had arrested Josef Cardinal Mindszenty.

5. Count Michael Riccardi-Cubitt (1920–); an old Amplefordian; during the war served as captain, Rifle Brigade, in the Near Eastern theater; in business in the Middle East.

The Royal Institute
of International Affairs
Chatham House
10, St James's Square
London S.W.1

18 January 1949

Dear Columba,

I was so glad to hear from you, though it was tantalizing that we were so near each other without being able to meet—but the old boys' meeting was obviously a first call on you, as you say.

I am also glad your ms. has gone to the printer. They are being quite prompt.

Yes, the unfriendly and even the uncomprehending reviews are the most enlightening and therefore the most useful. I have a file of them for use, and have got a lot out of them already.[1]

I am now in Part IX: the script of Part VII shall come to you as soon as Bridget has finished typing it and I have worked over it.

You ought to read the Zurich theologian Emil Brunner's 1947 Gifford Lectures 'Christianity and Civilization' (Nisbet).[2] He is a saintly man, and a modest one, as well as a strong clear intellect.

Your Belgian friend Father de Grunne[3] had lunch with me the other day. I liked him a lot, and hope to keep in touch with him.

God Bless you.
Yours affectionately,
Arnold

1. These provided the matter for "Reconsiderations," in *A Study of History*, vol. XII.

2. Emil Brunner (1889–1966); *Christianity and Civilization* (London, 1948); quoted in *A Study of History*, VII: 475, 486–87.

3. Dominic de Grunne, O.S.B. (1913–); a monk of the abbey of Maredsous, Belgium; for a time working at the chaplaincy in Oxford.

Ampleforth College
York

26 January 1949

My dear Arnold,

Thank you for your letter and suggestion to read Emile Brunner. I find reading that kind of book very stimulating; I am still reverberating to the *Golden Bough*, which perhaps I wrongly criticised in my last letter. But it does open up immense areas of religious ideas. I still cannot see how the myth of the dying God really began. It does not seem to fit to say that it is a reproduction of the vegetation cycle; if so for what? Is there not another theory that it represents the meeting of two cultures? But it is the King who usually gets killed, and in fact was it not usually the He, the herdsman—Shepherd king—who does the killing? You see I am befogged. If this death had ever been considered as redemptive, or a sacrifice for someone, one might see sense. I think you make that point; but by making it, prove the senselessness—as far as we can see—of the whole proceeding. Have you a key?

I have begun to study, at last, Henri Bergson's *Deux Sources*.[1] It is a great book, and I can see how it permeates lots of writings. I'll tell you more as I digest it more. At present I am delighted to recognise his insight into Catholic mysticism and its essential love content. I wish I had read this before *Law, Liberty, Love*. It fits.

The Chinese debacle is almost the last straw.[2] I had news of the Jesuits at Shanghai. They are staying and expecting martyrdom. Is the third great Christian effort in China going to be swallowed up like the earlier ones? Somehow I think not, as it is more in the blood now.

Yours affectionately,
Columba, O.S.B.

1. *Les Deux Sources de la morale et de la religion* (Paris, 1932), quoted frequently by A.J.T.; cf. *A Study of History*, VII: 511.

2. On 15 January 1949, Tientsin, and on 21 January 1949, Peiping fell to the Communist forces.

45, Pembroke Square
London W.8

3 March 1949

Dear Columba,

We sail on Saturday on the "Panthic" for the Institute for Advanced Study, Princeton, N.J., and back on the "Batóry", leaving N.Y. the 5th June and landing about the 15th June. You will be hearing from me while I am there; this is just a hasty line to say goodbye—though Princeton is really almost as near as Kensington is to Yorkshire.

Lawrence had a third daughter last week—one year and three days after the second![1]

He is doing well in his work and has been taken up by an apparently good London dealer.[2]

We are both of us well and happy.

My love to you,
Arnold

1. Clare Toynbee Huxley (1949–); cf A.J.T.'s letter of 11 December 1970, below.

2. The London dealer was Frederick Mayor, who held an exhibition of Lawrence's paintings; afterward Lawrence's pictures were handled by Leicester Galleries, which, early among London dealers, had dealt in Picasso and Cézanne.

Chatham House
10, St James's Square
London S.W.1

22 March 1949

Dear Rev. Father,

Before Professor Toynbee left for the United States he asked me to send you Part VII and Annexes of "A Study of History". He also wished me to say that he would like it back sometime but that there was no hurry about returning it.

Professor Toynbee did not have time to revise the typescript, or indeed to look at it at all before he left.

Yours sincerely,
Bridget R. Reddin

92 North Stanworth Drive
Princeton, N.J. U.S.A.

13 April 1949

Dear Columba,

We got back to this peaceful place to-day after two exhausting days in New York (tribute to my publishers, for whom I have to do a minimum of public speaking) and I found your letter waiting for me.

I am more pleased than I know how to tell you that, *im Grossen und Ganzen*, Part VII has not jarred on you, but, on the contrary, seems to you to be on the plus side of the account. For, while I know you would want to feel pleased with it, I also know that this would have no effect on your feelings if I were in fundamental discord with the Catholic point of view, and my wish, of course, is not to jar on anybody, but to help people of this generation, of different religions and points of view, to grope their way towards the light which we are all seeking in sorrow and hard labour.

At your leisure, do let me have your comments in general and in detail.

There are sure to be many points where I unintentionally put people off by some turn of phrase that has no essential relation to my argument, and I should be very grateful for help in changing offending adjectives and adverbs.

The Jung Annex[1] is also rather tentative and subject to modification. I haven't yet tried it on any of the psychologists, and I daresay they will tell me it is bunk.

As you know, I am through-and-through anti-rationalist, and this attitude comes out in my feeling about the religions. Brought up as you and I have been, within the Christian circle, how can we know that the other religions are not alternative roads to a single god? We know Christianity from inside; we haven't the same experience of Islam and the rest. Only God knows why he has put a number of different religions into the world, but Symmachus's conjecture is, I feel, a good human shot at finding the divine answer to the question.

However, this annex will no doubt have to be knocked about quite a lot.

O dear, Chicago next week! But, after that, a peaceful May here. (If one didn't go out a little bit into the blary world, one would quickly become incapable of it, and this would bring on old age. But it is a disagreeable form of psychological exercise).

I am sorry Lawrence looked ill. It may be the new baby, which has no doubt been a bit of a strain for him, though not to compare with the strain for Jean.

L. is doing well in his family, I think.

The whistling must have been for 'Dawn'[2] because when you suggested that, it immediately clicked in my mind. But we have to be patient—patience is the watchword in religion as well as politics in this chapter of history.

God Bless You.
Yours affectionately,
Arnold

1. "Higher Religions and Psychological Types," in *A Study of History*, VII: 716–36.
2. "The dog at Ganthorpe. In our walks together, 'Dawn' followed, got lost, and Arnold would whistle and call 'Dawn'—symbolic?" (C.C.E.)

27 April 1949 Ampleforth

My dear Arnold. You must forgive me for writing to you in this inhuman way.[1] I do it for two reasons, the first that I may have a record of what I have written in these very serious matters and secondly that I may show them here and there to Catholic thinkers whose opinion I respect and who will be for me a guarantee that I am neither being too narrow or too broad in my interpretation of Catholic ways of looking at things.

Thank you once again for a truly Arnold-like letter, the one dated 13th April. I agree that patience is all in all at the moment in these heart searching enquiries into man's relation with the Almighty, All-loving, All-knowing, God; it would be so easy to stir up anger and resentment. We all do it unawares. You will have received by now my first batch of notes and the letter which gives some references to 'jarring notes'. I do hope that my directness has not been offensive.[2]

1. In typescript.

2. Here follows a memorandum of thirty-seven typed pages, with specific comments on the script of Part VII and annexes of *A Study of History*: "Universal Churches," VII : 381–772. Many of C.C.E.'s comments are embedded in the published volume, usually under the formula: "A Catholic friend of the writer's comments . . ."; cf. A.J.T.'s letter of 18 June 1949, below.

The Institute
for Advanced Study
School of Economics
and Politics
Princeton, New Jersey

28 April 1949

Dear Columba,

Your Maundy Thursday letter[1] reached me on the wing to Chicago, and now your Easter Sunday letter,[2] with the notes, was on my table here when I turned up again this morning—after a battle on the shores of Lake Michigan with a Herbert-spencerian dinosaur called Frank Knight,[3] who believes that science and democracy have solved all problems and started a new age, were it not for cussed people like me who refuse to see it. I kept shooting Original Sin at him, but made no dint in his armour. I thought the species was extinct, but this specimen was vigorously alive.

To Frank Knight I appear to be a fatuous dupe of religion, while to others I look like Frank Knight.

Yes, do show the ms. to other members of the Community at your discretion, and also do get all the comments you can from Father D'Sousa.[4]

I don't mean, of course, to hurt people's feelings, and can no doubt largely avoid being offensive by changing or leaving out words. It is worth taking great trouble to do that, and I will. It may be that I shall also find myself changing more fundamental things, but there will, of course, be fundamental differences when all is done.

I don't expect to get down to revision for some time yet; I am making a push now to finish the whole thing in first draft, so there is plenty of time.

Now I have hurt you and caused trouble, and for this I am sorry, but it is worth doing this in order to be able to get the Catholic 'reaction' and digest it.

In Chicago I called on the Nestorian Patriarch[5] but eluded the Baha'is. The Nestorian Church throughout the world is governed from Chicago now instead of from Kurdistan. We were staying there with old friends: Quincy Wright,[6] the professor of International Law, and his wife, who is Secretary of the Chicago

Council on Foreign Relations. A witch-hunt for Communists was going on in the Illinois Legislature, and the University was in the dock. This vein of intolerance and persecution is a bit terrifying: the unforgivable sin is Communism today, but it might suddenly be something else—who knows what?

Yours affectionately,
Arnold

1. Missing.

2. Missing.

3. Frank Hyneman Knight (1885–1972); then professor of economics at the University of Chicago; *Freedom and Reform* (London, 1947); *The Ethics of Competition* (London, 1935).

4. Jerome D'Sousa, S.J. (1897–1977); delegate to the general assembly of the United Nations (1949); member, Indian Parliament; rector of Loyola University, Madras (1942–50); his family were Brahmins, Catholic for many generations. "His mother had taught him by heart the ancient Hindu Scriptures. Fr. D'Sousa was distressed by the harshness of Arnold's comments on the Holy Eucharist; I think Arnold softened his criticism as a result." (C.C.E.)

5. Mar Eshai Shimun XXI (r. 1920–73); "In our own lifetime the house-painting trade in Chicago has become a preserve of the Nestorian Christians; and, in consequence, has become the principal source of the Nestorian Church's revenue. Administrations gravitate towards the place from which their revenue comes; and today the Patriarch of all the Nestorian Christians of the world, who used to live in Kurdistan, has his residence in Chicago and administers the world-wide Nestorian Christian Church from that centrally situated North American city" (A.J.T. in *Christianity among the Religions of the World* [New York, 1957], p. 63).

6. Quincy Wright (1890–1970); then at the University of Chicago; in 1949–50 consultant to the U.S. high commissioner in West Germany.

Ampleforth College
York

23 May 1949

My dear Arnold,

As is the way, your letter arrived the day after I sent off my last. Yours was a great relief, though I should have known you would take all my remarks in the most patient spirit. It is a bit remarkable, really, that you should be so ready to submit to such a barrage of criticism. But, in fact, I enjoyed reading most of the MS. more than I can say. Of course, our views cannot yet coincide and you must say what you think.

How I should have liked to visit the Nestorian Patriarch with you; for me he stands for that amazing network of churches all over Asia in the days of Blessed John of Montecorvino.[1] Does he hold the same doctrine as those two Nestorian monks from Peking one of whom got to Rome? It would be interesting to know. And your Chicago Progress-dinosaur, he must have been fun.

I have just finished P. de la Vallée Poussin's book on Nirvana.[2] The best thing I have read on Buddhism to date; it is the first book which has made most things fit together. We cannot—I mean I have not so far been able to—realise how *fluid* is doctrine in these Eastern religions. Give them a couple of hundred years and they can turn some vital point upside down.

I am glad you are getting down to the first draft of the whole work. P. D'Sousa[3] is in Madras. It would be difficult for me to get his views unless I sent him the MS. But when I next re-read parts, I might jot down notes and queries to send to him.

In caritate Christi,
Yours affectionately,
Columba, O.S.B.

P.S. We have had a sad fixing of positions in the Irish situation. But after Attlee's initial blunder—I think—of including the guarantee in the Bill, he spoke very calmly.[4]

1. John of Montecorvino (1247–1328); Franciscan archbishop of Peking, one of the founders of the Catholic mission in China.
2. Compare C.C.E.'s letter of 7 November 1941, above.
3. C.C.E. had already shown Father D'Sousa portions of the manuscript of *A Study of History* that dealt with the Holy Eucharist.
4. On 17 May 1949, the British House of Commons recognized the independence of the Republic of Ireland but affirmed the status of northern Ireland as a part of the United Kingdom.

18 June 1949 45, Pembroke Square, W.8

Dear Columba,

Your letter followed me back here yesterday. It might well have found me still in America after all, for our passage had been booked since December on the Batóry—as it turned out, for the next voyage after Eisler's![1] And, till within four hours of the time she was due to sail the Monday before last, we didn't know whether the American authorities were not going to detain her. We couldn't have got any other passage for at least three months, so we were a bit anxious. However, they let her go, and we got home on Tuesday. We are happy to be back, though we also feel very much at home at Princeton, where we now have a number of friends, old and young.

As to your comments on the nonsense-book draft, you need never be afraid that I should take them amiss. Coming from you, they come with affection and complete sincerity, and who but a very benighted man would quarrel with criticisms of that kind instead of valuing them? I shall get great benefit from them when I come to revise Part VII.[2] Meanwhile, I am galloping ahead, with my eye on finishing the first draft of the whole thing. I am still on encounters between the West and other civilizations—I was doing the Crusades on board ship.

I wish we could have paid the call on the Mar Shimun[3] together. He expects to be coming to England before long, so I shall try to arrange it then. Yes, I think his doctrine is unchanged. He is perhaps slightly self-conscious about it, as he went out of his way to explain to me that the Christian Church in the Sasanian Dominions had not invented Nestorianism, but had merely seen no reason for condemning Nestorius when the news of the controversy over him in the Roman Empire spread to the Persian side of the frontier (he talked of it as if it had all happened the day before yesterday).[4]

I was interested in your impression of de la Vallée Poussin's book, which I too want to read. Perhaps that fluidity is the strength as well as the weakness of the Indian religions—as, conversely, the rigidity of the three Judaic religions may be their weakness as well as their strength.

Will you be coming through London at the end of the term? I hope so.

Yours affectionately,
Arnold

1. Gerhard Eisler had fled from New York in the Polish liner *Batóry* as a stowaway, while under sentence for perjury and contempt of Congress; he had refused to be sworn in before the House Committee on Unamerican Activities. He returned to East Germany to take the chair of social politics at the University of Leipzig. The returning ship was boarded on 5 June 1949 by the U.S. Immigration Service, and the passengers questioned. (*The Times* [6 June 1949])

2. Part VII and its annexes are studded with references to C.C.E.'s letters, especially to the memorandum of 27 April 1949; cf. *A Study of History*, VII : 430, n. 1; 456, n. 1; 484, n. 1; 502, n. 3; 503, n. 5; 722, n. 1; 723, n. 3; 734, n. 2.

3. Compare A.J.T.'s letter of 28 April 1949, above.

4. Nestorius (d. ca. 451) became bishop (patriarch) of Constantinople in 428; he was a zealous preacher who rejected the general application of the term *Theotókos* (Mother of God) to Mary, apparently lest it be taken to apply to Christ's divine rather than to his human nature; he apparently was accused of teaching that there were two separate persons in Christ, the one divine, the other human, in contradiction of the orthodox doctrine that Christ was a single person at once God and man. Nestorius denied this accusation, but he was deposed at the Council of Ephesus in 431. Eastern bishops who refused to accept a formula adopted in 433 eventually formed a separate Nestorian church with its center in Persia.

12 July 1949 — 45, Pembroke Square, W.8

Dear Columba,

I have been very negligent about writing, because I have been busy attending to all kinds of jobs that were waiting for me, but now the typescript has come back, and I have had your letter of the 8th July.[1]

All your comments, and those you have passed on from other people, will go into my revision of this Part, but at present I am pushing ahead to finish the first draft of the whole thing.

You didn't, I am sure, expect that what I wrote would turn out to be acceptable from the Catholic standpoint, but I shall at any rate be able to clear up ambiguities and avoid needless irritations, thanks to these criticisms.

I am very glad that the first proofs of '*Law, Liberty and Love*' are going through. I take it that Hodder and Stoughton will communicate with me about my signature, which I shall of course be glad to let them have.

I am greatly looking forward to seeing you the week-end after next, but can't you manage to come to lunch or supper on the Saturday (23rd) or Sunday (24th)? I am keeping 3.30–5.30 on the 23rd meanwhile, but do find the time, if you can, to come to something less meagre than tea. At that week-end we have so far no other engagements, and I shall keep it free till I hear from you again.

Looking forward eagerly to seeing you:

Yours affectionately,
Arnold

1. Missing.

Ampleforth College
York

15 July 1949

My Dear Arnold,

Yes I'll come along for dinner on Saturday evening. That would be grand.

No, I didn't really expect you to be in full agreement with me. But I did expect it to be nearer than it has proved to be. This was partly due to the pointers in vols. IV–VI particularly the recognition of Christ Jesus, Our Lord; and partly to the Burge lecture,[1] which David Mathew[2] always repeated was deceptive and I should not build too much on it.

However, the fact remains that even granted the differences—which of course make no difference to our friendship—I did and do expect you to *leave the roads open*. I thought the vol. was going to take a more factual turn; i.e. state what had been the relationship between religion and the birth, growth and death of Cultures; it has in fact become a bit apologetic and prophetic.[3] This is good up to a point, but perhaps should really wait until after the book is finished.

But no more now, I'll say it all on Saturday week.

Love to you both,
Columba, O.S.B.

1. A.J.T.'s "Christianity and Civilization," in *Civilization on Trial*, pp. 225–52.

2. Compare C.C.E.'s letter of 14 July 1944, above.

3. "Arnold was spurred on by his conscience, that thirst for ultimate Truth, to reach out beyond the religion of Christ to other higher religions, and in that search moved into a kind of syncretism that did not do justice to Catholic Christianity. Though my responses to this stance of Arnold's are not here detailed, the annexes in vol. VII of *A Study of History* in which Martin Wight, another Catholic friend of Arnold's, took up the challenge and answered Arnold's syncretic views represent mine also. The overall theme is that the Christian faith stands or falls by its historical foundations; it is not so much a theory about salvation as *something done* to give us salvation—namely, Christ's redeeming death and resurrection. Thus my stances correspond almost exactly with those of Martin Wight, which Arnold so generously allowed to be published in his own work." (C.C.E.)

Ampleforth College
York

16 September 1949

My dear Arnold,

I rang you up on my return from Spain but found you were up North. Really I have so much to tell you, the only solution is for you to spend a night or so here.

We—Fr. Maurus[1] and I—travelled all over from Irun to Algesiras and Salamanca to Segovia. We talked all the time to all kinds. The Franco regime has reached the middle stage of a crisis. I am no longer impressed by it. Something should be done, but the right thing, or we shall create a Communist Spain whether it be the government of Spain or merely the secret and organised opposition. But it is so big a subject we must talk. I am thinking of writing a little article to the *Spectator* (?) on my analysis and conclusions.

The page proofs of *Law, Liberty and Love* have arrived. I am dotting a few "i's" and adding a ½ page on toleration and the Church, condemning force as a means of producing faith. You won't object to that! Three times, a couple or three lines, I re-enforce, or repeat the Catholic teaching that as the Church and Christ are one in a grace-order-of-things, the voice of the Church is the voice of Christ, and so to obey it is in fact to obey God. You are not committed to the view of course, but I thought I had better tell you because it would not be fair otherwise. If you like, H & S could send you a copy before the final stage. But I don't see you objecting.

We saw Avila, and it required very little to see S. Teresa bustling about or going down to P. Bañez in the Dominican Priory in the plain below for Confession and advice. There is so much to tell you—

My love to Veronica; I hope you are having a real rest.

Yours affectionately,
Columba, O.S.B.

1. Anthony Maurus Green, O.S.B. (1919–) then teaching Spanish at Ampleforth; now at St. Mary's, Warrington; closely linked with the Focolari movement.

Ampleforth Abbey
York

21 September 1949

My dear Arnold,

A note:

(i) The Ortega lectures[1] occurred (reported) in Spanish Cultural Index, published by Cultural Relations Dept! Plaza de la Provincia, 1. Madrid.

Prof. Pastor, whom I met in Segovia, thought it your duty to contradict (in the *Times*!) the absurd views foisted on you by J. Ortega.

(ii) Here is the article;[2] I have another. I'm sending the original to the *Spectator*.

The boys came back last night.

Yours affectionately,
Columba, O.S.B.

1. José Ortega y Gasset (1883–1955); *Una interpretación de la historia, en torno a Toynbee* (Madrid, 1960); lectures held 1948–49, trans. Mildred Adams as *An Interpretation of Universal History* (New York, 1973).

2. C.C.E.'s "Alternative to Franco" appeared in the *Spectator* (7 October 1949). "It did create a stir. El Caudillo would not speak to Fr. Justo Perez de Urbel for a long time. He thought there was some connection. Not a bit of it." (C.C.E.) Compare C.C.E.'s letter of 23 December 1950 below.

21 September 1949 45, Pembroke Square, W.8

Dear Columba,

We got back here last night and I found your letter of the 16th waiting for me. As we passed through Raskelf[1]—we were coming from Edinburgh, I was looking at the hills, which were very clear, and following the branch railway with my eye towards the Ampleforth valley. I had had your card from Spain, written at an earlier stage of the journey. You have indeed been enterprising—especially considering that it was the hot season—and I am longing to talk to you and hear all about it. But now that I am back here I can't go off again, but must cope with arrears of work, and also, last time I stayed at Ampleforth, I found myself still too dangerously attacked by old memories. Time will help to heal this—yesterday, for the first time, I was able to look at the hills, which were unusually clear (Goremire, Sutton Bank[2] and the rest) without being devastated; but I must still give it more time. I am very sorry to have missed you when you were passing through London. Will you be here again at Christmas?

I am so glad *Law, Liberty and Love* has reached the last stage of printing. Don't bother to send me the proofs. I know I shall not be out of sympathy with the general spirit of what you say, and I don't think the reader will take my preface to mean that we agree *ad amussim*. I much look forward to seeing the book when it is out.

I wonder what the solution is for Spain. Though a constitutional monarchy is not in the modern Spanish tradition, it might be the bridge between all parties except the Communists and perhaps the extreme state-worshipping wing of the Falange. But we must talk about this when next we meet.

We are both much the better for a real holiday—nearly four weeks—the first since our fortnight in Westmorland last year.

Yours affectionately,
Arnold

1. Raskelf, a village on the railway that then ran between York and Gilling.

2. Lake Goremire lies close to Sutton Bank, the cliff face of which drops sheer to the water; cf. C.C.E.'s letter of 22 April 1940, above.

Ampleforth Abbey
27 September 1949 York

My dear Arnold,

I have just had a letter from Prof. Antony Pastor.[1] He is a member of the Consejo Superior de investigaciones Científicas of Madrid, and in charge of the English section. He asks me to find out unofficially whether you would go out and give one or two lectures at the Consejo—one for the general public, one to specialists—on history, and so have ample opportunity to answer your critics and of meeting them. You would be their guest of honour.

I rather hope you accept; it would be a helping hand held out to scholars in difficult circumstances; it would be new contacts and a chance of seeing Spain for yourself.

If you agree, in principle, then tell me and I could write to Pastor; or, of course, you could see him yourself. In fact, he would *very much like* to re-make contact with you. He is giving two courses at King's College, London, on Oct. 27, this year, and so you could write to him there, and tell him. His Spanish address is Serrano, 107, Madrid.

The *Spectator* has accepted my article on Spain. I hope sincerely it does good by reaching the ears of those who can do something.

Yours affectionately,
Columba, O.S.B.

1. Antonio Ricardo Pastor (1894–1971); scholar and banker; professor of Spanish language and literature, King's College, London University (1930–1945); cultural attaché to the Spanish embassy in London (1943–45); director of Banco Pastor in Madrid; founder of the Fundación Pastor de Estudios Clásicos of Madrid.

Ampleforth Abbey
York

9 October 1949

Dear Arnold,

Prof. Pastor says he will be "trouvable" at the Athenaeum, Pall Mall, from the 25th onward for about ten days, and seems very anxious to get in touch with you again.

His lectures are on "Ideals of Conduct in Spanish Literature"—I believe mostly about Spanish reactions to Drake & Co.

Yours affectionately,
Columba, O.S.B.

The Royal Institute
of International Affairs
Chatham House
10, St James's Square
London, S.W.1

11 October 1949

Dear Columba,

I have been slow in answering your letters of the 21st and 27th September, but I have read the copy of your article and I think you have managed to put your criticism of the present regime in Spain in a most tactful and constructive way.

This is fine, because the Spaniards are much more likely to pay attention to what is said by people who, like yourself, cannot be suspected of having any but friendly feelings towards Spain than to foreigners who have an ideological feud with the present régime and are simply out for its blood.

About your suggestion of my visiting Madrid, I cannot manage this for a good time ahead because I want both to break the back of the rest of the *Study* and to see our "*Survey of International Affairs*"[1] really on its feet again before I take on fresh commitments, even when they are things that in themselves are attractive, as this is.

We are putting off our next visit to America to next autumn, in order to be on the spot here, and I do not feel that I could arrange another trip abroad till about the spring of 1951. Meanwhile, the Duke of Alba[2] called on me three days ago to ask me to come to Madrid to give a talk to the Academy (I am not sure whether this is the Academy of History or the Spanish Academy: he seems to be a moving spirit in both) and I have accepted in principle while giving this answer on the question of dates. I wonder if I could not combine his invitation with Pastor's. Perhaps you might care to suggest this to Pastor, and anyway I will try to get into touch with him when he is at King's College, London, towards the end of the month.

As you know, Veronica and I have neither of us ever been to Spain and it would be a new world which we should both very much like to get a glimpse of.

Again, congratulations on the article. When will the book be published?

Yours affectionately,
Arnold

1. Publication of the *Survey of International Affairs*, interrupted by the war, was resumed with *Survey of International Affairs, 1938*; *vol. 2: The Crisis over Czechoslovakia January to September 1938*, by R. G. D. Laffan revised by V. M. Toynbee and P. E. Baker, with Introduction by A.J.T. (London, 1951); next came *Survey of International Affairs, 1939–1946: The World in March 1939*, ed. A.J.T. and Frank T. Ashton-Gwatkin (London, 1952).

2. Fitz-James Stuart, the seventeenth duque de Alba (1878–1953); descendant of James II and Arabella Churchill (tenth duke of Berwick); Spanish ambassador to Great Britain (1939–45); *The Great Duke of Alba as a Public Servant* (London, 1947).

Ampleforth College
York

17 October 1949

My dear Arnold,

Thank you for your appreciative words about my article on Spain. I hope the article does ultimate good; do you know of a dictator who has successfully withdrawn?

I am equally pleased that you have accepted at last 'in principle' the invitation to Spain.

Today I sent off *Law, Liberty and Love*—for the last time with all the last minute emendations. It is an odd feeling, rather like setting off on a journey and wondering whether one has packed everything, or locked everything up.

So the great work strides ahead. I am sure you are right to go on straight to the end. You must send me a line when the end arrives.

God bless you and the work,
Columba, O.S.B.

Ampleforth College
York

2 November 1949

My dear Arnold,

I hope you are persuaded by Professor Pastor, and go to Madrid by air next February. It would only take four days all told.

There are many things to be done about Spain and I am sure you are one of the people to do them. And time is an important factor. I think the going by air does make it more feasible.

You will be sorry to hear my book will now not be out till the Spring, owing to delay, here, there and everywhere. It would have appeared very suitably at this moment after all, after the *Times* leader the day before yesterday. But it will keep.

With the Abp. of Canterbury very low Church and the Cardinal too ill to take much part, the *Times* initiative[1] may come to little. I am very much in favour of a rapprochement; but, as you know very well, obedience is the core of it all. Perhaps misunderstandings can be cleared away and perhaps "Rome" might give way on disciplinary matters. But to enter discussions in the spirit of bargaining will get us nowhere. We want to fly over that into the realm of longing for re-union.

This morning I asked the Abbot if he thought I could write a little booklet on reunion;[2] and he thought I could. So when I am away at Beccles I hope to begin after Christmas, when there for a week.

Pray for inspiration for me; and if you have any ideas do, please write.

Yours affectionately,
In caritate Christi,
Columba, O.S.B.

1. This refers to the beginnings of the correspondence generated by the leading article "Catholicism Today" (31 October 1949); it called for a rapprochement among the churches, referred to the Catholic church as the "Mother-Church of Western Christendom," and pointed out that the Church in England and America lacked scholars whose work appealed to non-members. It was signed "a special correspondent," and the secret was kept for years: the writer was Aelred Graham, O.S.B. The letters continued over several weeks.

2. This finally resulted in *The Sheepfold and the Shepherd* (London, 1956).

The Royal Institute
of International Affairs
Chatham House

17 November 1949

Dear Columba,

My eye almost popped out of my head as it hit your splendid letter when I opened my *Times* yesterday morning.[1] I had been distressed, as I am sure you were, at seeing a promising correspondence gradually becoming small-minded and cantankerous. Your letter lifted it all onto a higher level, and I hope it will stay there till you have had time to buoy it up again with the book on re-union—it is very good news that you are to write that.

You have uncovered the heart of the matter: love and lack of love, and I am sure you are right that, if love can flower again, the stumbling block over obedience will disappear—we can't yet foresee exactly how, but I am sure it will be overcome.

I have had, I am sorry to say, to tell Pastor that I can't come to Madrid for those four days this February (I have had likewise to refuse four days in Lausanne in December, etc., etc.). It is not just the time, it is the momentum one loses, so I decided that my recent nine days in Holland, Hamburg[2] and Denmark must be my ration for this next twelve months, while I put all my energy into finishing the *Study* and breaking the back of our Chatham House history of the war, which are my two big commitments. If I go to Spain in the spring of 1951, I can spend rather longer there as I should like to do.

I am very sorry about the delay in your publication date.

Yours affectionately,
Arnold

1. C.C.E.'s letter to the editor of *The Times*, seeking an irenic approach to the efforts at reconciliation between the Catholic and the Anglican churches, was published on 16 November 1949; on 19 November 1949, E. G. Selwyn, the Deanery, Winchester, wrote that C.C.E. "has recalled this correspondence to a new level and outlook."

2. At this time T. S. Eliot was in Germany lecturing on *The Idea of a Christian Society*. A.J.T. informed C.B.P. that during this trip he only met Eliot at a station in Germany and was not making a joint tour with Eliot as reported by Eliot's biographers.

Ampleforth Abbey
York

17 November 1949

My dear Arnold,

I am snowed under. So excuse this note. I opened your letters first this morning as I wanted your reassurance.[1]

Thank you for your complete understanding.

God bless you.

In caritate Christi,
Columba, O.S.B.

1. "The bulk of the Catholic letters in response to mine in *The Times* and the 'feel' of many in the community were against it. So the reassurance of Arnold's letter helped." (C.C.E.)

Ampleforth Abbey
York

21 December 1949 (S. Thomas' Day)

My dear Arnold,

You will have seen in the paper that Fr. Stephen[1] died rather suddenly last week. He will go straight to heaven, but it seems to leave a very big gap behind. I hope I die before you do, but that, I suppose is very selfish, and I withdraw it.

Thank you very much—and Veronica too—for the Christmas card. I shall remember you both and all the family very specially during Christmas.

A Christmas article by me is appearing in the *Catholic Herald*. I am having a copy sent to you—you will see why when you read it.

Law, Liberty and Love is due out after Christmas. I am on the Rites controversy now and have found a great deal in vols. 32–34 of Pastor's lives of the Popes.[2] The Jansenist commotion in France was at the root of the opposition to the Jesuits. It is a cosmic tragedy.

The little book on Re-union will get begun as I travel about this Christmas and cannot take books.

On Jan. 3–5 I am attending a Re-union meeting at Hoddesdon, simply as an observer; apparently Rev. Angus Williams would like a Catholic there.

The 5th? No, I won't be there in time.

Love to you both and every blessing and enlightenment.

In caritate Christi,
Columba, O.S.B.

1. Stephen Marwood, O.S.B. (1890–1949). "One of the Ampleforth community and my closest friend, Fr. Stephen was also house master of Saint Oswald's, where Lawrence Toynbee was in the school." (C.C.E.)

2. Ludwig Freiherr von Pastor (1854–1928); *Geschichte der Päpste seit dem Ausgang des Mittelalters* (Freiburg, 1886–1933); trans. and reprinted in 40 vols. (1891–1953), with vols. 32–34 trans. by Dom Ernest Graf of Buckfast Abbey.

45, Pembroke Square
London W.8

23 December 1949

Dear Columba,

No, I hadn't seen the notice of Father Stephen's death: I am very sorry—not for him but for the world, which could not well afford to lose him so quickly. I admired him in all the aspects that I saw: as a schoolmaster and as a man; and I knew, of course, that there were depths behind which I hadn't penetrated, but which were the secret of the effect that his presence made on me.

I hope indeed you don't die before me, for you are a great deal younger than I am, though we may both often forget that.

I don't want to miss seeing you on the 5th January. Couldn't you stay the night (best of all), come to supper anyway if you can't sleep here, or at least look in on us at Chatham House that afternoon, which would at any rate give us a glimpse of you?

I am very glad you are making such good progress with the big work, and are able to write the re-union book with your other hand. I look forward to your article in the *Catholic Herald*, and, of course, to *Law, Liberty and Love*.

There is an exciting review in this morning's T.L.S. of Ronnie Knox's translation of the Old Testament.[1]

By the way, Blackwells have just reported to me the new edition of Ricci's *Opere Storiche*, but at the appalling price of £12-10-0! So I have asked them to send me titles and prices of the separate volumes. Which are the essential, important works?

I am now near the end of Part IX (Encounters between Civilizations that are one anothers' contemporaries). When that is done, I shall have written two-thirds of what still remains, and I hope to have the remaining third in draft within fifteen months from now.

I shall be thinking of you over Christmas, and hoping to see you on the 5th.

Yours affectionately,
Arnold

1. *The Times Literary Supplement* (23 December 1949), pp. 833–34, reviewed Ronald Knox's translation of *The Old Testament* (2 vols. [London, 1949]); cf. C.C.E.'s letter of 7 October 1941, above.

Ampleforth Abbey
York

St. Benet Biscop. (12 January) 1950

My Dear Arnold,

Raymond Lull[1] has been recently studied by Menéndez y Pelayo,[2] Rossello[3] and Obrador.[4] The titles of these studies I cannot find. In English Allison Peers[5] (pp. 1–454) wrote a life, presumably based on these, in 1929. Zwemer,[6] *Raymond Lull: First Missionary to the Moslems*, Pierre Charles[7] says is biassed, making Lull the first Protestant, etc., and the later work of the above writers confirms the view of the Bollandists,[8] vol. V of June, *Acta Sanctorum*, p. 732 "*praecipuis fidei catholicae athletis non immerito comparari possit*." He is beatified. Gairdner, based on Zwemer, Pierre Charles thinks poorly of.

Vols. 1 and 11 of Ricci's works[9] are the *Commentarii*, so I discover from vol. 1. It does not say what vols. following contain.

Les anciennes missions de la compagnie de Jésus en Chine, (1551–1814), imprimerie de la Mission Zi-Ka-Wei, Shang-Hai, 1924, par J. de la Servière, S. J. It is packed with facts. I have two exercise books full of them!

That I think covers the list of things I said I would do. You have already *Les paradoxes du Bouddhisme*, Taymans,[10] N.S.

Ortega's[11] lectures have now reached No. 10 in the Spanish Cultural Index (see No. 44 for September). The later ones refer to you quite a lot in a more friendly manner.

I was as always very happy to see you and stay with you. Was it imagination or did I really see a certain tiredness in you? Don't please, overwork.

As my bus nosed into Piccadilly at the Ritz, I thought I saw your figure thrusting through the park—Thursday, 9:30 A.M. I liked to think it was you. Would you have been going to Chatham House?

Ten days* in which to pick up again the China threads and then let them slip again. I must stop. God be with you to illumine your mind and heart.

In caritate Christi,
Columba, O.S.B.

My love to Veronica.
E. Gilson, *God's Philosophy*, Yale, 1941
E. Gilson, *Les Idées et les Lettres*, (pp. 171–196) J. Vrin, Paris, 1932.[12]
*i.e. ten days before the boys' return to school and end of extra-curricular activities.

1. Ramón Lull (ca. 1235–ca. 1315); "doctor illuminatus"; theologian, mystic, poet; martyred in his attempt to convert Islam.

2. Marcelino Menéndez y Pelayo (1856–1912); great Spanish scholar of medieval studies; catedrático of literature in the University of Madrid (1878–98); thereafter head of the National Library.

3. Gerónimo Rossello, ed., Ramón Lull's *Arbol de filosofía d'amor* (Palma de Mallorca, 1901).

4. Mateo Obrador y Bennassar, Editor, *Obras de Ramón Lull*, 8 vols. (1906–14).

5. Edgar Allison Peers (1891–1952); Gilmour Professor of Spanish at Liverpool University (1920–52); editor and translator of the works of Saint Teresa and of Saint John of the Cross; *Fool of Love, the Life of Ramón Lull* (London, 1946); *Ramón Lull, a Biography* (London, 1929).

6. Samuel Marinus Zwemer (1867–1952); missionary in Arabia (1890–1912); in Egypt (1913–29); professor of missions and the history of religions, Theological Seminary of Princeton; *Raymund Lull, First Missionary to the Moslems* (New York and London, 1902).

7. Père Pierre Charles, S.J. (1883–1954); *Les Dossiers de l'action missionaire* (Louvain, 1938), vol. 1.

8. The Bollandists are the Jesuit editors of the *Acta Sanctorum*, a series of scholarly studies of the lives of the saints; since 1882 these have been published in the *Analecta Bollandiana*.

9. Matteo Ricci (1552–1610); his collected works were edited by Pasquale M. D'Elia, S.J., as *Fonti Ricciane*, 3 vols. (Rome, 1949).

10. F. Taymans d'Eypernon, S.J. (1898–1956); Louvain University; Pontifical Seminary, Kandy, Ceylon; *Les Paradoxes du Bouddhisme* (Brussels, 1947).

11. Compare C.C.E.'s letter of 21 September 1949, above.

12. Étienne Gilson (1884–1978), neo-Thomist philosopher; founder of the Pontifical Institute of Medieval Studies, Toronto; *History of Christian Philosophy in the Middle Ages* (New York, 1955).

15 January 1950 45, Pembroke Square, W.8

Dear Columba,

Stay here again just whenever you can. If you like coming, you may be sure that we like having the chance of seeing you.

No, it can't have been I that you saw on Tuesday morning, for I was at that moment sitting in this chair in my study here, writing some of my nonsense.

As to looking tired, I am certainly at present working up to the full limits of my strength, but not beyond it. I have, though, of course, a tremendously strong purpose driving me, and I expect this does take it out of one a bit.

What were the results of your flat-hunting for your Mother? I hope you were anyway able to clear up her ideas about the region and the kind of flat to look out for.

Thank you for those valuable bibliographical notes.

I knew Samuel Zwemer: he was a considerable scholar and a far more considerable fanatic, so I am not surprised to hear that he ran off with Raymond Lull in his mouth and dropped him into the Protestant fold, in the conviction that every good *anima* is *naturaliter Protestans*.

His mission field was Cairo, and he told me once the story of the invitation he had to lecture at Al-Azhar[1]—a tribute to his Arabic scholarship, for they do not often invite unbelievers. He knew it was the opportunity of his life, and he took it. The subject he offered was 'The True Islam', and it wasn't till he had got about ¾ of the way through that it dawned on his audience that 'The True Islam' = 'Christianity'. When they tumbled to it, there was a hubbub, and the authorities had to bustle Zwemer out quickly. But he had shot his shaft.

Like all whole-hearted people, he was attractive.

Well, come again soon.

Yours affectionately,
Arnold

1. Al-Azhar; the chief theological seminary of the Islamic world; founded in the tenth century.

Saint Wilfrid's House
Ampleforth College, York

12 February 1950

My Dear Arnold,

Just a line to tell you I am still alive, and also to tell you one or two exciting things.

Fr. Paul for his jubilee, with the money given him by the Ampleforth Old Boys is going to Rome at Easter. He was taking Fr. Stephen, and he is now taking me—a poor substitute from his point of view because they were the closest friends, but wonderful for me. I had always hoped to go with you, and pray for the spiritual union of the world at the Confession of St. Peter.

You will have to be there only in spirit. I shall offer your book to God in the Centre of Christendom; find out the Tomb of St. Gregory and ask him to pray for you.

One can of course do all that here. But the knowledge that he lived there, that St. Peter died there, that so much has been done for us all from there, already gives me increased fervour at the very thought of going there.

The second thing is, that it looks as though Rome is coming down on the side of friendly approaches to those outside the Catholic Church. Thank God. It is a consolation to me.

We had Geoffrey Curtis[1] of Mirfield here the other day. He has been to Rome and seen the Holy Father, and was most impressed.

So, slowly the links are being made.

My love to you both.
Columba, O.S.B.

1. Geoffrey William Seymour Curtis (1902–82); University College, Oxford; an Anglican priest of the community of the Resurrection at Mirfield near Leeds; an early ecumenist.

16 Feb. 1950 45, Pembroke Square, W.8

Dear Columba,

I was thinking of you when I was reading in the *Times* about the new line of Vatican policy towards non-Catholic Christians—and Muslims too[1]—and hoping that this would re-open some doors through which you have messages to carry, and then your letter came, with the further news of your journey with Father Paul to Rome.

I am so very glad about this, and it won't prevent your going again one day with me.

The last time I was there, as I arrived at the doors of Saint Peter's, there was a pilgrim kneeling there, with wallet and staff. He must have come a long way for some great reason, and was giving thanks (as one could guess) for having been allowed to reach his goal. I have never forgotten him.

Yours affectionately,
Arnold

1. The new Vatican policy issued from the Sacred Congregation of the Holy Office.

5 March 1950 45, Pembroke Square, W.8

Dear Columba,

I was so very pleased to get the copy of '*Law, Liberty and Love*' that you sent me. When you stay here next, you must write my name in it.

I am going to send a copy of it to Bishop Bell.[1]

I was particularly glad to see the things on the jacket from Father d'Arcy[2] and Ronnie Knox.[3]

You could hardly have chosen a more auspicious moment for publication—just after the commencement of the new line of policy about clarifications between Catholics and non-Catholics. I hope this is going to open the way for you to do much more in this field, and meanwhile it is bound to wake people up to the importance of what you are saying in '*Law, Liberty and Love*.'

When do you start for Rome? I shall be thinking of you on your pilgrimage.

Yours affectionately,
Arnold

1. George Kennedy Allen Bell (1883–1958); bishop of Chichester; chairman of Central Committee of the World Council of Churches (1948–54).

2. Martin Cyril D'Arcy, S.J.; cf. C.C.E.'s letter of 30 July 1938, above.

3. Ronald Arbuthnot Knox; cf. C.C.E.'s letter of 28 September 1940, above.

Ampleforth College
York

Feast of S. Robert Bellarmino, 13 May 1950

My dear Arnold,

I have been back from Rome now two weeks and everything is more or less sorted out. It would have been so perfect to have been able to go to no. 45 and tell you all about it, but we merely passed through London.

It is a unique experience to walk up S. Peter's, which is like a world in miniature, and kneel like anyone else, for generation after generation, at the Confession of the Apostle. I felt that our history was present to me, with its triumphs and later its sad and bitter strife. All round were people from other countries, a Liberian priest whom we spoke with, some Chinese, French, Americans and so on. One felt at home and at peace.

Another day we went to S. Peter's for the Papal audience. It is a new idea, rather than have them in the vast rooms of the Vatican. There were at least 40,000 present. We recited the Our Father and Hail Mary and Glory be to the Father, in turn, in our various languages, and then all said the Creed in Latin. At Noon we sang the Regina Caeli, and, soon after, the Pope came in at the bottom of the nave. One could see a distant flutter of handkerchiefs. As he came up—carried, but with no or very few attendants—he motioned everyone to him, as though raising them up or drawing them to himself. Then, sitting before the Confession, he spoke to us all in our own languages, simply and blessing us.

The third time we went to S. Peter's was to say good-bye, on the last day of our visit to Rome. The huge church—it seems bigger every time you see it—was filling up with more pilgrims for another similar audience. A group of 20 Dominican nuns showed white half way up kneeling to the Blessed Sacrament Chapel.

S. Lawrence's, with its two churches and the tomb in the middle appealed to me very much. So did S. Paul's. There we got involved in a mass of French pilgrims crowding round the tomb. Perhaps the most wonderful place after S. Peter's is San Clemente, with its three layers, XI century, VI century and the House of S. Clement, and next door a temple of Mithras, five feet away, with its blood trough, its Apollo.

You and Veronica and the Book were ever in my prayers. England too, which humanly speaking is so important as the bridge between the Old World and the New.

We went to Monte Cassino and to Subiaco[1] from Rome, taken in a car by a kind Old Boy, half Italian, half American.[2] The former is already rebuilding. The framework of the church is completed; so is the vast refectory and the entrance section of the Abbey. The church is going to be decorated exactly as it was, pure baroque; I am sorry, as the design of the structure, as it is, is lovely.

Subiaco was not damaged and it still has a sense of the presence of our Holy Father St. Benedict. I did not forget you there either, he must have care of you, as you have so appreciated his spirit and work.

Florence was sight-seeing, but Fra Angelico is so spiritual that to see his frescoes is to pray. Venice I loved, particularly the ramshackle old San Marco, with its undulating floor and its uncertain pillars. We only spent two nights in each. Then we returned via Paris.

So you see I have had my wish: I have been allowed by God to pray at the Tomb of S. Peter and I have no desire to travel anywhere else, though doubtless I shall. My regret was that we did not share the pilgrimage.

God bless you.
Yours ever,
Columba, O.S.B.

Blackwell's has written for details of Ricci's work, and we are sending it.

1. When Saint Benedict (ca. 480–ca. 547) withdrew from the world, he first lived in a cave at Subiaco where he established his first community; in ca. 525 he founded Monte Cassino.

2. Count Filippo Senni (1908–); an Amplefordian who after two terms at Oxford had to return to Italy for army service; he served in the Abyssinian campaign (1935–38); fought in Yugoslavia; then was attached to Montgomery's army as a liaison officer; later a military attaché at the Italian Embassy in London; retired from service and spent twenty years with General Electric Co., retiring as chairman of its Italian subsidiary.

45, Pembroke Square
London W.8

15 May 1950

Dear Columba,

It was a great joy to get your letter this morning, and I don't know how you have managed to write me such a fine long one, for you must have been in a rush, starting the term after getting back. You wrote me a good one from Rome,[1] but I had been looking forward to hearing the next chapter of the story.

Well, evidently it fulfilled your hopes, and that was not easy: a longed-for goal of pilgrimage would be a very sad disappointment if it was a disappointment at all. Saint Peter's does, doesn't it, give one the feeling of being the centre of the world? I am glad you singled out San Clemente: it is history in three storeys, and I like the Irish monks who are in charge of it.

Subiaco I am longing to go to: perhaps we may still go there together: I imagine bare spurs of mountains overhanging a curving wooded valley. As for the Monte Cassino baroque, I do think that to restore baroque is wanton—one should be content with keeping one's hands off stripping it away when it is there. The nearest I have been to it is Circello and Terracina and Gaeta, on the coast—and I have not yet been to Florence, and I have been only within sight of Assisi, and as far as the porphyry emperors embracing one another outside St. Mark's, but no further (it was all locked up at 6.0 A.M.).

I am very glad that you had that audience with the Pope. From what you say, he seems to have the gift of making a personal link between himself and you, in spite of the huge numbers.

Some time, tell me what, if anything, you heard about the pre-Constantinian cemetery they have found under Saint Peter's? Is it true that they think they may have discovered the tomb of the Apostle? My sister Jocelyn who, as you know, is a Catholic and an archaeologist,[2] was in Rome not long before you, but seems to have been defeated by the Prelate Kaas,[3] who for some reason is in charge of Vatican archaeological affairs.

Well, what a lot we shall have still to talk about when we do meet next.

Yours affectionately,
Arnold

Thank you very much for sending particulars of the new edition of Ricci to Blackwells for me. I ventured to refer them to you because they seemed a bit incompetent about tracing it.

A.J.T.

1. Missing.

2. Jocelyn Toynbee (1897–1985); one-time fellow of Newnham College and professor of classical archaeology at Cambridge; in the event she had full access to the excavations and, with John Ward Perkins, published *The Shrine of St. Peter and the Vatican Excavations* (London, 1956).

3. Ludwig Kaas (1881–1952) was administrator of St. Peter's Basilica; not an archeologist but a scholar who had served in the Reichstag before the rise of the Nazi Party. See John E. Walsh, *The Bones of St. Peter* (London 1982).

Ampleforth Abbey
York

24 May 1950

My dear Arnold,

I enclose an article from *Life* on the Tomb of S. Peter. It is very cautious.

All kinds of rumours fly, one that the Pope has the urn of S. Peter's remains in his room. The most reliable information I got was that the excavations have not got to the precise point of the Tomb but all about, and the walls are covered with scribbled writings of pilgrims from the *very* earliest time, saying S. Peter pray for me, SS. Peter and Paul; SS. Paul and Peter pray for me.

The reason why progress has been slow is that there are no (!) foundations under S. Peter's, and water is everywhere.

Yes, S. Peter's *is* the centre of the spiritual world, as well as seems so. It is where reason and mystery meet, where certitude and liberation are symbolised. Solidity, spaciousness—how I saw it.

I am reviewing Wolfram Eberhard's *History of China*[1] for the *Tablet*. It would interest you. He looks at it all from the economic point of view, and he has sources of information untapped in the West—Hungarian and Turkish historians, particularly. Who is he? Is he a crypto communist, or am I imagining an under current? Perhaps you know him. It strikes me as excellent history, without its true, spiritual, point.

Yours affectionately,
Columba, O.S.B.

Could I have the article back some time.

1. Wolfram Eberhard, *Chinas Geschichte*, trans. E. W. Dickes as *A History of China from the Earliest Times to the Present Day* (London, 1950).

Saint Wilfrid's House
21 June 1950 Ampleforth College, York

My dear Arnold,

Three boys and I stayed up in my room last night—discussing the very point of your letter; and then behold your appeal.

Will it be heard? I think what we fear is unconditional surrender of our sovereignty. You should organise study circles for the circumscribing of rights. There is a sentence in my old friend the *Code of International Ethics*[1] which I think is the basis for a solution.

The powers of an authority are proportionate to the tasks it has to fulfill. No more and no less.

No more now. God bless you and your work.

In caritate Christi,

Columba, O.S.B.

P.S. I am going to Rome again in September on a flying visit for a Conference on Reunion.[2]

1. A publication of approximately 100 pages produced about that time by the Catholic social guild and later in U.S.A. (*Code of International Ethics* [Westminster, Md., 1953]).

2. "The Council on Reunion was a meeting, called by the Holy See, of priests interested in ecumenism; many countries were represented, including France, Spain, Belgium, Germany, the United States, and the United Kingdom. It was held in the beautiful and ancient monastery of Grottaferrata, outside Rome. Fr. Charles Boyer, S.J. was the chairman." (C.C.E.)

22 June 1950 45 Pembroke Square, W.8

Dear Columba,

Thank you very much for your letter—and I never wrote, as I had been meaning to, about yours on Spain, with which I was much in sympathy (Veronica and I are going there in April, on an invitation from the Duke of Alba:[1] I shall come to you for introductions, before the time).

What *splendid* news that you are going to Rome again in September, and on that mission, above all.

Well, the debate in the H. of C. on Monday night will be exciting,[2] but, like the *Times*, I doubt whether the Conservatives are sincere.

I expect, though, to see Schuman score a considerable success, and then I think the English will come trailing after the Continent.

Certainly we want, not unconditional surrender of national sovereignty, but an agreed subordination of all our sovereignties to a higher common authority. If we can't agree in that, we may keep the name of sovereignty but shall lose the substance.

Yours affectionately,
Arnold

1. See A.J.T.'s letter of 11 October 1949, above.
2. The debate concerned England's relations with the Common Market; on 9 May 1950, the French foreign minister Robert Schuman had proposed the Schuman Plan for the integration of the western European coal and steel industries.

Staithe House
Beccles, Suffolk

St. Lawrence's Eve (9 August) 1950

My Dear Arnold,

It is a long time since we wrote. Now you will I hope be resting up in the Pennines and able to read this at leisure.

Br. Kentigern and his "set" or year, were ordained priests at the end of term. It was a great day and a delight to me to see it happen. Unfortunately Fr. Kentigern has proved not very strong and has not been able to finish his course at Fribourg.[1] The last two months he has been taking things very easily.

Law, Liberty, and Love has received some quite good reviews, a particularly good one in *The Sword of the Spirit* [2] publication which understood what its aim was. H. & S. sent me an account up to the end of March, by when 1000 copies had been sold. This was before any review had appeared, so it is no indication.

You will be pleased to hear that I have finished my essays entitled "*Christ, the Heir*"[3] and Fr. Abbot is reading it now. The China book has been completely, 'first drafted,' but the 19–20 centuries are very sketchy. There is so much more activity. It is difficult a) to find the information, b) to see the wood for the trees.

The Reunion booklet[4] consists now of:

1. The mental outlook on reunion.
2. The idea of the Church as one in the N.T. from the symbols used of it: Bride, Temple, City, etc.
3. Peter and the Church.
4. Who is the Church. Various uses of the Term, and the confusions rising therefrom.

5. The early Church and the Church.
   The early Church and the Papacy.
   The idea here being that the Church clearly claimed to know its own mind, and in time the Position of the Papacy was clearly stated, and the Papacy always acted on that idea.

I have read two books of immense interest on all this. The first is Bivort[5] on *Anglicans et Catholiques*. Thrilling. The second Batiffol on *L'Église naissante*,[6] which is deeply learned. He now stands level in my estimation with Gibbon, in their separate worlds. It seems that Harnack had great respect for his learning.

To get back to the book. There is also a section on: the Church not impeccable.

I am going to write a section during the holidays on: prayers and reunion; and another on conferences and reunion.

There is a tedious and sad one on Anglican Orders.

So you see I have been busy. Meanwhile the school work goes on and the Exams were on the whole very much what I had hoped. If only one could find really suitable texts for boys to read. Why did not Columbus write a masterpiece on discovering America? or Cortes on Mexico? There are good plays by Calderón, but we are not always set them, while the old epics, they are old!

When you go to Spain you must meet the grand O.M. of Spanish scholarship Ramón Menéndez Pidal.[7] As an introduction read Starkie's[8] *Introduction*. It is very good.

You see I have not mentioned War III. Prayer is the only answer to that at the moment.

My love to you both,
Columba, O.S.B.

1. Fribourg University, Fribourg, Switzerland; a Catholic University served by the Dominican Friars.

2. The Sword of the Spirit; cf. A.J.T.'s letter of 10 October 1940, above.

3. The essays "Christ the Heir" appeared not as a book but in some early numbers of the *Life of the Spirit*, the Dominican monthly at Oxford; cf. A.J.T.'s letter of 16 November 1943, above.

4. This became C.C.E.'s *The Sheepfold and the Shepherd*; cf. C.C.E.'s letter of 2 November 1949, above.

5. J. de Bivort de la Sandée, *Anglicans et Catholiques*, 2 vols. (Paris, 1949).

6. Pierre Batiffol (1861–1929); *L'Église naissante et le catholicisme* (Paris, 1922). "My enthusiasm got the better in my comparing him with Gibbon; but his work had great value, as he with Msgr. Duchesne established the historical or positive theology in the Church, especially his studies of the growth of the papal power up to the time of Saint Leo. His work was done in Paris and Toulouse." (C.C.E.)

7. Ramón Menéndez Pidal (1869–1968); noted Spanish scholar of Castilian philology and especially Spanish epic and romances; *Flor nueva de romances viejos* (Madrid, 1928).

8. Walter Fitzwilliam Starkie (1894–1976); at that time British Council representative in Spain; scholar and violinist; *Spanish Raggle-Taggle* (London, 1934).

High Hall Beck
Killington
Kirkby Lonsdale
Westmorland

15 August 1950

Dear Columba,

I was so very glad to hear from you, and, as you guessed, we are here—for a couple of weeks: we go to Amsterdam and Paris for conferences towards the end of the month, and sail for America on the 30th September.

Is there any chance of your staying at 45 P. Sq. on your way north between 7 and 29 September? I should like to get a glimpse of you before this next three-months' absence.

A thousand sales before any reviews is really a splendid take-off, and, with the good review in the *Sword of the Spirit*, the book ought now to be sure of success.

What a spate of works! I had no idea that the Far East book was so far advanced.

I am much interested in the outline of the Reunion book. For touching the hearts of your non-Catholic readers—and, after all, you are preaching to the non-converted—I think the piece on the Church being not impeccable is the crucial one: no doubt also it is one of the most difficult bits to write: so much depends on emphasis and proportion here.

I have put down my pen for the moment half way through Part XI: 'Law and Freedom in Christianity and Paganism in the Roman Empire'.

I think we have it in our power, *if* we have the will, to make a decisively preponderant part of the World crystallise round America. But I don't believe this can be done except on a religious basis: I mean, I don't think anything except Christianity + Islam + Hinduism + Buddhism can defeat Communism.

The common platform of the religions is their belief (i) that Man is not God (ii) that spirit, not matter, is ultimate. These are two pretty big planks: can the religions stand together on them?

Yours affectionately,
Arnold

Staithe House
Beccles, Suffolk

21 August 1950

My Dear Arnold,

I visualise you perched up in the Pennines and relaxing the mind in the sweeping winds (and rain) of that lovely country.

The 19th Sept. I leave London: and, if I may, let us meet some time that afternoon. The train leaves 20.20 hrs. and I shall travel down from Ampleforth that morning. However, I shall give you more definite news later.

Your weighty contribution in defense of the Natural Law and the true nature of Freedom will be a tremendous help. I am delighted that the end of the Nonsense

Book is in sight. I hope you keep to the principle that you have used so well of picking out those things everywhere of which you approve. It is true, I think, that the Hindus and Buddhists have a belief in the distinction between creatures and God, but the former often slide into pantheism and the latter into nihilism,[1] and yet in spite of the thought of their greatest leaders. That is my general conclusion in *Christ the Heir*.

Every blessing and prayer on your efforts to group the world round America and to help America to be worthy of its destiny.

The rest when we meet.

God bless you both.
Love,
Columba, O.S.B.

1. "This criticism now sounds to me *simpliste*, even though at first sight some writings of Hindu or Buddhist origin might make a Westerner think that way." (C.C.E.)

23.8.50 45, Pembroke Square, W.8

I have had your letter of the 21st Aug. Will you arrive in London on the 19th Sept. in time to have lunch with us? And, if not, come in the afternoon, and have an early supper with us before leaving. Anyway, I will keep the 19th clear, from lunch on, till I hear again from you.

A.J.T.

26 August 1950 45, Pembroke Square W.8

Dear Columba,

How unlucky: I am taking my granddaughter Josephine to stay with my sisters in Oxford on the 16th–17th Sept., and I can't change the date, as it is a long-standing one, and it is also rather important for J. to have personal links with Philip's relations now that Philip's marriage has broken up.[1] I am most disappointed that I shan't see you when you are passing through London this time—when your plans were to bring you here as early as the Friday (15th). Well, there it is.

Yours affectionately,
Arnold

1. Philip's marriage to Anne Barbara Denise Powell was dissolved at this time; she married Richard Arthur Wollheim (1923–), then lecturer in philosophy, University College, London; that marriage was dissolved in 1967. As in the case of A.J.T., Rosalind, and Veronica, a friendly relationship continued among Philip, Anne, and his second wife, Sally; cf. Philip's *Part of a Journey* (London, 1981), pp. 191, 209.

Staithe House
Beccles

28 August 1950 (feast of St. Augustine)

My Dear Arnold,

It is only right that I should send you a letter on the feast of your true patron and example. I implored him to give you his insight, his courage, his humility. It came upon me that while his great work remains unassailable, rock-like, after one thousand and five hundred years, because it is a combination of reason and authority, will yours be? Will the men of the near centuries to come, let alone the men of 2400 A.D. be able to ground their lives on the synthesis you are creating with toil and tears? Yes and no. The Church will, as you know, remain of all the social organisms now functioning; that is, if men remain by then; and of the books of its youth and middle age there will be three outstanding: the *Civitate Dei*,[1] the *Summa Theologica*,[2] and, I know, *The Study of History*. But though you are as a city set on a hill, as a candle on a candlestick, you have not yet made the deepest synthesis of all—that between faith and reason, and the message will be blurred.

Yet from your remarks on my little writing on *Law, Liberty and Love*, it has been gradually borne in upon me that a slow revolution has been effected by God's grace in your heart.

You once used to say that many religions were more consonant with the majesty of God, but now I believe you would put them all, as I do, in an order: imperfect, perfect, natural and supernatural.

God bless you; and thank you for your kind hospitality.

Anything you write me on this subject I will destroy if you would prefer it for the time being.

Yours affectionately,
Columba, O.S.B.

I return to Ampleforth Saturday, and I hope you are enjoying a really good holiday.

1. Saint Augustine of Hippo, *De civitate Dei* (412–26); cf. "Saint Augustine," in *A Study of History*, X:87–91.

2. Saint Thomas Aquinas (ca. 1225–74); *Summa theologica* (1265–74).

Ampleforth Abbey
York

11 September 1950

My Dear Arnold,

We are just finishing a retreat given by the Abbot of Downside, a scholarly and holy man—a good combination! It has been most fruitful.

Your letter was something 'to offer up.' Well, we must not lose touch, but write to one another sometimes. You will, I hope, get an account of my second trip to Rome. You must join me in praying that enlightment does come concerning reunion. It seems madness that, in the face of the great danger, we do not have the sense to make herculean efforts to break the barriers. I know it is not by ignoring differences, but it should, with God's help, be possible to grasp the differences, and resolve many of them.

This great fuss about the Assumption;[1] it may, to a naturalist age, seem impossible and absurd, but I do not think it retards reunion. It will clarify the positions of many people. Those who cannot grasp the idea of flowering of truths, their unfolding, or of Tradition as being as vital to Christian thought as Scripture, will find themselves faced with those assertions. Then perhaps, with gentleness, the reasons for them will be forthcoming. I don't expect you to agree, but it is so good to know that you *understand*.

Sir Ernest Barker[2] has been staying in the vicinity. Fr. Paul was his pupil and has immense admiration for him. He spoke with affection of you and how he now saw more of you on various committees. I liked his review of vols. IV–VI, years ago. We had a very pleasant little chat, but he must have been disappointed in my 'learning.' He was almost shocked when he heard I had done French at Oxford.

My love to you both,
Columba, O.S.B., and
prayers in the City of
S. Peter

1. Pius XII was about to issue the formal definition of the dogma of the Assumption of the Blessed Virgin Mary; this appeared 1 November 1950 in *Munificentissimus Deus*.

2. Sir Ernest Barker (1874–1960); a polymath classical scholar at Oxford; medievalist and professor of social science; as the *Dictionary of National Biography* (Oxford, 1951), pp. 62–63, says of him, "He was perhaps happiest when 'dividing the swift mind' in discussing medieval history with, for instance, the headmaster of Ampleforth," his one-time student at Oxford, Fr. Paul Nevill.

12 Sept. 1950 45, Pembroke Square, W.8

Dear Columba,

I was so glad to get your letter of the 11th. It is sad that we shall miss each other both times you are passing through London between Ampleforth and Rome—at least, I take it you will not be coming home before the 30th September, which is the day we sail for New York.

As you raise the question of the doctrine of the Assumption, I will tell you my reactions, (which are probably typical of Western people with my Weltanschauung).

For me, the issue is not the one—put in the letter from the Archbishops of Canterbury and York—between the authority of the Bible and the authority of the living post-Biblical church. The idea of the flowering of truths is familiar and convincing to people like me; indeed, our hopes for the spiritual future of mankind on earth rest on this idea. On this fundamental point we are nearer to the Catholic church than to any version of Protestantism that takes the Bible, the whole Bible and nothing but the Bible for its foundation (I am sure, of course, that those two archbishops do not go to this extreme).

What troubles us is not that the doctrine of the Assumption lacks Biblical authority, and not that it is incompatible with our present Copernican physical cosmology. I am, myself, sceptical of all successive scientific accounts of the physical universe; and, while I believe that the pre-Copernican one, with a physical heaven on the rim and the earth in the centre, which the doctrine of the Assumption presupposes, is completely at variance with the true physical facts, I should also not be surprised to find our current physical cosmology likewise exploded by the further progress of scientific discovery.

What troubles me about the doctrine is that, whether physically false or true, it is in either case *irrelevant* to Religion: the nature of spiritual reality, the relation between God and man, the problem of good and evil, the status of the θεοτόκος herself—all these really important things are entirely unaffected by the physical question whether a material living human body did once leave the earth and go to some other part of the physical universe to remain there *in aeternum*. The fact that this—as it seems to me, childish and frivolous—physical question should be regarded as being one of momentous religious importance is what shocks me, because it seems to me to belong to the pre-Christian religious Weltanschauung in which physical cosmology was still mixed up with religion—the Weltanschauung that produced the myths of the assumptions of Heracles and Ganymede.

How does this strike you? I feel that this point of view is one that the flowering of truths (in which, like you, I believe) ought, not to ratify, but to discard, in order to liberate religion from irrelevant non-religious accretions. This, I think, is the crucial point for reunion. I should have been just as much put off if a doctrine about the physical disposal of the Theotókos's body which conformed to the latest theories of Western physical science had been promulgated instead of the present one, because this, too, would have implied the same misconception (so it seems to me) of what the things are with which religion is concerned.

Some time, let me know how this strikes you.

Yours affectionately,
Arnold

29 September 1950 45, Pembroke Square, W.8

Dear Columba,

When you write, send it to me at the Institute for Advanced Study, Princeton, N.J., U.S.A., as we are sailing to-morrow (arriving back about Jan. 13).

I am so glad the Rome expedition was fruitful—I am eager to hear about it.

This is just to say *au revoir* and send you my love.

Yours affectionately,
Arnold

Ampleforth Abbey
York

1 October 1950

My Dear Arnold,

Now I hope to have an hour to answer your good and honest letter about the Assumption of Mary, the Mother of God.

Your remarks about the growing in knowledge through the ages is one I like too, and in that point you and those you stand with are nearer to us than you or we realise. A strange paradox that the most 'advanced' and the most 'reactionary' should be so close. The very point that divides us is brilliantly illuminated by the doctrine of the Assumption. Let me explain. We advance, as you do, but we do not cast off what was once delivered to the saints.

Before going into your specific question let me tell you so that you can tell others. The Pope, in this particular instance, is not advancing one step further in development of doctrine. The Assumption is already the common Teaching of the Church. It is a holiday of obligation and has been in England since the IX century, I believe! The Pope in this instance is making a fuss about, or show about, something we have all taken for granted for centuries. You have rightly asked: why this fuss? Is it not irrelevant to true religion, is it not childish?

I think there are two answers, one with regard to devotion to Mary and her part in the Redeeming of men; the other to do with the precise doctrine.

Your attitude to Religion is, forgive me as usual, *Very Low Church* and spiritual. You would be rid of the anthropomorphisms and *earthy* side of religion. Your whole nature—it goes back to childhood—is de-humanized. But remember Pascal: 'l'homme n'est ni ange ni bête . . .'[1] But the religion of Christ was precisely an incarnation, the only incarnation. All the others were really divinizations—that is true is it not. God, as it were, took matter, earth, flesh, in both his hands and said we shall save man *through these things*, which he, poor little creature, understands. We shall lead him back, not in an etherial way, but humbly, simply, intelligibly.

Mary is part of that approach of God to us through his creatures. I grant that God could have done it your way: no symbols, no creaturely instruments. But I assert that if you look at the way God did come to us, it is through "the Word made *flesh*."

In the story of the Incarnated redemption, Mary is close to Christ, and Tradition asserts that she shares in this process, through and through. Consequently devotion to her is a natural and right thing. Now, the fact of the Assumption—if a truth—is a sign, symbol, visible mark, of her importance, her closeness to God, her perfection. Only a sign, yes, but we live by signs, we poor mortals who know in a glass darkly.

The Pope is defining it, not because he has discovered something new, but because he wants to focus our minds for a time on *one* of the elements of our redemption, the co-operation of creatures in it; because he wants to remind us of the resurrection of the body; because he wants to show reverence to the Body as such and probably lots of other reasons.

I wonder whether this makes sense. I pray God and Mary and all the saints that it does.

God bless you,
Love,
Columba, O.S.B.

1. For Pascal, see Lafuma, ed., *Oeuvres complètes*, *Pensées*, no. 678 (Brunschvicg no. 358).

Note of C.C.E.'s to letter of 1 October 1950
The Grottaferrata meeting

Gilling Station
Ampleforth Abbey, York

The contacts, it appears, with the 'Orthodox' are very happy and one hopes great things—but says very little, so says nothing. The Archbishop of Athens (Catholic, Uniat) spoke and also a most learned holy Dominican from Paris, P. Dumont, O.P.[1] The Père Boyer, S.J., Dean of the Theologican faculty of the Gregorianum in Rome was in charge.[2] He is one of those absolutely self-effacing Jesuits and very close indeed to the Holy Father. P. Congar O.P.[3] was there from France with a number of others. A young German O.S.B. from Maria Laach gave us a talk on activity there. During the war and immediately after it was promising, but things are less bright now. My talk on England was a mixture of cold water and hope. The French are over-optimistic. P. Boyer was kind enough to say he was grateful.

We saw the Pope privately at Castel Gandolfo. He spoke to each of us separately in turn and blessed us and all our friends—so you.

My general conclusions are that (1) we must create the desire for *union* by prayer, by private meetings in great sympathy with those who lead public opinion. In England much could be done; but we must not hide the difficulties, and yet be encouraged by every move towards understanding and real cooperation. I don't believe mass movements are good because the masses are ill-constructed.

Yours,
Columba

1. Christophe Jean Dumont, O.P. (1897–); founder of the *Centre d'Études Istina*; *Les Voies de l'Unité Chrétienne* (Paris, 1954); trans. by Henry St. John, O.P., as *Approaches to Christian Unity* (London, 1959).

2. Charles Boyer, S.J. (1884–1980); editor of *Unitas*; *Le Mouvement Oecuménique, les faits—le dialogue* (Rome, 1976).

3. Yves M. J. Congar, O.P.J. (1904–); French theologian; a *peritus* at Vatican II; *Jalons pour une théologie du laïcat* (Paris, 1953); trans., *Lay People in the Church* (Westminster, Md., 1957).

Ampleforth Abbey
York

All Saints (1 November) 1950

My dear Arnold,

I feel moved to write on this of all days partly because it stresses the communion of all men seeking God, partly because while I rejoice in the new dogma and have, as it were, enjoyed the party, you for me represent those outside who could not share it for one reason or another. And it pains me.

I do hope my earlier letter helped a little. There is so much to say: Our Lady in traditional and specially Patristic theology is the symbol of the Church. What is said of one is usually applicable in some way to the other. Her assumption is symbol of ours. The other thing I did not say is that her risen body is not to be taken materially—though it is her body—but spiritually: the complete Mary. Cf. the behaviour of Christ after the Resurrection.

Ampleforth is *en fête* today and 90% of all the boys have vanished already all over the countryside, as far as Scarborough and Harrogate. I have a chance to write a few letters.

If you have time to write, do tell me whether my book *Law, Liberty and Love* has appeared in America. The USA publishers have sent me advanced royalties, but so far no copy of the American edition. The publishers are The Devin-Adair Co., 23 E. 20th St. New York.

You will be glad to hear that my talk in Rome is being published in Rome in the Quarterly, *Unitas*,[1] and when you come back, I'll either give or lend you a copy. Meanwhile material is amassing for a book on Reunion.[2] Your help has been very great.

God bless you both and do lead (or help to lead) America along the path of justice and peace.

Yours affectionately,
Columba, O.S.B.

How is the book of books—for us.

1. *Unitas*, the Roman quarterly published under the editorship of Fr. Charles Boyer, S.J., of the Gregorianum. The talk was published in an English translation as *The Problem of Reunion in England* in *Unitas*; reprinted under the same title as separate pamphlet no. 6 in a series called *Unity Studies* (Garrison, N.Y., 1951).

2. C.C.E.'s *The Sheepfold and the Shepherd*; cf. C.C.E.'s Letter of 9 August 1950, above.

25 South Stanworth Drive
Princeton, N.J.

25 November 1950

Dear Columba,

I have been slow in answering two letters of yours, because I have been 'all out' finishing Part XI: *Law and Freedom in History*. I am writing now, before I get immersed in Part XII: *The Prospects of the West*. It is a good moment to write about these, and America, where the fate of the West is being decided—as far as human beings do decide their fate—is the right place. Meanwhile, we have had a great storm, and a falling tree has cut off our light and heat. Nature's practical jokes are very effective in a mechanised world.

I will now also write to your publishers; I have neglected that too, I am sorry to say.

Well, about the justification of the Doctrine of the Assumption: I have been trying to enter—imaginatively and sympathetically, if I can—into the common feeling that has made Catholics like you and Catholics unlike you (in being ignorant and simple-minded in the less complimentary sense) 'enjoy the party'—the phrase 'rang a bell,' because it put just what I, as an onlooker, had been conscious of. I suppose what was common to your joy was a sense that the Theotókos had been given an apotheosis, as Greeks and Romans would have put it. She had been paid honours on a par with the honours paid to Christ. As the Emperor Julian might have put it, Coelestis[1] had at long last been recognised again as being entitled to her traditional place on the same plane of worship as Adonis.[2]

Your note that the body is not to be taken materially, either in the Assumption or in the Resurrection, eases an intellectual difficulty but raises, I feel, a moral one. For you, as I now interpret it, the Assumption is really a traditional poetic formula for registering (what can't, I would agree, be registered in any other than poetic language) a conviction that a—the Greeks would say baldly 'a goddess,' the psychologists would say a personification of motherhood—is entitled to a particular degree of reverence and devotion which in fact has long since been paid to her. But what about the majority of the millions who, if I am right, sent telegrams to the Vatican begging the doctrine to be promulgated? Didn't a majority of these take the bodily assumption literally? And isn't the difference between this exoteric interpretation of the doctrine and your esoteric one a stumbling-block, so long as it is left undeclared?[3]

Perhaps it *has* been declared in the official texts, but I wonder whether the masses have understood it, all the same.

I look forward to seeing the print of your talk in *Unitas*, and am delighted that the book on *Reunion* is making headway.

I do believe a frank discussion of what we mean by the words we use will help reunion more than anything on the theological side. That wouldn't, in itself, dispose of the question of authority, of course, but it might make it easier to approach, by removing the fear of being compelled by authority to subscribe to what one didn't inwardly believe.

The American election was a bit disturbing to a West European.[4] Our goose was being cooked, and we had no finger in the pie. The lengths to which people here go in party politics are a bit alarming in a world governed by American politics, which has no margin left for playing the fool.

God Bless You.
Yours affectionately,
Arnold

1. Coelestis ($O\grave{v}\rho\alpha\nu\acute{\iota}\alpha$), the heavenly one, a cult title given Aphrodite.

2. Adonis, beloved of Aphrodite, a divinity of fertility, whose death was annually mourned.

3. ". . . The worship of the Great Mother had been withdrawn from Ishtar, Astarte, Isis, Cybele, and Inanna only to be paid, by Catholic devotees, to the same Mother of God under the name of Mary." But A.J.T. adds: "Catholic Christians, of course, did not admit the Protestant allegation that their adoration of Mary amounted to the worship of a goddess. According to the Catholic Christian doctrine, Mary was one of God's creatures . . ." (*A Study of History*, VII:467 and n. 1). In *Surviving the Future* (London, 1971), A.J.T. continued to hold that "she is really the ancient Neolithic goddess of fertility, the virgin goddess who was also a mother, surviving into the present day and receiving enormous reverence and devotion, . . ." even in her role as Kwan Yin (p. 126). "Ishtar—the goddess who was at the same time 'virgin, mother and queen'—lived for followers of the Mahāyāna in Kwanyin as well as for Christians in Mary, while Tammuz lived in Amitabha as well as in Husayn and in Christ" (*A Study of History*, VII:413).

4. The American elections of 7 November 1950 reduced the Democratic majority in both houses.

Ampleforth Abbey
York

2 December 1950

My dear Arnold,

I hasten to correct a misunderstanding. I hope that my understanding of *the bodily assumption* is the same as that of simple folk; they are right even if they cannot explain. I was only trying to point out that Catholic teaching on the "risen body" of anyone, Our Lord, Mary, us, is not material but spiritualised. I think the way to see it is to examine the behaviour of Christ after the resurrection: he appears and disappears, goes into a room, though the doors are locked. He has his body, it is his body, he is at pains to show it, by eating honey. But it is dematerialized in a certain sense, it ceases to obey the rules of matter. It is in this sense that all Catholics would say that the 'risen body' is a body with a difference. The elements in the facts, we would say, were not entirely in the natural order. We speak of a *glorified* body.

A second point. The Greeks used the word god or goddess, as far as I can see, very loosely; therefore to say we have turned Our Lady into a Greek goddess is not the same as saying we have turned her into the Hebrew God, Lord of the World, Creator, Judge, Wisdom itself. In fact a Greek goddess is not much catch! I should say we recognize Mary as very much better than that, NOT in any sense equal with Christ; no Catholic would hold with that. She was made by Christ in his Godhead; so honours *not* on a par with Christ, but much lower, are paid to her. It is because we are so sure where He stands: God-made-man, that we can praise his creatures.

P.S. All who reach heaven will be fundamentally like her, raised to likeness-to-God and with glorified bodies. But we shall still be creatures—receiving all.

Thank you very much for taking so much trouble over the American edition of L.L.L.

I am delighted that *A Study of History* is reaching completion. The prospects of the Western World would I think to a man on Mars appear to be nil. We have numbers and ruthlessness against us. But in the heart of the Western World is a faith which has not died. This will survive the impact of material destruction—if it comes—

and survive chastened. But it is not the Western World, it is something within it, and it is spread beyond it. You yourself have reached the same conclusion, I know, namely that the civilization which happens to exist is only the carrier of something more precious, namely a faith, a belief in God and the spirit in man, God's care of men, his saving of them. I hope you bring this out that the Western World, i.e. technology, our *form* of democracy, science, may suffer collapse, but that the child in the womb of the Western World, faith in Christ and his revelation, will be reborn of the travail of it. Give your readers the true hope that is in you, the belief in the spiritual; because they will certainly need that encouragement and re-stating of true values. You cannot yet see all the way, but the Catholic Church, I expect you recognise, is most fit to survive and bring through beyond the crisis the truths you believe in—though of course some others you cannot see—from your point of view not necessarily the most fitting, but still fit as a fact.

On the political plane, we over here are in a kind of mute fear; laughing, may be, as Figaro said, at everything to save ourselves from tears. As I see it the moral position is now clear: there *is* war and aggression; it is our right not only to defend but even to counterattack. We should, however, only do so if more good will come than harm. Korea is an unsatisfactory field for the contest. The enemy, the aggressor is really Russia; and if we are to fight anyone it should be Russia; or else she will be the *tertium quid*. I have no moral qualms about war in a just cause. The problem is, getting at the real culprit.

Let us hope that we shall not be forced to the last extremity and that we can get justice without recourse to arms.

My own part is to pray and I would willingly go to Russia to convert it to the Love of God if the thing were feasible. It is the real answer and will come.

Much love to you both,
Columba, O.S.B.

Ampleforth Abbey
York

23 December 1950

My Dear Arnold,

A note to wish you both a very happy Christmas and all God's graces. Please God we have a peaceful 1951.

I am not sure of your movements now. You must still be in the States, but due home soon, surely, as you are booked for Madrid this spring. I have warned P. Justo Perez de Urbel (4 Calle de Quiñones)[1] of your coming. He is away in Syria at the moment, but should soon be home.

You need make no further enquiries about LLL in the States. My first fan mail arrived last week, from a Chicago lawyer. He tells me he has sent a copy of his kind attack on it to you. Here is my reply. His point is an important one. As a matter of fact any is important if it holds up a mind. The scholastics would distinguish, I suppose, *in se* and *quoad nos*.

At last the London Library has been able to send me Eliot on *Buddhism and*

Hinduism.[2] So, having digested it this Christmas and incorporated useful ideas into *Christ the Heir*, I hope to send this to H. & S. in February at the latest.

Yours affectionately,
Columba, O.S.B.

1. Justo Perez de Urbel, O.S.B. (1895–1979); a monk of Santo Domingo de Silos; prior, Monastery of Our Lady of Montserrat in Madrid (1948–58); Franco's confessor; founding abbot of the Civil War Memorial Abbey of the Holy Cross of the Valle de Los Caídos (1958–66); a poet and historian; *Historia de la Orden Benedictina* (Madrid, 1941).

2. Sir Charles Eliot, *Hinduism and Buddhism*, 3 vols. (London, 1921).

107 East 70th Street
New York, NY

Christmas Eve, 1950

Dear Columba,

Here we are, staying over Christmas with our old friend Mrs. T. W. Lamont[1]—one of her sons, a doctor, and his four children are here too, so it is a happy Christmas party, the children all being too young for the world blizzard not to give their heads a miss: it passes over. Being in the house of a partner in J. P. Morgan and Co. is always slightly odd—though we are very much at home here—and New York, which is the apocalyptic image of the pagan modern world (though this house is a Christian oasis in it) is weird today. Here is New York, with its pride and shallowness of life still intact—a convex mirror in which we can all see the ugly features of our own faces—and yet, with this blizzard blowing, it seems impossible that it can stay intact. Even if the stones remain, something must be going to happen that will abash and mortify the spirit.

In America the crisis of the Western World—the incompatibility between the this-worldly ideal and the truths of Christianity—is, I suppose, sharper just now than anywhere, just because it *is* all still intact, whereas we have been losing it in installments since 1914. Hence the bitterness of the party recriminations that are so upsetting for all us non-American Westerners: it is a reflection, I think, of an unsolved conflict in American souls.

I wonder when we shall have a chance of seeing each other: we sail on the 5th January, and shall be home by the middle of the month.

I have no doubt that the true treasures are beyond the reach of atom bombs, and that, whatever does or doesn't happen, the truth and the right will still be right and true at the end of it all, so that the eggs that really matter are not in the crazy basket.

I read the Pope's appeal[2] this morning with admiration and assent, because he rose above partisanship and talked to the Communists as well as to the bourgeois as God's children. This may get no response, but, if any form of address could get one, this was it.

Well, we are back in the normal healthy condition of mankind, in which we can't deceive ourselves into fancying that we have the universe under neat comfortable efficient control. Γνῶθι σεαυτόν is, as always, the motto for us. (Our failure is within each of us.)

Yours affectionately,
Arnold

1. Thomas W. Lamont (1870–1948); chairman, J. P. Morgan & Co., Inc.; overseer, Harvard College; *My Boyhood in a Parsonage* (New York, 1946); Florence Corliss Lamont (1872–1952); cf. A.J.T.'s Latin poem (under the heading "ΦΙΛΙΚΑ") "*Florence Lamont*," 20 October 1942, in *Experiences*, pp. 387–88; and also A.J.T.'s tribute to Thomas Lamont in ibid., p. 73: "Thanks to Mr. Lamont's princely act, *The History of the Peace Conference of Paris* has been produced, under Chatham House's auspices, in six volumes."

2. The Christmas 1950 allocution of Pius XII.

SIX

1951–55

Philip's remarriage; the duke of Alba and Spain; A.J.T. pained by the "desecration" of the Mosque at Cordoba; the Gifford Lectures; Princeton revisited; A.J.T. speaks at an American Coronation service; C.C.E.'s pilgrimage to Rome; A.J.T among the panjandrums in Rome; the Teretina country; a visit to Castel del Monte; Pius XII; A.J.T. prays for C.C.E. at the Ara Coeli, "an auspicious place"; "the highest vision of God"; amplexus expecta*; vols. vii–x of* A Study of History *appear; responses to Douglas Jerrold's attack; A.J.T. on writing biography; "At Venice, Byzantium unbelievably meets Flanders"; C.C.E. a founder of the priory of St. Louis.*

Ampleforth Abbey
York

11 January 1951

My Dear Arnold,

Welcome home. Your last letter was a very great pleasure to me. I am glad you thought the same as I did about the Pope's Christmas address. He truly acts and speaks as the common Father of us all, as St. Gregory might have done.

Your words were so kind and sympathetic that I sent them off to one of his faithful lieutenants, P. Charles Boyer S.J.,[1] a dear holy little man who looked after the Reunion Meeting.[2] I asked him to tell his Holiness of your response.

On this coming Saturday I shall be in London for the Ampleforth dinner, with no time for anything but a phone call which I shall make about 6 P.M. just in case you are in.

Christ the Heir has gone off to Hodder and Stoughton. The *Reunion* book is progressing as my holidays have been fairly quiet. I would like you to see bits but we shall see.

Yours affectionately—in the peace of Christ.

Columba, O.S.B.

1. Charles Boyer, S.J.; cf. Note of C.C.E.'s to letter of 1 October 1950, above.
2. The Reunion meeting in Rome in 1950; see C.C.E.'s letter of 21 June 1950, above.

Ampleforth Abbey
York

Shrove Monday (5 February) 1951

My Dear Arnold,

It is a long time since I have written. Our last contact was the day you got home. And now you should be off to Madrid, Dr. Pastor,[1] the duque de Alba[2] and the rest. I am sure you will enjoy it; when you visit Toledo, besides remembering the scene before the battle of Navas de Tolosa,[3] and seeing those lovely El Grecos,[4] wandering also through the Cathedral, remember that San Juan de la Cruz[5] was imprisoned there in Toledo and wrote his greatest poems there. All that is left to remind one is the calle de los calzados, where the Carmelite monastery was. Pay your respects to his remains at Segovia, one of the most ancient cities in Spain. See Avila and Salamanca.

Philip, I see, is writing for the *Observer*, which means that your prayers have been heard—up to a point. The news he has is important but depressing. I hope you have looked at Patrick O'Donovan's book, *For Fear of Weeping*.[6] It could have been called: *In at the Finish*. *I Believed*[7] is, for all its publicity and the hysteria about it, fundamental. I think about it still, and it's days since I read it. Then there is something you would enjoy, and which I am reviewing for the *Tablet*: *Confucius, the Man and the Myth*, by Creel.[8] You probably know him (Prof. in the University of Chicago). My opinion is that it is full of ideas and scholarly. He discusses at length, too, the influence of China on XVIII century France.

My book on comparative religion, *Christ the Heir*, has been turned down by H. and S. The chief reason was that it was neither one thing nor the other, neither for scholars nor for the crowd. So I am now re-writing the more abstruse parts and making it popular. Also I am trying to confine it expressly: 1. to the attitude of men to God—primitive higher religions, etc.; 2. to particular representative persons or books, Confucius, the Bhagavad Gita. The trouble is that I have no one really to advise me. I think I'll imitate Msgr. Knox and fire off chapters at unsuspecting societies, to see what happens. (Have you read *Enthusiasm*?[9] It has a wonderful section on Jansenism—Wesley).

The international situation is improving slightly, it seems to me. But that is only incidentally; the background situation has reached an impasse. We can only truly destroy Communism by destroying the cause that brought it about, injustice followed by irreligion.

Your book, I hope, is shaping firm. It must be marvellous to see the end in sight. You must send me news immediately. You saw the little thing in the *Listener* on Historians, and how English ones go on refusing to see a shape in history. They mentioned you as being outstanding. There seems to be a fallacy that those who see a shape, put it there. A telling point in your favour is that the facts forced you, half way, to see a new shape.

We must unite in prayer during Lent, for peace and understanding. I like the bit of the Gospel which comes just before Lent: Lord, that I may see!

My love to you both,
Columba, O.S.B.

1. Compare C.C.E.'s letter of 27 September 1949, above.

2. Compare A.J.T.'s letter of 11 October 1949, above.

3. The battle of Las Navas de Tolosa (1212), in which the Berber dynasty of the Almohades was defeated by Alfonso VIII of Castile.

4. Domenikos Theotocopoulos, "El Greco" (1541–1614), lived in Toledo; his *Burial of Count Orgaz* is in Santo Tome, originally a mosque but rebuilt in the fourteenth century by Count Orgaz.

5. San Juan de la Cruz (1542–91); cf. C.C.E.'s letter of 16 June 1942, above.

6. Patrick Anthony O'Donovan (1919–83); the *Observer* correspondent in China when the Communists took Peking in 1949; *For Fear of Weeping* (London, 1950).

7. Douglas Arnold Hyde; *I Believed: The Autobiography of a Former British Communist* (London, 1950).

8. Herlee Glessner Creel (1905–); professor of early Chinese literature, University of Chicago; *Confucius: The Man and the Myth* (Chicago, 1951).

9. Ronald A. Knox, *Enthusiasm* (London, 1950).

45, Pembroke Square
London, W.8

8 February 1951

Dear Columba,

I am so sorry *Christ the Heir* has not been taken as it stands, and that you are having to revise it, but, at the cost of the extra work, you may succeed in getting it through better to your public—if the publishers know their business, and are giving you the right advice, as I daresay they are. Firing off pieces of a coming book in the form of lectures is a good plan, I have found personally.

I am glad you like Creel's book: I met him in November: he is a young man, with time before him to achieve things. There was a sincerity and straight forwardness about him, which I greatly liked.

I hope now to finish writing the nonsense book about April. If the Spanish visit comes off after that, it will be a pleasant interlude.

Am I right in thinking that the international temperature has fallen, or is this impression just the effect of coming home from America? I see you do think it has slightly improved. I agree, of course, wholeheartedly with your remedy for Communism—and this is a remedy that is in our own hands.

The news of Philip is good. He has done well for the *Observer*,[1] and they are taking him on permanently. He has felt the pleasure of making a success of a job and of being valued by the people employing him. He has married again—at Tehran—a girl called Sally Smith in the U.S. Embassy at Tel Aviv: she was secretary to the second in command there. I like her: she is straight forward and, I should think, stalwart. I am, of course, heartily sorry that his marriage with Anne broke up, but, as there was no mending that, I am not sorry about Sally Smith.[2]

Be sure to keep some time for us to see each other next time you are in London.

Yours affectionately,
Arnold

1. Philip's book reviews were to be of great importance to the *Observer* from this time until his death in 1981.

2. Frances Genevieve Smith (1923–), of Cleveland, Ohio; a graduate of Antioch College; see Harold Nicolson's characterization, "affectionate and gentle," in his *Diaries and Letters: 1945–1962* (London, 1968), p. 205; the marriage was a success: cf. Philip's *Part of a Journey*, passim; of this marriage were born A.J.T.'s only grandson, Jason Arnold (1953–), Warwick University, who works in a cooperative building group; Lucy Barbara (1955–), a psychiatric nurse; and Clara (1960–), formerly a clerk in the Gloucester County Court, now become a writer; in *Part of a Journey*, Philip preserves Clara's anonymity by referring to her as "Laura."

The Royal Institute
of International Affairs
Chatham House
10 St. James's Square, S.W.1

9 April 1951

Dear Columba,

Will you give me the references to 'deus absconditus'[1] (?Saint Augustine) and 'latens deitas'[2] (?an extremely well-known hymn by an extremely well-known medieval father).

By these questions you can measure the depth of my ignorance.

I am now in the straight before the winning-post—writing Part XIII and enjoying it.

When shall I see you next?

Yours affectionately,
Arnold

1. "Vere tu es Deus absconditus" (Isa. 45:15 [Vulgate]).

2. Perhaps a reminiscence of Thomas Aquinas' well-known Eucharistic hymn which begins: "Adoro devote latens veritas"; the Paris breviary has "Adoro te supplex."

The Royal Institute
of International Affairs
Chatham House
10 St. James's Square
London S.W.1

12 April 1951

Dear Columba,

Thank you so much for the references (I had missed 'absconditus' because the A. V. English translation of that verse is different from the Vulgate), and also for the letter from Dr. Wong Lien Ho,[1]—which I return herewith. I agree with all you say about it. It is a wonderful story.

I am sure he died a happy man.

I am so very glad to hear that you too are now 'in the straight'.

Yours affectionately,
Arnold

1. "It appears that this story of heroism was invented." (C.C.E.)

Ampleforth College
York

17 May 1951

My dear Arnold,

I got a message today from Rome via the Apostolic Delegate Archbishop Godfrey,[1] telling me that the Holy Father had been shown your comments on his Christmas address—the comments you wrote to me from America.[2] The message—which is from Monsignor Montini[3] his under secretary of State—runs as follows:

"You are at liberty to tell Professor Toynbee that the relevant sentence was made known to His Holiness and that the Holy Father appreciates the sentiments expressed and wishes the Professor to know that he prays that God may bless and guide him".

That should help you in completing *the book*. It is a real consolation to me. We had further news of the young Chinese scholar. He was tortured, beaten, burned, in order to make him renounce Christ, and finally shot. This is *all* very much between ourselves.[4]

On 1st June I am taking part in a Northern Region *view point* broadcast on Fountains. Rather exciting.

God bless you and your work, and Veronica, of course.

Columba, O.S.B.

P.S. Lawrence was here last weekend, looking well. Some of his paintings are hanging in the cloister. We like them a lot, specially his daughters and the railway ones.

1. William Godfrey (1889–1963); apostolic delegate in England from 1938; archbishop of Westminster (1956–63).

2. Compare A.J.T.'s letter of 24 December 1950, above.

3. Giovanni Battista Montini (1897–1978); later Pope Paul VI (r. 1963–78).

4. Compare preceding letter.

At the Quarry House
Dalhousie Castle
By Bonnyrigs
Midlothian

21 May 1951

Dear Columba,

I found your letter when I turned up here last night after a meeting of the Scottish Branch of Chatham House.

I had no idea, of course, that what I wrote to you about the Holy Father's Christmas address would ever come to his attention, and I much appreciate the message from Mgr. Montini. I shall have it in mind in finishing the book—which I hope to do before the end of June (We go back to London this next Thursday), except for a couple of annexes and a note on chronology.

I am so glad you are going on the air, and Fountains[1] is a good subject. I am involved at the moment in a series of talks on Asia in the Third Programme.[2]

My love to you, and Veronica thanks you for your message to her.

Yours affectionately,
Arnold

1. An "on the spot" broadcast (British Broadcasting Corp., North of England, Home Service, 1 June 1951) with Patrick O'Donovan and others. "We wandered about the romantic ruins of the Cistercian abbey, founded from St. Mary's Abbey, York, in 1132." (C.C.E.)

2. Printed as A.J.T.'s "The Impact of the West on Asia," *Listener* 45, no. 1160 (24 May 1951): 827–28, 840; and "Japan and the West," *Listener* 45, no. 1146 (15 February 1951): 258–59, 262.

Ampleforth Abbey
York

Corpus Christi (24 May) 1951

My Dear Arnold,

I hope you did not mind my sending on your appreciation of the Allocution. I made it plain to P. Boyer that I was merely copying out a sentence of your letter from USA to me and then asked him to ask the Pope to bless you and your work. I never dreamed that I was setting in motion the Papal secretariat, Apostolic Delegates and what not. It gives me deep satisfaction that you are linked with the Holy Father. He struck me as a truly holy man, besides all else.

I read your talk on Asia[1] and think you see it big and simple. Particularly I liked the explanation that we could now—with patience—give the underdog the benefits up to now only had by the élite. Your comparison between the atmospheres produced between Indians and us before and after independence is true of the few contacts I have had. The curse of the relations for the last 200 years has been that superiority in place of brotherhood in Christ. In a material age those who have the 'know how' are bound to be superior in their manner; it requires humility derived from some such notion as creaturehood or sin—*pace* Ld. Russell. Talking about his talks, it is exasperating to find one of his knowledge starting to refute a Christianity which is not the authentic. The fault is perhaps in us not succeeding in explaining clearly enough the True Teaching of Christ.

God bless you—

Yours affectionately,
Columba, O.S.B.

1. A.J.T.'s "The Impact of the West on Asia"; see A.J.T.'s letter of 21 May 1951, above.

Ampleforth College
York

16 June 1951

My Dear Arnold,

It was a thrill of contentment that I had when I read your little note of finality: "I have just finished the Nonsense book."[1] It is a work of such importance that it has been in my prayers all these years. Right or wrong, it shares and makes the great reputation you have, and its shape and theme will shape historical thought for many years to come. I conceive it specially as a return to true standards of importance: the saint above the philosopher, himself above the conqueror. Of course it also asserts a new unit, the complete culture.

I am glad you end with Fra Angelico, the perfect artist, because more than an artist, while that glorious litany[2] has been for years the epitome of history for me; and it links us with present heaven as well as past endeavour.

The book on *Reunion* has gone to Hodder and Stoughton. The chapter on prayer with it. I felt you were too busy to bother with it just yet. The "*Christ the Heir*" is in America with the firm which says it is publishing *LL&L* next September.

Let us in all things give glory and thanks to God.

My love to you both,
Columba, O.S.B.

1. Missing; in later years A.J.T. added two more volumes, XI and XII, to the Nonsense book (*A Study of History*).

2. C.C.E. here refers both to the liturgical *Litany of the Saints* and to the ecumenical extension of the *Litany* with which A.J.T. closes the *Study*, X: 143–44.

Hall Beck Cottage
Killington
Kirkby Lonsdale
via Cornforth

10 September 1951

Dear Columba,

It was a great happiness to see you again, after all that time. Meanwhile, I have read your talk on the non-Catholic English state of mind.[1] I should say that you had described it exactly, and in words that a non-English audience could understand. What happens next remains a mystery—and then the division between the different sects of Christianity is, after all, only a family quarrel. What about the future relations of Christianity with other religions that may perhaps express other sides of God's nature and of man's relation to God?

We got in here on Saturday, and I was hoping that we might be able to put you up if you could manage to come over; but our spare room here is full of furniture which can't be moved till our tenant's married son's bungalow is finished for taking it, and the farmer's wife next door is ill, so that we can't ask her to give us a bed, so for this time we are baffled. But there will, I hope, be many others, and one day I shall come to Ampleforth again. I won't venture at present, for fear of re-opening wounds, but I know that, in the end I shall be able to come with impunity.

I very much want you to see this place.[2] We are within twenty minute's walk of a corner of Yorkshire in the angle where two rivers meet, and our eastern skyline is the line of fells that make the county boundary.

I hope the two vols. of Grousset[3] reached you all right. I haven't yet read them, but I am sure it would be a good plan for you to read them in this last stage of producing your own book, as Grousset certainly has an eye for the shape of things on a large scale.

If you are passing through London at Christmas, we can always put you up in my dressing-room, even if our Austrian maid Nessie is with us then; so come if you can.

Yours affectionately,
Arnold

1. C.C.E.'s talk at Grottaferrata.

2. Compare A.J.T.'s letter of 19 June 1948, above.

3. René Grousset, *Histoire de l'Extrême-Orient*, 2 vols. (Paris, 1929); or, perhaps, *L'Empire Mongol*, vol. 1 by R. Grousset, vol. 2 by L. Bouvat (Paris, 1929).

Ampleforth Abbey
York

15 September 1951

My Dear Arnold,

Thank you very much for your note from the mountain retreat. As it happened I could not have come, even if the room had been available, as I have been made Prior. All I can say, inside, is *Deus vult*, because it is not the kind of thing one expects or wants. So the last few days have been busy as never before, digging my roots out of St. Wilfrid's and seeing to one thing and another. We have a broadcast coming off on the 23rd Sept, 9.30–10.15, and I am the "Thread voice."[1] So, you see, I could not write before. Thank you for the Grousset volumes which arrived safely. The Trigault translated will be sent off in due time.[2]

I am glad you liked the article on Reunion. Probably you are right, there are some interesting speculations in the philosophical order on the Nature of God, in Eastern "religions." The more one reads about them the less "bodies of thought" they seem to be, but hundreds of voices calling to one another in a mist, unsure. And yet we, so it seems to me, like the water diviner, can judge what is the real thing, because we have a coherent systematic revelation. This has now taken me 2 hours to write, so many people coming in; and I'm mixing metaphors! What I mean is that the world is full of good ideas mixed with bad, that the Church gives us enough Truth to go on with and for putting us on our guard against falsehood and positively helping us to discern the good.

What essential Truth, needed for our spiritual well-being, have these Eastern religions provided which is not already incorporated in the Catholic teaching?

I think they put the same thing in new ways sometimes—plus a lot of dross. I think too that the Indian thought is at times magnificent. But they all leave out a True Incarnation and, of course, the redemptive act and Christ's exclusive claim, his claim to finality and universality.

The above paragraph is really what I have been trying to say.

Say some prayers for me. I must stop.

Yours affectionately,
Columba, O.S.B.

1. Compare C.C.E.'s letter of late September 1951, below.

2. Nicholas Trigault, S.J., *The China That Was: China as discovered by the Jesuits at the Close of the 16th Century*, trans. L. J. Gallagher, S.J. (Milwaukee, Wis., 1942), Trigault's first book of Matteo Ricci's *De Christiana expeditione apud Sinas*. Compare C.C.E.'s letter of 22 April 1940, above, esp. n. 9 on Ricci.

Hall Beck Cottage
Killington
Kirkby Lansdale
via Carforth

17 September 1951

Dear Columba,

Well, what a piece of news. It doesn't surprise me, because the Community's feeling about you—and for you—which they have declared by electing you Prior,[1] happens to be the same as mine.

It is an honour because it is a hard task, but for you, I do believe, it will be as light a burden as it can be for any man because you will do it with love and humour as well as with zeal and disinterestedness, and you are therefore likely to have the consent of the governed—which matters, I expect, in a community vowed to obedience as well as among the children of this world.

It will be a wrench for you to leave those boys and that window like the window of the captain's cabin in the stern of a sailing ship, but I fancy that being a housemaster is something that is best done for not more than a limited spell of years.

Certainly you have, and will have, my prayers.

The cows are just passing under my window in their daily procession home from the pasture: you must see them one day: your visit is only postponed.

Ampleforth is something very special—perhaps unique. That makes your responsibility rather heavy but immensely worth while.

Yours affectionately,
Arnold

1. C.C.E. was not elected but appointed prior by the abbot after consultation with his council, in accordance with the Rule of St. Benedict, chap. 65.

Ampleforth Abbey
York

late September 1951

My dear Arnold,

My head is just beginning to come up above water; the change over, the broadcast,[1] the new year's work for the boys, the juniors' studies.

Your letter of encouragement is very precious to me. I mean especially what you said about Ampleforth—I am glad you still feel that way. Ernest Barker,[2] a friend of us both, wrote much in the same strain after hearing the broadcast.

There is to be an Overseas version on Sunday morning 8-15–8-30 and afternoon 4.45–5.15, on the 19 and 25 metres bands—if that makes sense to you! I have been answering letters ever since last Sunday on the subject.

Fr. Aelred sounds very happy in Portsmouth U.S.A.[3] We had a great simple profession ceremony on Tuesday, 8 novices. There are 4 new ones this year. Three from the school and one convert.

My love to you both,
Columba, O.S.B.

1. On 23 September 1951 (British Broadcasting Corp., North of England, Home Service), a morning service was broadcast from Ampleforth, preceded by an account of the life of the monks, by C.C.E. and others.

2. Ernest Barker: see C.C.E.'s letter of 11 September 1950, above.

3. Aelred Graham, O.S.B., was appointed, and later elected, prior of Portsmouth Priory, Portsmouth, R.I.

7 October 1951 — 45, Pembroke Square, W.8

Dear Columba,

Yes, I have never had anything but one feeling about Ampleforth. I didn't take long to form it, and it has never varied. It is one of the things about which I have no doubts.

I missed the broadcast[1]—I have never got the habit of looking out for what is on the air, and anyway our wireless was away being mended. Can you lend me a script?

We are off to Spain next week for a fortnight, under the joint auspices of the Duke of Alba and the British Council. I want to see Avila, Segovia, Toledo, Granada, Cordova, Seville, but everybody seems to be still away on holiday, so my itinerary remains a bit in the air.

We have neither of us ever been in Spain before. Will it be a new world or a replica of Turkey? As you know, it is for me a Carthaginian and Islamic country[2]—but I must not tell that to the conquistadores!

Yours affectionately,
Arnold

1. Compare C.C.E.'s letter of late September 1951, above.

2. "A.J.T. always refused to admit that Spain was part of Europe. I gave him some lessons in speaking Spanish before this trip." (C.C.E.)

Ampleforth Abbey
9 October 1951 York

My dear Arnold,

No, it should not be like Turkey. For one thing you will find a real, genuine, Christian revival. You will find churches lovely outside, and ruined with cheap baroque inside. You will find values change when you cross the "Pireneos"; among the people: valour, kindliness, heaven, hell. The saints, the Mass, count more than money. But among the proletariat of the cities the aftermath of hatreds, materialism. You probably will not see much of the last. But living in Alban luxury will make you conscious of the poverty. Things will have improved since I was there: at last a good harvest, and American money.

Soak yourself in the Counter-reformation* atmosphere of Avila—though the exterior is medieval. Think in terms of S. Teresa[1] trotting down to the Dominican friary outside the town to speak with her O.P. director, confessing and hearing the crucifix speak to her. It is still there.

Go see the Jewish meeting place in Toledo. Compare the two versions of the Apostles' portraits by El Greco, some in Toledo's sacristy, the others in his old house. You should really pause at Burgos: the cathedral, Las Huelgas, the Carthusian Monastery—Miraflores—where I was almost tempted to stay and hide, and half a day's journey off, the X century Benedictine monastery of Sto. Domingo de Silos.

I envy you your journey. Look up Dom P. Justo Perez de Urbel[2] the prof. of medieval history in Madrid. Get Prof. Marañón[3] to show you Toledo. I am sending him warning of your coming. I'll send you a copy of the script[4] on your return.

Adios,

Columba, O.S.B.

*In Spain it really was just a Catholic revival beginning before the Reformation.

P.S. I have written off to M. Émile Vaillancourt,[5] Canadian Ambassador in Peru.

1. Compare C.C.E.'s letter of 26 February 1947, above.

2. Dom Justo Perez de Urbel; cf. C.C.E.'s letter of 23 December 1950, above.

3. Gregorio Marañón (1887–1960); director de Patología médico en el Hospital General (Madrid); member academies of Language, Medicine, Sciences, and Fine Arts in Madrid.

4. Of the 23 September 1951 broadcast by C.C.E. and other monks; cf. C.C.E.'s letter of late September 1951, above.

5. Joseph-Jacques-Jonorier Émile Vaillancourt (1889–1968); Canadian ambassador to Peru (1950–55); interested in Canadian unity and recognition by Quebec of her French heritage. "I met him on a train journey returning from Rome, and we became friendly. The letter was no doubt connected with Arnold's visit to Peru." (C.C.E.)

[*Postcard*]

Granada, 27 October, 1951. Here we are taking a (strenuous) holiday in Andalusia, after 6 lectures in 6 days in Madrid,[1] Barcelona and Seville. I travel with the Poema del Cid in my pocket. The high point for me so far has been Avila: I don't know whether the mosque of Cordova will surpass it. We have also been to Segovia and Toledo. I lecture at Gibraltar on Tuesday and we fly home on Wednesday.

Arnold

1. A.J.T.'s lecture of 25 October 1951, in Madrid, appears as *Como la historia greco-romana ilumina la historia general*, trans. and ed. Antonio Pastor (Madrid, 1952).

45, Pembroke Square
W.8

4 November 1951

Dear Columba,

Well, here we are—as exhausted as if all the porters in all the railway stations and bus stations of Europe had jumped on our chests and hurled us about like bales—but it was worth the extreme exertion.

Who is the bishop of Córdoba? What is his history? As we were bearing down on Córdoba in a bus from Granada, we ran through a whole new city of working-class quarters rising on the south bank of the river and partly in occupation already, and we afterwards learnt that these were being put up by the bishop out of funds that he raises from the rich. This is notable, because I have nowhere seen so great a gulf between rich and poor as in Spain, or so little being done about it—with this one and remarkable exception.

Córdoba and Avila are my two high peaks: neither is convertible into terms of the other. Avila is the nearest thing I have seen to my notion of what Jerusalem must look like. The Mosque at Córdoba is the least unworthy place of worship of God that I have seen anywhere, not excepting the Ayia Sophia. Its great plain foursquare outer walls, like a Roman fortress, are as grand as the forest of columns inside, which were much more familiar to me from pictures. Of course, its desecration[1] made the painful impression on me as the desecration of A.S. used to make while it was still a mosque (Atatürk neutralized it, as I expect you know). As I stood before the mihrāb in that huge desolate building, I felt behind me the presence of the rows on rows of invisible former worshippers, and there went running through my head the lines of the poet Abu'l-Baqā of Ronda:[2]

> 'And where is Córdoba, the home of learning, in which many a great scholar rose to renown? . . .
>
> 'As a fond lover weeps at parting from his beloved, bitterly weeps the glorious Religion of Abraham.
>
> 'For desolate countries forsaken by Islam and peopled only by infidelity.
>
> 'Their mosques have become churches; there is nothing in them but bells and crosses,
>
> 'So that the mihrābs weep though lifeless, and the minbars mourn, though wooden. . . .'

There can be no more dreadful sight than violence done to one approach to God by the followers of another approach to the same God. The Turks, after nearly 500 years, had removed their own defacement of Ayia Sophia and have restored it, as near as possible, to its original state. I wonder if at Córdoba the Spaniards one day will do the same. Perhaps a day will come when, in both those great monuments to the glory of God, God will be worshipped by all His worshippers in common.

When will you be passing through London next? You were in my thoughts all the time on the journey—particularly at a moment when I was standing at the foot of the Alcazar at Segovia and looking up at the oratory where Saint John of the Cross wrote his poems.

Yours affectionately,
Arnold

1. The Great Mosque at Córdoba was founded in 786 by the Caliph Abd-el-Rahman; it was enlarged from time to time and is second only to the Kaabah in Mecca in size; since 1238 it has been a Christian church. Before it had been a mosque it had been a Christian church, itself built with the pillars of a Roman temple, still visible and used in the mosque that stands.

2. Abu'l Baqā of Ronda; (fl. ca. 1250); R. A. Nicholson, trans., *Translations of Eastern Poetry and Prose* (Cambridge, 1922), pp. 168–69; and cf. A.J.T.'s later, more extended quotation in *A Study of History*, X: 117. "Mihrāb": a niche pointing toward Mecca; "minbar": a pulpit.

Ampleforth Abbey
York

6 November 1951

My Dear Arnold,

Your letter was much as I expected it to be, the pang at seeing Córdoba I knew would be great. I could not face that desecration in the middle, though it was with as devout a heart as at any time in my life that I offered Mass in the far corner, at the Blessed Sacrament chapel, knowing all Islam round me and praying for reconciliation, understanding. Avila, too, I knew you would love. I think it the most complete thing in the way of cities that I know, and dominated by the spirit of Santa Teresa.

S. John of the Cross was carried back to Segovia by night from Úbeda in the south. There is a strange and veiled reference to this in Don Quixote,[1] when the fantastic knight meets the cortege in the darkness.

Perhaps at the back of the social work in Córdoba is Cardinal Segura of Seville. But I shall enquire. The Bishop of Valencia is, I believe, doing the same. I met an irate anti-clerical who was violently objecting to this activity of his as church-interference!

Just about when you were setting off I received an invitation—ultimately from the Holy Office—to go to a little conference in Geneva,[2] to do with Reunion. There are to be theologians not only us (i.e. 10 Catholics) but 2 orthodox, some "Reformed," a couple of Anglicans. In all, about 22.

I am staying with my niece, but could see you—I hope to—before starting, that is between my arrival in London and 6.30 when I am due at their home on 13th November.

Upon my return journey, I arrive late in the evening and go straight on, which is an unavoidable pity—and in any case an Old Boy has seized me for my brief scuffle through London to King's Cross.

Could I see you tea-time ish at No. 45 on the 13th?

My love to you both and God bless you.

Columba, O.S.B.

1. Cervantes, *Don Quixote*, pt. 1, chap. 19.

2. "This was in fact the first official—but completely secret—meeting of the Catholic Church as such with the World Council of Churches led by W. A. Visser't Hooft and regional secretaries from European countries, on the one hand, and Professor Journet (later Cardinal), Père C. Dumont, O.P., of Istina (Paris), Père Yves Congar, O.P., and others on the Catholic side. The Catholics later, many of them, became foundation members of the Secretariat for Unity set up at Vatican II with Cardinal Bea as its head." (C.C.E.)

7 November 1951 45, Pembroke Square, W.8

Dear Columba,

You wrote me a wonderful letter. I wish I had known that you had said Mass there. There were three people praying at that particular spot while we were there—the only other worshippers besides ourselves.

I am delighted that we shall be meeting so soon, and, still more, at the reason for it. Come here (45 Pembroke Square) from your train on Tuesday 13th: we shall be quieter here than at Chatham House. In the evening I have no engagement at C.H. till some time after 6.0. At lunch time I *may* have to take the chair at a meeting, but, if so, I will come round here immediately after, and, if you are before me, our maid Nessie (back again from Vienna) will let you in.

What a pleasure it will be to see you.

Yours affectionately,
Arnold

45, Pembroke Square
London W.8

26 November 1951

Dear Columba,

You were, of course, much in my thoughts during your expedition to Switzerland, and I have read your confidential account of what happened with the greatest interest—particularly the story of your two successive approaches and their different effects.[1] It looks to me as if, in the second approach, you did find the right opening, if, as I gather from your record, you then put your finger on Christian Love as the principal common *vestigium ecclesiae*. This might lift the debate above the level of legal argument: one sees the historical reasons why it fell to that level long since, but I also fear that, on the level of law, we shall not get the union of hearts that can only come through love. No doubt none of the parties is free to renounce its own legal position; but if we could leave the law in cold storage, that might give love this chance to find a way.

Yesterday I re-opened your comments on Part VII of the nonsense book, which I have had by me in an envelope since I opened them first in the spring of 1949 on the platform of Princeton Junction, waiting for a train to New York—not the best place for taking them to heart.[2]

I can see that I shall be able to deal with many of the individual points by modification or simple omission of sentences that would cause pain without being very material to the argument. But, when the red herrings have been thrown overboard, there remain more serious and difficult questions that you raise—particularly your reaction to my adoption of Symmachus's position—which neither my head nor my heart will allow me to abandon.

One thing I am doing: I am underlining the fact that my personal position is not the traditional and orthodox Christian one, and I hope this may clear the air.

Our meeting the other day was too short: I hope another opportunity may come soon.

Yours affectionately,
Arnold

1. This letter is missing. "My first 'approach' at the Geneva meeting was rather to point out the gaps in the churches of the Reformation and the second to recognize the riches they still possessed." (C.C.E.)

2. Compare C.C.E.'s letter of 27 April 1949, above and A.J.T.'s of 18 June 1949, above.

45, Pembroke Square,
London W.8

30 November 1951

Dear Columba,

I don't want any letters I write to you returned: I could not have them in better hands than yours.

I do not feel I have any knowledge about Christ and Christianity (the religion in which I have been brought up, and with which I have a familiarity that I have not with any of the others) that would warrant my saying *a priori* that Christianity (1) contains more of the light than any of the others (2) and is destined to prevail over them.

I guess that we are on the eve of a competition of rival religions, at close quarters, for individual souls throughout the World—as under the Roman Empire. Christianity *may* win again, but for me this is an open question, which only the course of events can answer. Again I *may* be right in feeling that 'God is Love' is the highest intuition of God's nature that I know, and that a God who becomes incarnate and suffers crucifixion for the sake of his creatures is the God who wins my heart. But my Muslim, Hindu and Buddhist brethren will say: 'How can you expect us to take this from you—a Christian born?' And to this I have no answer except to wait upon the outcome.

As a matter of fact, Christians—eager, as they are, to win non-Christians to Christianity—will, I believe, only move them by showing patience and humility instead of arrogance—for it *is* arrogance to say that one *knows* that one's own religion is a uniquely complete and saving revelation. It is an insidious form of egotism. '*My* religion is the best'. I say I base this claim on an objective historical fact. The others say the same, but in each claim the '*my*' betrays the egotism and the deadly sin of pride. God is enlisted to give *my* religion the precedence, when *I* am really the last person to make claims of this paramount kind for anything that is mine—including *my* religion.

I believe, in the coming stage of intimate contact, there will be, in each of the religions, a marriage of the Indian and the Jewish spirit: the two are complementary to one another. The next chapter after that is, I feel, impossible to foresee. Bounded, as I am, by my own Christian upbringing, I feel that Christianity has more to give to Mankind than the other religions have; but their followers feel the same about them. Who but Time can judge between us? Who would accept the advocate of one party as the judge in the case? Here, by the way, are several queries. There is no hurry about them, but I know you will be able—at your leisure—to give me the exact answers.

You won't agree with my attitude, but I think this letter may help to make it comprehensible.

Yours affectionately,
Arnold

Points for Verification

'modernistae . . . toti sunt in indagandis viis ad auctoritatem Ecclesiae cum credentium libertate componendam'.—Litterae Encyclicae S.S. D.N. Pii P.P. X: 'Pascendi dominici gregis . . .' (2nd May, 1877)

(this date must be wrong, as Pius X's pontificate was A.D. 1903–1914. Is the quotation wrong too?)[1]

'Si quis dixerit, fieri posse, ut dogmatibus ab Ecclesia propositis aliquando secundum progressum scientiae sensus tribuendus sit alius ab eo quem intellexit Ecclesia, anathema sit.' Concilium Vaticanum: De Ratione et Fide, Canon 3[2]

Could you give the Latin text, with references, of the Vaticum Council's pronouncement on Infallibility? (I want to quote it, as you suggest)

Could you give me the Latin text, with references, of that passage, written by Saint Thomas' research assistant, quoting his reply, when urged to finish the Summa, about its being like straw compared to the vision of God?[3]

1. The quotation was correct—the date, 8 September 1907.

2. See citation of "si quis" in *A Study of History*, VII : 456, corrected to read "quem intellexit *et intelligit* Ecclesia."

3. This text appears in ibid., p. 484n.

45, Pembroke Square,
London, W.8

19 December 1951

Dear Columba,

Thank you for finding all those things so quickly: I was a bit ashamed of asking you for them, considering the pressure on your time and those non-stop taps on your door. I now feel that at last I have the correct texts: I have put them all in, including both the version of the passage between Father Raynoldus and Saint Thomas,[1] because I couldn't bear to leave out either of them. I shall be writing to Father Barnabas tomorrow to thank him too, and I shall be sending you Denzinger back after Christmas, and *The Cid* a bit later, if I may—I have now read about half of the poems in the original. There is something very living, about it, perhaps because it is so concrete.

Going on thinking aloud in continuation of my last letter, I should say that, wherever one sees self-assertiveness, one can be sure that one is not in God's presence. *ἐκένωσεν εαυτὸν* as Saint Paul says in Philippians[2]—I believe this must be the nature, not only of the Incarnation, but of all God's dealings with His creatures. The creation itself is a supreme act of self-restraint, self-abnegation and patience—and, if God did assert Himself towards us, ever so little, the effect on us would be annihilation: the atom bomb to the nth power. Therefore I believe God acts in the World always unobtrusively and humbly, and this is one reason for the irony in human affairs, the confounding of the powerful and the wise by the lowly and the simple. God always incarnates Himself in a form in which no one expects Him and in which few human beings ever recognise Him. So we have to beware of taking it on ourselves to act for Him with a self-assertiveness that would never be shown by God Himself, because then we are in danger of alienating the Church—whichever it may be—in whose name we are self-assertive, we are in danger of alienating it from being an instrument of God's purpose and turning it, instead, into an instrument of our own egotism, which is more dangerous in its corporate form than in its individual form, because in its individual form we can hardly help seeing through it, whereas, in its corporate form, it may delude us into thinking that it is not the egotism that it nevertheless still is.

I must catch my bus, but shall probably continue this later.

My prayers will be with you for Christmas and New Year, with my thoughts on the Prior's talk, which is no light load.

Yours affectionately,
Arnold

1. Compare n. 3 of A.J.T.'s letter of 30 November 1951, above.
2. Phil. 2:7.

Ampleforth Abbey
York

Christmas Eve 1951

My Dear Arnold,

You are I think partly right and partly wrong about assertiveness; and it is a matter of meaning of words. What do you really mean?

Christ asserted yet remaining humble. "I am the Way." "I am the Truth."

Christ commanded his disciples to go and teach all nations.

St. Paul is incredibly assertive and exclusive.

You cannot mean that affirmations, clear and absolute, are signs of unGodliness. God is Truth. Although the manner of the Incarnation is unobtrusive it is almost unbelievably assertive: God-made-man.

A mathematician asserts all the time, without being assertive in your sense.

Therefore it seems to me, your "assertiveness" is no more and no less than the *motive* behind a particular assertion of a Truth. A truth may be asserted for its own sake, or because it is *your* Truth. In the latter case you have pride, in the former not.

The Catholic asserts—if he is a saint—without pride, but he asserts nevertheless Truths he has received. It makes martyrs, it makes apostles. He is not asserting his Truth but God's Truth. Of course a man may assert a real truth as *his* truth, but that is beside the point as to whether it is true or not. It only harms the teller and probably prevents the receiver of it from accepting it.

God surely could give us Truths and yet we retail them proudly. The Truths still remaining Truths, and they still needing to be passed from mouth to mouth, soul to soul.

You have attacked the manner and not the substance. The Catholic Church is, of course, the most open to this attack because it alone asserts absolutely among all the religions of the world—no, I suppose each sect of Islam and of Jewry does the same.

The fact of assertion is neither here nor there. I think one should examine primarily what is asserted and the credentials. Among the latter you would put humility, or non-assertiveness. I agree—in this you are looking for the note of holiness—but not to assert definitely at all, is not to have Truth, or if you have it, then to fail in charity. For good diffuses itself. A man who did not assert a truth, he knew to be for the good of others, would be selfish. A church which did not, would be selfish on a grand scale. In the matter of Truth, there cannot be anything but assertion. The manner will differ according to the love in the asserter's soul, according to the humility too.

If you accept Our Lord, you must accept all of Him. The humility of Him is most gloriously clear. But that is not the supreme virtue; and in Christ, so it seems to me, it is a preliminary to prove that when He does assert, and He does as no man ever has, it is not out of *self* assertion. He does not speak as the scribes and pharisees but as one having authority. "But *I* say unto you . . ."

A Catholic acts in two distinct roles. He receives Truth as God-sent. In that role non-Catholics call us slaves, craven, sub-human, giving up our free-will. He also gives out the message received, he acts as an instrument of the Church, which he holds to be animated—through grace—with the life of Christ. In this role he is accused of pride. He may be so animated, but this is not essential to the role. It should humble him, knowing his shortcomings. I shall be speaking in that role at midnight over the wireless.[1] God help me. There is, true enough, sufficient pride in me to ruin anything I say. But in his mercy God may do good in spite of that mist which will come between those listening and the Truths I am trying to state.

Do I convince, or am I being assertive? I am trying to prevent you overstating your case. I do believe that you are right fundamentally, in this sense, that humility and patience, gentleness, are the way into men's souls. We misuse Truth; that is human. The Church on its human side has often wounded in its use of Truth, instead of healed. But the Truth remained Truth all the same.

I wonder whether you reached to this point. Forgive my verbosity and self-assertiveness.

God bless us both *in caritate Christi*,

Columba, O.S.B.

1. The broadcast of the Christmas Eve Mass at Ampleforth.

Ampleforth Abbey
York

30 January 1952

My dear Arnold,

I go on thinking about the last problem you set me: the manner of enunciating Truth being a sign of God's presence. And we "concluded" that assertiveness was an adverse sign. Now I am doubtful: what of the Prophets of the Old Testament? That Prophetic absoluteness, certainty, almost violence against error. Christ's own condemnation of hypocrisy, of the cities of the Plain, a number of passages in S. Paul all lead me to a further elucidation. It is not assertiveness which is a sign of the devil, but *self*-assertiveness. Great Teachers are very assertive of the Truth, and should be self-effacing. St Thomas always was asserting—with no "perhaps", "I feel",—and completely self-effacing. I am sure that revealed Truth—not misty gropings—always creates that white hot need to tell it, and tell it as ABSOLUTELY True. The Church's pronouncements are in line with all that: insistent, assertive, uncompromising.

Yours affectionately,
Columba, O.S.B.

31 January 1952 45, Pembroke Square, W.8

Dear Columba,

Now I have had your letter of the 30th before I have answered your earlier one on the same point. I am ashamed, for I know I can't be as busy as you are—and certainly not as busy as you were at the New Year, when you managed to write all the same. I have been submerged by my part on encounters between civilizations, on which I had weighty comments on controversial topics (Russians *plus* Jews!) to wrestle with.[1] Anyway, I will shake it off and write now.

I think we have come to a formidable snag: the difficulty of distinguishing between self-assertiveness and assertiveness on behalf of God, Truth, or some other important cause that would be *not* oneself—*if* one could be sure that it wasn't a cloak for oneself.

Have you read C. Woodham-Smith's *Life of Florence Nightingale*?[2] It illustrates the snag. In her case her assertion of God's will (and I am sure she was right in believing that it was His will) that the wounded, sick and poor should be better treated by their fellow men, seems impossible to disentangle from her passion to exercise her power over important statesmen, and she is by no means peculiar in this. It is, of course, a common infirmity of great men. They are great enough not to let themselves succumb to self-assertion naked, so they dress it up (in good faith) as the assertion of God's will because, after all, they cannot bear not to assert themselves.

This is, I believe, one of the fundamental tragedies of human affairs.

How is any human being to be sure where the line between selfishness and altruism runs? The prophet feels sure that the message he feels constrained to assert has come to him from God, but it comes to the prophet's fellow human beings from the prophet, and they have to take it from him that its origin is divine; and, if they do take it, this gives the prophet enormous personal importance; even if they don't take it, his inward assurance that he is God's mouthpiece gives him an importance in his own eyes.

I think the remedy is for the prophet to confess to himself and the world that, while he feels constrained to give his message because it seems to him to be God's word, he knows that he too is only a fallible and sinful mortal, who may be mistaken, or may be influenced by egotism. This confession will disappoint the masses in the short run, because the masses, like children, want 'yes' or 'no' answers. But in the long run, I truly believe, if there is truth in his message, his admission that he may be mistaken will win more souls to the truth than an assertiveness in God's name.

Is there something in this?

Yours affectionately,
Arnold

1. In vol. VIII of *A Study of History*, esp. "The Modern West and Russia," pp. 126–49, and "The Modern West and the Jews," pp. 272–313.

2. C. Woodham-Smith, *Florence Nightingale* (London, 1950); Florence Nightingale (1820–1910), in her devotion to the wounded and dying during the Crimean War (1854–56), realized the inadequacies of old-fashioned nursing habits and reformed them.

Ampleforth Abbey
York

15 February 1952

My dear Arnold,

Half an hour presents itself and I want to answer your letter. How do people know whether God really wants them to say something or do something? You are right that often people think it is God pushing when in reality it is the Ego.

Obviously someone who is only claiming human knowledge should speak diffidently. We are all fallible.

The prophet. There have been a number of false ones lately, not least Hitler! He believes he is the mouthpiece of God. From the Catholic point of view the situation is peculiar. We believe that the *final* revelation came with Christ and his Apostles.

Therefore anything after will only be a stressing or deepening of what was once delivered to the Saints. All the 'revelations' to saints are of this kind. This simplifies matters as all such pronouncements of visionaries are checked by the Truth already revealed. Either it agrees or it does not. In fact the Church is extremely sceptical of all such private revelations; has exhaustive enquiries, damps enthusiasm. Years go by before it makes a pronouncement in favour and then it only says "This is in conformity with Catholic teaching". In other words the Visible hierarchic Church is very useful as a brake on the "Spiritual" Church. So often they are seen as opposites. All real mystics are childishly grateful for an authority to test their visions by. The devil can easily disguise himself as an angel of light. There is NO certainty in visions without the judgement of the Church. In Pre-Christian Jewry the Prophet had his message guaranteed by miracles. The trouble about the guarantee of holiness is that holy people can be self deceived. I know a case—a nun dead some 10–15 years ago. There are hundreds. We know more, too, than the ancients about the subconscious.

Action. It is very interesting watching *saints* set off on their gigantic activities. The most striking is S. Vincent de Paul[1]—an activist if ever there was one. Although he knew what should be done, he never made the first move until he was forced into it by circumstances or authority.

I must say that principle appeals to me. Obedience to God's call is usually—always—safe, and nothing else is, when circumstances throw the thing at your feet, and best when authority says "go". Remember S. Francis Xavier.[2] His activity was under obedience.

You are right that both the propagation of Truth and the doing of good works are full of pitfalls, and the only safeguard for the mover and for the recipients is authority, God showing his will and mind by inevitable circumstances or obedience to superiors, or by guaranteed revelation.

This cannot all seem right to you, but it does take the discussion a step further.

God bless your works and you.

Love,
Columba

1. Saint Vincent de Paul (ca. 1580–1660); founder of the Lazarist Fathers and the Sisters of Charity, the first congregation of women without enclosure, dedicated to care of the sick and the poor: "Monsieur Vincent."

2. Saint Francis Xavier, S.J. (1506–52); apostle of the Indies and Japan.

8 March 1952 — 20 St Stephens Gardens, W.2

Very Rev. Father,

I am enclosing an offering for Masses.

Oh what a tough job! The only ray of hope is the value and dependence placed in your friendship. It is very moving and *must* be significant.

I wonder if you saw the revise of Part VII, or heard any more about it. It's not quite finished yet, anyway.

I'm afraid I'm not doing my bit: the cold makes a coward of me—just when I ought to be doing my utmost.

I do hope you are well. Please remember me in your prayers.

Yours very sincerely,
Bridget Reddin

45, Pembroke Square
London W.8

3 April 1952

Dear Columba,

I took vol. vii to the printer the day before yesterday and am now returning herewith the *Poema*[1] and *Enchiridion Symbolorum*.[2]

I have read (more or less) about two-thirds of the *Poema* with the help of the modern Castilian translation. It reminds me of something north European, which I had not expected.

We are sailing for another visit to the United States on the 17th April, but shall be back towards the end of July. I am giving my first lot of Gifford Lectures[3] in October and November and immediately after that some Reith Lectures[4] for the B.B.C., but I hope to be able to ease off a bit after the New Year.

Yours affectionately,
Arnold

1. "I think this is the *Poema del mio Cid*." (C.C.E.)

2. H. Denzinger, *Enchiridion Symbolorum*, 1st ed. (Würzburg, 1854); frequently reedited; a historical "handbook" with scholarly texts of theologically significant creeds, epistles, decrees, and other *monumenta ecclesiae*; a major work of nineteenth- and twentieth-century scholarship.

3. *An Historian's Approach to Religion* (London, 1956) was based on A.J.T.'s Gifford Lectures delivered at the University of Edinburgh in 1952 and 1953.

4. Six lectures, published originally in *Listener* (20 November–25 December 1952) and later as *The World and the West* (London, 1953).

Ampleforth Abbey
York

Maudy Thursday (10 April) 1952

My dear Arnold,

I arrived back last night to find the parcel and your note. Thank you for both. If I had known you were off so soon I should have paused on my way through London. As it was I only had 30 minutes between Paddington and Kings Cross.

Thank you for the books.

The Denzinger reminds me of a letter I should have written to you about Our Lord's forthrightness on several occasions, both in act and speech; but today is not the day, "like a lamb he was led to the slaughter." It is sacrificing love that wins men, even if Truth has also to be stated clearly. I wish you a happy and fruitful time in America and look forward to seeing Vol VII, specially, in print. May it do nothing but good. I am glad you are giving the Reith Lectures, will they be an aperitif for the forthcoming volumes of the Study? You whet my appetite.

This weekend about 350–400 old Boys are coming to celebrate Easter and then the fact of Divine Providence that we have flourished here for 150 years (1802–1952). It will all be very exhausting but also rewarding and worthwhile.

The final revision of *Nestorians in China*[1] I hope has been achieved, but my time is so cut about I wonder whether the thing will ever get done.

Yours affectionately,
Columba, O.S.B.

1. Published as chap. 2 of C.C.E.'s *China and the Cross* (New York, 1957).

14 April 1952 — 45, Pembroke Square, W.8

Dear Columba,

I was so glad to get your letter, though I would have been still more glad to have a glimpse of you *en route*. You will probably hear from me next in Oregon.

'It is a sacrificing love that wins men, even if truth has to be stated clearly'. I can subscribe to that without any reservations or insincerity, and it is a grand directive for your mission of seeing what can be done to re-unite all Christians.

I am so glad the *Nestorians* are in their last stage, and I am sure you will get the book out all right, though a Prior's job is bound, I am afraid, to be a bit at war with an author's.

My love to you,

Yours affectionately,
Arnold

I am 63 today, but am not feeling old.

A.J.T.

6 Stanworth Place
Princeton, N.J.

18 May 1952

Dear Columba,

Well, we have been to Oregon and back since we wrote to each other last. The North-West was the one section of the U.S. that I had had no glimpse of before, so I was a good deal interested. The people are of quite a distinct type: there is something very simple and direct about them, which is attractive.

During the ten days that we have been here I have been making an assault on the first of my two sets of Gifford Lectures:[1] 'the dawn of the higher religions'. I got a provisional list of ten topics down on paper when we were in Switzerland in February. I now have notes for 8½ lectures out of the ten: no doubt these will change a lot as I carry them through the various stages that will end in print. My plot is: 'After Man had got the better of Nature, and so could not go on worshipping her, he had a choice between two other objects of worship: himself and God. This is the issue in the present religious crisis'—which has been 'on', I should say, since about 3000 B.C., after Nature-worship had lasted for many hundreds of thousands of years. I find—I suppose, not surprisingly—that, the more I think about Man-worship, the more horror I feel at it. It is a surrender to the egocentricity that is the moral and intellectual error in every living creature, but that is also the necessary condition for its having a separate life—which seems to mean that there is a tension in the very nature of life, or, in other words, that there can be no life without suffering. The worship of human power tries to defy suffering by main force; the Hīnayāna, more discerningly, tries to extinguish suffering by extinguishing life itself; the Mahāyāna and Christianity accept suffering as something that, by self-sacrifice, can be made an opportunity for Love, and they believe that this is not just a human fancy, but that God or the bodhisattvas have led the way for man to follow. Human beings couldn't 'take' the revelation of this until they had had an unusually severe experience of suffering themselves, and this is why, as a matter of history, the higher religions have all arisen in times of trouble. But why have they missed fire during their first few thousand years? I take as my text here the various miscarriages in the Parable of the Sower.[2]

Well, I shall show you all this at some stage, if I may.

The political temperature in America is happily much lower now than when we were here in 1950–1, at the time of the West retreat in Korea and the MacArthur affair.[3] I believe the Americans will learn to live with their troubles—which would be a heroic change from the impulse to cut knots which they acquired from clearing the continent by exterminating forests, bisons, Indians. But you can't dispose of, easily, the Asian Indians that way. Exterminate Gandhi, for example, and his soul goes marching on.

Send me a line to tell me how *Christianity in China* is getting on.

Yours affectionately,
Arnold

1. Compare n. 3 of A.J.T.'s letter of 3 April 1952, above.

2. Luke 8:4–15.

3. On 4 January 1951, the North Korean and Chinese forces had occupied Seoul in South Korea; on 14 March, the U.N. forces under General Douglas MacArthur reoccupied Seoul; on 10 April, President Truman recalled General MacArthur.

The Institute for Advanced Study
Princeton, New Jersey

22 June 1952

Dear Columba,

I have read the chapters, and am returning them herewith. My chief comment, as you will see from my scrawls in the margin, is: 'Avoid provocations that are irrelevant to your narrative': e.g. passing digs at China, the French Revolution, Democracy, Protestantism. These will be so many red herrings, distracting your readers from what it is your object to tell them, and alienating many unnecessarily, beyond a too narrow circle who are anti-Chinese *and* anti-Protestant *and* anti-Democratic.

Am I not right in thinking that Democracy has been officially pronounced to be no less compatible than Authoritarian Government with Catholicism? If so, why give it a passing dig? As for China and the mandarins, one's judgment on intolerance ought to be comparative. At the date when the Chinese Imperial Govt. was persecuting Christianity, what shrift did a Catholic missionary receive in England or a Protestant one in Spain? The 17th and 18th century Jesuits in China thought that she compared well with contemporary Europe, and she had, after all, succeeded in establishing the common govt., which Europe had failed to reestablish since the fall of Rome. China is comparable to Europe as a whole, not to any local European principality, and, even in the 19th century, there is less warfare, bloodshed and disorder in China as a whole than in Europe as a whole. Remember the mote and the beam.

Also, look back on the past history of relations between Catholic and Protestant missions in China in the light of the present, when both are in the same boat. If they can't feel charity to one another even in the face of Communism, their cause will be deservedly lost. This is all critical comment, but I do feel that you are in danger of doing less than justice to your subject by not giving enough free play to your natural large-heartedness.

Yours affectionately,
Arnold

Hall Beck Cottage,
Hall Beck
Killington
Kirkby Lonsdale,
Westmorland

9 September, 1952

Dear Columba,

How disappointing to miss you: your letter of the 4th[1] has just reached me here, and, as I haven't my address book with me, I must reach you at Beccles via Ampleforth. We come back to London on the 25th Sept., but I fear that, by then, you may already have passed through on your return journey. If so, we must talk by letter, but it is only a second best, for I should much have liked to see you.

I suppose Latourette[2] will give you the 19–20th centuries, but the non-Jesuit Catholic missionaries are more difficult, for the story seems mostly to have been written from the point of view of the Jesuits—and the J.'s have the beau rôle, in any case. What an opportunity lost! And how magnificent the Jesuits' plan was.

I now have 3 vols. out of 4 in the press, and the first of these almost all in galley, so I am getting on.

I am very sorry to have missed you in London.

Yours affectionately,
Arnold

1. Missing.

2. Kenneth Scott Latourette, *A History of Christian Missions in China* (London, 1929); *A History of Modern China* (London, 1954).

Gillingham Hall[1]
Beccles, Suffolk

12 September 1952

My dear Arnold,

Your letter reached me just as I was setting off from Ampleforth. I had guessed by that time that either you were not yet back or had moved up into your Pennine retreat. It was a great disappointment, but we'll meet before long I hope. Is it still impossible for you to come up and stay with us? So many would love to see you. I did not get in touch in July or August because I did not leave Ampleforth. The Prior is rather tied. As a matter of fact nothing is more peaceful than Ampleforth at that time.

I am staying with my mother who has sold her house and is living with friends very comfortably.

About the China book. Latourette[2] does provide a pretty good bibliography but it is hard to come by the books he mentions. I suspect that only The B.M. has them, Bodley[3] has not, at least not those on the Dominicans. A French Lazarist in Paris has sent me 3 vols of *Launay*[4]—the authority on post Jesuit Catholic missions—since I last wrote, and an 800 page diary of a *Chinese* priest 18th century (in Latin) Father Li (Ly). So things are looking up. But Fitzgerald's book on *The Taiping* I have not seen.[5] Have you a copy? I see in his book on China he has a chapter on the subject where he maintains that the *horrors* were perpetrated by Manchu soldiers. But did not the Christian Minister who instructed him—Roberts by name I think—join him and then leave him and his followers because of the atrocities? However, you are quite right, this episode is very important and I shall get down to it.

So the Nonsense book is to be 4 volumes more after all. It will give you more room. Does it include an index for the 10 volumes? Veronica will have a grand time on that. I am so glad the book is getting along so well. It must be extremely exhilarating to feel the end is so near.

To get back to China. I feel that the Protestant part is very much from the outside and does not convey the thrill they must have had in this missionary experience. Richards[6] strikes me as the most interesting person. But there again I have no solid work on him. Another point, I would like to be able to describe the Chinese reaction: taking the icing and not the cake, the scientific and democratic top without the doctrine. Another thing which I sense but can't prove is that the social inequalities in China were not faced and condemned by Christians as they are at least in word by the Communists. Only living there could perhaps make me competent in these latest phases. I am describing my sense of frustration on the subject.

Perhaps you can see a way out.

Yours affectionately,
Columba, O.S.B.

1. "Gillingham Hall, the home of Mrs. Todhunter, where my mother stayed for some time." (C.C.E.)

2. Compare A.J.T.'s letter of 9 September 1952, above.

3. The Bodleian Library, Oxford.

4. Adrien Launay, *Histoire générale de la Société des Missions Étrangeres*, 3 vols. (Paris, 1894); *Histoire des missions de la Chine, Mission du Kouang-Si* (Paris, 1903).

5. The T'ai P'ing Rebellion (1850–64); C. P. Fitzgerald, *Revolution in China* (London, 1952); *China, a Short Cultural History* (London, 1935).

6. Timothy Richards (1845–1919); Baptist missionary to China; secretary of the inter-denominational Christian Literature Society.

Hall Beck Cottage
Killington
Kirkby Lonsdale
Westmorland

22 September 1952

Dear Columba,

I wonder if Dr. Williams' library in London (the address will be in the London Telephone Book) would have any of the books you want. It is a specialized library on religious subjects. No doubt the librarian of the Monastery library could negotiate loans of books for you from them. Unluckily I don't possess Fitzgerald on the Taiping,[1] or I would have sent it along.

I have just finished revising my thirteenth and last proof for the press, and have nothing now to revise except a note on chronology and my acknowledgements and thanks—which are extensive, as you may imagine. So I ought to get Vol. X to press before going on the 23rd October to Edinburgh to give my first set of Giffords.[2]

I *shall* come to Ampleforth again one day, and, if I was the only person concerned, I would come now, without waiting any longer, for, sooner or later, the only way of discovering whether a wound is healed is to try—and my associations with Ampleforth are, after all, independent of my associations with Ganthorpe. The last time I came, though, it did re-open the wound, and then other people—first, Veronica—share the effects, and, after what she went through in 1942–1946, I should feel bad in going out of my way to bring further suffering on her (N.B. all this is my idea, not hers).

The other day, at a meeting of the local forestry society, I unexpectedly ran into George Carlisle[3] and Charley Morpeth,[4] and this gave me—foolishly—quite a turn, which was a danger signal.

But, as you know, my link with Ampleforth is one of my most precious spiritual possessions, so I shall never let go of it.

God Bless You.

Yours affectionately,
Arnold

1. Compare C.C.E.'s letter of 12 September 1952, above.

2. Compare A.J.T.'s letter of 18 May 1952, above.

3. George Josslyn L'Estrange Howard, eleventh Earl of Carlisle (1895–1963), cousin of Rosalind Toynbee.

4. Charles James Ruthven Howard, George Carlisle's eldest son (1923–); then Viscount Morpeth; now twelfth Earl of Carlisle.

Ampleforth Abbey
York

St. Edward's Day (13 October) 1952

My dear Arnold,

I was very happy to get your last letter with its affectionate remembrance of Ampleforth. You are much in people's thoughts and prayers, your old friends, Fr. Bruno Donovan,[1] Fr. Kentigern Devlin[2] (who is now over at Gilling) and all the rest.

Thank you also for the name of the Missionary library's custodian. When I have digested the Launay,[3] someone kindly sent from France, I shall get in touch with Dr. Williams.

The volume X is I expect now mostly complete and you will walk out onto a terrace as Gibbon[4] did and look out over the landscape and feel an immense content to have completed so vast an undertaking and in spite of so many hazards and troubles. May God bless it and give it the power to lead men's hearts back to himself, and no harm.

Your Gifford lectures will also be much in my prayers. Your subject is vital. Someone has sent me a book which would interest you on the comparative study of Moslem, Hindu and Christian mysticism. The book is from some lectures given at Cairo by Louis Gardet, preface by Louis Massignon, *Les Mardis de Dar EL-Salam*.[5] It is an acute analysis of the three approaches and it has cleared up several problems for me and confirmed me in many guesses or surmises. He was [prepared to] admit that Eckhart[6] was perhaps approaching mysticism from a Hindu angle—without knowing it—He does not try to equate all three, but says that to do so is to distort them all. Each is genuine and valuable as far as it goes etc. We had a "little brother of Charles de Foucauld"[7] staying here and he sent it me. This is a new order in the Church, founded just after World War II, in the spirit of C. de F. Some go into the desert—they all make their noviciate there. Already over 100 have been enrolled and taken vows. Most of them work in factories. They do not evangelise but live with the workers and in precisely their conditions. They do not drink or smoke or have any extra comforts. The rest of the time, not given to sleep, is given to prayer. They wish to be contemplatives in the world and bring Our Lord right up to the working man. It is having effect. The one we had was in a quarry near Leeds. He is French and educated—for 4 days no Yorkshire workman spoke to him or his companion.—Typical Yorkshire—then they thawed, asked what the little cross meant in his button hole. When he left, every single worker came and shook hands with him.

I believe this will prove the Franciscan movement of the XX century.

God bless you and love to you both,

Columba, O.S.B.

1. Bruno Donovan, O.S.B.; cf. C.C.E.'s letter of 8 April 1941, above.

2. Kentigern Devlin, O.S.B.; cf. C.C.E.'s letter of 21 April 1942, above.

3. See C.C.E.'s letter of 12 September 1952, above.

4. See *The Autobiographies of Edward Gibbon*, ed. John Murray (London, 1896), pp. 333–34; and cf. *A Study of History*, X: 102, where this passage is quoted in extenso.

5. Louis Gardet (1904–); lectured at the Cairo Muslim University; versed in Islamic theology; a disciple of Louis Massignon and Jacques Maritain; the article in *Les Mardis* was entitled "Recherche de l'absolu" (Cairo, 1951). He is now being cared for by the Brothers of Charles de Foucauld.

6. "Meister Eckhart" (ca. 1260–1327); Dominican mystic.

7. Charles Eugène de Foucauld (1858–1916); soldier and explorer who became a priest and hermit at the oasis of Tamanrasset in the Sahara.

Ampleforth Abbey
York

November 1952

My dear Arnold,

Real fan mail. All best wishes for The Reith Lectures which I see have begun. I have already read the Russian one.[1] You got your points across very well—most salutary for us. The most startling point was for me that Islam was a reaction to abuses of Christianity of the Prophet's day. I saw it as a reaction against Arabian polytheism and an acceptance of the simplest form of Jewish-Christian Theology. But I see what you mean, that once under way, Islam appealed to heresy-hunting weary Christians.

We have been reading in the refectory the new life of St. Francis Xavier by Fr. Brodrick,[2] and I am reviewing it in the *Tablet*. Perhaps the review will be published round about the date of the quartercentenary, 4th Dec., of his death on Sancian Island. He emerges as a man filled with divine love and love of men, but also sublimely unaware of what he was meeting. That was inevitable perhaps, being the first to travel through the Far East, Japan. But he was so convinced of the absolute superiority of the Catholic faith that all else was NADA, and worse than that.

I am hoping to go to Paris in January to delve into the library of the Missions Étrangères. If the plan works out, I'll let you know and try to meet you on my way through London.

God bless you and the Reith Lectures. How did the Gifford go?

Love,
Columba, O.S.B.

1. Compare n. 4 of A.J.T.'s letter of 3 April 1952, above; the Russian lecture appeared in *Listener* 48, no. 1238 (20 November 1952): 839–41; and subsequently in *The World and the West*.

2. James Brodrick, S.J., *Saint Francis Xavier (1506–1552)* (London, 1952).

5 December 1952 45, Pembroke Square, W.8

Dear Columba,

I have just had your letter of the 4th (returned herewith, with pencilled comments), as well as the earlier one.[1]

This is most exciting, and a great opportunity. I think your three divisions are the right ones, and I suggest your allocating 4, 8, 8 minutes to them respectively (allocation of time is crucial in a broadcast, I think).

You certainly must start (in an ex-Christian listening world) by placing the contemplative activity itself on the map, and showing that it is one of the distinctive and characteristic things in human nature: the true end of Man, in fact.

In 'Unity and diversity' you will be able to bring out what the activity is, and then you must keep at least 8 minutes for the revival of contemplation in the Western Christian Church. The dates of both the revival and the previous lapse would be worth placing in their historical setting, if you can find the time for that.

How I wish we could put you up for the night of the 18th. You must come to dinner, anyway, before the talk. We will have it at whatever time and place will be the most convenient. But, about the bed, we just can't be sure because my sister-in-law has had a sudden rather serious nervous break-down and is at present in a nursing home, having shock treatment. If, as we hope, this is going to do the trick, her brother will be coming down, just about the 18th, to take her to convalesce in his house in Cartmel and he will be staying the night with us, and we can't be certain of the date. In fact, all our plans are a bit in the air. But you must have dinner with us that night, and, if you go to Paris in January, you must stay with us en route both ways.

I hate the idea of your being here and not sleeping in our house, but there it is.

Yours affectionately,
Arnold

1. Missing.

The Royal Institute
of International Affairs
Chatham House
10, St James Square
London S.W.1

11 December 1952

Dear Columba,

Your script[1] arrived this morning and I have done what you asked: I have read it quickly, with my mind on general presentation and proportions, not on detailed points of words.

I am much struck, and of course also delighted, at your fraternal approach to the contemplatives of non-Christian schools. You have, I should say, managed to do this without leaving any doubt at all about your own line, and I think this is a very happy combination.

I feel that the first of the two alternative openings—bringing in Islam as it does—is decidedly better for your purpose than the second, because it strikes, right at the beginning, the note that you follow out in the rest of the talk. Also the introductory paragraph about Ampleforth comes in equally well on page 9, and this prepares the way for the last of the three sections of the talk.

There is just one question of words on the third sheet from the end which I venture to raise: for "follows as best they can" why not substitute "have taken for their guides." The second says no more than the first, but avoids seeming to be patronising. It is a tiny point, but worth thinking of all the same, as you want to be sure of carrying your non-Catholic listeners with you—the Catholics you will have with you anyway.

In haste,
Yours ever,
Arnold Toynbee

1. Script of the BBC talk on contemplation.

45, Pembroke Square
London W.8

19 December 1952

Dear Columba,

It was sad not to see you yesterday, and I didn't even hear you, as I was in a bus, going to my engagement, at the time when you were speaking. I hope you enjoyed giving the talk: if one feels that it is fun, one does it with much more zest, and this communicates itself to the listeners.

Well, we shall see you for the night of the 29th, and this is some consolation.

My brother-in-law took his sister off to his home in Cartmel this morning, and he seemed to be in good shape for the journey. I hope Veronica is now going to get a bit of rest, as she has been under a great strain.

With best wishes for Christmas, en attendant the 29th,

Yours affectionately,
Arnold

Istina[1]
Boulevard d'Auteuil
Boulogne sur Seine

31 December 1952

Dear Veronica and Arnold,

I am writing this on my return from my first visit to the library of the Missions Étrangères in the Rue du Bac. The archiviste, P. Monjean, is going to be most helpful.[2]

Thank you so much for your happy and homely welcome. I enjoyed all, the little dinner party at home and the one at the nearest to the Athenaeum I have ever been.[3]

The nuns turned out—in the train—to be as I expected, Irish, Little Sisters of the Poor, who spend their life looking after the aged infirm poor, an order founded last century in France. The 8 houses in Paris (they have 300 in France alone) are understaffed, so these had volunteered to spend the rest of their lives there. Not one of them knew any French. One of them was going later to Baltimore.

It is now snowing hard here and lying ominously. After leaving the Missions Et. I made a dive into the Lazarists headquarters across the road (rue de Sèvres) but the priest I hoped to see was out. The library in the Rue du Bac is just what I needed, and the archives, too.

A very happy New Year.

Yours affectionately,
Columba, O.S.B.

1. Istina is one of the great ecumenical centers of western Europe, started by P. C. Dumont, O.P. Its chief concern is links with the Orthodox Church, hence the name; compare C.C.E.'s note of 1 October 1950, above.

2. C.C.E. was doing research for *China and the Cross*; the Missions Étrangères had had many missions in China from the early nineteenth century on.

3. "This was in the women's annex of the Athenaeum, as Veronica Toynbee was present. It was, I think, on this occasion that A.J.T. invited Gilbert Murray to join us, and G.M. quizzed me on missions, saying their success, he thought, depended on political pressure or cultural superiority of missionaries. I pointed out the first three centuries." (C.C.E.)

45, Pembroke Square
London W.8

4 January 1953

Dear Columba,

We were so glad to have your letter. You seem to have struck the same weather in Paris as I did in November.

Come again soon to stay, and then I will take you to the men's annexe of the place we dined at last Monday.[1]

I am so glad you are finding what you hoped for in the Rue du Bac.

Your talk is in last week's *Listener*,[2] and I am sure it was as good to listen to as it is to read. You will find that your generous words about Muslims, Wesley and the rest will call out a response.

Just fancy the Irish Little Sisters working on that scale in France. The religious orders certainly haven't been worsted by nationalism.

Well, if I don't see you en route from Paris to Yorkshire, I hope your next visit will not be too long delayed.

Yours affectionately,
Arnold

1. The Athenaeum; cf. C.C.E.'s letter of 31 December 1952.

2. "The Contemplative Way," *Listener* (1 January 1953), pp. 17–18. C.C.E.'s address was criticized by H. D. Northfield as containing "a trace of that current nostalgia for the middle ages which is characteristic of so much Catholic thinking since the last century" (*Listener* [15 January 1953], pp. 103–4).

45, Pembroke Square
London W.8

15 March 1953

Dear Columba,

Well this is my last Sunday before sailing, and so practically my last chance of writing to you before we start, as I shall be engulfed from Monday morning till we take the train for the Medic at Liverpool on Saturday.

The penalty of having been in the news is that one gets busier and busier, and the pressure before sailing has become quite severe, this time. However, I have now finished my share of the maps for vol. xi (the other half is being done by a friend of mine, E. D. Myers, a philosopher at Washington and Lee University, Virginia), and the galleys of vii–x are about ¾'s through, so I can begin to see daylight.[1]

With an eye to a second edition of vols. i–vi, the Rockefeller Foundation have given Veronica and me a grant for visiting Mexico now and Peru and Japan in 1956. Mexico, both living peasants and archeological sites, is an unknown new world which excites me enormously. If you pass through London while the Mexican exhibition is still on at the Tate Gallery, do make a point of seeing it. You would be particularly interested in the influence of Christianity on Mexican folk art. It is difficult to think of a greater contrast than there is between the Canaanitishly cruel pre-Columbian Mexican religion and Catholicism, yet Catholicism has evidently captured the Mexican peasantry without stifling the strong creative force in them.

In October I am going to Rome for a sort of brains trust got up by the Council of Europe.

Veronica's sister is very decidedly better, I am glad to say, but Veronica is still suffering from the strain of last autumn, and shows it by her blood-pressure going up—not alarmingly, but enough to need paying serious attention to—when she exerts herself. She has had, and still has, an awful lot on her hands. I am hoping that the voyage will give her a bit of a rest.

My granddaughter Josephine[2] is all right again, I am glad to say.

Here am I, writing about pressure of work to you, who have many more pounds of it to the square inch than I have.

It is odd: when one is not well known, the world leaves one in peace to do the best work one can, but, as soon as one becomes a little better known, the world tries to pluck one away from doing serious work into all kinds of showing off. I resist this, but it is quite a struggle.

You are not absent from my thoughts when I don't write, as I am sure you know.

Yours affectionately,
Arnold

1. "Historical Atlas and Gazetteer," by A.J.T. and Edward Delos Myers (1907–69); in vol. XI of *A Study of History*. "E. D. Myers came to Ganthorpe later, and A.J.T. took him and me to the eighteenth-century terrace overlooking Rievaulx Abbey ruins, and slowly we walked its length, gazing down now and then on the (twelfth-century) ruins far below, at the points where the trees were cleared. The aim was to have the historical 'mystical' experience of twentieth-century man sinking back into his past, the eighteenth and twelfth centuries." (C.C.E.)

2. Josephine Toynbee, Philip's eldest daughter; cf. C.C.E.'s letter of 29 November 1939, above.

Ampleforth Abbey
York

16 March 1953

My dear Arnold,

I was very happy to get your letter, and strangely enough I started one to you the other day, and then tore it up. It was suggesting I should answer Douglas Jerrold's attack, on your broadcast talks, he did in a series of articles in the *Tablet*.[1] Then I thought it was waste of time. However I would willingly do so if you would like it and think it would do good.

I have read a great deal of Cortes's own account of his march to Mejico City and all his exploits. The cruelty of some of those conquistadores is unbelievable; and yet beside them were great missionaries. Your journey should be thrilling. Apparently an immense amount of new facts have come to light about the pre-Columbian periods, so you will be busy. Don't make Veronica climb the steepest crags! but I am sure it will all do her lots of good, unless she gets nightmares over the horrors of the Aztec religion!

Hurrah for the nonsense book. So it is now really complete. It has not gone all the way, but certainly a long way from XVIII C. Gibbon. I had hoped it would make the uniqueness of Christ clear. Your being dragged out into the public view, on show, as you put it, is not all bad. It forced you to make your ideas intelligible to many. It brings your ideas before a critical audience. It is at times humiliating and, that, rightly borne, does good to the spirit. It steals your time, yes, but God needs no time to have his work done. So if you accept for the right motive, He will look after the rest.

My love to you both, and both ever in my prayers, and the book.

Columba, O.S.B.

P.S. I may be in Rome in July. Shall I try to arrange a special audience for you with Pope Pius XII? You are sure to be able to see him anyhow, so any activity on my part is probably unnecessary.

1. Douglas Jerrold (1893–1964); chairman of the publishing house of Eyre & Spottiswoode; "Professor Toynbee, 'The West' and the World: Thoughts on the Reith Lectures, Parts 1–4," *Tablet* 201, no. 5882 (14 February 1953): 128–29; 201, no. 5883 (21 February 1953): 146–47; 201, no. 5884 (28 February 1953): 168–69; 201, no. 5884 (7 March 1953): 187–88; Jerrold later wrote *The Lie about the West: A Response to Professor Toynbee's Challenge* (London, 1954), which elicited a vigorous controversy; cf. C.C.E.'s letter of 1 May 1954 and following letters, below.

The Royal Institute
of International Affairs
Chatham House
10, St James's Square
London, S.W.1

18 March 1953

Dear Columba,

Yes, I certainly should like a special audience with His Holiness if this is possible to arrange. His recent words about European unity are really an anticipation of the job on which I am going to Rome. The Council of Europe is collecting four panjandrums—of whom I am one, and the most eminent is Schuman[1]—to discuss the idea of Europe under a sounding-board composed of a large number of high-brow publicists and journalists. Dates, October 13 to 16 or 17. The Italian Ministry of Foreign Affairs is the host, so the Vatican will have to contact them about arranging a time.

I hadn't seen Douglas Jerrold in the *Tablet*, and I am very grateful for your thinking of taking up the cudgels, but I am sure it is better not to, really.

D.J.'s charge reminds me of those ex-pagan French bourgeois in the 1890's who went Catholic because—I am sure very mistakenly—they thought Catholicism was a good foundation for ultra conservatism and nationalism. This seems perverse and unfortunate.

Well, you will be hearing from me. Bon voyage.

Yours affectionately,
Arnold

1. Robert Schuman (1886–1963); French foreign minister (1948–53); proposer of the Schuman Plan for the integration of the Western European coal and steel industries; in 1958, first president of the European Parliamentary Assembly.

[*Postcard*]

19 April 1953 Ciudad de Mexico

We visited this fortified monastery this morning. It was founded by Franciscans and taken over by Augustinians. Though fortified, it has an atmosphere of peace.

Just now we passed the shrine of Our Lady of Guadalupe, with vast Sunday crowds thronging round it.

Arnold

Ampleforth Abbey
York

June 1953

My dear Arnold,

Thank you for your card from Méjico. It must have been an exciting experience; and now you will have the "hang" of those strange and awful civilizations.

Mgr. Montini [1] wrote "Since it is not possible to give you a definite answer in this connexion at the present time, may I ask you kindly to mention the matter to me again, shortly before Prof. Toynbee undertakes his proposed journey. The necessary arrangements will then be made, if possible, for the granting of the audience in question" i.e. special audience.

So will you remind me four weeks before, and I'll write again 3 weeks before you are there. I should so hate to forget.

I go to Rome 20th. There are now 40–50 persons, Orthodox, Russian and Greek, Episcopalians, Anglicans, Wesleyans.[2] So say a prayer that grace will come.

God bless you both.

Love,
Columba, O.S.B.

1. Compare C.C.E.'s letter of 17 May 1951, above.

2. An ecumenical pilgrimage arranged by Barbara Simonds (1890–); an American Anglican "prophetess" living in Rome; cf. C.C.E., "An Oecumenical Pilgrimage," *Tablet* (25 July 1953), p. 92; Miss Simonds writes, "I should like to stress the importance of his [C.C.E.'s] power to listen and draw out the prophetic message" (letter of 4 August 1983 to C.B.P.).

Institute for Advanced Study
Princeton, N.J.

9 June 1953

Dear Columba,

I have just had your letter and hope this may reach you before you leave for Rome: you will have my prayers for union, as wide as it can extend.

I will let you know my exact Roman time-table nearer the date.

Did I tell you that I now have a grandson—Philip's child—called 'Jason Arnold'?[1]

I am working at Gifford [2] lectures and proofs of the nonsense book.

The Coronation [3] produced a union of hearts here; the Americans participated in our British feelings about it, and hundreds of Coronation services were held all over the country. I spoke at the one here in Princeton.

God Bless You in Rome.
Yours affectionately,
Arnold

1. Jason Arnold Toynbee; cf. A.J.T.'s letter of 8 February 1951, above; and Philip Toynbee's *Part of a Journey*, passim.

2. Compare n. 3 of A.J.T.'s letter of 3 April 1952, above. In the preface to *An Historian's Approach to Religion* (London, 1956), A.J.T. mentions "two happy visits to the Institute for

Advanced Study at Princeton, during which I was able to prepare the lectures, thanks to the hospitality of the Institute and the generosity of the Rockefeller Foundation" (p. vi).

3. The coronation of Her Majesty Queen Elizabeth II, on 2 June 1953.

Ampleforth Abbey
23 July 1953 York

My dear Arnold,

I have been to Rome and back. The pilgrimage was a great success. I am hoping to talk about it on the Home Service at 6:45 P.M. Wed. 29th July.[1] I would like to feel you were listening, as I can't explain it all in a letter. I can't over the air either, but some of the atmosphere should be.

Saying Mass at Subiaco in the Santo Speco[2] where St. Benedict spent his formative years, and surrounded by the heirs of his tradition, but heirs who had fought over the inheritance, was a moving act, more especially as they answered the prayers. We had a private audience with the Holy Father, and the monsignore who arranged it for us reminded me of your audience and of my having to write in September to put it "on the map" again. So they have not forgotten.

The discoveries under S. Peter's are staggering. There can be no doubt now about S. Peter's tomb, and these sceptical professors are now pretty sure about the bones. We were shown round by Prof. Ghetti[3] who discovered them.

Unfortunately, I shall not be in London in August. If I pass through in Sept., as I may, I'll let you know.

When is the Nonsense book coming out?

My love to you both,

Columba, O.S.B.

1. C.C.E.'s "An Oecumenical Pilgrimage" (*Tablet*, 25 July 1953, p. 92), contains the matter of the broadcast.

2. The cave at Subiaco in which Saint Benedict lived from ca. 500 to ca. 525; now incorporated in the Convento di San Benedetto.

3. B. M. Apollonj-Ghetti, "our guide to Saint Peter's grave" (C.C.E.); the official report of the excavations under St. Peter's was published as *Explorazioni sotto la confessione di San Pietro in Vaticano esequite negli anni 1940–1949: Relazione a cura di B. M. Appollonj-Ghetti; A. Ferrua, S.J., Enrico Josi, E. Kirschbaum, S.J.*, 2 vols. (Rome, 1951).

45, Pembroke Square
26 July 1953 London S.W.8

Dear Columba,

I believe I shall be able to hear you at 6:45 on Wednesday.[1] I have an engagement at 7:30, but close to Chatham House, so I shall arrange, if I can, to listen in there.

I have never been to the Sacro Speco yet, and can never have the experience that you have just had there. I wish we could meet sooner. I shall be here till about the 9th September, then for 2 or 3 weeks in Lunesdale, then to Rome (I want, first, to make an excursion to Venosa,[2] Melfi,[3] Monte Vulture[4] and Troia,[5] and perhaps the shrine of St. Michael on Monte Gargano[6]). I am very glad the possibility of an audience is remembered.

Though I shall hear you on Wednesday, this won't do instead of seeing you.

It sounds as if your pilgrimage may have opened up a new round.

Yours affectionately,
Arnold

The nonsense book is now all in print, and three-quarters in page, but it won't be published till September 1954!

1. C.C.E.'s broadcast account of the ecumenical pilgrimage to Rome; cf. C.C.E.'s letter of 23 July 1953, above.

2. The ancient Venusia, birthplace of Horace.

3. The first capital of the Normans in Italy.

4. The extinct volcano with a view, from its summit, of Apulia.

5. Founded as a Byzantine fortress, with a cathedral of mixed Byzantine, Saracenic, and Romanesque elements.

6. The Santuario di San Michele is in a grotto in Monte Sant'Angelo on the spur of Monte Gargano.

45, Pembroke Square
London S.W.8

30 July 1953

Dear Columba,

I was defeated of hearing you last night.[1] First, the distant strains that I had heard at Chatham House turned out not to be a wireless, but a tele-printer, and then, when I ran round to my Club,[2] and found the way to the bar (a hideous innovation there, which I had never set foot in before), the wireless was out of order.

Anyway, it would have been an incongruous place for hearing you.

Can you lend me a carbon of your script? It will be no substitute for hearing your voice, but it will be the next best thing.

I am much disappointed.

Yours affectionately,
Arnold

1. Cf. C.C.E.'s letter of 23 July 1953.

2. The Athenaeum.

Hall Beck
Killington
Kirkby Lonsdale

10 September 1953

Dear Columba,

We came here yesterday for a short late-summer holiday. We have been gathering firewood and piling billets of wood for our fire, and are feeling 'thoroughly relaxed' (the American description of the Earthly Paradise).

Well, my fourth visit to Rome approaches. I am planning to fly on Monday 5 Oct., stay one night, visit Monte Santangelo in Gargano (second only to Compostella in the 11th century) and Melfi (to climb to the top of the volcano Monte Vulture)[1] and be back in Rome by the evening of the 11th (Sunday).

I am thinking, of course, of that possibility of a special audience. My freest day, according to the present still provisional programme, will be Monday 12 Oct. when there is no engagement till 19.00 o'clock. From the 12th to the 16th inclusive, the sessions are 11.00–13.00 and 17.00–20.00 each day, leaving four hours in the middle of each day free, as well as after 20.00.

I am to be one of six panjandrums,[2] of whom Mr. Schuman is another (I am honoured to be in his company). It is a round table on Europe, got up by the Council of Europe, with the Italian Govt. doing the local honours.

On the afternoon of the 13th, I am to open the first public discussion on '*Le destin commun des Européens: (a) leur unité historique, (b) leurs perspectives au XXe siècle*.' It is a fine opportunity, and I look forward to it. Sixteen publicists are to tell the world what we say.[3]

We shall be here till Monday 28 Sept.

Yours affectionately,
Arnold

1. "He could not resist mountains anywhere." (C.C.E.)

2. The six were A.J.T.; Robert Schuman; Alcide de Gasperi, former premier and foreign minister of Italy; Eelco van Kleffens, former Netherlands foreign minister; Eugen Kogon, university professor and editor, *Frankfurter Hefte*; and Einar Lofstedt, former rector of the University of Lund.

3. See Council of Europe, Secretariat General, *The European Round Table Discussion* (Strasbourg, 1954). Denis de Rougemont was chairman; A.J.T.'s opening statement appears at pp. 19–25: "When we speak of Europeans we really mean, I believe, those inhabitants of the northwestern peninsula of the Old World, and of the adjacent islands, who are ecclesiastical subjects or ex-subjects of the Patriarchate of Rome."; and he referred to Saint Francis of Assisi as "the greatest European so far."

Quarr Abbey[1]
Ryde
Isle of Wight
(I am giving a retreat here)

14 September 1953

My dear Arnold,

Your note reached me here this morning. I have not forgotten and was wondering when you would send me word and particulars of your Rome visit. As soon as I get back to Ampleforth (Thursday) I shall write to Mgr. Montini, as he suggested, giving him all necessary facts. I think it would be well for you to send a formal note saying where you are staying, so that the invitation may reach your *quam celerrime*.

I am told in Rome that the Holy Father cannot guarantee an audience more than 24 hours before it happens, so do not expect a letter to await you. In your case it may be different.

I shall also now write to a young Monsignore[2] whom I met in Rome (half U.S.A. half Italian) asking him to keep an eye on the business—Mgr. Cardinale, a young and charming person who helped the unity Pilgrimage a lot.

The catalogues herald the arrival in 1954 of Vols. VII, VIII, IX and X. God bless them and make them do only good. I hope you have modified the section on the Holy Eucharist,[3] and I wonder what has happened to the psychological appendix?[4] The monks here are intrigued about you, some have read Vols. I–III and then an article in *Ami du Clergé*, which I have not seen, on your ideas. I tell them you would be a Catholic but for a deep fear of abandoning your liberty and too soft a place for eastern religions, and I tell them to pray for you. On the whole that is a fair enough summary; because the difference between your love of Christ and mine is that you cannot take the Church as a safe guide. You keep your private judgement all along the line. I know too that churchmen have often bogged us down, but that in the crucial pontifical statements the Church has saved the faith for humanity, and I accept the Church as from Christ, and in doctrine to be trusted.

I hope you will get down into the crypt and "fouilles" of S. Peter's, and see the pagan tombs, the Christian ones and the place of S. Peter's grave. Say a prayer at the Confession for me.

God bless you and lead you to the Visible Church as you have been led so far, so very far already.

Love,
Columba, O.S.B.

1. Quarr Abbey was established by the monks expelled by the anticlerical French government from Solesmes at the end of the nineteenth century.

2. Hyginus (Igino) Eugene Cardinale (1916–83); then undersecretary to Msgr. Montini the pro secretary of state; chief of protocol of the secretariat of state (1961–63); apostolic delegate to Great Britain, Gibraltar, Malta, and Bermuda (1963–69); papal nuncio to Belgium and Luxembourg from 1969 and the European Community from 1970; *Le Sainte-Siège et la diplomatie* (Paris, 1962).

3. *A Study of History*, VII: 530, 534–35.

4. It remains; see "Higher Religions and Psychological Types," in ibid., pp. 716–36 (A [iii] [*a*], annex 2).

Hall Beck Cottage
Killington
Kirkby Lonsdale
Westmorland

16 September 1953

Dear Columba,

I am very grateful. 'It is likely' (*sic*) that we shall 'be accommodated at the Hotel Hassler' in Rome, but this is subject to confirmation. I will let you know. Whatever hotel it is, I hope to arrive there on the 5th October, to be on my travels for the nights of the 6th–10th inclusive, and to be back in Rome on the 11th till I leave on the 17th.

Your description of me hits both nails on the head. I hold to my liberty to follow wherever the argument may lead me (and it may never stop keeping me on the move), and I am on my guard against hybris in the form of chauvinism in religion, as well as in politics, race-feeling, and all other group-feelings. But, for the revelation of the good of evil, the value of suffering, and the relation of God to human beings, I know of no greater one than has been given by Christianity. The attitude towards suffering is, for me, the acid test, and on this I am Christian, not Buddhist. Buddhism has largely denied its Buddhist principles in its Christian practice, I should say.

Well, God Bless you.
Yours affectionately,
Arnold

Hall Beck Cottage
Hall Beck
Killington
Kirkby Lonsdale
Westmorland

21 September 1953

Dear Columba,

After I had rushed off my line to you on Saturday, there has now come another—and I hope, the final—timetable, from the Council of Europe at Strasbourg, for our Rome round table, in which I read: '15th October in the morning, audience with the Pope.'

It doesn't say whether this is to be for 'the six' alone, or for the 16 publicists as well. If it is for the 22, some *improbus* journalist will probably hold the floor.

I hardly suppose that the Holy Father will be prepared to give me a private audience as well!

Meanwhile, the 12th October, from 11.0 A.M. onwards, has been filled up with 'preliminary consultations'.

I am sorry to be so inconstant-by-compulsion in my time-table.

De Gasperi [1] is to be the Italian member of 'the six'. With both him and Schuman it is going to be very well worth while.

Yours affectionately,
Arnold

1. Alcide de Gasperi; cf. A.J.T.'s letters of 16 May 1948 and 10 September 1953, above.

Ampleforth Abbey
York

21 September 1953

My dear Arnold,

Apologies to you for being such a nuisance. I thought I must have left the first letter in some book at Quarr, probably as a book marker. Then, having telephoned the wire to you—having spent a day hunting for it—there it was under a file of Spanish notes. . . . However Mgr. Montini will have got the information by this time; and let us hope the Holy Father is well enough to be allowed to see you.

You will find in this envelope a letter from a young man perhaps the most remarkable ever in St Wilfrid's, e.g. he took up Russian at Oxford, to convert Russia, if the occasion arises. He is a scholar of the House, and President of the Newman Society.[1] The rest explains itself. It seems absurd to ask you to do that talk, but it might be a new audience and a very keen one. So I leave you to decide and hope you say yes.

I liked your response to my little summing up. That kind of liberty you must have: fearlessly and humbly persistently, seek the Truth, until you find it. My remark though, had a slight implication that, even if the Truth were there, you might, the Adam in you, be loathe to abandon yourself to it. That is what I am afraid of for myself in so many ways, and pray for both of us on account of it.

With regard to the other point, I would always try to separate out the institution, or religious body, and the human instruments, the human element, within it. In the Catholic Church there is the divine element—as there is in much else in the world—and the human. We may condemn to our hearts content or sorrow the miseries of the poor human beings God came on earth to save, but we should recognise that Christ gave this divine element to the Church: of providing us with the knowledge of his mercies, with the means to reach to them, and with examples to follow. I would like to see you respond to the following:

You believe Christ was God.

You believe what He said—this follows.

[Have you looked at the Catholic arguments for the soundness of the Gospel records?]

Did He not found this visible-spiritual institution The *Body of Christ*—St. Paul, *passim?*

I like your approach through suffering, and treasure your remarks about our Lord. But why not now take the next step and see what He taught. There seems to be a stumbling block there. You are missing so much, the grace of sacraments, the peace and joy of the visible unity with Christ. The joy of being a little person in his Church. This is not pride. I would like all to be members, none excluded, not to prove I'm right, but because Jesus wanted it, did *all* to accomplish it.

Perhaps the sufferings of the Church today will bring you nearer than any argument. But a rational process is necessary as well.

How I long to see you one with Christ; not, I pray, to glory in the victory, but for your sake, it being all men's destiny, and for Love of Jesus.

My love to you both,

Columba, O.S.B.

1. A request by John Francis Stevenson (1933–), then president of the Newman Society of Oxford, that A.J.T. address the Society on 29 November 1953; Stevenson was a scholar at Christ Church, Oxford; then a monk of Ampleforth; and now a barrister-at-law.

Ampleforth Abbey
York

22 September 1953

My dear Arnold,

What a spate of letters. I have written a second to Monsignor Montini asking him, in spite of the audience for the group, to try to manage a personal one for you—that is asking a lot. I said you did not of course now *expect* a private audience, but I made a strong appeal that you should all the same. So we must now leave it at that for the moment.

The boys return today—much bustle. The day before yesterday I had to clothe 9 novices (postulants), the biggest batch for many years, and a promising lot, some direct from the school, some old boys and two from the world at large. Fr. Abbot is in Rome at a meeting of abbots.

Yours affectionately,
Columba, O.S.B.

Ampleforth Abbey
York

2 October 1953

My Dear Arnold,

I have heard from my friend Monsignor Cardinale. He says: a special audience will be possible—and says an official communication is to follow.

"Professor Toynbee would have to get in touch with the office of the 'Maestro di Camera,' where there is an English speaking official, the Rev. Brother Welsh, attending. Phone 555351 ext. 258. I will be honoured to assist the Professor in his contacts, but I shall be absent from Rome on Sat. 10th Oct. as from 1.30 P.M. and all Sunday 11th Oct." His address is Rt. Rev. Msr. E. Cardinale, Segretaria di Stato di Sua Santita, Vatican City, Rome.

As I thought, he has been instructed by Mgr. Montini to arrange and write to me. So I hope now all goes well and you get in touch early.

I am writing today to Prof. Ghetti[1] to see if he will show you the Tomb of St. Peter etc.

I hope my last letter (but *one*?) was not too violent.

Yours affectionately,
Columba

Pray for me at the Confession of St. Peter.

P.P.S. Talk anything but English to the Holy Father; and don't let him be merely polite; talk on what you really want to talk about—and meanwhile I shall pray for the success of the whole trip.

1. Compare C.C.E.'s letter of 23 July 1953, above.

Columba Cary-Elwes, a portrait by Simon Elwes, R.A., painted in 1967, in the Columba Cary-Elwes Library at the Priory

Rosalind Murray Toynbee, c. 1945

Ganthorpe Hall

Ampleforth Abbey Church

Amplexus Expecta, Ampleforth Abbey Church

Hawnby Hump

Arnold J. Toynbee and Columba Cary-Elwes, a running conversation on the Priory campus, 1961

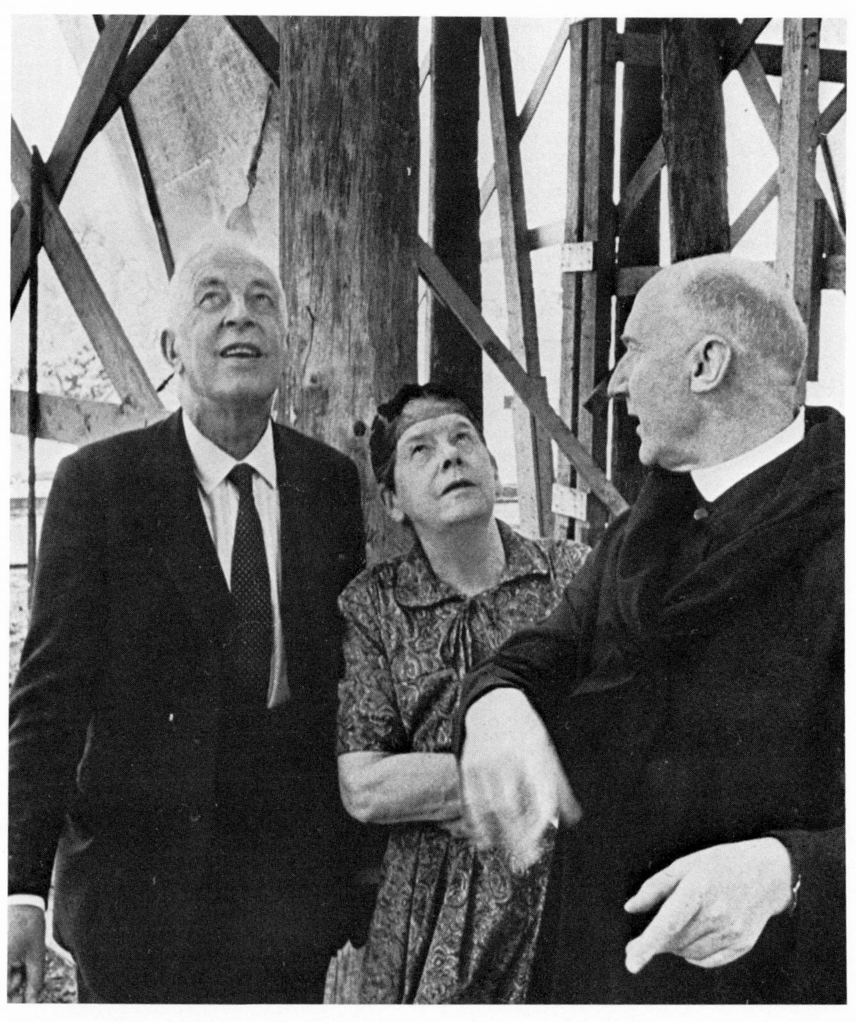

Arnold J. Toynbee, Veronica Toynbee, and Columba Cary-Elwes at the Priory Church during its construction, 1961

Columba Cary-Elwes, Ethel Peper, Arnold J. Toynbee, Abbot Christopher Butler, and Veronica Toynbee at the Peper residence in St. Louis, 1963

The *Ad Portas* reception at Winchester, 1974

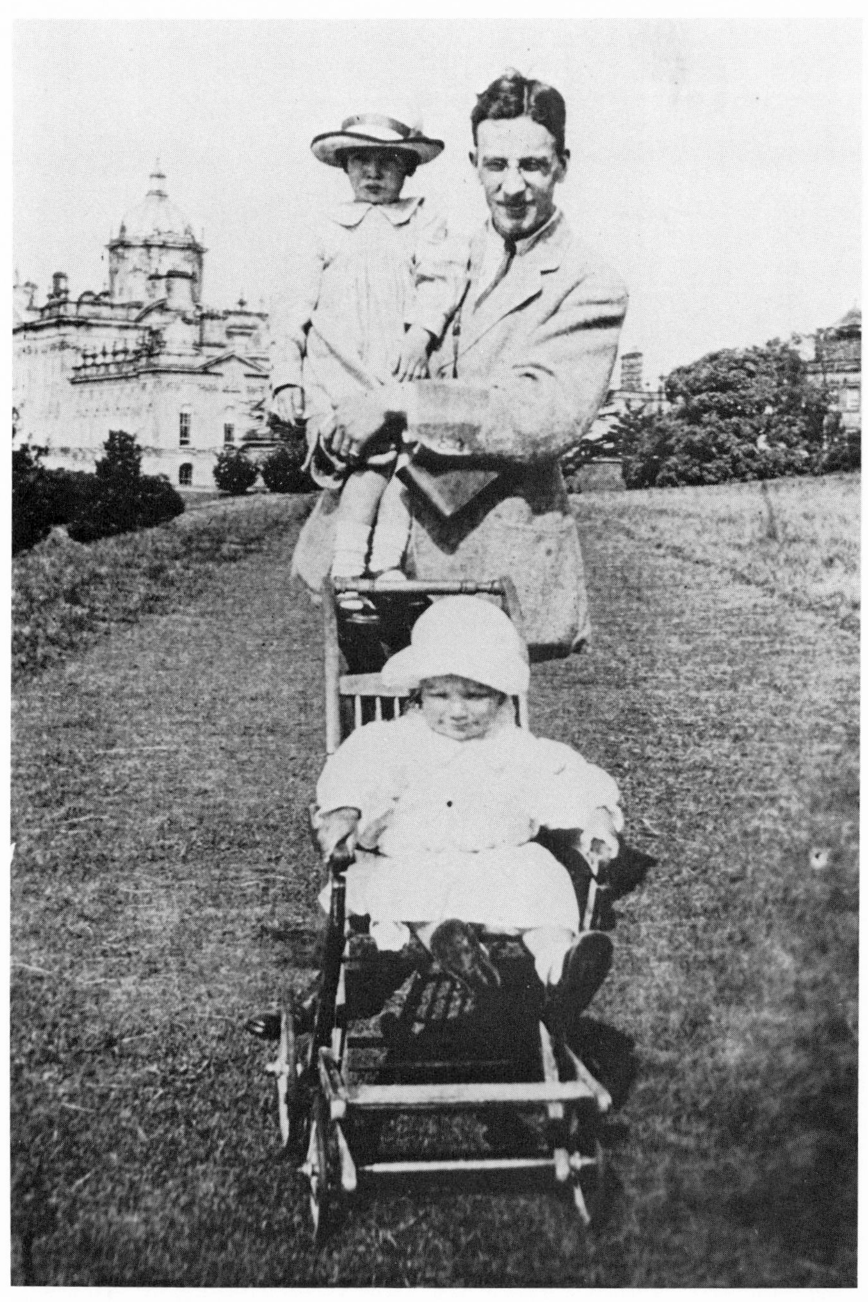

Arnold J. Toynbee holding Tony, with Philip in the perambulator, at Castle Howard, 1917

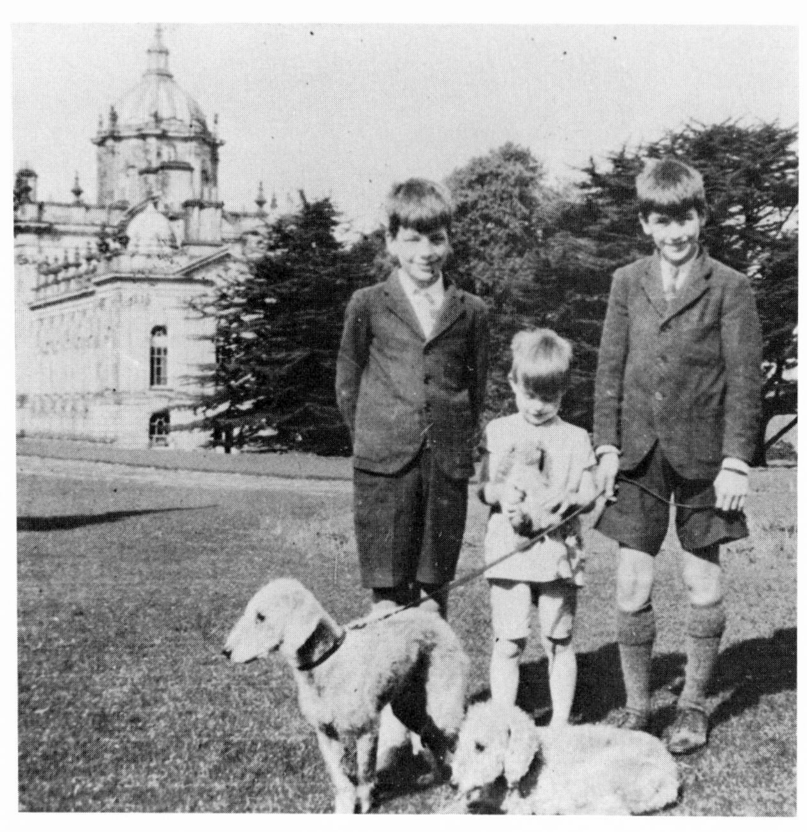

Philip, Lawrence, and Tony at Castle Howard, 1926

3 October 1953 45, Pembroke Square, W.8

Dear Columba,

Your letter of the 2nd has just arrived, and I am writing today a letter of thanks, and anticipations to Mgr. Cardinale, telling him I will carry out the instructions you have passed on to me.

After going over the preparations for this expedition, I am now looking forward to it—particularly, to climbing Monte Vulture, which I hope to do on Wednesday.

If Professor Ghetti would show me the tomb, that would be great.

My address in Rome is the Grand Hotel, Via delle Terme, 3. I spend a night there (5th) and then 6 nights (11th–16th).

On Monte Gargano I am hoping to see not only Monte Santangelo[1] but also father Pio of Pietralcina's[2] San Giovanni Rotondo.

No, your last letter but one wasn't too violent, though it may have been too sanguine.

Yours affectionately,
Arnold

1. Where an apparition of the Archangel Michael was reported in the fifth century.

2. Francesco Forgione (1887–1968); Capuchin friar; stigmatic since 1918; widely revered confessor; his cause for beatification is being advanced. In A.J.T.'s *Cities on the Move* (London, 1970), the two villages are included in the chapter on "Holy Cities": "The array of hostels for pilgrims at San Giovanni in Monte Gargano is as astonishing as it is at Fatima in Portugal" (p. 161).

[*Postcard*]

Albergo Cicolella
8 October 1953 Foggia

Mgr. Cardinale rang me up on Monday night, and I am to communicate with them again next Monday morning. I have come here via Naples, Salerno, Potenza, Melfi. I spent two nights at Melfi and climbed Monte Vulture yesterday. Today I have been to Frederich II's C. del M.[1] via Venosa and Minervino. Tomorrow I am going by bus to Monte Santangelo in Gargano, Saturday Sulmona via Pescara; Sunday Rome. What fun.

Arnold

1. Castel del Monte, the octagonal castle built by the Holy Roman emperor Frederick II Hohenstaufen (1194–1250); A.J.T. was interested in Frederick, the *Stupor mundi*, the "precursor of modern western secularism"; cf. *A Study of History*, VII: 537–39.

Ampleforth Abbey
York

St. Wilfrid's Day, 12 October 1953

My Dear Arnold,

Your card from Foggia gave me great pleasure—you have so obviously been enjoying yourself immensely. I wish I were with you.

By now (Monday) you will be back in Rome. I've notified Prof. Ghetti that your address is the Grand Hotel, but he may write to the other. So Mgr. Cardinale has already got in touch with you. I expect a full account someday both of Padre Pio and of Pius XII. You may be sure my prayers are with you throughout, not least for your lecture. I too have a deep and strong desire for the union which brings Peace.

Remember me in a little prayer at the Confession of St. Peter.

Love,
Columba, O.S.B.

Grand Hotel
Roma

12 October 1953

Dear Columba,

After all you have done, it is not going to come off. Following Mgr. Cardinale's instructions, I rang up Father Welsh this morning, and this week it is impossible—the collective audience for 'the Six' is wiped out too. The reason is that the Pope—like the Italian sheep, if you will forgive the association—migrates twice a year between Summer and Winter pastures, and this week he is moving down from Castel Gandolfo to the Vatican. As a result, he is inaccessible for more than a week in both winter and spring, and I have struck the unlucky season. This was explained to 'the Six' last night, but I rang up Father Welsh all the same, to make sure, and had the same answer. Well, I hope to be coming to Rome in September—not October—1954 for the International Historical Congress, so you must get me up to Castel Gandolfo then.

To-day was an unexpected holiday, because Signor de Gasperi's flight from the Hague was delayed by fog on the Alps. We each have a car at our disposal (!), and there was nothing till 4.0 P.M., so at 9.0 A.M. I got off to visit St. Benedict and Ciuso. As I knelt at the altar in the Sacro Speco,[1] I felt I was being admitted into the germ-cell of Western Christendom.

I then went on through the Teretina country[2]—Alife[3] and Alatri[4]—to Arpino,[5] and had lunch there: a lovely place, perched high above the Garigliano.[6] My charming driver did his best for me on our way back, but I was ½ an hour late, I am ashamed to say. But I don't really repent, for I came back with two *κτήματα εἰς ἀεί*.[7]

Schuman is a most delightful character: modest, sensible, and humourous, and I like de Gasperi too.

I have to kick off to-tomorrow afternoon by opening the first business session.

At Sulmona I blew my remaining money on lovely sweets for grandchildren, so I arrived in Rome on Sunday afternoon with the equivalent of $^{s}5/^{d}$ in one pocket, a penny to spare in the other, and half a slab of chocolate. The Protocol met my train but missed me, and perhaps it was just as well.

Yours very affectionately,
Arnold

1. A.J.T. recalls this visit in *An Historian's Approach to Religion*: "Here was the primal germ-cell of Western Christendom, and, as the pilgrim [A.J.T.] read the moving Latin inscription in which Pope Pius IX had recorded the names of all the lands, stretching away to the ends of the Earth, that had been evangelized by a spiritual impetus issuing from this hollowed spot, he prayed that the spirit that had once created a Western Christian Civilization out of the chaos of the Dark Age might return to re-consecrate a latterday Westernizing World" (pp. 150–51).

2. The Teretina was a tribal area in the valley of the Liris River, in which ex-Samnite praefecturae, such as Allifae, were placed. *Hannibal's Legacy*, I, p. 177, n. 6. Teretina named "*a flumine Terede*"; op. cit. p. 174 n. 2.

3. A.J.T. refers to the synoecism of the Samnite community of Allifae in a Roman municipium, *sine suffragio*. *Legacy* I, pp. 160, 248, 409.

4. Ancient Aletrium, east of the via Latina, approximately 7 miles from Ferentino. The remains of the pre-Roman fortifications, built in enormous polygonal stones, are outstanding. The ancient citadel still stands.

5. Ancient Arpinum, on a hill rising above the river Liris; a flourishing city in the time of the Roman Republic; famous as the birthplace of G. Marius and M. Tullius Cicero.

6. Modern name of the Liris River.

7. An adaptation of Thucydides' "*κτῆμα ἐς αἰεί*."

Grand Hotel
Roma

14 October 1953

Dear Columba,

It has happened after all: I had the audience at noon to-day. It wasn't a private one: there were about 30 people there, and he[1] walked round the circle. But I am the only one of 'the Six' who has been privileged, and it certainly was a privilege, as he is on the point of migrating from Castel Gandolfo to the Vatican.

When I reminded him that I was in Rome for the Council of Europe's round table, he immediately blessed me and my family and the round table. (Taking your advice, I talked, not in English, but in my rudimentary Italian).

I was much impressed by his straightforwardness and benignity.

Mgr. Cardinale—who has already won my heart by the charm of his voice over the telephone, is going to drive with me to-morrow night to a restaurant overlooking the Trevi Fountain. I am to fetch him in 'my' car after our coming session.

How preposterous to live in this worldly splendour. I had just time to get back from Castel Gandolfo via the Appia Antica to Cardinal Bessarion's[2] villa in order to be entertained at lunch by Prime Minister Pella.[3] I was next to de Gasperi, who is also one of 'the Six'. I like him and Schuman particularly.

I will tell you more later.

My love to you.
Arnold

1. Eugenio Pacelli (1876–1958), Pope Pius XII (r. 1939–58).

2. John Cardinal Bessarion (ca. 1400–1472); Greek scholar; accompanied the emperor John VIII Palaeologus to the Counsel of Ferrara and Florence and played a leading role in bringing about (in 1439) the short-lived union of the Eastern and Western Churches; in Rome he became an ecclesiastic statesman, translator of Aristotle's *Metaphysics*, and patron of Renaissance scholars. His villa has been restored and furnished in Renaissance style; the Commune of Rome uses it in receptions like that attended by A.J.T.

3. Giuseppe Pella (1902–81); a financial expert; became premier of the Republic of Italy 15 August 1953, after the resignation of de Gasperi on 28 July 1953; he was succeeded by Mario Scelba on 10 February 1954.

19 October 1953 45, Pembroke Square, W.8

Dear Columba,

I daresay this morning you will perhaps have had my air letter (posted Thursday morning!) telling you about the audience that I did have after all.

I had no chance to pray for you in Saint Peter's; for, though I skirted the eastern end of the Basilica in driving into the Vatican City in 'my car' to take Mgr. Cardinale out to dinner, I never had time to set foot inside it. So, instead, on Friday morning, when we were having our closing session in the Campidoglio instead of in the Villa Aldobrandini, I went a bit early and prayed for you in Santa Maria della Ara Coeli[1]—also an auspicious place. How ridiculous that *I* should pray for you. I was very happy to, all the same.

I liked Mgr. C. very much, and it was a bond that I happened to know Fondi and Terrecina from where his family comes. He told me something of his personal history, which was notable.

I flew back on Saturday, took Josephine and Polly[2] to Mdme Tussaud's yesterday, and go to Edinburgh (the Queen Hotel) on Thursday to give the first of my second batch of Giffords on Friday afternoon.

I am being bombarded by printer's queries. In haste.

Yours affectionately,

Arnold

1. Santa Maria in Aracoeli; founded before the sixth century, at the crest of the Campidoglio; "auspicious" because here Edward Gibbon first conceived the idea of writing the *Decline and Fall*; cf. A.J.T.'s letter of 30 October 1953, below.

2. Josephine and Polly, Philip's daughters; cf. C.C.E.'s letter of 29 November 1939, above.

Ampleforth Abbey
York

20 October 1953

My dear Arnold,

I somehow felt, even in the moment of great disappointment, that at the last moment you would see the Pope. And you have done. It pleased me more than I can say. Also, thank you for that prayer and that little pilgrimage up all those steps to the old parish church of Rome.

The English papers seem to have said nothing about your meetings. Will it be possible to read what you said? I am very keen to see it.

Mgr. Cardinale first charmed me with his voice. I am so glad you really met him. I shall write and thank him. Prof. Ghetti never answered my letters and presumably never contacted you. Next time I shall try Fr. Kirschbaum.[1]

Now for the Gifford Lectures.[2] I wish you very well with them, and hope to read them all soon. As the train passes South of Thirsk going to Edinburgh I have imagined once to have seen S. Wilfrid's House. So you may be passing very near us on Friday unless you go the west route.

Yours affectionately,
Columba, O.S.B.

1. Engelbert Kirschbaum, S.J. (1902–); one of the three archeologists working on the excavations under St. Peter's; *Die graeber der Apostelfuersten* (1957), translated as *The Tombs of St. Peter and St. Paul* (London, 1959); coauthor of *Explorazioni sotto la confessione di San Pietro in Vaticano . . .*; cf. C.C.E.'s letter of 23 July 1953, above. "He gave us—the ecumenical pilgrimage—a long talk about the excavations." (C.C.E.)

2. Compare A.J.T.'s letter of 3 April 1952, above.

The Royal Institute
of International Affairs
Chatham House
10, St James's Square
London S.W.1

21 October 1953

Dear Columba,

Your letter, after getting mine about the audience, came this morning.

I don't suppose there will be much in the press about our round table, as it isn't news, while Trieste[1] is. But I hope it may have long-term effects. If only it has convinced the Scandinavians that European union isn't a Catholic plot, it will have been worth while—and I do think they were impressed by Schuman's and de Gasperi's sincerity.

We go to Edinburgh to-morrow—the Queen Hotel, St. Coline St.—and come back on the 17th November. My love to you.

Arnold

1. Italy and Yugoslavia were at odds over the proposal of the United States and Britain to return Zone A to Italy and leave Yugoslavia in the central part of Zone B. Tito threatened to send troops into Zone A on any attempt by the Italians to enter it. The dispute was later settled by negotiation, and in 1954 Italy was accorded Zone A, which included the city of Trieste.

The Queen Hotel
St. Coline Street
Edinburgh

30 October 1953

Dear Columba,

Your sister and brother-in-law[1] are being most kind to us. We went to lunch with them yesterday and are to see them again next week. This is adding a lot to the pleasure of this visit to Edinburgh.

In this set of Giffords I am talking about the great secularising revolution in the West at the end of the 17th Century, and the effect of this on relations between the West and the rest of the World. For this I have found Bayle's *Dictionaire* a goldmine.[2] Have you ever grappled with it? Here you find the well-spring of all that is in Voltaire, Hume, and Gibbon.

Meanwhile, cross-references, imperious printer's queries, and sketches for maps rain down on me like an Edinburgh wet day, and keep me on the run. But, before the end of this year, I ought to have all this off my hands.

With very best wishes to you,

Yours affectionately,
Arnold

It was from the Ara Coeli[3] that came the chant of the Zoccolanti friars that set Gibbon off. But G. didn't, it seems to me, realise more than a fraction of the meaning of the experience that he was having.

1. Major Arthur Michael Cosmo Bertie (1886–1957); Inter Allied Military Control Commission in Germany (1920–23); in South African Defense Force (1940–44); Lilian (Crackanthorpe) Bertie (1902–); C.C.E.'s sister. Here A.J.T. met David Talbot Rice (1903–72); archeologist; professor of the history of fine art at the University of Edinburgh; *Byzantine Art* (London, 1954).

2. Pierre Bayle (1647–1706); *Dictionnaire historique et critique* (1695–97); this propagated the ideas of the Enlightenment.

3. See A.J.T.'s letter of 19 October 1953, above. This passage of Gibbon's *Autobiography* was a favorite of A.J.T.'s; see *A Study of History*, X: 98–107, esp. 103.

Ampleforth Abbey
York

St. Thomas' Day (21 December) 1953

My Dear Arnold,

A little note to wish you real Peace and joy at Christmas, and the childlikeness of heart and spirit that the children of God should have, together with the other virtues, of courage and compassion.

The text that fits this time is: God so loved the world, as to send his only begotten son;[1] and that other, not we have chosen God, but God has chosen us;[2] and the one how it is God who loved us first.[3] It requires faith to believe that the infinitely great can be concerned with the so small.

I gave a little sermon on Sunday trying to explain how Christmas is the making of all things anew, the new Adam, the second Eve, we reborn.

I shall be saying Mass for you at Midnight, and you must trust that God is prepared to give you all you need, if you are prepared to open the door wide. You must pray for me, please.

God bless you both.

Love,
Columba, O.S.B.

1. John 3 : 16.
2. John 15 : 16.
3. 1 John 4 : 19.

45, Pembroke Square
London

Christmas Day 1953

Dear Columba,

Thank you for your Christmas letter, and indeed you have my prayers—though, in praying for you, I am always abashed, because I am very conscious that the coin I offer is full of base metal, while your offering is pretty near to pure gold. So the fact that you care to have my prayers means much to me.

I saw Rosalind the other day—in hospital after an operation for too much thyroid, which has been affecting her heart. I am glad to say all has gone well. She went to the Grail[1] at Pinner yesterday.

Veronica and I are having a quiet and happy Christmas here.

Your sister was immensely kind to us at Edinburgh.

Yours affectionately,
Arnold

1. The Grail was an offshoot from a Dutch Catholic lay movement—women living in the world doing ordinary jobs, yet with vows.

45, Pembroke Square
London W.8

26 January 1954

Dear Columba:

I was most grieved to see the announcement of Father Paul's death[1]—though I know that members of the Order of Saint Benedict do not fear death, or repine at it, either for themselves or for one another.

In this world, though, there are few people alive at any time who carry the world on their shoulders for the rest of us, and Father Paul was undoubtedly one of those few.

One of the experiences that has had a lasting effect on me is turning up one day at Ampleforth, unannounced, at that time when Philip was in the monastery,[2] and there was some minor crisis about him, and Father Paul's amazing kindness to him and to me—serenely interrupting all his own business in order to give effective help to somebody in trouble.

Of course, if one were to look at him just in the external mundane way, his achievement in building up the school would have brought him the highest worldly recognition and honours if he had been in the running for that.

But all that, great as it is, is only the outward visible sign of the character of the inner man. In fact, Father Paul's work's relation to Father Paul himself is a symbol of the school's relation to the monastery, as I see it.

As I love the Community, I sympathise with you very deeply in your great loss.

Yours affectionately,
Arnold

1. "Father Paul Nevill (1882–1954) died of a heart attack sitting in his chair in the head master's room. He had been head master since December 1924 and had many qualities of mind and character that made him the great head master he was. He had great compassion for all in trouble, a clear grasp of problems, and was capable of taking infinite pains; he was a natural leader and had a very good mind, though no scholar. His interest was people, and his concern was to make Ampleforth an excellent school; in this he had a kind of boyish enthusiasm." (C.C.E.)

2. Cf. "Ganthorpe," in A.J.T.'s *Experiences*, p. 396: "And Father Paul, / Who cheerfully bears on his shoulders the burden of Atlas, / Took Philip into his fold and sped him again on his way / For the glory of God by the power of Saint Benedict"; and see A.J.T.'s letter of 23 October 1961, below.

Ampleforth Abbey
York

27 January 1954

My dear Arnold,

Your letter was something to treasure. It has helped to relieve my natural sadness at losing a dear friend. Nature submits to faith, but it does so with pain—and that is good for us. Death always gives me pangs, as though I were dying. So don't die before I do. Fr. Abbot was very moved by your letter. Yes, Fr. Paul was a giver all his life and this came from his love of Our Lord.

You will find a little appreciation by me in next Friday's *Tablet*.[1] It was written for his and my friends. How can one recall him to some one who never knew him.

Pray for us, we need wisdom in choice.

God bless you both.

Love,
Columba, O.S.B.

Monday 10 AM Oratory Mass with Monsignor Knox preaching.

1. *Tablet* (20 January 1954), pp. 114–15.

Ampleforth Abbey
York

St. Benedict's (21 March) 1954

My dear Arnold,

Just a note of sympathy over this campaign against Chatham House in the *Manchester Guardian*.[1] I don't suppose you are much personally implicated because you have been withdrawing these last few years to write the *Study*; but it must be distressing nevertheless.

Also a little note for the feast. St. Benedict was one of your favourite saints. I still read to people your little essay on him.[2] Fr. William is managing the school very well. Life goes on as ever. Fr. Paul's spirit still presides over much. His work cannot easily be forgotten—thank God.

My China book is once again at the publishers, and if it is refused again, I can't spend any more time on it. There are so many things one wants to do and write.

We are reading Hales' *Pio Nono*[3] in the refectory. It makes excellent, most interesting reading. You should have a look at it; it would appeal to you a lot.

My love to you both, and my prayers as always,

Columba, O.S.B.

1. The *Manchester Guardian*, on 8 March 1954, published a sharply critical article, "Chatham House, Reform in Head and Members?" suggesting that its overhead costs were unusually high, its junior staff neglected, and its publications dull.

2. A.J.T.'s "A Pair of Saviours" [Saint Benedict and Saint Gregory], in *A Study of History*, III: 264–69.

3. E. E. Y. Hales, *Pio Nono* (London, 1954).

30 March 1954 — 45, Pembroke Square, W.8

Dear Columba,

How like you to write about our bombardment.[1] Yes, I do mind, for Chatham House and for my colleagues, who are more personally involved than I am and who have not the consolations that a writer carries about inside himself.

Saint Benedict was, and is, one of my heroes, and another is Father Paul. It must be difficult to be his successor.

I do hope the China book will come into port this time: I expect it will.

Veronica and I have been in Uppsala and Helsinki for a fortnight: we flew back from Helsinki yesterday and it was a pleasure to find your letter waiting for me.

Yours affectionately,
Arnold

1. See C.C.E.'s letter of 21 March 1954, above.

Ampleforth Abbey
York

St. Joseph's Day (1 May) 1954

My dear head Publican,

I am delighted with your letter.[1] I think you put the point right; and I thought that it was "the approach," the attitude of mind, of some people that you were rightly resisting.

On the great question: how true is Christian doctrine, that, for one outside, must first be resolved by facts and of course—although we too rarely say so—by prayer and fasting—in the deepest sense of humility. Funnily enough I think that the Grand Master of the Publican's Guild does plenty of two and three, but has never really got down to the facts! A shocking accusation for one of your guildsmen to make.

The least of the publicans, or he would be, and yours affectionately,

Columba, O.S.B.

1. Douglas Jerrold had published his *The Lie about the West: A Response to Professor Toynbee's Challenge*. On 9 April 1954, *The Times Literary Supplement* (p. 225) reviewed this and J. B. de Beus's *The Future of the West* (London, 1954) in a leading review entitled "Counsels of Hope." This led to a series of letters, including those of the Aga Khan, Martin Wight, Jerrold, H. R. Trevor-Roper, and A.J.T.; these were reprinted as *Counsels of Hope* (London, 1954). C.C.E. refers here to A.J.T.'s letter to *The Times Literary Supplement* (30 April 1954) in which he said: "The publican is laying himself open to the possibility of salvation; the Pharisee is making himself fatally proof against it" (p. 281).

Ampleforth Abbey
York

3 May 1954

My dear Arnold,

I have written a letter to the T.L.S.[1] which should not cause you any sleepless nights. I had wanted to say how much I agreed with you and against D.J. on the main issue, and felt I must keep to one point.

The point of course is fundamental. In what sense are you prepared to admit the Christian revelation unique. I would have thought that you as a historian would have recognised its peculiarly historical, factual approach: this was done, that too, for man's saving. Then the very words of Christ claiming uniqueness.[2] We really should meet.

If my letter gets in, I should like you to set the ball rolling in that sense. Why not use the T.L.S. as a quiet arena.

My love to you both.

Columba, O.S.B.

"Qui videt me, videt et Patrem." (S. John's Gospel)[2]

1. Not printed; see Annex to this letter, below.

2. John 14:9.

[ANNEX TO C.C.E.'S LETTER OF 3 MAY 1954]

[Copy of letter to the TLS enclosed in preceding letter]

The letter in your columns from Professor T . . tries to imply that Roman Catholics are necessarily proud because of their exclusive claim for their Church. In spite of the obvious rejoinder *qui s'excuse s'accuse*, allow me to make some comment by stating the Catholic way of looking at the Church vis a vis the rest of the world.

If to follow Christ faithfully in his command to go baptise all nations and to belong to his one community is to be proud, then all Catholics are proud to be proud. But what kind of pride is this? Is it intellectual pride? The Catholic is submitting his judgement to that of Christ. He does not judge Christ's teaching by the yard stick of his own mind. He knows he needs a teacher and accepts him humbly. Then, what pride is it, if not intellectual pride? Was it proud of Christ to claim exclusive allegiance from all men? To say so would be to deny his divinity. If Christ is God, then he both has a right to make the claim, and if he did make the claim, it cannot be untrue.

Catholics are thoroughly aware that much truth is scattered throughout the world, not put forward as coming from Christ or his Church. These truths a Catholic will readily acclaim as true, and yet he, following his beliefs, will realize that they are in fact Christ's truths, for all the unawareness of their propagators, since Christ is the All-Wisdom of God. All truth is God's and so too Christ's.

Christ prayed that there should be only one fold; but he did expressly say that there were other sheep of his, not yet of his fold, which he would wish joined to it. A Catholic recognises in all good men and women, not visibly in the Church, those other sheep who truly belong to Christ, indeed in some sense to the Church, and who to the best of their ability are working for his Will.

We believe that they should be in the one Church, but do not deny them much good. Indeed I will readily affirm that many such respond better to the inspirations of God than one does oneself.

The Royal Institute
of International Affairs
Chatham House
10, St James's Square
London, S.W. 1

4 May 1954

Dear Columba,

I had your letter with the carbon of the one you were sending to the T.L.S. I am very glad indeed you agree with me on the main point. On the point you make in your letter to the T.L.S., there is, I think, a genuine difference of view between us. However, we each of us certainly aim at being publicans in as far as we are concerned individually and that carries one a long way.

I am enclosing now a carbon of a letter which I have written to-day and which I shall fire off at the T.L.S.[1] if they print yours (as I hope they will) this week and if they do not, then guillotine the correspondence.

If I am right, Jerrold's view, though compatible with Catholicism, is not very characteristic of Catholics at the present time. He looks to me like an English version of Charles Maurras.[2]

J.T.

1. Since C.C.E.'s letter was not published, A.J.T.'s was not; see Annex to this letter, below.

2. Charles Maurras (1868–1952); leader of l'Action française; cf. C.C.E.'s letter of 22 December 1939, above.

[Annex to A.J.T.'s letter of 4 May 1954]

45, Pembroke Square
London W.8

4 May 1954

The Editor,
The Times Literary Supplement

Sir,

My appeal to the parable of the Pharisee and the publican was not directed against those Roman Catholics and other Christians who think and feel as my friend the Prior of Ampleforth Abbey does; for all these are, I should say, unmistakable 'publicans.' I am not seeking to condemn our human impulse to advocate what we believe to be true and right; if I was, I should stand self-condemned, for I myself have, of course, been doing just that in my Reith Lectures and in this correspondence. The question is whether, in taking our lines, we take them in the publican's spirit or in the Pharisee's.

The distinction between Pharisees and publicans runs through the whole human race, and cuts across the divisions between religions and civilisations. But, subject to this fundamental difference of spiritual approach, there is, I believe, a difference of belief which once divided Symmachus from Ambrose, and which still distinguishes the Indian family of religions from the Jewish family. A publican-minded Buddhist or Hindu would, I imagine, go farther than a publican-minded orthodox Jew, Christian or Muslim would feel it legitimate for him to go in recognising (in Symmachus's words) that 'it is not possible to reach the heart of so great a mystery by one road only.' He would be publican-minded about himself, not only as an individual, but also in his corporate capacity as an adherent of a religious community.

Though, on this point, the Christian Church has, so far, followed in Judaism's wake, the plot of the tragedy of the New Testament—in which the Pharisaic Jewry of the day is the collective tragic hero—is a warning against the spiritual peril of believing that one's own religious institutions and beliefs are exclusively and definitively right. According to the traditional Christian reading of the plot, it was because the Pharisees thanked God that they were not as other men are that they failed to recognise God when they encountered Him incarnate. And this Christian tragic theme has a universal application.

The difference between the Jewish and the Indian view about the nature of creeds and churches has acquired a new importance now that the physical unification of the Earth by Western technology has made it impossible for us any longer to ignore Saint Paul's proclamation to the Athenians of the unity of Mankind through God. In our time—if possible, more than ever—the publican's spirit is the way of salvation. While publicans may differ among themselves over the question whether their churches are fallible, they will all agree that they themselves are; and, since all the representatives, on Earth, of all the churches are fallible human beings, the publican's spirit, as exemplified in Father Columba's letter, may still save us from running into new wars of religion and earning the death that is the wages of the sin of pride.

Yours very truly,
A.T.

Ampleforth Abbey,
York

Goremire Day (25 May) 1954

My dear Arnold,

Thank you so much for those two pamphlets. I treasure everything you send me. The Sheffield effort[1] was marvellously *secundum modum recipientis* in style. The American[2] one I found most interesting and liked not only yours, as always, but also Albright's. Fr. D'Arcy's was much along my old tracks and interesting that way. The more eastern stuff I can find, the better pleased I am. Some here. I was sorry your letter to me did not get in to the T.L.S. The editor wrote a kind letter of apology for not in the end printing mine, hoping, he said, that it was said in other letters. As a matter of fact, apart from your excellent finale,[3] I thought it ended not peaceably but in heat. That was a pity.

My love to you and to Veronica.

Columba, O.S.B.

1. "The Concentration of Power and the Alternatives before Us," delivered to the University of Sheffield, 3 December 1953 (Sheffield, 1954).

2. Missing.

3. A.J.T.'s final letter published in *The Times Literary Supplement* (4 June 1954) concluded, "The sin of which I feel that we Westerners need to repent is Pharisaism" (p. 361). C.C.E. here refers to A.J.T.'s letter of 21 May 1954.

The Royal Institute
of International Affairs
Chatham House
10, St James's Square
London S.W.1

26 May 1954

Dear Columba,

I am glad you approved my quotation from Pope Pius XI.[1] I feel that he was making a point of very great importance for the future as well as the past.

I hope it is the finale, as I dislike personal controversy and keep out of it except when there is something that I feel I can't allow to go by default.

I was very sorry that your letter didn't appear.

I, too, regret the heat, but I think this was generated by Jerrold, not by me. He has an unfortunate bullying manner: assuming that his opponent is a bad man, and trying to put him on the spot. I have no quarrel with him on this, as it gives his opponent an unearned moral advantage.

Jerrold's position seems to me to be, not Pius XI's, but Charles Maurras.[2]

He is, I think, making for the West the claim that the children of Zebedee made for themselves through their mother, because they hadn't the face to make it themselves to Christ.[3]

Individuals or civilisations that are Christian by profession can be unique, in virtue of Christ, only if they are unique in Christian practice: that is, in drinking the cup that Christ has drunk of; in taking up their cross and following Christ; in praying the Publican's prayer, not the Pharisee's; in seeing the beam in their own eye rather than the mote in their brother's eye.

I have tried to bring Jerrold on to this ground, but he has been silent about this, and has always repeated his claim that the Western Civilisation has got its uniqueness guaranteed, not in virtue of its own Christian practice, but in virtue of Christ's merits automatically.

Yours affectionately,
Arnold

1. On 21 May 1954, *The Times Literary Supplement* published (p. 329) A.J.T.'s letter, which responded to Jerrold's contention that "our Western civilization is unique in virtue of Christ's merits" by quoting the letter of Pius XI to Cardinal Gasparri of 30 May 1929, criticizing Mussolini's claiming "for a Western country a unique proprietary right in Christianity on the strength of Italy's being the owner-occupier of Rome."

2. Compare A.J.T.'s letter of 4 May 1954, above.

3. Matt. 20:20–28.

Ampleforth Abbey
York

30 May 1954

My dear Arnold,

Your last letter was very precious to me. It is so true that Christ's victory is only *applied* when the Christian accepts and lives by his precepts. It is a thoroughly Catholic outlook that the Christian salvation is not automatic but requires the consent of free men.

I thought D. Jerrold was trying to make an *amende honorable*.

I believe there is a uniqueness about the Christian revelation as well as in its fulfilment by every Christian. The nature of the salvation proposed is not disassociated from Christ. Salvation is not a technique, a theory, a moral code, but union with him—in the manner of St Paul's presentation of the mystery, particularly in Ephesians.

The world situation, on the surface, looks moderately calm, but I am inclined to think it ominous. We must pray, and each do his duty.

God bless you both.

My love to you,
Columba, O.S.B.

Glenstal Priory
Murroe
Co. Limerick

20 July 1954

My dear Arnold,

Here I am in Ireland for the first time. It has rained every day but one. I am giving the monks a retreat. They are almost all Irish, except for the remainder of the original founders who came over from Maredsous in Belgium.[1] The house is fantastic, a XIX century copy of Windsor Castle by Lord Barrington,[2] superb trees, a sub-tropical glen, etc. The boys live in the castle, the monks in the stable.

By chance—Providence—I have got on to someone who has been eluding me for a year or so, a certain Père Vincent Lebbe, who died in China 1940.[3] He is a character after your own heart, a second P. Ricci. His brother was a monk here, and they have some books. Get "*Pensées et Maximes du Père Lebbe*", (les Editions Universitaires, Paris-Bruxelles) ed. Léopold Levaux. It contains a short memoir of P. Lebbe, by Levaux and then P. Lebbe's maxims. The tragedy is that his work seems to have come too late. But I do not despair, remembering what the Diocletian darkness must have been like, and so many others.

On the political plane, I must say, the situation looks most serious, more especially as G. B. and U.S.A. are at sixes and sevens.[4] Violence has to be resisted by force, even though force is not the end. It is at times a necessary means. I am convinced that our trouble is this refusal to see communism as a threat wherever it is.

Do you know the Chinese proverb?

"If the tree falls, it is the worm at its heart."

"Si l'arbre tombe, c'est que le ver est au coeur." That would have been a good quote for the Decline of Civilizations. When does the Nonsense Book appear? The last volumes now make it sense.

My love to you both,

Columba, O.S.B.

P.S. Do you see anything of Archbishop David Mathew[5] now he is in England?

1. Glenstal Priory, founded in 1927.

2. The original house was built in the nineteenth century by Sir Matthew Barrington in thirteenth-century baronial style; Sir Charles Barrington sold it in 1926.

3. Vincent Lebbe (1877–1940); Lazarist missionary in China; he believed that the missionaries should make way for indigenous clergy; his plea was heeded by Pope Pius XI, who consecrated six Chinese bishops in 1926.

4. On 25–29 June, President Eisenhower and Winston Churchill conferred on these

differences in policy over Communist action in Southeast Asia: the results were announced in a "Potomac charter."

5. Compare C.C.E.'s letter of 14 July 1944, above.

27 July 1954 45 Pembroke Square, W.8

Dear Columba,

I am not sending this to Ireland, as you will probably be back by now. Will you be at Ampleforth in August? Having an American friend with us who drives, we have hired a car for a month, which will lengthen our tether, so the first thing that came into my head was that we might come down Wensleydale and pay you a visit. It would be fun if, by chance, you will be there.

We need a holiday; for Chatham House has been in the news lately, and this has taken it out of us.

I am very fond of Ireland, and the Irish missionary connexion with China is particularly interesting. I remember visiting the headquarters somewhere about 20 miles west of Dublin, of a missionary order that worked entirely in China, if I remember right. I am taking a note of Père Vincent Lebbe. As to his being too late, isn't it too early to tell? On a long view, I don't think Communism's prospects are good anywhere—it is a religion that offers nothing to meet the personal needs of human beings. And in China, above all, its dogmatism and fanaticism are very alien.

A set of Vols. VII–X is on order to go to you—publication day is—the 14th October, but I already have a bound set on my shelf, so I can't do a thing more to alter them now, and this is quite a relief. I am now at work on "*Religio Historici*".[1]

I am probably more optimistic than you are about the international outlook. I think the advantage that Communism is getting out of Asian and African revolts against European rule is only temporary. As soon as they have won their independence, I think they will be as anxious to defend it against the Russians as against us. Well, perhaps I shall see you in August.

Yours affectionately,
Arnold

1. A.J.T.'s *An Historian's Approach to Religion*; cf. the preface, with its reference to Sir Thomas Brown's *Religio Medici*.

Gillingham Hall
Beeches
Suffolk
(Till about 13th Aug.)

1 August, 1954
Feast of "St. Peter in Chains"

My dear Arnold,

I am seeing my old Mama for a few days. Your letter reached me there.

Thank you with all my heart for the promised 4 vols. How excruciatingly exciting. How will I prevent myself reading them day and night until completed. It is more or less how I read IV, V and VI.

I am delighted to hear you can come over to Ampleforth. Let me invite you to lunch tea and supper all of you, Veronica and your American friend's wife, if there is one. We can use the monastery guest room which is *always* open.

Now I suggest any day after the 17th and before the 27th as I am talking at a Catholic summer school that following week end (Union of Catholic Students). I may be back before 17th, but at the moment I cannot be sure. Fr. Abbot may say, go here, there, etc.

Here is an interesting article on you! by a friend of mine. I encouraged him to have it published, as I think it does record a fairish impression of your statements up to date. It should therefore be of use to you. Michael Richards[1] is a mod-language scholar of Cambridge now teaching with us and recently received into the Church. He was a very active minister of all reunion activities and still is. You would like him very much. I told him I would send you his article.

You must write your *religio historici* on your knees, at least metaphorically. Please let me see it before printing. I believe this may be the most important thing you write. The moment is coming for us all to face the world religions and find a way of crossing barriers. In a sense we are already across the barriers and do not realise it. That Penguin on Islam[2] for instance. Have you seen it. I should say it is epoch making. I only wish he (Guillaume) had dared to print more of these elusive early biographies of Mahomet.

Yes, in the long run Chinese Christians, Polish Christians, Roumanians, Hungarians and all the rest will raise their heads, "How long O Lord, how long".

Hasta la vista.

My love to you both, and prayers for the historian's religion,

Columba, O.S.B.

1. Michael Richards (1924–) was ordained and became editor of the *Clergy Review*; the article was printed in *Time and Tide* (17 July 1954), pp. 956–57; see A.J.T.'s letter of 2 August 1954, below.

2. A. Guillaume, *Islam* (reprint, London, 1976).

2 August 1954 45, Pembroke Square, W.8

Dear Columba,

Splendid: Let us know the day between 17th and 27th August, and we will come over—for lunch, it had better be. Our friend E. D. Myers'[1] wife is at home in America, looking after the children, so we shall be three.

I do look forward to this.

I am much interested in the *Time and Tide* article:[2] I think it is accurate and perceptive. I am feeling my way, and he is right in spotting changes in my point of view.

I am writing in haste, just before getting off. Our address, from next Saturday on, will be

Hall Beck Cottage,
Hall Beck,
Killington,
Kirkby Lonsdale
Westmorland.

My best regards to your mother.

Yours affectionately,
Arnold

1. Edward Delos Myers; cf. A.J.T.'s letter of 15 March 1953, above.
2. See C.C.E.'s letter of 1 August 1954, above.

Hall Beck Cottage
Hall Beck
Killington
Kirkby Lonsdale
Westmorland

10 August 1954

Dear Columba,

We will come on Friday, 20th August, as you suggest. We will start immediately after breakfast and come straight through. We ought to arrive between 11.0 and 12.0. To go to Rievaulx[1] in the afternoon, and possibly to tea at Gilling,[2] is just what we should like. There is the fourth place in the car, waiting for you to take it.

I am sure you will like my friend Myers.

Well, I do look forward to this.

Yours affectionately,
Arnold

1. Rievaulx Abbey; cf. C.C.E.'s letter of 22 April 1940, above.
2. Gilling Castle, the lower school; cf. C.C.E.'s letter of 25 October 1938, above.

Hall Beck Cottage
Hall Beck
Killington
Kirkby Lonsdale
Westmorland

21 August 1954

Dear Columba,

Yesterday was too short: the time went like the wind; so it was good to hear that there might be a chance of seeing you in London before long.

It was a very great happiness for me—as it always is—to get this glimpse of you again, and also to be again at Ampleforth, with Veronica sharing it this time. The monastery stands for breaking out of self-centredness and putting one's life to use for the glory of God and the helping of one's fellow creatures—and the whole of the law and the Prophets is contained in this, whatever doctrine one may or may not hold as well.

I haven't even this time, been able, without any self-regarding feelings, to see again the Sheepwalk and Stonegrave Wood and, above all, Hawnby Hump,[1] which I used to look at out of my study window. But I was not devastated, as I was last time (which, as you know, is what has made me keep away so long).

I have managed to 'put to work' a good deal of painful experience by transmuting it into the last volumes of the nonsense book, in faith that one will have made some use of one's life if one succeeds in helping other people to get infinitesimally nearer to a vision of God through history. And my feeling towards Rosalind—as I believe I can truly say, when I test it, as I was doing yesterday—is love combined with contrition at not having been able to give her what she needed.

I have exorcised much of my backward-looking pangs by putting them into some Latin verse which you will find at the beginning of the new batch of volumes,[2] but I am surprised at the strength of the feelings that objects in the landscape, like Hawnby Hump and Stonegrave Wood, call up in me. Something out of me has projected itself into them and animated them—I suppose this is the pagan worship of Nature. Perhaps it happened because human relations at Ganthorpe were never more than partly happy for Rosalind and me, so one's feelings ranged out and attached themselves to woods and hills. One must push on through them, for I am sure the road through them, as through all creatures, leads to God.

Well, till our meeting in London.

Will you tell "Father" Abbot how much I appreciated his coming in to join us yesterday?

Yours affectionately,
Arnold

1. Compare A.J.T.'s letter of 17 July 1947, above, and A.J.T.'s "The Broken Trunk," above.
2. "Scriptoris Vita Nova," in *A Study of History*, VII: xiii–iv.

Ampleforth Abbey
York

23 August 1954

My dear Arnold,

As you know, your long awaited return to Ampleforth gave me much rejoicing. And I was happy to take you into the church where you had so often prayed. It would have been suitable to have stayed there longer, but Prof. Myers was an unknown quantity. In any case you said your heart-felt prayer, I know, as you genuflected. The picture of your visit which strangely stands out most is that care you showed when Veronica might have slipped coming down the steps of the minor Temple. There was there so "tender [*sic*] a care",[1] it made me realise you were happy.

Hawnby Hump, the Stonegrave Wood, they are symbols of pain you so wished to be joy. They merely set off those reactions again. But you *are* master of that pain now. You have survived, offered it up in contrition. They will become symbols of God's victory in your soul; you had to learn by suffering, and you have learnt.

My very best love, and my small prayers.

Columba, O.S.B.

P.S. Do keep Veronica up to her promise of a chronology. A Hall Beck Chronicle; beginning BC 2,000,000,000 with the initial bang!

1. Gerard Manley Hopkins, "The Leaden Echo and the Golden Echo," in *Poems* (London, 1968), pp. 96–99.

24 August 1954 Hall Beck Cottage

Dear Columba,

I am delighted at your picture of Veronica and me at the temple, for I was quite unconscious of what I was doing, so it will, as you say, have been a true index of my feelings.

I love Veronica for what is, I think, the essence of what is lovable: the lovingness that takes no thought of self. This comes out in her all the time.

The highest vision of God that I know is Saint Paul's in the Epistle to the Colossians, ii, 5–8.

God Bless You.
Yours affectionately,
Arnold

Ampleforth Abbey
22 September 1954 York

My dear Arnold,

Thank you for the little blurb.[1] I liked it. It came straight out. The O.U.P.[2] one was a little more laboured, but I treasure the remembrance of the mound on Slingsby Moor,[3] having lain there with you one hot summer afternoon.

I read the *Spectator* article[4] this afternoon. I see you repeat your warning about the Chosen People. I should like to speak of the Chosen Truth and the Citizens of the City of God who are found the world over. Not all in the church will be saved, not by any means all those out of it cast into exterior darkness. But I cannot see how we can refuse to assert: this is right, this is wrong; this is more right, that less so. Any other method would paralyse judgement. I expect always you are attacking pride, not certitude; but at first reading it seems the other.

I can scarcely wait for VII–IX or is it X.

My love to you both,

Columba, O.S.B.

and God bless you.

I now have ½ China decently typed by an expert but feel very diffident and despairing.

1. "I think this was an advertisement for the volumes of *A Study of History* that were about to appear." (C.C.E.)

2. *A Study of History: What the Book is For; How the Book Took Shape* (London, 1954).

3. "The more southerly of the two round barrows on Slingsby Moor, on which I used often to lie on summer afternoons, . . . served as a physical receiving station for catching still unspent reverberations of waves of psychic events" (*A Study of History*, X: 235).

4. "The Teaching of History in a Shrinking World," a review of *History without Bias? A Textbook Survey on Group Antagonisms*, by E. H. Dance (London, 1954), *Spectator*, no. 6586 (17 September 1954), p. 329.

Ampleforth Abbey
York

17 October 1954

My dear Arnold,

I received the four volumes by post on Friday last. The first thing I did was to carry the parcel unopened into the church and lay it on the altar in the old Lady Chapel where Fr. Paul always used to offer Mass and where daily I have these many years said prayers for you and the book. Then and there I offered it to God to do only good with it, to prevent any wrong ideas harming and asked Him to enlighten you yet more. Of course, I lament you have remained in some of your positions; but I see it as a great effort to remain intellectually honest. God, who sees all our hearts, will surely take you to Himself, in spite of all your wrong-headedness. I hope He will do the same for me, who also must have just as, or almost as!, many wrong-headed views as you. In fact I believe many of your opinions on comparative religion, though at the moment not right, can be righted, more by prayer than by argument. Let us accept absolutely every good thing in every religion of the world, all good comes from God. Let us submit absolutely to Christ who was God and judge all by His standard, His Truth, not our own.

On my way out I passed by St. Benedict's chapel, and knowing your love of him, I linked him up with it all. Afterwards I opened the parcel in my room. So far, of course, I have only glanced at it, but here and now: *Thank you with all my heart*. The CCE made me very happy.[1] My old boys have a way of writing to me as Dear CCE. It would seem that pieces of our conversations by post have got into the book and I feel honoured. The passage on Ampleforth I treasure, so too the passage on the crucifix.[2] We had a young man photographing it a week ago. How it came out I have not heard yet. But I must get down to reading it all seriously, and I expect you will be getting "on reading A.J.T." in packages over a number of months.

My love to you and to Veronica.

Columba, O.S.B.

This is only a preliminary thank you.

1. "Acknowledgements and Thanks," in *A Study of History*, X: 242.

2. Ibid., IX: 634–35, X: 223.

18 October 1954 45, Pembroke Square, W.8

Dear Columba,

I was relieved, as well as delighted, to get your very understanding letter—fearing that, on some points, I might have pained you and so done something which would have been the last thing that I liked to do.

A book, even a big one, is only one piece of action; one moves on, has more happiness and more suffering, and, with God's help, grows.

Time Magazine has just arrived.[1] They start off with "*Amplexus expecta*" and with their photograph of the High Altar, which I am enclosing. Sometime, may I have this back. No hurry for that, but haste now.

Yours affectionately,
Arnold

1. *Time* (18 October 1954), pp. 54–58, 60.

Ampleforth Abbey, York
20 October 1954 Gilling Station

My dear Arnold,

Thank you for the cutting. I have another copy, so I return this, before losing it! I knew they would choose the photo taken from the opposite side.[1] The other side is extremely difficult to take. The light is wrong. Symbolic perhaps? You will be seeing it as time goes on more and more from the monastic side, my side (?).

I hope you are not distressed by the reviews. You must have expected something of the sort. I think the reviewers do not see it all in perspective, either of your own life or of the study of history in general. You are trying to be *fair* to all religions. One tends on those occasions to be unfair to one's own (family) (religion). The particular examples may be sometimes wrong, but the general idea of civilizations the unit, their progress, I think is established. C. Dawson's was the most understanding I have seen.

Yours ever,
Columba, O.S.B.

P.S. Wight[2] strikes me as very telling.

1. The *Time* photograph of the crucifix in Ampleforth Abbey church was taken from the viewpoint of the congregation, not that of the monks.

2. Robert James Martin Wight (1913–72); Chatham House (1936–38) and (1946–49); reader in international relations, University of Edinburgh (1949–61); professor of history, University of Essex (1961–72); a Roman Catholic; his comments on *A Study of History* are quoted in footnotes throughout vol. VII; his comments served "to turn my original monologue into a dialogue" (X: 238); *Power Politics*, Royal Institute of International Affairs, "Looking Forward" Pamphlet no. 8 (1946; reissue, Leicester, 1978); *Survey of International Affairs, 1939–1946: The*

World in March 1939, ed. A.J.T. and Frank T. Ashton-Gwatkin (London, 1952): several sections; see especially his *The Balance of Power*, ibid., pp. 508–31.

21 October 1954 45, Pembroke Square W.8

Dear Columba,

I am so glad you like Martin Wight's bits. I shall arrange, some time, for you and him to meet.

I am not distressed at the reviews; I am relieved to have got off so lightly—so far. Christopher Dawson,[1] of course, I liked very much—particularly because he was really reviewing the book as a whole. There is also a kind one by Denis Brogan in the *New York Times* Sunday book review.[2]

What you say about leaning over backwards from one's own religion in trying to be fair to the others is very true.

I was on television last night—the eighth of my ten hoops in England. I don't so much mind jumping through the American ones.

Yours affectionately,
Arnold

1. Christopher Dawson, "The Toynbee Philosophy of History," *Observer* (17 October 1954), p. 8.
2. Denis Brogan, "Time and Change and Mr. Toynbee," *New York Times Book Review* (17 October 1954), pp. 1, 50.

16 January 1955 45, Pembroke Square, W.8

Dear Columba:

It was exciting to read the announcement of your writing Father Paul's life. It is a splendid subject. You won't lack materials—you will have an embarrassment of riches. What may be difficult is to write a life of Father Paul that won't be a complete history of the school during his head mastership. His work was impersonal in the sense of being unself-centred, and at the same time intensely personal in the sense of being the work of a tremendous personality whose stamp printed itself, for good, on what he did.

I am now trying to recuperate, but am feeling the effects of accumulated fatigue and, for the moment, rather shying away from the pretty crowded agenda ahead of me. But no doubt I shall regain the necessary margin of energy. I can't really be too decrepit, as I took a party of eleven to the Circus on Friday. The number will increase year by year, as more grandchildren reach circus-going age.

Yours affectionately,
Arnold

Ampleforth Abbey
17 January 1955 York

My dear Arnold,

If you had not written a good review of the book on the h.m. of Winchester,[1] I would not be writing a book on Fr. Paul. It was your review which set Fr. Abbot and me talking, in the middle of which I discovered he thought I had already begun. But I had not. He seemed, six months ago, opposed, so I did nothing. In the meantime, all Fr. Paul's correspondence at this end has been destroyed.

Your letter of encouragement is a great help. There are people who say: not worth it. You help me to keep my conviction that it is.

Allow me to jot down a few ideas and perhaps you will comment.

What people will want to know about him will be the following, and it is those things I should write about.

1. his achievement, what he actually did. This will require a sketch of the *terminus a quo*.
2. How he did it.
    a. The apparent obstacles—the traditions of the Community, etc.
    b. The aids: his character, his lieutenants, friends.
    c. The fundamental ideas.
3. What makes a *Catholic* Public School and a *monastic* one distinctive.

I thought of giving his ideas on: religious instruction, boys and religion; games; boys and sex (tricky); parents; careers; the university, etc. . . any suggestions?

My view is that to make it 3 dimensional one must have incidents, anecdotes, and, in his case, laughing ones, he was full of fun.

What I have put down will surely set you thinking so I leave it. Among the saved letters strangely enough are yours years ago about Philip.[2]

About yourself. I am concerned that you have been overdoing it. Sorry! The Circus is the ideal remedy. What about coming up here for a time, or I could write to Downside; they would give you peace. But, of course, you do not know them as you know so many of us.

It is important to obey one's doctors in your state, so I hope you are doing so.

My life is pretty busy so I only had a few days to wallow in the S.O.H. and dived into Renaissances—here, there, and the examination system. No wonder the hornets rose in their thousands!

My love to you and Veronica.

Columba, O.S.B.

1. John D. E. Firth, *Rendall of Winchester* (London, 1954); Montague John Rendall (1862–1950); Trinity College, Cambridge; headmaster, Winchester (1911–24). For a picture of Rendall, see A.J.T.'s *Acquaintances*, pp. 37–42, and Kenneth Clark, *Another Part of the Wood* (London, 1974), pp. 60–65.

2. See A.J.T.'s letter of 23 October 1961, below.

18 January 1955 45, Pembroke Square, W.8

Dear Columba,

I am delighted that it was my review of Firth's book that decided you to write a life of Father Paul. Have you read Firth's book yet? You might find reading it a good start for your own work, as he really does deal in a masterly way with the problem of writing a headmaster's life. If you haven't a copy, send me a line and I will tell Blackwell to send you one on my account. I should like you to have the book from me.

My main comment on your ideas is that 2 (b) (The aids: his character, his lieutenants, friends) ought to be the heart of the book, and here I see a psychological difficulty. A monk suppresses his personality and, as one of Father's Paul's fellow-soldiers in the army of St. Benedict, you may perhaps find yourself writing, not so much a life of Father Paul as a history of the community's educational achievements in Father Paul's time through Father Paul's agency. Of course this is an important part of the book, and, in any biography of a great public figure, it is always a puzzle to find the right relation between the private element and the public element in the story. When your hero is a headmaster, this problem is particularly acute, because every great headmaster is both bound up with a school, which is a particularly strong form of public institution, and at the same time makes his effect on his boys through his personal character. Their feeling for him, I suppose, is a paradoxical mixture of awe and ridicule and, unless one can convey this, one will have missed something essential. So I am sure you are right in feeling that one must have incidents and anecdotes, and ones that are full of fun. Here, I think, you may find Firth's book particularly helpful.

Father Paul was, in my opinion, a greater headmaster than my own master, Rendall. Probably one reason for this was that Rendall's celibacy, which was a very strong vein in his nature, never found the positive outlet that Father Paul's found.

This brings one to your point 3 (What makes a Catholic Public School and a monastic one distinctive). Of the whole public element in your subject this, I myself feel, is the point that you should concentrate on, because, in my experience as a parent, the peculiar virtue of a Catholic monastic school is that the school is recognised by the boys as being a by-product of something that matters much more, and this saves the boys from feeling that the school itself is the centre of the Universe. I am sure this is very important.

But finally, going back to the question of bringing out the personality, you will have to try to perform a very difficult psychological exercise of imagining that, instead of being the Prior, you are somebody writing about Father Paul for an American popular magazine—this sounds vulgar, but it is a question of righting the balance. You have, after all, to look at a headmaster from the point of view of the boys, their parents and the public, as well as from the point of view of a fellow-member of the Order and the Community.

Well, I hope these rambling suggestions may be of some use.

Yours affectionately,

A.T.

Ampleforth Abbey
York

19 January 1955

My dear Arnold,

It was magnificent of you to write so fully on my work, Fr. Paul's life. I shall ponder all you say, especially the balance between the person and the history of the school—the latter should, I suppose, be second, and also the American journal style!

I am going to tell you a secret,* which will not be so long, but you are the first I've told. We have 24 hours ago accepted to make a foundation in the States, at St. Louis, having been invited by the Archbishop and a group of distinguished laymen and all the clergy of the diocese.

This, I am now going to suggest, may not appeal to you, but one of these laymen suggested that I might persuade you to write an article in *Harpers* analysing the significance of the event. It would help them in their "nation wide" appeal for funds for the building of an abbey and church worthy of the worship of God.

Of course, one would have to mention that there are two Priories of the English Benedictine Congregation already in the U.S.A., Portsmouth and Washington, but they are far distant from St. Louis and were not founded by us. I am thrilled by the idea and admit to having worked very hard to get others to see how good it would be to have an Abbey and school of our type there (it would start as a dependent priory, of course).

If you are feeling burdened, never mind, I would quite understand if you said no, but the idea might inspire you and not take long.

Yes, thank you very much, please tell Blackwells to send me Firth's book. I should read it.

Yours affectionately,
Columba, O.S.B.

* It is not meant now to be a secret, so you are not bound to secrecy about it.

Royal Institute
of International Affairs
Chatham House
10, St James's Square
London S.W.1

21 January 1955

Dear Columba,

I saw the news about St. Louis in the paper this morning after having had it in your letter.

I wish I could undertake to write something in HARPERS as you suggest, but my Doctor has told me to go slow for the present in order to recuperate from my last visit to America, so I really ought not to take on additional commitments. I am sure you will forgive me for this.

I have sent a line to Blackwell telling him to send you Firth's book on my account.

You don't need to write like a popular American interviewer so long as from time to time you have just a touch of his feeling for his subject.

Yours affectionately,
Arnold

Ampleforth Abbey
York

31 January 1955

My dear Arnold,

No, of course I don't mind, and fully appreciate that you must be kept free from all work except what cannot be avoided. I did not write before, hoping to be able to thank you for the Rendall book; but you must have forgotten! or Blackwell's run out of copies.

You will be glad to hear that I have received some interesting responses about Fr. Paul as the result of the 'press campaign'. The Bp. of Peterborough sent a particularly nice letter.

Well, keep quiet, mentally quiet, and embrace the little cross this is. When one compares the troubles of one's own life to that of millions East, one's troubles seem to fade away. Read *Freedom in China*, a Catholic Truth Pamphlet. I could scarcely believe the horror. No, I suppose you shouldn't read it at present.

The sight of our hanging crucifix has acquired new meaning and poignancy now. I am reminded always to remember you.

Yours affectionately,
Columba, O.S.B.

The Royal Institute
of International Affairs
Chatham House
10, St James's Square
London S.W.1

1 February 1955

Dear Columba,

I hadn't forgotten, but yesterday I had a card from Blackwell saying that Firth's book is now rebinding, so I am sending you my copy under separate cover, to keep, and telling them to send to me the one that I had ordered for you when it is procurable.

What you say about the crucifix touches me very much.

As to the Communist régime in China, when one thinks of the oppression and repression (I was hearing something about this, myself, the other day, from the former Librarian of the National Library at Peking) one has to remember three things: (1) This is the first stable and effective Government that China has had since Great Britain knocked the Manchu Government over in the Opium War (1839–42); (2) *all* Chinese are agreed in wanting to make China independent of

Western ascendancy of any kind; (3) ironically, considering (2), Communism is a Western import. It is something quite un-Chinese and un-Buddhist, and its fanaticism and tyranny, as well as its partly mis-applied but also partly genuine zeal for social justice, are part of Marx's heritage from the Jewish-Christian tradition in which he was born and brought up. So we Westerners have to take a lot of responsibility for Communism in the non-Western parts of the World.

I am sure you will enjoy Firth's book. It is really first-rate.

Yours affectionately,
Arnold

Ampleforth Abbey
York

2 February 1955

My dear Arnold,

The book—and its cheering inscription—have arrived. They could scarcely come separately. I am delighted with both. Thank you once again. Now I must make good use of the book.

Something of what you say about Communist China I have tried to instil into *China and the Cross*. The English are responsible for a lot, in fact all the Western Powers, but not U.S.A. (?). I sent the revised, enlarged, retyped 2nd ed. off to A. P. Watt today. This really is my last major effort on it.

Read Br. Lawrence on *The Will of God*.[1] Do you know it?

Yours affectionately,
Columba, O.S.B.

1. Brother Lawrence: Nicolas Herman (ca. 1605–91); Carmelite lay brother who wrote maxims, which were edited by the Abbé de Beaufort in 2 vols.: *Maximes Spirituelles* (1692) and *Moeurs et Entretiens du F. Laurent* (1694), which were published in English as *The Practice of the Presence of God* (London, 1926).

Ampleforth Abbey
York

17 March 1955

My dear Arnold,

Thank you for having Professor Heiler's article[1] sent me. I read it avidly straight through on opening the envelope, and found myself agreeing with almost every word.

There is a vast amount of God's truth strewn all over the world and in all ages, and we must recognise, welcome, worship it, wherever it is. It is God's truth.

How are you? I hope really resting and being the perfect patient and submissive husband.

Did I tell you Longman's have accepted *The Sheepfold and the Shepherd*,[2] and are really seriously considering *China and the Cross*.

The V.P.N.[3] material is almost all to hand, and I shall begin in the Easter holidays. For Holy Week, I shall be preaching in the University church, Dublin. I am a bit scared.

My love to you,
Columba, O.S.B.

1. Friedrich Heiler (1892–1967); he began life as a Catholic and studied Catholic theology, but in 1919 he became a Lutheran; later, influenced by von Hügel, his theology was more Catholic again, and he became an ardent ecumenist.
2. C.C.E.'s *The Sheepfold and the Shepherd* (London, 1956).
3. Material for the life of Paul Nevill.

20 March 1955 45, Pembroke Square, W.8

Dear Columba,

You won't be as much frightened, preaching at Dublin, as I have been the two times I have preached in Chapel at Winchester; for I remembered what we had said about the sermons when we were boys in the school, and you haven't been a student in Dublin at the National University, so you won't find it quite so hair-raising.

I am quite delighted at the news about Longmans. When they finally clinch with the China book, let me have a post-card, as I should get pleasure from knowing that it is all fixed up.

I am writing a paper on 'Men at Work in God's World' to be read in October to the Episcopalian Protestant diocese of Albany, N.Y. Saint Benedict is, of course, my central figure for this, and I shall be saying something about the Santo Speco (with Pius IX's inscription)[1] and Rievaulx, Fountains, and Jervaulx.

How fast you have got ahead in collecting the materials for the life of Father Paul. I shall be thinking of you in Dublin.

Yours affectionately,
Arnold

1. See A.J.T.'s letter of 12 October 1953, above.

Ampleforth Abbey
York

23 March 1955

My dear Arnold,

I have been in bed with 'flu' and last morning I took volume X and read what I could understand: I enjoyed it enormously, particularly *you* as a small boy grappling with the Persians and Chaldeans, and your moments of intuition; then too, Gibbon and St. Augustine. The end part, your thank-offerings, I had read before and had found them enlightening, too. Your mother, whom I met once, must have been a very wonderful person.

I am so glad you are thinking again on Benedictine lines. It is just possible that I may be in St. Louis when you are giving your address to the Episcopalians in U.S.A. This is *top secret* and may not happen. It depends on our abbatial election in April, but if I am, I invite you to visit us. Please accept!

Yours ever and affectionately,
Columba, O.S.B.

Still no news from Longmans about *China*.

11 April 1955 45, Pembroke Square, W.8

Dear Columba,

Thank you very much for *Gaudium Paschale*.[1] I found myself chiming in with the spirit of it, and I was especially delighted with the translation of Phil. ii, 3–11. It is the best translation I have ever read, and, as you know, this passage seems to me to be the heart of the distinctive Christian belief about what God is and has done.

My granddaughter Josephine's twelfth birthday fell on this Easter Sunday, so we spent the afternoon with her and Polly.

On Saturday we start on a month's journey: Stuttgart, Austria (lecturing), Asolo, Venice, Verona, Brescia (holiday).

The journey round the world in 1956–7 now begins to loom up. One must pray on the assumption that one may die to-day, but act on the assumption that one may be given time to take on board some more useful cargo and use it for other people's benefit.

With love to you,

Yours affectionately,
Arnold

My pen has made my writing even worse than usual.

1. Missing.

Ampleforth Abbey
York

Thursday, 14 April 1955

My dear Arnold,

I am so glad you liked the broadcast.[1]

Your version of the Ignatian attitude to life I agree with: pray on the assumption that death may be today; act on the assumption that time is given for more. Suppose you were taken ill, you will call for me, will you not? I think it good for you to give instructions to that effect.

This is really a line to wish you a happy journey and safe return. Do not let people make your life too strenuous. Do send me your thoughts, your encouragement and your advice. I would value it as one of my most precious heirlooms in America.

Say your good prayers too.

I suppose no passage in your forthcoming address in October[2] in which the O.S.B.'s appear could be used in our manifesto? I am intrigued by Asolo.[3] What is that?

Today I actually began the Fr. Paul book. It is flowing fairly easily so far.

My love to you both,
Columba, O.S.B.

and prayers for your safe return.

1. Perhaps a Mass from the Abbey.
2. Compare A.J.T.'s letter of 20 March 1955, above.
3. The little town overlooking the Venetian plain; the fief of Caterina Cornaro; scene of Robert Browning's *Pippa Passes*.

Ampleforth Abbey
York

30 April 1955

My dear Arnold,

I hope you have come back from your lectures and holiday refreshed.

There is some news for you; it means a separation in space—but no more. I am being sent, as I suspected and told you—to be the first superior of our foundation at St. Louis. I rejoice, and am afraid at the same time, rejoice because it means being able to give more up, and something resemble my patron, afraid and not afraid: of myself's inadequacies yes; of God's letting me down, NO. So I go forward pretty calmly. It does seem to me a tremendously good work we are aiming at, a fusion of the English Benedictine—the Ampleforth—spirit in both monastic and school elements with the American Catholic eagerness and life.

I gather that the American Catholics, without being exactly the American underworld—far from it—are intellectually behind their brethren, and as there are so many of them and they are spiritually so good, it would be an immense gain to help raise that standard. Then spiritually too I think we have something to give.

Like St. Columba I hope to remain; it would be a complete giving, or intent to give.

My love to you and Veronica,
Columba, O.S.B.

Ampleforth Abbey
York

13 May 1955

My dear Arnold,

This will be very short, but your note from Venice[1] will be one of my treasured possessions in St. Louis. You have a way of saying things which increases the value of the deed they refer to. As ever I am indebted to your great friendship.

Not least I was happy to receive the clear unequivocal statement of your religious position. I understand perfectly—or nearly!—and would respect your letter at the end.

Thank you for saying I may steal your words from the Episcopalian Bp. of Albany.[2] I shall write after October I suppose. Your 'lights' on Benedictines have also been gold to me, insights, inscapes, as Hopkins calls them.

Venice! I am envious. V.P.N.,[3] Fr. Terence[4] and I stayed in a very posh hotel opposite a lovely church over the canal, St. George's. Mass in S. Mark's. I had the same kind of sensation there as at Cordova, antiquity? difference.

My love to you and Veronica,
Columba, O.S.B.

P.S. Don't, like Abp. Garbett,[5] have to have a rest after your holiday!

1. Missing.

2. Compare A.J.T.'s letter of 20 March 1955, above.

3. Paul Nevill, O.S.B.

4. Terence Wright, O.S.B. (1904–57); contemporary of C.C.E.'s; procurator of Ampleforth Abbey (1948–57); Fr. Paul had chosen him as one of his companions on his jubilee journey to Rome.

5. Cyril Forster Garbett (1875–1955); archbishop of York (1942–55); *In an Age of Revolution* (London, 1952); in the House of Lords gave reluctant support to the manufacture of atomic arms; he, too, was given an honorary degree by Cambridge University on 10 June 1948; cf. A.J.T.'s letter of 19 June 1948, above.

15 May 1955 45, Pembroke Square, W.8

Dear Columba,

I was very glad to have your letter of the 13th. It is quite likely that you will be at my death-bed, for Chicago, as I said, is a likely place to die in at an advanced age, and it is no distance from St. Louis by air.

St. Louis has an almost extinct 'Old South' core, surrounded by a modern middle-western city. The river is noble, and the railroads—going to the ends of the Earth in all directions—are exciting. I think it is a well-chosen centre, as schools and colleges are much less thick on the ground in that section than in the N.E.

Perhaps your posh hotel in Venice was Danieli's. It occupies most of the Riva de' Schiavoni opposite St. George's. We took a little steamer from there to Malamocco, to see what the Lido is like when it is not buried under hotels and bathing machines.

On Friday, we woke up Brescia, saw Sant' Ambrogio and the Cenacolo and the Castello Sforzesco at Milan, and had supper in this house after skipping over the Alps.

At Venice, Byzantium unbelievably meets Flanders, and I am afraid Flanders has vulgarised Byzantium a bit. As soon as the Venetians drop their Byzantine moorings, they drift steadily towards Rubens, so it seems to me. I am glad to have seen this place at last, all the same.

Don't let me lose opportunities of seeing you in London before you go.

Arnold

[*Postcard from Ampleforth College, York*]

17 May 1955

You will be glad to hear that *China and the Cross* was accepted by Longman's two days ago. The conclusion of 25 years' work.

Thank you for your letter.

I must see you before final departure "the Fall," end Sept.

Yours,
Columba, O.S.B.

The Royal Institute
of International Affairs
Chatham House
10, St James's Square
London S.W.1

24 June 1955

Dear Columba,

I have just come back from a flying visit to Berlin [1] and have found your card from St. Louis. You didn't give your address, so I am sending this via Ampleforth. I do hope I shall see you before your final departure—which will be far from being a final separation between you and me, as I hope to go on paying visits to America, while you will be coming back here periodically, no doubt.

I wonder if any of the original nucleus of French Catholic population still survives.[2] They must have been very few, and have been swamped by Southern Americans even before the Civil War.

Last time I was in Berlin was in Feb. 1936—the time I saw Hitler,[3] the week before he went into the Rhineland. Driving down the Wilhelmstrasse was like coming back after 1,000 years. One felt the judgment of God. It was like something in the Old Testament: the Cities of the Plain, or Jericho.

My prayers for the prospering of your great undertaking.

Yours affectionately,
Arnold

1. Where A.J.T. delivered a lecture at the Freie Universität on 20 June 1955.

2. St. Louis was founded in 1764 by Pierre Liguest Laclède (1724–78), who was born in the parish of Bedous, Valle d'Aspe, diocese d'oloron en Bearn, France.

3. Compare A.J.T.'s "A Lecture by Hitler," in *Acquaintances*, chap. 22, pp. 276–95.

6 October 1955 45, Pembroke Square, W.8

Dear Columba,

I was thinking of you a lot these last days, especially yesterday, while Bun was painting me for Chatham House. I hadn't a chance of writing, though, for it was a non-stop performance. We did 20 hours' of sittings in 3½ days.

Well, it is a great enterprise that you are embarked on, and the people in power have perhaps more need of spiritual help than the rest of us. I believe the Americans will have the humility to take the help that you can give them, and this will make the enterprise immensely worth while.

I shall be praying for you. I wish I could visit you at St. Louis on this journey. But my 'schedule' is as full as I dare make it.

Send me your St. Louis address. But I see I have it. I must have taken it that day when we were lunching together.

Yours affectionately,
Arnold

Saint Louis Priory
Mason-Conway Rds.
St. Louis County,
26 October 1955 Missouri U.S.A.

My dear Arnold,

The whole little community, Fr. Luke Rigby,[1] Fr. Timothy Horner[2] and I listened in to your broadcast on one of the first evenings of our arrival.[3] Very many of our numerous friends here did so, too. Your voice sounded very young and alive. It was a joy to hear it. The matter was some of the best thinking you have done, it was straightforward, it had the A.J.T. sweep! it was to the point. I felt you were giving us a send off in *our* work, encouraging us to remember our own heritage, and we were all stimulated.

The little Priory is established in fact, though not in theory—we are not technically sufficient in numbers. But we say the Divine office much as at Ampleforth: Matins and Lauds, 5:20 A.M. After Compline all sing the Salve Regina.

Our friends, of course, are much on our doorstep and have an incredible generosity. The estate unfortunately has swallowed up several hundreds of thousands of dollars to buy (90 acres) and our building program will have to be cautious; and all the better for that.

Now I know what an Indian Summer means. This area is very wooded. The various kinds of oak, the maple and other trees have changed the color of their leaves in a wonderful dazzling way. I suppose one night a great wind will get up and all will be bare.

On several occasions I have had to make little speeches. It has impressed me how my audience responds to the idea of American responsibility and their need for DEPTH in education. These St. Louis leaders in the Catholic section are sick of vast expensive plants and 3rd rate teaching. They seem to have learnt the lesson that education is primarily a matter of the spirit.

In New York we contacted Fr. D'Sousa;[4] he showed us UNO and settled us in the assembly room on the first day of the voting for the non permanent members of the S.C. One sensed there and with tremendous impact, the deep division between east and west. Yet, I also felt that this orderly manner of disagreeing was doing the same work the Parliament at Westminster took several hundreds of years to achieve. The question is: are there any or enough common factors to make for the survival of UNO. We are all men. No room to run down that track!

My love to you both,

Yours affectionately,
Columba

1. Jerome Luke Rigby, O.S.B. (1923–); St. Benet's Hall, Oxford; prior of the St. Louis Priory since 1967.

2. Michael Timothy Horner, O.S.B. (1920–); Christ Church, Oxford; read Greats with distinction; major, Royal Artillery, M.B.E. (1940–46); headmaster, St. Louis Priory School (1955–74); pastor, St. Anselm at Priory since 1981.

3. A.J.T.'s address at Albany; cf. A.J.T.'s letter of 9 November 1955, below.

4. Jerome D'Sousa, S.J.; cf. A.J.T.'s letter of 28 April 1949, above.

Hotel Leamington
Minneapolis, Minnesota[1]

9 November 1955

Dear Columba,

It is tantalising to be so (comparatively) near to you and not to be able to see you, but already you have had experience of what life is like in America: one is stretched to the limit of one's time and strength, and has either to stop or perish when one reaches the line. Many American men perish at the age of 55 to 65 through wearing themselves out.

We go to Chicago tomorrow and sail from New York in the 'United States' on Tuesday (in New York on Monday our address is c/o Dr. Van Dusen, 606 West 122nd St.).

I have been thinking much of you and wondering how it is going. The Americans are humble about the things in which they find that other people have something to tell them, and this will be one of the keys, I believe, to the success of your mission.

At Albany, N.Y., on 19 October I spoke in the Episcopal Protestant Cathedral at their congress on 'the Church and Work,' and my theme was Saint Benedict.[2] When this was broadcast from Schenectady, I asked them to let you know, but the message may not have reached you. If you asked Bishop Richards of Albany, I expect he would send you a recorded copy of my talk.

I had a very large audience here: 8,000 people, including those in four overflow halls, and many thousands were turned away. This makes one feel abashed.

Well, I shall be writing to you as I go along. On 16 February I start on the round-the-world-journey, beginning with Peru and picking up Veronica at Panama on a boat from London to New Zealand. God Bless You.

Yours affectionately,
Arnold

1. On 6 November 1955, A.J.T. delivered a lecture at Minneapolis, which was published as *The New Opportunity for Historians* (Minneapolis, Minn., 1956).

2. Reprinted as A.J.T.'s "Man At Work in the Light of History," in *Man at Work in God's World: Papers Delivered at the Church and Work Congress held in Albany, New York, October 19–20, 1955* (New York, 1956), pp. 3–41.

Saint Louis Priory
Mason & Conway Roads
St. Louis County, Mo.

10 November 1955

My dear Arnold,

Your letter arrived this afternoon. I was delighted to get it. So near. . . ! Yes, your message about the broadcast reached us in time and the little community of three listened—so did half St. Louis. You will find a letter at home, written by me the day after. It is one of the best things you have done. I shall now get in touch with the Bishop of Albany for a copy.

As soon as I can settle down I shall get in touch again with the rector of St. Louis University and get him to suggest a date for Nov. (?) 1956 for you and a subject. I'm inclined to think: History is not bunk, or more politely: the uses of history. But I will get him to write to you.

We *are* settling down but how right you are. Our supporters arrive at breakfast-time, late in the evening, all during lunch. Their energy is inexhaustible, their generosity fathomless—I hope.

There is no doubt our job here, if we carry it out with success, could be of incalculable value. The Americans are so astonishly honest in admitting their need. I think it should be possible to do what we intend. Their architecture is symbolic. They have every gadget, every skill, all the ingenuity, but beauty, poise, seems to elude them. I think we shall build modern and put grace into it.

When you arrive, we shall be in the throes of plans—not yet of building.

Now, neither you nor Veronica must kill yourselves globe trotting. I suspect 8,000 + is audience enough for a month. How splendid, all the same.

God bless you both,

Love,
Columba, O.S.B.

The Royal Institute
of International Affairs
Chatham House
10, St James's Square
London S.W.1

28 November 1955

Dear Columba,

I waited to write till I was back from Ampleforth: I came back this afternoon from a very happy week-end there. I spoke yesterday to the Sixth Form on 'An historian looks at the world today', with a good discussion afterwards, and, the night before, I had a meeting, arranged by Charles Edwards,[1] with the boys who are just going to sit for history scholarships at the universities. I was able to look at Slingsby Banks and the Sheep Walk[2] this time without a twinge, but I did have a twinge whenever I passed your bow-window. This, though, you will allow, was a legitimate one, and quite healthy!

Father Robert met me in York, very kindly; in fact, he drove me both ways. I heard from him about his and Father Richard's reconnaissance to St. Louis in advance.[3]

Well, now the next hurdle is the tour round the world: a thoroughly good thing, but a bit formidable as one approaches it. I shall reckon on visiting St. Louis at the end of Nov. or beginning of Dec. 1957, en route from McGill University, Montreal, to the Rice Institute, Houston, Texas. When I do come, I shall have, among other things, to do something for Bishop Scarlett,[4] the Episc. Prot. Bishop of Missouri, who has been inviting me for years past. By then, the school will be fast rising towards university age, and you will be thinking about entrance to Harvard, etc. Veronica and I (supposing we survive the world tour) are immensely looking forward to the St. Louis date. It will be here in a trice, and can be repeated in more leisurely years in the future.

The penalty for having 'arrived' (as I now seem to have, at any rate in America) is being pre-occupied with engagements, correspondence, and the other petty cares of the World. When these keep me awake at night, that gives me an opportunity of trying to get things into proportion. I start by trying to visualise the original symbol for the Buddha—a blank circle, signifying detachment from material things, and then try to fill this negative circle with a positive turning towards God and a transfer of one's focus from oneself to Him. This is something very elementary for you, but not for me.

My prayers for your success. I believe it will be great and will bring blessings to America, England and the World.

Very affectionately
(American style without any
'yours'),
Arnold

1. Thomas Charles Edwards (1902–77); for many years in charge at Ampleforth of the scholarship VI form in history, "and very successful." (C.C.E.)

2. Compare A.J.T.'s letter of 21 August 1954, above.

3. On 7 December 1954, Ronald Richard Wright, O.S.B. (1907–69), and Francis Robert Coverdale, O.S.B., went to St. Louis on a reconnaissance visit. They returned to Ampleforth fully convinced of the value of the proposed foundations and of the solid support from the local community. This visit was decisive in many ways.

4. William Scarlett (1883–1973); Episcopal bishop of Missouri (1933–53). C.B.P. recalls a conversation with Bishop Scarlett, several years before the date of this letter, in which he disapproved of Rosalind's implicit criticism of her father in her *Good Pagan's Failure* [London, 1939].

Saint Louis Priory,
Mason Road
Creve Coeur, Missouri

4 December 1955

My dear Arnold,

I was delighted to get your letter recording your visit to Ampleforth; it gave me quite a sense of the abbey and the road under St. Wilfrid's window. I am so glad you could make the journey and even more that your soul has come to peace on some of the past. God be praised.

I am seeing the Rector of St. Louis University on the 8th, and I will mention to him that you have certain obligations of friendship with the Episcopalian Bishop of Missouri, and ask him how best we could save you and yet enjoy the pleasure of a talk. There is also the question of where you will stay, but I am taking it for granted that you spend one or two nights with us. When the time gets nearer I shall get in touch with the Bp. of Missouri, under your directions. We shall manage some suitable compromise.

By separate mail I am sending you a copy of our brochure. You are I am sure aware of these money drives. This brochure is part of it. The fortunate element is that the clergy do not have to be much mixed up in it, unlike their poor cousins the priests in England who so far have not cottoned on to getting the laity to do it all. It is interesting: what is done by government aid in England, in many instances is done in America by private subscriptions. A lot of it consists in giving a considerable proportion of what would simply otherwise go in taxes. But enough of that.

I am so glad you are praying—though this midnight time seems most unsuitable; you ought to be asleep. I admit to doing it a bit myself. This stillness and silence are conducive to the contemplative spirit: just as Constantine saw the cross over the sun, you see the cross in the void. We have to have the void to provide place for God and his Cross. I see no incompatibility between the earliest Buddhism as I see it and our Lord. The Buddha seems to have been a wonderful man, seeing beyond the unreality of material things. He was wise too in saying he did not know in what Nirvana consisted, but he knew it was perfect joy. St. Francis, the perfect disciple of Jesus, answers the Buddha across the centuries: perfect joy is the Cross.

Of course there are exaggerations in Buddhist expressions, but a deep truth lies there. It is a preparation for the coming of Christ.

So too Hinduism. If we can see the "incarnations" as longings of the human spirit for the coming of God, rather than historical facts (for India fact or fiction does not seem to be a distinction which has been faced), then basically Hinduism at its best can be a *preparatio animae*. We tend to minimise the significance of myth and they the significance of history.

All this . . . . when you wanted to hear about the Priory. Well, we are starting to build a small cloister building in Jan. to be ready by Sept. A good wooden barn at one end, already. There will be a temporary chapel, a building opposite with an arch as if going into a court-yard will be the entrance, and the space between will be enclosed by two rows of cells with an inside covered but open cloister. This all one storey but in brick with faint echoes of colonial style. This house we are in now will be school. Then when we burst at the seams, the boys will overflow into the cloister; the main monastery be built.[1] The site is splendid and we have 94 acres. We need books. Next time you are at Princeton, send us duplicates. You must have accumulated quite a lot there, and so you'll become a founder.

My love to you and Veronica,
Columba, O.S.B.

Don't overdo it. This may be my last before Christmas, so all God's blessings, Godspeed on the journey. What fun it will be. Give my love to Cuzco.

1. "This simple scheme came to nothing, because of cost. It was a godsend, as then we went straight into our final plan." (C.C.E.)

SEVEN

1956–60

A.J.T. goes round the world; Pitcairn Island to Australia; Abbot Sogen Asahina and Zen Buddhism; "there must be a spiritual vacuum in Japan"; war threatened over Suez; "we and France are now finding our true level;" A.J.T. visits the priory of St. Louis; "the Lebanese civil war . . . is a French legacy"; a formal correspondence on comparative religion; Buddhism and Christianity; "reality is in touch with all Its creations"; Rosalind's farming partner; A.J.T. at the University of Peshawar; "I think Scotland after the Forty-five must have been in about the same state as Western Pakistan today."

R.M.S. Rangitata
still three days
from Auckland

14 May 1956

Dear Columba,

Though there is no news on the Pacific, I am going to write to you now, because one is no sooner on land than one is in a rush. Veronica and I made our rendezvous all right—off Cristóbal, at the Atlantic end of the Canal.[1] I drove across the Isthmus the evening before: it takes only one hour and ten minutes on the North-American-built concrete road. I got on board early in the morning, so we went through the Canal together. The Canal itself, and the apple-pie order of the administrative and military headquarters of the Zone, at the Pacific end, give one a most impressive sense of the power and efficiency of the United States. On board, we have been having a much needed holiday. I have re-started writing a Home University Library history of Ancient Greek Civilization,[2] which I originally started in July 1914. Since August 1914 I have never managed to get back to it till now.

We have only seen three islands since we left behind the cluster at the Pacific mouth of the Canal: one of the Galápagos, Pitcairn, and a French one called Rapa—a cluster of collapsed volcanoes, with a fantastically jagged sky-line. At Pitcairn we anchored for a couple of hours, and the amiable and rather child-like descendants of the mutineers came on board to sell us their bananas and oranges. The surplus population emigrates to Norfolk Island: they are prepared to go a couple of thousand miles to find another island that is almost as remote as Pitcairn is.

I am eager to hear news of your trials and triumphs: no doubt you are having both: my address in Australia from 29 May to 18 August is c/o Miss Nance Dickins, Australian Institute of International Affairs,[3] 177 Collins Street, Melbourne C.I.

Victoria. This will be our headquarters, but we actually land at Sidney, and shall be staying there with a nephew of G.M.'s, Pat Murray,[4] who is a professor at the University of New South Wales. I am fond of him and his wife, and I haven't seen them for years, so I look forward to this.

It is odd, actually carrying out this great journey after having planned it for so long. The Andes were fascinating and vastly instructive for me. But I do also feel a distinct relief at having got my head out, undamaged, from between the feline goddess's paws. The savage power of Nature there is really terrifying: in the desert, in the jungle and in the mountains—I have sampled them all. Compared to the Andes, I expect New Zealand will feel like Surrey.

With my prayers for the prosperity of the Priory,

Yours affectionately,
Arnold

1. A.J.T. memorialized this trip in a series of articles written, en route, for the *Observer* and published as *East to West: A Journey Round the World* (London, 1958).

2. *Hellenism: The History of a Civilization* (New York, 1959).

3. A.J.T.'s Dyason lectures, delivered during this visit, were published as *Democracy in the Atomic Age* (Melbourne, 1957).

4. Patrick Desmond Fitzgerald Murray (1900–67); son of Gilbert Murray's brother Sir John Hubert Murray, who had been lieutenant governor of New Papua; Patrick Murray was then professor of zoology, University of Sydney (1949–60); *Bones* (Cambridge, 1936); *Biology* (London, 1950).

c/o Professor P. D. F. Murray
45 Vaucluse Rd.
Vaucluse, Sydney
N.S.W. Australia

4 June 1956

Dear Columba,

I was very glad to get your letter of 13 May.[1] Here we are, staying with Rosalind's cousin Pat, the professor of Zoology at the University of Sydney, and son of Hubert Murray, G.M.'s brother, who was Australian governor of Papua for many years and was notable for being a father to the natives.[2] Pat and Marjorie Murray were at Cambridge between the Wars, and I am fond of them both, so it is a pleasure to be staying with them. Oswald Wolkenstein sends you his very best wishes: he is now a wool-buyer in Sydney: most amusingly Australianised. We sat talking about Ampleforth as we looked across Sydney Harbour to the Bridge. Cristoph is now a G.P. in Winnepeg, with a French Canadian wife.[3]

I am very glad to hear your good news about the Priory and the School: it is a happiness to be doing something that is unquestionably good and worth while. You will enjoy teaching Ancient History. On the boats between Panama and N.Z. and N.Z. and here I was writing a Home University Library history of Greek Civilization (post-Minoan to 7th century of our era) which I began in July 1914. I was brought to a stop in August 1914 and have never got down to it again till now: of course it is working out rather differently from the original plan. When it is published, a copy will be coming to you. I am delighted that one of your two books is out and the other so well on the way.

Veronica and I had our blood pressures taken here the other day. Hers is down to 180 (from 220 (!) a week before sailing) and mine to 135 (from 180 when I crumpled up after my 950 miles drive in a land-rover along the Pan American highway in Peru).

An Historian's Approach to Religion[4] is being published in September, *Somervell* II[5] in the spring of 1957, and the *Gazetteer*[6] about the same time. I shall be sending you copies.

Sydney, with its two million inhabitants spread over 20 miles in every direction, is rather overwhelming. The city dwarfs the harbour, which does not seem so vast as I had imagined it from my old great uncle Harry's description of it. He used to come here in command of an East Indiaman in the 1850's.

Write to me c/o Miss Nance Dickins, Australian Institute of International Affairs, 177 Collins St., Melbourne, C.I. Victoria: this will find me till about 18 August.

Yours affectionately,
Arnold

1. Missing.
2. Compare A.J.T.'s letter of 14 May 1956.
3. Compare C.C.E.'s letter of 12 May 1940, above, telling of the internment of the Wolkenstein brothers, then students at Ampleforth.
4. *An Historian's Approach to Religion* (London, 1956).
5. D. C. Somervell's *Abridgement* of vols. VII–X of *A Study of History* (London, 1957).
6. A.J.T. and Edward D. Myers, *Historical Atlas and Gazetteer*, vol. XI of *A Study of History* (London, 1959).

The Australian Institute
of International Affairs
177 Collins St.
Melbourne, C.I. Victoria, Australia
(This will reach me till 17 August)

15 July 1956

Dear Columba,

I have just had your letter of 6 July (? or 7 June), following one of 24 May, and your card from Florida.[1] Once one is in the U.S.A., one gets on the move in a big way. You must have been nearly as hot in Florida as we were at Panama. I am so glad that *Sheepfold and Shepherd* is out and the China book so nearly out at last. I am also delighted that you are reviewing my *Religio Historici* in '*Books on Trial*'.[2] In the present state of the World we cannot, I think, expect agreement, but we *can* try to understand one another's different approaches. Your explanation, to Catholics, of my approach will be made with the patience and charity that are the saving virtues for the World in our time (perhaps for the World in all times). Where Pascal makes the same points as his secular-minded contemporaries, it is interesting, because it tells us what were the common problems that were exercising *all* the greater minds in Western Christendom in the late seventeenth century. As for the Indian religions and the Judaic ones, I think one has to equate our Judaic God with the impersonal Indian Brahma and Nirvana, and the Indian (and Greek) gods with the order of beings with whom, in the Christian hierarchy, exorcists are expected to be able to cope. The two facets of ultimate reality—personal and impersonal—that the Jews and the Hindus have perceived are, I am sure, only two out of an infinite number. They are to be equated, not only with each other, but with all those others that are beyond the horizon of our finite human minds. What are we turning to now? One has to look back behind our 17th century revolution, and to discover the causes of that, if one is to be able to look into our own future and—what is more important—to have a chance of influencing it. I think history will be important in this next chapter, because learning each other's history is an essential part of getting to understand each other better. But, as we approach towards mutual understanding, I believe our outlook will become less relativist, because I believe we shall come to see more of the underlying common ground between us.

Boddhisattvas seem less heroic than Christ and the martyrs. But then the Indian and Chinese experience of life has been less violent than ours at the Western end of the civilized world. Do you know the story of the Chinese nurse who took service with a cultivated and devout Christian family, whose house was full of reproductions of Italian old masters. She burst out one day that she could not understand how good and responsible parents, like these, could bring themselves to expose their children to these horrible pictures of a criminal being put to death by a form of torture that was happily unknown in the civilized World from which she came! The milder key of the Indian and Chinese part of the World has to be allowed for always.

Yours affectionately,
Arnold

1. The letters are missing; the postcard told of the acceptance of *China and the Cross*.
2. C.C.E.'s review appeared in *Books on Trial* (October 1956), pp. 63–64.

[*Postcard*]

The International House of Japan
2 Oct. 1956
By Air

We got here yesterday, on a French ship from Singapore, via Saigon, Manila and Hong Kong. The President of Vietnam is a fourth-generation Catholic. You would be pleased to see the Church in Vietnam with its Vietnamese bishops as well as priests. It has become a native plant—quite a large minority of the population.[1] We have come through six weeks of hard going in the tropics without mishap.

With our love,
Arnold

1. Compare A.J.T.'s *East to West*, pp. 61–62.

The International House of Japan
2 Toriizukamachi, Azabu
Minato-ku
Tokyo, Japan

15 October 1956

Dear Columba,

I came back here this morning and found your letter of 9 October.[1] I had been at Kamakura (the capital of Japan, virtually, from late 12th to early 14th century) visiting Abbot Sōgen Asahina of the Zen Buddhist Engakuji Monastery[2]—a notable man, full of life and purpose, which shine out through his dancing black eyes. He had called on me at Chatham House about a year ago, and I was pleased to see him again. If all Japanese Buddhist monks were of his kind, the ancestral religion of the Japanese would be helping them in their present need more effectively than it is doing (as far as I can make out so far). It will be interesting to get an impression of what the Hinayana is doing for Thailand and Burma. Six hundred new sects—Buddhist Shinto, and a few Christian—have sprung up in Japan since the War (I am seeing something of one or two of them). They can all raise money. This suggests that there must be a spiritual vacuum in Japan.[3] The crash of the old 'chosen people' militant ideology, at the end of the War, was enormous, and the younger generation rose up in arms against the past without having found anything positive to fill the empty place. In this younger generation, there is a very marked unstiffening. They are enjoying life much more than their elders have ever done, and, in itself, this is good.

What luck about the dates. We get back to England early in August, so we shall certainly meet then: I do look forward to this; it is sooner than I had thought possible. How you have covered the country—Florida a few months ago, and now 'the Coast'. I have been in California three times without yet having seen either the Grand Canyon or the redwoods. You have done it the right way—on your own wheels. This reconnaissance of the West will be valuable to you: it gives you the freedom of the city of America—a big city. I am so glad the two books are coming out soon. If there is still time, would you ask them to send *The Sheepfold and Shepherd* to me at Chatham House instead of No. 45, as No. 45 is let to tenants. I am glad you have been inoculated painlessly with television, for I am sure you will have to do a lot of it, and in America it is an important pulpit. I am glad, too, that you are teaching the boys Ancient History: it takes one out of one's own small time and place. Yes, you ought to include Eastern Asia, if possible. America is the chief representative of the West in Japan, and, sooner or later, she will play the same part in China again.

I am still furious with the Conservatives for having threatened to make war over Suez.[4] It now looks as if they won't be able to do it, but I shall feel uneasy as long as they stay in office. Cyprus was bad enough, by itself.[5] It is sad that we and the French should be clinging to the remains of our empires. It is also strange, considering how successful we have been in making friends with the Indians as a result of our great deed of giving them their freedom. Even the French, who tried to cling on, to the last, to their rule over Indo-China, are recovering the Vietnamian people's friendship now that they have limited themselves to cultural cooperation. On the whole, I do not expect a smash, but feel more melancholy, than before, at the silliness and badness of human nature.

Love from us both,
Yours affectionately,
Arnold

1. Missing.

2. Abbot Sōgen Asahina (1891 – 1979); the Engaku-ji monastery at Kamakura was founded in 1282 by Mugaku Sōgen (Wu-Hsüeh Tsu-Yüan); a graduate of Nippon University (1922); the abbot was president of the Engaku-ji school of the Rinzai sect; member Yokohama Unesco Cooperation Society; *A Comment on Rinzairoku* (Tokyo, 1935).

3. Compare A.J.T.'s *East to West*, p. 74.

4. On 26 July 1956, Egypt had nationalized the Suez Canal.

5. On 9 March 1956, Britain had deported Archbishop Makarios, the spokesman for the Greek Cypriotes who were demanding immediate internal sovereignty.

c/o The British Council
19 December 1956 Rangoon

Dear Columba,

This Christmas letter will not reach you till after Christmas, but I have been on the run, meeting and questioning Hinayana Buddhist monks here and in Mandalay, to try to find out what the Hinayana can do for human beings in the human race's present spiritual crisis. My findings are not very encouraging. The pick of these monks are spiritually noble, but aloof, like the Stoics. I do not for a moment think that Communism is going to hold the World. I believe Hungary is a turning point.[1] They have deprived themselves of their chief weapon, which was their pose as champions against imperialism. The Asian peoples have now seen through this. Judging by Japan, formal Christianity is not going to sweep the World either; on the other hand, the Christian approach to life is making great advances outside the official Christian fold in Japan. Perhaps this will be the next stage in Man's religious history.

Well, since we last wrote to each other we have seen 'the Fall of Britain' (it would be the fall of France too, if a country could fall twice over).[2] I am 100 per cent against the U.K. Conservatives, and on the side of UN and US. I believe UN, with American support, has won a very considerable victory in compelling a pair of middle-sized powers to withdraw. It could not have tried to push the Russians out of Hungary without starting a third world war—Russia being a much stronger power than France and Britain combined—but I do believe we have seen the beginning of the end of Russian imperialism in Eastern Europe as well as French and British imperialism in Asia and Africa. And UN, with American leadership and backing, might become the nucleus of a world government. If one is English it is shocking to see our reputation for good conduct and good sense come tumbling down. Do tell me what it has felt like in St. Louis. I believe the underlying fact is that we and France are now finding our true level, as Japan, Italy, and Germany have already found theirs. It is a painful process, and I am afraid the split in the U.K. will last long and will go very deep, as the issue is a first-class moral one, besides being materially important.

I had news today of one of your old boys, Foll,[3] who is now with the Burma Oil Corporation somewhere north of Mandalay. I was told that he remembered my coming to the House during your time there. I wish I could have met him.

I am making many new connexions and am learning a lot. I feel a great obligation to harvest all this in some way that may be useful to other people. On Saturday we fly to Calcutta: we are now headed westward, but we don't reach London till the beginning of August. I do look forward to seeing you, in England, soon after.

God Bless You.
Arnold

1. On 14 November 1956, Soviet forces had crushed the last rebel stronghold in Hungary.
2. On 30 October 1956, Britain and France had issued an ultimatum to Egypt and Israel to cease fighting and permit a French and British occupation of key points; on the next day U.N. Security Council resolutions to refrain from use of force were vetoed by France and Britain; on 6 November 1956, under pressure from the U.S. and the U.S.S.R., Britain and France acquiesced in a ceasefire; by 22 December 1956, British and French troop withdrawals were completed; the Suez Canal remained in Egyptian hands.
3. Cecil Foll (1923–); member of St. Wilfrid's House; Lieutenant Royal Naval Volunteer Reserve in World War II.

Saint Louis Priory
Mason Road
Creve Coeur, Missouri

14 April 1957

My dear Arnold,

I was thrilled to read your recent article in the *Observer* on Buddhist monasticism.[1] I do hope you are hoarding your experiences and will write a summary of your thoughts on eastern religions today. Did you have any intimate talks with really holy ascetics? It would be interesting to know the nature of their prayer.

This is written, Palm Sunday, and it might reach you in Eastertide; so I wish you *Gaudium paschale*, which is joy in the Resurrection and eternal life and the hope of our Salvation to attain those. It would be interesting to know whether the Buddhist progress is entirely on the natural plane or whether they teach—at least some representative ones—that the goal is beyond and above them and their own powers. Or whether the whole attitude of Buddhism is: there is the answer! it's yours for the picking.

As you know I shall be in England July 9th to August 19 about. The first half I shall be at Ampleforth, so letters will always reach me there; the 2nd half my headquarters will be Flat A, Clare Court, Henley Rd. Ipswich. The way things seem to be going with you, I can see you remaining east for months yet. But it would be a great disappointment if we did not meet.

How is the *Gazetteer*?[2]

We progress slowly. The great thing is that the Priory is established; the divine office is recited daily and we have a Sung Conventual Mass. The little school is winning good opinions. Then outside, we are designing monastery, school and church. The last is most exciting, but the ordinary folk are not, even in America, attuned to a modern style. I hope we have a circular domed church with the altar in the middle. Pier Luigi Nervi[3] of Rome has promised to help in the design. He came to visit us from Chicago where he was judging between 400 memorials for Fermi, the atomic scientist.

The world is in such confusion, the forces of right have so tied their hands, one wonders at times what can be the outcome. You must be particularly concerned at this hour, as the Middle East was your first love and the cement is falling out of that construction.[4] The riddle of the Sphynx remains; what to do in the face of force. God bless you and keep you moving towards Him. My love to you both.

Columba, O.S.B.

1. A.J.T.'s "Turbulent Monks of Burma" (7 April 1957), p. 11.

2. Compare A.J.T.'s letter of 4 June 1956, above.

3. Pier Luigi Nervi (1891–1979); architectural engineer noted for his mastery of new materials, especially reinforced concrete. In the event, the priory chapel was the work of Gyo Obata (1923–), a St. Louis architect, who had designed a circular building with (in the alternative) either triangular or parabolic arches; Nervi preferred the design with parabolic arches as being easier to carry into construction.

4. On 5 March, the U.S. Senate had approved President Eisenhower's request to use U.S. armed force in the event of Communist aggression in the Middle East (the Eisenhower Doctrine); the Israeli-Egyptian disputes over the Gaza Strip had only recently commenced to subside.

c/o Professor Nabih Amin Faris
American University of Beirut
Beirut, Lebanon

30 April, 1957

Dear Columba,

I was so very glad to have your letter. We shall be flying home from Beirut on or about the first August, so we shall certainly be able to see each other between 1 and 4 August.

We are leaving Montreal by train for Saint Louis on the evening of 28 November, en route for Houston, Texas. We should like to spend two nights in Saint Louis, and I will give a lecture if you would like me to. I have asked the New York branch of Wakefield Fortune travel agents to work out a timetable for me, and will let you know the exact times when I have them. I daresay we shall have to take a night train (i.e. on the second of the two nights) in order to arrive in Houston on 1 or 2 December. If we can manage to stay two days minus the second night, we will.

The Sixth Fleet turned up under our windows here this morning. We are off to Damascus tomorrow for our third journey in Syria.

God Bless you,
Yours affectionately,
Arnold

13 May 1957 St. Louis

Dear Arnold:

I was going to—am going to—write: to blazes with lectures. Whether you give one or not, what I want and lots want is a serious—cheerful—discussion in a well-chosen group—university and 2nd level—on the *Teaching of History*. Your book has led to that; and I believe it would be very useful and—why not—"epoch making." We still try to gather people from all over here at the priory 20 +, Catholic, Jew, Lay, Christian or not. It would be a discussion with some prepared and foreknown points.

Now! That means you will just have to stay *3* nights, one, when you arrive, that will be private, you being "acclimated", the second the lecture, the third the Discussion.

If you don't stay 3, then we will force you into the Discussion when you arrive. That would be very unfair; but I suspect you would enjoy it.

At all events we have time to prepare. So say yes to the Discussion and yes to 3 days.

Yours affectionately,
Columba, O.S.B.

(This is a very American-tone letter. You see I have progressed)

Saint Louis Priory
Mason Road
Creve Coeur, Missouri

Feast of St. Bede (27 May) 1957

My dear Arnold:

Perhaps it was an error to address letters to Beirut in answer to yours from there, as you, globe-trotter or flyer that you are, may well be in Timbuctoo by now. So I shall repeat and enlarge and send this to Chatham House.

1. Yes, absolutely delighted that you are coming our way. And we can put you

both up on the property, probably with the Sarmientos (Prof:[1] and wife, who have opted to join our "faculty".) His boy was at Ampleforth, and he professed Spanish at Cardiff. Try to stay 3 nights and we shall not overwork you, and do the last hop by air.

2. We are planning definitely a discussion group at the Priory with as many historians as we can muster to discuss: The Teaching of History.

3. After much discussion, I think the best way of getting you over to St. Louisans is for you to talk over their educational T.V. station, which is sponsored by the whole Community of St. Louis, i.e. the local government and especially the 2 universities, Washington Un. (not sectarian) and St. Louis Un. (which is Catholic). Does this appeal to you?

4. Let me know any individual you are particularly keen to get in touch with, and we'll see what we can do.

For the rest the program is still very fluid, and the T.V. talk is not fixed, awaiting your assent—or dissent. Subject too has been left; but I have one or two suggestions if you have not.

But don't let me turn this too much into an official reception. Let's enjoy ourselves.

In any case there is hope isn't there of our meeting in London. I shall be at Ampleforth 10th July–31st and Norfolk 1st Aug. to about 18th.

Affectionately,
Columba, O.S.B.

1. Eduardo Sarmiento (1907–); professor of Spanish, Cardiff University (1954–57).

c/o Professor Nabih Amin Faris, American University of Beirut, Beirut, Lebanon, till 1 August; then at Chatham House, 10 St. James's Square, London, S.W.1, till we sail for Montreal (McGill University) c/o The Principal and Vice-Chancellor) on 25 October.

1 July 1957

Dear Columba,

Here we are just back from Persia. I am giving the Commencement Address at A.U.B.[1] this evening.

I have had your letters of the Feast of Saint Bede and 13 May.

We are planning to come by train from Montreal via Detroit to St. Louis (CPR/CNR Pool 21; Wabash No. 3), leaving Montreal on 28 Nov. at 11:00 P.M. and arriving St. Louis 30 Nov. at 7:30 A.M. We will try to stay the three nights in St. Louis, (nights of 30 Nov. to 2 Dec.), leaving by Texas Eagle at 5:45 P.M. on 3 Dec. But I must ask the President of the Rice Institute, Houston, if this is all right for him, and if he does want me to arrive in Houston earlier than 4 Dec., I shall have to, I am afraid. However, my first lecture there is not till 6 Dec.

Be very English about it and keep formal engagements down to a minimum.

I should like to discuss the teaching of history and I will do the television.

I do hope we shall be seeing each other at home in Ampleforth.

Veronica went down with jaundice in Baghdad. She is better now, but it takes a long time to get over it.

Persia is marvellously beautiful. Love from us both.

Yours affectionately,
Arnold

1. The American University at Beirut.

14 July 1957 Ampleforth

My dear Arnold,

I have arrived! Temp. 45 rain, no sun—all to my taste. I left Chicago with its temp. at 100 and the plane probably 120. The crossing from Detroit to Prestwick took c. 11 hours, very convenient, but I must be like the cow that objects to the clock being tinkered with, as I felt quite dizzy for two days.

Thank you for your note. I have sent on the good news to Fr. Reinert. We shall prevent things getting too big.

My niece, Caroline Cary-Elwes[1] is going out to Beirut's British Legation in September. She is in that section of the F.O. and lips very sealed. Do prepare the way for her a little. She is unmarried, very young, intelligent and charming. What a "report".

Have you met Michael Cubitt out there?[2] He is "in" oil.

Everyone is enraged by the attack on you by T. Roper.[3] I do not propose to read it. The thing seems to be scandalous and blasphemous. It would be not for you to answer it. But someone should.

Yes, I am longing to see you. It seems probable that I will be in London c. 17th Aug. or 18th. When you arrive I shall write or phone you.

How miserable for Veronica. I do hope she recovers soon. Please give her my real sympathy.

Gilbert Murray's "reception" back into the church visible has caused a stir. I missed Fr. D'Arcy on the wireless, so cannot give you the facts.[4]

If he was conscious, I can believe a man would get insights as he prepared to break through the barrier. If he was unconscious, I can't see how this should have happened unless there had been indications of a change before.

Yours affectionately,
Columba, O.S.B.

1. Caroline Cary-Elwes (1936–); daughter of C.C.E.'s brother Eustace Thomas Cary-Elwes; married Stephen Loftus Egerton (1932–); Trinity College, Cambridge; British ambassador, Baghdad (1980–82); Assistant Under-Secretary of State, Foreign and Commonwealth Office (1982–86); British Ambassador, Saudi Arabia (1986–).

2. Michael Cubitt; cf. C.C.E.'s letter of 17 January 1949, above.

3. Hugh Trevor-Roper (1914–); *Arnold Toynbee's Millennium*, in *Encounter* (June 1957), pp. 14–28. "On the article as a whole, no comment" (A.J.T.'s *A Study of History*, XII: 574). He was among A.J.T.'s least sympathetic critics. He was Regius Professor of Modern History and fellow of Oriel College, Oxford (1957–80); became Baron Dacre of Glanton (life peer) in 1979; Master of Peterhouse, Cambridge, since 1980.

4. This has been questioned; cf. n. 2 of A.J.T.'s letter of 3 September 1939, above; in the *Listener* (22 August 1957), A.J.T.'s broadcast on Gilbert Murray is recorded: "His Catholic childhood had a negative effect on him that was apparent throughout the years during which I knew him. It made him rather sharply critical of religion in its traditional forms" (pp. 267–68).

22 September 1957 St. Louis Priory

Dear Arnold:

Things are getting under way.

1. We have found the ideal people to put you up—

Mr. and Mrs. Leicester Faust[1]
Thornhill
Chesterfield (St. Louis) Missouri

Their house is only 10 minutes away from us by car, on a neighboring ridge. They are kindness itself and would not *lionize* you. They will follow out instructions. Their house overlooks the Missouri River from a bluff—very wealthy but very simple and "homey".

2. The television program (sic) will be—if you are agreeable—you introduced by me, and the heads of the two universities in attendance. After you have spoken for 20 minutes or more, they and I will enter into discussion with you. "U.S. and the Non-Western World". (*Sunday evening*)

3. "The Teaching of History. A small panel of local historians is being gathered. This will be at the Priory *Sunday afternoon*.

4. Between 3 and 2 a *small* dinner party selected by Fr. Reinert,[2] (Pres. St. Louis University).

Saturday evening there will be a dinner party for our friends, again small.

The Leicester Fausts will entertain you on *Monday*, showing you the sights and are dining you.

Tuesday, quiet except for seeing the school and perhaps talking to groups very informally.

What do you think of that?

I so enjoyed our little dinner party at No. 45, and was happy to know that your visit to Palestine was rich in effects on your soul.

God bless you, affectionately,

Columba, O.S.B.

Sat arr. 7:30, taken by me to Leicester Fausts, Lunch.

Afternoon at Priory. Evening a dinner, not big. Sunday "Brunch" with friends 12 A.M.

Afternoon, Teaching of History at Priory

Evening, Guest of Fr. Reinert, Then T.V. Monday, quiet day w/ Leicester Fausts and dinner. Tues. at Priory, morning.

Afternoon quiet—and away 5:45.

Many are looking forward very much to your visit. A Fr. Daves of Rockhurst College,[3] Kansas City v. interested to have you visit there. Can it be done on the way back?

1. Leicester Busch Faust (1897–1979); his wife, Mary Plant Faust (1900–); generous benefactors of the St. Louis Priory.

2. Paul Reinert, S.J. (1910–); president, St. Louis University (1949–74); chancellor (1974–).

3. Rockhurst College, a Jesuit liberal arts college founded in 1914.

Saint Louis Priory
Creve Coeur
St. Louis, Missouri

29 September 1957

My dear Arnold,

Things move fast in the states, so do plans. So all I'll tell you this time is that at last—or rather unexpectedly soon—we have a tenant and you can after all be on the premises and comfortable right here. It was doubly lucky because Mrs. Faust has only just been "de-hospitalized" and Mr. finally put his foot down and said she must not entertain. So that was that, though they would both have loved to do it.

The T.V. is fixed for Monday and the little dinner before given by Fr. Reinert, President of St. Louis University, a very charming man.

Sunday still remains the discussion group here.

Saturday evening I am collecting some very typical Saint Louis men of all groups of interests, to give you a taste of Middle West outlook and reaction. It is being kept to twenty men.

The rest is gloriously fluid—as you asked. Some other things are brewing, but minor.

Martha Love[1] I think was your first love in the Persian Gulf.

Yours in haste and affectionately,

Columba, O.S.B.

P.S. Poor Americans they feel at a loss about Little Rock.[2] It is chastening them, and they are nervous. I say poor dears, as they are victims of circumstances. St. Louis has *much* of the south in its make up. It is something one senses and does not quite understand.

1. Martha Love Symington (1907–) and her brother were on the ship in which A.J.T. had crossed the Persian Gulf in 1929; they also traveled with A.J.T. in India.

2. At Little Rock, Ark., National Guards blocked black students from attending the all-white Central High School; a federal court on 20 September ordered the governor to remove the guards.

Saint Louis Priory
Mason & Conway Roads
Creve Coeur, Missouri

10 October 1957

My dear Arnold,

This is just to keep you up to date.

The TV appearance will be on Monday evening 9:15–9:45 P.M. The subject is as arranged, *The United States and the non-Western World*. The Chancellors of the two universities will be present, Ethan Shepley[1] of Washington University (St. Louis) and Fr. Reinert of Saint Louis University. I shall be in the chair to introduce the speakers. My suggestion is that you take 18 minutes and then they comment with you for the last ten.

Would it be a good thing if they had some warning of the line of your thoughts, so that they could comment extra specially intelligently?

The Sunday discussion on the teaching of History is coming on nicely too. We have four very good men (and a woman) from Saint Louis University and the head of History at Washington is bringing two or three. There remains the question of those from outside. I have not yet written to your friend Dr. Myers.[2] Would I have to pay for his journey? We can certainly find somewhere to put him up. It might seem an extravagance for us to do that. What do you think? The Chicago man I have no longer got, as I have mislaid the paper or letter I wrote his name and address on. If you think he would come, if I paid just his fare, would you please send it to me.

The small dinner with Saint Louis worthies (a few) is also going ahead. For the rest I am damping all other suggestions down as hard as I can.

I know you will be happy to hear that *China and the Cross* has been accepted by Éditions du Cerf in France for publication there.

We are very busy, two classes of high school, building projects, etc.

I am told that the November issue of *Forum*[3] is featuring our building plans, particularly our church. Its basic design was done by Pier Luigi Nervi, the great Italian architect.[4] All these things help our Drive for money—that endless problem. Fortunately in America the people who do all the work on this earthy subject are the lay supporters, God bless them.

I am only writing this thusly (as they say here) because I wanted a record and I shan't do it again.[5]

Yours affectionately,
Columba, O.S.B.

1. Ethan Allen Shepley (1896–1975); St. Louis lawyer; chancellor of Washington University (1954–61).

2. Edward Delos Myers; cf. A.J.T.'s letter of 15 March 1953, above.

3. *Architectural Forum* (November 1957).

4. The basic design of the St. Louis Priory Church was not by Pier Nervi; cf. C.C.E.'s letter of 16 April 1957, above.

5. This letter was typed.

As from Chatham House
10, St James's Square
London, S.W.1, England

20 October 1957

Dear Columba,

It is grievously disappointing! I am in the wars (I mean, my body is), and I shall not be able to come to St. Louis at the end of next month. I have got to have my prostate gland taken out this Wednesday, and they say it will be at least six weeks, perhaps two months, before I can travel. I only knew this yesterday morning, when they took an X-ray and found that my bladder is very far from emptying itself and that an operation is overdue. And they got on the track of this through the after-effects of an operation, which I had at the end of September, for a rupture that I got in the Asian journey. I knew I was going to have this, and it fitted into my 'schedule' all right; but this second, unexpected, one has shot the schedule up.

I am very thankful that neither thing blew up in the middle of the Pacific or in a corner of Indonesia or Persia. They tell me that both may suddenly become critical, and then one must be operated on within a few hours, or one will be for it. Mercifully I shall have had both operations before reaching the critical stage.

Don't give up hope of my being able to come over for a day or two from Washington and Lee University, Lexington, Va., in the spring or early summer. On the other hand, don't count on this, as, after the double operation on top of a long and strenuous journey, I may have to go slow for a time.

Give me your prayers—but I know you are always doing that. I imagine that the prostate operation is serious but not dangerous. However, I always try to live as if my soul had only till tomorrow but my working mind had till eternity. I find I am quite serene, but I am troubled about the strain on Veronica. The journey was too much for her, especially after she had had jaundice in Baghdad.

Well, you will be hearing from her or me about how I am getting on.

With love,
Yours affectionately,
Arnold

45, Pembroke Square
London W.8

28 October 1957

Dear Columba,

Your letter came today[1] and Arnold has asked me to thank you very much indeed for it. He is going on very well indeed—better I think, than the doctors expected—and has kept his strength wonderfully. He rang me up exactly 24 hours from the time of the operation! But he is naturally a lot weaker than after the first one and will need some time to recuperate after he leaves hospital before he is fit to travel and lecture.

He was very sad at having to cut St. Louis out of the schedule, but it is quite possible that we may be able to get over from Lexington, Virginia, during this spring. We can't of course tell yet how much of the programme at Houston he will be able to carry out or how they will feel about a truncated programme if that should be suggested.

It has been an anxious time, but fortunately the operation was quite straightforward and satisfactory and the trouble was just what they thought it was and should now have been cleared up all right. One can't help having a gnawing fear beforehand that it may be worse than they say. Arnold sends his love and will write himself when he can.

Veronica Toynbee

1. Missing.

As from Chatham House
10, St James's Square
London, S.W.1 England

5 November 1957

Dear Columba,

I was so glad to get your letter written on All Saints Day.[1] You needn't wish me to be in Heaven just yet. Anyway, I might not get there; but, if one had to wish every possible candidate to be removed from this world *quam celerrime*, this world would be a still less satisfactory place than it is.

I should have liked to do the article for you, but at present I am incapable of any work: I have the leisure, it is true, but I haven't the strength. I have been making a good recovery from this second operation, but it is more serious than the first and has come on top of it. At the moment I have an infection of the urine which is getting me up seven times a night. They think they have identified it, and say they will kill it. It is easy to get into hospital, but not so easy to get out again. It does one good thing to one—good, especially, at my time of life. It makes one realise one's mortality, and this helps one to see the universe, oneself, etc. in better proportion. I am not in the least losing hold on life, but I understand, better than before, that one's tenure of life in this world depends on a very fragile and imperfectly made material organism.

By now you will have had the foundation stone laid. It will have been a great occasion.

If I do manage to come in the spring, I shall be better equipped to write something about the school after seeing it.

Are the sputniks making a great sensation?[2] For the moment, anyway, the Russians have got ahead of the Americans in the Americans' own special field of technology. I wonder how the Americans are going to take this.

America (plus all the West) and Russia seem to me to be just like each other in the important—and very bad—point of putting nearly all their treasure in material achievements. A competition in ambitious saintliness would be better for the poor human race.

Veronica and I both send you our love.

Arnold

1. Missing.
2. On 4 October 1957, Russia launched *Sputnik I*.

The Royal Institute
of International Affairs
Chatham House
10, St James's Square
London S.W.1

2 January 1958

Dear Columba,

It was a happiness to have your card and the letter written in that scrap of time.[1] I felt bad at your having had none from me; I was just hibernating. I have now emerged with my strength restored.

We fly to New York this Saturday 4 Jan. and to Houston on 6 Jan. (c/o The President, The Rice Institute, Houston, Texas, till the end of the month).[2]

In New York I may be met by E. D. Myers.[3] You will remember what an impression Ampleforth made on him. He will have my 'schedule', and we shall then be able to see whether, and if so when, a visit to Creve Coeur[4] can be fitted in.

Whatever the right attitude about the different religions may be, it is clear now, I think, that our choice is, in some genuine sense, all to become brothers or else to blot ourselves out. This is, of course, a religious issue, not a political or military one.

This is the last rush, so I must stop.

Yours affectionately,
Arnold

1. Missing.
2. See A.J.T., W. V. Houston, R. A. Tsanoff, and Floyd S. Lear, *Conversation on International Affairs*, *Rice Institute Pamphlet* 45, no. 4 (January 1959): 71–81, a panel discussion, Houston, 19 January 1958.
3. Edward Delos Myers; cf. A.J.T.'s letter of 15 March 1953, above.
4. The St. Louis Priory was in this suburb of St. Louis.

Warwick Hotel
Houston, Texas

7 January 1958

Dear Columba,

Here we are: we arrived yesterday afternoon, after leaving London on the night of the 4th. It was hard going, but we have both stood it very well.

I have now seen my list of engagements at Washington and Lee.[1] During the period 2–23 May, I have nothing besides my one lecture a week on Friday evenings. Is that a possible month for you? If it is, should we aim at putting in a night or two at Creve Coeur between 2 and 9, or between 9 and 16 May?

I am provisionally keeping the W. and L. Spring holidays at the end of March and beginning of April for a dash to Guatemala, where we ought to have been at this moment according to our original schedule.

I have been overtaken here by an invitation from the St. Louis Council on World Affairs (a Miss Margaret Herrmann). I will not answer it, pending hearing from you, as I am afraid that, if I got entangled in it, it might swamp my doings with you, which are, of course, my reason for wanting to visit St. Louis. The C. on W.A. sounds high powered but low paying. If they had suggested paying our fares from Virginia and back, or part of them, that might have made them worth considering.

May I leave it to you to tell me what to do about this, or to deal with Miss Herrmann direct, if you prefer.*

Address from beginning of February: c/o Professor E. D. Myers, 301 Jackson Avenue, Lexington, Va.

Love from us both,

Yours affectionately,
Arnold

*I cannot answer her without letting her know that I shall probably be in St. Louis, but I can plead convalescence as a polite ground for refusing.

1. A.J.T. was visiting scholar in residence: "The Role of the Lawyer in a Changing World," XV, *Washington and Lee Law Review*, no. 2 (Fall 1958): 188–97 (a colloquy between A.J.T. and John J. McCloy).

c/o The President's Office
The Rice Institute
Houston, Texas

11 January 1958

Dear Columba,

I have had your letter of 9 January.[1] Splendid, let us aim at the days between 2 and 9 May.

Just in case I might be crossing the wires (I am pretty sure I am not), I am writing to E. D. Myers at Lexington, Va., who is keeping my schedule there, asking him to let you know if I have any engagement between 5.00–7.00 P.M. Friday 2 May and the same hour 9 May at Washington and Lee.

I am also asking him if he can find out from a travel agency in Lexington about the journey from L. to St. L. and back. I take it we shall have to go to Washington, D.C. and fly from there, but Roanoke, Va., might be an alternative.

I should doubt our reaching St. Louis by lunch time Saturday 20 [*sic*] May, but I haven't an idea.

I am writing to the St. Louis Council on World Affairs, excusing myself.

I am not yet American enough to talk to you by telephone, but I am losing no time in writing.

With love,
Arnold

1. Missing.

Washington and Lee University
Lexington, Virginia

7 February 1958

Dear Columba:

Following up my letter of 11 January, this is to ask whether you have an approximate date of the schedule that you would like for my visit during some of the days between Friday, 2 May and Friday, 9 May.

I gather from your letter of 9 January[1] that you would probably like us to come for the weekend, traveling on Saturday, 3 May.

I am writing now because I have had a renewal of an old invitation from the University of Louisville. Louisville is pretty well on the way between Roanoke and St. Louis and I should rather like to stop off there and keep this engagement—whether on the outward journey or on the return one. Incidentally, the fee would more than pay for our round-trip fare to St. Louis, which is a consideration.

So, if you could give me an idea of the dates you would like us to come so that, whether going or coming, I could stop off in Louisville on a weekday, I would then write to the Louisville people and suggest this.

If we are to come to you on the weekend, it looks as if stopping off in Louisville on the return journey would be the most convenient.

We had an agreeable journey from Houston here with stops at New Orleans and Atlanta, and are now settled into a lovely house with a view of mountains all around. We do enormously look forward to seeing you and to seeing the Priory.

Yours affectionately,
Arnold Toynbee

1. Missing.

Washington and Lee University
Lexington, Virginia

15 March 1958

Dear Columba:

I was so glad to have your letter of March 13th[1] except for the news about Father Ian.[2] I am glad he is now out of the critical state but no doubt it will take him sometime to recover. Please give him my sympathy and best wishes. I am so sorry about this.

I am enclosing a note of my ideas for the discussion on the teaching of history.[3]

Let me know if this does not meet your needs.
What fun it will be to be with you again.

Yours affectionately,
Arnold

1. Missing.
2. Ian Petit, O.S.B.; cf. C.C.E.'s letter of 16 June 1942, above.
3. A.J.T.'s note follows.

Notes for Discussion on the Teaching of History

The teaching of history in One World is a problem which we have to solve in our time, but it presents formidable difficulties.

In the days of local isolation, the field to be covered in the teaching of history was more manageable. We could concentrate on the history of our own country (e.g. the United States or China), take a side glance at the histories of other countries of the same civilization (e.g. the other Western countries or other East Asian countries), and peer back into our religious and cultural background (Israel, Greece, and Rome, or classical Chinese culture and Buddhism). The whole could be taught and learned as a single story in each case.

Today we all are vitally concerned with the other regions, civilizations, and religions of the World, and therefore also with their histories. East Asian students of history can no longer afford to ignore Western history; nor Western students to ignore East Asian history, and so on for all the principal religions, civilizations, and regions.

This need is a practical and a pressing one. But it requires a panoramic view, and this is difficult for both students and teachers to attain. There is a risk that our knowledge may be too superficial and our presentation too schematic.

This difficulty is sharpened by the current tendency of historical research. While the present-day world in which we live has been rapidly moving towards unity, the experts in historical research have been moving towards a greater division of labour and towards a breaking-up of their fields into smaller and smaller insulated units.

One cause of this tendency towards increasing specialization has been the rapid increase in our knowledge of details, owing to the opening of archives and the progress of archaeological discovery.

Thus, at the very time when, for urgent practical reasons, we have to broaden our field of historical study from some single country or region to the world itself, the overwhelming increase in our knowledge of detail is making it difficult for us to master the history even of a single province or parish.

Therefore our problem is to find some way of seeing history as a whole without seeing it only superficially and distortedly, and of mastering the details accurately without closing our eyes to the general picture.

What solution can we find for this rather formidable problem? My own suggestion would be that our education in history should now take the form of a combination of two approaches:

(i) We should teach world history with the broadest sweep—giving students a picture of the whole, though at the same time putting them on their guard against the risk of superficiality and distortion.

(ii) We should also teach the history of some special area in some special period, 'in depth',—giving the student an opportunity to master this fragment thoroughly and to learn something about the methods and the virtues of the expert specialists. At the same time we should put students on their guard against the risk of distortion that arises through artificially isolating a fragment of history from its context.

If we combined these two kinds of teaching, I think we could make each of them serve as a corrective to the drawbacks of the other kind, and this, in itself, would be a valuable intellectual training.

Washington and Lee University
9 May 1958 Lexington, Virginia

Dear Columba,

The time, which seemed so nice and long while I was looking forward to it, came and went in a flash. It was sad to have to leave, but I have come away with so much that will last, and I would not have missed this for anything. To see you again was the same happiness for me that it always is, and also to see 'you-all' (the Virginian second person plural), for you have certainly planted another Ampleforth at Creve Coeur, and the spirit is there whatever Father Bede may say about the landscape (to my mind the country is beautiful in its own way, and gives a fine setting for what you are building there).

I hope you won't be ground down by public relations, drives, and driving. These are unavoidable American institutions, but they do shorten American laymen's lives. I am amazed at the roots you have struck in so short a time. Educating the benevolent oligarchs, whose friendship and confidence you have won, is as important as educating the boys, and I suppose you are educating the oligarchs quite a lot, by example. It says a good deal for them that they realised that they needed what Ampleforth had to give, and that they took the initiative in asking for Ampleforth's help. You couldn't have started at a more auspicious moment, or have forseen what a favourable one it was going to be.

I suppose America is going to change her ideal. The post–civil war ideal of making one's private fortune in business and then partially repaying society by doing good works (which, like money, gives power) won't, I think, go on being satisfying, and it certainly won't appeal to the human race in general. So probably there will be a new version of the American way of life, and you will have a hand in shaping it. Didn't Roosevelt say, when he started 'lend-lease' that he was 'taking the dollar sign out of Anglo-American relations'? Perhaps you will be able to help the American people to take the dollar sign out of their own life, and leave the generous and idealistic traditions in American life to run on unalloyed.

We were kindly treated at Louisville, but we dropped out of the plane into a non-stop programme beginning with a TV conversation with one of those glamorous professional women that only exist in America. We are now back here in our lair, not the worse for the journey.

I shall be writing to Father Abbot.

God bless you and what you are doing, which is important for the World because it is important for America.

Yours affectionately,
Arnold

Saint Louis Priory
Mason & Conway Roads
Creve Coeur, Missouri

13 May 1958

My dear Arnold,

Thank you for coming: "*pleurs de joie*", Thank you for your enthusiastic and reassuring letter. Sometimes one wonders what is being created here. But if you see a beginning of a new Ampleforth, that is reassuring.

Even more important for your visit—you did enjoy it! I was afraid we did not guard you enough. I apologize for Sunday. But even that evening must have been an experience of America you don't often get; and it was my excuse for "using" you for our D Drive. The rest was just to give you a picture of our strange and fascinating and often absurd situation.

Had I to arrange it again I would have forced Fr. Luke to arrange quiet dinners down at the Gallagher house. But he already was expending himself to the limit. Yours to him he treasures, as well he might. And you treasure the memories of his labours. If ever a monk thought every guest was Christ, it is Fr. Luke.

The dollar atmosphere is depressing. But normally the lay folk fight it out among themselves. The trouble is, we are expected to be nice to those who will be "nice" to us. That is a revolting way of living. We try to be nice to all. Saint James' Epistle is salutary reading in our situation.

It was marvellous seeing you. But it passed so quickly, and so wastefully . . . these dinners! Now that you know the way, we must repeat the visit. I am sure Chancellor Shepley would love to have you lecture there at Washington University, even if Fr. Reinert is too timid. But come without lecture on your way to Los Angeles, or Honolulu.

Did you think there was anything in my thought of an exchange of letters on Christianity and world religions? *Be quite honest.* I am no match, but with time and help, I could say some things of value, and we would find much common ground and where the key difficulties were, if nothing else.

My love to you both,
Columba, O.S.B.

Washington and Lee University
17 May 1958 Lexington, Virginia

Dear Columba,

Well, if I am still in this world the one certain thing on my agenda is that I shall be coming to Creve Coeur again, and, I hope, more than once.

What you may be able to help to do, incidentally, is to help American boys to have a new ideal for a hero, and so to have at least an alternative to the ambition to go into business and 'make good' in that. The successful American business-man is obviously generous with his wealth and public-spirited in his ideas of how to use it: this is expected of him, and he expects it of himself. But his *first* aim is to make his fortune, and he thinks he has a right to use the power which his money gives to make America safe for her rich men. So his idealism is within limits, and I suspect that some of the startling unpopularity of this country in Latin America, and now in Canada too, is due to trade policies, forced on the Administration by business interests, which the American public is hardly aware of but ought to be aware of. Government by the rich with the consent of the governed (and they undoubtedly have their consent and respect and even admiration) isn't a system that will see America through.

What an opportunity you have with a school that is a consequence of a monastery. The possibility of the religious life is always present as an alternative to the business career. Of course the majority of boys wouldn't aspire to the religious life and wouldn't qualify for it. But they might leave the school with a kind of 'third order' ideal of how they might live in the world. And I am sure what America needs now in large numbers, abroad as well as at home, is a large number of Americans whose ideal of a secular career is service to God and man first and making one's living as an incidental necessity. I believe you will produce 'alumni' with some new American ideal on these lines.

The exchange of letters: it wouldn't be a question of who was a match for whom, as we should be debating, not to win, but to seek agreement in the Truth. If we try it, shall we find ourselves building a bridge or find ourselves getting dug into positions that can't be brought together beyond a certain degree? Well, one never ought to shrink from discussion for fear of its not turning out as one would like. So let us try, and you start, because the idea of the exchange of thoughts is in your mind. We can take our time, so we can give ourselves time to meditate on it as we go.

The news from Lebanon and Algeria is as bad as can be.[1] By this morning we may know whether Massu is going to do what Franco did. The Lebanese civil war, by the way, is a French legacy. In 1920 General Gouraud[2] in order to weaken Syria, doubled the size of Lebanon by forcibly adding to it a Muslim population as large as the original Christian one. The French policy is now coming home to roost, and it is the Lebanese Christians who are going to pay, poor wretches.

We are feeling quite sad that this visit to America is coming to an end, though it will do us good to have a long time in England with no publicity and no schedule. The Americans are a lovable people, and far the best of the possible candidates for taking the lead in the World. Do you think they will be able to rise to the occasion?

This time I am less confident about that than I have been up to now, but not less eager to see them succeed.

God bless you.

Yours affectionately,
Arnold

1. On 9–13 May 1958, there were riots in Beirut; on 15–19 July, U.S. troops landed in Lebanon. On 15 May 1958, the Algiers committee of public safety headed by Brigadier General Jacques Massu announced its intention of governing Algeria.

2. Henri Gouraud (1867–1946); conqueror of Mauretania; high commissioner of Syria after World War I.

Saint Louis Priory
Mason & Conway Roads
Creve Coeur, Missouri

27 May 1958

My dear Arnold,

Your reflections on the place of St. Louis Priory are so penetrating and helpful, I typed them out for the Fathers—and gave a conference to them on the gist of your thoughts. Thank you. I have, in fact, several times discussed with the boys: who is a great man. It opens my eyes—and theirs.

I am so glad you are prepared to cooperate in a series of letters. I am considering your remarks. They are basic to success, and after much more thinking I'll write you No. 1. It will outline themes, as I see them, and ask you for suggestions and comments.

But now is overfull of this and that. A retreat is in the offing, end of term too. So for the time being good bye—and a happy home coming to England.

Washington Un. would like you to lecture. I think I'll get wheels going for 1960.

De Gaulle![1] Like Napoleon on his return from Egypt? Like the calm before the tornado. After de Gaulle?

Adios,
Columba, O.S.B.

1. On 31 May 1958, at the time of troubles in Algeria, Charles de Gaulle (1890–1970) was named premier of France.

Saint Louis Priory
Mason & Conway Roads
Creve Coeur, Missouri

23 June 1958

Dear Arnold:

You remember when you were here in May I suggested we might carry on a slow-motion correspondence on a number of questions that arise out of your study of history and other writings. You agreed; so here is the first of the series, and like a preface it is almost impossible to write until the whole series has already been written. One has to take the plunge, so I will attempt to outline some of the topics without going into them in any detail and then you might comment on those before we get down to any of them.

The thought that instigated my suggestion was this: your study of history—of course it wasn't alone—has broken down barriers between the various parts of the world. Very many people now realise that we are all one world, very close to one another, and that we have to live together. That means understanding one another. The second great thing your book did, so it seems to me, was to make plain, after many years of materialism and refusal to accept the importance of religion, that the vital element in cultures, and therefore today, is the religion that underlies each culture. Now, as you show, we must understand one another across the world; therefore it is one another's religion that we must understand.

However, you go further and claim quite rightly that if we are to appreciate all the good that exists in other parts of the world, in some way or other these religions must come to terms. In fact one of them may supersede all the others, and from a purely historical viewpoint it might seem, on the contrary, that they might all coalesce. There are, however, other ways in which these religions might meet.

Now it is all this that I think we might discuss. I do not think we need to be afraid it would turn into an argument. A Christian, and a Catholic, has a great deal to learn in how to approach other religions, and there is certainly a great need for analyzing the relationship, for instance, between the Christian revelation and Greek thought, Christian revelation and the Confucian teachings, and then perhaps applying the same principles to Christian revelation and Hinduism, Buddhism, and Islam.

I think these are enough to begin with and perhaps you would now comment on that, and in my next letter we might agree to a plan.

Yours affectionately,
Columba, O.S.B.

Hall Beck Cottage
Hallbeck
Killington
Kirkby Lonsdale
Westmorland

12 October 1958

Dear Columba,

How awful: this is the date, and here is your letter of 23 June waiting at my elbow, unanswered, all this time. I am afraid this certainly has been 'slow motion' on my side. You and the letter have not been out of my mind, as you may imagine, but I have been engrossed in getting my volume of reconsiderations[1] under way; and, as the earlier part of this covers the same ground as our correspondence will cover, I haven't been able to write about the same thing in two versions at the same time. One thing that I will certainly do is to send you a fair copy of these chapters, as soon as I have one. Meanwhile, I will report the points that I have been thinking about.

(i) I have been trying to find a definition that applies to *all* the higher religions. I think the revolutionary new thing about all of them is that they have had a *direct* vision of absolute spiritual Reality, instead of seeing it, as it had previously been seen, through the medium of the economic and political life of some particular tribe. This has two effects: (i) religion becomes separate from the secular elements in culture, and sets up separate 'ecclesiastical' institutions of its own; (ii) it becomes universal: truth and salvation for all men, and its institutions become universal too.

(ii) I have been trying to define my own position. I think I am a 'trans-rationalist'.[2] I have tried rationalism and found it good as far as it goes, but also found that it can give no account of the spiritual presence, higher than man, behind the phenomena. It just has to ignore this, and to ignore the—rationally unverifiable—private personal experiences—from the prophets and founders of the higher religions onwards—on which the belief in the existence of this spiritual Reality is founded. I hold this belief (on the strength of just a touch of the direct experience) myself.[3] This links me with my fellow 'trans-rationalists' who hold the higher religions in their traditional forms. But I haven't gone back to any of the traditional forms, and seem unlikely to. All the same, I am definitely and, I expect, permanently, on the 'trans-rationalist' side of the line, and I believe this is a line that matters more than the other line between orthodox 'trans-rational' positions and unorthodox ones.

So much for the moment. Have you and the other Fathers been doing another enormous drive—to Hudson's Bay or the Isthmus of Tehuantepec? And how is the building getting on? And will your numbers this semester be 120 or even more? We have been here since the beginning of August—enjoying being sedentary, however much rain. I made a dash to Boston, Mass., at the beginning of last month, to speak at the 50th anniversary of the Harvard Business School[4]—leaving this cottage at midday on a Wednesday, and re-entering it the next Monday evening: ultra-American.

Veronica has been rather below par after gastric flu followed by a lingering cough. We have been having to keep her blood-pressure at bay with that Indian drug. She has also snapped a tendon in her top middle-finger joint, right hand, pushing a chair-cover down into a chair, and the finger is in plaster for six weeks.

My very best wishes to the Fathers. We both often look back, with happy memories, to our visit.

Yours affectionately,
Arnold

1. To become vol. XII of *A Study of History*.

2. Compare "The Issue between Trans-rationalists and Rationalists," in ibid., pp. 68–80.

3. Compare A.J.T.'s letter of 5 August 1938, above: "The recovery of a belief in God came through an experience of help in withstanding a very strong temptation."

4. The basis of A.J.T.'s "Thinking Ahead: Will Businessmen Be Civil Servants?" *Harvard Business Review* 36, no. 5 (September–October 1958): 23 ff.

16 October 1958 Saint Louis Priory

My dear Arnold,

Almost on the same day I got your letter and your new book.[1] So I have been enjoying myself travelling by proxy round the world, nosing about ruins, dreaming on top of ziggurats, peering through that veil at other religions. Congratulations, it really has the exhilaration of discovery, rediscovery and adventure. I think I chuckled most when at the last moment you did find a way up to the Cedars of Lebanon. I was impressed by your bare footed pilgrimage in Ceylon. Think of setting off on foot as the Nestorian pilgrims did from Peking in the Middle Ages to view and pray at the Holy Places. I thought your picture of the two of you "indomitable G.T. ers" going down to Aqaba perfect! The Indian, Chinese, and Japanese sections were full of the future. The trouble is that, what is now tiny will be big later, and we cannot see it. Curiously enough today I have a letter from Fr. Bede Griffiths, who is founding a monastery in Hindu India, living the life much as Ricci would have had him do. (Did you read his *Golden String*).[2] He fears a Communist ending to the present situation.

Many thanks indeed for a most delightful book. I have not begun to say all the things I liked about it.

Your letter will have to wait for a full think, though. When you next write please tell me which religions you are including this time in "higher religions." I have tried to do what you describe: find a definition. My difficulty is that whatever *definition* one gives, one has to push one of the great religions out. Buddhism is the most "slithery." God seems to be absent. Or is that an error on my part? Is it, Buddhism—or at least the Buddha—taking God as there and refusing to speak of him?

I would like to say that the higher religions are those that proclaim The One God and our obligations. That is a very Western way of putting it.

Your definition has this *excellent* element that it gives the purpose of it all: UNION WITH GOD. That is proclaimed certainly in a number of the Higher Religions. That fact may well be the bridge. All the sacraments, including the greatest—that of the Incarnation—are NOT ends in themselves, but means to *Getting Back to God*. Your life, if I dare say so, has been like Saint Augustine's, a search for the Absolute Beauty, God Himself. And He has been seeking you, especially when your quest flagged. The rational in us, after all, is only a means too, a ladder, and only one ladder. You have as you say "seen" beyond. All religion, worthy of the name, is a means to lead us there, before God's throne. But most of us, and all, most of the time, can expect the Vision only beyond. "Yonder," as Hopkins calls it.

God bless you both. Tell Veronica I shall keep her in my prayers. She is a heroine!

Affectionately,
Columba, O.S.B.

1. A.J.T.'s *East to West*.

2. Bede Griffiths, O.S.B. (1906–); pupil of C. S. Lewis; convert to Catholicism at Oxford; now head of a Christian Ashram, Shantivanam (forest of peace), near Madurai; *The Golden String* (London, 1954); *Christian Ashram* (London, 1966); see C.C.E.'s letter of 16 April 1973, below.

The Royal Institute
of International Affairs
Chatham House
10, St James's Square
London S.W.1

24 October 1958

Dear Columba,

I am so glad you like the book. I was thrilled at seeing with my own eyes so many places that I had cared about so long, and I wanted to communicate what I was feeling.

The question you are raising in your letter is whether the idea of personality is of the essence of the nearest approach that human beings can make towards a vision of Spiritual Reality. I do not think it is. I think 'It' with a capital 'I' goes deeper, and this vision is common to *all* religions and philosophies.

Reality is in touch with all Its creations, and must have a facet with which each of them can communicate with It. Since human beings are persons, It must have a personal facet looking towards them, as it has others for animals, vegetables, minerals, gases, and so on. But this facet gives us access at the cost of anthropomorphism—i.e. of a vision of Reality in *our* image, which is a very limited one. So it impoverishes Reality, and that is why the vision of It seen by the Judaic religions seems crude and childish to people in the Indian tradition—and also to people in the Chinese tradition, for here, too, the cable of personality was given up, for wireless communication with 'It,' at an early stage.

We do not know what the Buddha thought about Spiritual Reality, because he always refused to talk about it. He thought of metaphysics as escapism—a soft alternative to the hard task of getting out of sensuous existence into Nirvana by spiritual exercises.

We leave here tomorrow, go to Bonn for a week to stay with the Myerses,[1] and shall be back at 45 Pembroke Square from 4 Nov. onwards.

We went over to see Rosalind and her two farms the other day. Her American partner[2] is a very nice man indeed, and I should guess that she is now happier than she has ever been, which makes me happy.

My cousin Edward Frankland,[3] of Ravenstonedale, has just died of cancer. He died finely, thinking only of giving the least trouble possible, and taking pleasure in other people's affairs. I shall miss him greatly. He was about four years older than me. We had many interests in common.

Veronica is decidedly better than at the beginning of August. She has a greater reserve of strength. Her finger with the broken tendon will still be in plaster for another 3½ weeks. She is very gallant about doing things, nevertheless.

Love from us both,
Arnold

1. Edward D. Myers; cf. A.J.T.'s letter of 15 March 1953, above.

2. Richard James "Stafford" (1905–81); this name had been adopted by Richard Kehoe, a scholar at the Westminster Cathedral Choir School and at the Dominican School at

Hawkesyard; in 1927 he entered the Dominican Order and became a distinguished scriptural scholar at Oxford; like Matthew Arnold's scholar-gypsy, he left Oxford in mid-career; he became a shepherd and farmer in the Cumberland fells.

3. Edward Frankland (1884–1958); A.J.T.'s first cousin; cf. A.J.T.'s *Experiences*, p. 294, n. 1: "Edward fulfilled himself as a novelist, an artist, a gardener, a farmer, a forester, and a deservedly much beloved father"; cf. A.J.T.'s letter of 24 December 1946, above.

Saint Louis Priory
Mason & Conway Roads
Creve Coeur, Missouri

27 November 1958

My Dear Arnold,

Since your last letter we have been moving from one building to another, the new monastery. The process was exhausting, the result a delight. When that happened, Fr. Luke went off for a long break of two months. He has been overdoing it. So that leaves me with a lot. "Thanksgiving" has come round and here is a pause.

My point about Buddhism was that it left God out. Your comment, as far as I can make it out, is: no, it does not leave God out but sees with different eyes, and so not a Person but Id. This is the *via negativa*. It came west with the pseudo Denis.[1] Personally I do not think the two concepts are contradictory or irreconcilable, nor do I see that the *via negativa* is un-Christian, provided it is not exclusive. No matter what we posit about God: nature, person, goodness, beauty, power, wisdom, justice, mercy, all these are hopelessly inadequate expressions of the reality, and love too, *Deus caritas est*. I think the point one has to examine is, whether these ideas convey anything of God at all. I know not enough about Buddhism to be sure. You can correct me. In its philosophy, is not all the reality we know unreality? I know that in a sense a Christian might say the same. But we would not say: illusion—rather God said let there be light . . . and He saw it was good.

Is there not a tendency in the East to think of creation, created things, things, almost as a misfortune, a punishment, a prison—this reached into Greece. From that I suspect there follows the impossibility of seeing even the inkling of a positive knowledge about God. When Saint Augustine, in his own mind, conquered Manicheism, he set the scene for an exploration of the reality which is God, with the help of the knowledge we have of all that He made. If He made them there must be something of God, a *vestigium*, in each of them.

On the other hand the West needs the corrective of the East. God is not this, nor that. He is beyond this and that, NOT, however, by denying that He is all that, but by asserting he is All in an infinite and beyond human way, and without any limitation. It is this road that leads to God as love, wisdom, mercy, justice, and beyond all these.

If God gave us life, He must be life at and beyond its highest. The New Testament in order to explain the Redemption gave us knowledge of that life. We have put that in the form of Persons, in view of Christ's assertions of equality with the Father and yet distinctness from the Father.

Whether this knowledge is higher than the knowledge of God's nature, by the various ways, I do not know. It is all mysterious and all helpful, at various times. When I am in the presence of the Holy God, consciously, I do not by any means become always conscious of any Person. Yet, that we know of three Persons in God is a marvellous revelation and does help to explain the coming of Jesus Christ.

I wonder whether what I have written will be of any use to you. Your letter reminded me of the deep, impenetrable mystery of God. *Deus caritas est*—and with that, my love to you both.

Columba, O.S.B.

1. Dionysius the Pseudo-Areopagite; (ca. 500); probably a Syrian; in his treatise on the divine names posited God as τὸ ἕν, the One Being transcending all quality and predication, all affirmation and negation, and all intellectual conception; he sought a synthesis between neo-Platonic and Christian thought; his writings, once thought to be those of Dionysius of Athens, held great authority from the time of Gregory the Great through the Middle Ages; cf. C.C.E.'s letter of 26 June 1971, below.

23 December 1958 Saint Louis Priory

My Dear Arnold and Veronica,

I hope you are well again, and even game for another whizz round the world.

Thank you for that fascinating card, Charles I and his consort. Old Mr. Cave was one of those who rediscovered those bosses. You know his book.[1]

This, you will note, is written before Christmas, but I am afraid will reach you after. At all events, I wish for you a very happy one. Surrounded by children and grandchildren. How soon might it be great grandchildren?

We jog along at the break neck speed of American life. Scarcely are the monastery and Gym finished, and off we go on the Science Building. As the money is slowing up, so will our building, and I don't mind a scrap. Time is an important element in growth, and we need it.

As a historian are you picturing the future with the earth as the old world and other planets in outer space being the 'great powers.' Do you hope there will be so much space that men may cease to quarrel? I do, but expect the source is not without but within. Perhaps we shall find other creatures like ourselves with different modes of communication.

Are you not impressed by Pope John XXIII. It is so just for him to make much of the Lateran.[2] One finds St. Peters' (the building) a stumbling block to non-Catholics. I had forgotten it had been partly built on indulgences until an American Episcopalian friend reminded me, whereas the Lateran is common to us all.

My love—prayers to you both.

Affectionately,
Columba, O.S.B.

How goes the Gazetteer?

1. Charles John Philip Cave, *Roof Bosses in Medieval Churches* (Cambridge, 1948).

2. The Pope had visited the Lateran Basilica, the cathedral church of Rome and accordingly his seat as Bishop of Rome.

The Royal Institute
of International Affairs
Chatham House
10, St James's Square
London S.W.1

2 January 1959

Dear Columba,

I have two letters of yours at my elbow—27 Nov. and 23 Dec.—and my latest act has been to fill in a form under a seven-years' contract for a contribution to rebuilding the church at Ampleforth. This is a bet on the duration of one's life—but perhaps a more pardonable one than the foolish man's bet when he planned to build the big barn.[1]

I can well imagine that you are all being worked off your feet, and the temporary slackening in the arrival of funds is going to be a blessing. Expansion *does* take time to digest: this is an important point that Americans sometimes overlook.

Reality, I suppose, has a personal and an impersonal aspect and an infinite number of other aspects that human minds can't even formulate. Every aspect accessible to us is an avenue for us for communion with Reality. The Buddhists reach it in the form of Nirvana, Christians in the form of the Holy Spirit. What human being is able to say that the avenue opened to him by historical chance has any unique or exclusive superiority over the others? The different roads start from different points in the plain, but they all meet on the mountain top.

This is G.M.'s birthday; he would have been 93 today, and would certainly have been at the Christmas holidays' meeting of the Council for World Citizenship, at which I was speaking this morning: 2,500 boys and girls in Central Hall: secondary school sixth form: 3½ girls to 1 boy, but the male minority asked most of the questions. A happy New Year to you and the Community.

Affectionately, I ought to say, American fashion, with no yours,

Arnold

1. Luke 12:16–21.

5 January 1959

St. Louis Priory

My Dear Arnold,

Yours has just arrived. I shall have ascended the many roads up the same mountain—I always think of Robin Hood's look out at Goremire with that image—I just want to wish you, pray you, from the God of all life at least your seven years' bet. That was a kind action on your part, and also I suppose a little paying back of a debt, all the insights you have received in the Ampleforth church—not that one can pay back spiritual things except with spiritual integrity, and that you have shown over and over again.

I have been reading *The Novel out of Russia*:[1] my first impression is that here is a man who is seeing Christ with new eyes because of new experience. He sees him as the symbol, embodiment of LOVE and mercy, as the preacher of the INDIVIDUAL

PERSON. The writer's own experience has been a desert of love and a crushing of the individual. It is wonderful how Christ for him is contemporary. But I have not finished the book, and it may fade into nonsense.

Christmas for me is always the Epiphany, the Wise Men—I say always, only since it was explained to me. Jesus Christ was for all men and all times. The point was not that He was Saviour of the Jews but of the world. I had a long talk with a Hindu student out here (fem.). She had had no theological training, but by instinct knew her faith, charming, clear, humble. I was very impressed. Among the things which came clear was that Buddhism was "chased out" of India simply by being accepted into the Hindus' thinking. They would do the same with Christ—one Saviour among many. But I also discovered from her that all reality outside divinity, the absolute, will perish, that reality as we know it, *is* not real.

One wonders how much this is rhetoric, how much a firm belief. If it *is* now unreal, then all incarnations are not real, for them. Of course this world is 'unreal' compared with God, but we would say that it exists. The Buddhists, I believe, would say that if we could only persuade ourselves that it doesn't and that we didn't exist, then it and we do (would) not exist. So there is a gulf between East-West, speaking the same words but with great differences in meaning.

The traditional Christian teaching is that the world will dissolve, but that the spirit will go on, that our bodies will be spiritualized. I wonder what this will be like. The East—Hindu and Buddhist—would claim that all is dissolved, absorbed into God. I could believe the former possible. I find the latter intellectually impossible. God is absolute, infinite, you can't add to Him. I find these differences not ones of degree but simply plain contradictions between East and West and I suspect between Greece and Christianity.

So quite unpremeditatedly I find myself unexpectedly answering your mountain point. Are these not different mountains? No, I think the God is the same, as you said in your last, but the approaches cannot be entirely reconciled. *Do we exist? Shall we exist?*

My love to you both,
Columba, O.S.B.

1. Boris Pasternak, *Doctor Zhivago*, trans. Max Hayward and Manya Harari (London, 1958).

Saint Louis Priory
Mason & Conway Roads
Creve Coeur, Missouri

Saint Joseph's Day (19 March) 1959

My dear Arnold,

I am eager to answer fully your basic problem which you stated in your last; but I have not at present the peace to do it. Perhaps this will come after Easter. There is much afoot, I feel like rushing off to a Cartuja, as once I nearly did in Spain.

This is a business letter. An excellent master, Alexander Niven,[1] has been working for his Doctorate in History at the local University, Washington. The supervisor left, now they say they cannot find another. Saint Louis Un. on the other hand requires him to give up all teaching if he is to get their Doctorate. Alexander N. will be in London in a week or so and I am suggesting he try to do it (the doctorate) by correspondence with London University. I told him I'd write to you in case you could help, or had any ideas. He may call you on the phone. I enclose his record—which is quite distinguished, certainly varied.

You will be interested to know I have had to take a master's place teaching history, modern world. I took over at the Congress of Vienna and note it is Metternich's centenary—write an article in the *Times* and I'll read it to my class. These last 150 years seem to me to be the staggering of a giant who has crippled himself by throwing away his sight (faith). Now it is two blind giants eager in a kind of animal sense to destroy in order to keep alive themselves. The books do not emphasize enough the attempted destruction of religion in the 18th century, its partial revival: Newman, Leo XIII, Curé of Ars, Soeur Thérèse; now—so it seems to me—the scar left on the peoples made by the injustices perpetrated during the rise of the new industrialism. Politics seem so paltry and so slow to solve the problems. The other point I want to make is the entry of the rest of the world into our world. That is going to be quite hard. The "Study" is helping a lot.

Gaudium paschale to you both. Hope in God. My love to you.

Columba, O.S.B.

A. Niven's address will be Woburn Sq. London W.6.

1. Alexander Niven (1920–); first lay teacher at the St. Louis Priory (1958–62); a Civil War historian; now on faculty of St. Louis Community College.

6 April 1959 St. Louis Priory

My Dear Arnold,

A copy of *Hellenism*[1] arrived this morning with the little inscription from you. How kind of you to remember. I had already read it and enjoyed it. I can hear your voice and see you nod your head as just retribution falls on this or that actor on the scene. The Age of Agony might have been written for me as, when reading the *Study* I was always coming across the fact that Rome had alienated the internal proletariat—and this was how she did it. It was foolish of me, I expect, but I have reviewed it in a local Catholic paper[2] and pontificated critically rather on the religious thoughts at the end—though I say plenty of nice things too. I felt it was encumbent on me to tell the faithful the differences of view. That leads me to say sorry! I have not written for ages, much as I have been wanting to. We have had, still have, growing pains. They will disappear, but they hurt while they last and fill the horizon. You might destroy my last letter, which if I remember rightly, was pretty wild.

This summer will be very quiet for me, and I do hope to be able to face Symmachus' challenge fairly and squarely. There must be an element I miss in his way of looking at things, because the answer seems so simple. It is too simple, so there must be a blindness in me.

Have you seen Vincent Cronin's new book, *A Pearl to India, Life of Robert de Nobili S.J.*?[3] He excells himself, and you will rejoice with all your heart over Nobili.

The house is full of young men tentatively living the life with us. Not all of them, I think, are suitable. But we learn more quickly the secrets of the American way of thinking. Their Revolution, unlike the Rebellion over Magna Carta, is so recent that the spirit of independence is very strong—it is exhilarating and also quite tricky to manage in teenagers, and even too at novitiate age.

How are the *Reconsiderations* getting on? It is easy for people to have pot shots at you, but the monumentalness of the *Study* remains. One notices its influence all over the place, e.g. in Barbara Ward's new book, *Five Ideas that Change the World*.[4] She obviously is one of your fans. Then Koestler in his book on Copernicus, etc.,[5] is obviously using the *Study* much as an amateur theologian would use Saint Thomas: Let's see what A.J.T. says. He found very little! But that is not the point. What I mean is that the book has become a kind of framework within which people think. So your objective has been achieved. Next the younger ones will use your principles and find things you yourself never dreamed of. I believe you have reinstated religion at the centre of the state. The young will decide which.

How is Veronica—I do hope she has recovered. Give her my love and you have it too and many prayers.

Affectionately,
Columba, O.S.B.

1. A.J.T.'s *Hellenism*.
2. The local Catholic paper was the *Saint Louis Review*.
3. Vincent Cronin, *A Pearl to India: Life of Robert de Nobili, S.J.* (London, 1959).
4. Barbara Ward, *Five Ideas That Change the World* (London, 1959).
5. Arthur Koestler (1905–82); *Sleepwalkers* (New York, 1959).

7 July 1959 Saint Louis Priory

My dear Arnold,

At last I am free to think during long enough consecutive minutes and hours to write as I said I would. I am doing so as much for my own good as for yours! As this subject—Symmachus' challenge—needs to be faced. So I hope you will also have time to think on these thoughts and give your comments.

"There must be more than one line of approach to the heart of the great mystery of the universe".

The more I think about it the more I think that profoundly true. God has left his imprint everywhere on the things He has made. Each mind ponders on the universe—this or that or the other, and is moved to find the mystery behind. The astronomer sees the mystery as the mystery of the universe, its infinite space, its beginning (?), its order; the physicist peers into the 'infinitely small' as Pascal said, to find there also the mystery of the universe. God—or the Mystery—can be seen as a Mathematician, a Chemist, Physicist. The poet sees all these things differently, or other things, and his way to the great Mystery is his own too. Another may go as a child to its Father (your friend Sr. Thérèse), another go or follow after as a Knight his King. Yet another may see NOTHING but darkness, and wait in silence before the mystery, knowing it beyond all comprehension. Millions of others—in China—have accepted the 'infinite distance' between themselves and God, and got on with living as best they could together under the distant observation of the Lord in the sky. There are as many approaches almost as there are men, though I expect one could specify, put them into rough groups. But each man has his unique, complex experience. It is through his experience that he will most intimately search for an answer to the mystery, whether his experience is joy or pain or both, as it surely is.

It seems to me that it follows that those who have gone deepest may come back to tell the others. And this has happened over and over again. The greatest of these *returns* are the Eastern Religions, the multiple accounts of the Hindus and the Buddhists, etc. There is much of this in Christian thought too: the stripping off of all that is extraneous to immediate contact; the delight in all created things, as God's footprints, even natural ecstasy such as Newton's.

I believe that in all this we can learn arm-fulls, shiploads from the East. Every real experience of the Mystery is a contact with the Creator, That Which is. It is the natural ground of all religion, something the East has preserved; something the busy West has almost lost.

Please comment.

Yours affectionately,
Columba, O.S.B.

The Royal Institute
of International Affairs
Chatham House
10 St James's Square
London S.W.1

26 July 1959

Dear Columba,

Your letter of 7 July: my only comment is that I agree with all that you say in it. I have read it more than once, and would have answered before, but for preoccupations. *Retractationes*:[1] I finished the book this morning. I hope I have managed here to discuss with my critics, not to fight them or feel animus against them. I have tried to use their criticisms as opportunities for raising questions of general interest. Above all, I have tried not to fall into the silly position of defending my own past acts just because they happened to have been mine. Well, we shall see whether I have succeeded in all this when the thing is published and reviewed.

A greater pre-occupation, and anxiety, has been Veronica's health. I can't remember how long it is since I have written to you. Probably it is long, as we have been in the wars. Veronica had her appendix out in April. No warning, but fortunately we were in London; it was done within twelve hours, and done well. Then she went with a friend of ours, Margaret Carlyle,[2] to recuperate at Ravello, above Amalfi—a lovely place, high up, looking out over the sea, and over the mountains of the Sorrento peninsula. I picked her up and brought her home, and on the way back she got a 'virus', which sent, and still sends, her temperature up every day—not very high, fortunately, but high enough to pull her down and keep her down. She has been in University College Hospital for a fortnight, and there they tested her for everything they could think of. These tests all gave her a clean bill of health, and that is very good: there can't really be anything organically wrong. But they haven't been able to diagnose the virus, so she has to get the better of it through her own resources, and she hasn't, so far, the needed margin of strength.

At the moment we are with her sister[3] (address: Templand Cherry, Allithwaite, Grange-over-Sands, N. Lancs.) pending her being well enough to go on to Hall Beck. There couldn't be better conditions than here, and I hope she is going gradually to get the better of the thing, but it is worrying, and I hate to see her so tired and low in health.

We were both going to the University of Peshawar in November for several months, but we have decided that she had better stay at home, and I have cut down my own visit and put it off till March.

Two more monks will make a lot of difference, and I am delighted that there is a prospect of the Church.

The *Gazetteer* comes out in September.

Yours affectionately,
Arnold

1. Volume XII of *A Study of History*; *Retractationes* was Saint Augustine's title for his book of "Reconsiderations."

2. Margaret Monteith Carlyle (1896–1972); Lady Margaret Hall, Oxford; at Chatham House (1949–52); worked the Italian section at Oxford during World War II; a contributor to the *Survey of International Affairs* (see her "The Territorial Provisions of the Peace Treaty with Italy," in *Survey of International Affairs, 1939–1946: The Realignment of Europe*, ed. A.J.T. and Veronica M. Toynbee [London, 1955], pp. 453–80); *The Awakening of Southern Italy* (London, 1962).

3. May Boulter (1892–1975).

Saint Louis Priory
Mason & Conway Roads
Creve Coeur, Missouri

26 July 1959

My dear Arnold,

I decided to type the "serial letter" as easier for you to read, and it saves me time. If you think after these two, that the whole thing is a waste of time, or that I am barking up the wrong tree, don't hesitate to say. I feel that if you analysed the true nature of these other religions, correcting or confirming my generalizations, that would be valuable.

This evening I'm off to Saint Paul, Minn., to give two retreats of four days apiece. It will be interesting travelling up the Mississippi, through Fort Madison. I went to Saint Procopius—once a Slav (Catholic) monastery, now Americanized, but interested in Reunion, and Mass is sung there in one church every day in the Rite of Saint John Chrysostom.[1]

Nixon I feel has done some good in Russia.[2] We always take it for granted that people are sensible. But we've often been mistaken. People live in a dream world; and our friend K. is one of these, thinking that he can play around with atom bombs. I still think the situation is critical, but Nixon did penetrate through, that we mean business, i.e. retaliation. What a world. At one level planning annihilation, at another thin shell concrete churches, conversion of the Hindu world. A friend of mine at the Vatican said Pope John would be happy to receive a letter from me, so I wrote a plea for vernacular liturgy. So far no answer; but I hope that he will carry on the reforms Pius XII had in mind.

How are you both? My warmest greetings to Veronica.

Affectionately,
Columba, O.S.B.

1. St. Procopius Abbey, Lisle, Ill.; of the American Cassinese Congregation.

2. On 24 July 1959, Richard M. Nixon, then vice president of the United States, opened the American National Exhibition in Moscow and engaged in an informal debate with Nikita S. Khrushchev.

26 July 1959

Dear Arnold:

In a way my last letter was incomplete and not material for a discussion, but only for an unqualified assent, even though you probably could see which way the wind was blowing, and what port I was making for.

Before you write, let me then add the following. I think you will agree with me that the Indian and Chinese religions—Hinduism and Zen Buddhism, Mahayana Buddhism and the Hinayana Buddhism too, are all, even if in different ways, man's own effort to escape from this shell which is our human condition and so to reach beyond towards an absolute whose nature generally is wisely nameless. Some accentuate the burden of sin—Hinduism—some the power of human concentration—Zen—some the annihilation of self—Buddhism—some even claim that other men, Buddhas to be, when still on earth, merited for others so that they might find the way—a form of Mahayana Buddhism. In all this God himself, as far as one can tell, remained silent. That for me is the most astonishing and pertinent fact of all. There is no claim that God spoke, the Buddha thought it foolishness to discuss a matter so much above our heads. I will be interested to know whether you with your much wider knowledge will agree with me in this, that all this Eastern search is not so much God's search for Man as Man's search for God. Nor am I trying to belittle it. The more one reads and thinks on it, the more wonderful the achievement seems to me to be.

In my last letter I was explaining how noble and in a sense how fruitful a search it was. The main theme of the writings on this matter, I found, was on the natural plane and undoubtedly on this plane great discoveries have been made. We can by technique reach, be aware of, the ground of being. Aldous Huxley's PHILOSOPHIA PERENNIS[1] by his use of quotations from widely dispersed sources gives a proof of its general unity.

What then of the Jewish and Christian approach to the unknown God? There is certainly one thing in common, don't you agree, between the West and at least Hinduism and most forms of Buddhism, that is a realization that sin exists and that it has to be got rid of, expiated, not ignored. But as the East on the whole seems to keep to the natural plane, its response is quite different from the Jewish and Christian one. The former as far as I can see seems to hold that man himself by his own efforts can eliminate sin—even if this expiation lasts over a very long period of time, perhaps even thousands of years.

The Jewish tradition and the Christian tradition saw sin as a retreat from a condition of felicity infinitely above the dream of nature. Man before the Fall was a Friend of God, walked *with* God, God-like, talked *with* God. And this was no god with a small g, like that of so many ancient myths, but the mighty creator God, the being who made the whole universe as the earlier chapters of Genesis narrated. It is, to me, a wonderful thing, the grandeur of God in the first chapters of Genesis, of man's relations to Him and consequently the depths of the Falling away.

While in the Jewish Christian tradition men searched and still do, the new thing is that God also INTERVENED, not once but many times. And the occasions are marked in the Old Testament with great solemnity, for instance the one when the three messengers visited Abraham, the incident of Moses' encounter with God in the desert of Sinai, the name God gave of Himself. The new thing, and the first to differentiate the West from the East is, so I see it, the clear statement of the intrusion of God into his world, God's search for man culminating in "The Word was made Flesh." Now this is what Jews and Christians hold. I agree it is quite a different matter whether their contention is true. All I am saying at the moment is that the Western approach to Religion is basically different to that of the East on at least these two points: (1) the West thinks God has come Himself to show us the way and secondly that the object of man's striving and God's giving is *not* the Ground of being, but share in an above-nature life with God, something man by his own efforts could not attain, not merely because he had sinned, but because natural man cannot reach so high—man is man and God is God.

So I propose to ask you first whether you agree they have not the same goal? I suggest the mountain is not the same mountain but really different mountains.

Secondly let me ask you this. If the great God himself enters on the scene and if we can show this is so, what should all men do who up to then were groping for a way without being able to see the way?

Third, if a mountain is higher and is approved by God, shall all seek it or only a group; if only a group, which?

Fourthly, if the mountains are different, one group claims that theirs is beyond their own powers to attain and only God can grant it as a gift to them, and yet that He has offered this prize to all men, should all men accept his offer or not? If not why not?

So long as God has not spoken, every man must seek as best he may, but when God has come I put it to you, should he be ignored or followed? That is the Christian Claim: God has intervened but in a supernatural purpose. He might merely have said: man's end is to reach the ground of being, then we could all practise to reach it as best we could. He didn't. He said: I am the way, the truth, the Life, which means we are to be one with God, doubly impossible without his gift, both because it is above nature and because if we ever had grace we had lost it.

I am obviously not trying to make you accept the fact that God has intervened, but asking, suppose He has in this stupendous way, what then?

1. *The Perennial Philosophy* (London, 1946).

The Royal Institute
of International Affairs
Chatham House
10, St James's Square
London S.W.1

2 August 1959

Dear Columba,

I have been thinking about your paper of 26 July. The differences that you underline are certainly differences in words, but do these words—which are all necessarily used analogically—really have differences in realities corresponding to them?

If we think of the Absolute as a person, then one's relation with 'It' is, by definition, a two-way encounter or intercourse; if we think of 'It' as impersonal, by definition there is only one person involved. But does this mean that the Indian and the Judaic contacts with the Absolute are different in kind really? After all, the notions 'personal' and 'impersonal', applied to the Absolute, are just two bits of anthropomorphism, one positive, the other negative. We can't help it; we have to use the only means of thought and expression that we possess. But we must not take these literally when we are applying them in fields outside the field of experience, from which we have borrowed them for trying to explore a different field. In truth, surely, the Absolute is neither personal nor impersonal, though it is both these things, and an infinite number of other things as well, in the sense that it is all-embracing. 'God' and 'Nirvana' are facets which a human soul finds in the Absolute; it is able to find them because there is something in the soul itself that corresponds to each of these two ideas.

I also doubt whether this distinction between the soul's activity and the Absolute's activity (or inaction) has any real meaning when we are thinking of the relation between the soul and the Absolute. Nor do I think that there is a real difference between 'God' and 'the ground of being'. The picture of the Absolute as a person is a piece of Jewish anthropomorphism—legitimate, so long as we do not mistake the picture for the Reality. But the Buddhist picture of the Absolute is also legitimate—subject to the same condition.

Veronica seems to be recovering some strength, I am very glad to say.

Yours affectionately,
Arnold

The Priory
Saint Louis, Missouri

30 August 1959

My Dear Arnold,

I have been in retreat and so pretty busy since. Thank you very much for your last letter and its good news of Veronica. She must get really well before undertaking anything in a big way. Grand news also that your *Reconsiderations*—Second Thoughts—are in the press. Please don't fail to send me a copy, no matter who else has a "right." Have you seen Fr. D'Arcy's most perceptive and sympathetic almost defense of you—and all in his new book, *The Sense of History: Secular and Sacred*.[1]

I agree with your latest comments on Person and Ground as being attempted descriptions of the same Absolute; I agree that they both can be discerned by the human mind, unaided by 'revelation.' Indian thinkers found both at one time or another. But I think—though this is not my main point—that their importance is unequal. In a way 'Ground of being' has proved to be ambiguous, perhaps because arrived at by mystical experience, an experience which may not be more than one of the human being's own absolute self. We cannot, in fact, I would say, experience the Absolute of God Himself; we are on a different plane. I don't deny, though, that the Indian experience could be parallel to Saint Augustine's "*ictus Dei*." But being "within," it could simply be the experience of self and so cause sad confusion, e.g. identity of self with God, and eliminate love. Person too has its hazards, and is, as you say, used of God analogically, but it is fertile for us. Analogy need not mean it has less meaning. It could have more meaning, more true of God than of us. All that is limiting in 'person' we eliminate; all that is positive, God is infinitely. Person includes knowledge, Wisdom—logos—and love: *Deus caritas est*. How rich Person is. There must also be an infinity of other aspects of which we are ignorant.

That God is a Person made communication with us possible, and especially this appears in the O.T. and is brought to completion in the New. Of course, God communicated in this way outside the Judaeo-Christian framework. Job is an instance. Have you ever used St. Augustine's comment on this—*City of God*, Bk. 18 c. 47?

So far, I think, I have been agreeing with you, with some precisions that you may or may not agree with. The point, however, of all this is in the next step of the communication, i.e. *what* the communication was. Of course, God-made-man was a unique method; but was the message unique?

I would say it included all the good that went before, wherever it had been discovered, and then went on to perfect it and to go beyond what human expectation had proposed, or at least beyond what any human could hope for with nature only. It was: "Treasured promises, you are sharers in the divine nature." 2 Peter, 1.4, a theme which runs thro' the N.T.: New life, God's life, Christ's life, Now not I live, but Christ lives in me. It is to come not only through Christ but *is* Christ. In a way all the yearnings and myths of Mahayana Buddhism surely are fulfilled in Christ. Here is Nirvana partly disclosed. Here is the supreme example of Self Sacrificing love, God himself, made man to do it, dying on a cross out of sheer love, as St. Thomas says, to PROVOKE us to love. Is not this unique and yet the completion of all that went before. Is this a way to bridge East and West?

My love to you both,
Columba, O.S.B.

1. Martin Cyril D'Arcy, *The Sense of History: Secular and Sacred* (London, 1959).

10 October 1959 Hall Beck

Dear Columba,

Your letter of 30 August has been lying unanswered all this time, while I have been doing one thing and another. It has been turning in my mind. Uniqueness, as you point out, is the stumbling-block for me. You are right in saying that, up to that point, we practically agree; but, for me, as you know, uniqueness is unacceptable not only intellectually but morally. We know only a fragment of the universe, and that through a glass darkly, and we know nothing about the future. So, as I see it, both making the claim to uniqueness and accepting it is unwarrantable.

I am now having a bit of Jewish correspondence over things I have been publishing. I have taken the line that the Jews' destiny is, not to establish a state in Palestine, but to preach Deutero-Isaiah's message as a universal religion.[1] Some of the diaspora Jews, here and in America, seem to like this.

Veronica really is better now. I have been watching her recovering strength and proposing longer and longer walks. This has been a great happiness.

Rosalind and her farming partner Richard Stafford (Have you met him? American by origin; awfully nice) came over to lunch here, and we have been to see them.

What do you think of this election landslide?[2] It must be the industrial working-class vote that has done it. They want to be bourgeois. It is not altogether good; too much in terms of flesh-pots, like the American way of life—which the more strenuous and Spartan Russian way of life is now going to put on the run, I guess.

Do tell me what America is feeling about Krushchev[3] and co-existence now. As it has turned out, it is Russia, not America, that is negotiating from strength. It is lucky that the Russians want peace; I think there is no doubt they do.

Did the London O.U.P. send you one of my author's copies of the *Gazetteer* volume?[4] If they didn't, I will have one sent. (It should have been sent you by surface mail on Oct. 1, so it may not have arrived yet).

I am now writing a book on the economic and social consequences of the Hannibalic War.[5] I lectured on this at Oxford in 1913, and have had the book on the stocks since then. We shall be back in London on 15 October. I am giving a lecture in Rome to the Food and Agriculture Organization on Nov. 2.

Yours affectionately,
Arnold

1. "Isaiah, chaps. 40–55, often called 'The Book of the Consolation of Israel,' by an unnamed prophet, written toward the end of the Babylonian captivity. Here we have monotheism expounded and a religious universalism clearly expressed, and finally the supreme four songs of the suffering servant that specially appealed to Arnold." (C.C.E.)

2. A Conservative party victory at the polls.

3. On 15–27 September 1959, Premier Khrushchev toured the United States, conferred with President Eisenhower at Camp David, and agreed to hold further discussions on Berlin.

4. A.J.T. and Edward D. Myers, *Historical Atlas and Gazetteer*.

5. Published as A.J.T.'s *Hannibal's Legacy*, 2 vols. (London, 1965).

Saint Louis Priory
St. Louis, Missouri

16 October 1959

My Dear Arnold,

I am so glad to hear that Veronica is mending; for the first time I had a taste of hospital. It was flu, but it knocked me out for the time. Every one seemed to think it providential, as it gave me a good rest. Anyway I am as right as rain again.

Thank you for your last. I see you don't really want to go on discussing "uniqueness," so let's drop it. Le bon Dieu will look after you Himself, as I am sure He does anyway.

K. of Russia came and went. My impression was that the people round him hoped to teach him a thing or two and that to their surprise he growled and gave them quite a shock. He seems to have been so unpredictable that they were all terrified he would fly home in a huff, and who could know what then. The English elections were to be expected, but it always amazed me how, with almost equal votes, such unequal results. I personally do not like the 'class war' element in labour—any more than I like the causes that brought on the mood—but labour could do without it. The Liberals have my sympathy, and if Labour could be less doctrinaire and more liberal, they would have my vote. Yes, I expect the contented workers are going bourgeois. In England, if things economic go wrong, Labour is properly organized. America, so it seems to me, is still living in almost a pre *Rerum Novarum* atmosphere: free-for-all economy, badly or wrongly organized labour. Reading Schlesinger's book on the Collapse of the Old Order,[1] one wonders how in the early 30s the Communists failed to get control.

It shows how life has returned to 'normal' just as much as the election result, your writing on the effects of the Hannibalic wars. They seem so long ago. But I guess you are going to use them as a parallel to our age, so I await this with interest.

Thank you for the *Gazetteer*; I am sure it is on its way. If no sign in a week's time, I'll let you know. I await with even more interest the "*Retractationes*."

Suppose you were writing a history of the world, not as people want it, but as you think it should be written, putting the most important things first, what would be your scheme? I believe this is a valuable pass time for you, and a most stimulating gift for me.

Teilhard de Chardin's book on Man has come into my hands.[2] It is one of those books which suddenly illuminate the mind. I was thrilled and note that you had read it. He produced a pattern for man's development which made sense. He opened up the future also in a way that gave confidence.

My love to you both and prayers,
Columba, O.S.B.

P.S. I did not know Rosalind had married again.[3]

1. Arthur Meier Schlesinger, Jr. (1917–); *The Age of Roosevelt: The Crisis of the Old Order* (Boston, 1957), vol. 1.

2. Compare A.J.T.'s "Vision of Unity," a review of Pierre Teilhard de Chardin's *The Phenomenon of Man* (*Observer* [22 November 1959], p. 21).

3. She had not.

The Royal Institute
of International Affairs
Chatham House
10, St James's Square
London S.W.1

20 October 1959

Dear Columba,

I do hope the rest has outweighed the flu, and has left the balance on the credit side. The whole enterprise must have been a tremendous strain—all decisions and responsibilities pulling on you—and you have had no let-up. Dealing with those big business men, alone, must be anxious work—nice though most of them seemed to me to be.

Krushchev seems to be persevering: he has now drawn soft words even from Adenauer. If the U.S. would be less unfriendly to Peking, that would relieve Krushchev of what must be a serious embarrassment for him.

As for politics here, we need a non-ideological, non-class-label other party, so that we can deal with politics in terms of more or less, and then the floating vote will grow bigger again. It is unhealthily small, now, and the great effects of a small turnover of votes are undemocratic.

About uniqueness, probably we have each said about all that we can say, and here we are discussing something that is at, or beyond, the limits of human understanding. A scheme for a history of the World, putting first things first: I say without hesitation: a continuous series of meetings with God. These meetings are between individuals and God. Only souls, not committees or nations, can have spiritual experiences. The encounters with God in our public affairs are repercussions, at second-hand, from the individual ones. Of course, I am merely describing the scheme in the Bible.

If the *Gazetteer* doesn't come, let me know.

Yours ever affectionately,
Arnold

The Priory
Saint Louis

23 October 1959

My Dear Arnold,

You can be sure that I am better for my trip to hospital and feel very well.

The long awaited *Gazetteer* has arrived. Thank you with all my heart. What an undertaking. It would almost be a worthy life work for any ordinary man. That Appendix on the Hittites, I expect that will be of immense help to historians in that field; and I can see it as the fruit of your long stay in Turkey. You were quite right to load that map with names, because those who turn to it will want to know where x is, and that is the purpose of most maps. Some of the maps have been well kept free of places when your aim was something else: cultural overlapping, etc. Islam is the most startling disclosure. I mean the extent of it and its central position. This is very clear in 9. 11 is good too, showing the "rain" of Aryans pouring down from the north. Your favorite, I suspect, is 12 B with its vents and "thresholds." What a good word, "Roundabout" 21 B. Of course, it would have benefited by colouring giving configuration, but that would add to expense and make the names illegible. I can't believe there should be so few +s[1] in your 29 map. None in England. I'm glad to see Lastingham (35). What is that Hatfield? Was it the scene of a council? I don't understand your Crusades (41) to Ireland, Norway? In 47 you only put Yarmouth.[2] Fr. Augustine pointed this out. Is it because the people of Yarmouth feared the coming of the Mongols? I have faint recollections of Gibbon mentioning something of the sort. The Mongol empire wins for size. Why did you make France brown? I'm not objecting. 64–65 a lesson in ups and downs of history. 70 reminds me of your clamberings 2 (1?) years ago in Guatemala.[3] Some of the maps are marvels of delicate precision, e.g. 54. What industry! One of the little tags of information I pride myself foolishly on is that once upon a time the Oxus flowed into the Caspian. Was this pre all this?

You made two wonderful points in your letter. The first that politics in England should get back to the political principle that it is all a matter of 'more or less' and not one of black and white. The other much more important—your picture of history—I could not agree more. Some of these individual contacts with God we only know of by their residue. But the main ones are pretty clear. Primitive man must have had insights. Even those who denied knowledge (the Buddha) in a sense had insight. Mahomet, one feels had, and then went wrong, had too many! Where would the basic inventions come in your scheme, and how treat the titanic, but often wicked men: Napoleon? Do go on talking about this.

Yes, we've come to near the end on comparative religion. I believe now that if

God gave you the grace to believe with wholeness in the absolute Divinity of Christ, the bonds would be broken. But I still would not force the issue. God's dealings with each of us is his secret too.

May He bless you, Veronica, all of us.

Columba, O.S.B.

1. The symbol for a Christian church.
2. As a Western city-state.
3. Map no. 70 was of the monuments of the Mayan and Yucatec civilizations.

The Royal Institute
of International Affairs
Chatham House
10, St James's Square
London S.W.1

10 December 1959

Dear Columba,

Your letter of 23 October has been lying at my elbow while I have been getting the 'reconsiderations' volume ready for press. The pressure always mounts at the end. There are outstanding queries—often trivial, but they have to be settled. However, I have finished this morning, and shall be taking it to Amen House tomorrow.

There is a lot in it about the Jews; I wanted to make sure of doing them justice. It is extraordinarily hard, isn't it, for us to see them just in themselves, and not in relation to Christianity, which, in their view, is irrelevant to Judaism. But when one has had a Christian upbringing, it is difficult to see the Jews except through a Christian lens. This is irritating to them, and it does, I think, prevent one from seeing them straight.

I suppose the key to the Jews is that they have not yet resolved the conflict between religion as nationalism and religion as the worship of God with a capital G. They found God, but couldn't bear to give up nationalism.

There is a very liberal-minded Jewish scholar, Rabbi J. B. Agus[1] of Baltimore, with whom I have been in correspondence. I think you would appreciate him.

As to the *Gazetteer*, it was a mistake of the O.U.P. not to allow me colours: those patches of brown were the most that I could coax out of them. Colour would have made it more expensive, but also so much more clear and useful that I believe it would have paid for itself in larger sales.

Veronica is all right now, I am glad to say, but she hasn't much margin of strength, so I am sure we have been wise in deciding that she should not come with me to Pakistan, etc.—though it is sad. I fly on 23 Feb. to Karachi. Early in February we are going to Portugal for a week: I am giving a lecture for the Chief of Staff, a rather jolly man called Pina.[2]

The other day I was lecturing at the U.N. Food and Agricultural Organization at Rome,[3] and unexpectedly got into the news. My subject was food and population. I was careful not to suggest anything that was incompatible with the Catholic

Church's line—at least, am I not right in thinking that the church does not condemn, in principle, taking thought to limit the size of a family, but only condemns certain particular ways of achieving this?

Yarmouth—see Matthew Paris, *Chronica Minora*. In the years in which the Mongols invaded Russia, herring prices slumped in the international herring market at Yarmouth, because the continental buyers stayed at home to protect their families.

Yours affectionately,
Arnold

1. Jacob Bernard Agus (1911–); then rabbi of Beth El Congregation, Baltimore; *The Meaning of Jewish History*, 2 vols. (London, 1963); A.J.T. reviewed this and other works ("Judaism: The Field of Force," in *Judaism* 16, no. 3 [Summer 1967]: 373–76); Agus's comments on A.J.T.'s references to Judaism are printed in *A Study of History*, XII: 664–69.

2. Luiz Maria de Camara Pina (1904–70); chief of the Portuguese General Staff.

3. Delivered 2 November 1959, at a plenary session; published as *Population and Food Supply* (Rome, 1959).

The Royal Institute
of International Affairs
Chatham House
10, St James's Square
London S.W.1

5 January 1960

Dear Columba:

I was tempted to ring you up this morning to say goodbye again, but didn't: answering would have been just one more thing to be done before starting for the air-port. So I am writing instead, thinking of you now just about taking off. Unexpected pleasures are some of the best, and hearing your voice from Norwich, and then seeing you yesterday, was one of these. How nice the Chapmans[1] are, and what a kind welcome they gave us.

Well, we shall be seeing each other, I hope, next spring, and even at your age, let alone mine, a year is no time. In fact, time depreciates automatically, as money seems to do.

I get a lot of happiness from thinking of what you have been planting, and of the fruit that it is bearing already: so soon. You are doing the very thing that Europe can and should do for America: what is also encouraging is that the St. Louis community should have realised that Ampleforth could do this for them, and should have asked the monastery to do it.

Au revoir.
Yours affectionately,
Arnold

1. Michael Chapman (1912–); University College, Oxford; director of Associated Portland Cement Ltd.; Antonia (née Crackanthorpe) Chapman (1926–); C.C.E.'s niece, daughter of Mrs. Bertie; cf. C.C.E.'s letter of 30 October 1953, above; Michael also a relation on another side.

Saint Louis Priory
16 January 1960 Saint Louis, Missouri

My dear Arnold,

The English interlude has closed over like the sea over a stone. But it is a most happy memory, only half real. It was grand seeing you and Veronica.

You are invited once again for Spring 1961, and we'll have you meet some more business men and a few historians, but again see to it that life is calm and unruffled most of the time.

The Jews are a kind of persistent miracle, in their pre-Christian existence, carving their monotheistic way through the jungle of many-godded fancies and, after Christ, are a witness, willy nilly, of the prophesies about their own doom. The greatest people on the earth. I am longing to read your account of them.

Don't worry about the to-do over the Rome meeting.[1] When I next write to his Holiness—apparently, his secretary wrote to me, he would like letters—I will assure him you did not say or intend what the papers produced. Next time you are in Rome do try to see him privately. There is something very attractive about his personality, don't you think?

I go on thinking about this real world history of those seeking God. *If* you are not going to write it, give me an outline and a few books and over 20 years, if that is still my life span; I might write something which would set others on the same trail and deeper and better. This may all be fanciful, and so was *China*. It would be fun to work it out, even if it only got as far as a plan.

Your words of encouragement on our work do help. Sometimes one wonders, with the defeatists, whether we are making headway. If you ever go to Ampleforth or write to Fr. Abbot, do say much as you wrote to me last.

Snow is falling. The roads are icy. We may be cut off for a day or two. *Pax.*

My love to you both,
Columba, O.S.B.

1. Compare A.J.T.'s letter of 10 December 1959, above; *The Times* (2 January 1960) reported that, addressing the conference on "Peace and Population," A.J.T. had said regulation of the birth rate required "thousands of millions of individual decisions" and that "we have not much time to spare before the present explosive growth of populations through the continuing lack of any control of the birth rate will produce catastrophe if it is left unchecked by us human beings."

Saint Louis Priory
2 February 1960 Saint Louis

My dear Arnold,

As I told you, I wrote to his Holiness, enclosed in a note to Mgr. Cardinale. By return I get a letter from the latter. Here is an extract as it concerns your good self: . . . "I am sending you an immediate answer as I want to tell you that the Holy Father will be pleased to receive Prof. Arnold Toynbee while in Rome next spring.

"When Prof. Toynbee has decided the date of his passage here, he can write direct to the Holy Father and enclose his letter in an envelope addressed to me and I shall take care of all. The rule is that the interested party should make the request, and that is why I am suggesting this procedure; but you can tell him from now that the Audience will be granted.

"I remember meeting him when he stopped in Rome some years ago. We also corresponded a few times but then discontinued because of our mutual ceaseless activities. But I kept remembering him all the time.

"The press did make a lot of fuss about his statement at FAO meeting in Rome, but we all know that press-reports are hardly reliable."

So it is now up to you. I hope you do not feel I have gone too far! It would be easy for you to back out, should you wish; but I feel pretty confident that you and the Holy Father will have plenty in common.

Address Rt. Rev. Mgr. I. Cardinale
Segreteria de Stato
di Sua Santita
Citta del Vaticano, ROME

In some haste,

Affectionately,
Columba, O.S.B.

The Royal Institute
of International Affairs
Chatham House
10, St James's Square
London S.W.1

6 February 1960

Dear Columba,

Here are your letters of Jan. 16 and Feb. 2 still unanswered. We have been for 5 days in Portugal (first visit). I was lecturing for a very nice man, General Luiz Pina,[1] who is chief of the General Staff. I had an hour with Dr. Salazar:[2] a most impressive and most likeable man: completely straightforward and without self-conceit or pomp.

Alas, I shall not be in Rome this spring. On 19 Feb. I whizz straight through from London to New Delhi.[3] When Veronica and I were planning to go together, and to go in November last, we planned to stop off in Rome, en route, for the FAO lecture; but, when our plans had to be changed owing to her illness, I did the FAO expedition in November separately.

I am writing to Mgr. Cardinale to explain and to tell him that I hope I may have a later opportunity of being received by his Holiness.

Asia is now rushing towards me, while Africa is now erupting in a way that pleases me. You will be hearing from me, and you can always reach me via Chatham House.

Affectionately,
Arnold

1. Luiz Maria da Camara Pina; cf. A.J.T.'s letter of 10 December 1959, above.

2. Antonio de Oliveiro Salazar (1889–1970); premier of Portugal (1932–68).

3. A detailed account of this journey appeared in A.J.T.'s *Between Oxus and Jumna* (London, 1961).

Chancellor's Guest House,
University of Peshawar

10 March 1960

Dear Columba,

This campus is on the plain between Peshawar City and the Khyber Pass. West, north and south there are walls of mountains, but, east, the plain stretches all the way to Calcutta and beyond. The Grand Trunk Road from Calcutta to the Afghan frontier skirts the campus. I am very happy here, except for being away from Veronica, and I think I can do something for them. They are intellectually starved, and pathetically eager for help. I am here till 30 March. I then go back to India for 3 weeks (universities in Rajasthan), fly from New Delhi to Kabul on 20 April, travel round Afghanistan with our Ambassador there for a month, and, in June, come back by road from Kabul to Peshawar—and then travel along the Pakistan side of the frontier, first up to Chitral, and then down to Karachi through Baluchistan. From Karachi I shall be jetted back to London in about 8 hours (it took only 11½ hours to jet me from London to New Delhi last month).

I started by giving the second series of memorial lectures provided in honour of Maulana Azad: a Muslin theologian, who was the first Minister of Education in independent India. Azad died in 1958; and the first set in the series was given last year by Pandit Nehru. It is very nice (considering that we put Azad, as well as Nehru, in prison) that they should have asked an Englishman to give the second set, and I took it very kindly that they thought of asking me.[1]

So far, my most interesting experience has been at Multan: an old-fashioned city that is now being ringed round by new properties. The old city centres on the Tombs of four saints. I was the guest of the Shiʿite one of the four. He came to Multan from Gardez, in Afghanistan, about 900 years ago, and I was staying, a stone's-throw away from his Tomb, in the guest-house of one of his descendants (Headmaster of a secondary school, and prominent in the world boy-scout movement). I met many members of the family (having a saint, with a tomb, for one's ancestor keeps a family in existence). There was every degree of mixture between ancient and modern.[2]

Dr. Munawwar Khan, the head of the History Dept. here, is a Yusefzai Pathan from an independent village in the Swat valley. He took me to his village the other day, and I met his father and his uncle (feudal lords; they had just won a case against 15,000 subjects of theirs who had been striking against paying their feudal dues). The uncle has introduced poplars and orange-trees (very profitable) into Swat. As a young man, he ran away to sea, and got not only to Cardiff but to Yokohama. Another young Swats Khan who ran away at the same time got to California, and has made a fortune there. At this moment he is on his way to revisit Swat for the first time in 40 years.[3]

I think Scotland after the Forty-five must have been in about the same state as Western Pakistan today. Even since I was here in 1957, I can see changes. For instance, the Afridi bus service has increased its fleet of buses and lorries.

Well, you will be hearing from me again. In New Delhi, 1–20 April, I shall be c/o the British Council, Old Mill Road, New Delhi 2. So write to me.

Affectionately,
Arnold

20 April–end of May, c/o the British Ambassador, Kabul.

1. A.J.T.'s lectures were published as *One World and India* (New Delhi, 1960).
2. Compare A.J.T.'s *Between Oxus and Jumna*, pp. 14–16.
3. Compare ibid., pp. 17–18.

New Delhi
India

2 April 1960

Dear Columba,

What a pleasure: when I got here yesterday there was your letter of 24 March[1] waiting for me, and also two from Veronica (the second of these, 30 March). Really the world is becoming one small city. I am sorry Albany was so inclement. Veronica and I once went to a conference there on religion and work. It is quite an old city, because it was the head of navigation for seventeenth-century Dutch ocean-going ships. Your news of the school all sounds good, and I am *very* glad that *China and the Cross* is on the way of publication. *Reconsiderations* has gone to press and will be published in the spring of 1961.

Yes, I have been seeing the Himalayas and the Hindu Kush glistening in the sun, from the Peshawar University guest-house windows, on the rare days on which the March weather in Peshawar has not been like a wet August in Westmorland. The poor nomads, on their way to their summer camping grounds in Afganistan, were having a hard time. They were more concerned for their camels than for themselves. The camels and their foals were wearing sackcloth coats, but the children were plodding along barefoot, and the tents looked mighty draughty.

Yes, the Pathans are living between two worlds: I should say that they are in about the same stage, today, as the Scottish highlanders about 1760. In religion they are fundamentalists, and therefore are perhaps exposed to the danger of swinging over to the opposite extreme. Their attitude towards Islam suffers a lot, I should say, through being mixed up with such irrelevant things as national and personal *amour propre*. I tease them by suggesting to them that they may have something to learn from Hinduism and Christianity. This always arouses a lively discussion at the end of my lectures.

Tomorrow I am off for a week or ten days to Rajasthan[2]—a vast city of refuge in semi-desert, where people have silted up after being driven out of the fields of the

Panjab and the U.P. I was in Jodhpur long ago—1929,[3] and was eager to see it again, and some of the other ancient cities too. Even in Rajasthan I expect I shall find that the old order is dissolving.

Macmillan seems to be doing well at Camp David.[4] The chances for disarmament have never looked so good, I think. I am also encouraged by the strength of the world-wide reaction to the South African shootings. It is particularly good that the U.S. Government has spoken out about this.[5]

Well, you will be hearing from me further as I go along. I am flying home from Karachi on or about 1 July.

Affectionately,
Arnold

1. Missing.

2. Compare A.J.T.'s *Between Oxus and Jumna*, pp. 31–35.

3. See A.J.T.'s *A Journey to China*, pp. 135–39.

4. On 28–30 March 1960, Prime Minister Harold Macmillan was in Washington discussing nuclear tests.

5. On 21 March 1960, Pan-Africanists had demonstrated at Sharpeville, Vereeniging, against the pass laws; desultory shooting in the morning ended in a mass stoning of armored police cars, which in turn evoked bursts of firing of Sten guns; the mob scattered, leaving scores on the ground; on 22 March, the U.S. State Department said that "it cannot help but regret the tragic loss of life resulting from the measures taken against demonstrators in South Africa" (*The Times* [23 March 1960]).

2 June 1960 As from Saint Louis

My dear Arnold,

I am in fact writing this in the boys' infirmary at Portsmouth where I have been wafted by jet; the occasion is the opening-dedication of St. Gregory's Priory's new church.[1] Quite an event in these parts. The architect is Beluschi[2] of M.I.T. and the designer of the crucifix ensemble is Lippold.[3] The church is in stone, redwood and tiles; the crucifix silver gilt, but all round it wires and bars of metal hanging. The wires come in to it from all directions except below, and the effect is 3/multi-dimensional and mysterious. The symbol is of the Holy Trinity. Now I must get back. The day began in mist, now the sun has come out; there should be little difficulty.

Much has happened since we last wrote. Is it possible that power is getting out of the hands of the Communists into that of the generals? There is always the possibility that a general may not be doctrinaire. The summit was, it appears, never meant to be taken seriously by the Russians, because the plane incident could easily have been dealt with in another fashion.[4] Then your friends in Turkey,[5] have they all been put in prison? Were they so dictatorial as all that? I say: your friends, but I of course don't know which party you approved of over there. Here in U.S. the people are slowly waking up for a presidential election. The religious issue is still low powered, but once Kennedy is elected—if he is—I am sure it will be a repetition of

Al Smith—if not quite so general. From the Catholic angle it is not as easy as Kennedy makes out. There are many issues which have not only political but also moral implications, and while morals are part of the natural law and K. could say that natural reason could guide him, the Church is always ready to put its oar in to bolster up or rectify private judgement, and I presume that many a U.S. president has abided by his own interpretation or his church's interpretation of the Bible.

Our church plans are now out to bids, and we are anxious, as it appears the architects in a comparable building were low on their estimates. So we wait and see. The bids are opened in four week's time.

You will be interested. Three of our boys were accepted at Harvard, 5 at Yale, 2 or more at Brown (R.I.) and a number at other Eastern colleges. The local Saint Louisans are jubilant. We wait the reaction of the lower clergy. I am sure we have the archbishop with us. But on the whole the local church opinion is much what Manning's was—against Newman—on the Oxford argument: should Catholics go or not? Once we get over this year's excitement, and the boys do not disgrace themselves, we should not have any trouble in the future.[6]

My love to you both,
Columba, O.S.B.

1. St. Gregory Priory, Portsmouth, Rhode Island.

2. Pietro Belluschi (1899–); dean, School of Architecture and Planning, Massachusetts Institute of Technology (1951–65); he designed the whole of Portsmouth Priory's modern campus.

3. Richard Lippold (1915–); sculptor; professor, Hunter College, New York (1952–67).

4. On 1 May 1960, a high altitude U.S. reconnaissance plane, a U-2, was shot down over Soviet territory; Khruschev then broke off the Paris Summit conference and canceled his invitation to President Eisenhower to visit Russia.

5. On 27 May 1960, military officers seized control of the government of Turkey as a junta called the Turkish National Union Committee.

6. "The American church policy up to this date had been that Catholic boys should go to Catholic colleges; this added to the segregation of Catholics from the broad river of American life. Cardinal Ritter, of the St. Louis Archdiocese, favored prudent intellectual integration." (C.C.E.)

Priory of the Annunciation
Bismarck, North Dakota

12 June 1960

My dear Arnold,

Here I am 1000 miles+ from base giving a retreat to some Benedictine nuns. They have built themselves a beautiful convent overlooking the Missouri and row upon row of low straight hills is their view. It is very quiet, no aeroplane, scarcely a car on the roads, and wooden farm houses in 50–100 acre lots, trees only in the bottoms; and the Benedictine life is as at home here as in Italy, England or France. There are 200 nuns, mostly from the area, and I found many spoke with a German accent. The whole of this part, it appears, was settled by Germans 70 (?) years ago, coming from S. Russia where they had been settled 100 years before that. They speak here about the rather wretched soil as black earth!

I am only here for the inside of a week, but the quiet and complete break with the proximity of the turmoil of Saint Louis have done me good. Prayer is the heart of life and I breathe again more freely. How far away too from this vantage point is all the hubbub of the Russians. Please God He holds the hand of the wicked and leaves us in peace.

All this international breakdown must have been, and must still be, very distressing to you who have done so much to help maintain the precarious peace. It should make you more and more put your trust on God.

On my way back through Chicago a friend is hoping to arrange a meeting for me with Professor Pelikan[1] who wrote a book on the Catholic Church, which I am sure he thought irenic, but which I found far from so, and then with the anthropologist, Prof. Eliade,[2] whom I admire much via his books. If this comes off, I'll let you know.

The convent here, like the Abbey church at Collegeville was designed by Marcel Breuer.[3] It is somewhat like our building, but with more stone and to that extent better. Our church is out to bids. We shall know the result June 30.

My love to you both—and prayers.

Columba, O.S.B.

1. Jaroslav Jan Pelikan (1923–); Lutheran theologian; then at the University of Chicago (1953–62); professor of ecclesiastical history at Yale University (1962–); dean of the Graduate School at Yale (1975–78); *The Riddle of Roman Catholicism* (London, 1960).

2. Mircea Eliade (1907–86); professor, University of Bucharest (1933–39); University of Chicago (1956–85); *Patterns in Comparative Religions*, trans. by Rosemary Sheed (London, 1958).

3. Marcel Lajos Breuer (1902–81); pupil of Gropius at the Bauhaus and teacher with him at Harvard; coarchitect of the Unesco building in Paris.

Saint Louis Priory
13 August 1960 Saint Louis, Missouri

My Dear Arnold,

No news from you for quite a time; knowing your tendency to behave on mountain slopes as though you were under thirty, I hope you have not overdone it. On the other hand my fears lead me to think you may be caught up in pre W.W. III activities. I did notice a review of yours in the *Observer* pleading for a pacific approach to such a challenge.[1] I must say the present prospects are gloomy from a this world angle. In S.L. one could easily—and in London—wake up next morning in the next world. There is even a mood over here of a preventive bomb dropping. The Communist successes—Cuba—have made people more jittery. We however go quietly about our job, *opus Dei*, and on the 15th of this month expect to see the builders start on our round church. Everything is set—including even 99/100 of the money. So when you next come and when is that?—you will perhaps find the shell up. I have made yet a third attempt at a life of Fr. Paul.[2] Whether anything will come of it I do not know. Now I'm resting a little and enthralled by Abercrombie's life and work of Edmund Bishop.[3] It has so much to interest me: the English Benedictine Congr. emergence fin. XIX century, the liturgical discoveries of E.B., his curious character, Gasquet, Anglican Orders . . . I wonder as I write whether English will before long be introduced into the Mass. My guess is yes, after the Council. Meanwhile we are going to have a restoration and rationalization of the shape of the Mass. How are you both, and all the family and what of the "*Retractationes*" and other multifarious works? Keep on praying for peace and for this little island seeking true peace, as I do for you.

Affectionately,
Columba, O.S.B.

1. A.J.T.'s "Power and the State," a review of *Nations and Empires*, by Reinhold Niebuhr (*Observer* [17 July 1960], p. 28).

2. Father V. Paul Nevill, O.S.B.; compare A.J.T.'s letter of 26 January 1954, above. "My first version was judged too outspoken, and the second rejected, partly because it revealed a deep division between him and Fr. Ambrose Byrne, the elder brother of Abbot Herbert Byrne, whose memory the latter venerated. There was also considerable difference of opinion between the Abbot and Fr. Paul, all charitably managed; nevertheless, Abbot Byrne was unwilling to allow it to come to light. The third version foundered on the same rock and doubtless for other reasons that did not come to light." (C.C.E.)

3. Nigel Abercrombie, *The Life and Work of Edmund Bishop* (London, 1959).

Hallbeck Cottage
Killington
Kirkby Lonsdale
Westmorland

19 August 1960

Dear Columba,

For ages I have had two letters of yours on my desk. When they reached London in June, I was travelling along the Pakistan side of the Pakistan-Afghanistan frontier. Now here is your letter of 13 August. My long silence was not due to any mishap—unless it is a mishap to have to make out an overdue income tax return. But that is an annual torment. At last I have got abreast of my letters (I was more than 4 months on my travels). I did travel very hard, but I enjoyed it enormously, and I don't mind dry heat. A dry 121 in the shade at Sind in Baluchistan did not bother me, but a damp 104 at Karachi almost laid me out. However, I came back home in the pink of health, with a lot of New Knowledge, and also some new friends, in my bag.

You have a number of things to be happy about: I do congratulate you on the boys who have been taken by Harvard, Yale and Brown (I know Brown too, fairly well). Also on the new church getting under way. I am shocked at your news that people are even playing with the idea of a 'preventive' atom attack. It would be the biggest public crime in history, besides being the last event in history. I don't think it is going to happen, but it is another bit of evidence that, in our collective life, we are still juvenile criminals. I have just finished reading the first proofs of '*Reconsiderations*' (680 pages, including bibliography, but not including index, which Veronica is making at this moment 3 feet away from where I am). I also have finished a book of travel sketches of this latest journey.[1] (hence my messy address on this aerogram: I started writing to the Ambassador in Kabul about some photographs that he took, then remembered that I must send my letter to him by F.O. bag, as letters by Afghan post are not quite certain to arrive).

We shall see each other in a few months. Veronica and I are sailing to New York on 31 December, going to McGill, Montreal, till the end of January, and then to the University of Pennsylvania from the beginning February till 18 May inclusive. Shall we pay you another visit at Creve Coeur? I have been making out a fair copy of my schedule up to date to look for big enough blank spaces (the blanks fill up alarmingly fast). My main fixture is a world seminar at Philadelphia on Thursdays 2.00–4.00 P.M. I see there are still four full complete blanks between one Thursday and the next: March 3–8; March 31–April 5; April 28–May 3; May 5–10. As we shall be flying (I imagine there are lots of flights between Philadelphia and St. Louis), probably one of the two later dates would give us greater security against being delayed by bad flying weather. What fun to be going to see each other again so soon. A tenth granddaughter—Philip's wife Sally's daughter[2]—was born on 25 April, so now I have 11 grandchildren. I have clothed nine of them with sheepskin coats, embroidered coats or waistcoats, and gold-thread shoes.

Much love to you,

Yours affectionately,
Arnold

1. A.J.T.'s *Between Oxus and Jumna.*
2. Clara (1960–); cf. A.J.T.'s letter of 8 February 1951, above.

The Royal Institute
of International Affairs
Chatham House
10, St James's Square
London S.W.1

31 October 1960

Dear Columba,

Our visit to the Priory: dates. We have provisionally fixed May 5–10, as you will remember. Is there any possibility that we could change it to some period between May 18, the date of my last seminar at the University of Pennsylvania, and June 9? The reason I ask is that I have just had an invitation from Haverford College, Pa., to give the Commencement Address there on June 9 and, in this connexion, to spend a week on their campus at some earlier date ('in the spring').

It depends, of course, on *your* dates at the School. If a later date than May 5–10 would be impossible, or, short of that, be awkward, let us leave the dates as they stand now, and anyway leave them as now provisionally. But it would help me to decide between 'yes' and 'no' to Haverford if I knew whether the later date that I have now suggested for you was a possible one for you or not.

We have had a quiet nine weeks in Westmorland, and are now having a spell in London before sailing on December 31.

Yours affectionately,
Arnold

The Royal Institute
of International Affairs
Chatham House
10, St. James's Square
London S.W.1

8 November 1960

Dear Columba,

I have just had your letter of 4 November.[1] That is very kind indeed of you and Father Timothy. We shall be delighted to accept for a week (or perhaps even a day or two longer) beginning about May 19 or 20. I have just heard from the man in New Zealand who is taking 45 Pembroke Square furnished, that his date for the end date of his tenancy can be adjusted to our dates, so everything now fits.

I should, of course, like to see something of the boys and also to do anything that might be useful in the way of lecturing or bull-sessions. The earlier part of the week beginning Monday May 22 would, I expect, be the most convenient time for this, as it would be furthest from the end of term.

Yes, I too, think Kennedy is going to win. I very much want him to. By the time this reaches you, we shall know.

Pope John and Archbishop Fisher are indeed doing well.[2]

'*Reconsiderations*' comes out on May 4.

Well, we do look forward to seeing you. The Priory will be a haven after a busy semester in Philadelphia.

Yours affectionately,
Arnold

1. Missing.

2. On 31 October 1960, it was announced from Lambeth Palace that early in December Geoffrey Francis Fisher would pay "purely a courtesy visit" to Pope John XXIII in the Vatican, the first such visit since 1397. *The Times*, 1 November 1960.

Saint Louis Priory
Saint Louis, Missouri

19 November 1960

My Dear Arnold,

I had lunch with the Consul yesterday, George Merrells.[1] He had with him a friend of yours Robin Cecil,[2] who travelled with you to Sicily, last year (?). The latter wants you to lecture here under his auspices. He runs British information in N.Y. So

I said that was all right. You apparently had agreed and referred him to me. It does not seem to matter whether this organization is mentioned—possibly advisable if it is not. The chief advantage seems to be that you get your journey and keep! This struck me as eminently reasonable. So we discussed ways and means. The suggestion that pleases me is for you to speak to one of the universities or both jointly and on such a topic as: the need for history Study in U.S. (particularly in the Mid West!). Robin Cecil thought it a good subject. I would feel inclined to approach Fr. Reinert,[3] President of S. Louis University and get him to stage the lecture but invite Washington University too. My reason is that the former needs to have visiting lecturers of standing and so rarely gets them, whereas W. Un. gets quite a number. If this pleases you, please send a line and I'll go ahead.

Otherwise I have as yet made no plans. But I expect we should gather a few historians much as last time (subject?) and also have a dinner with local celebrities. We shall see. But more important, we can talk.

It is good news that the *Reconsiderations* are coming out in the calm of the spring.

Just to hand, your article on Education.[4] I like the point that everyone need not be educated to the same level—not an easy thought for democrats of the U.S. kind.

What do you think of the gun-boat diplomacy round Cuba.[5] How inevitably history repeats itself.

My love to you both,
Columba, O.S.B.

1. George L. Merrells (1915–); British consul at St. Louis (1959–62); afterward serving in the Foreign Office in England.

2. Robert Cecil (1913–); director general, British Information Services, New York (1959–61); counsellor, British embassy, Bonn (1957–59); *Life in Edwardian England* (London, 1969).

3. Paul Reinert, S.J.; cf. C.C.E.'s letter of 22 September 1957, above.

4. A.J.T.'s "Conclusions," in Edward D. Myers, *Education in the Perspective of History* (New York, 1960), pp. 269–89.

5. On 28 October 1960, the United States in a note to the Organization of American States, charged that Cuba was receiving significant arms shipments from the Soviet bloc. The missile crisis was to come in October 1962.

The Royal Institute
of International Affairs
Chatham House
10, St James's Square
London S.W.1

23 November 1960

Dear Columba,

I have just had your letter of the 19th. I am so glad that Robin Cecil's proposal does not seem to cut across any plans of yours. I asked him to take it up with you in order to make sure about that.

His wife, by the way, is a Catholic, and I should guess that he will be one, if he is not one already by this time.

St. Louis University, with Washington University associated if they like, would be fine—unless you would like it to be under the Priory's auspices.

Whatever we do about that, I shall of course do for the boys anything that you and Father Timothy may think useful.

I have a lecture on 'The Use and Value of History.' Perhaps this would fill the bill if I give it a topical turn, with a Mid-West audience in mind.

For date, we shall have to allow ourselves time, after the 18th May, to clear up our furnished apartment at Philadelphia and come along to St. Louis.

This will be a great pleasure and relaxation.

How unwise of the rich Germans to be so unaccommodating to America when she needs their help.[1] America reacts very strongly to anything that smells of ingratitude. Germany ought to remember China and think again.

Love from us both,
Yours affectionately,
Arnold

1. Germany had refused a request that it contribute $600,000,000 to defense costs, mainly through support payments for U.S. forces in Germany.

Christmas time 1960 Saint Louis Priory

My Dear Arnold,

This is to wish you a very happy, peaceful and God filled Christmas. It struck me today that the liturgy does exactly what you are so keen on: create an appreciation of contemporaneousness with past events. Christmas: the coming of Christ, and the second coming in our souls. We are in a spiritual sense not so much heirs of the apostles as going through the same experiences as the Apostles, the experience that God has visited his people, does, after all, care, does love. I always think we don't appreciate enough that God could love us. Of course He must if he made us, but we are pretty small fry aren't we. But big with his promises.

You, I, Fr. Reinert, Chancellor Shepley did our turn again before Saint Louisians last night, so I heard this morning. That little colloquium goes the rounds I believe.[1]

"Inc."[2] i.e. our friends are very keen that the Priory accepts your offer of lecturing under our steam. Quite how it will be managed.I don't know. But let us keep the lecture you suggested unless something else you would like to speak on occurs to mind in between.

I do hope Veronica is well. Do give her my love.

Did I tell you *China and the Cross* will soon be in Chinese.[3]

My love to you and many prayers.

Yours affectionately,
Columba, O.S.B.

P.S. Isn't Rusk[4] a friend of yours?

1. "This was the television discussion on world affairs the four of us had before the local television camera." (C.C.E.)

2. "Inc." is the familiar name for the group of supporters of the priory, which incorporated itself under the title "Catholic Preparatory School for Boys, Inc."

3. "The first portion only, through the Franciscan chapter. I think the Franciscan publishers in Hong Kong were a little afraid the later chapters could be used by the Chinese Communists for propaganda, as Western imperialism pops up here and there, especially in the nineteenth century." (C.C.E.)

4. Dean Rusk (1909–); secretary of state under John F. Kennedy and Lyndon B. Johnson (1961–69).

EIGHT

1961–66

The Peace Corps; A.J.T.'s recollections of Paul Nevill; Philip publishes Pantaloon*; A.J.T. in Egypt: "The most beautiful thing in Egypt is the countryside itself"; Vatican II; Grinnell College; the Priory of St. Louis revisited; prophets; A.J.T.'s analysis of Muhammad; Vietnam: "The American people are committing, pretty heavily, the sin of pride"; A.J.T. and Gibbon; A.J.T. attends Good Friday services in Addis Ababa; to Greece for the seminar on ekistics; C.C.E.'s recollections of A.J.T.*

University of Pennsylvania
Philadelphia 4
The College
Department of History

10 February 1961

Dear Columba:

Here we are at the University of Pennsylvania[1] after a strenuous but most interesting and enjoyable three weeks in Montreal.[2]

We have gradually been getting our schedule into order. Our last engagement on the campus here in Philadelphia is on the afternoon of Thursday, May 18, and we shall need a day or two to clear things up after that. We could probably fly from here to St. Louis on Sunday 21st, or Monday the 22nd, if that would be more convenient to you. Our next engagement after St. Louis is with the British Consul General at Denver. I give a lecture at the University of Colorado on May 30th,[3] so that we should be leaving St. Louis either on the 29th or 30th of May.

I am letting you know these provisional dates now, so that you can make sure that they will fit in with any arrangements that you may be making.

We are enormously looking forward to seeing you again.

Yours affectionately,
Arnold J. Toynbee

Post Script

While this was being typed your letter of January 30th came in.[4] I should be glad to give the talk on the "Use and Value of History" for Father Reinert, and I will certainly talk on current affairs at the dinner of the Priory Society. I am all for Kennedy,[5] in fact I am quite enthusiastic for him.

A.J.T.

1. Where A.J.T. delivered lectures published in *America and the World Revolution: Public Lectures Delivered at the University of Pennsylvania, Spring 1961* (London, 1962).

2. Where A.J.T. had delivered lectures published in *The Present-Day Experiment in Western Civilization: The Beatty Memorial Lectures Delivered at McGill University, Montreal, 1961* (London, 1962) and had engaged in a debate with Yaacov Herzog, the Israeli ambassador to Canada, on Arab-Israeli relations.

3. A.J.T.'s lecture "Does History Make Sense?"

4. Missing.

5. Then commencing his administration.

University of Pennsylvania
Philadelphia 4
The College
Department of History

22 February 1961

Dear Columba,

It was very good to get your letter of February 16.[1] We are in a pleasant little apartment (4016 Pine St., Philadelphia 4, tel. Evergreen 6 7650). My office at University of Pennsylvania is Room 213, Bennett Hall (Ev. 6 0100, ext. 408). Life is being pretty strenuous, but happily we have both been standing up to it pretty well so far.

I agree gladly all the arrangements that you have made with the Jesuits. I look forward to this. I am letting Robert Cecil know, as I gathered from him that he was proposing that we should go partly under his auspices (travelling expenses, etc., as you say).

The cottage sounds most restful, and we shall be very grateful for the rest.

About dates: would it be all right for you if we came from here to St. Louis on Tuesday May 23 and went on to stay with the Consul at Denver on either Monday May 29 or Tuesday May 30? (This would depend on the engagements that he is thinking of for us there). I suppose the first thing to settle will be the date with the Jesuits. For a choice of subjects I suggest: Does History make Sense? Effective Citizenship Today; The Rise of Nationalism in non-Western Countries; The Outlook for the West To-day.

We certainly should like to see Martha Love,[2] if you can arrange it. There are also some young friends of ours, the Howard Reeds,[3] now working at the Danforth Foundation in St. Louis. I have asked him to get into touch with you, but I do not know if he has yet.

One has to settle these business details, but of course what has been in my mind all the time has been your Mother's death. I am very sorry indeed. At whatever stage in one's mother's life or one's own this parting comes, one is bound to feel it in a very special way. Perhaps no other parting is quite like this. I will certainly remember her as you ask.

Yours affectionately,
Arnold

1. Missing.

2. Martha Love Symington. "During this visit she arranged a dinner in St. Louis for A.J.T. at

which Arthur Holly Compton (1892–1962), atomic physicist, then chancellor of Washington University, James S. McDonnell (1889–1980), founder of McDonnell Aircraft Corporation, and I were present. A.J.T. asked Mr. Compton if he still held his Wesleyan faith. He replied 'Yes, with a difference.'" (C.C.E.)

3. Howard Alexander Reed (1920–); delegate in Greece, World Studies Relief (1946–47); instructor, Princeton University (1949–50); assistant director, Danforth Foundation (1960–64); professor of history, University of Connecticut (1967–).

University of Pennsylvania
Philadelphia 4
The College
Department of History

26 March 1961

Dear Columba,

Your letter of 23 March was most welcome.[1] I have never set foot in Africa, though I have visited a number of Asian countries, as you know. If the S.L.P. Society will not mind my speaking from only second-hand acquaintence, I will speak on Africa with pleasure. It is a good subject, because it raises all the main problems: mixed populations, the need for preparation for self-government, and so on.

We expect to be flying from here to St. Louis on Tuesday 23 May. We need a few days at the end of the stay here for cleaning up.

If my talk can make a little money for the Priory, I shall, of course, be delighted.

We are both heavily up against an exacting schedule. One starts with the intention of keeping the schedule within bounds, but this is a forlorn hope.

It is a most interesting time to be in this country, isn't it? My enthusiasm for Kennedy continues to grow.

What do your boys think of the Peace Corps?[2] *Some* new device for breaking through the barrier that hedges in Americans abroad is, I am sure, a most urgent need. This was impressed on me by what I saw in Pakistan and Afghanistan last year.

Love from us both.

Yours affectionately,
Arnold

1. Missing.

2. The Peace Corps was established 1 March 1961 by executive order of President Kennedy.

University of Pennsylvania
Philadelphia 4
The College
Department of History

28 April 1961

Dear Columba,

I was so very glad to have your letter of 21 April.[1] I believed that I had told the O.U.P. to send you a copy of the book on my account.[2] But, in the whirl of my schedule I may have muddled it. So I am very glad you have had a copy from the Post-Dispatch, and I am quite delighted that you are reviewing it and that you liked it.

The proposed activities all sound very nice, not least the blank Friday. I take it that Jesuits ad lib, means lecture, with attendant festivities, at St. Louis University.

With love from us both,

Yours affectionately,
Arnold

1. Missing.
2. Volume XII of *A Study of History*.

c/o H.B.M. Consul
Denver, Colorado

30 May 1961

Dear Columba,

You will have heard from Father Luke about our fourth (!) case of mechanical breakdown on a plane during this trip. We were rueful about wasting an hour of Father Luke's time, but he was our life-line. There were moments when it looked as if we should just be returned, undispatched, to the cottage. However, they held the second plane for us at Kansas City, so all was well in the end.

These have been very happy days for us. There is no pleasure like seeing one's friends, and when they are building up something splendid, and it is progressing, the happiness is complete. The time fled fast, but, as you said, the effects are lasting.

I am now looking forward to hearing that you will be giving that TV talk—some time, I hope, between 19 June and 25 July, when we shall be in London.

This last week has been the high point of this visit of ours to America.

Well, may we see each other soon again.

Yours affectionately,
Arnold

St. Louis Priory
St. Louis, Missouri

6 June 1961

My dear Arnold,

All the Graduation excitement is over, the speeches and the dances, and dinners and prizes, hand shakes and now the N.N.T. arrives this morning; so it is an added incentive to write. Very many thanks. I've dived about already.

Much, much too short your visit, far too full of this and that, making me want to curse or at least kick myself. It is so refreshing to pick up the old themes again and new ones. I felt nearer to you in thought and sentiment than for a very long time, as though you had got a lot off your chest and felt liberated. As you say, meeting makes one hungry for more. When? How? The Good Lord will arrange it. I leave for England Friday and will be at Ampleforth by Monday 13th, before you return. This will have to await your arrival.

I thought you were both very alive, but both pretty tired.

My love to you both and thanks for all you did for the Priory.

Columba, O.S.B.

At Thurton Hall
Near Norwich
Norfolk

17 July 1961

Dear Arnold,

I am forwarding you a copy of the magazine which 'carries' our meeting in Saint Louis. It talks the usual rot, but one or two of the photos are good, one or two funny. And Veronica also may be interested.

I have now been in England over a month, first at Ampleforth and then here. I shall be with my sister near Ipswich (Crepping Hall, Stutton, Nr. Ipswich) next week and then a few days in London. I go to U.S.A. Aug. 2 if B O A C are in operation again by then. Is there any chance that you will be in London between July 29 and Aug. 2? and we could meet.

The atmosphere over here is curious: a combination of fear that the Americans are not wise enough to handle the explosive situation—who is?—and a fatalistic attitude—'It's bound to come sooner or later.' But I think those who think more deeply hope that every one will work for a compromise. The thing that stands out is the obvious fear of the E. Germans that they are going to be let down for good.[1]

I have had a very quiet and restful time this last 10 days and am beginning to want to get "back to business." Fr. Luke writes that our church tower (wood frame) is up.

Love to you both,

Columba, O.S.B.

1. On 15 August 1961, the East German government was to begin to build the Berlin Wall.

St. Louis Priory
St. Louis, Missouri

20 October 1961

My Dear Arnold,

The local newspaper has just last week sent me your travel book[1] for review, which I have done enthusiastically. How do you do it? It is a splendid piece of work, so full of life and verve, and the inquisitiveness of it. I am so glad you got to Balkh. It has for long interested me and I was amazed to read how immense it once was. The Nestorians had a great See there. Doubtless Alopen went through and also those two Nestorian monks from Peking going to Jerusalem. Your comparison between the British outpost and the Roman wall was good. I can see you persuading the driver to avoid the tortoises. I must say the local government did you proud. They were determined—I guess—to land you back on the frontier at the finish alive. My only criticism—not voiced in the Globe Democrat—was that your map did not really help. But I got out my historical atlas and off we went.

The study club you attended one evening at the Peper home is back at work. They are each buying a copy of Zaehner's "*World's Living Religions*"[2] and each will take one religion, beginning with Hinduism. My line is that God has revealed Himself through all these religions, and we can learn something from each of them. It will be interesting to see whether they find they think they discover anything fundamentally new, or only restatement of what they knew already. Some Buddhist teaching will contradict their faith, and that will be obvious, but the Zoroastrian and Hindu insights are interesting too. When I said "reveal" above, I meant it in a general sense because as far as one can see these revelations or insights are practically all—or all one accepts—on the rational plane, within the framework of what reason might discover.[3] We shall see how it goes.

The church is up, not the floors, nor the windows but the whole concrete framework, tower and cross above. It is lovely inside. I'm not quite sure about the outside. The opening is May 1962!

It was sad your being out of London when I was there, as in fact just before my return I had 3 days there, and one afternoon listened to Mr. Macmillan propose the Common Market.

My love to you both,

Columba, O.S.B.

P.S. Get a visa for Kashgar, Cherchen, Samarkand and the rest. You've really only done half that world!

1. A.J.T.'s *Between Oxus and Jumna.*

2. Robert Charles Zaehner (1913–74); Spalding Professor of Eastern Religions and Ethics, Oxford, from 1952; received into the Catholic Church, 1946; *The Catholic Church and World Religions* (London, 1964); *Drugs, Mysticism and Make-Believe* (London, 1972).

3. "I no longer believe that but am prepared to believe that God could and no doubt did and does reveal, beyond reasoning, insights to non-Jews and non-Christians as to Job and others before and since." (C.C.E.)

The Royal Institute
of International Affairs
Chatham House
10, St James's Square
London S.W.1

23 October 1961

Dear Mr. Speaight,[1]

I have just heard from Father James Forbes of Ampleforth that you are going to write a life of Father Paul Nevill, and that you are asking old boys and their parents to send you notes of their personal memories of Father Paul. Father James suggested that I should send you a note of mine. I am doing this with very great pleasure. Father Paul was a great headmaster because he was a most human person. It would have been a loss if some account of him had not been put on record at a time when there were still plenty of people alive who had known him personally; and now, most fortunately, you are going to provide this.

Please feel free to use, or not use, the following notes of mine. You will almost certainly have more materials than you can make use of. I send mine just on the chance that they might fit into the plan of your book. I have only one stipulation—an obvious one—that, if you do use them, you will not mention names. My son Philip is now a very good father of a family, and quite a distinguished writer—and he might not have been either of these things now if Father Paul had not gone out of his way, as he did, at a moment's notice, to help Philip to get onto the rails again at a critical moment in Philip's early life when he had run off them.

Philip, at the beginning of his last year at Rugby, had run away to join a Communist cell that had been started by Lady Churchill's nephew, Esmond Romilly, to propagand the public schools. (Against all his anti-bourgeois principles, Esmond became an R.A.F. Bomber Command rear-gunner in the second World War, and was killed).

Philip was inevitably expelled from Rugby. My wife and I, who were neighbours of Ampleforth and knew Father Paul, told him, over the telephone, what had happened, and, in that same telephone conversation, Father Paul said he was going to ask Father Abbot if he would take Philip as a guest in the monastery, and volunteered, supposing that Father Abbot agreed to this, that he, Father Paul, would coach Philip personally for a scholarship at Oxford.

Father Abbot did agree, and, as a result of Father Paul's coaching, Philip got a history exhibition at Christ Church. (The subject of the essay in the scholarship paper was the same as that of the last essay that Philip had written for Father Paul. Father Paul was a first-class professional, incidentally). Of course, the coaching and the getting of the scholarship, important though they were for Philip, were not so important as the effect on him of being at Ampleforth at a time when he was very much at sea. Father James, then a very young monk, was given the job of looking after Philip and giving him companionship, and I am everlastingly grateful to James as well as to Father Paul.

Father Paul was taking a risk, because Philip, in the mood in which he then was, might have been a Communist cat among the pigeons in the school if he had found a chance. It was characteristic of Father Paul, and of Ampleforth, that they did take this risk, and made their decision straight away.

Philip was provocative. He used to come into the refectory wearing a flaming red tie. An old monk once muttered: 'I'd like to throw a plate at his head', but was reminded by his brethren that it was part of a monk's duty to put up with annoyances that would drive people in the world into retaliating.

Philip was restive and, at one moment, looked like breaking away from what was, at the time, his one chance. I rushed up from London to Ampleforth to see what could be done, and found that Father Paul had already done it. He had persuaded Father Abbot to let Philip have a motor-bicycle at the monastery as an outlet for his energies—an unheard of thing.

That evening I went to bed in the guest-room, all in, and had just got under the bed-clothes when Father Paul came in with a whiskey-and-soda in his hand and put it to my lips. I was supposed to be a grown-up responsible parent, but, in an ordeal, the child who needs a grown-up person's human kindness comes out, I suppose, in most human beings. Father Paul had realized this about me. The whiskey, the motor-bicycle: he was always resourceful. But his human kindness was the big thing in him. I have never forgotten my feelings at that moment, and never shall forget them as long as I live. That visit to me in bed by a very busy man, with a thousand things to see to, may sound like a trivial incident, but it wasn't.

Philip is just publishing the first volume of what looks as if it might be his magnum opus. So, at this moment, I look back to that turning-point in his life—in 1934 at Ampleforth—and my feelings go out, in gratitude and love, to Father Paul.

I am very glad indeed that you are writing this book, and I wish you the success, that I am sure you will have, in painting a picture of Father Paul that will bring him alive to people who did not know him personally, as well as to those who did.

Yours sincerely,
Arnold Toynbee

1. This letter is substantially the same as that written to C.C.E. (now missing) when C.C.E. was undertaking Fr. Paul's biography. Robert Speaight (1904–76); actor and writer; *The Life of Hilaire Belloc* (London, 1957); performed the part of Becket in the first production of *Murder in the Cathedral*.

The Royal Institute
of International Affairs
Chatham House
10, St James's Square
London S.W.1

10 November 1961

Dear Columba,

I was so glad to have your letter of 5 November [1] and to hear that the copy of the book reached you all right. You had already sent me a copy of your very kind review.

The present world situation gives one a horrifying picture of human nature that has neither love for God nor awe of him. By 'God' I mean a spiritual presence higher than Man. Man cannot be the highest. Left to itself, or, rather, having itself to itself, human nature seems to be mastered by a lust for power. This lust is so strong that, rather than see our human opponent's power prevail over our own, we are willing not only to commit suicide but to liquidate the human race. I am appalled at the wickedness of our behaviour: it is irresponsibility that amounts to wickedness. We are threatening the lives of hundreds of millions of innocent human beings: women with child, children in their infancy. And we are also threatening to deny to countless possible future generations the gift of life that we ourselves have received. We are using our new power—mere brute material power—to play at being God, and to take decisions that no human beings have any moral right to take. If suicide is a usurpation of God's prerogative, genocide must be, *a fortiori*. I find this horrifying, as I say.

Personally, we are well and prospering. I was lecturing in Cambridge yesterday, and we were seeing my granddaughter Josephine, who is a freshman.[2] Philip has just published the first installment of his magnum opus. Title, '*Pantaloon*:'[2] it is the reminiscences of an old man, in free verse, interspersed with critical second thoughts in prose. It has been having a mixed reaction, which is not surprising, as it is a new genre. I am very much hoping that it will win through to being a success. Your comments on '*Reconsiderations*' will be very valuable to me, but do not press yourself to produce them: you have far too much to do, as it is.

With love from us both,

Yours affectionately,
Arnold

1. Missing.

2. Josephine Laura Toynbee (1943–); daughter of Philip and Anne Toynbee; cf. A.J.T.'s letter of 29 November 1939, above.

3. Philip Toynbee's *Pantaloon* (London, 1961); the sequel, *Two Brothers* (London, 1964); and see *A Learned City* (London, 1966); *Views from a Lake: The Seventh Day of the Valediction of Pantaloon* (London, 1968).

Saint Louis Priory
Saint Louis, Missouri,

20 December 1961

My dear Arnold,

Thank you for your letter and both of you for your good card and good wishes. I too wish you a happy Christmas, and please God peace in the New Year.

The latest shock to world peace was in the papers last night: Diu and Goa:[1] Symbols they were of European domination, but it is the old, old story of ignoring the machinery for peaceful settlement. Stevenson[2] takes this event as an indication that the U.N. like the League before it has become a sham. This seems to me a pity. Nations behave like children, and while now and then they go overboard, in general they want peace.

America is moving towards a much sterner frame of mind. It would I think retaliate with atom bombs. This is too awful to contemplate, and the reason for this I think is that over here there is little of the Lord Russell kind of action.

I can see and agree with all his arguments, but I cannot quite agree in the last analysis with the conclusion of unilateral pacifism. *L'esprit de géométrie et L'esprit de finesse*[3] seem to come in.

Is each government responsible for seeing that women and children are evacuated from great cities? Or is this quite unrealistic?

What a dreadful Christmas letter to be writing. It shows what a pass we have come to. You would say: better put the world back three thousand years into slavery than the holocaust required to prevent it, and you may be right.

My love to you both.

Columba, O.S.B.

1. On 18–19 December 1961, Indian troops invaded and conquered the Portuguese territories of Goa, Damao, and Diu.

2. Adlai Ewing Stevenson (1900–1965); then representative of the United States at the United Nations.

3. See Blaise Pascal's *Oeuvres complètes*, ed. Louis Lafuma (Paris, 1963), Pensées, no. 512 (Brunschvicg no. 1).

45, Pembroke Square
London W.8

27 December 1961

Dear Columba,

Your letter of the 20th came this morning by the first post-Christmas post. We got back from Egypt on the 22nd: a very strenuous three weeks, but very much worth while. Being a state guest gives one a taste of what kings and queens have to go through, every day of their lives, poor things: formal calls, and being shown many things, like fertilizer-plants and power-stations, that one does not understand. Unlike kings and queens, I was lecturing as well.[1] All the same, we did manage to see an awful lot of people and things that we wanted to; and one's first visit to Egypt is anyway an event in one's life. The most beautiful thing in Egypt is the countryside itself, so exquisitely cultivated and with all the people and animals so busy. The big thing that is happening now is a social revolution—drastic but bloodless. For the first time, I suppose, since before the pyramids were built, something is being done now for the ordinary people, not just for a privileged few. Ancient Egyptian architecture knocks one down, of course, (we got as far south as Ramses II's colossi at Abu Simbel in Nubia). But the art is monotonous, except for the portrait statues of the Old Kingdom and Akhenaton's short burst of naturalism. The beautiful architecture—and this in several styles—is that of the mosques in the medieval parts of Cairo. Well, here we sit till we make a brief sortie to Puerto Rico in February.

I feel as you do about Goa. I blame Portugal as well as India. When both Britain and France had voluntarily given up their Indian holdings, it was preposterous that Portugal should have refused to do the same. Yet it was very wrong of India to take Goa by force, since every use of force takes us a step nearer to an atomic world war. Every country goes on putting its own sectional interests before those of the human race, though every country will be annihilated if the human race commits suicide.

Your account of American feeling is alarming. You call the mood 'stern', but doesn't sternness imply an understanding of the dire consequences of what one is doing? And, if I am right, the American people does not even begin to understand what an atomic war would be like. If they did, they wouldn't be thinking in terms of shelters (i.e. in terms of a war like the last one). It is not surprising, because they haven't had a taste of war in their own country since Sherman's march through Georgia;[2] and human nature is unimaginative. But it is alarming. If America made an atomic war, I think her morale—and every other country's, too—would collapse in a few minutes. Happily, the President evidently does have the imagination to understand; and I pray that Kruschev does too. But the politicians on both sides may become prisoners of their own past propaganda.

I also agree with you about Bertie Russell.[3] I admire him for caring so much, at his age, about the future. But unilateral disarmament of Britain is beside the point. Only agreed Russo-American simultaneous disarmament can serve us, and we know how difficult that is.

The commencement of the oecumenical council[4] is a ray of light.

Love and best wishes from both of us for you and the Priory and the School and the World.

Arnold

1. A.J.T. delivered seven lectures during this visit; four were published as *Importance of the Arab World* (Cairo, 1962).

2. General William Tecumseh Sherman (1820–91); in 1864 marched through Georgia to the sea, ravaging the country, destroying crops and railroads.

3. Bertrand Russell had publicly supported unilateral disarmament.

4. Vatican II was formally convoked by Pope John XXIII on 25 December 1961. It opened on 11 October 1962.

16 January 1962 Saint Louis Priory

My dear Arnold,

Your description of the Egyptian situation was most reassuring. It is confirmed by a book—sent me for review:—about the Nubian Nile dam scheme. At last the little men may live in modest comfort and justice there. Russian money!

If Puerto Rico,[1] why not Saint Louis on the way back. This time absolutely incognito, if only for a couple of nights, or as long as you wish. We have not the cottage available as Fr. Luke's secretary has moved in, but the ¼ of the house near by where the Barrys[2] live.

I went by car to Washington D.C. after Christmas to attend and assist at the blessing of the first abbot of S. Anselm's[3] there—an English Benedictine foundation. Fr. Augustine[4] and Fr. Ian[5] went with me. It was hard going: to Saint Vincent's Abbey, Latrobe[6] (Penn.) the first day. S.V.'s is the oldest OSB house in the States; then Washington by 6 PM next day. We came back by a more southern route, through Virginia, and stopped over the river from Cincinnati at Covington Priory[7]—nuns. Then the next night at Gethsemani,[8] and so home the third day. I was tired. How Americanized can one get? Not much more.

The church construction is being held up by very cold weather c. 15° below zero (new style).

Is the Common Market going to happen for U.K. It would be sad if political manoeuvering hindered it. England used to be part of Europe and really is still. It would be good for both parties. I must admit E. is pretty unstable, beginning with France. But economic stability—which seems on the way—goes a long way to bringing political stability, would not you say?

I have nearly finished a little book called *Both And*, an ecumenical discussion. The title should give you the key to the contents. I haven't sent it to a publisher yet. What are you at?

Love to you both,
Columba, O.S.B.

1. Where A.J.T. delivered the lectures published as *The Economy of the Western Hemisphere* (London, 1962).

2. Brian Barry (1924–) and his wife and children; Amplefordian; Royal Naval College; then instructor in Mathematics and physics, now in charge of computer science, at the Priory school.

3. St. Anselm's Abbey; cf. A.J.T.'s letter of 24 September 1942, above.

4. Augustine Measures, O.S.B. (1927–); Ampleforth monk; then at the St. Louis Priory; now on parish duty at St. Benedict's, Warrington, England.

5. Ian Petit, O.S.B.; cf. C.C.E.'s letter of 15 March 1958, above.

6. St. Vincent's Archabbey; the first permanent Benedictine foundation in the United States; founded in 1846 by Bavarian monks.

7. A Benedictine convent, in Covington.

8. A Trappist monastery (reformed Cistercian monks).

The Royal Institute
of International Affairs
Chatham House
10, St James's Square
London S.W.1

24 January 1962

Dear Columba,

I have just had your letter of 16 Jan. (the P.O. officials here are 'working to rule', as you know). Alas, we can't put in a visit to St. Louis on this trip. We shall just be the one night in New York each way. We have a spring journey in S. Italy and Sicily looming up—part of the work on my Hannibal book—and we must sit tight a bit, in between. But on 1 Feb. 1963 we shall be arriving, for a whole semester, at Grinnell College, Iowa, pretty well next door to you, so we shall have easy opportunities of meeting then—unless, of course, before that, you have Americanised yourself to death, which I hope you will resist doing. That last journey of yours sounds like a nightmare.

We had a circus party of 27 people (including grown-ups) last month: quite strenuous too, in its way.

With love from us both,
Arnold

19 April 1962

Saint Louis Priory

My dear Arnold,

I have been meaning to write for weeks and things flooded in. Now I have a few moments before the great ceremonies of Holy Week and a retreat I am giving to c. 20 undergraduates who are being housed here and there on the property.

Gaudium paschale and a feeling of victory through Christ who has won for man peace with God. I pray that more and more you and I come to love and reverence Christ and follow his meekness and courage and love. It is this time of year that is so lovely and springlike at Ampleforth. So it is here, the New Life is symbolized all round us.

It is wonderful news that you are to be in U.S. next fall and winter. Can you be here for the consecration of our church, Sept. 7, 1962. We hope the Cardinal will do it.[1] He had a scruple, there were no walls to consecrate. But the Congregation of Rites reassured him that "wall" has to be taken in the broad sense!

Doubleday wrote today provisionally accepting a MS. on ecumenical matters, but says they must have 65,000 words, so I shall have to scribble a lot more. There are still plenty of ideas in my head, but do put a few down which you think basic.

We hope to send two novices over to England in Sept. They should do well. Two have already "stuck" over there. Soon, I hope, we'll have our noviciate here.

The bells are in the tower, the windows are in, all is ready for the plasterers. The altars, of granite, are being made, the carvers (sculptors)[2] are at work on the crucifixes. It now remains to be seen whether everyone finishes on time.

The world seems to totter along as usual, but I believe with you that every year that a major clash can be averted the less likely it is to come.

Kennedy has won a major victory over big business.[3] The retreatants arrive.

My love to you both,
Columba, O.S.B.

1. Joseph Elmer, Cardinal Ritter (1892–1967); bishop of Indianapolis (1934–46); archbishop of St. Louis (1946–67).

2. The sculptors were: Leslie Thornton, Doris Caesar, William Schickel, Hillis Arnold, Gerhard Marcks, Clark Fitz-Gerald, Luis Sanchez, Robert Adams, and Wolfgang Behl.

3. Within a fortnight after having secured a noninflationary wage pact, U.S. Steel informed John F. Kennedy of a proposed substantial increase in steel prices; Kennedy immediately issued a public denunciation, ordered an antitrust investigation, and persuaded other steel companies not to match the increase; within seventy-two hours the price increase was rescinded.

The Royal Institute
of International Affairs
Chatham House
10, St James's Square
London, S.W.1

25 April 1962

Dear Columba,

Veronica and I came back from Palermo yesterday and your welcome letter of 19 April came this morning.

I do wish we could be with you on the great day, Sept. 7, 1962, but we must take a full holiday to be fresh for our strenuous programme of next winter and spring.

We find that we have to ration our travelling now. We could easily put ourselves to a premature death by doing all the journeys we should like to do.

We kept our Easter at Palermo in the Martorana Church[1] (Greek rite; local Albanians) and in Monreale Cathedral.[2] This was the end-up of a five weeks journey in Southern Italy and Sicily. On the mainland we were the guests of the Agrarian Reform Organization,[3] who are doing a notable job.

I am so very glad about the progress of the church and also the novices who are the heart of what you have been doing.

I am afraid the retreat will have been no holiday for you. Love from us both.

Arnold

1. Santa Maria dell'Ammiraglio, a Norman church founded in 1143 by George of Antioch, admiral of Roger II; presented in 1433 to a convent established in 1194 by Eloisa Martorana.

2. Santa Maria la Nuova, the Norman cathedral, rich in mosaics; erected (1172–76) by William II, the son-in-law of Henry II of England.

3. A.J.T. made this trip under the auspices of members of the Facoltà Agraria of the University of Naples, the officers of the Instituto Agrario of the University of Palermo, and others. "The agrarian reform in present-day Italy throws light on the Gracchan reform in the second century B.C. Once again an attempt is being made to change the face of the Mezzogiorno and to make life better for its people by breaking up latifundia into small holdings." *Hannibal's Legacy*, 1 : vi.

The Royal Institute
of International Affairs
Chatham House
10, St James's Square
London, S.W.1

22 June 1962

Dear Columba,

Would a visit from Veronica and me about 24 May, 1963, be a possibility for you?

We are going to be on the campus of Grinnell College, Grinnell, Iowa, for the second semester of 1962–3. Among other invitations, I have had one from Lindenwood College, St. Charles, Mo., which seems to be on the threshold of St. Louis. I have offered them May 23 for the date—I do not know whether it will suit them, but, if it does, I thought we might perhaps come on to the Priory from there.

I seem always to be refusing to do things and always finding that I have too much on hand. Since the autumn we have been in Salzburg, Egypt,[1] Puerto Rico,[2] Calabria, Sicily, Morocco; Texas looms up, for a week in October, then Greece and Turkey, then Venezuela, then Iowa.

We do want to see the church pretty well complete.

Meanwhile, I am starting on vol. ii of the economic and social consequences of the Hannibalic War.

I do hope you are standing up to your still more strenuous life. Now that I am getting old, I find that time counts again, as it does when one is a child.

This is rather a hasty letter.

Love to you from us both.
Arnold

1. Where in December 1961 A.J.T. delivered lectures published in *The Toynbee Lectures on the Middle East and Problems of Underdeveloped Countries* (Cairo, 1962) and *Importance of the Arab World* (Cairo, 1962).

2. See C.C.E.'s letter of 16 January 1962, n. 1, above.

The Royal Institute
of International Affairs
Chatham House
10, St James's Square
London, S.W.1

2 July 1962

Dear Columba,

Now your second letter has come:[1] this is something to look forward to. By that stage we shall be in great need of rest and quiet.

If you *can* put us somewhere together, I shall be glad. I should love to sleep in the Monastery, but I think Veronica might feel a little bit forlorn, however hospitably entertained, if she was by herself.

We are off on Friday for a sedentary three months in Westmorland, which we need. 'Hannibalic' was the word, as you guessed. My handwriting, never good, is degenerating.

I do look forward to seeing the church—and you.

Yours affectionately,
Arnold

1. Missing.

407 North Eighth Street
St. Louis, Missouri

21 August 1962

Dear Mr. and Mrs. Toynbee,

Father Columba has told us that you are intending to spend a week in Saint Louis in May of 1963, and Mrs. Peper and I should be delighted if you could be our guests during this period. You will remember the library portion of our house; it also includes separate living quarters where we think you would be most comfortable. As you know, we are only two miles from The Priory. We also have an extra car which we shall be glad to place at your disposal so that you may come and go at will. We shall do our utmost to protect your privacy.

We hope that you can be with us.

Yours very sincerely,
Christian B. Peper

The Royal Institute
of International Affairs
Chatham House

26 August 1962

Dear Mr. Peper,

My wife and I have just had your and Mrs. Peper's most kind and hospitable letter of August 21. We should like very much indeed to accept your invitation. At Grinnell College, Iowa, where we shall be, classes end on Saturday, May 25, and their Commencement, at which I am giving the address, is on June 7, so we could come at any time between these dates, on whatever days were most convenient to you and Father Columba.

Thank you, too, for your considerate offer of the use of a car. Unfortunately, neither of us drives a car, but my legs are still good for carrying me those two miles and back as often as I want.

We do look forward to staying with you.

Yours sincerely,
Arnold J. Toynbee

I apologize for this awful typing. We are away in the country and our old typewriter here has suddenly started to behave like this.

A.T.

26 August 1962 Hall Beck

Dear Columba,

We have just had, and accepted, a most hospitable invitation from Mr. and Mrs. Peper. We have told them that we could come for any days that suited them and you between about 25 May, when classes at Grinnell end, and 7 June, when I have to be back at Grinnell to give the commencement address there.

My idea of combining the visit to Lindenwood College, St. Charles, wouldn't work, as this would be too late in the season for them, so I have had to put the Lindenwood College lecture on April 18. On the same expedition, I may possibly also be lecturing, on April 17, at Washington University, St. Louis, so we might get a preliminary glimpse of each other then, perhaps.

The Pepers have offered us the use of a spare car, so I have had to confess that we are neither of us drivers. However, I have also told him that my legs are still good for carrying me the two miles' round-trip as many times as I want—and this will, no doubt, be often.

I can see the church complete in my mind's eye, but I expect the reality will surpass my imagination of it.

We are sitting rooted here for three months, and this is going to do us good—though we have been a bit the worse for a kind of nervous breakdown that my sister-in-law, who lives not far off, has had. Happily this seems now to have been cured by electric shock treatment, but it has been rather gruelling for Veronica, unfortunately.

I am pushing ahead with vol. ii of my consequences-of-Hannibal book. When I have finished that, I shall be at the end of an agenda that I have had since 1916. This will be a curious sensation—except that the agenda is sure to sprout.

I hope you are not letting America kill you by inches—or, rather, by sets of seven leagues—by working you to death.

Yours affectionately,
Arnold

The Royal Institute
of International Affairs
At Hall Beck

18 September 1962

Dear Columba,

I have just had your letter of 13 August.[1] Meanwhile, Veronica's sister has had electric shock treatment, which has had a remarkable effect, so she is now back home in her bungalow again and is, I am glad to say, apparently recovered.

The Pepers are being very kind. A week is a long invitation. We will stay for the inside of a week. I have just accepted an invitation from the U.N. Food & Agriculture Organization to be one of their speakers at a Congress of theirs which opens on 4 June at Washington, D.C., so perhaps we might come just before that, and go straight from St. Louis to Washington, without returning to Iowa in between?

I am so glad the church is complete, and consecrated. You are right: the Taj Mahal is still the latest sensation in India, but nothing, however beautiful, is likely to go on being that for long in America.

Our retreat here at Hall Beck is indeed refreshing. The processions of several sets of cows, several times a day, that pass our windows, are soothing. We are threatened with one of those new speedways within a few hundred yards off. The threat has been hanging over us for 14 years, and may still materialize. There are, though, alternative possible routes that would not cut up so much good agricultural land.

On 5 Oct. we have to pluck up our roots and fly for a week to Houston Texas for Rice University's jubilee, and then we go to Greece and Turkey for the British Council. These engagements keep one alive, but are also exhausting. We enjoy the quiet here while we can.

Funny that you should have thought of a history of the world for me. I have been meditating one, Home University Library size,[2] as my next item after finishing 'The Consequences of Hannibal', and I am now nearly half way through Vol. ii of that.

Our love to you,
Arnold

1. Missing.
2. A.J.T.'s *Mankind and Mother Earth: A Narrative History of the Earth* (London, 1976).

The Royal Institute
of International Affairs
Chatham House
10, St James's Square
London S.W.1

2 December 1962

Dear Columba,

Your letter of 23 Nov. was very welcome.[1] I have never been in Dallas—only in the air port—and I should never have thought of Hungarian Cistercians being there. We were in Austin and Houston for a week, early in October,[2] and came back ten days ago from five weeks in Turkey and Greece, where I was lecturing for the British Council. We did a lot of travelling too, and I put some important new country on my map, eg. Eastern Macedonia and S. W. Anatolia (I was ten days in a landrover, south of the Meander, with two old Turkish friends of mine, but I dissuaded Veronica from doing that). We are now here till Jan. 26, when we fly to Carácas en route for Grinnell, Iowa, via Jacksonville, Florida.

We were in Athens during the most critical days over Cuba,[3] and the news merely told us what the President had done, without giving the reasons why, so it looked like very arbitrary and provocative action. It was a pity that the reasons only came out afterwards. I hope everybody is now sobered into a more accommodating frame of mind. We can't afford to continue in relations in which we might again come so near to the brink as that. I feel particularly bad about it when I see my grand children—I was seeing some of Lawrence's children yesterday at Oxford. We were staying with Lawrence and Jean: I was speaking to a *joint* meeting of the Oxford undergraduate Jewish and Arab societies. I agreed to give a talk to each if they would have a united meeting, so they did, and we are going to have at least one more. I feel I have achieved something useful.

Well, the Vatican Council[4] will probably be better organised, in its next session, for getting down to business.

I am much looking forward to seeing you.

Yours affectionately,
Arnold

1. Missing.

2. The lecture delivered at Rice University, Houston, was published as "The Changes in the United States' Position and Outlook as a World Power during the Last Half-Century," in *Man, Science, Learning and Education*, ed. S. W. Higginbotham (Houston, Tex., 1963), pp. 1–20.

3. The Cuban Missile Crisis of 22–28 October 1962.

4. Vatican II (1962–65).

Saint Louis Priory
Saint Louis, Missouri

Sunday 23 December 1962

My dear Arnold,

This would have been written a week ago, but I was caught by a kidney stone last Monday night and have been in hospital ever since. Don't worry, pain is a great grace, particularly this kind as it is not lethal; it reduces one to the atom that one is. I am full of gratitude to God for having given me this taste of what true suffering is. Of course there are depths beyond this, like the loss of friends; but I leave what He gives to his own judgement.

The doctors looked after me well, and this morning I return to the Priory.

The book I took with me, apart from the New Testament and a detective story was your *Reconsiderations* which I love to dip into, with its sweet potatoes, its comments on your classical education, etc. This time I read the part on Law and the empirical method.[1] It amazes me how many people criticized without reading the whole work and without knowing that the hypothesis had to come first. Then I re-read the part on Relativity in dealing with Religion and approve your word transrationalism.[2] I find this a humble approach. The word verifiable is one that some day I would like to talk with you about, for instance—and I think one has to use a concrete example—the case of the Resurrection: against the natural order of things, I should say! and yet "verified" by many people of the N.T. And then, to use your own cautious approach to scientific generalizations, why should there not be an exception? But how gentle and winning your effort is to bring the two sides together.

I came upon the little "poem" about buses and trams by RAK and to test dear Veronica's thoroughness I looked in the index—I often do—and sure enough there it was p. 241 n. Give her my love, and tell her I keep her in my prayers as I do you; not only because she looks after you so well, but for her own dear self too.

The Council, I believe, has won through; that is, the mind of the Council has shown itself for renewal; it has brushed aside the rather feeble efforts of the Curia to make it a rubber stamp affair; the 9 months to come with the new Commissions at work, should produce the principles on which the saints of the next age will *act*, as those, like Ignatius,[3] Francis,[4] Charles,[5] Philip,[6] did after Trent. It is interesting to me that the Holy Spirit can be hindered at a Council, as I feel He was at Vatican I up to a point, whereas in the Bible He governed; I mean that the action of God in the Church does not eliminate the wilfulness of man except to avoid error and even that only in General Councils, etc.

A very happy Christmas and thank God we are all still alive.

Love to you both.
Columba, O.S.B.

P.S. When do I see you next.

1. *A Study of History*, XII: 235–50.

2. Ibid., pp. 68–102.

3. Saint Ignatius Loyola; cf. A.J.T.'s letter of 25 July 1939, above.

4. Saint Francis Xavier; see C.C.E.'s letter of 15 February 1952, above.

5. Saint Charles Borromeo (1538–84); active at Trent; cardinal and archbishop of Milan; a true shepherd during the great plague.

6. Saint Philip Neri (1515–95); spiritual adviser; a gentle saint; founder of the Congregation of the Oratory (secular priests living in a community without vows); the Oratorians were introduced into England by Cardinal Newman.

The Royal Institute
of International Affairs
Chatham House
10, St James's Square
London S.W.1

27 December 1962

Dear Columba,

I came back to Chatham House this afternoon. I am most concerned, as Veronica will be when I take it home for her to read. I gather that you have now been 'cut for the stone' as Pepys puts it. But the pain must have been grim. I have not, so far, had any fearful physical pain, but I have had bad spiritual pain, as you know. Losing a human being—Tony one way,[1] Rosalind another[2]—is bad pain; feeling that one has perhaps done wrong before God is much worse.

What pleased me most in your letter, of course, is your feeling for Veronica for her own sake.

N.B. Pepys's diary begins with his being cut for the stone[3] (without an anaesthetic) and ends many years before he died; so you will probably live as many years after this operation as Pepys did. Only, immediately after, you must go at an English, not an American, pace.

We shall see each other, I hope, when Veronica and I come to Washington University on 17 April and to Lindenwood College on 18–19 April, and then again for a week from 25 or 29 May on.

Well, you are always much in our thoughts, now you will be particularly there during convalescence.

With love from us both,

Yours affectionately,
Arnold

1. Compare A.J.T.'s letter of 19 March 1939, above.

2. Compare A.J.T.'s letter of 25 February 1943, above.

3. *The Diary of Samuel Pepys*, edited by R. Latham and W. Matthews (London 1970), Vol. I, p. 1.

Grinnell College
Grinnell, Iowa

13 February 1963

Dear Columba,

I do hope you are now completely recovered. Your convalescence sounded rather strenuous. We got here last Sunday, via Venezuela and Jacksonville, Florida. Both the college and the town are most attractive, and we are sure we are going to be happy here.

I am writing now about dates. Do you think it would be convenient for the Pepers if we came on Sunday May 26 or Monday May 27, and left (for Aspen, Colorado) on the morning of Friday May 31? We want to be sure not to trespass too much on their hospitality, or to suggest anything that might be inconvenient for them.

We anyway hope to see you before that, as, on the evening of April 16, we are flying to Washington University, St. Louis, staying there over April 17, going from there to Lindenwood College, St. Charles, on the 18th, and leaving again for Grinnell on Friday the 19th. I hope we may get at least a glimpse of each other then.

After London last month it is a comfort to be warm indoors.

Yours affectionately,
Arnold

Grinnell College
Grinnell, Iowa

8 March 1963

Dear Columba,

I have just had your letter of March 6.[1] We are both all right. This is a charming little town and the faculty and students at the College are particularly nice. It has a more or less nation-wide clientèle, not just a local one. We are in a very handy warm apartment, within short walking distance of everything.[2]

I do hope we can see each other on April 17. The schedule is tight, as you guessed. We are arriving in St. Louis on the evening of April 16 by B.N. 233 at 8.35 P.M. I have not heard from Washington University where we are spending the night but I am lecturing there at 11.0 A.M. on April 17, and then we are being carried off after lunch on the 17th to Lindenwood College, St. Charles, Mo., and are taking B.N. 234 on April 18, leaving St. Louis at 5.15 P.M. for Des Moines. I seem to have a pretty full schedule at St. Charles. I suppose there will be some kind of a lunch at Washington University after the lecture. Couldn't you come to that? Or, if there isn't one, couldn't we come to lunch with you that day and get ourselves picked up that day after lunch at the priory instead of at Washington University by Lindenwood College?

The Professor in charge of us at Washington University is Irving Litvag, Director of Special Events (I must be one of these), so he is probably the man for you to get in touch with.

In May, I am afraid I ought to agree to have a meeting with the Grinnell alumni in St. Louis, as I am on their campus. I shall refuse anything else that is not your own suggestion.

Our very best wishes,
Yours affectionately,
Arnold

1. Missing.

2. A.J.T. held the Heath Visiting Professorship at Grinnell College; cf. the preface to vol. 2 of *Hannibal's Legacy*, where he praises the library: "At Grinnell I enjoyed the luxury of having an excellent classical library within ten minutes walk of where I was living."

711 Seventh Avenue
Grinnell, Iowa

2 June 1963

Dear Columba,

Well, those were very very happy days for Veronica and me. We were sad when they came to an end—and the time passed quickly—but we came away refreshed.

I do like having these glimpses of what you are building up—it is something so well worth building.

We ran into a thunderstorm on Friday before reaching Denver, but fortunately it was fine when we skimmed on from there to here (Aspen) in a two-engined plane. We were supposed to skim out again tomorrow morning en route for Washington, D.C., but today the clouds have come down, so we shall probably have to make an early start tomorrow and go back to Denver by road to catch our plane there.

Here we have been among business men: it is quite instructive to listen to them talking.

Well, if we do not see each other again before the autumn of 1964, we shall certainly manage it when we are at the University of Denver then.

Our very best wishes to the fathers.

The Pepers were amazingly kind to us, and made us quickly feel like old friends.

God Bless you.
Yours affectionately,
Arnold

The Benedictines
of Westminster Abbey
Mission City, B.C.

14 June 1963

My dear Arnold,

As you see from the address I am perched up on a minor mountain overlooking the Fraser River and Mount Baker away to the south, a fine sight. I've been giving the monks here their yearly retreat. Since 1939 they have been in the area and since 1954 actually on this spot, about 30 monks now, abbot and all. They stem from the American Swiss congregation and run a diocesan seminary. The M.C. of today's ceremonies is an old Downside boy, entering the priesthood out here.

Thank you for your note, but so much more for coming; it was a wonderful thing to be able to be together and talk leisurely. After you left I felt some sense of guilt at not having brought up the subject of the Church and what your position is. But now I think we did right. It was not the time, and you are fully aware of the situation. But time *is* running out, and while we may meet in the Fall of 1964—I hope you do repeat the visit—it is always possible that God may call one or both of us. Meanwhile I pray that we both have insight to help one another.

Please do not forget a *little* bibliography for a possible ecumenical approach by me to Buddhism etc., though it seems ridiculous at times considering I do not know these religions first hand. But a beginning has to be made. The question always arises: for whom is one writing the book? If for Christians, then it has to show the good in Buddhism, Mahomedanism, etc., if for the others, then what?

I think I am more interested immediately in the Prophetic idea, but no harm to accumulate material for the other.

Do keep up with Abbot Butler.[1] He quite obviously was delighted to meet you and to find you all and more than he had hoped.

Saturday I set off for Mount Angel Abbey near Portland, and I am going to do it by bus, then across the Rockies to Bismarck and so home.

It was very good to see Veronica, and, whilst I thought she looked very tired, she perked up as the days went by, and unless Washington was back to the whirlpool perhaps on arrival in England she will have the energy to go flat hunting.

God bless you both.
Yours affectionately,
Columba, O.S.B.

1. Abbot Basil Christopher Butler, O.S.B. (1902–); Scripture scholar; then Abbot of Downside; now Bishop Butler. During the Council he was raised to the episcopate, assistant to the Archbishop of Westminster; he had edited Dom Cuthbert Butler's *The Vatican Council (1869–1870)* (1930; reprint London, 1962). Bishop Butler and A.J.T. attended a meeting of the Priory discussion group held at the Peper residence during A.J.T.'s visit to St. Louis; A.J.T. was interested in Bishop Butler's account of the Vatican Council, then in midcourse.

The Royal Institute
of International Affairs
Chatham House
10, St James's Square
London S.W.1

22 June 1963

Dear Columba,

Your letter of 14 June was waiting for me when we got home on 20 June. What a lovely landscape—and you will have been through more beautiful country on your way to Portland.

Now that our American schedule is all performed, we do feel tired, and are finding it hard to take up all the things that were waiting to be dealt with here. In the present-day world, one cannot 'relax', even after nominal retirement.

Yes, one may die any day: I am very conscious of this, as people younger than me keep on dying, now, just from old age. Anything that I can accomplish now I am thankful for, as a bonus.

My position is the same as before, and will, as far as I can foresee, go on being the same so long as I am alive. It would be practically impossible for me to enrol myself as a member of any organised religious community, just because I reverence so much what I believe to be the essence of all the religions. I am sure you will understand this, and that it won't in any way make a barrier between us: I should be sad if it did.

This morning's news is splendid. May Paul continue what John has begun.[1]

I shall be sending you the bibliography on a prophetic view of religions—but not just yet, I am afraid. I have a lot of dull but necessary business (e. g. income tax return) to catch up with.

My very best wishes to all the members of the Community, and to the Pepers.

Yours affectionately,
Arnold

1. On 22 June 1963, Giovanni Battista Montini (1897–1978) was elected Pope (Paul VI).

The Royal Institute
of International Affairs
Chatham House
10, St James's Square
London S.W.1

3 July 1963

Dear Columba,

We are now just getting our heads above water again, so I have been able to make for you the following list of books on the relations between the several higher religions. Smith and King are both notable.

1. Zaehner, R. C.: *The Convergent Spirit: Discourses on Dialectics of Religion* (London 1963, Routledge).
2. Smith, W. Cantwell: *The Meaning and End of Religion: A New Approach to the Religious Traditions of Mankind* (New York 1963, Macmillan).
3. Tillich, Paul: *Christianity and the Encounter of World Religions* (New York 1963, Columbia University Press).
4. Parrinder, G.: *Upanishads, Gita, and Bible* (London 1963, Faber).
5. Parrinder, G.: *Comparative Religion* (London 1963, Allen and Unwin).
6. Brandon, S. G. F.: *Man and his Destiny in the Great Religions* (Manchester 1963, University Press).
7. Van Dusen, M. P.: *One Great Ground of Hope: Christian Missions and Christian Unity* (Philadelphia 1961, Westminster Press).
8. Kraemer, H.: *World Cultures and World Religions: the Coming Dialogue* (London 1960, Butterworth Press).
9. Bhaganan Das: *The Essential Unity of All Religions* (Wheaton, Ill., 1946, Theosophical Press).
10. Neutigin, J. E. L.: *A Faith for this One World?* (London 1961, S.C.M. Press).
11. King, W. L.: *Buddhism and Christianity: Some Bridges of Understanding* (Philadelphia, 1963, Westminster Press).
12. Smart, N.: *A Dialogue of Religions* (London, 1960, S.C.M. Press).
13. Neill, S.: *Christian Faith and Other Faiths: The Christian Dialogue with Other Religions* (London, 1961, O.U.P.).

Bhaganan Das and Kraemer are at the opposite extremes of the gamut.
I hope this may be of some use.

Yours affectionately,
Arnold

Encounter of Religions,
J. A. Cuttat
Desdée & Co. (New York)

8 July 1963 Saint Louis Priory

Dear Arnold,

I have to thank you for two letters. No, as you say, it makes no difference—your being stuck—to my affection for you. I respect your conscience. You *have* to follow what it proposes. In fact I can see in the rather obscure ways of Providence that your position is a help to the ultimate marriage of all minds. Some one has to be a bridge, and so long as he can't see himself as walking across it instead of being it, he is serving a very useful purpose. My own aim would be, while remaining a loyal Catholic, follower of Jesus, to embrace all that is good in all the other religions "Only one is Good, God", and so all that is good comes from Him.

Thank you very much for that most up to date list of books. I shall take special note of King and Smith.

Your visit was all joy and already it is receding into a distant past, so different from the usual humdrum of St. Louis life.

I hope you keep up with Abbot Butler. He was obviously most drawn to you.

Fr. Luke is hard at work supervising the pouring of concrete for the extension of the refectory. I'm giving a retreat to a group of whom Chris P. is one, Thurs–Sun. next. Then I go away for 6 days.

We still have 3 of the 4 postulants.

My love to you both.

Affectionately,
Columba, O.S.B.

How is the flat hunt progressing?

Saint Louis Priory
St. Louis, Mo.

17 December 1963

My dear Arnold,

To both of you a very happy Christmas with children and grand-children and all. I shall be remembering you and all your works at midnight Mass c. 6 A.M. by your time.

Much has happened since I last wrote; and if you have not been in U.S. recently, the mood is changed. The murder of Kennedy[1] seems to have been like a sudden flash in pitch darkness and certain figures suddenly standing out starkly. The figures that did stand out were all the hate-mongers. It came as a salutary shock to the ordinary man. But even here in "Saint Louis" people toasted the deed in champagne. So, something is seriously wrong. That was the exception.

The Council seemed to get bogged down, but I do believe only 'seemed,' partly because the meetings proved a vast educative drive on the Bishops themselves. Even if they did not understand the debate, they did lots of home work, listened to Rahner,[2] Congar,[3] de Lubac[4] and others. So the liturgy will be made intelligible, the Church presented for what it should be, a mystery and agency of love and mercy. The Curia? Ah! That is a problem. But there again it seems the end of the old regime is in sight. Abbot Butler's letters from the Council were most illuminating,[5] tho' not on his own big part. He was elected the other day onto one of the main Commissions. Dear David Mathew[6] on the other hand is sad—or ill—and has retired to Stonor. He was the last of "Recusant" Bishops.

Here we thrive. Our 3 new novices from S.L.P. are doing well at Ampleforth; that is a good sign.

I am poised to begin on prophetic figures in—and out of the Church: Joan of Arc,[7] de Lamennais,[8] Savonarola,[9] Newman,[10] Luther,[11] Catherine of Siena,[12] Soloviev.[13] Who would you think stand out as great witnesses as having unusual insight? Of course there are always the giants, S. Francis of Assisi,[14] S. Augustine.

Has the Hannibalic war book come out? What of the Simple History of the World?

I've completed my Ecumenical book and now must seek a publisher.

Much love to you both and many prayers.

Columba, O.S.B.

1. On 22 November 1963, John F. Kennedy was assassinated in Dallas, Texas.

2. Karl Rahner, S.J. (1904–84); German theologian; a *peritus* at the council; edited *Encyclopedia of Theology* (London, 1975).

3. Yves M. J. Congar, O.P.J.; [cf. C.C.E.'s letter of 1 October 1950, above].

4. Henri Cardinal de Lubac, S.J. (1896–); French theologian; a *peritus* at the council; *Catholicisme* (Paris, 1938), translated as *Catholicism* (London, 1950); *Aspects du Buddhisme* (Paris, 1951).

5. Abbot Christopher Butler, O.S.B.; cf. C.C.E.'s letter of 14 June 1963, above.

6. David Mathew; cf. A.J.T.'s letter of 14 July 1944, above.

7. Joan of Arc (1412–31); canonized in 1920.

8. Félicité Robert de Lamennais (1782–1854); religious and political author; a youthful Ultramontanist; later a forerunner of the Modernists.

9. Girolamo Savonarola (1452–98).

10. John Henry, Cardinal Newman; leader of the Oxford Movement; cf. C.C.E.'s letter of 6 April 1940, above.

11. Martin Luther (1483–1546); cf. *A Study of History*, IX:93; *An Historian's Approach to Religion*, pp. 111, 171; A.J.T. shows little interest in Luther.

12. Catherine of Siena; cf. C.C.E.'s letter of 19 January 1943, above.

13. Vladimir Soloviev (1853–1900); Russian philosopher and theologian; sought to restore communion between the Orthodox and Roman Catholic churches.

14. Francis of Assisi (1181–1226); cf. A.J.T.'s letter of 10 September 1953, n. 3, above; his letter of 22 November 1965, below.

The Royal Institute
of International Affairs
Chatham House
10, St James's Square
London S.W.1

23 December 1963

I shall be thinking of you at six A.M. the day after tomorrow.

Dear Columba,

Your letter of 7 December, arriving just before Christmas, was good to have, and I am delighted that all goes well with you and the fathers: my best wishes to them all. The three novices are perhaps your best gains of all for the Priory, because they are so many growing points.

There seems to be an all-round thaw in the World's affairs: the Pope's visit to Palestine, and the Oecumenical Patriarch meeting him there;[1] the temporary opening of a door in the Berlin wall;[2] the improvement in Russo-American relations;[3] the slight signs that the new German government has begun to realise that it cannot get reunification unless and until Germany and America together do something to convince Russia that she is not going to be invaded by German armies again.

Your prophetic figures sound exciting. If you are leaving out the giants, there might be room for Joachim of Fiore[4] and Blake[5] (an even more unorthodox prophet).

We are now in the middle of moving from 54 Pembroke Square, which we have sold, with many twinges, into a flat, 95 Oakwood Court, W. 14, which is going to be very nice (old-fashioned, with thick walls and plenty of room). Going from four floors to one seems wise at our age. It is going to save Veronica a lot of fatigue, I hope.

Vol. i of 'Hannibal's Legacy' has gone to the publishers, and Vol. ii will go next month. Then, from Feb. to the middle of April, we are going to Nigeria, Sudan, Abyssinia, Egypt, Libya. After that, I shall begin to think about the simple history of the world.

You have finished the Ecumenical book at a good moment. I am glad you are optimistic about the Council. This was my impression too—following it without your inside knowledge.

'Toasted the deed in champagne'. It shocks me through and through. I do not think one would find hatred like that over here. Perhaps we exported our fanatics to New England in the seventeenth century.

This is a most un-English clear cloudless sunny day. Outside my window, here at Chatham House, they are building a tall building to bring Chatham House some rents. We shall have our circus party for the grand children from the new flat (closer than the house is to Olympia) on 18 Jan.

Yours affectionately,
Arnold

1. On 4 January 1964, Pope Paul VI and the Ecumenical Patriarch Athanagoras were to meet in Jerusalem.

2. From 19 December 1963 to 5 January 1964, on permission of the East German government, over 500,000 West Berliners visited relations in East Berlin.

3. On 5 August 1963, the United States, Great Britain, and the Soviet Union had signed a limited nuclear test ban treaty.

4. Joachim of Fiore (ca. 1132–1202); Cistercian mystic and philosopher of history; cf. *A Study of History*, IV: 358, where A.J.T. refers to him as "a Calabrian intellectual revolutionary."

5. William Blake (1757–1827); poet, visionary, and artist; cf. *A Study of History*, VI: 161, citing Blake's "To see a world in a grain of sand" and concluding that "the poet who has this vision of the transfiguration of This World by the Kingdom of God must also be something of a prophet."

Royal Institute
of International Affairs
Chatham House
10, St James's Square
London S.W.1

18 February 1964

Dear Columba,

Thank you and the Fathers ever so much for the Council Album.[1] Besides being very amusing, it is a serious part of the 'documentation' of an historic event which is going to go on working and growing, now that it has started.

To-morrow we fly to Lagos on a two-months African lecturing tour (Nigeria, Sudan, Abyssinia, Egypt, Libya). I can be reached via Norah Williams here.

Meanwhile, we have moved from 45 Pembroke Square (which we have sold) into a flat: 95 Oakwood Court, W. 14. This has a lovely view over the S.W. corner of Holland Park, and it saves Veronica a lot of fatigue, so it is good that we have done it while we were still not too old to face it.

Veronica will be 70 in Addis Ababa and I shall be 75 in Benghazi. We are fortunate in still having our health and faculties.

Vol. ii of 'Hannibal's Legacy' has now gone to press, and vol. i will follow in May, after we get back. I am lucky to have been able to finish this huge book at this age.

You will be hearing from me on our travels, if I have any time to write.

Yours affectionately,
Arnold

1. A privately printed compilation (edited by C.C.E.) of copies of the *Drawings of the Second Vatican Council* by Frederick Franck (1909–); cf. Franck's *Outsider in the Vatican* (New York, 1965).

Tuesday in Low Week (7 April) 1964 Saint Louis Priory

My dear Arnold and Veronica,

I had been meaning to write to you when you reached Benghazi for your birthday, and then what with one thing and another, including a short bout in hospital, I put it off. Still I have remembered you both in my prayers: 70 and 75 are respectable ages, even 60 I think is a mile stone. So God bless you both and keep you going merrily—and prudently.

This African experience must be intensely interesting—here are the successor states cropping up under your very noses. But how new as well—this economic incompetence; this tattered native tradition and simply a jumble of undigested ideas from the old empires a hair withdrawn. Do you think they will "make it," I mean these new nations?

I've had a week's pause, with the boys away, and plenty of rest. I lay on my bed a lot and read right through the great life of Mahomet—one of *my* prophets—by Ibn Ishāq.[1] Once I got into my stride it read like a drama, or nearer, a tragedy. At first he was so clearly inspired. Then it all got tangled up, I was almost going to say, in revenge. The trouble was that he went on 'hearing' the answers to his problems and one answer was *fight*. So, he did. There seems to be a squeamishness about allowing that he personally fought—not always. On one occasion he seems to have taken a hand in beheading 800 Jews. Yet underlying all the political unification is a man, with compassion, with belief in the one God. Then I reread your Appendix on the subject and found you had ended on the note *prophète manqué*.[2] An interesting comparison would be Gandhi. A curious point emerged that tho' M. conquered Mecca by a show of force his headquarters remained Medina; another, that Heraclius is supposed to have warned his generals that Palestine could not be defended and withdrawal was wisest; another that the Negus was early converted to Islam, I mean in M's life time. Is that true?

Another area I've been scouting around is the very early Church and finding how important prophecy was—ending with excesses of Montanists—but this explains the position *after* the Apostles, of the prophets in the Litany of the Saints.

All are well here. We shall have 200 boys in Sept., rather a lot with no increase in the Community. Four novices went over this year; your young friend, Jack Winkler and all the others doing well; also a nephew of mine.

Have a look at the new-old species of man dug up at Tanganyika by Dr. Leakey?[3] That will complicate our genealogy.

A very happy Easter time and God bless you both.

Yours affectionately,
Columba, O.S.B.

1. Ibn Ishāq; born at Medina ca. A.H. 85; died at Baghdad A.H., 151; he collected all the accounts he could of the facts of Muhammad's life; in writing his Sīrat Rasūl Allāh, life of Muhammad, he preserved in his text all the sources that he used; this unique work was translated with notes by Alfred Guillaume (London, 1955).

2. See "The Political Career of Muhammad," in *A Study of History*, III: 466–72, and "Islam's Place in History," in ibid., XII: 461–76.

3. Louis Seymour Bazett Leakey (1903–72); archeologist; discoverer in the Rift Valley of the skull of *Australopithecus boisei*; with W. E. Le Gros Clark, *The Miocene Hominoidea of East Africa* (London, 1951).

The Royal Institute
of International Affairs
Chatham House
10, St James's Square
London S.W.1

23 April 1964

Dear Columba,

We got back yesterday from Tripoli and found your letter. I am concerned about your being in hospital. I hope whatever it was was just due to your perpetual overworking, and that having a rest has cleared it up. But I will be grateful for more news of your health. Yes, Veronica was 70 at Addis Ababa, and I was 75 at Benghazi. Life is full of inequalities. Here are we, travelling hard for nine weeks on end, and, at Lalibela in Ethiopia, going three hours up and three hours down again on muleback, to see some rock-cut churches:[1] and this morning I was looking at the unconscious face of a school fellow of mine, David Davies,[2] whom I have known for 62 years. He is six months younger than I am, but he was losing his wits, and now he is dying.

Muhammad is, for me, a tragic figure:[3] a genuine prophet who started by risking his life disinterestedly for his vision of God, but ended by falling to the temptation—which Jesus resisted—of accepting from Satan the kingdoms of this world. An unsuccessful prophet and a successful statesman: it was the wrong way round. If one were an environmental determinist, one would point out that Jesus lived inside the Roman Empire, so he had no chance of founding a political empire of his own, while Muhammad lived in a no-man's land outside the Roman Empire. But, then, many would-be Jewish messiahs did take up arms all the same, and Jesus was perhaps unique among them in refusing to do that. Gandhi seems to me to be the prophet of the Atomic Age: he found out the spiritual means of bringing about revolutionary changes without violence.

I am very glad that the school is increasing, and the community with it, but I am anxious about how you are standing the immense strain of building up a new institution from the start, so do tell me more about how you are.

Africa was enormously interesting. The saddest spot was the Southern Sudan. There is a latent quarrel between Christian (and pagan) Negro Africa and Muslim Arab Africa. The Sudan and Nigeria are the key countries, because they straddle these two different Africas.[4] With much love to you,

Yours affectionately,
Arnold

1. Compare A.J.T.'s *Between Niger and Nile* (London, 1965), pp. 51–52.

2. Sir David Davies (1889–1964); Winchester, New College, Oxford; King's Counsel 1935; Judge of County Courts (1937–47); commissioner, under National Insurance Acts (1946–61).

3. "Tender-hearted Muhammad, who art also one of the weaker vessels of God's grace, pray that His grace may inspire us, like thee, to rise above our infirmity in our zeal for His service (the "Litany"). A.J.T.'s *Study of History*, X: 143.

4. Compare *Between Niger and Nile*, pp. 120–25.

Saint Louis Priory
Saint Louis, Missouri

28 April 1964

My dear Arnold,

Thank you for your very interesting letter. I shall be taking your line on Mahomet.

The Buddhist insight of *Return* we can already say went back to the Buddha himself. I like his humility. He was a seer (even tho' he professed to *see* nothing).

It is a pity there is no *person* among the Hindus. Râmânuja,[1] would he fit? But he's not typical. Gandhi seems more Christian than Hindu. So, who for Hinduism?

I hope to get down to all this in the summer. The Council has talked quite a bit about the prophetic office within the Church and how it should be fostered. But of course it is the fate of the prophet to be stamped on, and perhaps the best sign of his genuineness is *how he takes it*.

I have prostatitis i.e. a chronic condition of slight infection which causes a slight irritation, a kind of uncomfortableness, and occasionally it flairs up and makes passing water difficult. The doctor and I are not particularly concerned. The only trouble is that there seems no assurance of a cure, only an assurance of control.

I enclose a letter which explains itself. Now, if you can spend a few days in the Fall, it would be very easy for you to talk to this group, i.e. the undergraduates of S. L. Un. I suggested to them to ask you to talk on the place of U.S. in the world today, but see they've left it open. So it is!

There is an ancient track running right across Africa, E. & W., south of the Sahara. I wonder whether you came across it. Veronica will be cursing me—in a very lady like way—for putting it into your head, as next time you'll be for setting off on a camel. I was told by an old Amplefordian who explored it during the war that it was only "open" in the non-rainy season.

Ethiopian Christianity sounds Hebraic, at a distance. Did you find it so? One can't help thinking of Candace's[2] minister. . . .

Love to you both,
Columba, O.S.B.

1. Râmânuja (fl. ca. A.D. 1118); founder of the Śrî Sampradâya sect.

2. Acts 8: 27.

The Royal Institute
of International Affairs
Chatham House
10, St James's Square
London S.W.1

18 May 1964

Dear Columba,

I am concerned about your prostatis. Hadn't you better have the operation? Though it is a nasty one, it has the merit of being once for all. It might catch you out suddenly by flaring up on a journey, for instance. Anyway, the longer you leave it, the more it is likely to get you down. I was much relieved at having it behind me. Don't let your doctor be too casual about it.

I wish I could accept the invitation from James Heidenry[1] of Saint Louis University, for it would give me a chance of seeing you. Unfortunately, I don't see how we can get to St. Louis on this coming trip. We have to be in Denver[2] by 12 September, so we shall be flying out, with perhaps a minimum break in New York. If we tried to fit in Saint Louis University then, it would probably be too early for them, and it would mean an awkwardly early start in September for us. From Denver we go to the state University of New Mexico, then Sarasota, Florida, then Mexico City, then home: all in the wrong direction. It will be sad if we don't manage to meet this time, but it looks difficult.

I got back from Africa just in time to see my school fellow and oldest friend, David Davies, still breathing but unconscious. He died that afternoon.[3] We had been friends since our first day at Winchester, which was in September, 1902. Life is very unequal in the last chapter. So far, I have been kindly treated: I have kept my physical vigour and my wits. But every day of life is a bonus, and this all through, and not only when one is old.

My very best wishes to the whole community. Do something about the prostatis.

Yours affectionately,
Arnold

1. James J. Heidenry (1944–); then student director, Great Issues Lecture Series; now an attorney in St. Louis.

2. In Denver A.J.T. participated in a discussion published as "Dialogue: The Inspiration of Historians," *University of Denver Magazine* 2, no. 2 (December 1964): 4–9; he also delivered lectures that, together with those delivered at New College, Sarasota, Florida, and at the University of the South, Sewanee, Tennessee, formed the "starting point" for *Change and Habit: The Challenge of Our Time* (London, 1966).

3. A.J.T. delivered the address at the memorial service for David Davies held at St. Peter's, Eaton Square, London.

Saint Louis Priory
8 June 1964 Saint Louis, Missouri

My dear Arnold,

Forgive me for not answering your last sooner, considering it recorded the death of your life long friend. No matter how expected the end, it comes as a tragic shock. So I have kept you and him very much in my prayers, particularly in my Mass. You yourself have certainly been blessed with astonishingly good health, all for a Providential purpose. I too seem to have recovered from the infection. It was not an enlarged prostate, which would just have to be taken out. If it recurs I shall certainly take your advice. The doctors it is true seem very adverse to operating.

I gave a talk on the Prophetic Gift to our group—the Peper one, you know—and it was so well received I feel encouraged to write it down at some length. In the end St. Thomas[1] gave some useful leads, and I can not only see the facts but am groping now towards a coherent theory. I also read the Symmachus Saint Ambrose "brush"[2] and felt that S. got the better of the argument, partly because St. A. wandered off the point.

I am very disappointed at your not being able to visit us next fall. But I agree that it would be a mighty rush, and far better wait for a more convenient occasion.

Friday I drive with Fr. Augustine[3]—in a car some friend wants East—I to Philadelphia to give a retreat, he to Osterville where he stays a few days before embarking for England for good, to take on Sr. Classics Master, as Fr. Patrick[4] is the new head master. Fr. Bernard[5] is Newman chaplain at York University, Fr. James[6] goes to St. Benet's Oxford. So changes are occurring.

My love to you both,
Columba, O.S.B.

1. Saint Thomas Aquinas, *Summa theologiae*, II II, 171–76.

2. For A.J.T.'s interest in Quintus Aurelius Symmachus' controversy with St. Ambrose, see *Study*, XII, p. 625; and his letter of 24 December 1946, above.

3. Augustine Measures, O.S.B.; cf. C.C.E.'s letter of 16 January 1962, above.

4. Noel Patrick Barry, O.S.B. (1917–); headmaster, Ampleforth College (1964–76); elected Abbot, 1984.

5. John Bernard Boyan, O.S.B. (1910–); now at Cathedral House, Liverpool.

6. James Forbes, O.S.B.; then Master of St. Benet's Hall, the Benedictine "private hall" at Oxford; cf. C.C.E.'s letter of 18 February 1941, above.

25 July 1964 S.L.P.

Dear Arnold,

Your letter was most welcome. Yes, we must keep in touch by letter. It is a great disappointment you will not be here in the Fall. How marvellously agile you seem to be in spite of spending most of your life reading and writing. It has been the walking that has kept you fit. An end comes sooner or later. In my 61st year I recognize the signs more of mortality and the need to be and do all one can for God's kingdom.

. . .

My book. You write cautiously. I may be taking on more than I can chew. May I send you the chapters as they get written if they do? That is one problem. Every day is broken up into little pieces and the mind too. It might be better to take simply a pious subject and jot down 'meditations.' But there has been so much of that. I am beginning with the hardest nut, while my 'élan' is still there, the Buddha. Obviously he was a pathfinder, a seer. The trouble is, *what* was his message?

Have you seen a marvelous little book, *The Catholic Church and World Religions*, by Prof. Zaehner?[1] It is 98% about the World Religions; I have found it so good, it has almost made me say, why write my book. Do get a copy. You'd enjoy it tremendously. If you do read it, give me your impressions. It is one of a series, most of which are not in the same class with this. (Burns & Oates).

We are "enjoying" temp. c. 93–100, for a week. There are now 7 S.L.P. monks and 1 postulant going over this September.

Love to you both,
Columba, O.S.B.

1. R. C. Zaehner; cf. C.C.E.'s letter of 20 October 1961, above.

Hall Beck
Killington
Kirkby Lonsdale
Westmorland

6 August 1964

Dear Columba,

I was very glad to have your letter of 25 July, which arrived this morning, together with the rather alarming news of the U.S. retaliation against Northern Vietnam.[1] This will not lead Russia into war, but I am not so sure about China. At the same time, the President could hardly have turned the other cheek, especially now that he has Senator Goldwater[2] on his tail.

What is dismaying about Goldwater is that he should have got the Republican nomination and that the Party should have accepted his platform. That platform, if it were to become the policy of the U.S. Administration, will mean an atomic World War, and I think Goldwater really means what he says. So it is good news that labour is going to oppose him.

I did not mean to be cautious in what I wrote about your book. It is *the* subject. I am going to get Zaehner's book; I read an enthusiastic review of it somewhere in the T.L.S., I think it was. I like everything of his that I have read.

Philip has been getting good reviews of the second volume of his epic. This volume is about him and Tony, but it is less autobiographical than the first one, and has more shape to it.[3] He is now getting recognition as a distinguished writer, which is a very happy thing.

It is not 100° in the shade here, and never will be, but we are enjoying being in the country—busy though we are—before our American trip begins.

With much love to you,
Arnold

1. On 2–4 August 1964, North Vietnamese torpedo boats attacked a U.S. destroyer in international waters; on 5 August, U.S. planes retaliated by destroying air and naval installations on the North Vietnamese coast; on the same day the Tonkin Gulf Resolution was passed by the U.S. Congress, authorizing the president to "take all necessary measures to repel any armed attack against forces of the United States."

2. Barry Morris Goldwater (1909–), Senator from Arizona since 1973, was the Republican candidate for the Presidency; he was considered an extremely conservative anti-Communist.

3. Compare A.J.T.'s letter of 10 November 1961, above.

Saint Louis Priory
Saint Louis

17 August 1964

My dear Arnold,

Your letter from the cool wind-driven Pennines almost cooled me in a Missouri heat wave of 90–103 for a month. However an occasional descent to air-conditioning—which I dislike—allowed me to do some reading and writing. I hope I've broken the back of the Buddhist chapter.

My scheme is to spend 10 years—if God gives me that—on this book. I would like you to keep a distant, or close eye on it, will you? By the end that would make you 85, why not?

The Buddha chapter seems to come out as follows:

1. The life, culminating in the enlightenment. (Thomas)[1]
2. The originality: not the enlightenment, but the attitude toward it: middle way—like S. Benedict—and that it is natural.
3. An examination of the essence of the enlightenment: The Self aware, some of and all that implies. Here I follow Dumoulin,[2] Zaehner[3] and specially a critical essay by Thomas Merton.[4] (*Continuum*, a Chicago periodical.)
4. The method: sound morality, the 9 commandments.
5. Possibly a footnote, Annex on: belief in God?, in future life?

I feel that at the time the B. came, this simplification was a tremendous thing, and the assurance of a hidden absolute.

If what I say is true it makes the Buddha a very peculiar "prophet," but not in the sense of a seer.

How does this seem to you?

My "firm" list are: The Buddha, Zoroaster, Confucius, Mahomet, Gandhi, Moses, Jeremias, St. Bernard, Erasmus[5]/Luther, Newman, John XXIII.

Doubtful: St. Francis/Joachim,[6] Savonarola, St. Gregory, Pascal.

The great Liturgical week starts Mon. next, 1st English Mass in U.S. I hope it won't be long before *all* is in English including the Divine office.

A young Benedictine Historian from Worth Priory U.K. was here, Edward Cruise.[7] He is very keen for you to visit them. I said write!

Yours affectionately,
Columba
Love to Veronica

1. Edward J. Thomas, *The Life of Buddha as Legend and History* (London, 1927).
2. Heinrich Dumoulin, *Technique and Personal Devotion in the Zen Exercise* (Tokyo, 1963).
3. Compare C.C.E.'s letter of 25 July 1964, above.
4. Thomas Merton (1915–68); monk of the Trappist monastery, Gethsemani, Kentucky; *The Seven Story Mountain* (New York, 1948); cf. C.C.E.'s letter of 16 January 1962, above.
5. Desiderius Erasmus (ca. 1466–1536); humanist and seeker of peace in the Reformation.
6. Joachim of Fiore; see A.J.T.'s letter of 23 December 1963, above.
7. Edward Cruise, O.S.B. (1916–); later at Worth Abbey's Foundation in Peru as Prior, in one of the poorest quarters of Lima.

The Royal Institute
of International Affairs
Chatham House
10 St James's Square
London S.W.1

23 August 1964

Dear Columba,

We should be glad of some of your 103°: it has turned windy here; but we shall be boiling in New York on 9–10 September. I, too, always keep the air-conditioning turned off. I dislike the noise, and dislike sudden changes of temperature: I would rather keep to nature's temperature, whatever it may be.

I like your sketch for the chapter on the Buddha. His moderation and common sense are indeed like Saint Benedict's. Your Point 5 will be the difficult one, because, on principle, he would not discuss metaphysical questions with his disciples, so, except for the all-important belief in Nirvana, it is hard to be sure what his personal beliefs about ultimate things were.

Your list: If I were making it, I should promote three 'doubtfuls'—Saint Francis, Saint Gregory, and Pascal—to 'firm', and should demote Moses, Erasmus, and Newman. Moses was probably historical (his Egyptian name suggests that he was), but we really know nothing about him. Newman, though immensely attractive, doesn't seem to me to be of this nature. Erasmus is humane and enlightened, but his spiritual stature is below his immense intellectual stature. Joachim is, of course, very attractive, and has great spiritual perception and imagination; Savonarola is worthy in context but is too militant for me, so I should leave both those where you put them.

Live to 85? Well, if I keep my strength and wits, and if Veronica is still alive. I try to will to be the survivor, and I do wish it with my mind, but with my heart it is difficult to be to that degree unselfish. At this stage of life, I am seeing a lot of bereavement, where people have been very close to each other. This is the inevitable price of the love of which human beings are capable. There is no help for these personal sorrows in the progress of technology or even in such morally splendid things as the abolition of war would be. Impersonal public gains don't cure personal losses.

Well, one's end is not in one's hand. Veronica and I—and Rosalind too—have been fortunate, so far, in our old age.

Yours affectionately,
Arnold

c/o Professor George Curry
4223 Bay Shore Road
Sarasota, Florida

23 December 1964

Dear Columba,

We were delighted to find your letter of 14 Dec. when we arrived here last Sunday.[1] This change of feeling between the different religions—which you are doing so much to help on its good way—might be a turning-point in history. When the Pope is enthusiastically welcomed by a Muslim crowd at Amman and by a Hindu crowd at Bombay,[2] this must mean that the world's religious temper is changing. It is something unprecedented, I think. I imagine that these crowds felt that the Pope truly cares for all human beings, including those who are not part of his own flock, and this touched their hearts.

Eight American monks already is a lot. You have planted the Ampleforth tradition in American souls—which is what the St. Louis Catholic community hoped that you would be able to do. But I am sorry another bout of fund-raising is looming up.

Hannibal's Legacy will come out in August. I shall be sending you a copy. I passed the last bit of the revised footnotes yesterday.

We are both all right. Veronica will benefit by having got rid of the index and having come down from 5000 feet to sea level (we have cut out a projected visit to the University of Mexico). But it is strenuous—the hospitality much more so than the work. Last week, en route via Albuquerque, Las Cruces, and El Paso, I did 5 lectures + one bull-session in 5 days, and El Paso was like London in November, with the fog sitting on a landscape like Waziristan.[3]

I wish we could see you, but we just can't make it on this trip.

God Bless You.

Yours affectionately,
Arnold

1. Missing.
2. On 2–6 December 1964, Paul VI attended the Eucharistic Congress in Bombay.
3. Compare A.J.T.'s *Between Oxus and Jumna*, pp. 152–61.

New College
Sarasota, Florida

24 February 1965

Dear Columba,

It is more than a month since I had your letter of 17 January.[1] I got back late last night from the *Pacem in Terris* Convocation (I was one of the speakers yesterday morning,[2] with Senator Fulbright in the chair).[3] The best of the chairmen was Barbara Ward.[4]

My main impression was that Pope John's love and concern for his fellow human beings has broken through all barriers. Communists, Asians, Africans all spoke about him with affection and gratitude, and I am sure they were being sincere. This is one of those timely acts that cannot be undone. Pope John has 'made history', I should say, in the deepest sense.[5]

My second impression is that the American people are committing, pretty heavily, the sin of pride, and are thereby drawing on themselves the moral disapproval of the rest of the world. They are refusing to admit that they may have made a mistake, that mistakes have to be paid for, and that America cannot be—and ought not to be—always 100 per cent victorious. The choice before them, and this in the near future, is either a compromise over Vietnam or the McNamara's 1 to 7 million American casualties,[6] but they do not seem to be facing the choice. Certainly they are not in our 'blood and tears' mood of June, 1940. This is very disturbing in a nation which has mankind's fate in its hands.

The students here (all 110 of them, all straight out of high school) are of a very high level, and are very much worth trying to help, but we don't like this part of Florida. After Denver, where we were very happy, it seems un-genuine.

Veronica didn't come to the Convocation, I am glad to say; the pace and pressure were formidable, even for this country: I am still half dazed by it, but am recovering.

Love to you from us both,

Yours affectionately,
Arnold

1. Missing.

2. A.J.T.'s speech was the basis of "Change—Minus Bloodshed," published in *Rotarian* 106, no. 6 (June 1965): 40–41.

3. James William Fulbright (1905–); U.S. senator from Arkansas; active in opposition to the Vietnam policies of the administration.

4. Barbara Ward; cf. C.C.E.'s letter of 5 February 1940, above.

5. On 10 April 1963, John XXIII had issued the encyclical *Pacem in Terris* seeking a world community of nations to ensure peace.

6. Robert S. McNamara (1916–); secretary of defense (1961–68); president, World Bank (1969–80).

New College
Sarasota, Florida

1 March 1965

Dear Columba,

Your letter of 24 Feb. has just come.[1] No, we are certainly not out of the wood.

I should have very much liked to be with you over Easter, but, alas, the 'schedule'. On Maundy Thursday we shall be approaching Washington, D.C., and on the morning of Easter Sunday we shall be landing in London airport.

Do you have dealings with St. Leo's Florida?[2] A rather nice English lay monk from there, called Harry Gill,[3] came here to see me today.

What is wrong with American views on America's mission is that they identify freedom and democracy with American power and prestige. I *never* hear the Vietnamese or Chinese points of view discussed. The Asian peoples might just not exist—not be human. I think that, bad as we had been in the past, we began as early as about 1917 to stop thinking of our fellow human beings as 'natives'.

It is grand that you will be home next summer. We shall be in London all this June—come and stay at 95 Oakwood Court. We shall be in Greece from about July 11 to the end of the month.

Well, in spite of the schedule, we shall be seeing each other again before long.

Yours affectionately,
Arnold

1. Missing.

2. A Benedictine monastery at St. Leo Florida; a village in itself, with mayor and postmaster, all monks.

3. Harry Gill (1902–); as a civilian worked with HMS Admiralty; was sent to the United States in 1943; remained and became a distinguished professor of political science at St. Leo; was never a monk.

c/o Dr. George Curry
New College
Sarasota, Florida

12 March 1965

Dear Columba,

Splendid: you will be coming to 95 Oakwood Court on 10 June; stay as long as you can spare. I ought to have known that Archbishop Cardinale is in London now. Is he Papal Nuncio there?[1] Anyway, give me his style and title and tell me what alternative dates, beyond 10 June, we can give him, and I will invite him. I liked him very much, and shall be very glad to be in touch with him again.

We got back last Tuesday from a trip to the University of S.C. and back via Charleston and Savannah—both of which were well worth seeing.

Yours affectionately,
Arnold

1. At this time he was Apostolic Delegate to Great Britain.

New College
Sarasota, Florida

5 April 1965

Dear Columba,

I have just heard from Archbishop Cardinale that he will come to dinner on *11* June. I wish you could stay with us for longer than that one night but I realize that your time is short, and that there are very many people who are eager to see something of you while you are in England.

Though the students at New College are good, in every sense, we shall not be sorry to leave Sarasota: you have here the worst side of American life: frivolity combined with militant conservatism.

We have fixed provisionally to come to the University of Pennsylvania in or after the Autumn of 1966.

Yours affectionately,
Arnold

Royal Institute
of International Affairs
Chatham House
10, St James's Square
London S.W.1

5 August 1965

Dear Columba,

It was a jolly evening last night. The only drawback was that you and I did not have a chance to talk to each other much in that affable company. Well, if you do not come home again next summer, we shall make a point of seeing you at Saint Louis in the first half of 1967.

The Archbishop's combination of Italian with American know-how is a pretty strong bond which will carry him far. If he had not been ordained I am sure he would have become at least Mayor of New York. What is the equivalent in the Church? He will soon be friends with everyone of any importance in the World.

The Vietnam War is being escalated fast now. Are American mothers willing to give their sons' lives for this?

It was very good to see you again, even just this glimpse.

Yours affectionately,
Arnold

As from Hall Beck Cottage
Kirkby Lonsdale
Westmorland

18 August 1965

Dear Columba,

It was good to have your letter of 9 August,[1] and I am so glad you like the Africa book.[2]

Yes, we were more tired than we thought, but Hall Beck is restful: no 'schedule'.

It would be a fairly safe bet, I think, that the first non-Italian Pope since Martin V (?) (no, there was Charles V's Fleming, Adrian) will be an Italian-American one, and that would give Archbishop Cardinale a high place in the running. As he is young, he may be, say, the next Pope but two.

I have suddenly started writing some reminiscences—not, of course, intimate personal ones, but things of more general interest, such as peace conferences, Greece, Hitler.[3]

By the way, we stayed with Bun and Jean at Ganthorpe last May, and I am very glad to say that I found I could do this without a pang. My feeling was pure pleasure that they and the children were having the benefit of the place. This indicates that I am, long ago, healed of my wound, and I am healed because I am happy.

Next month I am going to be anathema in the U.S. because I am publishing an article in a magazine called *Fact*, urging the American people to think again about Vietnam.[4]

'Affectionately' without the 'yours', what an Americanism.

Arnold

1. Missing.
2. A.J.T.'s *Between Niger and Nile*.
3. A.J.T.'s *Acquaintances* (London, 1967).
4. Published as "The Failure of American Foreign Policy," in *Fact* (September–October 1965), pp. 3–7, and reprinted in *The Best of Fact* (New York, 1967).

Saint Louis Priory
Mason Rd.
Saint Louis, Missouri

11 November 1965

My Dear Arnold,

I am typing (so called) because I want to have a copy. The time has come for me to attempt to write this book on Prophetic Insight. I cannot quite decide which to take of all the figures of the past that loom up, so I'm asking your help. 1. I want to take the ancient world, or shall we say, the non-Christian world. So my present suggestion is

a. the nameless prophets, i.e. those who had insight in primitive times: to invent sacrifice, to penetrate into the inner man (Hindu).

b. the great figures: Zoroaster, the Buddha, Confucius—treat them together, and show what a tremendous progeny they have had.

c. Mahomet. Or should I link him with b?

A comment. I do not necessarily want to choose those who came through their experience with complete success, but just as much, perhaps more, to find prophets who had difficulties, even who failed, to do their job right. Another kind of failure of course is almost a sign of true prophecy.

The Old Testament. At this point examine the nature of prophecy and take—here I can't make up my mind—Ezechiel, Osee, Moses.

N.T. Chiefly show, from the N.T. and earliest Fathers, that prophecy is still meant to exist in the Church.

Modern Times A.D. 33—
I really cannot decide who in the early (Patristic) period best suits my book. In a sense every saint is a prophet. Any ideas? Possibly: the three Francises: Assisi, Xavier, de Sales. Certainly: Joachim of Fiore,[1] Peter the Venerable,[2] Ramon Lull,[3] and P. Ricci,[4] Hus,[5] Savonarola, Erasmus—each with insight, but something went wrong, not necessarily all their fault. Pascal, Newman, de Lamennais (Possibly Galileo) ditto. John xxiii, Teilhard de Chardin and who third? Lincoln, Gandhi and a third wanted. Or is there a trio of pacific people of Gandhi's stature? I notice that in the past I have toyed with: Leo xiii,[6] Wesley,[7] St. Joan,—no.

So you see, I'm not quite asking you to write my book for me, but to give me some help in definition.

I hope all goes well with both of you and that the summer proved a real rest. What of all your writings?

The news has just announced the withdrawal of Rhodesia.[8] It is going to be very wrong, but to fight over it would probably—certainly—produce even more wrong in its train. So, please God, the evil is suffered. This seems to be the lesson we have to learn today. As the Council comes to its end the impression I have is that the Church must go to the poor, and that is the missionary action all wrapped up in one, that Christ would have done, would do with us. I feel a bit tied up here; but shall press for this in every way I can.

My love to you both and many prayers.

Columba, O.S.B.

1. Joachim of Fiore; cf. A.J.T.'s letter of 23 December 1963, above.

2. Peter the Venerable (ca. 1092–1156); abbot of Cluny; the first to have the Koran translated into Latin.

3. Ramon Lull; cf. C.C.E.'s letter of 12 January 1950, above.

4. Matteo Ricci, S.J.; cf. C.C.E.'s letter of 12 January 1950, above.

5. John Hus (Huss) (ca. 1369–1415); Bohemian reformer.

6. Vincenso Gioacchino Pecci, Pope Leo XIII (1810–1903); Pope from 1878; reversed his

predecessor's (Pius IX) policies and attempted to bridge the gap between the papacy and the modern world.

7. John Wesley (1703–91); cf. A.J.T.'s letter of 22 November 1965, below.

8. On 11 November 1965, the Rhodesian government issued a unilateral declaration of independence.

The Royal Institute
of International Affairs
Chatham House
10, St James's Square
London S.W.1

22 November 1965

Dear Columba,

Your letter of 11 November has a lot in it to think about. I have been turning it over in my mind, and here are some first thoughts.

First of all: prophets are creators, innovators, rebels, revolutionaries. Their inspiration comes from an unconventional source. Whatever else God may be or may not be, he is certainly not conventional-minded, so his revelations through human prophets are always shocking. Prophets are lucky if they win converts posthumously after, and because, they have suffered martyrdom for the sake of their disturbing and therefore unpopular visions. For a prophet to be successful in his own lifetime is a great test of his character. The Prophet Muhammad is the arch example. It would have been better for his message—and he had a great one—if the Quraysh had succeeded in killing him before he became a successful refugee politician in Medina.

For this reason, I don't think either Lincoln or St. Joan was a prophet. They were noble characters, but they worked on the level of politics and they used war as their instrument. Lincoln (here playing politics) deliberately put the lesser political cause of preserving the Union above the greater moral cause of abolishing slavery.

I don't think Francis de Sales and Erasmus were prophets either. They, too, were admirable, but they lacked the prophet's fire.

Here is a shot at a list:

(i) *The Buddha and Confucious*

(ii) *The Old Testament Group*: Deutero-Isaiah far away at the top; Jeremiah, Amos, Hosea (though these three were a bit tarred with politics); Zoroaster, Muhammad (they both belong to this group).

(iii) *The Early Fathers* seem to me to be in the Erasmus category; not prophets but intellectuals, apologists, interpreters, translators of Christianity into terms of Greek philosophy.

In this age the Christian prophets are the heretics; Montanus,[1] who revived the first Christian generation's 'speaking with tongues'; Marcion[2] who was revolted by the omnipotent creator god, and refused to identify him with the self-sacrificing god. (Cp. William Blake).

(iv) *Western World, mediaeval*: Francis of Assisi, far away at the top; by far the greatest soul that has appeared in the West so far. Then Columba,[3] Joachim of Fiore, Ramon Lull, Hus, Savonarola; (Xavier and Ricci seem to me to be not prophets but interpreters, doing for the East Asians what Clement of Alexandria[4] and Origen[5] did for the Greeks).

(v) *Modern World, world-wide*: Gandhi[6] and John XXIII[7] at the top. Then Pascal, Teilhard,[8] Blake, Tolstoy,[9] Wesley,[10] Marx,[11] the Bāb[12] (Marx is a teaser for you, but he is an undeniable prophet, and he had the luck to be unsuccessful in his lifetime, though posterity has done its worst for him by giving him dazzling posthumous success, and this in politics. Marx is posthumously another Muhammad. Both M's are in the stream of the Jewish Christian tradition).

Marx rejected Christianity because, in his time, the Christian Church was doing nothing for the new industrial working class when it was being ground down. Organised religion always tends to be captured by the rich minority as time goes on. I am sure you are right in feeling that Christianity must now try to jump clear of this compromising alliance and must address itself, again, to the poor majority.

The Council's resolution about the right to freedom of conscience and to religious liberty is a landmark.

We are both all right and are staying here till the beginning of July. My *Hannibal's Legacy* is out in England, but perhaps not yet in the U.S.A.

Rhodesia: In the Atomic Age (and in all ages) it is wrong to resort to force till one has tried every alternative with all one's might. But it would also be wrong to put up with 217,000 whites trying to make themselves independent in order to go on oppressing and exploiting four million Africans. Economic sanctions—*à outrance*—are the first thing to try. If this were to fail, force would certainly be used, and the conclusion that force is the only effective thing in human relations would soon lead, in the Atomic Age, to mass-suicide.

Love to you from us both,

Yours affectionately,
Arnold

1. Montanus of Phrygia began to prophesy in the late second century that the Heavenly Jerusalem would soon descend. Tertullian, a Montanist, described its members as *pneumatici* or spirit filled.

2. Marcion of Pontus (fl. 140–160) distinguished between the Demiurge of the Old and the God of love of the New Testament. A.J.T. was fascinated by Marcion; he wrestles with him throughout "The Freedom of Human Souls That Is the Law of God," in *A Study of History*, IX: 395–405, where he also quotes William Blake as a Marcionite ("anima naturaliter Marcionita").

3. Saint Columba (ca. 521–97); Irish abbot and missionary who established a foundation, Familia Columbae, in the island of Iona; a leader in A.J.T.'s "abortive far Western Christian Civilization"; cf. *A Study of History*, II : 322–40.

4. Saint Clement of Alexandria (ca. 150–ca. 215); philosopher and theologian.

5. Origen (ca. 185–ca. 254); biblical exegete, theologian, and student and successor of Clement; a voluminous writer.

6. Mohandas K. Gandhi (1869–1948); "a Hindu statesman-saint" (*A Study of History*, VIII : 546–48); A.J.T. and Philip Toynbee, *Comparing Notes* (London, 1963), p. 38.

7. For A.J.T.'s assessment of John XXIII, compare *The Greeks and Their Heritages* (London, 1981), p. 105.

8. Pierre Teilhard de Chardin, S.J. (1881–1955); *The Phenomenon of Man* (London, 1959); cited in *A Study of History*, XII : 8, n. 3.

9. Leo Tolstoy (1828–1910); cf. A.J.T.'s acknowledgment of *War and Peace* in *A Study of History*, X : 225.

10. John Wesley is invoked in the "Litany": "Blessed Francis Xavier and Blessed John Wesley, continue Paul's work of preaching the Gospel in all the world." *A Study of History*, X : 143.

11. Karl Marx (1818–83); A.J.T. insisted on the Judeo-Christian origins of Marxism; cf. ibid., V : 177–80 and esp. 179: "If this archaic Futurism is the distinctive Jewish element in the Marxism faith, the distinctively Christian element is an Oecumenicalism."

12. Bāb-ud-Din, Gate of the Faith, the name assumed by Sayyid ʿAlī Muhammad of Shīrāz (executed 1850), who revealed a new holy book; the precursor of the founder of the Bahāʾī sect; A.J.T. noted the "spirit and cult and practice of gentleness" of this sect (cf. ibid, pp. 174–75).

14 December 1965 — Saint Louis Priory

My Dear Arnold,

Your long and carefully thought out reply to my letter on candidates for the Prophetic Insight book was most welcome and so typically kind of you. Thank you. Before I get any further with that—a very happy Christmas, and I pray that all of you and all of us over here receive a deeper and deeper insight into the significance of the Coming of 'the One who was to come.' I like the title, Pontifex, the bridge-maker between God and us. I like 'heir of all things;' but all those biblical titles are so much richer than the 'theological conclusions.'

I am in accord over, Confucius, the Buddha and Zoroaster—though of the last I know little as yet. I agree very much over the 2nd Isaiah, Osee, Amos and Jeremiah (I meant Jeremiah in my letter and put Ezekiel by mistake). How about Origen instead of Montanus—towards whom I have not all that sympathy. Columba, to be frank, I hadn't seriously thought of him. Do you mean his revulsion from the use of force?

I am cooling towards Joachim, as his influence seems very obscure and not particularly helpful, unless one can prove a line between him and Francis. Excellent about St. Francis and Ramon Lull. I am glad you agree about Huss (I've got hold of Vooght) and about Savonarola. Marx, I will go along willingly over him, provided you can prove that he did not propose that his ends should be gained by hatred. But as far as taking over the prophetic office concerning the injustices to the poor which the Church should have taken up, yes. Who is the Bab? I'll find out. Blake I'll have to enquire into more. The others of the moderns I'm in complete agreement about. Tolstoy perhaps would be an appetiser for Gandhi. I am particularly delighted you agree about Pascal.

No, the great book, *Hannibal's Legacy* hasn't yet come, nor have I seen any US review of it; but then I don't see all that many. I am longing to get my hands on it, and I'm sure it will be a great success.

Columba, O.S.B.

The Royal Institute
of International Affairs
Chatham House
10, St James's Square
London S.W.1

5 February 1966

Dear Columba,

I have been a long time answering your letter of 14 December—in fact, it may not have been your last, for I remember hearing from you that 'Hannibal' had reached you.

Evidence for East-West contacts ca. 100 B.C.–A.D. 250: there is a lot. The contact was mainly by sea, from Alexandria by ship-canal to Suez, or from Egypt's Red Sea ports, to the Indus delta. We have accounts of how, in the last two centuries B.C., Alexandrian navigators learnt to use the monsoons for sailing straight across the open sea, instead of hugging the Arabian coast. We also have, in N.W. Pakistan, a mass of monuments of Greco-Buddhist art. Intercourse must have been active, and not just commercial.

I am in a low state, which I hope to struggle out of. At bottom, no doubt, it is the difficulty of coming to terms with old age. I don't dread death; too many of my contemporaries were killed in 1915–6; but I do dread staying alive without being still able to use my capacities at full stretch. At the moment, with one book in the press and two others finished and being typed, I have no agenda—for the first time since 1913! I find this disconcerting because I am an American-like Western man. If I were an Indian I should feel that I now had my opportunity for contemplation—i.e. for the proper use of life. Then our friend and pillar, Norah Williams,[1] has got Parkinson's disease (don't refer to this in writing, as she doesn't, herself, yet know what it is, poor thing).

Well, no doubt I shall come up again, but at the moment I am a bit up against it, and public affairs don't help—they are pretty glaring evidence of the reality of Original Sin.

Much love to you from us both.

Yours affectionately,
Arnold

I used to be amused at Gibbon's not knowing what to do next after he had finished the *Decline and Fall*; I feel less supercilious about this now.[2]

1. Norah Williams (1903–72) had worked at Chatham House as clerical assistant (1947–63).

2. Compare *A Study of History*, X:102, where A.J.T. quotes in extenso Gibbon's famous account of the moment when he "wrote the last lines of the last page."

The Royal Institute
of International Affairs
Chatham House
10, St James's Square
London S.W.1

6 March 1966

Dear Columba,

By this time you may have heard from the Pepers that we saw each other last week when they were heading for home through London. We were very glad to see them again. We often think of their kindness and hospitality to us and how nice they both are.

Yes, Gibbon had the same experience. He couldn't think what to do next, after he had written the last words of the *Decline and Fall*. He lived for six more years, and was bothered by his situation. I always thought his difficulty was rather ridiculous, till I was overtaken by it myself.

I have taken your advice, and started writing about the ultimate things. It is best to use the medium to which one is used, and I can probably meditate better with a pen in my hand than in a yogi-posture.

I am very fortunate—particularly in having kept my health and wits till now. I am more and more conscious of being exceptional in my generation in having had this length of life. I think more and more of my contemporaries who were killed in 1915–6, with their life-work hardly begun. If one could be a Westerner for the first half of one's life and an Indian for the second half, that would be convenient. But one can't swap heritages at half time.

With love to you from us both.

Yours affectionately,
Arnold

Saint Louis Priory
Mason Rd.
5 April 1966 Saint Louis, Missouri

My Dear Arnold,

Just a note to wish you a happy Easter, by which I mean for you a sharing in the power of Christ won by him on the Cross. We all need this hope, as Pope John was never tired of telling us. Gloom is there, but we mustn't let it overpower us. So in the hope of the Resurrection somehow we carry on. S. Augustine must have felt very down at times; he kept going. So we have to, that is how I feel. I mention Augustine because we have been reading in the refectory an excellent (not new) book on him as Bishop, by van der Meer.[1] He must have read every word he wrote as well as being an archaeologist.

So England has a government which can rule as it wishes.[2] I hope it is not going to be too doctrinaire. There are plenty of realities it will have to face, insolvency and the rest.

Fr. D'Arcy[3] has been staying with us; I like him more every time we meet. He talked at various places, and a lot here among us.

The Holy Week services in English are good, especially the Passions, as it forces us to abandon the theatrical and just listen to *what happened*. This has all become far more meaningful to me because I find I am not alone among theologians in the church who do *not* hold that Christ had the beatific vision all the time. Though He knew he was the Son of the Father, in his human consciousness there really was obscurity. "My God, my God" really meant what it said.

Do tell me how your meditations are getting on. The great thing about meditating is keeping it up.

We are all well, 3 possible postulants for novitiate next September; and even possible we shall have it here. Say a prayer that wisdom is given.

My dearest love to you both,

Columba, O.S.B.

P.S. I'm glad you managed to see the Pepers. It so delighted them.

1. Frederik G. L. van der Meer, *Augustinus de Zielzorger* (Utrecht, 1947), translated by Brian Battershaw and G. R. Lamb as *Augustine the Bishop* (London, 1961).

2. The 31 March 1966 elections had given the Labour party a majority of ninety-seven in the House of Commons.

3. Martin Cyril D'Arcy, S.J.; cf. C.C.E.'s letter of 30 July 1938, above.

The Royal Institute
of International Affairs
Chatham House
10, St James's Square
London S.W.1

13 April 1966

Dear Columba,

I came back the day before yesterday from Ethiopia and found your letter of 5 April. I was giving some lectures and having some bull sessions at the University,[1] and, in return, I was taken on some more expeditions, by landrover and Cessna plane, into back parts of the country. I was eager to see these, and was also set up by finding that I can still stand a 15-hours day in a landrover, travelling over non-roads, though I shall be 77 to-morrow.

I went to the Good Friday service in three pre-Chalcedonian churches in Addis Ababa,[2] and then back to one of those for the Easter midnight service. They had two choruses of singers who, at climaxes, sang together. They celebrate the mass at midnight, but the celebration of the Resurrection itself is at about 11.00 P.M. For this we circumambulate the church (two concentric rings, with a holy of holies in the middle) with lighted candles. The singers were not inhibited, as Western Christian celebrants might be. They were unaffectedly merry (though they had been fasting completely since Thursday evening and had been singing since 3.00 P.M. Saturday) at the joy of the Resurrection, for which they were praising God. I found this very moving. The joy was expressed physically too in a kind of dance, accompanied by drums.

I was mighty glad to see Veronica again. We are getting too old not to suffer from being separated, even for a short time. But this was an opportunity that was not to be missed, as my friend Dr. Myers[3] is leaving the University of Ethiopia next month to become cultural attaché in London again.

Very much love to you from Veronica and me.

Yours affectionately,
Arnold

1. Compare A.J.T.'s *Between Niger and Nile* (London, 1965), p. 118, for an account of Haile Selassie University.

2. The Council of Chalcedon (451) was a crucial event in the history of the Monophysite dogma concerning the nature of Christ; the Coptic churches of Ethiopia are Monophysite; cf. *A Study of History*, II: 258, VIII: 444–45.

3. Edward D. Myers; see many earlier references.

The Royal Institute
of International Affairs
Chatham House
10, St James's Square
London S.W.1

1 July 1966

Dear Columba,

I have been slow in answering your letter of 12 May and card of the other day from St. John's Abbey.[1] We have had a quiet winter and spring, ending up with six weeks in Westmorland. We hadn't been there in the spring before and were astonished at the wealth of wild flowers in the hedges, and, in general, the genial look of the country—but the weather was exceptionally good.

The day after tomorrow we are going off to Greece (the annual Symposium on the World-city of the future);[2] then from mid August to late September we are to be guests of the govts. of Brazil, Argentina (but there has been a military coup there, since), Uruguay (quiet and respectable) and Chile. We were to have gone, in January 1967, to the Annenberg School of Communications at the University of Pennsylvania, but it has fallen through (they thought they had the money, but they hadn't).

I have been told by doctors to take things a bit easier, as I have a slight irregularity (not a dangerous one, apparently, if I am provident, as I mean to be) of the heart. I don't want to leave Veronica solitary, and, also, I find that, after all, I have a number of bits of work to do that were right at the back of my mind and have now emerged from there since my conscious agenda was finished. I have just written a booklet on *Constantine Porphyrogenitus*. Apart from these strong holds on life, I shouldn't be sorry to leave this world. I like it less and less: the make-up of the girls; Vietnam; the laziness and economic folly in this country. But one has a stake in the future of the human race beyond one's own life time, so one must go on living as long as one has the physical strength and the wits to do something useful.

Love to you from us both,
Arnold

1. Both missing.

2. A.J.T. had attended the first International Seminar on Ekistics in Athens on 20–24 July 1965; in the 1967 meeting he presented a paper published as "Town-Planning in the Ancient Greek World," *Ekistics* 24, no. 145 (December 1967): 445–48; his interest culminated in *Cities on the Move* (London, 1970).

St. Louis Priory
St. Louis, Missouri

19 July 1966

Dear Arnold,

Yes, this is quite an official letter.

Fr. Aelred Graham,[1] whom of course you remember at Ampleforth, and who is now Prior at Portsmouth, Rhode Island, is thinking of doing an eucumenical tour of the Far East—an approach to the 'Other Great Religions' such as Vatican II wants. He says he is no professional scholar but is keenly interested and still learning. He hears that the Guggenheim Foundation might be ready to give him a travelling fellowship; but they would need the names of four 'experts' who would be prepared to say that his scheme makes sense. I think it does, and I am pretty sure you will think so. When he writes to you I am sure you will let him use your name.

Less official. I am so sorry to hear that your heart is showing signs of wear and tear. Veronica, I am sure, will keep a close eye on your mountain climbing propensities.

God bless your South American tour. I am convinced that some wise words from you will help them to grasp their problems and find solutions.

Love to you both.
Columba, O.S.B.

1. Aelred Graham, O.S.B.; cf. C.C.E.'s letter of 19 January 1940, above.

Royal Institute
of International Affairs
Chatham House
10, St James's Square
London S.W.1

25 July 1966

Dear Columba,

We got back yesterday from Greece and found your letter of July 19th. Of course, I will gladly testify to the Guggenheim Foundation about Father Aelred—but why do you say he is not a professional scholar: no, I see *he* says this, not you. Anyway, I will testify with the greatest pleasure.

The doctors urge to be sensible and you can go on working: with Veronica's loving care, I have been almost completely sensible in Greece (very difficult there; easier in South America, where not every mountain is historic).

We are both all right, though the conferences-cum-sightseeing likewise is quite hard work.

Yours affectionately,
Arnold

Saint Louis Priory
Mason Road
Saint Louis, Missouri

17 November 1966

My Dear Arnold,

Are you still on the same land mass as we are? I hope the excursion in S.A. went well and that you encouraged the leaders to carry out social reforms before it becomes too late. I also hope you really resisted the temptation to climb any Andean peaks! This thought of our possible parting—who knows either of us is quite likely to die soon now—makes me pray all the harder that we both cling to the truth we know and live by it during the shortening days. I have just received your latest book—which I bought, to boost sales!—and find it as always, engrossing, like a renewal of our conversations.[1] No, I don't think the great religions can coalesce in one exactly, though I think we (Catholics) can learn plenty from the thought of India and beyond. I don't think, though, that we are talking quite about the same thing, even though we seem to use much the same imagery. Perhaps that is not quite accurate. We *do* cover the same ground at a certain point, but from then on diverge. The Hindus and Buddhists seem to keep firmly to the natural order, and we Christians (Catholic, at least) launch out into something beyond. Is it fair to call them preparations for Christ, even Mahomet? That is a wrong way of putting it to Hindus and Buddhists. Is there any way of putting the relationship which would be theologically and historically true and yet not *hurt*?

My book on *Monastic Renewal*[2] will be coming out in U.S. (Herder & Herder) and B.O.W. in England in March; and the publishers asked whether they could send a proof copy to you, apparently to get a friendly comment for the dust cover. I said I thought you wouldn't mind. So about January this may happen. I hope that is not imposing on you.

The Americans are so dug in out in Vietnam there seems no way for them to extricate themselves. I can see only misery for the S. Vietnamese either way. War machines always want to try out their latest. We used to do it on the N.W. frontier. But now the toys of last century are world destroying.

You'll be interested to hear that Eden Seminary[3] (Evangelical) has asked me to be one of their speakers on a weekly seminar they run for their students on Sacraments. If ecumenical work came my way I think I would enjoy it. This is a beginning.

. . . Interruption. One of our barns caught fire—it was ½ full of hay which must have internally combusted. Fortunately no serious damage.

When can you come and visit us. 1967 I think you must.

My love to you both and prayers for good health.

Columba, O.S.B.

1. A.J.T.'s *Change and Habit: The Challenge of Our Time.*

2. C.C.E.'s *Monastic Renewal* (New York, 1967).

3. Eden Theological Seminary; the successor to a seminary founded in Missouri in 1849 by members of the German Evangelical Church.

95, Oakwood Court
London W.14

26 November 1966

Dear Columba,

I was very glad to have your letter of 17 November. We have been home four weeks today, but still haven't fully recovered from the hard labour (entertainment, not the lecturing) of being 'state guests'. I was not in danger of death, except perhaps for a few hours when I was 'dehydrated' at Brasilia, and my blood pressure threatened to drop to zero. I am considerably nearer death than you are (the difference in our ages counts at this stage, as it does in childhood). Ever since 1915–6, when half my contemporaries were killed, I have felt it odd to be still alive. I have now had a fifty-years' bonus-time to do what many of them would have done if their lives had not been cut short. So, since then, I have constantly had death in mind, and I fancy to myself that I am prepared for it when it comes, though one never knows beforehand whether one is going to live up to one's expectations of oneself.

I suppose the adherents of each of these religions feel that their own religion is the perfect one and that the others are approximations to it. Also, the distinction made by Jews, Christians, and Muslims between the natural order and a supernatural one perhaps would not be accepted as valid by Hindus, Buddhists, and Confucians. There is no authority, recognized by us all, to judge between us, so I think we have to coexist, loving each other and working together for good against evil, while recognising that the claims that we each make for our own religions are not convincing to our neighbors.

Of course I will read the proofs of the book and will write a few lines for the publishers, if they want them.

We are going to be at Stanford University for the spring quarter of 1967, beginning of April to June 8. I long for another meeting before too long, but I fear it is unlikely that we shall get to Saint Louis this time. South American fatigue has warned us both that we must keep long distance flying within limits at our age. This is something that Americans find hard to understand, but it is common sense.

Yesterday I wrote a statement about Father Aelred for the Guggenheim Foundation. It was easy to write. I do hope he will get the award.

I am glad the barn had an escape.

I find the Vietnam War harder and harder to bear. The killing and destruction are frightful, and the deliberate 'escalation' can only end in an atomic World War unless the American people can overcome their pride (the arch sin) and can bring themselves to admit that they may have taken a wrong turning and that they had better have second thoughts. If one will not admit that one may have been wrong, one is in a spiritually desperate state. This is true of people collectively as well as individually.

Well, my love to you.
Arnold

17 December 1966 — Saint Louis Priory

My Dear Arnold,

I must write even though I am up to my antlers—as Wodehouse would say—with thank-you letters—as your friendship means very much to me. How many years is it since you stayed at Ampleforth that Christmas and I showed you the

Codices room?[1] I have learnt so much, especially an open mind to world religions and a recognition of the riches that are there and which I must acclaim. It now seems to me that if I can only have the time simply to learn and write down all the insights of people like the Buddha, this will be a beginning of a mutual understanding. There is absolutely no sense in not recognizing Truth wherever it is. But meanwhile I've been talking to the diocesan clergy on the Sacraments, 12 talks; next term I'm sitting in on a seminar, also on Sacraments, at an Evangelical seminary (Eden); this holidays is eaten into by a retreat up at Benet Lake.[2] So, like the China book, it may take 15 years to do the Prophetic one; and 15 years now is a toss-up. . . . However, I do believe I may get a respite from running the Priory, and like Fr. Aelred have a time to think and pray, so important. I'm always amazed how you have tidily completed all your main tasks.

I was fascinated by your new book.[3] The style is now completely geared to the "educated layman." You also have your "travelog" style. What next? The whole argument of the book is very telling. Will humanity be wise enough to take your advice? It looks as though Russia is coming out of the isolationish, agin-the-world mood. Or is this only one more *volte-face* for expediency? How does one know? You will say: by their restraint. And I expect you are right.

You startled me by producing the imperial decree of intolerance;[4] did it have any power in Western Europe in the Middle Ages. Peter the Venerable's open-mindedness on the Mahommedans was what drew me to him.[5] Was there any positive persecution of other religions in the Middle Ages?* e.g. in the Jerusalem Kingdom, apart from obviously political rivalries and fear. I know that in Spain after the Reconquista there was, but at Toledo in medieval times wasn't it all light and understanding?**

I shall remember you and Veronica specially at Midnight Mass and always in my prayers.

My love to you both,
Columba, O.S.B.

* yes, I know, the Albigensians[6]
** This is probably very ignorant; so ignore it. Your ch. X was very telling, but I still think one religion can be more right than others. Your plea, though, is so right, one of our human rights is the right to learn . . . . to the end. Then we shall, please God, see Him face to face.

1. Compare the Annex to this letter.

2. Benet Lake, a Benedictine Monastery in Wisconsin.

3. A.J.T.'s *Change and Habit*.

4. Theodosius I established Christianity as the official religion of the empire (ibid., pp. 45–52).

5. Peter the Venerable; cf. C.C.E.'s letter of 11 November 1965, above.

6. Compare *A Study of History*, IV: 369, IX: 305.

Annex to C.C.E.'s Letter of 17 December 1966

One morning, possibly in 1936, I was waiting in the head master's room for him to come and discuss some business—it was Fr. Paul Nevill, already a friend of Arnold Toynbee. As Fr. Paul was delayed in coming, I took down from his shelf vol. III of the *Study of History*, where I came on the heading "The Saviours of Europe." They proved to be Saint Benedict and Saint Gregory. This was so unexpected and so perceptive that immediately I was enthralled. This led on to further reading, so that when the author of that passage himself came to stay in the monastery for a few days, I already felt atuned to his spirit.

One evening we came together, as he was interested to examine our codices room in the library. Myself having been for a number of years librarian, we had a common interest. We spent a happy hour or so, I pulling out this and that, he handling each with care and vast knowledge, and ever since I remember particularly his delight to have in his hand a very early printed edition of Thomas S. Stapleton's translation of Saint Bede's *Ecclesiastic History of the English People* with a forward to Princess Elizabeth, Queen of England (Antwerp, 1565). A very bulky tome, an incunabulum in some Germanic dialect, had puzzled me for a long time. So out it came from its shelf for Arnold to scrutinize. In a fraction of a minute he was musing aloud, tentatively as sometimes he did: Provenance, the Brothers of the Common Life: *Lives of Saints*, a Baltic coast German dialect, no doubt printed at Lübeck before the turn of the fifteenth century. I replaced the volume later and leafed through it once again. There hidden between the pages was a thin slip of paper, a memorandum from the British Museum; and its suggestions were identical in content with Arnold's few words. (It was later found to be by Lucas Brandiss [Lübeck, ca. 1480]).

I discovered that by the time we knew each other, while he had vast knowledge of secular history, his whole mind was already concentrating on its significance for the spirit of man. Religion, in the widest sense, was the heart of the matter for him. He was always searching for a deeper grasp of the ultimate reality.

In the early days of our acquaintance, 1937–39, we used to go for long walks in the woods and the bottoms, to the pasture land with cattle grazing to the east of Ganthorpe Hall. The dog we took with us invariably would follow a scent and lose us, following its own hunting instincts. Then Arnold would call out endlessly "Dawn, Dawn:" and the name of the dog began to have a symbolism of its own. The light was always just below the horizon, sometimes deep down.

Once after the catastrophe of the first marriage, he dared to go back to his old home with its overpowering memories. He took me there, strolling fiercely through the woods following a track he had gone along when he was almost driven to despair over the break with Rosalind. We went right to a canal where he had resisted the temptation to smother that despair by oblivion. He told me this as we stood there, and I realized something of the victory that he had won.

But his favorite corner was the prehistoric barrow of the "Old Man" near Slingsby Bank. In the summer's heat he would lie there on top of the barrow, silent, listening to the sounds of the wood and the stirring of the cattle round, he communing with his most ancient ancestor, crossing the vast stretch of time by silence, until we were surrounded by the cows and the calves who were too curious to leave us alone. Then up we would get and stride back for tea, talking of saints and particularly his favorite, Francis, the Poor Man.

Rereading those hundreds of letters that passed between us, and recalling those many visits to Ganthorpe and to his house in Pembroke Square in London, it has come upon me how generous Arnold was with his time and his thoughts, hopes and fears. His integrity and humility, his wholeness, remain preeminent. He was no mere scholar, though perhaps the greatest of his time; he was a man in the world of affairs, a citizen of the world.

He taught me to see beyond national history, beyond politics, beyond the economic factor in history, to realize—what must have been instinctive in me—that the deepest, most lasting and most important history is the history of religion, of men's relationships with God, with the ultimate reality. For a time his star is low on the horizon, but before long scholars and thinkers of the future will realize that mankind needs to return to its spiritual roots. Arnold opened wide the door to the world of comparative religion. We still have to discover the true relationship between the insights of the great religions. His books are stacked with insights, of course not all of them are true, but many leading the way.

(C.C.E.)

95, Oakwood Court
London, W.14

21 December 1966

Dear Columba,

It was like you to make time to write your letter of 17 December in spite of all that you have in hand. It always gives me joy when I see your handwriting turning up in my mail. Yes, like Father Aelred, you ought to get a break from administration. Building up the Priory and the School has been a long haul, and then there was the housemastership—also very exacting—before that. And, as I found during the war, it is difficult to combine administration with thinking and writing, even if one has the time, because it means a change of psychological rhythm. In administration, one has to be accessible, at any moment, to any person or thing that may turn up with a right to your attention, whereas, for intellectual work, you need stillness and peace. My travelling style? This very afternoon, en route from Chatham House to Oakwood Court via the American Embassy, I delivered '*Between Maule and Amazon*' to the Oxford Press. How have I completed my main agenda? Because I have schooled myself to write every day, whether I am in the mood or not, and because, each morning, since about the age of 16, I have started bent forward to run the hundred yards when the pistol goes off—i.e. at 7.00 A.M. (a late hour by your standards). Since we came back, wrecks, from being 'state guests' in those hectic American countries, this habit of mine has been costing me my sleep. In old days I woke up with a maid bringing Rosalind and me a cup of tea before we got out of bed. Nowadays, I am off, like a greyhound after the electric hare, to make the breakfast before Veronica (who does all the rest of the housework still at 72) is up. No, not quite all the rest; I have now taken on dusting six of the rooms at week-end.

Of course, some religions are better than others. In the Latin America book that I have just delivered, I have a piece on the gods coming to life again in Mexico, and I think, quite as strongly as you do, that if this really happens, it will be a spiritual catastrophe. To the Aztecs, the Spaniards' suppression of human sacrifice was a tyrannical interference with a rite that made the world go round. But the Spaniards, being now the masters, had the responsibility of taking the decision, and it would be hard to argue that they did not choose right.[1]

About the Russians, if one imagines oneself in their position, one cannot doubt that they are sincere in wanting now to come to terms with America, and one can also see that they cannot do this without America's changing her policy in Vietnam. The Russians cannot make peace with America without getting acceptable terms for *Ho Chi Minh*[2] as well as for themselves. If they were to sell him down the river, this would be giving the Chinese reason for saying that they were traitors to their fellow Communists. In my belief, Ho Chi Minh would like to be extricated from China's menacing embrace, but only Russia and America, acting in concert, can do that for him. Short of that, he must continue to be China's unwitting prisoner (euphemistically called 'protégé').

About Theodosius I, whom I deplore: I think it was lucky for the West that the Roman Empire collapsed there within eleven years of his death. Even so, I wouldn't have liked to be a Cathar or Lollard[3] in medieval Western Europe.

At midnight before Xmas Day I shall be thinking of your Mass.

With love to you from
us both,
Arnold

1. A.J.T.'s *Between Maule and Amazon* (London, 1967), in which "The Gods Come Back to Life" is on pp. 127–35.

2. Ho Chi Minh (ca. 1890–1969); president of North Vietnam (1945–69).

3. The Cathars were known as Albigenses in Southern France; cf. "Paulicians, Bogomils, Cathars," in *A Study of History*, IV: 624–34, and *Constantine Porphyrogenitus and His World*, Annex IV, The Paulicians and the Bogomils, pp. 652–98. The Lollards were followers of John Wycliffe (ca. 1329–84).

NINE

1967–72

Rosalind's death; "I can't imagine how Death can have had the audacity to take her"; "I love Rosalind with all my heart, and I love Veronica, too, with all my heart"; C.C.E.'s return to England; Muhammad as a prophet; A.J.T. at the Acherusian plain; Humanae vitae*; C.C.E. in Kenya; the Masai; A.J.T.'s "limits of belief"; A.J.T.'s coronary thrombosis; A.J.T.'s twinge at his not receiving an O.M.; Rosalind's will; A.J.T.'s granddaughters; an essay toward his biography; Christ and the Buddha; Francesco and Pietro Bernardone; "every living creature is a temporary splinter of the ultimate reality";* A Study of Toynbee.

95, Oakwood Court
London W.14

11 February 1967

Dear Aelred,

I don't know how you found time to write before leaving: you had a non-stop schedule. Your letter made us both very happy.

As for the information that I was able to give you, the only use, and pleasure of acquiring that, or anything else, is to make it serve other people in some way or other, so doing what I could to help you was very enjoyable for me—apart from the personal pleasure of seeing you again after all this time.

I believe I forgot to give you the letter for Shigabana Matsumoto [1] of International House, Tokyo, so I am enclosing one to him now. Of course you have your own connections in Japan, and there is also the British Council, but International House is a valuable centre for meeting Japanese—and my friend Shiga is particularly good at putting foreign visitors in touch, quickly, with the kind of people they want to see.

Well, God bless you. And let us continue to keep in touch with each other.

Yours ever,
Arnold Toynbee

The Very Reverend the Prior, Portsmouth Priory, Portsmouth, R.I. U.S.A.

1. Shigabana (Shigeharu) Matsumoto (1899–); graduate, University of Tokyo (1924); student at Cambridge, England; lawyer; editor in chief, Domei News Service (1939–43); managing director (1943–45); chief managing director, Kokusai Bunka Kaikan (International House of Japan, Inc.) (1965–); edited *Arnold Toynbee's Lesson of History* (lectures in Japan) (Tokyo, 1957); *A*

History of the World, 1945–61 (in Japanese) (Tokyo, 1962). He had welcomed A.J.T. and Veronica to the International House during their 1956 visit and was the first of their many Japanese friends.

273 Santa Teresa
Stanford, California

2 May 1967

Dear Columba,

Your Easter letter[1] had travelled far before I found it waiting for me here[2] last night, on getting back from an expedition to Pasadena and Santa Barbara (at Pasadena a public dialogue—not dog-fight, with Allan Nevins,[3] for the American Friends Service Committee; at Santa Barbara, a day at Robert Hutchins' Centre for the Study of Democratic Institutions).

I am very glad your 'Monasticism' is now so near to being launched. You have so many spiritual and administrative calls on you, and these, being personal, are imperious, and have to be attended to *instanter*, like parliamentary questions, whereas the spirit within us which creates things—as for instance, a book, needs to concentrate, and is rather grievously interrupted when the telephone starts ringing.

How I wish I could see you while we are on this side of the Atlantic this time. But the doctors have warned Veronica and me seriously to restrict our activities. During the first three weeks of this visit, we were on the move and were exhausted—our blood pressures went up inordinately (they are now down again, since we have been stationary on the campus here. But we have been warned).

In the course of nature, you ought to be a good way farther from death than I now am; but—already at birth—death is close, and we have both of us contemplated it, and tried to make it influence our lives in the right way, for many years past. It has been my constant companion since 1915–16, when about half of my closest friends were killed before they had reached thirty.

Death stares at me in a formidable way now, for I have just heard from Philip that Rosalind—about whom we have all been rather concerned for some months past—has been diagnosed as having cancer in the lungs, and that the doctors do not expect her to live for more than three to five months longer.

I shall see her, still alive, when we get back. As you know, since very soon after her and my marriage broke up, relations between her and Veronica and me have been wholly affectionate. The last time she came to see us in London—not so many months ago—she seemed still full of her old vigour and alertness.

I think freedom from animosity (perhaps taught to us by Gandhi) is one of our generation's successes, to set against its many dreadful failures. Anyway, thirty years of marriage is an unbreakable bond, even when it is actually broken. I have not yet absorbed the shock.

This is confidential, because Rosalind has not been told the facts. It was a difficult decision, because she had always insisted that she did want to be told if the situation arose. But she is no longer quite herself, so, after all, she might not be able to take it.

She is at home at Low Holm, Cumwhitton, Cumberland, and was very happy to come home from hospital. Of all living people, Richard Stafford[4] is, I suppose, the closest to her, and is perhaps the only person who has even half come up to her expectations. He is like an adopted son, and has done for her, I should say, the equivalent of what Veronica has done for me. The bereavement for him will be greater than even for Philip and Lawrence and me. She has, I imagine, done a great deal for him, too, in a situation in which he must have been in very great need of help.

I wonder whether the Buddha is really obscure—or is only obscure to us, because our Jewish-Christian-Muslim imagery of ultimate spiritual reality is perhaps more naïve and crude than the Indian. Anyway, the Buddha was moved by love. He deliberately postponed his own exit into Nirvana out of love for his fellow sentient living beings, including the non-human ones, like Saint Francis. He stayed to teach them the way.

Don't you think that, at bottom, all the religions are trying to help the individual living creature to do what is against the nature of life, and is therefore so hard, though so necessary—I mean, to transfer the centre of one's concern from oneself to the true centre, by whatever name one may call this. Nirvana = extinguishment of self-centredness—, in Judaic theistic terms, the transfer of one's centre of attachment from oneself to God (but we need not use the anthropomorphic imagery of a personal God to mean what the Buddha meant—and what Jesus meant too).

'Saint Francis of Assisi and Saint Francis de Sales'[5]—my poor father, who lived for many years after going out of his mind, used to repeat the two names over and over again. My family were Anglicans, as you know, but the Fioretti and an anthology of Saint Francis de Sales' dicta were always on the bedside table in my parents' bedroom when I was a child.

If the two Francises had been contemporaries in this world, I believe each—being wholly a saint—would have understood, admired, and loved the other, but their respective followers, being on a lower level, would have failed to appreciate the other saint's qualities; the Salesites would have found the Assisian saint naïve, and the Assisian-ites would have found the Salesian saint living at too low a tension. And both ites would have been missing the mark.

Well, my mind goes back to Rosalind. She will have your prayers.

With much love,
Arnold

1. Missing.
2. A.J.T. was at Stanford University delivering lectures to students for credit.
3. Allan Nevins (1890–1971); American historian; *Ordeal of the Union*, 8 vols. (New York, 1947–71).
4. Richard "Stafford"; cf. A.J.T.'s letter of 24 October 1958, above.
5. Saint Francis de Sales; cf. C.C.E.'s letter of 10 September 1940, above.

Stanford University
Stanford, California,
273 Santa Teresa

11 May 1967

Dear Columba,

Your letter of 9 May[1] has just come and has given me very great help and consolation—except for the last paragraph. Please do not be cryptic with me; for my love for you is too great for this not to make me anxious. If your 'providence' means a new posting, which comes to monks as it does to soldiers, that is one thing. If it means some serious prospect about your health, it is another matter. Do let me know.

At the moment I am particularly susceptible. Yesterday morning a cablegram was telephoned through to me: 'Mummy has died: Philip and Bun.' My last news had been a letter of 3 May from Philip, telling me that there had been no change. He and Sally were just back from a conference in Vienna, which Rosalind's doctors had told him *not* to cut, because death was not imminent, and he had advised me, for the second time, not to come home, as she was expected to live for from three to five months. So the end must have been sudden, unexpectedly. No doubt I shall soon get a letter, telling me more.

Philip's letter of the 3rd. also told me that Richard had now come round to the view that Rosalind ought to be told, and that it was being arranged that this should be done by the local priest,[2] whom she liked. I do hope, first that she *was* told in time, to give her the chance of facing death and trying to prepare her soul for it, which is, I think, one of the 'basic human rights'. My second hope is that, if she was told, she did have time, but not more time than necessary.

Yes, I love Rosalind with all my heart, and I love Veronica, too, with all my heart, because the heart can give the whole of itself to more than one person; this is one of the things in which love is unique and in which the First Epistle General of Saint John speaks one of the ultimate truths when it identifies love with God.[3]

I do not know how I should have got through yesterday without Veronica, who is completely understanding and, what is more important and much more difficult, completely un-self-regarding about this as about everything else. If I could stand back, as an outsider, and make an objective comparison between Veronica and Rosalind, I should, I suppose, guess that Veronica is the nearer of the two to the Kingdom of Heaven, but when one loves someone—as, e.g. I love Rosalind, their weaknesses and frailties, do not make one love them less.

The one happy thing for me is that, for many years past, Rosalind has been in complete love and charity with Veronica and me, *et invicem*. The worst of all our sins, as I see it, is to have even the least touch of malice, hatred, and uncharitableness towards any other living creature.

About myself, the telephoned telegram hit me like a bullet, and, all yesterday, I felt as if I had received a physical wound. Not to have seen Rosalind again; not to have been with her at the moment of death; not to have been—or have had the right to be—the person who was doing for her what was being done by Richard and his sisters: this hurt a lot; but what hurt more was the flood of the return of the life that we had shared for thirty years, and contrition—welling up, as strong as ever, after a quarter of a century—for my failure to save our marriage from eventually breaking down.

To face one's failures and repent of them is, I know well, the beginning of salvation—at least, there is no hope of salvation beginning unless one has done that, and every good thing has its cost.

I had to give a lecture at 1.00 P.M. yesterday and managed it all right—borne up by my concern not to fail the University which had engaged me, and the students in my class, who are dependent on this course of mine for earning some of their credits. This duty was a help. But Veronica and contrition were my chief helps.

My love to you,
Arnold

I remember, at the time of the break, you rightly reproved me for having, as I had confessed to you, felt towards Rosalind more as if she were a goddess than as if she were the human being that she was. I must still have some of this feeling left, because I can't imagine how Death can have had the audacity to take her.

1. Missing.
2. Francis Gerard Sitwell, O.S.B. (1906–); monk of Ampleforth; priest of Warwick Bridge; one time Master of St. Benet's Hall.
3. 1 John 4:7–16.

273 Santa Teresa
16 May 1967 Stanford, California

Dear Columba,

Your letter of 18 April,[1] delivered to Chatham House, has now followed yours of 13 May[2] in answer to mine about Rosalind's death. Your answer was a great help to me.

I am greatly relieved that the cryptic thing—explained in your April letter—has nothing to do with health, but of course I feel much concern for you, and I am particularly sorry if there is even a touch, as you hint, of any feeling on the other side that hurts. I know well, from experience, the difference between criticism made with complete kindliness and charity (such as I used to have from my dear pugnacious Dutch friend and critic, Pieter Geyl,[3] who died several months ago; he criticised utterly without malice) and criticism with even the slightest grain of animosity in it; this gives one pain unavoidably. Monks are human, and small and close-knit communities—e.g. Oxford and Cambridge senior common rooms—do lapse into animosity, though, in my belief, it is a very considerable sin to let oneself stay at all out of charity with any fellow human being.

Administration is a thankless job compared to, say, teaching, discussing, writing, or doing the kind of work that you will be doing if you do now go into the ecumenical field as your principal job. There is so much to be done there that can make for love to replace hostility, and this is just in your line. Will you be working with Archbishop Cardinale? I imagine that you and he see eye to eye about this.

I remember, during the War, Lord Samuel[4] (for whom I had an affection and admiration, as you see from 'Acquaintances') said to me that it was very good for me to have to do a stint of administration, and so it was, but I was much relieved to be able to lay down the burden, and the research and drafting work that I did for the F.O.[5] as a young man during the first war were more rewarding personally, though I dare say my second-war job of getting professors to work for civil servants was more useful. However, it was like the game of croquet in Alice in Wonderland, and I suppose all administration is like that.

When I was talking with Aelred[6] about his coming travels, I could see how much rejuvenated he was feeling at the prospect of laying down his 'priorship'. You will, I am sure, feel the same when the change has been made and is behind you; but it is a pity if there has been any unpleasant atmosphere; there shouldn't be; and it is bound to hurt, however much one tells oneself—endlessly—that one must not mind it too much, and that, as you say, there is probably more love than vindictiveness on the other side.

I have had no more news from home yet since that telephoned cablegram. No doubt they are all very busy. I get waves of grief, but am carrying on all right, thanks to Veronica, and also because, in writing and in having 'bull-sessions' with students, I feel I am putting out something for other people. I feel for these American students very much. They are sheep without a shepherd, and, for many of them, the question of conscience—shall I or shall I not allow myself to be inducted into the army?—is very acute.

With very much love and the sympathy that you know you can be sure of in me.

Arnold

1. Missing; C.C.E. had written that he was being transferred from St. Louis to Ampleforth.

2. Missing.

3. Pieter Geyl (1887–1966); professor of modern history, University of Utrecht (1936–58); A.J.T. wrote an obituary of Geyl (*Encounter* 28, no. 5 [May 1967]: 34–37; *The Times* [7 January 1967]); cf. *A Study of History*, vol. XII, passim.

4. Herbert Louis Samuel, first viscount (1870–1963); British high commissioner in Palestine (1920–25); *In Search of Reality* (Oxford, 1957); cf. A.J.T.'s *Acquaintances*, pp. 302–4.

5. Cf. *Comparing Notes*, pp. 116–7 for a reference to A.J.T.'s work during World War I, cf. A.J.T. and Philip Toynbee, *Comparing Notes: A Dialogue across a Generation* (London, 1963).

6. Aelred Graham; cf. A.J.T.'s letter of 11 February 1967, above.

Stanford University
Stanford, California
273 Santa Teresa

26 May 1967

Dear Columba,

Your letter of 23 May came yesterday.[1] I am very glad my letter was a help. It came from the heart, and from a bit of experience of my own, too. 'Torn but happy'.

When Epicurus was dying of some painful disease, he wrote to a friend: 'I am in physical agony but am blissfully happy'. Spiritual pain is harder to bear than physical, but it, too, is compatible with happiness.

Yes, I have now heard from both Philip and Lawrence. They did (I forget whether I told you) fortunately decide—before being taken by surprise by Rosalind's dying, so long before the doctors had predicted—to let her know that she was going to die, and they arranged for the parish priest, whom she liked, to tell her. This must have been done, about a week before her death, which was time enough, but not needlessly long. Lawrence had a talk with her on Thursday 4 May, when she was still more or less herself (I think she must have died on the 8th.), and found that she already knew, was surprised, said she would have loved to live a little longer, as she was very happy (this has given me great comfort, incidentally), but she was evidently reconciled to death by then. Philip did not get back to Low Holm till she was in a coma—partly produced by drugs, given her to overcome physical pain—so, to his sorrow, he never saw her again *compos mentis*. I feel the same sorrow that I was not there and could not even do the little that a man can do to help in the nursing. Providing for this was difficult; Richard's two sisters came, and were evidently wonderful.

I have had a cable from Richard: 'All my sympathy and love'—which has touched me greatly. Since he and I first met, I think we have had a spontaneous feeling for each other, the bond being a common feeling for Rosalind. Of the living, I feel more concerned for him than for any of the rest of us. Rosalind did, I suppose, save the situation for him in a great crisis in his life by taking him into partnership with her; he was like an adopted son; and, having been freely chosen by her, he was perhaps the only man with whom she was ever intimately associated who came up to her standards. I remember, one day when Veronica and I were at Low Holm, she asked Richard to keep an eye on the leg of mutton in the oven to see that it was not over-cooked. He forgot about it, as any one would do, and it was cooked to a frazzle. If it had been Philip or Lawrence or me in times past, she would have told us that this was just one more illustration of the wretched inadequacy of our moral character; so I held my breath, but she took it like a lamb, though Richard was quite offhand about it. A trivial thing, but it showed how good their relation was.

I know she has made adequate provision for him in her will, but that does not solve the personal question. Of all of us, he is the most bereaved, and I am anxious to find out what his plans are—whether or not he will go on farming Low Holm. Happily, Philip's and Lawrence's relations with him are as good as mine are. This is important, because, unlike me, they are concerned in what happens to Rosalind's estate.

Well, your coming back to England means, I hope, that we shall be seeing more of each other again.

With love,
Arnold

1. Missing.

Kyoto Sangyo University
Kyoto

12 December 1967

Dear Columba,

This is the last night of our month's stay in Japan;[1] tomorrow we fly to Taipei, and on 16 December we sail in the P. and O. SS 'Cathay' from Hong Kong to London—round the Cape; five weeks; we reach London on 25 Jan., and hope to see you soon.

This is my third visit to Japan (my first was in 1929) and Veronica's second (we were here in 1956). We will tell you all about it when we see you. The technological development is astounding, but a number of deeper-minded Japanese are disturbed about the spiritual vacuum. Christians are, as you know, few, but the influence of Christianity radiates beyond the formal membership. One of the professors who has been looking after us is a Catholic and an authority on patristics. His little son is named Ignatius (after Saint Ignatius of Antioch).

We have to get up at 5:45 to catch our plane tomorrow morning at Osaka, and it is now past ten and I have been talking since 10.00 A.M., so I must go to bed, but I can't go before scribbling this line to you.

Yours affectionately,
Arnold

1. A.J.T. had lectured at Kyoto Sangyo University: *Impressions of Japan*, annotated by Tsuyoshi Amemiya (Tokyo, 1968).

Hotel Merlin
Kuala Lumpur,
Malay

22 December 1967

Dear Columba,

Your letter[1] has crossed with one to you from me. I got yours at Singapore the day before yesterday. The O.U.P. met us, brought us here by road for me to give a lecture at the University last night, and have a press conference this morning. They are putting us on board the Cathay again tomorrow at Penang, and we are to dock in London on 25 January.

Two good bits of news: Your appointment to be one of the observers,[2] and the India possibility; I will keep this confidential. (I guess that Keralese monks don't mix well at Bangalore because they are virtually foreigners there—Malayalam-speakers in a Tamil-speaking country (Indians are now unfortunately becoming language-conscious).[3]

Of your four alternatives, I would advise against Nobili's[4] line: (a false shortcut) it was seed on stony ground, both in India and in China. The contemplative life in India for Westerners would be like carrying coals to Newcastle. We of course need to recover contemplation in the West (the concluding point of my last night's lecture), but in India they need other things more urgently. So I would opt for education, combined with *some* work for the poor of the poor, to demonstrate that you are not aloof from India's awful material misery. At present, I fear, Indians seek education, not for its own sake, but for winning a diploma which may or may not win them a job. Persuade them to value education (i) for its intrinsic interest, (ii) as an instrument for helping the less fortunate majority of their fellow human beings.

The *Pensées*. I have them on board in my bag, together with Saint A's Confessions, Homer, Dante, the Quran, and the Golden Treasury. But I am not well enough up in Pascal to be a possible contributor. So much minute work has been done on him and his historical setting, and I am not *au fait*.

But you *must* rope in a Japanese connoisseur of Pascal, Professor Maeda[5] of the Imperial University, Tokyo.

In haste to catch the post,

Yours affectionately,
Arnold

1. Missing.

2. Apparently from a missing letter; observer to the British Council of Churches. "There was speculation as to the possibility of my going to India to help one of the monastic ventures starting there. All very exploratory, but A.J.T. took a keen interest." (C.C.E.)

3. "The Keralese are from Kerala, in the southwest of India. Many of their families have been Christian since the second-century A.D.; and so, for the Hindus generally, they had become almost a separate caste. In 1981 I visited the monastery founded near Bangalore Asirvanam, and it was flourishing." (C.C.E.)

4. Robert de Nobili, S.J. (1577–1656); missionary to India; adopted the mode of life of the Indian Brahmins; Fr. Bede Griffiths, O.S.B., of Prinknash has established in Shantivanam a Christian but Hindu style ashram or monastery, near Tiruchirāpalli, not far from Madurai, where Nobili had worked.

5. Yoichi Maeda (1911–); graduate of Tokyo Imperial University; the Sorbonne; professor, University of Tokyo (1949–72); managing director, Kokusai Bunka Kaikan (International House of Japan, Inc.); *Christian Apologetics of Montaigne and Pascal* (Tokyo, 1949); *Commentaries on Pascal's Pensées* (Tokyo, 1980). There was then talk of a massive edition of the *Pensées* for the English reading public. In a letter of 16 November 1984 to C.B.P., Maeda remarks: "I am surprised and feel honored that Arnold Toynbee remembered even my name, because I have had the pleasure of talking with him only once during his visit to Japan in 1956."

Ampleforth Abbey
York

20 January 1968

Dear Arnold,

Welcome home.

We had an old Wykehamist, the Bishop of Whitby,[1] preaching to the boys on Friday, as part of our Unity Octave day of prayer. He was very good, all 6 ft. 7 of him.

I enclose Fr. Aelred's latest interview that he specially asked me to send on to you. It seems to me that ex President, Radhakrishnan has mellowed in the years.[2]

How are you? I hope, both of you, rested by the long sea voyage. Did you land at Cape Town?

What is puzzling me at present is this: the N.T. has little about organization and authority—certainly not in terms like "sovereignty;" the Middle Ages went mad on it, in the West, legalizing the Church almost out of recognition. What is essential, what not? Obviously some organization, authority is necessary; but how much is scriptural, how much human (if useful), how much is transmuted from love into law and so on. This is one of the key questions and still needs an answer. The Orthodox have something to teach us, but they don't get things done. You see how my mind is working. Love to you both.

Columba, O.S.B.

1. George D'Oyly Snow (1903–77); Winchester; Oriel College, Oxford; suffragan bishop of Whitby (1961–71); *The Public School in the New Age* (London, 1959).

2. Sarvepalli Radhakrishnan (1888–1975); philosopher; president of the Republic of India (1962–69); cf. Aelred Graham, *The End of Religion* (London, 1971), pp. 140–47; cf. *A Study of History*, VII:735–36, quoting Radhakrishnan's *Eastern Religions and Western Thought*, 2nd ed. (Oxford, 1940).

95, Oakwood Court
London W.14

10 February 1968

Dear Columba,

I was very glad to have your letter of 20 January enclosing the script of Father Aelred's conversation with Dr. Radhakrishnan. It is most valuable—as it was likely to be, since they are two first-class minds (and souls). As it was I who gave Aelred the introduction, I am particularly pleased that it has had this result.

We got back on 25 January after more than five weeks at sea,[1] and, though there were 61 under-twenty-ones on board, out of 192 passengers, we have come home rested: our blood-pressures are impeccable, which they certainly wouldn't have been if we had flown.

I don't think it is surprising that the N.T. has so little about organisation and authority. Jesus and his disciples and the evangelists—any way, Mark and John—were politically null. They were 'natives' under a colonial regime: Saint Paul, who was a Roman citizen, does have something to say about organisation and authority in his epistles.

Speaking, for the sake of the argument, in purely mundane terms, have you ever thought of the effect on Jesus's and Muhammad's respective careers of the fact that Jesus, living as a subject inside the Roman Empire's frontiers, had no opportunity of going into politics, whereas Muhammad, living in a turbulent independent city-state, had no opportunity—any more than Dante had—of keeping out of politics. Muhammad had to perish or accept the invitation to become podestà (the medieval Italian name for his post) at Yathrib, so, instead of being put to death for preaching his unpopular convictions, he became a flaming political success, to his own and Islam's great spiritual disadvantage. It was only in the West, where the collapse of the Roman Empire left a 'power-vaccum', that the Church went ultra-organisational and legalistic. It didn't in the East till the East Roman Empire fell. The

Makarios-type of Eastern Orthodox prelate is a product of the Τουρκοκρατία,[2] when clerics were the only leaders, for all purposes, that the Greeks, Serbs, and Bulgars still had. In French Canada the Church has played the same part for the same reason. The true political chief of Quebec province is not the provincial Prime Minister; it is the Father Superior of the Petit Séminaire which educates the teachers who train the parish priests, who are all little local Muhammads-at-Medina. When Makarios was making himself a nuisance to H.M.G.,[3] someone complained, in a letter to the *Times*: 'Why can't he behave like the Archbishop of Canterbury?' This man evidently knew no history. Henry VIII: no power-vacuum there.

When shall we see you? We shall be here now most of the time till the end of May, at least. I hope we shall see each other again soon.

Yours affectionately,
Arnold

Are you still a prior and 'Very Reverend'? Not that you would care, but I should like to get it right.

1. A.J.T. was returning from Japan; cf. A.J.T.'s letter of 12 December 1967, above.
2. Under which the Greek Orthodox patriarch was an ethnarch over his own people.
3. Archbishop Mouskos Makarios III (1913–77); in 1959 he became president of Cyprus after years of struggle for independence.

Ampleforth Abbey
York

13 February 1968

My dear Arnold,

Welcome home. It is good news that your hearts are in good shape. Go slower. That is good advice. My love to Veronica.

I am sure Aelred will be happy to hear how much you appreciated the recorded conversation. Where he is by now, I haven't the slightest idea, so cannot tell him, but I shall when he "surfaces" again.

Your letter to the *Times*[1] was the first sure sign I had that you had landed. It was well timed and I am sure gave many a signal to pause and consider the Common Good.

Yes, your comments on the N.T. and Muhammad are pertinent. Perhaps when the chapter on M. is typed, you would be happy to read it? I've also finished Confucius and Pope John. The Buddha is half way. I've been reading Isaiah Berlin on Marx.[2] He certainly had the dedication of the prophet and the occasion; but he had not compassion for people. It is easy to throw stones from the peace and moderate comfort of a monastery.

You will be glad to hear that our Indian Novice, having been recalled to India by the Government arrives back today, having disinherited himself they let him come (he is the eldest son of a Raja). He has been wonderfully brought up in the best Hindu tradition. He then discovered Jesus and became a Catholic. Age, c. 27 yrs.[3]

Yours affectionately,
Columba, O.S.B.

P. S. I've written an article for *The Times* on corporate reunion. They've said "nihil" so far. I am giving a retreat in Wimbleton May 3–12. Perhaps we can meet then. We must. No, I fled from titular titles and was left in peace. So Rev.![4]

1. On 10 February 1968, A.J.T. wrote to *The Times* that he had just returned from Japan, where "the Japanese people have earned this boom by working hard and living hard, but they are not resting on their oars. . . . The national interest . . . am I right? . . . is, in Britain, still being subordinated to sectional and factional interests, and this by people of all incomes and of both the major political parties.".

2. Sir Isaiah Berlin (1909–); Chichele Professor of Social and Political Theory, Oxford (1957–67); president, British Academy (1974–78); *Karl Marx: His Life and Environment* (London, 1939).

3. "The Indian novice left; the cultural change was too great; he found the Old Testament Psalms, particularly their warlike spirit, difficult to transmute with love. He had much to give." (C.C.E.)

4. "Later I was almost bullied into accepting one—prior of Durham, a purely honourary title." (C.C.E.)

95, Oakwood Court
London W.14

February 1968

Dear Columba,

We shall be in London all through May, because our Japanese friends are coming sometime in May, so we are sure to be able to meet between May 3 and 12—more than once, I hope.

I shall be glad, of course, to read the Muhammad chapter.

I guessed that you might not be partial to titular titles, but I wanted to get it right.

If the portrait of you[1] is as good as the photograph of it is, it must have been a success.

Yours affectionately,
Arnold

1. The portrait of C.C.E. by his cousin, Edmund Vincent Paul Simon Elwes, R.A. (1902–75); now at the St. Louis Priory; Simon Elwes was the son of Gervase Elwes, the singer, and Lady Winefride Feilding, daughter of Rudolph, eighth Earl of Denbigh and Desmond; he studied at the Oratory; the Slade School; lieutenant colonel in the Royal Hussars in 1944.

Ampleforth Abbey
16 February 1968 York

Dear Arnold,

Here it is.[1] I am always ashamed of the shoddiness of my writing; I don't seem to have the energy to re-write for the 3rd, 4th times; and I hear St. François de Sales' motto ringing in my ears "well enough is soon enough," but still I don't listen. So, if you can bear it, do criticize as well as you can.

Yours affectionately,
Columba, O.S.B.

P.S. Yes, the portrait is supposed to be the best male one he has done (?).

1. The chapter on Muhammad.

21 February 1968

Dear Columba,

I have just read your Muhammad chapter and am returning the script herewith.

Crucial point: Revelation. This is something that, we all agree (whatever we may hold to be its ultimate source), wells up into consciousness through the subconscious without deliberate volition and, as you point out, in Muhammad's case (? here make a comparison with the story of Jonah), very much against his will originally, because (i) he was an honest man and he was not sure, at the beginning, whether he was truly receiving revelation from God and (ii) he foresaw that, if he were to be convinced that it was true and were therefore to feel in duty bound to proclaim it, he was going to have a bad time with his fellow Meccans.

I agree with you that M.'s original experiences were genuine. You rightly stress M.'s probity. I also think that when, instead of being lynched by the Quraysh (which would have made Islam a religion of suffering, like Christianity, if Islam had survived, as it might have in Abyssinia), M. received his spiritually disastrous call to take on a political job at Yathrib, (the temptation that Jesus rejected), M.'s revelations were probably self-induced, because, at Yathrib (I mean 'Medina'—'the City' [of the Prophet]), M. turned out to have enormous political ability, and he had to take a politician's day-to-day snap decisions on 'one damned thing after another'. I do not believe that, in the Medina period, any more than in the Mecca period, M. was ever consciously fabricating revelations. There are parallels to this psychological question about M. in the life-histories of some modern spiritualist 'mediums', and, for all that we know, Harold Wilson[1] and L.B.J.[2] believe that decisions of theirs that seem to us to be flagrant acts of *Realpolitik* are charismatic intuitions.

For that matter, M.'s vision of Gabriel as a gigantic figure appearing at a bowshot's distance had been anticipated in the vision of a Syrian Christian monk whose description of it, recorded by himself, is still extant. (I can't find the reference[3] and just cannot spend more time searching for it. But you might find it in *The Encyclopaedia of Islam*, s.v. Gabriel. Anyway, read Richard Bell: *The Origin of Islam in its*

Christian Environment (1926); Tor Andrae: *Les Origines de l'Islam et le Christianisme* (1955); Tor Andrae: *Mahomet, sa vie et sa Doctrine (1945)*.) The visual form of M.'s own vision must have been determined by this precedent; the resemblance is too close to have been a coincidence. M. perhaps heard the story by word of mouth when he was in Damascus on business as a young man. (It is most unlikely that M. knew enough Syriac to be able to read hagiographical works in Syriac, though he must have talked good enough pijin-Syriac to have been able to do business within the frontiers of the Roman Empire.) But this is *not* evidence of fabrication; it is evidence of the human mind's well-known trick of believing that something that it has heard or read long ago is an original idea of its own (or an original inspiration). E.g. I myself thought in 1927 that I was inventing the phrase 'challenge-and-response', but in about 1943 I found the phrase, to my astonishment, in Browning's poem 'Master Hugues of Saxe-Gotha', which I had read at school in about 1905.[4]

But what irony there is in the sequel. The Quraysh wanted to liquidate M. because they assumed that, if M. were to discredit the trinity of goddesses in the Ka^cba (a trinity that had seeped into Arabia from the Fertile Crescent before Judaism and Christianity), the annual pilgrimage, which was also an annual fair, would stop and they would be ruined commercially. (Trade and the pilgrim business were, and are, Mecca's sole sources of livelihood.) Instead, M. made the fortune of the pilgrimage through resisting the temptation to betray his mission by declaring, against his own convictions, that the trinity of goddesses were God's daughters. Second irony: M., the prophet who became a successful politician,—'*travaillait pour le roi de Prusse*'—i.e. for his bitterest enemy among the Quraysh, the business-woman Hind, whose son, Mu^cāwiyāh—an even more able politician than M.—became M.'s fifth political successor (Khalifah) and founded a dynasty. M.'s cousin and son-in-law, ^cAlī (a hopelessly bad politician) and M.'s grandson Husayn were assassinated. M.'s own descendants never succeeded in becoming caliphs. The Caliphate was wrested out of the hands of Mu^cāwiyāh's descendants by the descendants of M.'s uncle, ^cAbbās.

Two points of terminology—important, because they might create prejudice, which you are scrupulously trying *not* to do.

(i) Drop Machiavelli's and Carlyle's cliché 'Prophet with the Sword'. It is a truth, but only part of a complicated truth. The Sword, without inspiration and conviction, would never, by itself, have made Islam's fortune. The cliché is therefore unfair and misleading. On this, read Sir Thomas Arnold's *The Preaching of Islam*.

(ii) For 'Allah', substitute 'God' throughout. The transliteration of the Arabic word 'Allah' in a European language, suggests that, like 'Yahweh' or 'Chemosh', it is the proper name of a tribal god who is not the same as 'God' in the Jewish-Christian-Muslim sense of the solely real One True God. Remember what a heroic spiritual effort (or, alternatively, what tremendous inspiration) it required in the series of Israelite and Judahite prophets, from Amos to Deutero-Isaiah, to replace 'Yahweh' by 'God' in our sense.

Now, in Arabic, 'Allah' (al-ilah) means '*the* god', i.e. 'God' in our sense. I know no

Syriac, but I believe (please verify) that, in the Syriac versions of the Christian creeds and scriptures and liturgy, the Greek word ὁ Θεός is translated 'Allah' (this being a Syriac, as well as an Arabic word).[5]

I must stop. I have a pile of stuff to deal with.

Yours affectionately,
Arnold Toynbee

1. Sir James Harold Wilson (1916–); Jesus College, Oxford; leader of the Labour party (1963–76); prime minister and first lord of the Treasury (1964–70 and 1974–76); now Baron Wilson of Rievaulx.

2. Lyndon B. Johnson (1908–73); then president of the United States.

3. "A.J.T. met me in London; we went to a library to find the reference. For once, after long research, he could not find it again." (C.C.E.)

4. Compare *A Study of History*, X: 231–32.

5. Among A.J.T.'s many references to Muhammad, see ibid., VII: 160–61, 289–90, 464–65, and passim, and *An Historian's Approach to Religion*, pp. 110, 129.

Convent of Marie Réparatrice
Elie House
Elie
Fife, Scotland

26 February 1968

Dear Arnold,

I put you to an immense amount of trouble. Thank you very much. Your comments are invaluable.

Allah, yes, I will avoid giving any offense there. Curiously enough, in Malta, I learnt enough Maltese phrases to say the responses in Maltese, and *Dominus vobiscum* comes out as *Il Muley makom*, and *agnus Dei* as *Allah*. . . . ? (I've forgotten), which at the time gave me great joy, i.e. to be using the Muslim word for God.

I'll find a better title for the chapter; I will stress the honesty of Mahomet throughout, and try to hunt down the Syrian Monk's story. What an amazing double irony you point out—worth bringing in.

Yes, what is the test of Revelations? Holiness, I suppose, is the only one that would be acceptable to the modern mind. Do we have an instinct for holiness? If so, that is very interesting. Do all peoples share the same idea of holiness? My answer, I think, would be, that all peoples understand the holiness of true love. Would you agree?

I'm here for 3 days, giving a retreat to "old" ladies, and return to A. to give one to the boys—a change of gear.

Thank you, once again. God bless you both.

Love to you both,
Columba

P.S. I go on putting Prof. A.J.T. That is correct is it?

Ampleforth Abbey
York

2.3.68

Dear Arnold,

I am a little anxious, as you said you were returning the text of my Mahomet and it was not in the envelope. So I thought I would drop you this line before I got submerged into the Boys' Retreat.

Thank you once again. I am tempted to think your letter would be more useful than my chapter. So, it will be incorporated, after, I'm afraid, a transmutation.

Yours ever,
Columba, O.S.B.

The Royal Institute
of International Affairs
Chatham House
10, St James's Square
London S.W.1

29 July 1968

Dear Columba,

Your letter of 9 July[1] was written the day before Veronica and I left for our annual town-planning conference in Greece,[2] so this is why I haven't written earlier.

Bury your bones in East Africa? Of course you won't. Why, the Wednesday before last, Veronica and I went down into the oracle of the dead where Odysseus raised the ghosts,[3] and we came up again alive, though we had to scramble over a wall to get there. Cocytus and Acheron[4] were flowing just below (now drained by petrol pumps to feed sprinklers on fields that were once the Acherusian Lake). How indignant Dante[5] and Milton[6] would have been at their horrific infernal rivers being turned into public utilities. Perhaps, though, we may bury our bones in Eastern Turkey, where we are going in October. However, in expectation of surviving, we have now to do the unpleasant job of negotiating a new lease for our flat. . . . Luckily we have made some post-war savings, on which we shall now have to draw, and I do not expect that we shall outlive them.

I have written about a third of a book on death that is being published by Hodder & Stoughton.[7] I shall be sending you a copy when it is out. I am very glad that you are to have an interlude for coping with the prophets. Considered as an Arab of his generation, Muhammad was humane, but, as a prophet for the present and future world, he is entirely a stumbling-block.

I do hope we shall see each other before you go to East Africa. Persuade Father Abbot to let you go by sea round the Cape, and you will then have time for some more meditation and more writing.

Yours affectionately,
Arnold

I have again looked, without success, for the ref. to the Syrian monk who had Muhammad's vision of Gabriel before Muhammad.

1. Missing. C.C.E. was going to East Africa to give retreats to the Mill Hill fathers and others throughout Kenya, Uganda, and Tanzania and to explore the possibility of establishing a Benedictine foundation in Africa.

2. Where A.J.T. took part in the discussions; at the final meeting of the Delos Six Symposium, held in the ancient theater on Delos, he remarked: "The human race is very unwilling to be regimented. . . . We must have freedom and participation and self-order and discipline too." *Ekistics*, 26, no. 155 (October 1968), p. 320.

3. *Odyssey*, 10.512–15.

4. The river Acheron in Southern Epirus enters the Acherusian plain where a lake lay in ancient times; the entrance to Hades was said to be at the confluence of the Cocytus and Pyriphlegethon rivers, which joined the Acheron below the lake. (Pausanias, *Description of Greece* 1.17.5; *Aeneid*, 6.295–97; Plato, *Phaedo*, 112–13).

5. *Inferno*, 31.122 ff.; 32, 33, 34.

6. *Paradise Lost*, 2.574–86: "four infernal Rivers that disgorge / Into the burning Lake their baleful streams."

7. A.J.T.'s *Man's Concern with Death* (London, 1968).

11 August 1968 — 95, Oakwood Court, W.14

Dear Columba,

I have had your letter of 5 August.[1] I have been reading in the correspondence in the Times about the Encyclical[2] (the Times says it has received 2000 letters).

The most evil use to which the pill can be put is to give impunity to adultery and to promiscuous sexual relations before or outside marriage, so, as I see it, the most necessary response to the invention of the pill is to promote the institution of marriage, and to do everything possible to encourage and help married people to lead a good married life. Now the Encyclical does nothing to discourage promiscuity and adultery, but it does lay a burden on respectable marriages, so, apart from the issue over the substance of the Encyclical, I feel that married couples are the wrong target for the Pope to have shot at. His sincerity is not in doubt, but his wisdom is, I should say. The Encyclical has come at a moment when the collegiality of bishops, the participation of the laity, and reconciliation with other religious communities are all on the march. I guess that the incidental issue of Papal monarchy will turn out to be as explosive as the immediate issue of the use of contraceptives in marriage.

Veronica and I are going up to Hall Beck on 20 August. We are both all right, I am glad to say.

I am afraid the Encyclical must be putting a strain on you.

Yours affectionately,
Arnold

1. Missing.

2. On 29 July 1968, Paul VI had issued his controversial encyclical *Humanae vitae*.

Ampleforth Abbey
York

27 August 1968

Dear Arnold,

A card giving me your Tel. no., sent by the G.P.O. reminds me you are one up. It also shows me I've been addressing you wrongly all these years. I'll conform.

Oct. 15 I take the mission-plane from Amsterdam to Entebbe, and for a year have a feel of what I wrote about in China.

Yes, the Pope's encyclical was a seismic shock. Part of the bother is that the weight of an encyclical is not clear, nor that of a Papal pronouncement which is not *de fide*. This one is not. I am still sorting out the bits, partly for myself and especially for others. I believe in their case I must go as far as I dare and yet be duly obedient. For myself I feel, the problem is so differently solved by important minds that my own view can't be all that positive, tho' I leaned very strongly in favour of the pill in certain circumstances. But for the consciences of others, I would say something like this. "You think you are not doing wrong, in fact right, to use the pill. Have you seriously studied the Pope's decision, given it the weight it deserves?" Yes. "You still think you are right?" Yes. "Then follow your conscience. You must, and carry on in the Church."

If the Papal doctrine had been the summary of the view of the consensus of all the Bishops, theologians and people of God, I would have said its 'weight' would have been mighty great. But in fact it is the consensus of one school, but also *his* personal view, so not to be ignored or turned down, in fact very weighty.

I'm not in favour of this newspaper publicity; it can do much damage. It seemed to me that the Bishops were caught unawares (2 days' warning?) and acted hastily.[1] This is another sign that the decision was a lone one. Had it been *de fide*, it would have been different.

In general I feel H.V. is part of the curial struggle to free itself from Vatican II, and I'm sorry Pope Paul has got involved in that. I wonder how all this somewhat critical view seems to you.

I hope you had a nice sunny spell up in your mountain retreat. I'm off Oct. 15.

Love to you both,
Columba, O.S.B.

1. In *The Times* (30 July 1968), a "spokesman" at the archbishop's house, Westminster, is quoted as saying the encyclical is "clearly an authoritative statement" but "does not appeal to infallibility."

Ampleforth Abbey
York

2 September 1968

Dear Arnold,

Your book on death has come back to mind. Fr. Peter[1] was found dead on the stairs in the Junior House, Wednesday last—or rather he died Wed., was found

Thursday morning. He was a lovely character, full of kindness to the last day. There is the breaking of bonds when someone you love dies. It is worse with those very close relationships, mother-son, husband-wife. This is a physical agony as well as a spiritual one; and even though one believes absolutely in a future life. Then after a time, as with my mother, and with Fr. Peter and other close friends, the reality of an ever-present triumphs, as also the joy that they are at peace. We know almost nothing of what that peace is; and how we would like to know. "Eye hath not seen. . . ."[2] But St. John did write that we would see God as He is. This almost frightens me. God . . . so immense. Only the thought of Jesus Our Lord makes me realize that God will be bearable and Lovely, Truth. The justice and power of God at other times are overwhelming.

I am longing to read your book.

St. Francis' end: Welcome Sister Death. So like him. I've just been reading *Bishop Moorman's*[3] account. You can't go far wrong with St. Francis. But he has done it beautifully.

I've now written: Confucius, Muhammad, Buddha, Jeremiah, Francis, Ramon Lull, Huss, Pope John, Teilhard de Chardin. I still have Isaias II, Pascal. The introduction (mostly done). Lincoln ½ done. But time is running out. I want to fire off some of these in seminaries etc. in E. Africa. There are so many others one wanted to add: Wesley, de Lamennais, I still think Newman. But one has to come to an end. Yes, I've done Karl Marx.

The Belgian Bishops have been brave and I think wise.[4] Perhaps the U.K. Bishops will be gentler than heretofore.

Love to you both,
Columba, O.S.B.

1. Peter Utley, O.S.B. (1906–68); Ampleforth monk; he had just relinquished being head of the Junior House at Ampleforth; as a young man he had played for Hampshire and The Gentlemen at cricket.

2. I Cor. 2:9.

3. J. R. H. Moorman, *The Sources for the Life of St. Francis of Assisi* (Manchester, 1940).

4. The Belgian bishops had responded to the encyclical with an approval that included a statement that "we are not held to absolute and unconditional support of the sort which is required for a definition of dogma" (*The Times* [2 September 1968]).

Hall Beck Cottage
Hall Beck
Killington
Kirkby Lonsdale
Westmoreland

5 September 1968

Dear Columba,

I have just had your letter of 27 August after Bank Holiday delay. Will you be leaving for Amsterdam from London on 15 Oct.? If you will be, I do hope we shall be there. We are due to go to Turkey for three weeks about 10–15 October, but haven't yet heard the date. I hope it may be just late enough for us to see you off, and, if we are still in London, I hope you will take off from Oakwood Court.

Veronica's nephew Hugh Boulter[1] and his wife are pretty certainly going to Uganda next year to teach in a school there—not in Entebbe, but Uganda is a small place, so you may come across them. Christianity has had a relatively long history in Uganda. I believe you will find that there are a lot of things worth doing for you to do there.

By the way, we come back to London on 27 September, so if you are going to be in London before you actually leave, stay with us then, anyway.

Your imaginary dialogue at the top of the other side of your letter is just what I should say if I were a priest. I am more sorry, if possible, for priests than for married couples, for I suppose a priest's paramount duty is to give spiritual advice to the busy laity according to his conscience, and this may be irreconcilable with his duty of obedience to authority. I am particularly sorry for Archbishop Cardinale.[2] The very day on which the Encyclical was published he was being interviewed by the B.B.C. It must have been as grim a moment for Nuncios as Suez Day was for British Ambassadors.

The Pope, unlike Eden,[3] did at least warn the local ecclesiastical authorities in advance, but the letter, published in Yesterday's *Times*,[4] shows that he didn't give them much time or much latitude either. There have been very great differences in the line taken by different bishops in national groups of bishops, all the same.

I am afraid you are likely to be right in guessing that the Encyclical is entangled with power politics in the Curia, which are, I dare say, as fierce as they are in the Kremlin. De Gaulle's word 'participative' seems to be the key one: participation of bishops and parish priests and lay men and women in the taking of decisions that affect them all.

With love from us both,

Yours affectionately,
Arnold

1. Hugh Boulter (1940–); Corpus Christi College, Oxford; director of the worldwide education service of the Parents' National Education Union.

2. *The Times* (30 July 1968) also expressed its sympathy: "There will be considerable private sympathy among liberal Catholics for a prominent churchman whom they tended to number among themselves—the Apostolic Delegate to Great Britain, Archbishop Cardinale."

3. In the Suez crisis of 1956.

4. On 4 September 1968, *The Times* published a letter by Cardinal Cicognani, Vatican secretary of state, to papal diplomatic representatives, telling how hard it was for the Pope to decide on *Humanae vitae* and asking them to present the teaching in its true light: "Like them [the religious] he is informed of the ideas and practices prevalent in contemporary society."

Ampleforth Abbey
York

5 October 1968

My dear Arnold,

As always my visit was full of joy. Thank you and Veronica very much. It must have been quite a labour for her.

You are very kind to agree about a preface.[1] I have written off to Chris Peper to tell him; and that if and when galley sheets are ready, you must be sent a copy and then your bit will be written. I know this little book isn't worthy of its recipient, but I would like to dedicate it to you. Quite what a dedication means I don't know, except bearing witness to a friendship and a great debt of gratitude.

It all began years ago in the codices room in our library, when I showed you some of our precious books, and I hope a friendship lasts in heaven too. S. Thomas More certainly thought so, always speaking of "meeting merrily in heaven."

I quote for you from Daniel 7 even though you know it, as I find it so interesting that at the crucial moment Our Lord should think of that passage—when before the high Priest—

> "I gazed into the vision of the night,
> And I saw, coming on the clouds of heaven,
> One like a son of man.
> . . . .
> On him was conferred sovereignty,
>   glory and kingship,
> And men of all peoples, nations and languages became his
>   servants"   (vv.13–14).

My love to you both and prayers,

Columba, O.S.B.

1. To C.C.E.'s work on prophets.

c/o D. A. Goodall, Esq.
P.O. Box 30465
Nairobi (very soon)

14 December 1968

Dear Arnold,

I'm not yet in Nairobi but in an area near Kisii[1]—I think Kisii is a town/village, an area and a tribe—in the S.W. corner of Kenya. Here, at the minor seminary where c. 140 boys are being trained, I'm giving 3 retreats of 3 days each to ⅔ of the priests. There are 30 all told, so 10 for each retreat. 17 are Mill Hill Fathers and Brothers (mostly Dutch), the rest 14 or 13 local African clergy, tho' the Rector of the Seminary is from Toro, W. Uganda. I'm learning far more than they; in fact I find it not a little absurd for me to be lecturing them. But we have fruitful discussions.

For nearly 2 months I was in Uganda, mostly near Kampala[2] with its Western splendours—hotel and banks—and its native squalor. But I went to Fort Portal and stayed with the Bishop (McCauley)[3] an American and visited four of the outlying missions. Before very long—he has cancer—he will retire and an African—a cheerful Vicar General, all expect—will take his place. But the Holy Cross Fathers will stay on in a subordinate position.

Then I went north to Lira for a consecration of an African Bishop. Everyone was there, including the President, Dr. Obote,[4] tho' a Protestant; it is all part of the eagerness to Africanize the Church. It was a peculiar mixture of Roman Ritual and African spontaneity, cheers and banners.

Then south I went to Masaka[5] and a day journey to a lovely spot, Mbarara,[6] in the S.W. My general impression from these journeys, talking and seeing, is that round the Lake (Victoria), where the Baganda[7] are, the Church is strong. These people have had a strong culture for a long time and Christianity "took." At Fort Portal[8] the same; but in the North and N.E. it is very patchy. One tribe is too keen on drink, another on women, another lazy. But time is required for establishing the Church.

Of course the bishops would love to have us out there, to help run a seminary, or 2ndary school, or a retreat house. But here in Kenya the lack of priests is even worse than in Uganda. I'm off tomorrow to a parish 7000 ft up: 130,000 people, 20,000 Catholics, the rest pagans with their witch doctors, their many wives and endless children—and only two priests.

The climate is marvellous, rain now and then, but cool. I believe it is hotter in January.

My love to you both and a very happy Christmas,

Columba, O.S.B.

1. The bishop, Maurice Otunga (1923–). "Later during my stay he became (and remains) archbishop of Nairobe; he was made cardinal in 1973. His father, a great chief with 100 wives, became a Catholic when Maurice was made cardinal." (C.C.E.)

2. The capital and financial and commercial centre of Uganda.

3. Vincent McCauley (1906–82); of the Congregatio Sanctae Crucis of Notre Dame, Indiana; appointed bishop of Fort Portal by John XXIII in 1961; in 1972 he resigned in favor of an African successor, Bishop Serapio Magambo.

4. Milton Apollo Obote (1924–) is an Anglican but went as a sign of approval that a Ugandan priest, not a foreigner, had been appointed bishop; president of Uganda (1966–71); deposed by a military coup; reelected in 1980; and since then again deposed.

5. Masaka is the heart of the Baganda tribe and very Catholic.

6. A small beautiful town with strong Catholic life.

7. The Baganda had a dynasty of monarchs extending to the fifteenth century; they were the first to receive both Protestant and Catholic missionaries in the late nineteenth century; they produced most of the Ugandan martyrs, both Catholic and Anglican.

8. Fort Portal, a trading town near the Zaire border; former headquarters of Tooro.

The Royal Institute
of International Affairs
Chatham House
10, St James's Square
London S.W.1

19 December 1968

Dear Columba,

I was delighted to have your letter of 14 December. Your travels in Uganda! They beat Veronica's and my second in Eastern Turkey. We have been as far south in the Sudan as Juba (head of navigation on the White Nile), and this is not so far from your northernmost journeys in Uganda. I suppose the Baganda[1] and the Kikuyu[2] are ahead of the other peoples in Uganda and Kenya in modernisation—hence a great deal of trouble. Don't destroy yourself by overwork: high altitudes on the Equator are treacherous climates. There is going to be so much demand on you that you might be tempted to try to do more than is humanly possible. It is exhilarating to be wanted, but sad that the need is so desperate and the supply of people to meet it is so short.

I have just been reviewing the modern-most volume of the New Cambridge Modern History for Father Alberic.[3]

Veronica and I are very lucky in still keeping our health and wits. I expect I told you that in April we are going to New York. There is to be some kind of beano there for my eightieth birthday.

One very good thing about Uganda which comes out in your letter—if I am right—is that there is a lot of cooperation and friendly feeling across the dividing lines between religions and nationalities. East Africa is not so rich as West Africa and does not have as many people with a modern education, but, so far, except in Ruanda-Urandi, it is stopping short of genocide.

I shall be thinking of you on Christmas Day. Write me when you can again. Is c/o Mr. Goodall a permanent address?

With love to you,
Arnold

1. Compare C.C.E's letter of 14 December 1968, above.
2. The Kikuyu are the major tribe in the center of Kenya and around the capital.
3. John Alberic Stacpoole, O.S.B. (1931–); Ampleforth monk; onetime soldier; at that time editor of the *Ampleforth Journal*, in which A.J.T.'s review of vol. 12 of *The New Cambridge Modern History* appeared (74, pt. 1 [Spring 1969]: 94–95; now senior tutor at St. Benet's Hall, Oxford.

c/o R. Rector Kibosho Phil.
Seminary, P.O. Box 3041
Moshi, Tanzania

4 February 1969

My dear Arnold,

I saw with much pain the account of the violent reactions to your article on Mahomet;[1] you cannot be held responsible for this fanaticism. Truth is paramount;

and I'm sure you expressed it with moderation. As you see I'm moving on into Tanzania.

I am sure you would like to hear something of my expedition into the Masai[2] country all along the southern border of Kenya. This is the great high plain that the Rift Valley seems to spill out into. This is not to say there are no hills, some are enormous; but the general impression is of a mighty wilderness full of astonishing game, gazelles, elephants, gnus, lions, giraffes.

Msgr. Davies,[3] the Vicar Apostolic took me in his car together with his mother and the Masai secy. for Catholic schools. The last is one of the most distinguished converts from this most un-convertible of tribes. He has travelled widely in England, Germany and especially the United States where he followed courses at Harvard and in Texas. Our tour lasted ten days. We started from the Ngong Hills just south of Nairobi where Msgr. has his episcopal 'palace.' The car a V.W. is good and strong.

The first lap of the journey was really round the Masailand taking the northern route via Kericho[4] and reaching Kilgoris[5] at the extreme western limit late that afternoon (c. 220 miles). There the country is hilly, long ranging mountains with broad plains in the easterly direction. This is the edge of Masailand. The men and women come in from the silent plains to receive help from the excellent little hospital set up there by Dutch Sisters. I went round their maternity and childrens' wards, spotlessly clean. Standing about outside or lolling in the shade were Masai relations in their earth coloured blankets waiting for news.

The Mill Hill Fathers[6] had also set up a school; this too the Masai will take. But their way of life is so effectively ingrained into them, by the persistent training of their young for all their youthful life, that it will be very difficult to persuade them that their customs (some of them) should give way to better. Their food is milk (with a dash of cows blood and its urine). They rarely eat meat. They believe that it is against God's will to break into the earth with spade or plough; on the other hand their own religion is noble without superstitions: they believe in the one supreme God, the sky God who governs the rain and health; to Him they pray in emergencies, not at other times.

But their morals are unsatisfactory, if at one time ideally suited to their way of life—there is the rub. For centuries they had to fight for their lives and their ways. So they established a warrior class, boys of 14, to early manhood. These are not allowed to marry, but are allowed complete sexual license with young girls, who have no rights against them, except that pregnancy is frowned upon. This period over, the young men (now elders) marry but like Abraham and other worthies of the O.T. could take several wives. They still do all these things. For them they are not wrong. But such a situation makes it difficult, if they wish to be made Christians, to baptise them. Here we have two cultures, ours and theirs, running parallel but in different Ages of Man.

From Kilgoris we made daily expeditions to outlying mission posts, small chapels where little groups of Masai come to Mass; near by, a small school. A Dutch journalist passed thru' with a friend and got lost in the wilds, spent the night in the car and walked 15 miles back in bare feet to the mission, very shaken.

We then went on to Narok,[7] another centre. From there too we ranged around, visiting the tiny mission schools and chapels atop mountains, up remote valleys. On one occasion I concelebrated in Swahili with the bishop. We would pass men and boys by the roadside, gaunt, silent; the boys controlling herds of cattle, one hundred strong, boys of 6, 7 to 10 years of age. The warriors dress fantastically, in strange head gears, mud and ochre, plenty of beads . . . The women bind their arms, ankles and legs with iron rings.

The most notable missionary, Fr. Gogarty[8] who lived right in with them in their very low huts, drinking their food and talking cattle day and night, I hear, has just gone to the Mater hospital in Nairobi, exceedingly ill. That is sad. A real rapport had been established.

We did not get to the eastern end of the Masailand N. of Kilimanjaro, but returned to Ngong. 1,700 miles covered.

Your devoted friend,
Columba, O.S.B.

1. In his tribute to Mahatma Gandhi entitled "Relevance of Gandhian Creed in the Atomic Age," A.J.T. said, "Muhammad gladly seized the opportunity of becoming a political leader," and he "suffered spiritually from his political success"; this article appeared in the *Statesman* on 26 January 1969, and on 31 January, Muslims demonstrated in Calcutta before Statesman House; Hindu-Muslim riots followed, in the course of which four died and scores were injured (*The Times* [1 February 1969]); see A.J.T.'s letter of 10 February, below.

2. The Masai, a pastoral people living in the Great Rift Valley area of northern Tanzania and southern Kenya; numbering in Kenya approximately 150,000.

3. Colin Davies (1924–); Mill Hill missionary; prefect apostolic to the Masai (1964); bishop since 1977; his prefecture covers 15,000 square miles.

4. Now the center of the tea plantations in Kenya.

5. An old center of the Masai tribe.

6. Founded by Cardinal Vaughan, Archbishop of Westminster. "The British government at the time—when there was tension in East Africa between French and English interests—demanded English Catholic missionaries. Although the centre of the Mill Hill fathers is at Mill Hill in London, the majority of the members today are Dutch and Irish." (C.C.E.)

7. The chief center of the Masai.

8. Father T. Gogarty, M.H.M. (1936–); still serving in Kenya. "Very few missionaries have the physical stamina to live as the Masai live. He is exceptional." (C.C.E.)

The Royal Institute
of International Affairs
Chatham House
10, St James's Square
London S.W.1

10 February 1969

Dear Columba:

I was so very glad to have your letter of 4 February. You are certainly seeing the World; it is a great opportunity, and you will be able to turn it all to good account.

The poor Masai are, I am afraid, going to have a head-on collision with the modern world, whereas the Kikuyu, being agriculturalists, have been adapting to modern life and consequently have become, and will remain, dominant in Kenya. In real life, Cain murders Abel *and* gets away with it. Pastoral nomads, like the Masai, are, of course, on a much higher level than food-gatherers like the Amerindian natives, yet they find modernization almost equally difficult. However, Arab pastoral nomads have been succeeding in becoming technicians in the American oil cities in Saᶜudì Arabia.

I am much distressed that there have been deaths in Calcutta as a result of my contribution to Dr. Radhakrishnan's symposium volume commemorating the centenary of Gandhi's birth.[1] Of course there was nothing in my reference to the Prophet Muhammad that would reasonably have given offense. The furore is, I think, a symptom of the present sense of frustration among Indian Muslims in particular and Muslims in general. Islam, though noble and rational, is another historic way of life that finds it difficult to accommodate itself to the modern world.

The rather formidable April birthday celebrations in New York are now bearing down upon us, but we are bearing up.

With love from us both,
Yours affectionately,
Arnold

1. A.J.T.'s "A Tribute," in *Mahatma Gandhi: 100 Years* (New Delhi, 1968), pp. 375–80; and see C.C.E.'s letter of 4 February 1969, above.

Diocese of Moshi
P.O. Box 3011
Moshi, Tanzania

1 March 1969

Dear Arnold,

I am sitting in an old German mission house built like a schloss under the shadow of Mawenzi, the lesser of the two peaks of Kilimanjaro; out of my window I can see the eastern part of the Masai country of Kenya. The mission, Rombo (Mkuu)[1] is one of the three oldest c. 1895: Kilema, Kibosho, Rombo. For a day or two I'll be on a rather strenuous series of journeys back to Kampala and beyond (to Peramiho)[2] via Nairobi, Kericho, Tororo; and know that you too will be in a great flurry in April; I thought I'd write my congratulations and joy early; and you'll have them as a little feast of pleasure, I hope.

First, I thank God that we met all those years ago now at Ampleforth, was it 1935[3] (?) and that from then on we became firm friends; that I resolved ever to keep you in the forefront of my prayers. There has been no difficulty about that. And during April, at holy Mass, I shall join you (and Veronica) with myself in union with Christ, the Perfect Man—Son of God, before the Father of us all, in a very special way.

Secondly, I am so grateful to God, and you his son, for making you an instrument of His Truth, especially in the *Study* where you portray, establish man's relations with God, and man's relationship of love and justice with one another, as the heart of history; so that the history of Religions and of God-like people is the summit of the human story. I believe too you have helped to make us all recognize the foot print of God in all religions.

Thirdly, I am grateful for your courage in speaking even in unpopular causes, especially for the Arabs, but often. I feel that instead of being more tolerant, the modern mind is tending towards fanaticism.

But, of course, being human, I rejoice specially in our long friendship; and let us together praise God for it.

May your celebrations not be too exhausting. You will, I know, like my cousin Gervase Elwes,[4] the singer, be saying, as the world's applause rings in your ears:

"Non nobis Domine, non nobis
sed nomini Tuo da gloriam."

I've just visited an old sister (Dutch) 92, who has been all her life in the missions, 50 years at Kilema, knew the old saint who founded it, Fr. Auguste;[5] then an old Alsatian, Holy Ghost Father, Pere Hubsch,[6] aged 84, who evangelized the Usumbara[7] nations on foot, occasionally on horseback (but only on the heights).

August 31 I'll be back perhaps.

Love to you both,
Columba, O.S.B.

1. Rombo Mission, founded in 1896 by the Holy Ghost Fathers.

2. Peramiho and Ndanda were two abbeys founded by the Otillien Benedictine Congregation in 1896 and 1906 (and both created as abbeys nullius in 1931); the abbeys were governing dioceses, the abbots having episcopal powers (abbas nullius). Now both dioceses have indigenous bishops drawn from the local diocesan clergy.

3. 1936.

4. Gervase Elwes (1866–1921). "During World War I, my family stayed in his home during the holidays; and I, aged 14, asked him once what he thought on the occasions when the whole audience in the Albert Hall would give him an ovation. He replied smilingly what I quoted to Arnold." (C.C.E.)

5. Auguste Gommengingen (1857–1943); Holy Ghost father who founded the mission of Kilimanjaro, Kilema, in 1890.

6. Franz-Josef Hubsch (1885–1971); Holy Ghost father; in those days the missionaries walked from the coast, Mombasa.

7. The Usumbara dwellers in the mountains east of Kilimanjaro.

95, Oakwood Court
London W.14

March 1969

Dear Columba,

I treasure your birthday letter. How strange is the apparent accidentalness of our first meetings with those other human beings who have made all the difference to one's life. I met you apparently by chance, and something new, of transcendent importance for me, came into my life through our friendship. We are indeed very close to each other.

'The heart of things is love.' We both believe this with all our heart, and the words have, I believe, truly the same meaning for each of us.

I think love includes humility, because there can be no genuine love without this, and, if it is not included, it should be added.

Detachment: I doubt whether this is compatible with love, and this is why there is a third spirit at the heart of things: suffering voluntarily incurred at the cost of any amount of self-sacrifice: in traditional Christian terms, immolation and crucifixion. But we do have to have some detachment—not pushed to Buddhist extremes—from even the best and most beloved fellow creatures, because no creature, however lovable, is the highest spiritual reality—the ultimate reality: I am putting it in these Indian-like negative terms, which express the sure and sincere extent of my beliefs. Of course 'creature' implies 'creator', but, if I used this personal word for the ultimate reality, I should be going beyond my limits of belief.

I am enclosing Syllabus, Part II,[1] with a sheet of notes about it.

It is very good news that you are going back to Nairobi Seminary. There is clearly so much need for you there. But remember that malaria once you have had it, is apt to come back to you. Consult Jean[2] about this—prophylactics or, if possible, a cure.

With much love from us both,
Arnold

1. The outline of C.C.E.'s proposed lectures on church history from the Reformation to the twentieth century; A.J.T.'s comments appear in the annex to this letter.

2. Jean Constance Asquith Toynbee (1920–); daughter of the Hon. Arthur Asquith (third son of H. H. Asquith, prime minister (1908–16); later the Earl of Oxford and Asquith); and Betty Constance Asquith (daughter of the third Lord Manners); wife of Lawrence; Somerville College, Oxford (B.M., B.Ch., 1948); a physician in active practice in Ampleforth Country.

[Annex to A.J.T.'s letter of March 1969]

Syllabus: Part Two

I should be inclined to cut down on 1–3 and 8 [the Reformation and the 30 Years War], and to enlarge on the rest, especially on persons whose goodness will make an impression across racial and cultural barriers (for me, Charles Borromeo,[1] François de Sales,[2] Philip Neri,[3] St. Vincent de Paul[4] stand out) and on persons who have carried Christianity out into the wide world, beyond the narrow bounds of the Western World, because they felt a concern (in the Quaker sense) for all human beings (Ricci[5] and Nobili[6]: bring out their eagerness to get out of their constricting Western skins).

1–3 and 8 might seem to Africans like irrelevant and unintelligible—and therefore boring—inter-Western domestic family quarrels—only edifying because they bring out the deplorable consequences of failure to live up to charité.

I should enlarge on charité which is something of which every human being has some direct personal experience, whereas truth is disputable, and disputes about it may become uncharitable.

In 9–13, the industrial revolution, science, and social reform will 'ring a bell' in Africa, because, though these are originated in the West, they are making a World-wide impact.

The humanitarian saints should be stressed, especially those who loved and served Africans. Who was the man at Cartagena in Colombia who cared for the newly arrived slaves? (?Peter Claver).[7] Las Casas:[8] rather delicate for an African audience: he was so much concerned for the native American Indians that he condoned the enslavement of the physically tougher Africans.

1. Saint Charles Borromeo; cf. C.C.E.'s letter of 23 December 1962, above.
2. Saint François de Sales; cf. C.C.E.'s letter of 10 September 1940, above.
3. Saint Philip Neri; cf. C.C.E.'s letter of 23 December 1962, above.
4. Saint Vincent de Paul; cf. A.J.T.'s letter of 15 February 1952, above.
5. Matteo Ricci, S.J.; cf. C.C.E.'s letter of 12 January 1950, above.
6. Robert de Nobili, S.J.; cf. A.J.T.'s letter of 22 December 1967, above.
7. Saint Peter Claver (1581–1654); from 1610 to his death ministered to the slaves in Cartegena, Colombia, then the slave mart of the New World; declared himself "the slave of the Negroes forever."
8. Bartolomé de Las Casas (1474–1566); a lawyer with a degree from Salamanca, he accompanied the Spanish governor to Hispaniola in 1502; became a priest (later a Dominican) and an inveterate defender of the cause of the Indians against colonial oppression; *Brevísima Relación de la Destrucción de las Indias* (Seville, 1552).

As from Catholic Mission
P.O. Peramiho, via Songea
Tanzania

10 May 1969

My dear Arnold,

On the very day of the great Birthday dinner party in New York I received (in Kampala) the invitation, which had gone all the way round by sea to Mombasa and then chased me through Kenya and Uganda; and also the request to send you a letter to be included in the volume. The latter I would have liked to have had the honor to share.

Then, the day before, I got a letter from Chris Peper to say he had visited you in London, only to find you struggling to shake off the flu. I hope that the N.Y. venture was in the event not too much for you.

Thank you very much for your helpful suggestion about the MS. in *Prophets*. Letters have not caught up with me, so I know no more.

At Easter time I was busy giving retreats and talks, first in Tororo[1] (U.) then Jinja,[2] then near Kampala; finally at the Pastoral Institute at Ggaba,[3] nearby. At

Ggaba I got to know a Fr. Shorter,[4] old Downside boy, now a White Father, the only missionary I've so far met who is doing serious field anthropology, chiefly at the moment among the Karamajon,[5] a tribe akin to the Masai and far more primitive or untouched by the outside. One soon learns that generalizations about African tribal customs are almost meaningless, from the uses of drums to marriage lore. This makes liturgical adaptation a very delicate affair, and the approach to marriage problems a *terra incognita*, e.g. when do most tribes think a marriage is absolute? When it works? Then are tribal Christian marriages only truly Christian when they work?

I am on my way to Peramiho. The first 80 miles from Kampala to Katigondo[6] I did in a "communal" taxi, 12 persons; the next 100 miles in a V.W. "baby"; we went through a flood and at one point water went right over the top. Bukoba[7] was where I stayed. It looks out E. over L. Victoria. From there I took a 200 mile bus-night ride with an African priest to Mwanza[8] near where Speke first guessed he had found the source of the Nile.[9] Then 100 miles by bus to Shinyanga[10] where Americans (Brs. and priests) run a newly subdivided diocese; so, on by bus (120 miles) to Tabora,[11] of slave memories, and once a German centre. The town is dominated by the cathedral, the T.T.C. put up by German and Dutch Catholic funds, by a new Aga Khan mosque. The Abp.[12] is a wonderful, gentle person. The major Seminary Kipalapala[13] is 6 miles away. I stayed there. Mother Teresa (of Calcutta fame) has a home in Tabora for the 'unwanted,' the blind, orphans, derelict old people. It is the admiration of all. At Bukoba a native Catholic brotherhood, spontaneous and lay, the Banya Karoli,[14] are doing something similar. I visited them. With no money, but trusting Providence, they have collected a no-legged man, a blind boy, two crippled old women, an arthritic old man and care for them, for the love of Christ. All over the Bukoba diocese they are simply helping those not capable of helping themselves.

At Kipalapala I gave the seminarians a talk on monasticism. When I told them what I was to speak about, they laughed as tho' it was quaint and old fashioned; when I explained that it was the great contribution of Africa to the Church, they became interested. At the end two young men (one of them outstanding) came and said "When are we going to start?" They felt that this was needed now for the deepening of Christian life in Africa. One was from Bukoba, grandson of a famous catechist, the other from Kilimanjaro, where the Wachagga[15] live.

The distance from Tabora to Mbeya[16] I had to do by plane and the next journey to Songea too. Mid June I'll be in Dar[17] talking to the Bps. on Nyerere's socialism[18] of which I heartily approve, then to Nairobi and on to Ggaba for the Pan-African Bps.' conference, where I'm going to translate for the French speaking Bps. into English. End Aug. I hope to be home.

Love to you both,
Columba, O.S.B.

1. Near the Kenya border near Mt. Elgon; the center of a small diocese with a native bishop; suffered during the period of Idi Amin's rule.

2. At the north end of Lake Nyanga (Victoria), where the Nile escapes by a great waterfall, now made a hydroelectric dam.

3. Near Kampala where the Pastoral Institute for East Africa had been set up. The mission began in 1900 with Mill Hill Missionary fathers.

4. Aylward Shorter (1932–); then (1968–75) lecturer at AMECEA (Association of the Members of the Episcopal Conferences of East Africa) Pastoral Institute, Ggaba, Uganda; also lectured in anthropology at Makerere University, Kampala; professor of moral theology, Kipalapala Seminary (1978–80); *African Culture and the Christian Church* (London, 1973); *African Christian Theology* (London, 1975).

5. The "left behinds" of the Masai nation in their ancient trek south to where the Masai now live.

6. The famous old Catholic mission center in the Baganda country west of Lake Nyanza with its old seminary and sun-baked brick church.

7. Bukoba has a seminary for philosophy on the cliff overlooking Lake Nyanza to the east; the mission was founded in 1910.

8. At the southern end of Lake Nyana; the mission was founded in 1907.

9. John Hanning Speke (1827–64); African explorer who reached (with Richard Burton) Lake Tanganyika and alone discovered Victoria Nyanza; the first European to see the Nile flowing out of Lake Nyanza.

10. Near the diamond mine.

11. The great meeting place of the slave tracks from the south, west, and north, all of them from there leading on to the coast at Bagamoyo.

12. Mark Mihayo (1907–); archbishop of Tabora.

13. A large senior seminary for most of the Catholic dioceses of Tanzania, near Tabora.

14. Brothers of (Saint) Charles; a spontaneous lay group eager to cooperate in the life of the parishes; 40,000 strong in 1912, but by 1969 it had dwindled.

15. "The most lively tribe of Tanzania, partly because, being on the mountain, they were well nourished. The Germans divided the mountain into sections. The Catholic one when I was there had 300,000 members." (C.C.E.)

16. "The diocese selected as a prefecture in 1938 and a diocese in 1949. The Tanzanian bishop, M. Rev. James Sangu, took me with him to the furthest limit of his diocese." (C.C.E.)

17. Dar es Salaam: The talk was never delivered, crowded out by other business.

18. Julius Kambarage Nyerere (1922–); president of Tanzania (1964–1985); chancellor, University of Dar es Salaam (1970–); *Uhuru na ujamaa* (Freedom and socialism) (Dar es Salaam and London, 1968).

As from 95 Oakwood Court
London W.14

20 May 1969

Dear Columba,

I am addressing this to you at the Catholic Mission P. O. Peramiho, from which you wrote on 10th May, on the chance that this letter will reach you there or will be forwarded if you have already left. What travels you are making, and how tough the travelling is. I do hope you are standing it all right.

Instead of going to New York I had a coronary thrombosis. It was lucky that this did not happen in America. I am making a good recovery, but a slow one—at least, it seems slow to me, for I fell ill on 26th March. My doctor is pleased with my progress, but warns me to go slow, and of course I am obeying doctor's orders. It is very surprising suddenly to be laid by the heels without warning. I might have been struck dead; instead, I am having another lease of life, with an opportunity—not sought, but valuable—for meditation.

With love from us both, and looking forward to seeing you when you are back in England in August.

Yours affectionately,
Arnold

c/o Br. Marcel, P. O. Box 2133, Dar es Salaam (I'll be there 23–29 June);
c/o D. Goodall, P. O. Box 30465 Nairobi, Kenya (after 29th June, off and on)
Whitsunday (25 May) 1969
My dear Arnold,

Your note was a tremendous shock. One always knows that such an attack and the dangers it includes are possible; when they come, then, a sudden illumination of how intimate one's links are. What a tremendous disappointment it must have been to you and all your many friends. And there was I, completely unaware that you had not flown the Atlantic, that the dinner had not taken place, right up to last night. Three of us, a Swiss O.S.B. priest, a German Brother and I had gone off to an outstation in the late afternoon. The Father had a handful of mail for the local group. He handed the letters round after supper. He handed me your dispatch 20th, 4 days before. Thank God you are recovering and Veronica is there.

I can't help being reminded of Pope John. He too took the prospect of death gently and realistically, his bags he said, were packed. He did not trust in his own greatness, as though he had done anything, but in the love God had for him, and yet he had spent himself in the good cause. So I believe with you, my dearest of friends, you have spent yourself searching for Truth with love and humbly.

Now that the attack is under control and you are prepared to "obey doctor's orders" *you should get strong again*; and, as soon as I can, I shall visit you. There is no possibility of my leaving earlier than 25th August, as the last retreat I give ends that A.M. On the other hand Fr. Abbot wants me at Ampleforth that evening (if possible!) so as to be at our Chapter, and I could obviously make a contribution on the Missions. It looks as though I shall have to rush across London on arrival and take the first train to York. But exact times of arrival I have not yet got clear. I'll let you know. This would be very sad, If I could not even spare ½ hour.

My first week here in Peramiho was spent grappling with malaria; not a bad attack, but sufficiently so to make me feel wretched. Now all is well and it is an ideal place to rest, at the moment a lovely climate.

It has to be seen to be believed—immense, almost as big as Ampleforth—"ruling" an area ⅓ as big as England, with huge mission stations, lovely churches, schools, hospitals all over. At the eastern end of the southern frontier, another vast abbey, Ndanda,[1] doing the same. The day you wrote, an African Bishop was installed to replace the Abbot-Bishop; and all the missions were handed over to him; almost all have African secular priests as parish priests, the German monks serving under them; the end of an epoch.

All my prayers are linked with your recovery and God's will for you both. My love as always to you both.

Columba, O.S.B.

1. Compare C.C.E.'s letter of 1 March 1969, above.

95, Oakwood Court
31 May 1969 London W.14

Dear Columba,

Your Whitsunday pastoral to us has just come. I am so glad my aerogram caught you before you were off again. What pleased me most was your enquiry after Veronica herself. She has a double load of anxiety on her shoulders: beside me, her sister, who is no longer fit to live by herself and is in the betwixt and between stage between normality and dotage at which people are most difficult to manage. As you may expect, Veronica is showing marvellous fortitude, serenity too, and, above all, of course, love. I had a night-nurse for six weeks, and this relieved Veronica's anxiety about me during the night and so made her able to sleep. I have diminished her chores a bit now by having all meals in the kitchen, washing and dressing myself unaided, and doing the drying (sitting down) as before, when she washes up. My ambition is to get back to making a breakfast again and bringing her a cup of coffee before she has finished dressing, but this depends on the doctor, who is cautious.

You are right: if it had happened in the U.S. I should not only have lost my lecture-fees (as I have) but should have had a serious 'hospitalisation'. If it had happened in Eastern Turkey last autumn, probably I should not have survived, and it would have been a frightful experience for Veronica.

I am very lucky to be recovering, and to be a writer who, like a snail, can carry his work with him wherever he goes. The suddenness has been disconcerting. Over night I was changed from a bird into a tree; I hope and expect to change back from a tree into a dachshund. The lesson for me has been humility ('I have said, ye are gods, but ye shall die like men and fall like one of the people').[1] I had been guilty of 'the pride of life'—not in the gross sense, but in the assumption that I was invulnerable. It is a fine line between pride and proper self-respect earned by doing one's business well and promptly and efficiently, but there *is* a distinction, as I have now discovered. I have not faced death since my contemporaries were killed in 1915–6, but I have greatly feared incapacitation, and I am fortunate in having been spared a stroke, which is an alternative way in which Nature might have pulled me up short as she was bound to do, sooner or later, in one way or another. It seems unlikely that I shall live much longer, and most likely that Veronica will survive me, and this makes me anxious about her future. Happily, my deferred royalties and other savings since the war ought to be enough to see her through, and, if she wants, she knows she can have a home with either Philip or Lawrence or two American friends (but America is not the place for old age). Meanwhile I have goals that are worth while: to transfer as little as possible of my own human load onto Veronica's and other people's shoulders, and to go on working in ways that won't demand strenuous physical exertion.

Peramiho is most striking: the mission planted in that beautiful country is a new source of spiritual life. Your travels are unceasing. These experiences, and the friends whom you will have made, will be a permanent possession for you and will lead on to other things on which you will be able to take satisfaction.

I hope we shall see each other soon after you are back in England in August. Archbishop Cardinale has been transferred to Belgium: I had a very warm-hearted letter from him.

With much love from us both,
Arnold

1. Ps. 82:6–7; for "people" read "princes."

c/o D. Goodall
P. O. Box 30465
Nairobi, Kenya

11 June 1969

My dear Arnold,

From a circular letter sent from U.S.A. and including your so characteristic letter of apology and ponderings to the disappointed guests, I gather that you are pulling through and regaining strength—thanks be to God. I am trying to arrange that I leave Nairobi P.M. 24 August so that the A.M. of 25th will be free and I can see you and chat at leisure before setting off for York. But what David G. has succeeded in doing I don't yet know.

I remembered after posting my last that you were supposed to be writing me a preface.[1] That is out of the question. You must have no work hanging over your head. Of course if it is already done, well and good; but perhaps Veronica could drop Chris Peper a note, because he would have to tell publishers.

Ndanda, where I am till Monday, is the other O.S.B. missionary centre, inland from Lindi. The situation is different from Peramiho where, all over the countryside, 70%–75% are Catholic. Here in the Ndanda diocese 70% at least are Moslem and all, Moslem, pagan and Catholic and very high Anglican, are matriarchal: i. e., the wife's brother rules the family. How it works I don't know. (The only stage I have not yet seen are the "stone age people", the Karamajon.)[2]

Relations between the U.M.C.A. (Trevor Huddleston[3] was Bishop here) and the Catholics are extremely cordial. The people cannot see why there should be any separation and most of the local clergy. The theologians and Canonists make union difficult.

The people are extremely poor and at the same time happy. There is food and the soil is fertile, but the African is not energetic. The Government is caught in the mesh of international finance and trading. Everything that Tanzania can sell is either more cheaply made artificially (sisal v. artificial fibre) or is on a quota, coffee, so it has little money to encourage agriculture. The monks have agricultural schools and trade schools. The best carpenters in T. come from Peramiho.

I hope Msgr. Cardinale knows of your plight and has come to see you.

Dear Veronica, how are you managing? I pray for you both and hope to see you in 2 months' time.

Love to you both,
Columba, O.S.B.

1. To C.C.E.'s book of prophets.
2. Compare C.C.E.'s letter of 10 May 1969, above.
3. Ernest Urban Trevor Huddleston (1913–); Bishop of Masasi, Tanzania (1960–68); Bishop of Mauritius and Archbishop of the Indian Ocean (1978–83); active in the anti-apartheid movement; *Naught for Your Comfort* (London, 1956). U.M.C.A.: Universities' (Oxford and Cambridge) Mission to Central Africa.

95, Oakwood Court
London W.14

25 June 1969

Dear Columba,

I have had your letter of 11 June. I *do* hope you will be able to leave Nairobi on 24 August and see me here on 25 August before going on to York. We should love to have you here for the night, and this would be a matter of course in normal circumstances, but I can't yet tell in advance whether Veronica will be able to manage—your enquiry about her touched my heart. She has had a double anxiety—over me, and over her sister, who is becoming senile, but we believe we have found a place now for May[1] in a home for old ladies. I shall be in touch with you between now and 24–25 August. We are going to be at Ganthorpe from 2 July to 22 July—then here again.

The preface: the Pepers were here just before I fell ill. At my suggestion, he went to see Hodder and Stoughton about the book, but I have no news of the result, and they went back to America the day after. I have been waiting to write the preface till I heard who was publishing the book. Have you had news from Mr. Peper about this? If you have, let me know, and I will write the preface during the summer.

I am making a very good recovery; my doctor is pleased about it. I am being prudent, and this is difficult, but there is no doubt about its being right. I now get into Holland Park—right up to the crown of the hill. I look forward to going to Chatham House and the B.M. reading room again—but I may be forbidden to travel by bus, and I haven't quite reconciled myself to the prospect of taking taxis like a landlord.

Are you going to write another—quite different—book about your travels? You ought to. You have seen a lot and seen it from the inside at a crucial time of transition.

Love to you from us both,
Arnold

1. May Boulter; cf. A.J.T.'s letter of 26 July 1959, above.

Ganthorpe (now Hall, but my hand wants to write House, on the same principle as being 'Mr.' not 'Sir')
18 July 1969

Dear Columba,

Your letter of 3 July[1] has reached me here. Lawrence and Jean are being very good indeed to us. Veronica is getting a let-up from housekeeping, and one anxiety has been partially lifted. Her sister May has been taken into a Lancashire County Council home for old people near Burrow-on-Furness. The choice was May's, which is important, and, though she lacks privacy after having had a house of her own, she won't any longer have to feed herself—and what was particularly worrying was that she had become incapable of looking after herself in her bungalow. As for me, I have been recuperating splendidly here, and shall now be able to get about again in London—with less bus and more taxi, I expect, but taking taxis makes me feel unordinary and guilty, apart from the cost.

When you arrive on Sunday morning 24 August, come straight to us at 95 Oakwood Court, and then see how you feel. Though you do not cross so many time-zones in the diagonal flight from East Africa as you would, going an equal distance due east and west, the time-displacement is quite enough to tell on even so hardy a traveller as you are; so there will be a bed for you in London if it seems better for you to take a night's rest before going on to Ampleforth. How about your malaria? Do they now have drugs that can checkmate it? It used to have an unpleasant trick of recurring.

The Buddhist supplement (an essential one) to the Christian love is refraining from 'tanhâ' (from 'grasping').[2] Writing that poem[3] helped me to un-clutch my fingers from Ganthorpe, and I now take pure pleasure in Bun and Jean being here and making such good use of it. Two days ago I had a twinge when an historian—not me—was given the O.M.,[4] Veronica Wedgwood.[5] She must be about 20 years younger than me, and, I suppose, is not of my calibre. But 'refraining from grasping' has fortunately unclutched me now from coveting the O.M. which, for some reason, I have been perhaps wanting, to force the English reluctantly to give me the recognition that I have had in other parts of the World. This is trivial, and was therefore humiliating till I got rid of it. I do not cling to life—I have been so much more fortunate than my contemporaries, and very much so in living long enough to do what I wanted to do. I do dread incapacitation before physical death, and, above all, I dread bereavement (i.e. I dread the possibility of outliving Veronica, though I am ashamed of not being able to make myself want to take the pain of bereavement on myself).

Your message for Veronica was the best, for me, of the many good things in your letter. She is made of love and fortitude, and she seeks nothing for herself.

Our African travels almost join on to yours, but not quite. We have not got farther S.E. than the southernmost airport in Southern Sudan, on the Upper White Nile.

Well, we shall be writing to each other again before you come.

With much love,
Arnold

1. Missing.

2. See *An Historian's Approach to Religion*, p. 2, where A.J.T. quotes the Upādāna-Sutta: "With the ceasing of craving, grasping ceases; with ceasing of grasping, coming into existence ceases."

3. "The Broken Trunk"; cf. A.J.T.'s letter of 17 July 1947, above.

4. The Order of Merit; A.J.T. had been awarded the C.H. (Member of the Order of Companions of Honour) in 1956; Lawrence recalls that, after World War II, A.J.T. had been offered the K.C.M.G. (Knight Commander of the Order of St. Michael and St. George) for his services but had declined because the honor was not for work in his own field.

5. Dame Cicely Veronica Wedgwood (1910–); *The King's Peace* (London, 1955); *The King's War* (London, 1958); "I think she is admirable and most enjoyable to read" (*Comparing Notes*, p. 77).

Ampleforth Abbey
25 August 1969 York

My dear Arnold,

It was a relief and joy to see you looked much more fit than I had expected, though as you said, mortality and final sickness is our common fate. That shan't prevent me from praying and hoping that the end will be merciful for all of us.

Those letters, which I hurried through, were a marvellous and real testimony to your friendship and wisdom, far deeper and more worth-while than any O.M., tho' of course this should have been yours years ago. But the real reward is the good you have done through your writings and through *being* who you are; replacing the spiritual values at the top of the list: love and compassion.

I caught the train all right; it meandered north, stopping at all kinds of places that ordinarily one goes through so quickly, I was surprised to find they were on the line at all—Newark. Today we had our Chapter and I was bombarded with questions on Africa; but so far with little immediate desire to go. Perhaps that is too strong. Desire, yes, but obstacles even greater. It now remains to be seen whether the African Bps. think a one year offer is worth while; I'm not sure I would.

Please thank Veronica for giving me so nice a meal, and for taking all that extra trouble.

Love to you both,
Columba, O.S.B.

Theobalds
Blackheath
Guildford[1]

9 January 1970

Dear Arnold and Veronica,

I had better write now, as I may find myself in the grip of continuous complicated organizational work on arrival.

It was a great relief to see you both more rested. Keep away from America. But we all have to grow old and die. It is only a beginning; but the beginning of what? If we believe in a merciful God, or benevolent Will, it must be bliss *if we trust*.

I like the way you keep going, undaunted, and look forward to your latest Byzantine volume. One can't keep up! There seem to be two, between it and *Experiences* which I've never heard of before.

The book of yours I carried away so brutally I find has a chapter by you as well. It is, I think, an extract from a volume I've already seen, but no harm to reading it again. We must start with tolerance, then understanding, mutual respect, mutual recognition, but still maintenance of Truth, finally perhaps drawing towards a unity. It will need lots of hard work.

You will be happy to hear *Il Portico*[2] was an unqualified success. My sister seemed to know exactly what to choose from the menu and the Chianti did the rest.

God bless you both,

Love to you both and many thanks for those rich few hours,

Columba, O.S.B.

1. The home of C.C.E.'s brother, Colonel Oswald Cary-Elwes.

2. "A little restaurant in Kensington High Street frequented by A.J.T. and Veronica and suggested to my sister, Mrs. Bertie." (C.C.E.)

95, Oakwood Court
London W.14

Sunday 8 March 1970

Dear Columba,

We were very glad to have your letter of 20 February.[1] You certainly have your hands full, as happened on your last journey, but anyway this time you are not so furiously on the move. The spiritual directorship alone sounds like at least one job and a half—and, the more you succeed in it, the more it will grow. But I should think that this would be the most necessary work of all. They must be bewildered by the double change of social and mental environment. I am not surprised that liturgy goes over—it can jump over barriers of race and language, and is something present and actual. The historical part must be the most difficult to put across: Hellenists v. Hebraists, Qumran, etc. It must be difficult to bring to life a world of ideas that is so remote from Black Africa's own past.

The Essenes:[2] perhaps the Christians ignored them because they felt that there might not be room in Judaism for both these 'deviationist' movements. The Gospels would not have mentioned 'Simon the Zealot' if they had been afraid of getting into trouble through being associated with the Jewish equivalent of present-day Palestinian Arab Al-Fatah.

There was a letter by Bishop Butler in the *Times* the other day, sketching the outline for a possible conversion of the Anglican Church into a Uniate Church.[3] I hope it comes off. The Anglican liturgy is in the melting pot. Today we have been to the christening of Veronica's great nephew Jonathan (son of her nephew Hugh Boulter)[4] and there was not a recognizable sentence from the 'order of common prayer' in the entire service. We are fond of Hugh and his wife; straight-forward, well-behaved, responsible people in that generation give one comfort. He is no. 2 in the local education offices at Slough—now a pretty big industrial town, full of Welsh, Sikhs, Pakistanis and West Indians, and therefore full of educational problems.

If you were to tune in to the BBC, this evening you would hear a talk,[5] which I recorded some days ago, on 'Has Religion a Future?' My answer is that being human involves having religion of some kind, and that the pertinent question is 'What kind?' As usual I brand the worship of human power as the most prevalent religion today and as a very bad one. Other speakers in the series are Charles Davis[6] and Marshal McCluhan [*sic*].[7]

We are both all right (I, thanks of course to Veronica). I am physically feeble—can't walk nearly as fast or as far as before March 1969—but my mind is still alert and I put in a full days intellectual work, sitting at my desk at this window looking out to Holland Park. My biggish book on 'Constantine Porphyogenitus and his World' is making headway. I have had it in mind since about 1910. I hope to finish it, but I should not repine if death overtook me first—unfinished business is incidental to mortality. I seem to be all right again, but no doubt my heart might give out, without warning, any time. I don't flinch from sudden death, but do wish one could die without causing distress to the people whom one loves—and whom one does not want to leave, even if one has had enough of wars, income tax returns, strikes, demonstrations and inflation.

With love from us both.
Arnold

1. Missing.
2. A Jewish ascetic sect that arose in the second century, B.C., and disappeared in the second

century, A.D.; it is referred to, not in the Bible, but in Philo, the elder Pliny, and chiefly in Josephus.

3. Basil Christopher Butler, then auxiliary bishop of Westminster; as a *ballon d'essai*, had suggested full ecclesial communion under the primacy of the successor of Peter: the pope, the patriarch of the traditional Western rite; Canterbury, patriarch of the English; cf. *The Times* (5 March 1970), reporting an article in the *Tablet*; cf. C.C.E.'s letter of 14 June 1963, above.

4. Hugh Boulter; cf. A.J.T.'s letter of 5 September 1968, above; Jonathan was born in November 1969.

5. In *Listener* 83, no. 2140 (2 April 1970): 439–40.

6. Charles Davis (1923–); theologian; *Liturgy and Doctrine* (London, 1960).

7. Herbert Marshall McLuhan (1911–80); Canadian media analyst; director of center for culture and technology at University of Toronto (1963–80); *Understanding Media: The Extensions of Man* (London, 1964).

St. Thomas' Seminary
P.O. Box 30517, Nairobi

21 May 1970

My Dear Arnold,

I gave my last two classes this morning: Sacraments was one, Liturgy the other. Exams follow and then, June, the seminarians go off to their various missions from Mombasa in the east to Eldoret in the west, Meru in the North. I shall remain in Nairobi most of the time; but two of us intend to visit the missions round Eldoret for a week. I think the term (4 months) has been a real success; the place is surely afloat, and only a handful of students have left or been sent away. We still have 123, the number we started with, as a few have been added.[1]

In history I've done the Dead Sea Scrolls; Jewish v. Gentile churches, Gnosticism and Irenaeus' reply. The Martyrs: Peter and St. Paul, Polycarp, the M M of Scillium, SS. Perpetua and Felicity. And we are poised to start the Church and Greek thought: Origen onwards and monasticism. I expect we shall reach Cluny or O.S.B. It is amazing how much of early Ch. history is *African*.

Someone gave me your BBC talk on the future of Religion.[2] They might have kept Paisley off the page! I was very glad to see you condemn our worship of human power, of nationalism. Poor Kenyans accepting these things as part of the treasure of the West, and half-heartedly taking Christ's message as being part of the Colonial legacy.

No, I don't, of course, quite agree that it is the impersonal God (god) who will triumph, partly because it is less true, partly on your own earlier writings that *Love* is what men need. Not much of eastern religion really is directed to an impersonal god, is it? One half of Buddhism has swung over to the personal, and ninety per cent of Hinduism is to many a personal God(s). On the other hand, in a way, the Christians do recognize the truth underlying what you say: namely that *person* in a human sense is a limitation, and we only use it with the proviso that we should eliminate the limiting element. God is beyond the beyond.

The Church—as you rightly see—is going through growing—or awakening—

pains. It is fascinating and one cannot foresee the outcome, except that the Spirit of God is astir.

My love to you both. Please give me detailed news of you both.

Columba, O.S.B.

1. "For a year—an extra year—I helped to salvage the one major seminary (theology and philosophy) in Kenya, just outside Nairobi, at the pleading of Archbishop Otunga and Bishop de Reper, as the whole philosophic and theological staff had withdrawn back to the United States over a misunderstanding with the bishops. Three of us had to carry much of the load for two terms." (C.C.E.)

2. Compare A.J.T.'s letter of 8 March 1970, above.

The Royal Institute
of International Affairs
Chatham House
10, St James's Square
London, S.W. 1

30 May 1970

Dear Columba,

We came back from Ganthorpe yesterday, and I was overjoyed to find your letter of 21 May. I had been becoming anxious about you—expecting that you were just being overworked, and feeling, at the back of my mind, that you might have cracked up. Last Sunday we went over to Ampleforth, so I started hunting for news of you, and finally made contact with Father Hubert,[1] who gave me some. But your own letter is none the less welcome.

Do be a bit careful of yourself. Even you are now not still quite young, and, until the body rebels, we have a hubris in taking such liberties with it (I speak from experience). After a gruelling tour, strenuous hard travelling—and at a considerable altitude—might be just too much.

This was my first sight of the church since it was completed. It is all good, but the interior is the best: very noble simple austere lines.[2]

A cricket-match at Ampleforth makes one feel for a moment as if we were back in pre–1914. But no doubt both the community and the boys have changed; and it would be disturbing if they hadn't; I mean, changed at the level at which one has to change in tune with the world; I am not talking about the deeper levels that are timeless.

Yes, the early Church is very African, and I hope the Negro Africans haven't become so racial-minded that they feel 'Caucasian' Africans—Clement of Alexandria, Origen, Saint Augustine—to be 'whitey' aliens.

Though I deprecate more distant travels to even higher altitudes, I wish you could get a glimpse of Ethiopian Christianity—the wholehearted austerity of the monks at Debra Libános, and the church walls covered with pictures which educate the illiterate.[3] Perhaps you will get there. There is an important Catholic community in Eritrea, and they might put you in touch with their pre-Chalcedonian neighbors.

Veronica and I are all right, but age does tell. However, we are both still keeping going.

With love,
Arnold

1. Eric Hubert Stephenson, O.S.B. (1911–71); parish priest at Ampleforth (1949–69).

2. Ampleforth Abbey church, completed in 1961; Perigordian, with shallow domes and early pointed arches; the architect was Sir Giles Gilbert Scott (1880–1960), whose masterwork was the Liverpool Cathedral (Anglican); he was the grandson of the designer of the Albert Memorial, Sir George Gilbert Scott.

3. Compare A.J.T.'s *Between Niger and Nile* (Oxford, 1965), pp. 56–57.

P.O. Box 30517
Nairobi, Kenya

29 July 1970

My Dear Arnold,

My plans for returning to U.S.A. via London have now taken a fixed shape up to a point.

I shall spend one night in London for certain: October 22–23.

The Goodalls[1] who have been so kind to me out here (He is an old Amplefordian, in my old House, and in the Br. High Commission here, now back at the F.O.) are putting me up. But we arranged that they would invite you both to dinner that evening. They live a few hundred yards from you. Please manage to come.

34 Addisland Court, Addison Rd. W.14. If you can hold that date it should be a wonderful evening. You will like them both very much.

The plan as it stands is for me to go to Malta, where my sisters are, via Rome, then from Malta to London.

Fr. Aelred Graham has had a seizure—not very bad, so I hear now—in U.S.A. somewhere. If I can locate him, I shall then fly there, and so on to St. Louis via Washington, arriving at S.L. as little later than 26th as I can manage.

Reading up about the States, it really does seem to have taken a dive for the worse. But America always has to go right to the bottom before it can pick itself up. So I'm still hopeful.

Out here everyone is storming about the S. Africa arms sale—even though it hasn't happened. It shouldn't happen. What a lot of good will has been sunk by this gesture. I can see why, but it was not worth it. On the other hand, money is at the root of most moves, and I don't expect Kenya will cut the links.

How are you both? Not doing too much I hope. Your advice to me is being carefully followed. I am coasting home—

Love to you both,
Columba, O.S.B.

1. Arthur David Saunders Goodall (1931–); a member of St. Wilfrid's House at Ampleforth College; Trinity College, Oxford; head of Chancery, Nairobi (1968–70); Minister, Bonn (1979–82); deputy secretary of the Cabinet (1982–84); since 1984, deputy under-secretary of state, Foreign and Commonwealth Office.

As from 95, Oakwood Court
London W.14

4 August 1970

Dear Columba,

I have had your letter of 29 July, and we have noted 22 October, 34 Addisland Court. The widow of a schoolfellow of mine lives there, so we know our way. We do look forward to having this glimpse of you. You will be glad to see your sisters. I hope Malta is being a success for them.

I am very sorry about Father Aelred, and this makes me glad that you were not posted for life (which might have meant 'for death') at St. Louis. St. Benedict's Rule is a stronger Maginot Line against the American way of life than the non-religious (I mean 'religious' in the technical sense) have, but even this is liable to be overrun by air-travel and conferences and parties.

You are, I am sure, right about arms sales to S. Africa. Money is at the root of it. A few people in England make the money, and Black Africa, as well as Arab Africa, is pushed into the Russians' arms. Just what the Russians must have hoped for, and what capitalists would do according to Marxist theory. I am afraid Douglas-Home[1] is a bit of an ass. For the U.K. in 1970 to launch out on naval competition with Russia in the Indian Ocean: he is living in *1870*.

Veronica and I are all right, but are hard pressed. She has had no help in the house since the winter, and my unfortunate secretary has collapsed and I have had to change her. She keeps house for three modern daughters, besides trying to do a part-time professional job, and, as I know from Lawrence's daughters, 1 daughter means at least three young men, too, about the house.

I am also in anxiety about the effect of Rosalind's will, and gifts (e. g. Ganthorpe) before her death, as between Philip and Lawrence. She was extremely partial to Lawrence. Both L. and P. are behaving well over this, but it has, I am afraid, inflicted a permanent psychological wound on Philip. With Bun's full agreement, Veronica and I are trying to right the balance in our wills as far as possible, but I am grieved at this posthumous effect of R.'s acts. It is very sad to be remembered for injustice. I begged her to divide equally, as I wanted to do, but I could not persuade her.[2] Well, we are going to Hall Beck on Thursday for a bit of a let-up for us both, though less for V. than for me.

With love,
Arnold

1. Alexander Frederick Douglas-Home (Home of the Hirsel) (1903–); fourteenth earl of Home; foreign secretary (1955–60); gave up the title to become prime minister (1963–65);

secretary of state for foreign and Commonwealth affairs (1970–74); created life peer as Baron Home of Coldstream; *The Way the Wind Blows* (London, 1976).

2. Rosalind devised the Gelt Bridge farm to Philip, the Moorthwaite, Low Holm, and Hornsby Cumwhitton farms in Cumberland to Richard Stafford, and the residue of her estate, including several farms, to Lawrence, expecting no doubt that A.J.T. would provide for Philip; in the event, A.J.T., after a life estate to Veronica, left three-fourths of his estate to Philip and one-fourth to Lawrence. Rosalind had given Ganthorpe to Lawrence several years before her death.

P.O. Box 30517
Nairobi

26 September 1970

My Dear Arnold,

It is ages since I wrote and I have your letter on my desk. Now the work is coming to an end. I've warned the students of the likely "theses" or questions in their exams. Oct. 17 I leave—go to Rome and so to my sisters in Malta, then London, where I shall be seeing you both, God willing and hi-jackers.

Your letter was from up in the Pennines. I do hope your holiday proved a real refreshment. Also, it was a shame that you've had to change secretaries.[1] I hope your new one can pick up the threads.

Since I last wrote I made a rush (over a long week-end) to Mombasa[2] via the Taita Hills, where a remarkable tribe lives, rather like the Wachagga on Kilimanjaro, not far off: most industrious and intelligent.

At Mombasa I visited the frightful Portuguese Fort Jesus;[3] and I bought some post cards to send you—but left them somewhere! It, the fort, is a huge construction, facing inland and looking out to sea. The island of Mombasa is on three sides protected (or threatened) by the main-land. The distance across is only a few hundred yards. Portugal is still very much present—down the coast—and in men's minds. Our world is explosive. Only charity will bring peace.

Love to you both,
Columba, O.S.B.

1. At this time Louise Orr (1913–) became A.J.T.'s confidential secretary and remained with him until his death.

2. Mombasa, an ancient Perso-Arabic settlement of the twelfth century; under Portuguese control as a trading depot from time to time until the early nineteenth century.

3. Fort Jesus; made of coral from the reef; at one time a slave depot.

23 October 1970 95, Oakwood Court, W.14

Dear Columba,

Well, it was a short glimpse of you—long looked forward to—but I hope we shall see a bit more of each other from Easter onwards. The Goodalls were extremely kind and hospitable, and it was a very happy evening.

I shall be thinking of you even more than usual while you are at St. Louis. I am glad you are breaking the journey at Washington, for the first moment of return may be queer—as it was for me when I first went back to Ganthorpe, but now I have got over that, and I feel nothing but pleasure in seeing the house so well used and so much enjoyed by Lawrence and Jean and the children.

This letter is about nothing in particular—just a wish to communicate again while you are still here.

With much affection,
Arnold

30 October 1970 95, Oakwood Court

Dear Columba,

We have been thinking of you, arriving at the Priory, with 7 November approaching. You will enjoy seeing again your many friends, not only your brethren in the Priory, but in the city too. How are the Pepers standing their terrible ordeal?[1] Gradual foreseen death is more of a strain but less of a shock. I have just lost a much loved American contemporary of mine, Quincy Wright[2] (Professor of International Law of Chicago for many years). In September he and his wife were here, and he seemed as well as ever. On 17 October he died—arteries and heart. He had only a fortnight's illness; it is his poor wife who is the sufferer.

Though I can't bear the thought of parting from Veronica, I also cannot rise to the unselfishness of wishing to outlive her, so that I, and not she, may take the pain of bereavement. I can will it with my mind, but not with my feelings.

I had a spate of continuing deaths of contemporaries in 1915–6, and now the not untimely deaths are nevertheless painful.

He hath ta'en Rowl of Aberdeen
And gentle Rowl of Corstorphine.[3]

My refrain, though, is not William Dunbar's

Timor mortis conturbat me.

It is

Timor orbi fiendi conturbat me.

The next letter that I shall be writing is to the son of a (dead) school fellow of mine. The son is now in his early thirties, progressively incapacitated by a mysterious paralysis that they can't diagnose. He is serene and cheerful and this is really sublime courage.

Veronica and I are all right, but I wish we could find some help for her in cleaning this large flat. We need it to house my books and papers, but she pays the price: and my amateur attempts do not do much to lighten her work.

My greetings to all my friends at St. Louis and love to you from both of us.

What would you do if you had a grand daughter[4] living with a man (a very likeable, suitable man) without any intention of being married? There is no legal obstacle. He is a widower. I treat them with the affection that I feel, and I show my disagreement with them in a way that does not put them off. Am I condoning what I feel to be wrong? If I made a Victorian gesture and broke off relations with them, the effect would, no doubt, be 'counter-productive', and a piece of affection and love would be killed. I should be making a 'demonstration' in the present-day sense, which I deprecate more and more. My priority is: do not cut off a section of love; this would be the greater evil. But I am unhappy about this.

Arnold

1. Ethel Peper was suffering from cancer, later, *Deo gratias*, cured.
2. Quincy Wright; cf. A.J.T.'s letter of 28 April 1949, above.
3. "Lament for the Makaris," in *The Oxford Book of Scottish Verse* (Oxford, 1966), pp. 103–7.
4. Celia (Toynbee) Caulton (1948–); daughter of Lawrence; she married the man in question, Jeremy Caulton, director of opera planning of the English National Opera Company; cf. A.J.T.'s letter of 9 July 1948, above.

All Saints (1 November) 1970 Washington

My Dear Arnold,

I got your note before I set off. It was so nice of you. I told the Goodalls how much you enjoyed the little dinner party. I too would have liked a quiet hour or two or three with you on our own. But we must arrange that on my return from the States, God willing.

I arrived here 7.30 last night, c. 2 A.M. by U.K. reckoning. So we did not stay up late. I am staying one night with Donald Cape (Counsellor) and an Ampleforth Old Boy[1] and one night at St. Anselm's Abbey,[2] then I'll be in a fit state to face the St. Louis reception. It will be strange returning to a life now past; but I hope I can help people to have more self confidence *under God*. One of America's idolatries has been self confidence *tout court*. Now the hollowness of that is so apparent, they've gone to the other extreme: no confidence at all.

My love to you both,
Columba, O.S.B.

1. Sir Donald Cape (1923–); K.C.M.G.; Brasenose, Oxford; counsellor at Washington, D.C. (1970–73); ambassador and U.K. permanent representative to the Council of Europe, Strasbourg (1978–83).
2. St. Anselm's Abbey; cf. A.J.T.'s letter of 24 September 1942, above.

St. Louis Priory
5 December 1970 St. Louis, Missouri

My Dear Arnold,

I should have answered your letter weeks ago. I've been selfish—so many people, so much visiting, being visited. It is dying down.

I am sure you are doing right about your grand daughter. She knows how you feel, and the fact that you stretch out a loving hand in spite of it all will touch her heart, in the long run, far more than a gesture of disapproval. I think it different with parents of young children; the apparent disregard of poor behaviour could lead the young to think little of it too. But you are free of that problem. I am sorry for your grand child; it sounds as though she is building up sadness for herself and others in this life.

The Pepers were so very, very happy to have your message and to know how much you were linked to them in their distress. Ethel is very brave, but this axe over her head is psychologically shattering at times. I've been over several times, and see them at Mass here, so try to give courage and consolation. No matter how much one may believe in the future life, the sheer physical event is something stupendous with all the human ties that are broken at its coming.

Dear Veronica, woman that she is, she is more able to survive you than you her—I'm sure she will be happy to carry that burden for love of you, should God so decide.

But we must not take the bridge before we get there, and put all these mysteries into the hands of God, however we describe him. He certainly can't be less than human and so concerned, even if we cannot fathom how. *Deus absconditus*. How can we expect to fathom infinity? This is part of our novitiate in "littleness."

This may prove the last letter you may get from me before Christmas, as everyone is talking of a post-office strike.

Chris is going to write you of a plan of his, that he and I might combine to write something on you. I told him that I would love to help, but left it to him to write officially. I can see many problems and in my case many others more competent, though none more loving, Veronica excepted, of course.

Love to you both, and real happiness at this time of Christmas.

Columba, O.S.B.

95, Oakwood Court
London W.14

11 December 1970

Dear Columba,

We were very glad to get your Christmas letter of 5 December. I am answering quickly, in the hope of getting ahead of the threatened post-office strike that you mention. At the moment our electricity is on, but it may go off at any moment.

I think much of the Pepers, and of three other American friends of mine, two of whom have lost a husband, and one a wife. I am still bound to life by love of Veronica and you and my friends, and the happiness and courage that their goodness gives me. I have a young cousin and godson, Roger Frankland,[1] who cannot pass examinations but is a well-spring of love for his fellow creatures: he wants to be a probation officer—work in which someone who cares for other people can help them most effectively. I think of him when I am despondent about my grand daughter, Clare,[2] who is a year or two older. I feel sad about her. I do not know whether nowadays 'stripping' would debar one from afterwards getting a respectable job, or would deter a man from wanting to marry a girl. But the serious damage is inward. To sell one's ability to titillate male lust must injure one's soul. But it is complicated. She has done it to pay off an overdraft. Her mother sent her a cheque for covering this, and Clare returned the cheque. This was good. She wanted to stand on her own feet and not to scrounge on her parents, but then she made her money in this way.

Making money at any price seems now to be almost universal. Money has become the test and symbol of success, so even the highest paid people have now begun to press for rises, though these are entirely cancelled by surtax, and, at all levels, they are cancelled by inflation. 'Private enterprise', of which 'the Free World' is so proud, has come to mean extorting the utmost for oneself, in terms of money, at whatever price to one's neighbours and to the community. This is such a bad ideal that our society seems to me to be condemning itself to catastrophe unless it has a change of heart. I always come back to St. Francis and his reaction to his father, who was, I suppose, a precursor of John D. Rockefeller, Sr. The luckless Pietro Bernardone has had the same role as Pilate. He has become a symbolic figure. Yet most of the people who condemn Pilate and Pietro behave as they did.

I still feel as much concern about the future and as much curiosity about human affairs, past and present. I have zest for life, and that, as well as love, binds me to the World. Yet I hope not to be condemned to live to Bertie Russell's[3] age.

My love to you and to my friends at the Priory and to the Pepers.

With much affection,
Arnold

1. Roger Frankland (1951–); son of Noble Frankland; he has accomplished his wish and become a probation officer; cf. A.J.T.'s letter of 24 December 1946, above.

2. Clare (Toynbee) Huxley (1949–); the daughter of Lawrence; the stripping episode made the press; a graduate of Somerville College, Oxford; she married Andrew Huxley, a barrister, formerly fellow of Trinity College, Oxford; later tutor at the University of the West Indies; now at School of Oriental Studies, University of London.

3. Bertrand Russell (1872–1970); cf. C.C.E.'s letter of 20 December 1961, above.

19 December 1970 Saint Louis Priory

My dear Arnold,

Your grand daughter Clare has done a sad thing; but I expect she did not realize the implications, not half of them, Money, money, money, this is the idol. In her case, it was a necessity, and you have put your finger on our world's weakness: it has become the supreme necessity. St. Francis still beckons us in all his ways: poverty, love of the poor, of peace, of unity, supreme love of God from which it all sprang in him. Clare must be dear to St. Clare.

I've been reading your book on Death.[1] Yes, I was overjoyed not long ago when a doctor told me I might have cancer. It proved untrue. There was a sense of fear, but an over riding sense of coming fulfilment. How I would take death with pain I don't know; I shrink from it; also how do I know that in the breakdown of one's physical strength, I will be strong in heart to trust in the mercy of God. I don't believe my own activities or "goodness" (for what it is worth) will be my salvation, but truly God's mercy in spite of my failures.

Yes, it is true that I look forward to meeting all those I love: parents, friends, the saints, the many Francises, Benedict. . . . I look forward to being enlightened in the Vision of God. All this talk about separate existence is probably inadequate because we will be swept up into union with that which is, the Beyond all Being.

All this talk about bodily resurrection is of course based on the fact—take the word as you will—of Christ's Resurrection. It is a central element in the Christian story; but its form is mysterious even in the N.T. telling of it.

By the way, Mark 10, could Christ have been egging the rich young man on: Why do you call me good, only God is good. He never said he was God, but he was always edging people towards it.

Fr. Mark[2] told me how he and you sat on the terrace at Ampleforth for ½ hour, not speaking. And at the end you said: "Death is a mystery," and he, from bashfulness, said never a word!

I repeat with Thomas More, "I pray we shall meet merrily in Heaven," changed yes, annihilated, no. But I hope to meet you long before that.

My love to you both,
Columba, O.S.B.

1. A.J.T. et al., *Man's Concern with Death* (London, 1968).
2. Mark Haidy, O.S.B. (1907–77); a member of the community of the St. Louis Priory from 1970 until his death.

December 16, 1970 St. Louis

Dear Arnold,

Father Columba and I have been toying with the idea of collaborating in an attempt to write your biography. We fear that you may consider this not only temerarious but also superfluous in view of the myriad of autobiographical passages embedded in text, footnotes and appendices from Volume I of *A Study of History* through *Hannibal's Legacy*, and your later works. "*Si monumentum requiris* . . ." However, we think these in themselves are tantalizing glimpses and building blocks of a consecutive biography which surely will someday appear.

We are not sure that this serious work is within our capabilities; indeed, we suspect our reach may exceed our grasp, and we are prepared to recognize this and confine our attempt to a more specialized treatment of a more limited segment. We also realize that this field may long since have been pre-empted by others, or that you may have other plans. Accordingly, we welcome any suggestions you may make and should be prepared to enter any smaller province you might outline for us.

In our more ambitious moments we contemplate a full-length book: commencing with ancestry and youth; continuing through Oxford; your walking tours; the chair of Greek History at London; your World War I years; your career as Director of the Royal Institute; the origins of the *Study of History*; the *Study of History* I–VI; its publication; a brief and objective study of its influences and critical reactions; the World War II years; Part VII to X of the *Study of History* with a similar brief synopsis of its influence and critical reactions; the world-wide lectures and University visits; trips and later books; *Hannibal's Legacy*; later activities; family and friends; a chronology and a bibliography.

This task may not require the talents of a professional historian or biographer, but I think those undertaking it should have, at the very least, some familiarity with the ancient world and with the higher religions both of the East and West, and, above all, a deep concern with your life and work. Father Columba and I have not been captains of the Hampshire grenadiers, but the experience of a monk and a lawyer may not be useless to the task of the biographer.

The sources which immediately suggest themselves would be: your books, articles and prefaces, including the official publications of the Royal Institute; such letters as are available; manuscripts such as the MSS. of the *Study of History* in Mr. Houghton's possession; available records of Chatham House; Universities; fellow historians; and other materials you might be willing to make available. We suspect there may be a vast corpus of your writings not formally attributed to you.

Ethel and I are hoping to come to Rome, Sicily and then London in January; and perhaps, if you have not rejected our project out of hand before we come to London, it would be possible then to discuss it with you. Father Columba has approved this tentative.

Two basic questions remain to be resolved. Are we able to accomplish something of this sort? Would you like us to undertake it?

Yours very sincerely,
Christian

95, Oakwood Court
London W.14

24 December 1970

Dear Christian,

I am very much touched by your letter of 16 December, 1970. Your and Columba's wish to write my biography is a mark of affection and regard that is very precious.

As it happens, I have been thinking a lot, during the past few years, about a biography: not my own, but Gilbert Murray's. I am his surviving literary executor, and I was his son-in-law till my first marriage broke up.

G.M.'s biography is now—thirteen years after his death—in the first stage of being written by Francis West, who has already published an admirable life of G.M.'s elder brother Hubert.

A biography will not do justice if it is not frank, and it has to be frank about the subject's personal life as well as his professional work. These two sides of life are inseparable. A biography ought to be based, not just on documents, but also on living people's first-hand acquaintance with the subject. This raises the question of timing. If the biography is written too soon, the writer will be inhibited by having to consider, too much, the feelings of people, still alive, whose lives were bound up with the subject's. If too late, everyone who knew the subject intimately will be dead. Finding the right moment is particularly difficult in the case of a subject who died at an unusually high age, but, on the whole, I think Professor West and I have found, in G.M.'s case, about the right moment for doing the job.

You point out in your letter that there is a lot of autobiographical stuff scattered through my published work, but you will notice that this is limited to my intellectual history and to my views about public affairs (including religion as well as politics). I have deliberately not published anything about my personal inner life or about my relations with my children and my first and second wife. A biography would be incomplete if it kept silence about the subject's inner life and his most intimate personal relations. For the reasons that I have given, I do not think that a frank and comprehensive biography can be written till about ten or fifteen years after the subject's death (his age at death will affect the timing).

There is quite a large amount of material on paper which Veronica is gradually sorting out. At 81, I have already lost a number of my intimate friends (I lost about half of them as far back as 1915–16). How many of them will survive me cannot be guessed. But, if a biography of me is written, I am sure this ought to be posthumous.

Well, this is about all that I can say now. I want Veronica to have the last word if she is still alive when the time comes. My other literary executors and my sons would also have a say. Whatever is eventually decided, I shall have the warmest feelings about your and Columba's present suggestions, though I feel sure, as you see, that to try to do the job would be premature until I have been dead for some years.

We do look forward to seeing you and Ethel here in January.

Yours very sincerely,
Arnold Toynbee

Ampleforth Abbey
York

6 April 1971

My dear Arnold and Veronica,

First, I must say once again how much I enjoyed our last meeting, at the flat and at Il Portico.[1] That was a real success in spite of the guitarist, who I think began to realize we were not too keen on his noises.

It is so good to know that you are busy producing books. This latest: *The 70 Questions*,[2] I am longing to see. Did I tell you, I've abandoned hope on my *Prophetic Vision*. Chris Peper sent it round to any number of publishers—lots of nice letters, but no acceptance. Lots of good books on the subject are coming out, so no matter.

Meanwhile I'm at work collecting material for 8 talks to Anglican Seminarians on the Spirituality of Christians in various ages: N.T., 1–3 centuries; Monastic; Patristic; Medieval, Reformation period: Spanish, French—as a help to one's own spiritual life—life in the Spirit.

Lincoln Theological College[3] also wants me to talk about the theology of liturgy. I find that a funny way of expressing it. Presumably they mean: what is liturgy about and why.

On Spirituality I toy with an alternative scheme, of simply following individual themes thro' history: devotion to the Holy Trinity, Christ, Eucharist—good works, prayer, asceticism. It is bad to wobble, one doesn't get down to it!

A very happy birthday and the grace to accept these trials of old age with peace, not least the anxiety over death itself and the troubles for others it might entail. If you go first, Veronica will not feel entirely bereft because she will be still concerned, lovingly, with your thought, and that is you. So will I. But who knows who goes first?

Easter is the sign of resurrection, not I'm sure in a simple return to what we were, but an establishing of the whole of us in the oneness and multiplicity of God and his creation.

My love to you both and many prayers.

Columba, O.S.B.

1. Compare C.C.E.'s letter of 9 January 1970, above.

2. *Surviving the Future* (New York, 1971), a dialogue between A.J.T. and Professor Kei Wakaizumi of Kyoto Sangyo University.

3. An Anglican Theological College in Lincoln, England, that over a number of years had a Roman Catholic presence for a term.

95, Oakwood Court
London W.14

10 April 1971

Dear Columba,

We were so glad to have your letter of 6 April. Our evening together was very good.

I had feared that *Prophetic Vision* might not win a publisher. If anyone could have found one, it would have been Chris Peper. I feel bad because, after a long wait, I have just had my 'Constantine Porph.' O.K.'d by the O.U.P. But we are both of us getting plenty of requests to do new things, and these are good tonics.

For your talks (and, I hope, an eventual book) on the spirituality of Christians in different ages, I think your alternative scheme of following individual themes might land you in difficulties, because, in the lives and feelings and thoughts of the outstanding spiritual Christians, these individual themes have, if I am right, been indissolubly inter-connected with each other.

'The theology of liturgy'. I should have thought that liturgy was the emotional, physical, and visual expression of theology, but I cannot think of liturgy as having a theology of its own.

I don't feel anxiety about death, with the big exception that you mention—posthumous anxiety for Veronica and for my grandchildren, who stand for all the future generations. As long as Veronica is there and also as long as I have jobs that I want to do, I am glad to stay alive, but, if death were to catch me with jobs unfinished, I should not repine, because I have been immensely fortunate in living to finish a lot.

With much love from us both,
Arnold

Ampleforth Abbey
York

Saturday, 26 June 1971
(Written from Lincoln)

My dear Arnold,

I've been meaning to write to you for so long, and keep on putting it off—laziness!

Monday I shall set off again for Ampleforth. I feel as though I have been constantly travelling—*instabilitas*!—for the last three years, and want, as a migrant bird must feel after a 1000 miles, to be at rest—*quies*.

This College[1] is very worth while, not partisan i.e. evangelical or anglo-catholic, but representing pretty nearly the broad gamut of Anglican opinion, in tolerance. The Warden is a charming person and genuine to a degree. You may know him, Alec Graham,[2] one time chaplain at Worcester, Oxford, N.T. scholar. On the staff there is also a Methodist O.T. scholar, David Deeks,[3] a young man, and one imagines, spiritually, very much in the tradition of John Wesley. I like him.

Of course most of the students are married.

The cathedral that overshadows us is still in the world of Trollope, but the Chancellor is first class—Victor de Waal, Dutch-Austrian in origin.[4]

My talks were not a very great success, though some seemed to enjoy them very much. All the same—with the experience of talking over the various subjects—I can see my way better to what kind of a book would be valuable on spirituality through the centuries. One can concentrate too much on the Dionysiuses[5] and the Eckharts[6] and forget the normal Christian—good works and the normal ways of prayer. We must discuss it all when we meet.

Has your Japanese Question book come out yet?[7] I am longing to see it. Fr. Aelred's book[8] is out and I've read it. Have you? It is full of good things, lots of provocative things and nicely written. I've told him that I don't agree with the unity of religious experience there expressed, but with much, much else.

The Pepers came here for a week-end. They are heroic in their love and determination not to be broken by prospects of parting. A dear (f) cousin of mine—or really "in-law", a sweet person, died a month ago. She seems almost by prayer and will power to have delayed her death in order, as she said, to come to terms with it, to know exactly what she was doing. Her peace at the end was such that all her family were at peace, tho' they loved her very much.

Fr. Abbot writes to say he would like me to be stationed at Ampleforth. I am happy about that. God bless you both, and my love to you both.

Columba, O.S.B.

1. Lincoln Theological College.

2. Andrew Alexander Graham (1929–); warden of Lincoln Theological College (1970–77); bishop of Lincoln (1973–77); bishop of Newcastle since 1981.

3. David G. Deeks (1942–); Downing College, Cambridge; Theological Tripos (M.A.); ecumenical lecturer at Lincoln Theological College (1970–74); tutor, Wesley House, Cambridge (1980–); coauthor, *Doing Theology* (London, 1972).

4. Victor Alexander de Waal (1929–); chancellor of Lincoln College (1969–76); dean of Canterbury since 1976; *What Is the Church?* (London, 1969).

5. Not the Areopagite of Athens (Acts 17:34), or the bishop of Corinth (ca. 170), or Dionysius the Great of Alexandria (d. ca. 264), but the followers of Dionysius the Pseudo-Areopagite (ca. 500); cf. C.C.E.'s letter of 27 November 1958, above.

6. Meister Eckhart; influenced by the Pseudo-Areopagite; cf. C.C.E.'s letter of 13 October 1952, above.

7. *Surviving the Future* (London, 1971).

8. Aelred Graham's *The End of Religion* (London, 1971).

95, Oakwood Court
London W.14

3 July 1971

Dear Columba,

We were very glad to have your letter of 26 June, 1971. If the talks were enjoyed, they can't have been unsuccessful, and anyway they were part of the evidently happy relations between you and the people at the College. You made a human link that will last.

However, as you say, you have been on the go for a bit too long, and I am happy at your being pleased at Fr. Abbot's wanting you to be stationed at Ampleforth. You will, I hope, now have a bit of leisure to think and write and to give the much that you have to give to your brethren and to the boys. It is very much indeed, and it will be appreciated and valued.

A copy of '*Surviving the Future*' (the Japanese question book) is on its way to you. I haven't seen Father Aelred's book. Have you read Zaehner's '*Concordant Discord*'?[1] I guess that his criticism of Father Aelred would be the same as yours.

I do not think that there is unity of religious experience, but I think that these diverse experiences may all be experiences of the same multi-faceted—infinitely multi-faceted—ultimate reality.

The Pepers are brave; two days ago I met another pair with the same tragic prospect: the wife doomed by cancer; the husband thirty or forty years older, and still hale and hearty. He is Admiral Sam Morrison[2]—perhaps the only professor of history who has also been an admiral. He must be 84, at least, but he is still travelling about, locating the land falls of the earliest European discoverers of the Americas. His wife, like Mrs. Peper, is brave.

Two days ago the son of one of my school fellows died at about the age of 33 after years of being incapacitated by an incurable disease.[3] Nature is inequitable—not, I believe, out of malice, but out of partial incompetence: I think she does her best. Man-made evil is blacker: Eastern Bengal; Vietnam!

With love from us both,
Yours affectionately,
Arnold

How do I address the envelope? Are you Prior Emeritus, and Very Reverend? I am putting the simple form, as I would for myself, till I hear from you that it is incorrect, but I should like to get it right.

1. Robert Charles Zaehner; cf. C.C.E.'s letter of 20 October 1961, above; *Concordant Discord: The Interdependence of Faiths*, Gifford Lectures, 1967–69 (Oxford, 1970); Zaehner's most important work; the title is from the beginning of Saint Francis de Sales's magnum opus, *The Love of God*; C.C.E. reviewed it in the *Post-Dispatch* while in St. Louis.

2. Samuel Eliot Morison (1887–1976); American historian at Harvard University (1915–55); *Admiral of the Ocean Sea*, 2 vols. (Boston, 1942); appointed official historian with rank of lieutenant commander, he wrote *The History of United States Naval Operations in World War II*, 15 vols. (Boston, 1947–62); he served aboard eleven ships and retired in 1951 as rear admiral.

3. Compare A.J.T.'s letter of 30 October 1970, above.

Ampleforth College
York

8 July 1971

My dear Arnold,

If you must, the correct address is V. Rev. If you forget, I shan't pine. But that reminds me, should I write Dr. Arnold J.T.? or Dr. Arnold T.? rather than Prof.? because, while you still profess *occasionaliter* and by book, you don't, not steadily.

Pain, suffering, illness, death, agonies of mind and body, all these are inexplicable by reason alone. I believe, and you also, in a different way perhaps, I feel obliged to posit a creating Being, and by revelation a Good God; yet part of the evidence does not fit, or put it this way, we can't see how it fits.

Was that one of the reasons why Jesus Christ accepted the Passion and death He did? Doesn't his death give us the beginning of an understanding of suffering? You yourself have more than once claimed that as individuals and as a race or a culture we have learnt by suffering.

Fr. Aelred[1] in his book thinks that the Buddha was wiser than Christ in not forcing the issue, and dying a natural death. But the death of Christ, besides being, as I believe, redeeming, was such a sign of love, that, as St. Thomas wrote in the *Summa*, it provokes us to love in return.[2]

Here I am back at Ampleforth and, apparently, for good. I am very glad to be quiet. But in the last week of July I shall be in London staying with David Goodall[3]—the family will be up at Ampleforth as, excitement of excitements, they have bought a cottage there. Will you then be perched up in your Pennine eyrie? If not, I'd love to see you c. July 27–8.

Yes, I've read with keen interest and agreement Zaehner's *Concordant Discord*. He confirms my hunches. I like what he says about the Gita. That seems to be the crux for him. On the other hand he is maddeningly irresponsible on a number of irrelevant subjects. One suspects that his audience, though good "stayers," must have found some of the lectures a little soporific, and he may have wanted to provide light relief. A very good book.

Much love to you and Veronica. Look after each other! Many prayers for you and your friends.

Columba, O.S.B.

I'm looking forward to the parcel and will have read the book before we next meet.

1. *The End of Religion*.
2. "Per hoc [Christ's passion] homo cognoscit quantum Deus hominem diligat, et per hoc provocatur ad eum diligendum," Saint Thomas Aquinas, *Summa theologiae*, III, 46.3.
3. Compare C.C.E.'s letter of 29 July 1970, above.

95, Oakwood Court
W.14

10 July 1971

Dear Columba,

Your letter of 8 July has just come. What a pity: we are going north on Tuesday 13 July: first to Ganthorpe and then to Hall Beck. It is sad that we shall miss seeing you in London. It is not a bad thing, though, to miss seeing more Yugoslavs, Russians, Japanese, and Americans (mostly armed with tape-recording machines).

I don't think Christ forced the issue, and I do not think the issue arose for the Buddha. Given the idea of a Messiah, and the Jewish people's and the Sanhedrin's and the Romans' expectations of what a declared Messiah would try to do, the Sanhedrin had the choice between forcing Herod to put Christ to death and risking a popular revolt in his name that would have provoked the Romans into taking savage reprisals. The Sanhedrin decided that it was expedient that one man should die for the people, and Christ decided to give himself up and not 'go on the run', which would have led to many Jewish deaths. This, I believe, was the agonizing choice that he made. His temptation was to act the conventional part of a Messiah; the Buddha's temptation was to make his exit into Nirvana, now that he had found enlightenment, instead of staying on in a world of suffering in order to teach the way to other suffering creatures. So I do not think the two situations are comparable.

I am glad I asked you what your correct title is. I wanted to be sure to get it right when I was writing to you at Ampleforth. Mine? I feel most comfortable with Esq., but tolerate Dr. Since I retired, I am technically no longer Prof.

Well, I wish I were going to see you on July 27. But we shall be at Ganthorpe from evening July 13 to morning July 19. Do ring up Jean and arrange to come over while we are there, or for us to come to see you at Ampleforth.

Much love from us both. Veronica looks after me, and I a bit, after her, but we are reaching a stage when both us need looking after by someone younger; and who is to be found for this?

Arnold

Hall Beck Cottage
Killington
Kirkby Lonsdale
Westmorland

20 July 1971

Dear Columba,

It was very good to see you—the more so as we shall miss seeing you in London at the end of the month. I am very glad you have found that house for the Goodalls; you and they will enjoy seeing each other quite a lot, as you now will.

Sunday was a very happy day for Veronica and me. It was good of Father Abbot[1] to find the time to meet us at lunch, but he will have liked to do this for you. He is a striking person. 'Αρχὴ ἄνδρι δείξει[2] was inscribed on an ancient bed in which the head of the school at Winchester kept a stock of ground-ashes for beating Juniors (no doubt, long ago abolished—but the Greek dictum remains there).

We had an easy journey yesterday with one Mr. Capstick[3] of Sedburgh, a good friend.

If we break the journey again at Ganthorpe, early in September, we shall see you again then, unless you happen to be away taking a retreat or holding a seminar.

With much love,
Arnold

1. Georges Basil, Cardinal Hume, O.S.B. (1923–); Abbot of Ampleforth (1963–76); since 1976 Archbishop of Westminster.

2. A.J.T. refers to this phrase in *Surviving the Future*, p. 16: "Translated into English these were: 'Rule (meaning power) will reveal the man', that is, will show what kind of a man he is. . . . It is a good motto for any ruler."

3. A trusted (and very cautious) chauffeur.

Ampleforth Abbey
York

23 July 1971

My dear Arnold,

Thank you for your kind note. I am so glad you both enjoyed your visit. I was afraid you were a bit tired at the end. Fr. Abbot was delighted to meet you. Your Greek quote I see is in the book. Yes, a very penetrating three words' worth.

The book has arrived.[1] I am devouring it, and find it after 60 pages, among the very best I've read on our predicament. If only the young and "rulers" would read it, we might see the growth of the change of heart.

What you say on Love is *profoundly right* and surely you penetrate there to the centre of religion. St. Francis I see is still your 'darling,' as the Americans might say;

he is rightly so. There is our dilemma. All the money in the world cannot transform man's heart. How produce a St. Francis! Yes, perhaps prepare the ground by seeing that the Gospel truth is known, that true values are taught, Buddhist and Christian. Then when the grace of God strikes, the human soul so caught will not be a freak fanatic, but a really holy man.

Thank you also for the excellent analysing of the situation/predicament Jesus found himself in. I agree. (your earlier letter).

Tomorrow I pass very close to you, as I go to Warwick Bridge[2] for the week-end. We are having rain, so perhaps you are, on the roof! I mean you are getting roof-rain water.

Three days I was at Croft Hospital,[3] run by Brothers of St. John of God (+1550). They look after incurables, paralytics, spastics, broken-spined people, the blind. I got talking to these and pushing their wheeled-chairs. I was amazed how happy they were, with a humble peace of mind. I was amazed.

My love to you both,
Columba, O.S.B.

1. *Surviving the Future.*
2. A parish served by the monks of Ampleforth.
3. St. Cuthbert's Hospital, Hurworth, near Darlington, County Durham.

Hall Beck Cottage
Killington
Kirkby Lonsdale
Westmorland
(in Yorkshire)

20 August 1971

Dear Columba,

Here is our full address in Westmorland. I have had your letter of 26 July[1] at my elbow while I have been answering the second batch of Japanese questions (101, this time).[2]

About ceasing to exist, I suspect that 'before' and 'after' have no meaning for the spiritual aspect of our 'psychosomatic' human selves, but only for the empirical aspect.

In this set of questions, there is a lot about industrialization and pollution, and this has made me think of the effect of *Genesis* i, 28 ('subdue it') on the Royal Society's agenda[3] and on the consequent Industrial Revolution a century later. The East Asian precept that man should not try to subdue nature, but try to live in harmony with her, may have its innings next.[4]

There is too much nasty news. I have a hunch that the present mounting anarchy is going to somersault into stabilization at the price of an unpleasant dictatorship—something like the political unification of China in 221 B.C.

After having arrived here in a water-famine, we now have water again in the taps, even upstairs, but coping with the drought took it out of Veronica, and she is still very tired.

It is pleasant here, among the cows and sheep dogs and we enjoy seeing my tribe of cousins, the Franklands,[5] who live round about.

With much love from
us both,
Arnold

We shall be at Ganthorpe again, 2–9 Sept. This is a help to Veronica—breaking the journey. I hope we shall see each other.

1. Missing.
2. Compare *Surviving the Future*.
3. The Royal Society of London for Improving Natural Knowledge, chartered in 1662; it took as its motto *Nullius in verba*: "They assumed that an advance in technology would necessarily be an advance in welfare as well. They did not perceive that power of all kinds . . . is ethically neutral and that it can be used for evil as well as for good" (A.J.T. and Daisaku Ikeda, *Choose Life* [London, 1976], p. 294).
4. Ibid., pp. 293–300.
5. The Frankland family is described in A.J.T.'s *Experiences*, pp. 293–97.

Ampleforth Abbey
York

St. Martin's Day (11 November) 1971

My dear Arnold,

A long time since news has passed between us. How are both of you? Have you found a helping pair of hands.

The world you know so well has changed as it has not changed for a very long time: England (sorry U.K.) once again IN Europe; China in the U.N., but sad Taiwan out. It should not have been so arranged. The dancing of the Third World with delight was very significant. China has given much to Tanzania etc. and not (yet) required her pound of flesh. Your insight looks like coming true. China will be the knight in shining armour serving the poor maiden in the grips of dragon Capitalism. I wish you'd write a short article for the *Journal* on those lines.

Then what of Russia and France linking hands? The trouble is that no one trusts anyone, yet we should try to live by trust as much as others will allow.

The Roman synod[1] was not very significant except the maintenance of celibacy, a brave gesture. We can all *talk* about helping the Third World. What should really be done short of abolishing the profit motive as the steam for the engine? I'm thinking it just has to be abolished, and how? Can it only be by revolution?

The BBC are in among us doing a programme on discipline. Three others they're doing: school (infant) discipline; military discipline and Borstal.[2]

My love to you both,
Columba, O.S.B.

1. The Roman Synod of representative bishops called to implement Vatican II; it reaffirmed the role of a celibate clergy.

2. The generic term for a government school for delinquents; being sent to Borstal meant being sentenced to a period in one of many establishments for young offenders.

95, Oakwood Court
London W.14

15 Nov. 1971

Dear Columba,

Your letter was very welcome. I had been feeling, like you, that it was a long time since we had talked to each other. We do now have help in the flat—since last week. She is quite a nice person, and a good cook and diligent cleaner. Anyway, if this one doesn't last, the precedent has been established. It was hard for Veronica to capitulate, but, as she is both good and sensible, she has recognised that she must.

I don't think revolution will abolish the profit-motive. I think people's disgust with mechanised work may become stronger than their thirst for profit, and then the assembly lines at the conveyor-belts will disappear for lack of new recruits. But this would be a very negative way of de-industrializing ourselves. I think the profit-motive can only be overcome by a stronger motive. This might, of course, be an even worse one—e.g. greed for power or the hatred of one's fellow men, but it also might be a better one. The Industrial Revolution has consecrated greed instead of executing it, but greed has always been there, and the only worthy victor over it is love. So we are back at the issue between Saint Francis and his proto-capitalist father.[1] It is as unlucky to have been Saint F.'s father as it is to have been Judas or Pilate.

I think the important practical decision now is not between Communists and pro-entrepreneurs, of whom the trades unionists are now the most aggressive; it is between the minority (which includes Russia) that has committed itself to the conveyor belt and the majority that is still uncommitted. I hope the Chinese are going to find a way of alleviating the poverty of peasant life without turning the peasantry into an urban proletariat.

If you want a short article for the *Journal* on this theme, I shall be glad to do it, but not just yet, as I am in a jam getting a new illustrated abridgment of '*A Study of History*'[2] to Press.

Love from us both. Veronica is, I am glad to say, definitely better.

Yours affectionately,
Arnold

1. Pietro Bernardone, a wealthy cloth merchant, had opposed Francis's vocation.

2. The one-volume illustrated *Study of History*, abridged by A.J.T. and Jane Caplan (London, 1972).

Ampleforth Abbey
York

17 December 1971

My dear Arnold and Veronica,

It was a joy, and so unexpected, to see you both the other day, in the company too of the Pepers. They are so brave. We went on together to Oxford next morning, as they wanted a "raid" on Blackwells, and wanted me to share the spoils.

On Paddington Station we met four Buddhist monks from Thailand, dressed in their saffron robes, all quite young—perhaps one was elderly?—also going to Oxford, as far as we could gather, to bring the good news to the University. They were financed by their government. A perfect example of your premonition years ago of the counter-apostolate.

It was grand to see you so full of life too, especially with the A.J.T. exhibition of MSS. that should be of great interest to many people.[1]

I'm at Burnham[2] giving a short retreat and tomorrow (Sat.) I make for Exeter and go by car to Bideford to give another end-of-year mini-retreat. Then I make my way back to Ampleforth. But the Christmas–New year ten days I shall be at Richmond (Assumption Convent).[3] Yes, acting as chaplain and in complete quiet. I'm looking forward to it.

You will be much in my prayers during the Christmas season, so that God may give you strength and peace of mind and joy, whatever is in store for us all.

Much love to you both,
Columba, O.S.B.

1. See C.C.E.'s letter of 10 March 1972, below.

2. Burnham, in the diocese of Oxford; a small community of Anglican nuns living the contemplative life under enclosure; their rule is based on that of Saint Benedict with Cistercian elements.

3. Assumption Convent at Richmond.

Ampleforth Abbey
York

20 January 1972

My dear Arnold,

It was good to see you both the other day. I thought: suppose you get ill? Let Veronica tell me immediately. If I can, I will come, should it be the end. In any case I would then be close to you both in prayer. And let me say categorically that I will of course make no move whatever to turn you at the last moment into an R. C. or anything else. You have followed truth as you see it—and, in my terms, God already loves you infinitely for that.

Here is the name of the book: *A New Charter for Monasticism*, ed. J. Maffitt, London and Notre Dame.

In fact it is all about Christian-Eastern religious contacts. Read the articles (i) of a

Catholic sister living in a Hindu Ashram, (ii) Fr. Jacques Amyot, (iii) Fr. Enoniya Lasalle.

Love to you both,
Columba, O.S.B.

P.S. The BBC are with us (Monks not school) in force—a 50 minute broadcast in a series on 'Obedience'—military, approved school and otherwise.

95, Oakwood Court
London W.14

25 January 1972

Dear Columba,

We were so glad to have your letter of 20 January. Suppose I get ill? Very pertinent. At my age, and after a coronary, any serious illness would be likely to bring death, and my contemporaries (the survivors) are now dying rapidly: e.g. my school-fellow and bosom friend Theodore Wade-Gery,[1] Emeritus Professor of Ancient History at Oxford, and, a few days later, Rosalind's one surviving aunt, Aurea Macleod[2] (only six years older than Rosalind was).

It is always in my mind that about half my contemporaries were killed in 1915–6, and that my uncle Arnold[3] died at thirty, so being still alive at 82 is, for me, a freak of chance, and death is familiar and is merely surprisingly tardy in my case.

Yes, indeed I should be sad to die without having seen you again, and I have complete trust that you will not try to turn me, when defenseless, into something that I am not. In truth, you and I are not far apart, as you say.

We both believe that love is present, behind the phenomena, and not only in ourselves and in our fellow human beings, where we know love by direct experience.

My conception of the inconceivable ultimate spiritual reality is no doubt more Indian (i.e. less in terms of a personal god) than Judaic, and I am also a Marcionite[4] in believing that love is not omnipotent, whereas you are presumably an Irenaean.[5] (I cannot reconcile omnipotence with beneficence). I believe in the Agony in the Garden and in the Crucifixion, but not in the Resurrection (I am using all these words in the symbolic sense). In general terms, I believe that every living creature is a temporary splinter of the ultimate reality, and is re-united with this at death. 'Reunited' covers several superficially different beliefs: e.g. personal immortality, personal annihilation, and nirvana. I am content with 're-united.'

With love,
Arnold

1. Theodore Wade-Gery (1888–1972); cf. A.J.T.'s letter of 22 February 1948, above.

2. Lady Aurea Macleod (1884–1972); Rosalind's mother's sister; she was an earnest tee-totaler; in middle life she took up the inspection of slaughterhouses and reported on their condition.

3. Arnold Toynbee (1852–83); fellow of Balliol; an economic historian interested in social

problems; *Lectures on the Industrial Revolution in England*, posthumously published from "popular addresses, notes and other fragments" (London, 1884); *Toynbee's Industrial Revolution* (a facsimile reprint) (Newton Abbot, 1969); *The Industrial Revolution*, Preface by A.J.T. (Boston: Beacon Press, 1956); Toynbee Hall was founded in his memory; cf. A.J.T.'s *Acquaintances*, pp. 21–22, 33–36.

4. Marcion; cf. A.J.T.'s letter of 22 November 1965, above.

5. Saint Irenaeus (ca. 130–ca. 200); Bishop of Lyons; the first great Catholic theologian; he emphasized the unity of Father and Son in the Redemption.

Ampleforth Abbey
York

2 February 1972

My dear Arnold,

Many of your letters are specially precious to me; none more than the last. Yes, "The inconceivable ultimate spiritual reality," which we call/know to be Love is our ultimate goal. To that we hope to be reunited. I have been brought up to think in Personal terms, but that can only mean that at least the Ultimate knows and loves as (?) we do. But then again "Not this, not that"—always beyond this or that.

You have been providentially educated in the Greek tradition and find the Eastern akin: body, soul: prison, freedom from it. In the Hebrew tradition it is just the whole me that survives, not of course as we are, the whole universe too, and if we follow Ep. to Colossians 1.15–20, a mysterious insight which might reconcile Love—infinite and the agonies of this mortal time.

Of course, quite truthfully, I cannot, nor I suspect could Irenaeus,[1] *see* how all these infinites fitted together: justice, mercy, love, punishment. We have scraps of information and we put it together as best we can. In the end we will be "oned".

¡Oh noche, que guiaste!
¡Oh noche amable más que el alborada!
¡Oh noche, que juntaste
Amado con amada,
Amada en el amado transformada!

S. Juan has put it in a way that is true for all.[2]

Love to you both,
Columba, O.S.B.

1. Compare A.J.T.'s letter of 25 January 1972, above.
2. Saint John of the Cross, *The Dark Night of the Soul*.

Ampleforth Abbey
York

10 March 1972

My dear Arnold,

I am reminded of your exhibition or rather of the exhibition of you and your doings, by the *Times* today.[1] I hope it all goes very well. I thought the article in the

Times was very good. It did not mention A.J.T. the traveller and his "travelogues" which I enjoyed so much.

These events are likely to be tiring and all that I can think is: Veronica is on guard and will hold you back a little!

Love to you both and prayers and wishes for a happy Easter, even if your interpretation of survival is not quite mine.

Columba, O.S.B.

P.S. I'm saying a few words in St. Gregory's Minster (Kirkdale) Sunday, at Matins, on St. Gregory and am reminded your words on him in Vol. iii of the Nonsense Book were the first of yours I ever read and they've held me ever since.[2]

1. The Oxford University Press and the National Book League displayed an exhibition entitled "A Study of Toynbee" at 7 Albemarle Street, London, 9–23 March 1972; it included notes, letters, and publications carefully annotated by a series of autobiographical comments; *The Times* article appeared 10 March 1972.

2. Compare C.C.E.'s letter of 3 November 1939, above.

14 March 1972 95, Oakwood Court, W.14

Dear Columba,

Yes, I was very grateful to the *Times*,[1] and it was a happy occasion—but an exhausting one, as we followed up with a sandwich lunch at Chatham House for grand children and for aged retired Chatham House colleagues, who got there by heroic efforts—so did the widows of three of my school fellows: this touched me very much.

I have never been so frightened about speaking: first, because the thing was centred on me, and second because I was feeling very acutely for my contemporaries, and for my Uncle Arnold, whose lives had been cut short, while mine, by accident, has been long-drawn-out.

I had five minutes, and I overshot my time, unprofessionally, by 1½ minutes. I was able to mention 5 persons: one living (a colleague of V.'s and mine on the Survey), three killed in 1915–6 (all three fellows of New College, two of them my school fellows), and my Uncle.

We included in the exhibition[2] my Uncle's book[3] and some sheets of the MS. of his notes for lectures, given in 1880–1, out of which the book was produced for him after his death by friends and pupils. He died on 9 March, 1883.

I also held up for view the title page of my school fellow Guy Cheesman's one little book (published in 1914): '*The Auxilia of the Roman Imperial Army*.'[4]

As you will see, it was a considerable strain, but also a happiness to have this opportunity of mentioning the dead who are constantly in my mind.

'Not quite mine' is, if correct, a meiosis. But can you be sure? The ineffable is like the infinite (perhaps they are just two words for the same thing). Here parallel lines can meet.

The exhibition was splendidly set out by the National Book League and the O.U.P. and my marvellous secretary, Louise Orr. Veronica and I fished out some amusing early stuff: e.g. an essay on tenth-century Byzantine history in a drawing-book of 1903—69 years before the proofs on *Constantine Prophyrogenitus*, which are now coming in: some are here in my table now.

As Alice found, things become 'curiouser and curiouser.'

Love from us both,
Arnold

1. *The Times* (10 March 1972).
2. "A Study of Toynbee."
3. Arnold Toynbee; cf. A.J.T.'s letter of 25 January 1972, above.
4. George ("Guy") Leonard Cheesman (1884–1915); Winchester; New College, Oxford; first-class honors in classics; killed at Gallipoli; *The Auxilia of the Roman Imperial Army* (Oxford, 1914); cf. A.J.T.'s *Acquaintances*, p. 24; and *A Study of History*: "had he lived, he would have become the greatest Roman Historian in his generation" (X: 30, n. 2). Cheesman has left an unpublished diary of his last two years at Oxford; he writes: "a short walk with Toynbee in the afternoon was a revelation of his industry and my idleness (7 February 1913)."

Ampleforth Abbey
York

26 April 1972

My dear Arnold,

I've been up at Pluscarden Priory[1] giving a retreat to a nice lot of monks—from Prinknash,[2] from Caldey—I enclose a card. It was a ruin—the Order of "The Valley of Cabbages" somewhere in Burgundy, later O.S.B., then suppressed. It is near Elgin.

Your birthday must have passed when I was up there. God be praised for it and keeping you among us.

I also enclose a sheet about our Ecumenical meeting in July, just to show you I've not been idle. It looks as though it should be good. We shall see.

Tell me: (i) do you think the Christian writers on prayer in their descriptions are writing about the same thing as the Hindu and Buddhist even though their terminologies are different, and consequently their analyses appear to be saying that the experiences are different; (ii) or do you think they really are different? (iii) Or is it impossible to say?

A missionary from India was holding view (ii) with me two weeks ago. I'd like to know what you now think.

Love to you both,
Columba, O.S.B.

P.S. Please don't say (iii)

1. Pluscarden Priory (now an abbey), founded originally in 1230; near Elgin in Morayshire, Scotland.

2. Prinknash Abbey, founded by an Anglican community on the Isle of Dogs, removed to the Isle of Caldey; became Catholic in 1913 and was transferred to Prinknash Park in Gloucestershire in 1928; in 1947 Prinknash sent a colony to occupy the abbey of Farnborough, now autonomous.

95, Oakwood Court
London W.14

30 April 1972

Dear Columba,

I was so glad to have your letter of 26 April (N.B. there were no enclosures).

I am sure the July Ecumenical meeting will be very much worth while—as evidently the retreat in Scotland has been.

I believe (i), not (ii) because I believe that every human being has a relation to an ultimate spiritual reality which is the same for each of us, though each individual, or each religious community, expresses its intuition of this reality in different words. Though the differences of expression are great, I do not think that they refer to different things. Our vocabulary for describing spiritual things is very very inadequate. It is all derived from our vocabulary for describing material things. This is direct and precise. Our spiritual vocabulary is entirely analogical (e.g. spirit = 'breath', to describe something that is no more like breath than it is like rock). All this analogical language is clumsy, and much of it is actually misleading, but we have no other.

This is why I believe the different descriptions refer to identical experiences. My postulates are the uniformity of human nature and its universal intuition of what I believe to be one and the same reality.

My birthday: I have much that still attaches me to this world, e.g. concern for my family and friends and also for the vast majority of people, now alive or not yet born, whom I shall never know personally. I am also fortunate, so far, in being physically and mentally still compos, and in having undiminished curiosity about the universe and about the reality behind the phenomena. At the same time, I am glad that I do not have an unlimited liability to life in this world, and, if I believed in re-birth, I should be as eager as any Buddhist to make a permanent exit into Nirvana from the sorrowful round.

I am more and more impressed and grieved by the perversity of human nature.

For the last 30,000 years, what human beings have suffered from non-human natural forces (earthquakes, floods, droughts, sharks, bacteria, etc.) is small compared with the suffering that we have inflicted on ourselves.

We do know this, and know that we ought to do better. I think this is another way of saying that every human being has religion, even if he believes that he doesn't have it.

Love to you from us both,
Arnold

95 Oakwood Court
9 May 1972 London, W.14

Dear Christian,

Your letter of May 2, enclosing the clipping,[1] gave us both the greatest pleasure. It is by far the fullest, and kindest, of any published account of the exhibition that we have seen. We are very grateful for it.

I do hope Nixon, in his desperation, isn't working up for a confrontation with Russia.[2] The lesson of President Kennedy's diplomatic victory over Russia about Cuba is that such victories can't be repeated. The First World War happened because Germany tried it once too often.

Our love to you and Ethel.

Yours ever,
Arnold

1. C.B.P. had visited the exhibit and written an article about the "Study of Toynbee," published in the *St. Louis Post-Dispatch*, 30 April 1972.

2. President Nixon was to visit Russia from 22 to 29 May 1972.

Ampleforth Abbey
14 May 1972 York

My dear Arnold,

Your lament over human behaviour was sadly exemplified by Nixon's frantic behaviour. Fr. McKenzie[1] of the excellent 1 vol. *Bible Dictionary*, was speaking in Nairobi when I was there and must have been in your frame of mind as he attacked us humans for being less than other animals in this that at least *they* do not kill their own kind.

The strike is *laissez-faire*, but on the other foot.

Here is the programme for our Ecumenical meeting. Will you be around. If so COME, an honored guest.

Thank you for your thoughts on my question and three possible answers. Yes, I'm glad you chose the first, though I have some doubts.

In the first place I agree that the Ultimate Spiritual Reality is the same Ultimate Reality for all of us; and that we have the same humanity. But—and this is where I think we have to be careful to avoid confusions, distortions—that Ultimate Reality is *infinite*, will have unimaginable depths of being (or beyond being). Therefore, though we are the same, we can each of us, or each culture or religion, approach it/ Him from different angles, and at different depths. The latter, I think, may be more important. So, while I believe all are "in touch with God," I think this may be at very different levels. This is borne out by the experiences of the mystics (S. Teresa and S. John) who have attempted to express this journey.

How true that our expressions are inadequate. Interesting that English and Greek and Hebrew use this image, breath (inspiration). Or is it that they are all derived from the Hebrew through LXX, through vulgate . . . ?[2]

Are you going to your hide out this year? If so, you'd better take a strong arm or two, and a strong back!

Love to you both,
Columba, O.S.B.

P.S. How is the reduced "Study" progressing?

1. John L. McKenzie, S.J. (1910–); *The Two Edged Sword* (Milwaukee, Wis., 1955).
2. *Ruach* (Hebrew); πνεῦμα (Greek); *spiritus* (Vulgate).

95, Oakwood Court
London W.14

19 May 1972

Dear Columba,

I was very glad to have your letter of 14 May, 1972. I should much have liked to come to the July meeting, but we shall be in Greece. We may perish on the expedition, but it is the last of Doxiadis's[1] series of ten annual conference-cruises, and we could not bear not to be taking part.

We are all right. Veronica is benefiting decidedly from now having some help in the flat, and I am standing up to getting two books to press simultaneously.

In approaches to infinity, can there be different depths? Measured against infinity, aren't all depths equally far away from the bottom?

I hope we shall get to Hall Beck in August, but this depends on the state of the water-supply.

Love from us both,
Arnold

1. Constantine A. Doxiadis (1914–78); architect and city planner; gave A.J.T. his "third" Greek education: in ekistics, a word coined by Doxiadis (from οἰκιστική) to denote the whole subject of human settlements; A.J.T. acknowledges his indebtedness in *Experiences*, pp. 40–45; cf. his *Cities on the Move* (London, 1970); *Cities of Destiny* (London, 1967); and *The Greeks and Their Heritages*, p. 266.

Ampleforth Abbey
York

8 June 1972

My dear Arnold,

Have a splendid time in Greece. No, don't perish in the attempt. Come back safe and sound and refreshed. Veronica, now, I am sure, can hold you back from climbing Mt. Olympus and such like.

I am not sure I agree with you about different depths in the divinity. Yes, of course I agree that God is infinite; but it is the receiving end which is not. Just as in one's own life there are moments and periods even of deeper insight, so I think we can see this in a comparison of an Eckhart and a San Juan de la Cruz or a St. Catherine of Genoa.[1] Perhaps then this is true, by and large, of religions; and the reason would be in the capacity to receive—allowing always of course for God's paramount power to do as He will, as S. Paul reminds us. So in a way I suspect that an inadequate philosophy or theology could cramp one's insight. I wonder whether I've made myself clear?

As for not wanting to live "for ever and ever," I agree! But we are always being caught out by language. Personally I don't believe it is for ever and ever, like an interminable road, but an absolute present; an infinite ecstasy without a hangover. This of course is as hopeless an effort at expression as the other. I'd better stop.

My love to you both,
Columba, O.S.B.

1. Saint Catherine of Genoa (1447–1510); *Vita e dottrina* (1551); cf. F. von Hügel, *The Mystical Element of Religion as Studied in St. Catherine of Genoa and Her Friends*, 2 vols. (1908; reprint, London, 1927).

10 June 1972 95, Oakwood Court, W.14

Dear Columba,

Well, I go far, but not quite the whole way, with you. I agree that some religions create, where prevalent, a more favourable spiritual climate than others for—here comes my reservation—people with particular kinds of character and temperament. But characters and temperaments differ, and I believe some kinds are likely to get farther in an Indian (i.e. Buddhist or, indeed, Hindu) milieu than in a Judaic one, and that, in the Judaic field, Judaism or Islam may be more helpful than Christianity for some kinds of people—and, of course, the other way round for other kinds.

A practical ethical precept on which all the higher religions agree is very much to the point. They all warn against the snare of 'growth' (in the present-day usage of the word, to mean the maximum satisfaction of greed for material possessions). The present-day world is taking its cue from Pietro Bernardone, not from Francesco, but I believe Saint Francis's and the Buddha's precepts and practice are even more to the point today than they have been in the past (they are right, of course, always and everywhere).

I find the present state of mind in this country very painful. Greed is producing the still worse evil of mutual hatred among the people who are scrambling for the material spoils.

Spiritual wealth, being infinite, can't excite this rancorous competition, but, at present, spiritual wealth is at a discount.

Even allowing for the well-known jaundiced view of the old, I believe I am right about this objectively.

Our love to you,
Arnold

Ampleforth Abbey
York

23 June 1972

Dear Arnold,

I was at Ganthorpe the other day. Three of us—two Portsmouth monks and I—set off for Castle Howard, and found it shut against us. So we dropped in at Ganthorpe, and both Lawrence and Jean were there, who received us with open arms and a delightful bottle of wine. Then she telephoned and we were granted permission to wander round C.H., tho' not in it. Both Lawrence and Jean looked remarkably well, he particularly, as he had just retired from his London job.[1]

The answer to religious-fittingness is for the great religions to learn from one another. Fr. Aelred is doing his bit. His new book is selling well in the States.[2] The world being a village, this process is bound to take place, and of course the *Study* has been part of the general drawing together.

Lawrence says you are a household word in Japan. That is good news as the Japanese came into the 20th century feet first and need a head and even more a heart to guide them; I mean a philosophy and religion of life.

The trouble you wrote about in your last letter, especially our industrial unrest and American acquisitiveness pervading all, is our appetite gone wild because there is no higher aim; nor is there any adequate sanction against complete, ruthless selfishness. In ancient times the Few could gorge all wealth and tyrannize over the rest, now a whole continent can gorge and keep the rest of the world starving.

We have just had visiting a priest who has been on a papal or episcopal commission of enquiry in S. America on conditions. He says that the responsibility of the rich countries is appalling. Most S. Americans live in "miseria" or *abject* poverty. *Quid Faciendum*? The only solution is a world government capable of controlling for the good of all the world's wealth which is for all. But first we need a *change of heart* and a not-seeking this world's wealth. Then World Govt. will be unnecessary! In any case a World Government can also be tyranny.

I hope you have a most rewarding time in Greece.

Love to you both,
Columba, O.S.B

1. Lawrence had been director of art and of the gallery at Morley College, London; Morley College was an adult education center, specializing in music; Lawrence during his tenure had organized loan exhibitions, including one from Castle Howard.

2. *The End of Religion*.

August 1972

95, Oakwood Court
London W.14

Dear Columba,

Since I had your letter of 23 June, 1972, we have been to Greece, and, what is more, have got back alive. We were most tenderly looked after there, but it was too much for us. Veronica got bronchitis on return, and, the Monday before last, I fell over backwards in the kitchen from sheer physical fatigue (X-ray shows that I haven't injured myself, but I stiffened into helplessness, and I am only just finding my feet again, thanks to skillful massage).

We can't do that again, but we would have been grieved to miss this last of the ten Doxiadis conference-cruises. I gave the opening talk in Athens on Philópappus hill, which overlooks, from the south, the Areopagus as well as the Acropolis. I also spoke the last words, in the theatre of Delos. I invoked Apollo (Delos is his island) to move us Westerners to follow Francesco Bernardone's example, instead of following his father Piero's example, as we have been doing so far.[1]

As you say in your letter, the need is for a change of heart that will move us to change our objective. The ruthless competition for material wealth is evil in itself, and it creates unhappiness, in the long run, for everyone—including the few who succeed in robbing the many.

There is much emphasis now on voluntariness, and it would indeed be an extra misfortune if the restraint of greed had to be imposed dictatorially. But we do have inspiring examples of the voluntary renunciation of material (not of spiritual) wealth in the Christian and Buddhist monastic orders. Saint Francis renounced a lucrative family business; the Buddha renounced the heirdom to a kingdom.

At the Doxiadis conference there were some of the leading people from the Stockholm conference. Increase in material wealth is bound to stop, because the 'biosphere'[2] is rigidly limited. This is just a thin film round the surface of a single planet, and it could easily be made uninhabitable. On the other hand the 'noosphere' (in which Teilhard, I take it meant to include the spiritual, as well as the intellectual, universe) is infinite.[3]

The sad thing now is that the trades unionists, having acquired power, are using this to satisfy their greed at the expense of their fellow human beings—including fellow trades unionists. And the plutocrats continue to set the same bad example.

I must stop. My strength is limited. In October I shall be sending you a copy of the new illustrated abridgement of the Nonsense Book.

Love from us both,
Arnold

1. The address, an "Envoi to the tenth and last of Constantine Doxiadis's Delos Conferences" in the form of a prayer to Apollo, was published in *Ekistics* 34, no. 203 (October 1972): 292–93.

2. Compare *Mankind and Mother Earth*, p. 5, where A.J.T. adopts Teilhard de Chardin's term.

3. Pierre Teilhard de Chardin, S.J. (1881–1955); *La Place de l'homme dans la nature* (Paris, 1956), pp. 115–73; Teilhard therein refers to A.J.T.'s "oeuvre monumentale," p. 124.

15 August 1972 As from Ampleforth

My dear Arnold,

Your letter arrived only today, as I am acting chaplain for a week at a Carmelite Convent at Quidenham, Norfolk.

The news is disturbing. I can see you are both utterly exhausted. Thank God you are on the mend. But no more Greek cruises. How wonderful the last one must have been all the same, and worth it.

Yes, Saint Francis is still our symbol. Nor must we expect everyone to follow. It is a mistake to expect all to be in step, enough if a few take the right road, clearly and unmistakably. But even in his day the two Cities lived side by side; and today it is the same, except that the City of the World is becoming monstrously powerful.

One of the plagues of our world is greed for wealth; another the itch for ever more pleasure; another the snatching at power as the cure all; another lying to reach one's ends. They all are resolved in selfishness; the world may be despoiled, but after I'm dead, is the underlying assumption.

As you pointed out in the *Study*, religion, faith is the basis of civilization, and with the collapse of religion comes the collapse of a decent way of life.

I am very excited to hear that the Nonsense Book is coming out under your guidance, illustrated and reduced; my guess is that you have almost re-written it. I shall certainly re-read it word for word; and I wish it enormous success. Thank you for promising to send me a copy.

I've just been re-reading—as you probably have guessed—the City of God, this time in the excellent Penguin translation. I wish you and St. Augustine could have met. I think you will yet!

Poor Veronica, she must be terribly tired too. Give her my special love. Of course you will not be able to go to the Pennines hideabout this year. You must be very quiet and recoup your strength, both of you.

I'll be back at Ampleforth Saturday next, so do keep me informed of how you are.

People underestimate Teilhard de Chardin. He had vision.

Our Ecumenical meeting was a great success, many friends were made, many prejudices melted away in the peaceful atmosphere.

My love to you both,
Columba, O.S.B.,
and prayers

Ampleforth Abbey
York

28 August (S. Augustine's day) 1972

My dear Arnold,

Thank you so much for sending me your prayer to Apollon, god of light. I see no reason why you should not so pray if you feel that he is the same God, only under a different name from that of Christ or Muhammad; after all, the attributes of the God of the O.T. were not all appropriate, and we all see the Light through the faulty prism of our minds.

I would like you to write another prayer as though you were standing below Assisi and appealing to the God of Francis, the God of love and beauty and meekness and poverty and for the same western minority.

The very attitude of suppliant that you took is the beginning of conversion/

change of heart for Western men and women, who, having been self-reliant, are now at a loss, but have forgotten how to pray. You have not, and what a gift of God that is.

Now, on a lower level, I shall be passing through London on two days, one going, 26th Sept. Tuesday, one coming back, 4 Oct. Wednesday. One day is engaged already, but you choose which one you can manage best and let's meet for lunch (sandwiches at the flat?). I hope you can manage this.

Much love to you both and many prayers for your well-being.

Columba, O.S.B.

P.S. I return the MS. in case you need it. Otherwise do send it back.

95, Oakwood Court
London, W.14

29 August 1972

Dear Columba,

I was very glad to have your letter of 28 August. You are tolerant and understanding. Yes, for me Apollo (though at times he behaved disgracefully; see Euripides's indictment of him in the *Ion*) is a less fallacious image of Ultimate Reality than Yahweh—or than Zeus. The god of Francis is the god who has voluntarily been crucified and who communicates his stigmata to the rare human beings who are worthy to receive them. I think—though you can hardly agree—that Francis's god is more like Marcion's 'stranger god' than like the god of orthodox Christian theology, who submits to become incarnate and to be crucified, yet is all the time also omnipotent and immortal and is therefore assured, in advance, of coming to life again. I think this orthodox theology lapses into docetism—the voluntary crucifixion of an omnipotent immortal god is not the absolute and irretrievable act of self-sacrifice, without reservations, as the voluntary crucifixion of an ordinary mortal man—above all, if he does not believe that he is immortal.

Well, dates: definitely 4 October, not 26 September, if 4 October is still all right for you. The Oxford Press is making it very awkward for us to get away from London, but we hope to go to Ganthorpe on Tuesday 12 September and then, if we feel up to it, to go on from there to Hall Beck for about ten days (or alternatively stay on for those ten days at Ganthorpe). If you are going to be at Ampleforth till 26 September, we shall be able to see you in Yorkshire before that, as well as in London on 4 October.

When we have got the tiresome TV publicity date in London settled with O.U.P., New York, we shall be able to let you know our exact time-table.

Anyway, we shall be meeting at least twice, I hope.

With much affection,

Arnold

O U P London have just rung up to fix 11.00 AM. on Monday, 11 September for the TV, so I hope we shall be able to go to Ganthorpe on Tuesday 12 September.

Oulton Abbey[1]
Stone
Staffordshire

1 September 1972

My dear Arnold,

Thank you for settling the date. I shall come to the flat as soon as I can on the 4th October probably between 12.30 and 1 P.M. I'll ring Ganthorpe after you have arrived. I am giving a retreat here, nice and quiet and friendly—Benedictine nuns, part of the English diaspora of 16th–17th centuries, first Brussels, then Ghent, then here.

Yes, even St. Thomas couldn't see his way to allowing Christ a completely human 'like us in all things' except for sin, as Ep. to Hebr.[2] lays down. He had to claim that he had the beatific vision from the start. I don't believe anyone was quite so sure of this until S. Thomas, and few theologians of today (not yesterday) hold to it. Certainly Scriptural Scholars (R.C.) go along with others asserting Christ's lack of knowledge, growth in understanding of his mission in his earthly life. It makes sense of so much. It also makes the Passion and Death of Christ the Man—though one with the Divinity—real, as you would want it. It explains the "My God, my God why have you forsaken me."[3] In his human knowledge, under the stress of agony and death He had no intellectual, conceptual, immediate awareness of God. Can this be explained in an orthodox way? Probably not, because the union of natures in one Person is unexplainable. It is possible, I think—I say gropingly—that such a oneness could exist in which the human intellect of Christ was not able to concentrate, be aware of that union, even if at a deeper level it was known. But you see I am babbling. However the point of those words "My God . . ." is to make us appreciate that the agony and death were real. It is a kind of Monophysitism to deny a real death and of Nestorianism to say that He ceased to be God at the crucifixion—both efforts to avoid the Death of God. He died in his total humanity.

If Christ allowed Himself to be completely human, then in his human knowledge—kept separate from his divine knowledge—He only *by faith* believed he was immortal. As man He went through our agony of dying.

Now, I don't think we should treat Him as a hero, exactly. His death was not simply the heroic act, and the less He gained from it, the more heroic. His death had other aspects, part of the Incarnation-meaning. I think S. Irenaeus' "recapitulation" explanation gives quickest what I mean. Christ died and rose again to be our death and our new birth. He is a new creation, a re-making of man, and we are one-d in Him. God became man, that man might share in the Godhead. He took our fate to defeat it by facing death *as a true man* with tranquility and love. He made up for our lack of love.

But I'm getting obscure and am tiring you. I like S. Thomas'[4] saying that Christ chose so harsh a death so as by his love to provoke us to love in return.

Much love to you and Veronica. Every success with the T.V. show.

Columba, O.S.B.

1. Oulton Abbey, founded by Benedictine nuns from Ghent in 1853.
2. Heb. 4:15.
3. Matt. 27:46.
4. Compare C.C.E.'s letter of 8 July 1971, above.

Ampleforth Abbey
York

Monday, 9 October 1972

Dear Arnold,

I got back last Thursday from Acton Burnell to find a non-forwarded letter from Jean in my room. It had been my intention to write you at the week-end, but I had to "whisk" over to Parbold[1] where Fr. Alban Rimmer[2] is ill. It was unavoidable that we did not meet as you passed through G. on your way back to London. I would have liked to know how your holiday went. The weather further south was gorgeous.

I've had a firm request from Glenstal[3] to join their venture in Kenya, Fall 1973. I feel inclined very strongly to put it to the Abbot. What do you think?

Love,
Columba, O.S.B.

1. The parish at Wigan served by the monks of Ampleforth.
2. Alban Rimmer, O.S.B. (1911–84); monk of Ampleforth; active in parish work.
3. Glenstal Abbey, established, with a college, near Limerick, Ireland, in 1927, by the monks of Maredsous in Belgium.

Ampleforth Abbey
York

20 October 1972

My dear Arnold,

Your precious volume arrived the very day of publication, and I must admit I spent most of that day pouring over its pages; its marvellous maps; its gorgeous illustrations and their little apposite notes; and the very text itself, rushing to those points which I wanted to examine to see "where you had got to."[1] Your little chapter on the eremitical life is a masterpiece and was a great help to me. I shall show it to Fr. Aidan in his hermitage at Hawnby.[2]

Then your final paragraph has come to rest on a peaceful solution or statement of the Greatest Question in Our World. I agreed with it, and said "journey's end." I do believe we are all seeking the same infinite Ultimate Reality and each has found an aspect of the Same but a different aspect and we can therefore learn from one another. (I see there is a good book on Nicolas of Cusa out, but in German—no good to me. He was 400 yrs ahead of his time. Nikolaus von Kues . . . Ld. Rudolf Haubot, Mainz: Mattheis Grinende—Verlag, 1971. pp. 224).

I am so glad to see you have tucked Black Africa into the Study of History; it will give many so much pleasure.

Off at another tangent. You were too late for Leakey?[3]

Your gentle defense of religion I thought telling. But as you know, I find your Marcionism a bit dated! Though understandable.

Which illustrations struck me? The world—that glistening child's marble, the Nestorian monk, the ship coming to the Japanese port, the drawing of the shouting revolutionary crowd (Caruso) the first steps of the Virgin, S. Francis holding up the Lateran, the two Mongols having a chat—or a quarrel?—p. 90 Endless Death or Eternal Life. But I must stop. Thank you with all my heart.

My African prospects have dissolved, as I got in touch with the Abbot of Glenstal to find out the exact situation, and his account was slightly different from that of one of the pioneers—the future superior. The Abbot seemed to be confident that 4 of their monks would be able to go; and for me that meant I was not absolutely necessary, as 4 was enough to go on with. However the situation is fluid.

Now I await impatiently for your mini-study and your world history. I would like to be inside your brain as you disentangle the second, because as you see history repeating itself, it must be hard to find a flow. I remember your simile of the cart and the wheels and slowly climbing the hill.

You must tell us whether men in Asia and Africa and America really were cut off, or whether they had means of communication, e.g. stone implements seem to be the same everywhere, going through the same evolution. Was it an accident that the Buddha, Isaiah, Zoroaster, Confucius all came about the same time?

You could write a world religious, economic, social, scientific history. Politically, what you said years ago is true "Vain repetitions . . ."

c. Dec. 15 I shall go to St. Louis for a month on a cheap ticket to see all my old friends.

My love to you both—and all my encouragement for the World History.

Columba, O.S.B.

1. The one-volume illustrated *Study of History*.

2. Aiden Gilman, O.S.B. (1927–); he was living, for six years, the life of a hermit at Hawnby Hump; now chaplain to the Benedictine Convent, Stanbrook Abbey, Worchester.

3. Louis Seymour Bazett Leakey (1903–72); the discoverer of the skull of *Proconsul Africanus*; cf. C.C.E.'s letter of 7 April 1964, above.

Ampleforth Abbey
York

Eve of All Saints
(31 October) 1972

Dear Arnold,

I realized, on seeing you in London, that I had hurt you a little by "taunting" you with being a Marcionist. It was only foolishness. And you could have retorted that I believed in an even older, a Mosaic cosmology! In fact of course your objection to the O.T. is a very real and unanswerable one: it is brutal and crude and it gives an inadequate answer to the problem of evil, which seems even more monstrous today than it ever did. We try to answer your first objection by saying that the revelation of God is refracted in very opaque glass, and your second by admitting—I wish we would more regularly—that evil is a mystery.

I shall always treasure this volume as your last expression of your great themes in the *Study of History*. You have always clung to your vision and mission to seek the truth. This is the message; and everyone who reads your book will learn it—or should—and set off on their pilgrimage in their turn.

It is good to read over again the chapter on the Papacy, especially as we are approaching the moment in ecumenical discussion when the place of the Papacy must be faced by us all. Your fearless criticism and compassionate appreciation should be part of the healing process. History cannot be reversed; but history-known may for once be able to restore an essential element in our world. We need a centre of unity, a beacon. The Papacy is that natural focus.

My love to you both,
Columba, O.S.B.

I hope you liked my cousin Roderick Chisholm.[1]
P.S. We have Prof. Steiner[2] here. He gave a talk to the boys contrasting Miriam's song[3] and dancing triumphantly over the drowned Egyptian army, and Odysseus' restraint of his old nurse in her gloating over the suitors' death.[4] He claims this last is the first time ever.

1. Roderick Aeneas Chisholm (1911–); air commodore; D.F.C. (Distinguished Flying Cross) and D.S.O. (Companion of the Distinguished Service Order) (the originator of night aerial fighting in the early days of World War II); Ampleforth; Imperial College of Science and Technology; Royal Air Force (1940–46); *Cover of Darkness* (London, 1953); his mother, Edyth, the sister of C.C.E.'s father.

2. George Steiner (1929–); then extraordinary fellow, Churchill College, Cambridge; *Tolstoy or Dostoevsky: An Essay in the Old Criticism* (New York, 1959); *The Death of Tragedy* (London, 1961).

3. Miriam, sister of Aaron (Exod. 15:20–21).

4. *Odyssey*, 22.410–18.

Ampleforth Abbey
All Souls Day, (2 November) 1972 York

My dear Arnold,

I have now read 'The Challenge of Disintegration'[1] and I simply thank God. This is the most wonderful chapter you have written; not only do you distil the message of the Christian God as perfectly as I know, but you link it in a constructive, unifying way to all that is best in the Far East. I shall read it many times. I so agree about Jesus' way of revealing the Passion, about the need for pity, compassion in Buddhism, found in the Mahayana, that the Ultimate is Love—This chapter brings all the great work of the *Study*, all the Non-sense, to 'Divine Sense.'

Many pages of the book I have not yet read, but I can't believe any will reach the summit or depth of understanding of these. Let us praise the God of love together who has opened up his secret to you and to me partly through you.

Love and gratitude,
Columba, O.S.B.

Feel no obligation to answer.

1. The one-volume illustrated *Study of History*, pp. 249–54.

Royal Institute
of International Affairs
Chatham House
10, St James's Square
London S.W.1

6 November 1972

Dear Columba,

I was just trying to answer your first letter when the second one came. I am so very glad that you feel as you do about my piece on 'The Challenge of Disintegration'—particularly, that you find that I have seen a harmony between the Christian and the Buddhist approach.

This has given me very great pleasure and happiness.

Yours affectionately,
Arnold

TEN

1973–75

C.C.E. in Cameroon and Nigeria; the cottage at Ganthorpe; Philip's communal farm; animadversions on Adam Smith; Rosalind and Richard Stafford; "we shall vote Liberal"; A.J.T. returns to Winchester; his ad portas *oration; the final stroke; A.J.T.'s last words to C.C.E.*

Ampleforth Abbey
York

19 January 1973

My dear Arnold,

Back once more to our island home. I must say I enjoyed the visit to St. Louis very much. I suppose it was partly because every one was so pleased to see me and clamoring for me to stay. The situation seemed, in general, less disturbed than two years ago, I mean both in the Church and politically. All this talk about the young throwing overboard the structured church was not mirrored in the huge crowds of young people at Mass at the Priory and neighboring churches. Politically they are all a bit stunned, voting for Nixon whom they dislike, but being even more frightened of McGovern. It is amazing how a war can be carried on with, one suspects, the majority of the population against it.

I hope you have a chance to read a most perceptive and I think just account of your "wider ecumenicism" in that excellent publication, *The Journal of Ecumenical Studies*,[1] current number. He, the author, claims you were before your time and only now are we ready for your message.

How are you both? and how is the world history progressing?

The Pepers were as usual in excellent spirits—she is a brave person—and we had a meeting of the old group at their house one evening, and recalled the time you and Bp. Butler[2] both spoke of Vatican II—still I think in progress. They of course asked after you both.

When do you take up residence at Ganthorpe?

Love to you both,
Columba, O.S.B.

1. L. Stafford Betty, "The Radical Pluralism of Arnold Toynbee: Its Implications for Religion," *Journal of Ecumenical Studies*, vol. 9, no. 4 (Fall 1972): 819–40: "As for Toynbee's pluralistic

vision as a whole I believe that in many ways it is more significantly prophetic than any other ecumenicist I have read"; but Betty doubts that A.J.T. knows "how to pray." The reader of these letters may not share this doubt.

2. Compare C.C.E.'s letter of 14 June 1963, above.

95, Oakwood Court
London W.14

23 January 1973

Dear Columba,

I have had your letter of 19 Jan., and now I have read your letter in this morning's *Times*.[1] You have dispelled a bogey. Your setting-out of the facts is clear, and it should be very helpful.

I knew, of course, that you would get a splendid welcome at St. Louis. But you do not say whether, in the next stage, you are going to be there or at Ampleforth. In which place do you feel that you could be most useful? For selfish reasons I hope the answer is Ampleforth.

The plans for our cottage are now being drawn professionally, for running the gauntlet of the planning authorities.[2] There doesn't seem to be any reason why they should reject them, and the builders at Terrington are keen to do the job. Though the move will be a formidable operation—especially the books—the cottage will be a shelter from the storm: within a few yards of Lawrence and Jean, and we shall no longer be at the mercy of shark landlords and London traffic.

I haven't seen the article in '*Ecumenical Studies*.' I have just had a letter from a Japanese, discussing whether my 'spiritual presence behind the universe' is the same as the Buddhist conception of ultimate reality. I think it is.

We are both all right in health, but are finding the present-day world very detestable—above all, its greed, and the dishonesty and insincerity that are the further vices that greed breeds. We are *all* greedy, without distinction of class or race or party.

Under separate cover, I am sending you a rather posh 1973 diary that I have had from a Spanish publisher for whom I have done some jobs.

Love from us both,
Arnold

1. C.C.E.'s letter in *The Times* (23 January 1973) stated, "The Papacy and its claimed infallibility stand as one of the chief obstacles to union" with the Anglican church; only two popes had ever claimed to be infallible. "The Papacy is not a mechanism for infallible pronouncements. It is rather a rallying point for the Flock of Christ."

2. Lawrence had made available to A.J.T. a plot of ground in Ganthorpe within a few yards of the Hall, adjacent to the cottage that Rosalind had made into a Catholic chapel; Lawrence designed his father's cottage.

Ampleforth Abbey
York

16 April 1973

My dear Arnold,

I enclose a little Easter present, because I expect you have not seen this *Tablet* article, and it is so good, you should read it. Besides Fr. Bede [1] is someone who really should know.

I haven't heard from you for ages—nor you from me, either. I've been to Spain to give a retreat (in English) in Madrid.[2] It was ecumenical, as an Anglican and a Presbyterian minister also took part. It was arranged by an Old Amplefordian working out there (in Unilever), one who had tried his vocation here years ago.

A Mr. Todd of Longman, Darton & Todd has tentatively asked me to sketch out a book relating O.S.B. spirituality and modern trends and needs. I think the headings he has in mind are: prayer, commitment, conversion, poverty, community, especially the last. I am tempted to try, but my knowledge of the young is scrappy.

How is the History [3] getting on? How is your cottage getting on? How *are* you both.

A happy Easter and my enduring love to you both,

Columba, O.S.B.

1. Bede Griffiths, O.S.B.; cf. C.C.E.'s letter of 16 October 1958, above; the article, "Erroneous Beliefs and Unauthorized Rites" (*Tablet* [14 April 1973]) pointed out, inter alia, that the spiritual riches of Hinduism were such that a convert to Christianity was in danger of living at a lower spiritual level.

2. The retreat in Madrid was given partly in a Catholic hall, partly in the hall of St. George's Church (of the British Embassy).

3. The work published, posthumously, as *Mankind and Mother Earth*.

95, Oakwood Court
London W.14

27 April 1973

Dear Columba,

I haven't answered your letter of 16 April, 1973, before because we were away, staying with Philip.

An ecumenical meeting in Spain would, I suppose, have been inconceivable only a few years ago. Things are moving, in this field, in a good direction.

Father Bede's article is splendid,[1] both for its point of view and for the clarity and exactness with which he makes his points. I agree one hundred per cent.

I do hope you will accept the invitation to do that book for Longman, Darton, and Todd. It is very relevant to mankind's present plight. It is true that the young change while you watch them, like chameleons. I daresay young monks change to some extent. The Order of Saint Benedict has often, hasn't it, taken stock of the World's changing needs, and has exerted itself to meet them. The Cluniacs were not satisfied with the unreformed houses, and, after two centuries, the Cistercians were not satisfied with the Cluniacs. At each stage the Order did give something new and pertinent to a changing world.

I have now got to 1420 in pre-Columbian America and to 1099 in Western Christendom. I can write with some confidence about other civilizations—believing that I know the solid points—but, in dealing with Western Christendom, I am not sure of my ground—and still less sure from the seventeenth century on, when the Westerners dethroned religion (deservedly under a cloud at the time) and put science and technology in its place.

The plans for the cottage are now with the county authorities. No difficulties are expected. The builder in Terrington does good work, and is keen to undertake the job.

Though I have been born and brought up in London, I shall be relieved—to my own surprise—to get away from the traffic and from the shark landlord.

Is there any more news of your future posting? Africa? Missouri? Ampleforth? I hope you will be asked to go where you feel that you could do the most for other people, but, selfishly, I hope this will turn out to be Ampleforth as a base of operations for ecumenical work.

Going back to Father Bede's article, that interaction between the revelation of Christ and the non-Christian religions that he foresees is already noticeable in Japan for anyone who has a Christian background. The number of converts to Christianity in Japan is tiny (though some of them are in key posts) but what Christ stands for (as distinct from the mixed bag of good and evil that Christianity stands for) has influenced the Japanese very widely without their being aware of this. If events keep you at Ampleforth to your own spiritual satisfaction, this will be a great piece of good fortune for me.

Arnold

1. See C.C.E.'s letter of 16 April 1973.

Ampleforth Abbey
York

11 May 1973

My dear Arnold,

I was sure you would be happy with the Bede Griffiths article. It is splendid. It must have reached you near your birthday, which as always I forgot!

So the cottage is gradually taking shape. That is good. Whether I shall be here to welcome you is now a real question mark: Africa, U.S.A., everything seems to be possible. But my experience of the last few years seems to point to status quo, tho' not the portents. I'll keep you up to date. The Pepers were here yesterday. It was cold, but we were happy in the car chatting away and travelling to and from

Ripon/Fountains, lunching and "teasing". It is wonderful the way they courageously and joyously squeeze every ounce and minute of the few years left. I was delighted you had them to lunch at the Athenaeum, and they told me shortly of your joint-possible-plan for your books at Oakwood Court.[1] As you must know, I *find that lovely*; and if I am there, even more so; but at present it has a sombre flavour. We don't want to lose you.

The History is going to interest me more than I can say. Of course you can't see your way in the modern Western world, because it has lost its way; you can only follow us poor lost sheep over the mountains and down the ravine; each "doing his own thing" as they say today. The Watergate episode is symptomatic.

But there are some marvellous things and these in time will be the significant part of our history. But the good things make little noise at the time.

My love to you both,
Columba, O.S.B.

P.S. My sister Irene is better. She has had two heart attacks.

1. A project proposed by C.B.P. to create an Arnold J. Toynbee room in the Columba Cary-Elwes Library at the St. Louis Priory and, after A.J.T.'s death, to bring his private library to St. Louis. In the event, A.J.T. bequeathed his basic historical library in the Toynbee room at Chatham House to the Royal Institute of International Affairs, the rest of his books (mostly at Oakwood Court) to his trustees; the bulk of the books bequeathed to his trustees and to Chatham House were acquired by the University of York; C.B.P. arranged the acquisition by Harvard University of the manuscripts for books other than *A Study of History*; A.J.T. had sold the latter during his lifetime to Arthur Houghton.

Ampleforth Abbey
York

13 July 1973

My dear Arnold,

The African venture is *on*. The Abbot and Council more than acquiesce, they send me as our little contribution to the 3rd World. The monk in the Cameroons finally "surfaced" and gave me some idea of his plan. He and I assemble at Bamenda[1] in old British Cameroon to launch a tiny seminary for a new African bishop. Then at Easter we two monks and another—who will have come from Nairobi—will go into Iboland and arrange for a mini-monastery in or near Nsukka.[2]

I shall be leaving, I expect, early September, so hope to see you then; but will also be in London c. 30 July–3 Aug. and perhaps we could meet then, if you propose a series of dates and times to choose from. My two sisters are arriving from Malta c. 2–3 Aug. so when they arrive I shan't have much time.

Drop me a note to Haye Farm, Mappleborough Green Studley, Warwickshire, where I'll be most of next week.[3]

So we shall not meet at Ganthorpe till my return! and when will that be, one year's time? Three? or ten? Who knows? Ten would make me near 80, and you would be 93! But I will keep writing to let you know how I'm getting on; and you will have to do the same.

Love to you both,
Columba, O.S.B.

1. A market town; center of a highland cattle breeding area.
2. A small village on the northern edge of the Ibo country, which, shortly before the civil war, with help from American universities, became a leading university center in Nigeria; in 1973 it was slowly recovering from the war.
3. The home of Basil King, brother of Fr. Henry King, O.S.B., of Ampleforth.

95, Oakwood Court
London W.14

14 July 1973

Dear Columba,

I am *very* glad about your news. In Africa you will be able to spend all your powers—spiritual, intellectual, but be careful about too much physical—on doing a job that is valuable without any question, and this is the fulfilment of life. And I am much more glad that you are going to have this opportunity of fulfilling yourself (by expressing yourself) than I am sorry (I am, as you will realise, very sorry) that we shall not be having frequent meetings with each other in Yorkshire. If you were staying at Ampleforth, I do not see any present opening for you there of comparable value to the African enterprise.

30 July–3 August: my only engagements will be the mornings of Monday 30 and Thursday 2 at Chatham House, so come and see Veronica and me during that week for as much time as you can spare. I shall try to keep that week free. Also, we shall be here in early September, and may see you again then, if you fly from London.

You will certainly be coming back to England from time to time, but of course you may not find me alive. At present, there is no indication that I am going to die in the near future, but at 84 one may die any day. I have been used to the idea of that since 1916, when so many of my contemporaries were killed.

Meanwhile, we will write to each other anyway, and will meet if we have the chance, when you are on visit to England.

Work has begun on our cottage at Ganthorpe, and we hope to have made the move by the early summer of 1974.

Well, God bless you: you have both the experience and the enthusiasm for doing the African job, and that combination is the key to success.

Much love from us both, and we greatly look forward to seeing you here from 30 July to 30 August.

Arnold

The Royal Institute
of International Affairs
Chatham House
10, St James's Square
London S.W.1

18 September 1973

Dear Columba,

Veronica and I have been thinking about you a bit anxiously ever since the day you started. I expect the flight to Duala was good and relatively easy. I do hope the overland transport from there to Bamenda has worked out all right, and that the three of you are now assembled and are installed in your quarters in Bamenda. You must have a 'boy'. The Apostles found by experience that they needed to have deacons in order to be able to do their own work.

You will find West Africa partly familiar and partly very different from the Africa that you already know. But all Africa needs the kind of help that you have given in East Africa and will now be giving again.

I pray for your safe arrival, and I add a small prayer for your baggage that has gone by sea.

We are just off to Ganthorpe to see how the cottage is getting on. We shall miss not seeing you in Yorkshire.

With much affection
and concern,
Arnold

Final address till Jan. 1974
P.O. Box 56
Bamenda, Cameroon

2 October 1973

My dear Arnold,

Thank you for your most welcome letter. They take ages to get here, almost the end of the road, and a poor one. You are right about the diaconate. We shall have a boy in Enugu. Here we share the staff and "Mess" of the other professors, so no problem.

On Friday next our bishop[1] is off to Nigeria to the installation of an Ibo bishop. He is taking me with him, so I shall have a chance to see and hear for myself. But all say that the Ibos mean business and when they want something, they really want it.

We live comfortably in a beautiful climate so far—the tail end of the rainy season, lovely great mountains all round. In the mornings the other OSB and I go off in one of these wild taxis to Bamenda (9 m. away) and teach in a little-girls school to help pay for our enterprise and help the poor nuns out. This is exhausting.

There is some hope we shall get into Nigeria in January. But this all depends on my visa.

I feel we are marking too much time and energy here. The other Fr. Columba[2] has gone down with a touch of malaria. He is not strong. So we'll have to watch him.

The third member of the party will arrive from Nairobi in November.

I'm so glad you've been up to Ganthorpe. That means the cottage is progressing. Yes, I would love to be there to receive you.

Cameroon seems to have its "Ibo" tribe which likewise, in part, is somewhat volcanic. Even a Bishop got involved in gun running,[3] believe it or not, and is languishing in gaol, poor man. But all is peaceful. Of course, like most African countries the loyal opposition does not exist. Nyerere thinks opposition should only be *within* the party.

Love to you both,
Columba, O.S.B.

Excuse my sending this via Ampleforth. Postage is fearfully expensive.

1. Paul Verdzekov (1931–); bishop of Bamenda in 1970; Verdzekov means "born in the forest" as he was, in the course of a sudden persecution of Christians.

2. Columba Breen, O.S.B. (1917–); monk of Glenstal Abbey; now remaining at Ewu; a classical scholar trained in biblical studies.

3. "Albert Ndongmo (1926–); made bishop of Nkongsamba in North Cameroon in 1964; accused of joining plot to overthrow the one-party government; denied that he had planned violence; imprisoned for life; later released, and retired to Quebec. My term 'gun-running' was inaccurate." C.C.E.

P.O. Box 56
Bamenda, N.W. Cameroon

14 October 1973

My dear Arnold,

You must forgive my last scrappy note. Here at least is a full account of the long journey, and, I hope, a turning point in our progress. I'm sending it to Ampleforth, but thought you'd like a copy.

5th October till yesterday I spent travelling to Nigeria, and in it and back. Bp. Paul of Bamenda drove me and Bp. Pius[1] of Buea to Ogoja[2] in E. Nigeria for the installation of their friend Bp. Ukpo.[3] Bp. Paul only got his exit permit at 5. P.M. that day; so our journey to Mamfé[4] near the border was mostly in the dark. Right in the forest we got stuck in the mud. Trying to get the car out we were up to our calves in it. I only had one pair of trousers and one pair of shoes. Against all probability a taxi passed and stopped c. 7.30 and dug us out.

The installation was a gathering of 17 Nigerian Bps. and one Irish one who was handing over the diocese. Of course immense delight. Almost all the N. Bps. were under 40. We concelebrated.

At the luncheon (300) we ate jolif rice—which upset my tummy—and twelve spoke. Two regional governors present, not the Ibo one who had sided with the West and was anti-Christian. One of those present made a surprising speech: the State was above the Church; the Church's part in education was over. The State was grateful, but was now taking all over. The new Bp. followed. Very gently he said that the Gov. could not expect him to agree entirely and that the question of Church and State had been answered long ago.

Bp. Okoye of Enugu[5] was present and he told me to join him in a journey he had to make to Makurdi on the Benué river—and we could talk about the proposed foundation. I had no taste for more road travel, but it would give me a great opportunity for intimate discussion. Of course I accepted. He is a short plump Bp., jovial and dynamic, said to be a holy man. We sat in the back of the car and talked.

Yes, he was keen that we should come. When? I said as soon as we can be released from Bambui. He said the only real problem was visas. But he would get working from his end and we should from ours. If we had friends in Nigeria in the government it would make it easier. As missionaries it would be impossible, as teachers, it could be done. He hoped we would do a little teaching at the university, or major or minor seminaries. He would provide a house, or build one. It should be in the Nsukka Un. area.

He said we could either follow the missionary money system or the S.J. and O.S.B. one. The former received all from the diocese and put all in to the diocese. Every 6 months they would render an account to the diocese of all receipts and all expenditures. Any surplus was handed over to the diocese. So all expenses, travel, medicinal, cars, etc. were paid by the diocese. The S.J.s and O.S.B.s in the past had kept what moneys they received, had borrowed for building from Bp. and in time paid it back. He said we could choose. We are discussing it.

The Makurdi[6] diocese is run by English (Lancs. and N.E. almost to a man) Holy Ghost Fathers. It has been going c. 30 years. They have built 230 schools; they have a minor seminary c. 125 students. We said Mass there. The Bp. preached for 30 min. The church was built by the rector and the seminarians and two masons; no blue print; only a week to week advice of a neighbouring Italian architect. Its design is like St. Louis Priory and Warrington—more the latter.

At Nsukka University I met the senior chaplain. He has 900 to Mass on Sundays. He thought I could come and teach Mod. Lang. I said preferably social theory of Church; Church history etc. He said at the Dept. of General Studies I might find a niche. Ditto Fr. Columba Breen. After the war he came back to find his house absolutely empty, no notes, bedding etc. The roof of the church blown off.

The amazing thing about Iboland is that apart from a few destroyed bridges one would not know there had been a civil war.[7] Of course in the mind it is still there, and the Ibos don't get good jobs, nor places in the army—which is made up mostly of men from the North, i.e. Moslems. But the Ibos are getting on with making money, restoring their great market on the Niger. Children are like ants, thousands and thousands. Half the population, they say, of Nigeria is under 21.

The Catholicism of the Ibos is most remarkable. It seems to be in the blood. But they are not the only ones. The Tivs now—and they seem to be their mortal enemies—are taking to it too in the Makurdi diocese. The seminary (major), which I visited, is bursting. Beds in dormitories are only 2 feet apart; tiny rooms with bunks on top of each other; class rooms stacked tight with desks. 460 students there, for the Eastern states this year. Enugu had 70 entrants for this year's class. Only 20 could be fitted in.

Bishop Okoye sent a little truck to the frontier with me in it. There a Kiltegan priest drove me across the Cross River bridge. I found a taxi for Bamenda. At Mamfé a missionary almost dragged me from the taxi, said I had to spend the night with him. It was already 5 PM. Thank God I did. I reached Bamenda 6 PM next evening, thanking God I had made it. I've done some journeys but never quite so non-stop.

I've taken the liberty of using your name as one of three references for the university post. By the way they remember your visit.

You were very kind to write. It must be exciting to see the cottage progressing. God bless you both.

Love,
Columba, O.S.B.

1. Pius Suh Awa (1930–); bishop in 1971; See of Buea on Mt. Cameroon in 1973.
2. Diocese of eastern Nigeria near the Cameroon border.
3. Joseph Ukpo (1937–); bishop in 1971; of Ogoja in 1973.
4. An old town on the way from the Nigerian frontiers into the mountains and the old provincial capital, Bamenda; site of a Catholic school and mission.
5. Joseph Okoye (1913–77); bishop of the second port of Nigeria, Port Harcourt, 1961; translated in 1970 to Enugu in East-Central Nigeria.
6. A large town astride the Benué River, which flows from the mountains into the Niger.
7. On 30 May 1967, the Republic of Biafra, of which Enugu was the capital, seceded from the Nigerian Federation; the civil war that followed was ended by the victory of the federal government in January 1970; this was a victory of the Moslem north over the largely Christian and more prosperous Ibos of the south and east.

P.O. Box 56
Bamenda, N.W. Cameroon

6 November 1973

My dear Arnold,

Today I am 70. I find it difficult to believe; but I'm grateful to God to allow me more time to help people, as well as to prepare for the next world. But I wonder whether I get any "better." We just have to trust in the loving mercy of God.

Here we are in a kind of suspended animation, waiting and hoping for visas. My guess is that we may succeed in crossing the border c. Feb. or March—everything is very slow.

We gather that we will be eligible to teach at the university—not yet decided—and preferably in General Studies (1st year courses) because then we have an audience of up to 200 students. I don't know what to choose (1) monastic/medieval history? (2) Ecumenism? (3) intro. to comparative religion? (4) Christian political philosophy. I'm inclined to (4) (2) (1) in that order as most likely to attract interest. What do you think? Any ideas?

N. W. Cameroon is a little out on a limb, tucked away in the mountains; happy enough, but dead politically. Apparently they tried a democratic local federal government, but it became so corrupt that quite willingly they handed themselves over to the central French government at Yaoundé.[1] But that is dictatorial. However, intelligent people say that the W. form of democracy simply doesn't work in an uneducated [unsophisticated] African setting. The one thing these same people regret is that Yaoundé does not rule through the chiefs as the British did. They are the only authority the people can stand. The old tribal structure is dying of inertia.

I gave a week's retreat 30 miles from here to a ¾ African Community of Cistercian monks, the monastery poised in a typically monastic setting, superb mountain scenes—more Benedictine than Cistercian—many of the monks are Ibos. One young Ibo told me that when he was a youth in his Biafran village, they all went naked, yes, and the girls. And this was the very opposite of a problem. No girl was ever pregnant. This was not done. After puberty they [the girls] were given a single girdle; before marriage, a dress!

So much for our pruderies. Very odd. But the conversations were mostly about Africans and the monastic life, and an Ibo foundation. There was unanimous approval of the latter. I was reminded that the Ibos have no words of politeness, please, thank you. It is gestures that show the feeling. So, if an Ibo says "no" bluntly to a command, he is just as likely to go off and do it as not!

How are you both. *Not* I hope wearing yourselves out packing. You will have to have some young arms and heads to organize that.

Much love and
union of prayers,
Columba, O.S.B.

I'm longing for news—how is the house shaping, and the book History of the World—what is the next on the stocks?

1. The capital of Cameroon; formerly capital of French Cameroun; a business center; site of a Catholic seminary; Mont Fébé Monastery overlooks the city from a hilltop.

P.O. Box 56
Bamenda, N.W. Cameroon
W. Africa

10 November 1973

My dear Arnold and Veronica,

A very happy Christmas indeed. And I suspect at Ganthorpe, so I am addressing the letter there. My love and best wishes to Lawrence and Jean, too. Of course, you may not have risked going up as it may be cold there. But they should have wood and living an 18th century existence, perhaps meeting you at York with a horse and trap—after all they are "Carriage folk", an old snobbery perhaps come back to life.

By the time you get this, the three "monk-ateers" will be in Yaoundé, staying at the Swiss (Franco-phone) monastery of Mont Fébé for Christmas and in between times trying to persuade the Nigerian Embassy to forward our petition for resident visas in their country. This is the crunch!

We've just read a wonderful and striking passage from Jeremiah's *Book of Consolation*—during Evening Prayer, that we sing and say with the seminarians—

ch. 30 v 21—God is speaking thro' Jeremiah about "The one who is to come", "Who else indeed would risk his life by coming near to Me?" It struck me that Jesus by keeping near the Father lost his life; and the saints, they're prepared to lose their lives. And I? We must be brave and follow the Truth, regardless, because the Truth *is* the ineffable God. This is my prayer for you both and for myself.

And I hope the Western world may be enlightened by its predicament. One is afraid it will only encourage them to find ways and means at any cost to restore their supremacy. On the other hand, I find the Arab technique unacceptable. They are basically in the right, as it seems to me, over Palestine. But does this justify crushing the whole western economy? I could not help remembering Vitoria's (the 16th century O.P.) one and only argument which he thought valid for the Spanish intrusion into America, namely that the resources of the world should be for all the world, all peoples. And this would justify Western intrusion into Libya and the Gulf States. *But*, the same principle should force the West to share the lion's share it has of the world's goods with the third world.

It is interesting, the seminarians are all on the Arab side, partly because of African solidarity, partly they are against Jewish aggression, partly they enjoy seeing the West not having it all its own way. They don't see the moral and don't become Western-like. This still dazzles them.

This little world is a triple culture all muddled up; native pagan, Muslim (little) and Christian, e.g. they still have an eight day week.

Thank you for your last letter, about the crisis.[1] I'm so glad Thompson[2] is coming up to promise.

My love to you both and prayers, especially at Christmas and New Year.

Columba, O.S.B.

1. Missing.
2. The local Ampleforth village builder.

16 November 1973 — 95, Oakwood Court, W.14

Dear Columba,

I have been so glad to have your letters of 2 and 14 October and 11 [*sic*] November. I have been remiss in not answering before—especially when I have been conscious that you are having a trying time, waiting in uncertainty—though, fortunately, in a good climate.

I have been taken up with writing articles and giving interviews. Nowadays, enough happens in a single hour to fill a whole lifetime: the war, the precarious cease-fire, the oil-embargo, Nixon, the multiple economic and financial trials everywhere.

I think the so-called 'undeveloped' countries are going to fare best. They are still based on agriculture and animal-husbandry, and these ways of human economic life are probably the best balance between mankind and non-human nature. In the

Industrial Revolution, the 'advanced' countries upset the balance; we are now going to have partially to de-mechanise our life, and this will be difficult and painful. For instance, there will be a shrinkage of manufacture and use of motor-cars. Railways, and perhaps even horses, will re-appear.

At Ganthorpe the roof is almost on to the cottage, and then they will be able to finish the work in all weathers. Joe Thompson of Ampleforth, who is building it, is first-rate. We have also got an assignee for the lease of 95 Oakwood Court—subject to his references being all right; we haven't yet heard about that. We expect to make the move in March; I hope the storm will not yet have broken in full force. It is going to be a real blizzard.

Of your options for teaching-subjects, I would agree with you in putting first Christian political philosophy and second Ecumenism. I think monastic medieval history would be a bit exotic for Africans—unless you concentrated on Monophysite monasticism in Ethiopia (this was, and still is, very austere). Comparative religion might become undesirably controversial.

I have just had a letter from Christopher Dawson's daughter Christina. She is writing a life of her father, and wants to see me about this—which I shall do with pleasure, for I liked and admired C.D. a lot.[1]

Well, I do hope this difficult time of waiting will soon be over. I am sure that, when you get into Ibo-land, you will have more than enough of worth-while things to do.

Much love from
Veronica and me.
Arnold

I hope you will be able to decipher this letter.

1. Compare *A Study of History*, IX: 12, 21, 30–31, and passim (where A.J.T. cites Dawson's *Religion and the Rise of Western Culture* [London, 1950]), and XII: 16, 74, 78, 83, 95, 100, and passim (where A.J.T. cites his *The Dynamics of World History* [London, 1957]).

95, Oakwood Court
London W.14

23 December 1973

Dear Columba,

This Sunday morning there was a Christmas-time post (and an opening of the butcher's shop for me to go and buy a chicken). Your aerogram of 10 November (!) was in the batch of letters—a welcome surprise.

I am sure the Francophone Swiss monastery will give the three Anglophone monks a happy Christmas. Francophone Swiss Catholics? From Canton Fribourg? From the Valois?

I am sorry, but not surprised, that the Nigerian Embassy is stalling over the visas. Xenophobia (anyway towards Whites), bureaucracy, a hang-over of war-time suspicions and controls: a powerful combination of road-blocks. Yet, *inside* Nigeria, the wounds of the civil war seem to be healing. In last week's T.L.S. there was a review of two books, published in Nigeria in English, by Nigerian authors who, in the civil war, were on opposite sides.

We haven't gone to Ganthorpe for Christmas. It will be full of grandchildren + the great-granddaughter, and we are reserving ourselves for a visit in January to see how Joe Thompson the Ampleforth builder is getting on with the cottage.

We are in deep trouble with Philip, who has broken off relations with both Lawrence and me because we are not giving him £50,000 for starting a communal farm.[1] Of course I couldn't begin to raise capital for him. Veronica's and my main source of livelihood is income from annual installments of accumulated royalties, which pay tax as the installments are released to me by the publishers. Unhappily, Philip has a burning sense of injustice from Rosalind's indeed most unjustly unequal division of her estate[2] between Lawrence (not L's fault), Philip, and 'Richard Stafford' who turns out to have been not only R's farming-partner but her lover (in the sexual meaning). This trouble is difficult to mend.

Yes, Jesus lost his life for doing what his father had appeared to have told him to do. It was not part of the plan that his life should be saved. In the agony in the garden, he overcame the temptation to 'go on the run' like the present-day Palestinian guerrillas or Provisional I R A gunmen. This was the conventional course for anyone who had allowed himself to be acclaimed as the Messiah, and the Sadducees had a good case for judging that it was expedient that one man should die for the people. Jesus does not seem to have dissented from this.

The oil-embargo: the Arabs are using oil as a military weapon (like the British Navy in the two world wars and like the United Nations against Rhodesia now). But the inventor of OPEC is the Shah of Iran, and the Shah learnt from John D. Rockefeller I and from the British trades unions the trick of forming a ring to cover an indispensable commodity and then raise the price. Probably this will wreck Japan, Europe, and the U.S.; but it was Adam Smith who whitewashed self-seeking by arguing that this was socially beneficial. This thesis is manifestly untrue, but we have all swallowed it because it makes self-seeking seem respectable. Consequently, the edifice built on greed since the Industrial Revolution is going to collapse. Francesco, not Pietro, Bernardone has the last word, after all. Philip is, in part of himself, an idealist who wants to found a fraternity dedicated to Poverty, but, in another part, he is a Howard who expects capital to be provided by other people. In fact, like his grandmother Lady Mary,[3] he is an aristocrat. Veronica and I, being matter-of-fact middle-class people, are trying to meet the crisis by reducing our material standard of living.

Christmas wishes to you and your two fellow adventurers. May Christmas bring the visas.

With love from
Veronica and me,
Arnold

1. Philip describes the latter days of his communal farm in *Part of a Journey* (London, 1981); he refers to his "greedy anxiety" when the project was being liquidated; "it is alarmingly like my father's almost pathological obsession with money" (p. 219); Jessica Mitford describes Philip's *Barn House Community* in *Faces of Philip* (London, 1984), pp. 124–44.

2. Compare A.J.T.'s letter of 4 August 1970, above.

3. Lady Mary Murray, Rosalind's mother; cf. A.J.T.'s letter of Saturday, March 1910, above; "the social distinction between my parents was something of which both were keenly, though seldom openly aware" (Philip, in *Part of a Journey*, p. 89).

P.O. Box 56
N.W. Cameroon
W. Africa

12 January 1974

My dear Arnold,

A happy New Year, in spite of all the turmoil, family and otherwise. Do what you think is right and be at peace, even though there is bound to be anguish as well. God will look after Philip too.

I felt in your last letter great pain, not only over the Philip situation, but also over Rosalind. I can understand your feeling. But, these situations are so complex, I'm sure you do not judge, but wait one day, as I am sure (you're not quite) when we will understand and be re-united in all that is best.

About the money, it surely is good to help the poor who have nothing; and there are plenty of those, but to help somebody to become poor; I don't quite see it. I'm reminded of S. Francis of Sales who somewhere wrote how strange that one had to produce a fat "dot" in order that a girl could make a vow of poverty: all a bit topsy turvy. No, I feel Philip had far better get on with working as best he can. If he wants to burn his boats, let them be his boats. But of course there is danger that he might get into a financial morass and then hope you will pull him out. So firmly, I would make it plain that this would be impossible.

Yes, I know that will of R's was lopsided, but you, if I remember, are trying to rectify that by yours. Of course, that does not help P. now; and your first concern must be Veronica. Be sure of my prayers, I hope more useful than the above.

The African Chronology[1] by Freeman-Grenville, an old friend, has been sent me to review (!) by the O.U.P. at his request—very kind of him. Of course, it has not yet reached me. But I am reminded that he and his Lady wife live at Sheriff Hutton and would very much like to contact you when you reach "haven".

Your writing has reached such minuscule proportions that I can scarcely read. Please enlarge, for *your* eye-sight's sake and mine. The date of my last letter "11", should, I think, have been "12". It took me several days to get around to changing. Apologies. So probably my letter started from here 10th Dec.

The world situation is very strange, almost unreal for me, perched up in these remote mountains, with the Fulani[2] passing thru' as they have always done going south, burning the mountain-side grass behind them, so that these are all aglow at night, and the simple people, women and children carrying loads of bananas etc. on their heads to market, or large pails of water from the streams and wells. No trains, no aeroplanes, but yes TAXIS on the dust covered roads. These are gentle people. Not so the traders—mostly Ibos in the maze of a market in Mankon (Bamenda); there Piedro B. is still alive, and in the East the Western powers struggle to control the economy with France an easy winner. We need not a world government, but world controls, if only those in power were not even more selfish than the rest. Then oil and wheat and all should rightly belong to all. I don't believe the Sheiks have any more right to the world's oil than the British had to world trade.

But how can this be brought about. I'm not for "a back to the land" movement, as tho' machinery were in itself wrong. It would be a modern version of Stoicism, emotions are wrong—no, only wrongly used. Poor Francis, he began with himself and this is the only way. But how many really followed? This is our fate, to be forever beginning again.

My special love to
you both and prayers,
Columba, O.S.B.

1. G. S. P. Freeman-Grenville, F.S.A., F.R.A.S. (1918–); overseas civil servant (1951–64); professor of history, State University of New York (1969–74); *Chronology of African History* (Oxford, 1973); *Chronology of World History* (London, 1975).

2. A widespread tribe of Muslim herdsmen who travel north and south with their cattle; cf. A.J.T.'s *Between Niger and Nile*, pp. 12–13.

95, Oakwood Court
London W.14

20 January 1974

Dear Columba,

I was so glad to have your letter of 12 January. David Goodall had very kindly sent me a photostat of your letter of 23 December. I will try to write bigger. At school I used to annotate the margins of Greek and Latin texts with a triple-H pencil, and I seem to be reverting to this minute script. When I come across bits of my handwriting written 20 or 30 years ago, I am abashed at the deterioration.

Yes, I have been, and still am, in distress—wanting to help Philip within reason—that is to say, without endangering the provision that I have made for Veronica after my death, which is, as you say, my first concern; fearing that, instead of helping Philip to get over his justified sense of grievance, I may find myself in a permanent quarrel with him through my refusing to meet all his demands; above all, finding myself resentful and disillusioned towards Rosalind. I remember I once said to you that I had treated her like a goddess, and you said, very sensibly, that this had been very bad for her. She did spellbind me, and Philip and Lawrence too. The reaction is proportionate, but one ought not to feel resentment towards the poor dead, since they can do nothing more in this world to put right what they have done wrong—whereas the living can still repent and reform.

I am so sorry you are still stuck at the frontier. The successor-states of European colonial empire have gone in for red tape in a big way, and no doubt this has been aggravated in Nigeria by a legacy of suspicion from the civil war.

I should like to see the Fulani on trek. I have seen treks of nomads in Turkey and Afganistan. This is a relic of a simpler and more straightforward world that is now being snuffed out. The more sophisticated part of the world is wrecking itself by the pursuit of *sacro egoismo*. Adam Smith[1] has a lot to answer for. He was a respectable man, and he made selfishness look respectable, and everyone was delighted to be taught this agreeable but false and fatal doctrine. I am afraid we are going to go on like this till we are pulled up short by a disaster. It will need a big disaster to teach us our lesson.

My handwriting has been dwindling again. But I will write in large letters—love to you from Veronica and me.

Arnold

1. Adam Smith (1723–90); increasingly regarded by A.J.T. as the eighteenth-century compeer of Pietro Bernardone; cf. A.J.T.'s letter of 23 December 1973, above.

P.O. Box 56
Bamenda, N.W. Cameroon,
W. Africa

12 February 1974

My dear Arnold,

Thank you for a very recent letter. You are having your fill of troubles. I can, like you, see Philip's point: he has to wait for his 'inheritance' through the unevenness of Rosalind's will, so late that it does not help him in his crisis. Your point still remains valid that your first care is Veronica, and he is not disabled (is he) and can really fend for himself. I am sure you will do what you can. But upsets are not always one's fault, and you'll have to bear it in peace.

I scarcely venture into Rosalind's last phase, as I know nothing except what you have written. I do wonder whether she was having pity on this—at one point—psychologically broken priest; and felt that she was free to marry him. I'm not saying she was right, but I can imagine a situation where *she* could *feel justified*. Amen.

We are being inflicted with a drift of sand in the air from the Sahara. We can't see the surrounding mountains; it all drops not as gentle dew from heaven but as fine dust on everything. When the wind changes, the rains will start.

Meanwhile we have heard from the Bp. of Enugu, and for the first time he sounded positively hopeful. His secretary is pressing for a decision at Lagos, and he thinks he has the right grounds for our entry—specialized teachers for his seminary. There's many a slip. However, we are praying. If it comes off we'll send an advance party after Easter.

I've just been giving another retreat at Mbengui—the monastery—to sisters from Nigeria. The monks are worried: the oil for lighting, grinding nuts, working the carpenters' shop, for the truck taking cattle, has gone up 100%, so has cement. I find that the average rise is 75% on almost everything. Unemployment is already bad in Cameroon; the country people will survive and be happy; the towns will be hit. Yes, Adam Smith didn't see where his shiny principle would lead. Isn't it true that he was using self-help against government interference with trade. Others later applied it to government interference between employers and workers at a time when the former had the whip hand. I can see this being quite central in your history of the last chapter. But when did acquisitiveness become a passion? Was it the Fuggers?[1] Was it when the currencies collapsed with excess gold in the 16 century? Was it the great Trading Companies of the Baltic?[2] St. Francis saw it as a threat in city life, with many uprooted people who had lost their traditional way of life. This precise thing is happening in the Third World. Hordes are going to the towns, in spite of warnings. In the villages they are supported by custom and or by Christian missionaries. In the cities they have little work, and the rich become completely materialistic. We need thousands of St. Francises.

You must be soon making your way north. God speed. May I suggest you find a copy of K. Rahner's *Theological Dictionary* (English or German).[3] It is more like "Pensées" and has some wonderfully penetrating and consoling ideas.

My love to you
both and prayers,
Columba, O.S.B.

1. The Fugger family of Augsburg, bankers of the Habsburgs; fl. early sixteenth century.
2. The Hanseatic League; fl. thirteenth to fourteenth centuries.
3. Karl Rahner, S.J., and Herbert Vongrimler, *A Theological Dictionary*, ed. Cornelius Ernst, trans. Richard Strachan (New York, 1965); cf. C.C.E.'s letter of 17 December 1963, above.

95, Oakwood Court
London W.14

22 February 1974

Dear Columba,

I was so glad to have your letter of 12 Feb. 1974, with the more hopeful prospect of your being allowed entry. It is hard to be kept waiting all this time when you have valuable work to do, and you really can't be politically suspect. Recently liberated countries are tempted to assert their power, and I suppose the civil war still makes the Nigerian Government particularly obstructive. I do hope you will get your visas at last.

Jean told me about R's sexual relations with 'Richard' when I asked her the direct question. R. had told Lawrence under pledge of secrecy, and, after R's death, Richard, when drunk, blurted it out to Philip, which gave Philip a great shock. What shocked me was that R. continued, to the last, to be implacable about her sister Agnes's[1] and her granddaughter Celia's[2] having had sexual relations outside marriage. As Philip puts it, R. had a capacity for believing *bona fide* that she herself was always a special case, and that what she chose to do was 'holy'.

I do think that she did this out of charity. I guess that Richard has strong sexual passions, and that he did find it difficult to live on intimate terms with R. without having sexual relations with her. Apparently he had no inhibitions about this, but did have them about marrying, because he had been (? still is) a monk.[3] This seems irrational and tortuous, but most of us have some queer kinks in our character.

R.'s implacability towards Agnes and Celia is what distresses me. I have no personal feelings. I divorced her, and thereby left her free.

Unhappily, Philip has broken with Lawrence over the unequal division of the inheritance. Philip, like the N. Irish Catholics and the Palestinians, has a genuine great grievance, but to be obsessed by wrongs suffered by oneself is unprofitable and unhappy. Veronica has done her best, via Philip's wife Sally, to make peace between the two families. V. and I are determined to remain on good terms with both.[4]

Yes, the sophisticated top layer in the economically backward countries is going to suffer most from the increase in the price of oil. As you say, the people who are still living the agricultural and pastoral life are less exposed—except, of course, to the ravages of Nature. That Sahara sand that is being blown into the Cameroons means drought and death for people and cattle farther north.

Things here are depressing. In this crisis, the British people are coming out badly by comparison with their performance in 1914 and 1940. Everyone agrees that things are as serious now as they were then, but they also agree, pessimistically, to refuse to suspend their irrelevant and unedifying quarrels. Every individual, private organization, and state is now pursuing its short-term selfish interests at the expense of mankind's future—and of the sinner's own, too, on a longer-term view. 'The nation's necessity is the merchant's opportunity' is the slogan on which we are all acting. So I fear there is likely to be a world-wide catastrophe. We shall vote Liberal at the election, in the hope that the Liberals may have a counting vote in the new parliament.

The myth of automatic progress, meaning growth of material wealth, is being exploded; the traditional view that Man is sinful is being confirmed. What happens next?

Well, I do hope your next letter will be from the other side of the frontier.

Love from us both,
Arnold

1. Lawrence recalls that his mother had been troubled because Agnes had been living in the South of France with a man without benefit of clergy. Gilbert Murray wrote to A.J.T., "She [Agnes] had amid all her escapades and naughtiness a wonderfully loving and generous nature and she lit up our lives for us" (Francis West, *Gilbert Murray: A Life* [London, 1984], pp. 165–66).

2. Compare A.J.T.'s letter of 30 October 1970, above.

3. Richard Stafford was not a monk; he was a friar preacher, a Dominican, O.P.; cf. A.J.T.'s letter of 24 October 1958, above; he had not been dispensed from his vows but was not in a state of contention with his brethren, who paid visits to Low Holm.

4. Compare A.J.T.'s letter of 4 August 1970, above.

P.O. Box 56
Bamenda, N.W. Cameroon
W. Africa
As from the seminary

7 April 1974

My dear Arnold and Veronica,

Welcome to Ampleforth Country and Ganthorpe. I hear you arrived on March 25th, the day the world had a new beginning—the Annunciation—and I would love to have been part of the 'reception committee'. Now it will be easier for you both to live peacefully, meditatively, as the world always has till our Western daemon took hold.

Myself, I'm a bit like a cork on a bumpy sea; as 4 days ago I came to the rescue of this Benedictine Convent and associated parish or mission in E. Cameroon, at Bamete.[1] It is one of the oldest missions, but at the time of "the troubles" most of the population went 3 m. away to *Mbouda*[2] where the military were. In fact this is the heart of Bamiléké[3] country, and like the Ibos, the market is the thing: they have one every 4 days in Mbouda (eight day week in these parts!). The people are profoundly religious, belief in the One God, but pretty materialistic too. So they are slow to move. For instance, you might get a regular attendance at Sunday mass of 800, but only 130 or so are baptized.

The nuns are Swiss Benedictines; they've been in E. Cameroon since the late '40s, but for a group of reasons have failed to attract local girls—2 so far! I suspect they are far too European; and the Bamiléké can't see the point of the contemplative life. I'm living in the chaplain's house, and the pidgeons live and move in the roof.

The rainy season has begun, so let's hope the famine up north is for the time over. But it has been going on for years now, the drought, so that I'm told Lake Chad is simply wet mud, with the fish dead. The old Bishop, now retired, a Dutchman, told me the other day that U.S.A. offered $300,000,000 for relief; but when the oil scare came, there was no further mention. He also said that that money should be used not for shipping food from across the Atlantic but for increasing the yield here, 200 m. south, with its massive rains and good soil.

I'm glad you voted as you did. I think I would have done, as the Conservatives seemed to have become unusually ideologues. But the problems are deeper than mere politics or economics. I'm not impressed by the way some activists are attempting to swing so many Catholic religious movements into political pressure groups. I'm sure that this economic world of ours needs to change radically, but this will only happen when men's hearts—ours—have changed. It seems to me that if this world is the be all and end all, materialism will flourish, and with it selfishness, and, for the unlucky ones, want. A totally otherworldly attitude is equally harmful. It is the twin love, of God and neighbour, Christ's special message, that could bring a world of peace. I'm inclined to agree with you and your old friend Lionel Curtis that some one, on that Christian Oasis, should work out a politico-economic structure to maintain it.

The Middle Ages, for all their brutalities, did have embryonic structures, e.g. the Guilds, which were in the right direction. So have we, but these great industries are more powerful than Countries.

Holy Week is beginning two days from now, and I must get off my hobby horse and return to the *unum necessarium*. I wish you all at Ganthorpe a happy Eastertide—a time of Hope, Renewal, and Resurrection—not endless succession but an infinite Present.

Love to you both,
Columba, O.S.B.

P.S. Have you F. Grenville's *African Chronology*. One for me is still on the high seas. A very happy birthday. Special greetings to Lawrence and Jean and their chaplain,[4] whose name I've forgotten.

1. St. Benedict's Convent (Benedictine nuns); founded from Sarnen, Switzerland; transferred from South Cameroon to Bamete in 1968.
2. A large market town in Cameroon.
3. The Bamilékés are the largest of the tribal groups; more than 600,000 strong; speaking similar (Bantu) languages and sharing common customs, they inhabit the high grass lands; many are Christian.
4. Douglas H. N. Carter (1905–); Winchester; Oriel College, Oxford; a retired priest living at Ganthorpe Hall; a convert to the Catholic Church after Oxford; taught at Ampleforth; served on the commission for the beatification of John Henry, Cardinal Newman; translator of vol. 3 of Grandmaison's *Jesus Christ: His Person, His Message, His Credentials* (London, 1934); portions of the Jerusalem Bible; he was Lawrence's parish priest at Oxford; and they went to Rome together in 1950 and became close friends.

Chapel Cottage
Ganthorpe
Terrington, York

17 April 1974

Dear Columba,

Veronica and I were so glad to have your letter of 7 April, 1974. It must be irksome for you and your brethren to be still halted at Bamenda, but meanwhile, you are finding good things to do locally, so some Africans—though not yet your future flock—are benefiting already by your presence.

We have survived the move and have completed the assignment of our lease of 95 Oakwood Court. We are still with Lawrence and Jean, but the plaster in the cottage has now dried out, so we shall be able to move in in about ten days from now.

Yes, our troubles go deep, and also fairly far back. That well-meaning man Adam Smith made self-seeking look respectable by declaring (this is, of course, demonstrably untrue) that selfishness is socially beneficial. This was such an agreeable doctrine that everyone, from 'developers' to trades-unionists, has adopted it eagerly, as soon as each, in turn, has acquired the power to turn the screw on society.

Have you seen the original version of Solzhenitsyn's letter to the Soviet Government?[1] It is Byzantium, reprimanding the West. I haven't yet seen Sakharov's reply, putting the case for Western Liberalism.[2] I agree with many of Solzhenitsyn's points, but he is surely naïve in thinking that if autocratic government in Russia is de-westernized (meaning de-Marxised) it can be made benevolent.

Life is very sociable and genial here. Troops of young men and women spring up, over night, out of the earth and then vanish again, as suddenly. Jean is, of course, the presiding genius. Her daughters' rejects still come back to Ganthorpe to visit, not them, but Jean.[3]

We shall be in the cottage in about ten days from now. The plaster has at last dried out. It is lovely, and is roomier than we had expected.

Much love to you
from us both,
Arnold

1. Aleksandr I. Solzhenitsyn (1918–); *Pis'mo Vozhdi͡am Sovetskogo soi͡uza* (1974), trans. by Hilary Sternberg as *Letter to the Soviet Leaders* (New York, 1974).

2. For Sakharov's reply, see Donald R. Kelley, *The Solzhenitsyn-Sakharov Dialogue: Politics, Society and the Future* (Westport, Conn., 1982).

3. See A.J.T.'s praise of Jean in *Surviving the Future*, p. 129.

Chapel Cottage
Ganthorpe
Terrington, York
England

17 April 1974

Dear Ethel,

It was a great pleasure for Veronica and me to have your and Christian's letter of 10 April 1974. We have survived the move, and have had very happy birthdays. Veronica is now eighty, and I am eighty-five.

At the moment, we are in Lawrence and Jean's house, but the plaster in ours has now dried out and the paint is being laid on and a parquet floor being put down, so we expect to be installed in about ten days from now.

I am looking out of the window across Lawrence's garden at the cottage, watching the painters at work.

We have heard again, as I expect you have too, from Columba, still stuck at Bamenda, but finding some worthwhile things to do there.

Love from Veronica and me to you and Christian.

Arnold

P.O. Box 56
Bamenda, Cameroon

16 June 1974

My dear Arnold,

Below is a copy of a "last minute bulletin." You will see how erratic our course is. But I am more hopeful than ever before, except for the rather absurd course we were persuaded to take.

We shall see.

The picture changes every few days. We spent a long time trying to reach Nigeria as specialized teachers. This got through the central government at Lagos, but the minister of education at the local level of E. P. State [1] (Iboland) refused his permit. So about three weeks ago the Bishop with inexhaustible energy and imagination thought he saw a way through by the ministry of health and suggested we present ourselves at the Consulate in these parts as Social Workers. We were somewhat loath to do so unless encouraging young men to live a good life through following the Rule of S. Benedict might be said to be conferring a social benefit on the country. So we went to Buea and filled in a new form or rather an individual letter, which is what they then required. We came back and were awaiting events. Then suddenly we hear through missionaries passing over the frontier to here that suddenly the Nigerian government, taking fright at the lawlessness of the young since the restrictions on missionaries and Christian schools, has let in a flood of missionaries as such, a quota of 190 priests. So now we wait to find out whether we have missed the boat by taking on a disguise. Anyhow, we have decided to go over on temporary visas and take our impedimenta with us, books, etc. and find out. Everyone here says that now it should be easy for Bp. Okoye to get us in, and are very hopeful. Fr. C. Breen goes over on Monday, the advance guard; Fr. Tinsley [2] goes over in two weeks time. I accompany him with the luggage in a VW bus and the Rector [3] who has offered to drive to the frontier (5 A.M.–11 A.M.) there we shall be met by Fr. C. B. with a van and we will transfer all the packages at the Nigerian customs from the one to the other. Then Fr. Rector sets off back to Bambui (29th June). I will go on with F. Ambrose, pass through Enugu to hear what the latest news is, and go on to Ibadan [4] (300 miles) where I'm giving a retreat 20–27 July. I shall extend—if allowed—my tourist visa to the full three months and settle at Nsukka until we hear the results of all our efforts.

If the answer is negative, then we shall all make tracks for home. But we do not think this time it will be negative.

The address on receiving this is *PO Box 302 Enugu, Nigeria*, between 16th July–20th you would catch me at Ibadan during my stay there 20–27th, address there P.O. Box 1476 Ibadan Nigeria. The mail probably takes just under one week.

Many thanks for your most recent letter. Wilson seems to be doing better than expected, though at the last moment in Ireland we are faced with violence everywhere as an instrument of policy. But all is not dark. The Near East uneasy peace is an extraordinary achievement. Even there it was submission to force, or economic pressure.

I've just received Freeman-Grenville's chronology of African history—quite fascinating and astonishing industry. I'm not the one to know how accurate it is in detail—who is?—but as an overall picture a most useful piece of work. Since you've settled up N. have you seen him? Please salute him from me. And how do you feel in your cosy little home? I hope much rested. Let yourself enjoy a more contemplative life now; you deserve it.

Much love to you both,
Columba, O.S.B.

P.S. I hope you are inviting Alberic Stacpoole over. He would love it.

1. Eastern Provincial State.
2. Ambrose Tinsley, O.S.B. (1942–); monk of Glenstal Abbey.
3. Christian Wiyghan Tumi (1930–); bishop of Yagoua in 1980; founder and rector of the Major Seminary at Bambui.
4. The capital of the western state of Nigeria; site of a university.

Chapel Cottage
Ganthorpe
Terrington, York

27 June 1974

Dear Columba,

Your last-minute bulletin of 16.6.74 came this morning. You are having a frightful time—seeking nothing except to help your fellow human souls, yet being met with suspicion and obstruction. This is, I am afraid, characteristic of the state of all mankind today. Here, the ruthless self-seeking, the readiness to inflict suffering on unoffending other people, and the refusal to work together, are lamentable. The great majority still (amazingly) have no inkling of what is coming to us by next winter, at latest. A spiritual revival—the only remedy—seems as far off as ever.

I am sending this to Enugu, which I remember well. We are in the cottage; we slept here for the first time last Friday. We are utterly exhausted, but we shall gradually recover, and I think we are here for the rest of our lives. Whatever happens, we are unlikely to be evicted, and there is not much reason for billeting people on us.

Is Freeman-Grenville the Swahili scholar at Sheriff Hutton?[1] He has lent me a master's gown (Oxford) for being received '*ad portas*' at the College of St. Mary de Winton prope Winton the day after to-morrow. I shall be welcomed in Latin and shall reply in it—great fun and a rare honour. But I wish there had been a longer interval between this and the move, for I shall be intimidated by the Warden and the Head and Second Masters, though they are babes compared to me—inside gate, I shall feel like a junior school boy again.

My greetings and sympathy to your two fellow-intrepid adventurers. I do hope your move into Nigeria will result in your lasting establishment there.

Very much love and sympathy from Veronica and me.

Arnold

1. Yes; cf. C.C.E.'s letter of 12 January 1974, above.

P.O. Box 19
Nsukka

6 July 1974

My dear Arnold and Veronica,

Yours was the first letter any of us had since we arrived here, 30th June, and it was specially welcome.

The situation has changed very much for the better. We can stay here six months at least on tourist visas; but all say that will not be needed as the Govt. has suddenly relented and granted a new quota of 190 more missionaries, plus auxiliaries, such as we are, come to train local people. So we think it all may be settled in a month. Anyway, we have had two sessions with the local bishop. He is providing a house in the near future, and we shall have ample opportunity to get ourselves known in the University and elsewhere. Lectures? Probably occasional or a series, but no regular employment there. Age! and lack of university teaching experience are two counts against me. But we are free, and poorer—no bad thing.

I was guessing about St. Mary's—at first I thought it must be York, and then I realized your alma mater, Winchester, was honouring you. Tell me more when you next write. I'm glad it (W.) is dedicated to Mary; she will have had care of you, even tho' you may have rarely, if ever, thought that way. She was humble and wise and seeking always God's will.

So, at long last your pilgrimage too has reached a term. Nothing more exhausting than "moving house". I hope after your trip you keep very quiet for a month, basking in the simplicities of the English countryside.

Iboland[1]—the defeated side—struggling as only Ibos can to restore prosperity. The central Govt. does not help much. The bridges are still down and make-shifts up; the roads are shocking, at least to springs. The schools were all taken over from the missionaries; but the substitute teachers are very inadequate and very few. Even here at Nsukka, in the two schools within 100 yds. of here, play is the order of the day. Once I saw one master taking a class. Of course, no religion is taught, or only morality based on air, which will collapse under selfishness. The Catholic Church is incredibly strong, and the parents are organizing religious instruction, separate quite from the schools. In the Muslim north 600 Russians are coming in to help in the schools.

Italy and its economic collapse is a portent; but as you say, people close their eyes, so that they will not see.

Freeman-Grenville (also let him know I've arrived) was out in E. Africa in Colonial Service, did some exciting explorations (archeological) on the islands of that coast and found early medieval Arab trading posts, Chinese pottery, etc.; friend of Gervase Mathew;[2] his wife in House of Lords—both Catholic. Yes, he is/was Prof. of Swahili at York. You've seen, I suppose, his splendid *Chronology of African History*, O.U.P.

We came over the mtns. of Cameroon in a V.W. bus with 2 iron boxes, one trunk, my 9 cartons of books; the other two had 6 suitcases; I had 2; a large African seat and drum—presents. We got stuck in mud twice; we were hauled out by a lorry. One of us, already in Nigeria, just made it to the frontier with a pick-up; and we transferred all. The Lord was good to us.

Much love to you both and all at G.

Columba, O.S.B.

If you have the energy telephone Goodall at Ampleforth Village (see book) and say I've decamped.

1. Compare C.C.E.'s letter of 14 October 1973, above.
2. Compare A.J.T.'s letter of 14 July 1944, above.

Chapel Cottage
Ganthorpe

11 July 1974

Dear Columba,

Your aerogram had more good news in it than I had dared hope. It offset one from some American friends of ours, retired, who have actually been discussing with their sons the possibility of suicide as the only way out of a life that has become impossible for them (he senile, she crippled, both refused admittance into an old people's home, their house burnt down, nowhere to go; none to help them).

Veronica and I are very lucky. Yesterday Lawrence finished putting up our pictures; we now feel we have a home again.

Your account of Iboland is sad, but there will be work for you to do, and the Ibos are indomitable. They are worth helping.

The College of Saint Mary de Winton prope (i.e. outside the walls of) Winton was founded to feed the college *ad* (i.e. inside the walls of) *Oxon*. (New College). The founder meant his pair of colleges to give opportunities to peasants' sons for becoming parish priests. He disapproved of monks, so, at the foot of his alabaster effigy in the cathedral (I re-visited it), there are three little monks chortling over his death. The *θεοτόκος* was not popular with us, because, Saturday being her day, we had a (compulsory) extra service in her honour on Saturday afternoons—four centuries after the Reformation. We also sang hymns in Latin, because we had remained outside the jurisdiction of the Ordinary. For the rest of England, Latin had been forbidden in the Liturgy.

Above the gate at which I was received, there were three niches. In 1902 they were empty; by 1907 the middle one had been filled with a statue of our patroness that did not tone in with the 14th century architecture. Today, all three niches have in them weather-worn statues which, if fakes, are remarkably convincing ones. Perhaps they really are the original ones, banished at the Reformation and re-discovered. I didn't have time to ask about this.

It was a formidable ceremony: three sides to 'Chamber Court' lined with 600 boys; a pack of V.I.P.'s behind me; the head of the school facing me. He made a short speech to me in Latin, and I answered in Latin. I spoke for a quarter of an hour (I had said it to myself every night in bed for several weeks, so I had learnt it by heart).

A school-fellow one year older than me (bishop emeritus of Truro) was looking on from a window, and I was able to greet him in the course of my speech—a very great pleasure for me.[1]

I used my speech to commemorate my school-fellows who were killed in 1915–1916—recalling them in the place where I had first come to know them.[2]

Veronica and I have not yet quite recovered from the fatigue. It was a rash expedition, but I could not have borne refusing to make it, when invited. I was wearing Freeman-Grenville's doctor's gown. Since then, he has told me that he has heard from you.

Well, continue to give me news of your mission and of yourself.

Much love to you
from us both.
Arnold

1. Edmund Robert Morgan (1888–1979); had given A.J.T. and Veronica a wedding service at Winchester in the Cloisters of College; cf. A.J.T.'s letter of 3 October 1946 above; Bishop Morgan's presence at the window had been staged; Lawrence recalls experiencing "vicarious agonies of excitement" as he witnessed A.J.T.'s performance. Veronica reported that this was one of the two honors conferred on A.J.T. that he had appreciated most; the other was his appointment, in 1968, by the French Academy to occupy Sir Winston Churchill's fauteuil at the Institut de France.

2. A.J.T.'s reply was published in *The Wykehamist*, no. 1230 (10 July 1974), pp. 368–69; the permission of the Warden and Fellows of Winchester College to include this is gratefully acknowledged. The following, with minor rectifications, is from the text at the Bodleian.

AD PORTAS SATURDAY 29TH JUNE 1974. PROFESSOR TOYNBEE'S REPLY.

Ab imo corde gratias ago tibi, Aulae Praefecte, vir egregi—immo, vir clarissime, tu qui potestatis plenitudinem praetorio praefecti potestati fere parem exerces. Domine Custos, Domine Custos Collegii Sanctae Mariae Wintoniensis ad urben Oxonium, olim aulae praefecte, ceterique Domini Gubernatores collegii nostri, Domine Informator, Domine Hostiari ceterique Domini Magistri, vos omnes grato animo saluto.

Studii generalis praeclari ad urbem Lugdunum Batavorum discipuli hunc morem observant. Quicumque eorum examinatoribus satisfecit, is in academiae illius pariete nomen suum inscribit, haec verba addit: "Hic sudavi, sed non frustra". Nos quoque in collegio nostro sudare discimus, praesertim quamdiu iuniores sumus. Non frustrane sudamus? Frustrane sudamus? Hoc, ut opinor, nemo de se ipso revera dinoscere potest. Quod ad me attinet, hoc tantum scio, mihi diu sudare licuisse, quia diu vixi.

Hoc reputans, aliqua tristia recordari moveor. In hoc collegium per hanc portam ingressus sum, vir novus, anno secundo huius saeculi. Hodie, post annos paene septuaginta duo elapsos, hic sto rursus, senex. Sed pauci ex sodalibus meis usque ad hanc diem vixerunt. Mehercle, unum eorum hic praesentem video, virum valde reverendum Edmundum Robertum Morgan, urbis Truronis episcopum emeritum. Edmunde mi, te aspiciens gaudeo. Nos—tu et ego—sortem eandem adepti sumus. Ambo diu viximus. Sodales nostri nobis aequales erant aetate, longaevitate non aequales.

Eorum permulti bello absumpti sunt iuvenes—bello ecumenico primo. In duobus bellis ecumenicis—generis humani istis duabus diris cladibus—decerptus est flos iuventutis paene totius terrarum orbis. Tot iuvenes intempestive exstinctos plango. Omnes maereo, omnium gentium, sine discrimine acierum quae in bellis his quasi civilibus inter sese concurrerunt.

Ex hac innumerabili multitudine iuvenum atrociter trucidatorum, tres iuvenes citabo. Hi nostri collegii alumni erant, Domino Edmundo et mihi condiscipuli, unus eorum ex pueris commensalibus, duo ex scholaribus, quorum unus aulae praefectus fuerat, ambo postea Collegii Sanctae Mariae Wintoniensis ad Oxonium socii facti sunt. Ecce volumen longum anni tertii huius saeculi. Hic illa tria nomina impressa invenietis.

Leslie Whitaker Hunter, tu, si tot annos vixisses quot vixi ego, tu litteris Graecis et Latinis interpretandis lumen ingenii tui docte adhibuisses. Unius scriptoris Graeci opus recognovisti, emendavisti. Hoc post mortem tuam edidit sodalis. Edendi tempus tibi ipsi defuit. In Gallia vallum hostile inexpugnabile expugnare iussus, ultro in mortem missus es.

Guido Leonarde Cheesman, tu si tot annos vixisses quot vixi ego, tu rerum Romanarum historiam sollertia eximia explorasses. Unum librum scripsisti, et hunc praestantem. Sed plura scribendi tibi tempus defuit. E nave in Chersonesi Thracicae litus desiliens statim occisus es.

Roberte Stafford Arture Palmer, tu si tot annos vixisses quot vixi ego, tu re publica gerenda cursum honorum illustrem perfecisses, bonum publicum magnopere auxisses. Sed tibi quoque tempus defuit. Letali vulnere ictus, in Babylonia mortuus es.

Amici misere mihi adempti, perpetuo in memoria mea vos vivide vigetis.

Nunc ad minus tristia me revocabo. Rogeri, in carmine nostro "DOMUM" nuncupati, officio mihi benigne functus est gener meus, neptis meae maritus, nuper aulae praefectus, Dominus Josephus Pennybacker. Is mihi caballos tulit—caballos celeres, naphtha Arabica fortiter animatos. Sic me ad hanc urbem Ventam Belgarum vexit a domo mea, quae sita est in Brigantium agro, fere duodeviginti milia passuum ultra urbem Eboracum.

Eboraci, anno aevi nostri ducento undecimo, mortuus est imperator Romanus Libyphoenix Lucius Septimius Severus. Die qua moriturus erat imperator, tribunus, ut solitum, mane ei adiit, signum diei ("password") poposcit. Quaerit imperator: "Antecessor meus, Publius Helvius Pertinax, die qua mortuus est ille, quid signum dedit?" Respondetur: "Divus Helvius signum dedit 'Militemus'." "At non sic ego," inquit Lucius. "Non do signum 'Militemus'; do 'Laboremus'." Lucius, saeva necessitate ipse bellator, omen infaustum posteris legare nolebat. Bella futura prospiciebat, perhorrescebat; virtutem civilem colere suadebat; laborare, sudare, non militare, trucidare monebat.

Di deaeque omnes, vos obsecro; huic suboli, precor, parcite. His sortem duram, sortem iniquam, quam sodalibus meis decrevistis, ne decernite. Di, invidere desinite. Hos saltem iuvenes everso saeculo nostro succurrere ne prohibete. Iampridem satis luimus.

Caulis huius senescentis, ab holitore carissimo Montacuto Rendall Hostiario olim assidue exculti, oratiuncula ad finem vergit. Sed unum superest. Omnem hominem occidentalem bene eruditum utraque lingua facundum esse oportet. Marcus Tullius noster, quandocunque litteras dictabat, sermoni patrio Latino verba Graeca creberrima inserere solebat. Ciceronis exemplo fretus, ultima verba mea Graece loquar, *μὰ δὲν θὰ σᾶς ὁμιλήσω αὐτὰ ποῦ μαθαίνομε ἐδῶ στὴ σχολὴ αὐτή. Θὰ σᾶς μιλήσω, ὄχι τὰ ἀρχαῖα, τὰ Ἑλληνικά. Θὰ μιλήσω τὰ Ῥωμέϊκα, τὰ δημοτικά.*

Λοιπὸν, πρῶτον λέω. Ἄς σεβώμεθα τὴν κηδεμόνα τῆς σχολῆς μας, τὴν Παναγίαν Θεοτόκον, ποῦ ἡ εἰκών της ἔστεκε—και τώρα πάλι στέκει—ἐκεῖ ἐπάνω στὴ πόρτα αὐτή. Δεύτερον λέω. Ζήτω ὁ ἀοίδιμος κτίστης τῆς σχολῆς μας, ὁ δεσπότης—ἔτσι λένε οἱ Ῥωμαῖοι τούς ἐπισκόπους των - ὁ δεσπότης τοῦ κάστρου Οὐέντης, ὁ μακαρίτης Γουλιέλμος ὁ Οὐικχαμηνός. καὶ τρίτον λέω. Γιὰ τὴν ὁμάδα τῶν πνευματικῶν υἱῶν τοῦ Γουλιέλμου, ἡμῶν τῶν Οὐικχαμιστῶν, πολλὰ χρόνια, multos annos, çok yaşa.

Κύριε Ἔπαρχε τῆς Αὐλῆς, σᾶς εὐχαριστῶ πάλι πολύ—πάρα πολύ. Domini, iterum vos saluto, iterum vobis gratias ago. *καὶ οἱ φίλοι μου ὅλοι· χαίρετε. χαίρετε.* Dixi. Peractumst.

Translation by C.B.P.

From the depth of my heart I thank you, Prefect of Hall, you outstanding—indeed, most distinguished—man: for you exercise a plenitude of power almost equal to that of the praetorian prefect. I thankfully greet all of you: Mr. Warden, Mr. Warden of St. Mary's College of Winchester at the City of Oxford, (New College) once Prefect of Hall, other fellows of our college, Mr. Headmaster, Mr. Second Master and all you other masters.

The scholars of the renowned University of Leiden in Holland observe this custom: every one who has passed his examinations inscribes his name on the wall of that academy and adds these words: "Here I have sweated, but not in vain." We also in our college learn to sweat, especially while we are juniors. Do we too sweat "not in vain?" Do we sweat in vain? This, I think, no one can truly discern about himself. What pertains to me, this at least I do know, that I have been permitted to sweat for a long time because I have lived for a long time.

When I consider this, I am brought to recall sad events. To this college, through this gate, I entered, a young man, in the second year of this century. Today, after the lapse of almost seventy-two years, I stand here again, an old man. But few of my schoolmates have lived to this day. Indeed, I see one of them here, the right reverend Edmund Robert Morgan, late bishop of Truro. My Edmund, I rejoice to see you. We—you and I—have attained the same lot. We have both lived a long time. Our schoolmates were equal to us in age, but not in longevity.

So many of them in their youth were destroyed—in the first world war. In the two world wars—those two dire calamities of the human race—the flower of the youth of almost the whole world was plucked. I weep for so many youths destroyed before their time. I grieve for all, of all nations, with no discrimination between those who belonged to different battle lines which clashed in these almost civil wars.

From this innumerable multitude of young men so cruelly slaughtered, I shall mention three. These were alumni of our college, fellow students with Edmund and myself: one of them was a commoner; two were scholars, of whom one had been prefect of hall; both afterward were made fellows of St. Mary's College of Winchester at Oxford (New College). Examine the long roll of the third year of this century and there you will find imprinted these three names.

Leslie Whitaker Hunter, if you had lived as many years as I have, you would have brought the scholarly light of your genius to the interpretation of Greek and Latin texts. You revised and emended the work of one Greek writer. This was published by a friend after your death. The time to publish it yourself was taken from you. Ordered to attack an unassailable enemy trench in France, you wantonly were sent to your death.

Guy Leonard Cheesman, if you had lived as many years as I have, you would have explored the history of Roman affairs with superb skill. One book you wrote, and this outstanding. But there was no time to write more: as you leapt from a ship to the shore of the Thracian Chersonese (Gallipoli) you were cut down.

Robert Stafford Arthur Palmer, if you had lived as many years as I have lived, you would have completed an illustrious career in government and would have greatly augmented the public weal. But for you also time was lacking. Stricken with a mortal wound, you died in Babylon.

My friends, sadly snatched from me, you flourish always, living in my memory.

Now I recall myself to less sad matters. Mr. Joseph Pennybacker, my grandson-in-law, the husband of my granddaughter, recently Prefect of Hall, kindly played the role of Roger in our song "Domum"; he brought me horses—swift horses—fiercely fired by Arabian petrol. Thus he brought me to this city, Winchester, from my home in Yorkshire almost eighteen miles beyond the City of York. At York in the year 211, the Roman Emperor Libyphoenician Lucius Septimius Severus died; on the day of the Emperor's death, a tribune came to him in the morning and, as was the custom, asked for the password of the day. The Emperor asked: "What password did my predecessor, Publius Helvius Pertinax, give on the day of his death?" The answer was: "The divine Helvius gave the password 'let us fight on.' But not so I," said Lucius; "I do not give the word 'let us fight' but rather 'let us work on'". Lucius, himself a warrior through bitter necessity, was unwilling to bequeath an ill omen to posterity. He was foreseeing future wars, and was shuddering; he was urging the cultivation of civil virtues: he warned us to work, to sweat and not to fight and slay.

All you gods and goddesses, I beseech you; I beg you, spare this generation. Do not condemn them to the harsh, the unjust lot you decreed to my companions. Begrudge them no longer, gods. At least do not prevent these young men from succouring this twisted world of ours. Enough have we suffered for too long a time.

Now the little speech of this aging cabbage, once so assiduously cultivated by that dearest of gardeners, Montague Rendall, as Second Master, approaches its end. But one thing remains. Every well educated Westerner should be fluent in either language. Our Marcus Tullius whenever he composed letters, used to engraft Greek words liberally into his native Latin speech. Relying upon the example of Cicero, I shall give my final words in Greek.

But I shall not speak to you in the same words which we learn here in this school; I shall not speak to you in the ancient, the Hellenic language; I shall speak in the Romaic, the demotic language.

So first I say: let us revere the Patroness of our school, the Most Holy Mother of God, whose image stood—and now again stands—there above that very gate.

Secondly, I say: May long flourish the founder of our school, the "despot" of blessed memory (thus the Byzantines name their bishops) the "despot" of Winchester, the blessed William of Wykeham.

And thirdly, I say: to the company of the spiritual sons of William, to us Wykehamists, may there be many, many, many years.

Master Prefect of Hall, I thank you again deeply, most deeply.

Gentlemen, again I greet you, again I salute you, again I thank you.

All my friends, farewell, farewell I have spoken. It is done.

5 August 1974 Nsukka, E.C.S. Nigeria

My dear Arnold,

Thank you so much for your last letter; very refreshing to get it, and its good news that you are thoroughly settled in Chapel Cottage; also that you survived and obviously enjoyed, the ordeal of "S. Mary's outside the walls"—most interesting too for me. Why do grown-ups make the young do their praying for them? You should at least have been given some extra buns on Saturdays, and you might have sung the antiphons more lustily.

Since I last wrote, we made the epic journey from Bamenda to here, complete with about 35–40 items—boxes of books, trunks, suit-cases, African stool, drum. These were transferred to a second pick-up at the frontier. We arrived at Abakaliki covered from head to foot in mud, as we got stuck twice and had to push—ineffectually—while the wheels buzzed round.

Here we are on the edge of a Catholic hospital housed in small, disused doctors' houses, fairly comfortably, but all very noisy.

Six months ago the convent was held up by armed robbers—they infest the neighbouring forests—and all the month's wages, including builders' ditto, were taken. Now the compound is guarded at night by Hausas.[1] They are never sure of Ibos being in league or being browbeaten. Two Hausas talk away under my window till 11 or 11.30 P.M. I don't like to move them on; they are a protection! This robber problem is all over. People are particularly frightened of a night car breakdown between Benin City[2] and Ibadan.

Two weeks ago I went to Ibadan by public transport to give a retreat. What with one thing and other, it took 3 days. Onitsha[3] on the Niger has been very badly hammered during the war and its roads are impassable. But the great market has been rebuilt, also the cathedral and Bp.'s house by the side of the river. It looks so sluggish and hot and enormous. Benin City is overshadowed by an immense Guinness factory which no doubt syphons off any wealth the locals have. The factory is the "new king's" compound, tho' the old red mud walled one of the old king is still there;[4] and so is he, hidden away for fear of evil spells.

Ibadan is one vast market for the Yorubas.[5] They buy and sell all day and night, in every street, in every house; then, on one side, is the old colonial quarter, so clean and utterly separate.

Visa news: Fr. Ambrose went to Lagos from Ibadan when we were both at the latter. Our documents were at the top of the pile. They would be signed next day! any day now! But, still no news. So we are in a quandary, and not sure what to do as tourist visas run out. We're trying meanwhile to extend the latter, or even temporarily, we may flee back to Cameroon. God's will is very obscurely being unfolded in this complex situation.

My letter to the Goodalls (at Greystone Cottage, Ampleforth, see telephone) complements yours. You should exchange news.

Love to you both and all at G.

Columba, O.S.B.

P.S. Sorry about the messiness of all this—the heat perhaps.

1. The most numerous people of the northern states of Nigeria; farmers and traders; their city-states in northern Nigeria were established around the thirteenth century; their language is widely diffused.

2. The ancient capital of the Empire of Benin; famous for its traditional arts.

3. Onitsha was shattered by artillery bombardment from across the Niger while it was in Biafran hands.

4. The king (oba) in Benin had been worshiped as a god; cf. J. G. Frazer, *The Magic Art and the Evolution of Kings* (New York, 1935), vol. 1, p. 396; Montserrat Palau Marti, *Le roi-dieu au Bénin* (Paris, 1964), pp. 62–95. The "old king," the oba, sans power, still lived on, as a recluse, in 1974; the "new king" refers to the manager of the Guinness factory in Benin.

5. Farmers and traders living in the western and Lagos states of Nigeria; the Yoruba language is spoken by more than 10 million; rich in poetry.

Purey Cust Nursing Home
York

16 August 1974

Dear Columba,

Your letter from Nsukka was brought to me here from Ganthorpe. I think Mr. Freeman-Grenville has already written to you and told you that Arnold had a stroke during the night of 2–3 August. It happened after quite a normal day, but I suppose was probably to be explained by the unusual strain of the *Ad Portas* ceremony at Winchester following so soon after the long strain of the prolonged move into our new house.

It is of course very difficult to tell at present what his future will be, but there is no doubt that he is making slow progress at present. Though his speech is affected, I do not think his brain is. (It is the left side that is partially paralyzed, and that is said to be a good sign), and though he was sometimes very miserable at first, he cheered up a lot after a few days when he was given a pen and a pad of paper and found that he could write (it was definite words, not very legible, but by no means a soufflé). So I think it reasonable to look forward to a distant future when he may be able to come home, even if he has to use a wheeled chair and can't do much in the way of intellectual activity. I do think he understands most of what is said to him, allowing for his deafness, and must think us all very stupid that we don't understand what he says! This must of course apply particularly to me!

I expect you know about this nursing home. We were lucky to be able to get him a room here almost at once, for it is all quite excellent—Doctor (a Balliol man) Matron and Nurses. And we have belonged to a Private Patient's association (B U P A) for a long time, and that will cover a great deal of the cost. He will have to be here a long time, and I am prepared for this. I have been sleeping in odd places in York (full of tourists in August of course) but Matron has told me that she is trying to fit me into a room on the top floor where the juniors who have not yet taken their training, sleep. This would be a great convenience. I was thinking of sleeping at home and coming in and out by bus to the spot, about 4 miles from Ganthorpe where they used to meet the younger girls when they were at school in York.

I do hope you will be able to stay in Nigeria and not be pushed back again into the Cameroons. You have been having a very difficult time.

Arnold would send his love if he was able to understand that I am writing to you. At the moment he is asleep, though he opens an eye occasionally.

Veronica

P.O. Box 302
Enugu, Nigeria

6 November 1975

My dear Veronica,

I hope and pray you are rested and restored a little, though the huge vacuum remains. I do not know your beliefs and so do not know whether you can receive consolation from Arnold's continued existence in another life and his continued love for you. Let me give you a little picture of my own feelings.

Now that the cloud of debris of those last months has blown away, all that period seems to me insignificant except for the struggle to be calm. The most precious words I heard were: "I don't want to hate." And then for me the other words were the naming of the Holy Trinity. I shall never use that publicly as a sign of "conversion"—something he was so anxious should not be "imposed" on him; but personally it seemed like an answer to a life-long prayer for him.[1]

But apart from these two facts, and the love he showed—and especially to you at the end—I revert to when he was fully alive, and remember his gentleness and humility and moral courage. I hope you too can now climb back over the debris to the real Arnold. God bless you. I've expressed myself very badly.

The African world is closing in round me: the great struggle between the old paganism and the Christian faith; the secular power with money as the driving force and the Church. All these very simple people with astonishing faith are reminders of how "the Good News" must have seemed to the early Christians.

Perched on our hill the heat is bearable; go down into the plain, and it is not quite!

Love to all at Ganthorpe
and yourself,
Columba

1. "During our last meeting (18 September 1975), during which he was incapable of clear speech or writing, suddenly he said very distinctly the words, 'In the name of the Father and of the Son and of the Holy Ghost,' and then fell back into silence. As I wrote before, I do not use that to prove anything to the general public. It may have been an act of courtesy to me on his part, as Veronica suggested. For me it was the answer to prayer!" C.C.E.

Benedictines, Eke
P.O. Box 302
Enugu, Nigeria

18 December 1975

My dear Veronica,

The 17th is over,[1] I hope and pray it went well, and that you were satisfied.* I was present all these thousands of miles away. Now too I hope you can see all in some perspective. You will never know what a marvellous support in love you were to Arnold, especially in those critical days and years of the break with Rosalind. I know something of it because he told me. Of course he must have told you.

I loved him, too, as a kind of second father, elder brother, great friend. He had a wonderful humility to accept and listen to my babblings over so many subjects about which he knew almost infinitely more. He was also always ready to come to the defense of any one, even though he was outrageously one-sided (I mean Mr. X).

He once said to me he was always falling over backwards to be fair to other religions, because he was only inside Christianity. I believe that in the Providence of things it was beneficial that he remained uncommitted, as all were prepared to listen, whereas, if he had, in fact, accepted Catholicism, he would have been written off.[2] But I don't think, in one sense, he was ever very near, because he also said to me—unusually fiercely!—that he must keep his freedom of mind.

Now dear Veronica, enter into the peace of Christmas and let Jean and Lawrence coax you into resting. God bless you, and a happy Christmas to you and all the family and Fr. Carter[3]—I hope that is his name—Love,

Columba, O.S.B.

*How can one be "satisfied"? at least content to have done one's best.

P.S. Do let me know your plans.

1. The memorial service at St. James's Piccadilly, 17 December 1975; Philip read the lesson; Lawrence wrote the bidding prayer; Noble Frankland gave an address.

2. Compare A.J.T.'s statement of 5 August 1938, above.

3. Compare C.C.E.'s letter of 7 April 1974, above.

INDEX